Business & Professional Ethics

for Directors, Executives & Accountants

5th Edition

Leonard J. Brooks

Professor of Business Ethics & Accounting
Executive Director, Clarkson Centre for Business Ethics & Board Effectiveness
Joseph L. Rotman School of Management
University of Toronto

Paul Dunn

Associate Professor
Department of Accounting
Brock University

SOUTH-WESTERN
CENGAGE Learning

Australia • Brazil • Japan • Korea • Mexico • Singapore • Spain • United Kingdom • United States

SOUTH-WESTERN
CENGAGE Learning™

Business & Professional Ethics for Directors, Executives & Accountants, Fifth Edition

Leonard J. Brooks, Paul Dunn

VP/Editorial Director: Jack W. Calhoun

Editor-in-Chief: Rob Dewey

Sr. Acquisitions Editor: Matt Filimonov

Developmental Editor: Heather McAuliffe

Marketing Manager: Kristen Hurd

Sr. Content Project Manager: Martha Conway

Production Technology Analyst: Emily Gross

Sr. Frontlist Buyer, Manufacturing: Doug Wilke

Production Service: Macmillan Publishing Solutions

Sr. Art Director: Stacy Jenkins Shirley

Internal Designer: Juli Cook

Cover Designer: KeDesign, Mason, OH

Cover Image: © Getty Images/ Photodisc

Text Permissions Manager: Bob Kauser

For product information and technology assistance, contact us at **Cengage Learning Academic Resource Center, 1-800-423-0563**

For permission to use material from this text or product, submit all requests online at **www.cengage.com/permissions** Further permissions questions can be emailed to **permissionrequest@cengage.com**

ISBN-13: 978-0-324-59477-5

ISBN-10: 0-324-59477-1

South-Western Cengage Learning
5191 Natorp Boulevard
Mason, OH 45040
USA

Cengage Learning products are represented in Canada by Nelson Education, Ltd.

For your course and learning solutions, visit **academic.cengage.com** Purchase any of our products at your local college store or at our preferred online store **www.ichapters.com**

Printed in Canada
1 2 3 4 5 6 7 13 12 11 10 09

B *usiness & Professional Ethics for Directors, Executives & Accountants* is focused on deepening the understanding of how best to incorporate ethical values into governance, strategies, and actions to the benefit of us all.

Our preparation of the Fifth Edition has been enriched by the contributions of many, but none more than our wives and families who have supported and encouraged us, and to whom we dedicate this work. It is with great pride, thankfulness, and love that we acknowledge Jean and Kathy, and our growing families.

Leonard J. Brooks
Paul Dunn
Toronto, Canada
November 2008

Leonard J. Brooks is Professor of Business Ethics & Accounting at the Rotman School of Management of the University of Toronto. He is the Executive Director of the Rotman School's Clarkson Centre for Business Ethics & Board Effectiveness, Director of the University's Master of Management & Professional Accounting Program, and Director of its Diploma in Investigative & Forensic Accounting Program.

Professor Brooks served for fourteen years on the Editorial Board of the *Journal of Business Ethics* and continues to serve as a reviewer for that as well as other journals. He has published articles on ethics issues in the *Journal of Business Ethics, Accounting Organizations and Society, Business and Society,* and has authored or coauthored/edited the research monograph *Canadian Corporate Social Performance* and books or publications entitled *Business & Professional Ethics for Accountants, 2e; Principles of Stakeholder Management: The Clarkson Principles;* and *Ethics & Governance: Developing and Maintaining an Ethical Corporate Culture, 3e.*

Before joining the University of Toronto, Professor Brooks obtained his Chartered Accountant (C.A.) designation in Canada and subsequently became an audit manager and Director of Manpower for Touche Ross & Co. (now Deloitte & Touche) in Toronto. He has served as a member, then Chairman, of the CAs' national Board of Examiners, and Chairman of their national Syllabus Committee. Professor Brooks became a Fellow of the Institute of Chartered Accountants of Ontario in 1982.

Professor Brooks consults to individuals, corporations, governmental and nongovernmental organizations, and serves as an expert witness and frequent media commentator. He is also a former Director of the Canadian Centre for Ethics & Corporate Policy, and a former President of the Canadian Academic Accounting Association.

Paul Dunn is an Associate Professor of Accounting at Brock University. He attended the University of Toronto, graduating with a BA in philosophy (1972) and then a MA in philosophy (1973). Entering the workforce, he became a Chartered Accountant, working with Clarkson Gordon (that later became Ernst & Young), in the finance division of the Canadian Imperial Bank of Commerce, and in the accounting department of a private computer company, and finally with a not-for-profit. After working in downtown Toronto for over fifteen years, Professor Dunn returned to school, receiving his doctorate in accounting from Boston University in 1999.

Dr. Dunn's research interests focuses on issues in corporate governance, corporate social responsibility, and business ethics. His work has been published in a variety of scholarly journals including the *Journal of Business Ethics, Teaching Business Ethics, The Journal of Management,* and *Business & Society.* He is the Treasurer for the Social Issues in Management division of the Academy of Management, and Chair of the Audit Committee of the International Association for Business and Society. He is also a seminar leader at, and writes cases for, the School of Accountancy that is run by the Institute of Chartered Accountants of Ontario. Recently he has returned to his roots by writing philosophical papers.

CONTENTS

PART 2

ETHICAL BEHAVIOR | 141

PART 3

ETHICAL GOVERNANCE, ACCOUNTABILITY & MANAGEMENT | 239

CHAPTER 6 Professional Accounting in the Public Interest, Post-Enron 343

PART 4 SIGNIFICANT ETHICS ISSUES FACING BUSINESS & THE ACCOUNTING PROFESSION | 461

CHAPTER 7 Managing Ethics Risks & Opportunities 462

Challenges and Opportunities

Expectations for appropriate business and professional accounting behavior have changed dramatically. The demise of Enron, Arthur Andersen, and World Com triggered the U.S. Sarbanes-Oxley Act of 2002 and galvanized reforms in the accountability and governance of both corporations and professional accounting. These reforms and the subsequent subprime lending fiasco have influenced business and professional ethics around the world, and they will continue to bring new challenges and opportunities for directors, executives, and professional accountants.

The reforms in accountability and governance frameworks have recognized that corporations and professional accountants are more broadly accountable than prior tradition evidenced. The crisis of corporate reporting credibility that Enron began, Arthur Andersen fostered, WorldCom capped, and the Sarbanes-Oxley Act (SOX) sought to remedy heightened the awareness that corporations and the accounting profession must have the support of many stakeholder groups to achieve their strategic objectives.

That support requires trust—trust based on the expectation that the corporation and professional accountant will do the right thing, that their actions will respect the interests of the stakeholder group. Earning and maintaining that trust requires changing the strategy, risk management, planning, operations, and decision making of the corporation to take account of the interests and expectations of stakeholder groups in addition to shareholders. A new accountability framework is required that focuses on indicators of performance related to stakeholder expectations for both internal and external reporting.

Governance must focus on this new, broader accountability framework in order to ensure that stakeholder trust objectives are met. Such a change will not happen by itself, and directors are in danger of not fulfilling their risk management, due diligence expectations to shareholders if they ignore this duty. Some directors have understood the value of an excellent reputation and have been including risks to reputation in their risk management programs. Now that the linkage among ethics, reputation, and trust is clear and better understood, it is vital for corporations to upgrade their accountability and governance frameworks to ensure continued support. Shareholders and other stakeholders have come to expect more than they did pre-SOX—and the bar continues to rise.

Professional accountants can and should provide a critical element in the trust-oriented accountability and governance system. First, professional accountants can be important agents for ensuring trust. They are expected to serve in the public interest, and must do so to preserve the trust placed in them by a society that expects them to behave as professionals. This expectation, which applies to professional accountants in public practice as well as those employed by corporations, requires a rededication to their role as a trusted fiduciary. Second, professional accountants are well placed to understand the role of trust in internal control and accountability frameworks, and in the governance frameworks that provide direction and oversight to corporate activities. Third, good professional accountants are expected to display a level of professional skepticism and duty that should enable them to recognize the red flags of potential problems and report or remediate them.

Perhaps most important, these new governance and ethics expectations have reached the academic launching pads for new directors, executives, and professional accountants. The interest in newly created directors' governance education programs is startling. In 2004, the accreditation body for business schools worldwide published an Ethics Education Task Force Report that called for business students to be educated about (1) the responsibility of business in society, (2) ethical leadership, (3) ethical decision making, and (4) corporate governance and ethics.[1] Moreover, many jurisdictions are requiring compulsory ethics courses for accounting students before they are considered ready to write their qualifying exams for professional accounting designation. Accordingly, ethics and governance coverage is penetrating the curricula of far more business schools than in the past—which bodes well for the future.

Understanding these trust expectations and the interrelationship to ethics and governance will resolve challenges and present opportunities for directors, executives, and professional accountants. More important, it will provide the essential foundation for ensuring their support—and that of corporations—in the future.

Purpose of the Book

The crisis of corporate reporting credibility became so severe in mid-2002 that drastic measures were required to restore that credibility and relieve the gridlock that froze capital markets and dampened economies around the world. In fact, the financial disasters in 2002 accelerated and crystallized the impact of pressures for enhanced corporate accountability and a supportive governance framework that had been growing for years. As governance reform based on sound ethics takes hold around the world, there is an increasing need to understand the historical precursors involved, the responsibilities expected, and the techniques available for the satisfaction of those expectations.

Telling the story of ongoing pressures for more trusted governance and of the contributions of the disasters at Enron, Arthur Andersen, and WorldCom is important to the development of an appropriate understanding of the new SOX world for directors, executives, and accountants. Just as sound governance has recently incorporated the need for a risk management process, now the risk management process must be broadened to involve awareness of factors that can erode the support of stakeholder groups.

The reputation of corporations is recognized as being connected with the degree to which stakeholders trust that corporations will do the right thing. In other words, there is now a concern for both what a corporation does and how it is done. At certain times in the past, the emphasis was so strongly on achieving profit that little attention was given to how the profit was earned. Now that the support of stakeholders is recognized as critical to success, understanding how to build their expectations into corporate behavior, accountability, and governance is an important second objective of the book. Extending this discussion to the new era for professional accountants, and reviewing their potential roles, is a third objective.

Directors, executives, and accountants need to understand how to make ethical decisions they can defend to stakeholders. Codes of conduct cannot cover all situations, so organizational cultures need to be developed and decision processes utilized that are based on sound ethical decision-making frameworks. *Business & Professional Ethics* covers these topics as well as the development of an ethics risk management process, strategies for dealing with and reporting to stakeholders, and strategies for ensuring ethical behavior in the workplace and during the management of crises.

In a nutshell, *Business & Professional Ethics* examines the background and nature of the new stakeholder-support era of corporate and professional accountability and governance and

---

 1. The Association to Advance Collegiate Schools of Business, *AACSB Ethics Education Task Force Report*, June 2004, available through the BPE website at **www.cengage.com/accounting/brooks**

provides insights into the development of sound patterns of behavior on the part of directors, executives, and accountants. Successful management of ethical risks and the development of ethical competitive advantages depend upon the mastery of the subjects discussed. Professional accountants must understand the issues covered as a foundation for the fulfillment of their role as fiduciaries and experts in accountability and governance.

Applicability

Business & Professional Ethics is intended as a sourcebook for directors, executives, and professional accountants on post-Enron/SOX accountability and governance, and on appropriate decision making, behavior, and ethics risk management in the new era. Blending text, readings, and cases, it can be used as a stand-alone book in courses in business and/or professional ethics, or in governance. It is also very useful for independent study, or as an adjunct to traditional strategy, governance or accounting texts to provide access to interesting, real-world dilemmas. The material in the book has been used very successfully with MBA and Executive MBA students as well as accounting students.

The book has been organized into relatively freestanding chapters to facilitate custom publishing of a selection of chapters and/or cases. For example, Chapter 2, which covers the Enron, Arthur Andersen, WorldCom, and Sarbanes-Oxley developments, has been well used to start off Executive MBA programs. Similarly, directors and executives or MBA students wishing to focus on conflict of interests could benefit from Chapter 2 and 3, plus cases from other chapters. Chapters 1 and 4 have provided a fundamental platform for understanding current business ethics expectations and defensible approaches to ethical decision making for business students beginning their studies. New Chapter 8, which covers the subprime lending fiasco, provides an essential understanding of the current business challenge gripping us all worldwide. Professional accounting students should be familiar with all chapters.

The coverage provided is largely North American (N.A.) in orientation. Examples, readings, and cases are drawn with that perspective in mind. Basic ethical problems and principles are the same throughout North America, since they are shaped by the same concerns, markets, and similar institutional structures and legal strictures. Where points of difference are noteworthy, they are dealt with specifically. It should be noted that the increasing globalization of capital markets has extended North American expectations and problems to large companies around the world. Several new cases covering problems of large European companies and doing business abroad are included to provide a global perspective.

Because of the prominence of N.A. capital markets, and the significant impact of the N.A. practices of the Big Four professional accounting firms, the N.A. governance frameworks for both business and professional accountants around the world will serve as a benchmark for developments in other jurisdictions. In addition, domestic and foreign expectations for behavior will be increasingly intertwined because the practices of multinational corporations or firms will be increasingly scrutinized globally by stakeholders active in major consumer and capital markets and in regulatory arenas around the world.

Ethical behavior in international operations and international accountability are specifically explored, however, because differing cultures call for somewhat different ethical behavior. In addition, the recent emergence of global ethical accounting standards under the auspices of the International Federation of Accountants (IFAC) is covered extensively to prepare readers for the global harmonization process that is occurring.

Authors' Approach

To the greatest extent possible, *Business & Professional Ethics* focuses on the development of a practical understanding of the ethical issues driving the development of emerging accountability and governance frameworks, and of the practical skills required to deal with them effectively. Of necessity, this means providing a learning experience embedded with real-life cases and examples. At the same time, these real-life problems are interpreted through exposure to classic positions and articles that have had a lasting impact on business ethics in general and the accounting ethics in particular. The authors' experience as directors, executives, and professional accountants, plus substantial experience in the teaching of and consulting on business and accounting ethics, management control, and similar governance-related subjects, contributes significantly to the development of the issues and discussions offered.

Organization of the Book

To facilitate the purpose of the book, it is presented in four parts, each with two chapters that include a total of 84 cases and thirteen seminal readings and appendices, as follows:

		CASES	READINGS
PART 1	**THE ETHICS ENVIRONMENT**		
Ch. 1	Ethics Expectations	12	3
Ch. 2	Enron Events Motivate Governance & Ethics Reform	5	—
PART 2	**ETHICAL BEHAVIOR**		
Ch. 3	Philosophers' Contributions	3	1
Ch. 4	Practical Ethical Decision Making	5	2
PART 3	**ETHICAL GOVERNANCE, ACCOUNTABILITY & MANAGEMENT**		
Ch. 5	Corporate Ethical Governance & Accountability	17	2
Ch. 6	Professional Accounting in the Public Interest, Post Enron	29	2
PART 4	**SIGNIFICANT ETHICS ISSUES FACING BUSINESS & THE ACCOUNTING PROFESSION**		
Ch. 7	Managing Ethics Risks & Opportunities	9	3
Ch. 8	The Subprime Lending Fiasco	4	—
		84	13

Part 1 provides an understanding of concerns that have been driving the development of ethics expectations both pre- and post-Enron.

❙ Chapter 1 deals with concerns traditionally felt by a range of stakeholder groups, and how these concerns produced a broadened stakeholder-oriented accountability expectation.

❙ Chapter 2 tells the story of how the Enron, Arthur Andersen, and WorldCom fiascoes precipitated the corporate reporting credibility crisis that led to the Sarbanes-Oxley Act, which crystallized ethics expectations into new frameworks for accountability and governance for corporations and professional accounting. Both provide a useful foundation for later chapters.

Part 2 facilitates how a director, executive, employee or professional accountant should respond to the emerging ethical expectations by taking decisions and actions that will be considered both right and defensible when codes of conduct do not precisely fit the circumstances. It presents both concepts developed over the centuries by philosophers as well as practical frameworks for their application.

▌ Chapter 3 covers important contributions by several philosophers to provide a background from which to reason ethically.

▌ Chapter 4 presents several practical approaches to ethical decision making—really the core of ethical behavior—that facilitate the development of strategy as well as day-to-day decisions business people must face.

Part 3 examines how corporations and professional accountants can develop sound ethical accountability, governance and management systems that respond to the new ethics expectations.

▌ Chapter 5 covers those issues, expectations, and ethical culture-promoting systems that directors and executives should understand in order to discharge their duties successfully in the modern era.

▌ Chapter 6 deals with the roles and functions of professional accountants in the new accountability system for corporations, as agents of ethical accountability, as experts in the development of ethical accountability and governance mechanisms, and as professionals who should be demonstrating professional skepticism. Both Chapters 5 and 6 cover the identification, assessment, and management conflicts of interest, and other key elements of a modern ethics-oriented governance system.

Part 4 deals with a set of extremely important issues that directors, executives, and professional accountants need to understand and develop a facility with in order to avoid serious pitfalls and to take unique opportunities that others will miss. The last chapter of the book provides an overview of one of the most pressing ethical and economic problems of our lifetimes that we will all suffer from, and all should learn from.

▌ Chapter 7 deals with the super critical areas of ethics risk and opportunity management, effective stakeholder management, corporate social responsibility performance and reporting, workplace ethics, motivation and avoidance of fraud and white collar crime, ethics for international operations, and ethical crisis management.

▌ Chapter 8 written in November 2008, reviews the *subprime lending fiasco* and presents an ethical analysis of this latest ethical disaster to influence the world negatively. Lessons drawn from the ethical analysis are presented to provide a platform for discussion and learning so that future problems can be avoided. In its own way, this chapter provides a summary application of the material covered in earlier chapters.

Each chapter presents an interesting selection of cases, a selection of very significant readings, and a useful list of references. The combination of text, 84 cases, and 13 readings provides a much richer learning experience than books that present just cases, or text plus a limited number of cases and no seminal readings.

In addition, numerous references are made in the margin where a website link/reference or a downloadable file is available on the *Business & Professional Ethics* website at **www.cengage .com/accounting/brooks.** The *BPE* website is updated continuously with new information, notes, and website links of interest.

Improvements to the Fifth Edition

Building on the strong foundation developed in the earlier four editions, the new edition has been thoroughly updated, benefiting significantly from:

▌ The contributions of a new coauthor, Paul Dunn.

▌ A new chapter (Ch. 3) on Philosophers' Contributions to Ethical Behavior.

▌ A new chapter (Ch. 8) on the Subprime Lending Fiasco that has triggered a credit freeze that has led to a downturn in economies around the world.

▌ Full integration of international (IFAC) ethical standards to which the world is harmonizing in Chapters 4 and 6.

▌ Enhanced treatment of Corporate Social Responsibility in Chapter 7.

▌ New section on Fraud and White Collar Crime in Chapter 7.

▌ 32 new cases, raising the total to over 84 plus 5 illustrative applications.

▌ New or revised material on:

  • The globalization of business and professional ethics

  • Enron updates

  • Philosophers' contributions to ethical behavior

  • Modifications and improvements to practical decision making approaches

  • Examples of philosophical and practical decision making approaches

  • Ethical corporate cultures

  • Alternative governance theories

  • Integration of international (IFAC) ethical standards

  • Corporate social responsibility

  • Motivations for fraud and white collar crime, including an analysis of a real case.

The fifth edition includes 32 new cases and 2 new illustrative applications including the following:

Ch. 1 Ethics Environment

▌ China's Tainted Baby Milk Powder: Rumored Control of Online News

▌ Should Porn be Sold by Cell Phone Companies?

▌ Virgin Mobile's Strip2Clothe Campaign: Exploitive, Risqué and Worthwhile?

▌ The Ethics of Bankruptcy: Jetsgo Corporation

▌ Bausch & Lomb's Hazardous Contact Lens Cleaner

▌ Magnetic Toys Can Hurt

Ch. 3 Ethical Behavior

▌ Dealing with Disappointed Apple iPhone Customers (also in Ch. 4)

▌ Terrorist Payments

▌ The Case of Cesar Correia

Ch. 5 Corporate Ethical Governance & Accountability

▌ Spying on HP Directors

▌ Manipulation of MCI's Allowance for Doubtful Accounts

▌ A Minority-Controlling Shareholder: The *New York Times Company* and the Ochs and Sulzberger Families

▌ Stock Options & Gifts of Publicly Traded Shares

▌ The Ethics of Repricing and Backdating Employee Stock Options

▌ Siemens' Bribery Scandal

▌ Société Générale' Rogue Trader

Ch. 6 Professional Accounting in the Public Interest, Post-Enron

▌ Livent—When Maria . . . When?

▌ Strategic Roles to Consider

▌ Biker Nightmare

▌ Budget Conflict

▌ An Exotic Professional Accountant?

▌ Freebie Services for Staff

▌ Summer Camp Holdback

▌ Theft Reimbursement, Twice

▌ Marketing Aggressive Tax Shelters

▌ Providing Tax Advice

Ch. 7 Managing Ethics Risks & Opportunities

▌ Walt Pavlo's MCI Scams/Frauds

▌ The Need for Skepticism, Courage & Persistence

Ch. 8 Subprime Lending Fiasco—Ethics Issues

▌ Mark-to-Market Accounting and the Demise of AIG

▌ Subprime Lending—Greed, Faith & Disaster

▌ Moral Courage: Toronto-Dominion Bank CEO Refuses to Invest in High-Risk Asset-Backed Commercial Paper

▌ The Ethics of AIG's Commission Sales

 Importantly, the *BPE* website, **www.cengage.com/accounting/brooks**, is constantly expanding to include helpful references such as video clips of major events, and brief summaries of key books on ethical matters.

As well, the BPE Instructor's Manual, which is available online, has been augmented to provide sample examinations and the discussion of successful, innovative usage of the book by satisfied instructors.

Acknowledgments

By Len Brooks

I have been fortunate to receive excellent suggestions for improving this and earlier versions of *Business & Professional Ethics* from Graham Tucker, Alex Milburn, Bill Langdon, Peter Jackson, Michael Deck, Curtis Verschoor, Lyall Work, and John Grant. But, as in the past, I want to acknowledge specifically the searching and insightful contributions by David Selley and particularly Ross Skinner. In addition, I want to thank Miguel Minutti, whose research enriched many of the book's cases and discussions. These contributors should rest easy, however, as I did not accept all their suggestions and therefore take responsibility for any errors or omissions.

To my former colleague, Max Clarkson, I owe a debt of gratitude for providing the initial platform and encouragement for development and exercise of my ideas in the classroom and as a consultant, and the stimulation to search for new ideas to contribute to our discipline.

To my mother and my father, who was a CA, CGA, CMA, and CPA, I owe my understanding of values and my interest in pursuing them.

To my wife, Jean, for her continued support, and for their forbearance my children, Catherine, Len, Heather, and John, their spouses or significant others Christina, Gabe, and Rob, and to my grandchildren Bianca, Willow, Mya, and Owen, I owe my love and respect.

By Paul Dunn

I am grateful to those who taught me so much in university, in particular, Larry Lynch and Edward Synan at the University of St. Michael's College in Toronto, and James Post at Boston University. They provided me with the grounding I needed in philosophy and business; they showed me how good teachers motivate and encourage learning in students; they also graced me with their friendship. Ross Dunn's life demonstrated how ethics and business could be successfully linked together. I have been fortunate to have received extremely helpful suggestions on many of the new cases in this volume from Alan Gardner and Paul Singleton, as well as Peter Thor and the discussions with his family at the Cottage.

My wife, Kathy, has been by my side for over thirty years. I am grateful for her love and support, as well as the love and encouragement I have received from my three children: Ryan, Heather, and Megan and her partner Todd. They have each provided me with strength and love. Thank you.

The End of the Beginning

Amid the tragedy created by the Enron, Arthur Andersen, and WorldCom fiascos, there is a silver lining—the acceleration and crystallization of stakeholder-oriented accountability and governance frameworks for corporations and professional accountants. The subprime lending fiasco is sure to further stimulate these processes. Awareness of these developments, and what they require to generate and maintain stakeholder support, provides the foundation for the roles, responsibilities, and future success of directors, executives, and professional accountants. We have entered an era wherein appropriate values upheld and applied hold the key to ethical behavior, reputation, and sustained success. *Business & Professional Ethics* provides an orderly development of the issues and skills involved and the understanding necessary to use them effectively—hopefully for the benefit of the business community, the accounting profession, and society as a whole.

Leonard J. Brooks
Professor of Business Ethics & Accounting
Executive Director, The Clarkson Centre for Business Ethics & Board Effectiveness
Joseph L. Rotman School of Management
University of Toronto

Paul Dunn
Associate Professor
Department of Accounting
Brock University

The disasters at Enron, Arthur Andersen, and WorldCom and recently the subprime lending crisis have fundamentally changed expectations for the behavior of directors, executives, and professional accountants. Good risk management practices must now incorporate ethics risk management, accountability, and governance practices that ensure the reputations of individuals, corporations, and firms are protected, and that the support of stakeholders is strong enough to facilitate success. Leaving the development of ethical boundaries to trial and error—risking bad practice—is no longer acceptable.

Corporations and business professionals are now part of a new post-Sarbanes-Oxley Act era of broadened stakeholder-oriented accountability and governance. Directors, executives, and professional accountants, now realize this necessitates considering the impacts and risks of their decisions on the public interest—certainly on more than the traditional short-term set of shareholder interests. Some businesspeople and professionals will want to go beyond developing a good defensive accountability and governance system to develop a competitive advantage where customers, employees, and others will be attracted by distinctly higher levels of trust based on commonly respected values such as honesty, fairness, compassion, integrity, predictability, and responsibility.

Unless directors, executives, and professional accountants develop effective accountability, governance, and risk management processes that incorporate ethics,

▌ Directors will be unable to fulfill their due diligence requirements.

▌ Executives will be unable to develop sound competitive business models and protect their emerging legal liability.

▌ Professional accountants will be unable to fulfill their role as fiduciaries and as leaders in the development of accountability and governance systems.

▌ Corporations and the accounting profession as we know them will be further discredited and regulated.

Business & Professional Ethics provides an understanding of why ethics has become a critical success factor, the nature and role of the Enron/Sarbanes-Oxley developments, how ethical behavior can be guided, how ethical decision making can be improved and made defensible, and how special problems—including the subprime lending crisis—facing directors, executives, and the accounting profession can be dealt with. This is accomplished in the following four parts and eight chapters:

Part 1	**The Ethics Environment**	
Ch. 1	Ethics Expectations	
Ch. 2	Enron Events Motivate Governance & Ethics Reform	
Part 2	**Ethical Behavior**	
Ch. 3	Philosophers' Contributions	
Ch. 4	Practical Ethical Decision Making	
Part 3	**Ethical Governance, Accountability & Management**	
Ch. 5	Corporate Ethical Governance & Accountability	
Ch. 6	Professional Accounting in the Public Interest, Post Enron	
Part 4	**Significant Issues Facing Business & the Accounting Profession**	
Ch. 7	Managing Ethics Risk & Opportunities	
Ch. 8	Subprime Lending Fiasco—Ethics Issues	

The Ethics Environment

Introduction

Unless an individual has developed a rather extraordinary interest in business and professional ethics, and has been able to pursue it daily, it is probable that he or she has not developed an adequate awareness of ethical issues to combat the challenges presented by the increasing complexity of business and professional ethics problems. Remedying that deficiency is the purpose of Part 1.

Chapter 1 provides a guide to the rest of the book. It begins with a summary of the forces responsible for the changes in the public's expectations for corporate ethical behavior, and in turn, in the public's expectations of accountants who audit those corporations as well as those who serve in the management of the corporations. Responses to these forces and related developments are reviewed including; the new mandate; frameworks for governance, stakeholder accountability, and ethical behavior; new techniques for the management of reputation and ethics risks; and new perspectives on accountability and business ethics.

Chapter 2 examines the profound changes brought by the Enron, Arthur Andersen, and WorldCom debacles, including the Sarbanes-Oxley Act recommendations and related U.S. Securities and Exchange Commission pronouncements, all of which are changing corporate governance and the accounting profession around the world. These two chapters are intended to provide an up-to-date perspective on the changing expectations for ethical behavior for directors, executives, managers, and professional accountants.

1

ETHICS EXPECTATIONS

Purpose of the Chapter

Business and the professions function within a framework created by the expectations of the public. Enron and the subsequent Arthur Andersen and WorldCom fiascoes have triggered a "sea change" of new expectations for business governance and the accounting profession around the world. These new behavioral expectations are based on an acceleration of business and professional ethics trends that have been long in the making. Business and professional ethics have become key determinants of success, and the focal points of research and corporate change.

This chapter explores the changes that the ethics trends have brought to the expectations framework, as well as the developments that have arisen in response to those changes. It also begins to consider what the changes in expectations mean for the professional accountant. As such, this chapter provides an introduction and overview for the book.

The Ethics Environment for Business: The Battle for Credibility, Reputation & Competitive Advantage

During the last twenty-five years, there has been an increasing expectation that business exists to serve the needs of both shareholders and society. Many people have a "stake" or interest in a business, its activities, and impacts. If the interests of these stakeholders are not respected, then action that is often painful to shareholders, officers, and directors usually occurs. In fact, it is unlikely that businesses or professions can achieve their long-run strategic objectives without the support of key stakeholders, such as shareholders, employees, customers, creditors, suppliers, governments, host communities, and activists.

The support for a business—and business in general—depends on the credibility that stakeholders place in corporate commitments, the company's reputation, and the strength of its competitive advantage. All of these depend on the trust that stakeholders place in a company's activities; trust, in turn, depends on the values underlying corporate activities.

Stakeholders increasingly expect that a company's activities will respect their values and interests. To a large extent, this respect for stakeholder values and interests determines the ethical standing and success of a corporation. Consequently, corporate directors are now expected to govern their company ethically, which means that they are to see that their executives, employees, and agents act ethically. Moreover, the corporation is increasingly expected to be accountable to stakeholders in a transparent or ethical manner. Performance assessment now extends beyond what is achieved to encompass how ethically those results were achieved.

As a result, the emerging governance and accountability regime for business and the professions has become far more concerned with stakeholder interests and ethical matters than has been the case in the past. Directors, executives, and professional accountants, who serve the often conflicting interests of shareholders directly and the public indirectly, must be aware of the public's new expectations for business and other similar organizations, and must manage their risks accordingly. More than just to serve intellectual curiosity, this awareness must be combined with traditional values and incorporated into a framework for ethical decision making and action. Otherwise, as was the case with the Enron and Arthur Andersen debacles, the credibility, reputation, and competitive advantage of capital markets, the organization, management, professional, and the profession will suffer.

What has produced this change in public expectations for business governance, behavior, and accountability? Several factors appear to share causal responsibility as indicated in Table 1.1.

| Environmental Concerns

Nothing galvanized early public opinion about the nature of good corporate behavior more than the realization that the public's physical well-being, and the well-being of some workers, was being threatened by corporate activity. Initially, concern about air pollution centered on smokestack and exhaust pipe smog, which caused respiratory irritation and disorders. These problems were, however, relatively localized, so that when the neighboring population became sufficiently irate, local politicians were able and generally willing to draft controlling regulation, although effective enforcement was by no means assured.

Two other problems associated with air pollution that were slower to be recognized were acid rain, which neutered lakes and defoliated trees, and the dissipation of the earth's ozone layer. In the first case, the sulphur in exhaust gases combined with rain and fell to the ground far away from the source, often in other legal jurisdictions. Consequently, the reaction by politicians in the source jurisdiction was predictably slow, and many arguments were raised about who was responsible and whether the damage was real or not. Ultimately, however, the level of awareness of the problem became sufficiently widespread to support international treaties and more stringent local regulations.

The dissipation of the earth's ozone layer has been more recently recognized as a serious threat to our physical well-being. The release into the atmosphere of CFCs, once the most common residential and industrial refrigerant, allows CFC molecules to use up molecules of ozone. At the same time, the cutting down of the rain forests in Brazil, which were a main source for replenishing ozone, has contributed further to the depletion of the ozone layer around our planet. This layer was our major barrier from the sun's ultraviolet rays, which contribute to skin cancer and damage our eyes.

The timing of the recognition of water pollution as a problem worthy of action has paralleled the concern about our depleted ozone layer, partly because of our limited ability to measure minute concentrations of toxins and our inability to understand the precise nature of the

TABLE 1.1	Factors Affecting Public Expectations for Business Behavior
Physical	Quality of air and water, safety
Moral	Desire for fairness and equity at home and abroad
Bad judgments	Operating mistakes, executive compensation
Activist stakeholders	Ethical investors, consumers, environmentalists
Economic	Weakness, pressure to survive, to falsify
Competition	Global pressures
Financial malfeasance	Numerous scandals, victims, greed
Governance failures	Recognition that good governance and ethics risk assessment matter
Accountability	Desire for transparency
Synergy	Publicity, successful changes
Institutional reinforcement	New laws—environment, whistleblowing, recalls, *U.S. Sentencing Guidelines,* OECD antibribery regime, Sarbanes-Oxley Act (SOX) reforms, professional accounting reform, globalization of standards (IFAC, IFRS) and principles (Caux)

risk of water-borne metals and dioxins. Corporations asserted that they did not have the technical solutions to the elimination of air and water pollution at reasonable cost and therefore could not do so and remain competitive. However, once the short- and long-term threats to personal safety were understood, the public, led by special interest groups, began to pressure companies as well as governments directly to improve safety standards for corporate emissions.

Government reaction, often prompted by disasters, has been significant at all levels. Locally, no-smoking regulations have been enacted and local ordinances tightened. Environmental regulation has been the subject of international treaties. In the United States, the United Kingdom, and Canada, environmental protection acts have been put in place that feature significant fines up to $1–2 million per day for the corporation convicted of environmental malfeasance. In addition, personal fines and/or jail terms for officers and directors have focused the attention of executives on programs to ensure compliance with environmental standards. Nothing has energized executives in the United States and Canada more than the statement of a judge in regard to the promulgation of the U.S. Sentencing Guidelines on November 1, 1991. He said that the "demonstrated presence of an effective program of environmental protection would constitute an adequate 'due diligence' defense which could reduce the level of fine from $2 million/day to $50,000/day." Although this reaction may be viewed as defensive, the "due diligence" movement should be viewed as only one phase, the codification phase, of the movement toward corporate environmental responsibility.

Moral Sensitivity

During the 1980s and 1990s, there was a significant increase in the sensitivity to the lack of fairness and to discrepancies in equitable treatment normally afforded to individuals and groups in society. Several groups were responsible for this heightened social conscience, including the feminist movement and spokespeople for the mentally and physically challenged, for native people, and for minorities. To some degree, the public was prepared to entertain the concerns of these groups because unfortunate events had brought the realization that some special interest groups were worth listening to, as environmentalists, consumer advocates, and anti-apartheid supporters had shown. Also, for most of the period from 1960 onward, disposable incomes and leisure time have been sufficiently high to allow members of the public to focus on issues beyond earning their livelihood. In addition, as a result of the advances in satellite communications that have allowed virtually "live" coverage of worldwide problems, the thinking of the North American public has become less inner directed and parochial, and more sensitive to problems featured by wide-ranging investigative reporters.

Evidence of public pressure for more fairness and equity is readily available. The desire for equity in employment has resulted in laws, regulations, compliance conditions in contracts, and affirmative action programs in corporations. Pay equity programs have begun to appear to readjust the discrepancy between the pay scales for men and women. Consumer protection legislation has been tightened to the point that the old philosophy of "buyer beware," which tended to protect the large corporation, has been transformed to "vendor beware," which favors the individual consumer. Drug tests for employees have been much more carefully handled to minimize the prospect of false findings. All of these are examples in which public pressure has brought about institutional changes through legislatures or courts for more fairness and equity and less discrimination, and therefore will be virtually impossible to reverse. Indeed, the trend is unmistakable.

Moral sensitivity is also evident to international issues as well as domestic. The campaign to boycott buying from corporations that engage in child or sweatshop labor in foreign countries provides ample testimony to this, and has resulted in the creation of codes of ethical practice for suppliers, and compliance mechanisms to ensure they are followed. Organizations such as the

Social Accountability International and AccountAbility are developing workplace policies, standards, workplace auditor training programs, and reporting frameworks.

Bad Judgments & Activist Stakeholders

Directors, executives, and managers are human, and they make mistakes. Sometimes the public, or specific groups, take offense at these instances of bad judgment and take action to make the directors and management aware that they do not approve. For example, the decision by Shell UK to scuttle the Brent Spar Oil Storage Vessel in a deep part of the ocean rather than take it apart on shore led to demonstrations in support of Greenpeace, which tried to stop the scuttling, and to the boycott of Shell gas stations in Europe. Nestle products were boycotted in North America and Europe to stop the free distribution of baby formula powder to African mothers who were mixing it with contaminated water, thereby killing their babies. Nike and other companies' products were boycotted through the efforts of concerned individuals and groups to stop the use of sweatshop and child labor, particularly in foreign countries. The recall of Firestone tires was ignited by the media, beginning with a television show in Houston, Texas. North American corporations were extravagantly overpaying their executives—including several above $100 million per annum—or not reducing executive pay when profits declined, so CalPERS, the California Public Employees Pension Fund, called for the establishment of compensation committees consisting of a majority of independent directors. Activist stakeholders were clearly able to make a difference—one most people thought was for the best.

Two other kinds of activists also made their appearance in the late 1980s and early 1990s: ethical consumers and ethical investors. Ethical consumers were interested in buying products and services that were made in ethically acceptable manners. Consequently, books such as *Shopping for a Better World, The Ethical Shopper's Guide*, and *Conscious Consumption* were published in the United States, Canada, and in the United Kingdom. They provided ratings of companies, their affiliates, and their suppliers on different performance dimensions, such as hiring and treatment of women, environmental management and performance, charity, progressive staff policies, labor relations, consumer relations, and candor at answering questions. Ethical consumers were then able to "vote with their checkbooks."

Ethical investors took the view that their investments should not only make a reasonable return, but should do so in an ethical manner. Originally pioneered by large pension funds such as CalPERS and The New York City Employees Pension Fund, as well as several church investment funds, the movement has been augmented since the early 1990s by several ethical mutual funds. These ethical mutual funds employ screens that are intended to knock out companies from consideration that are involved in so-called harmful activities—such as producing tobacco products, armaments, or atomic energy, or misusing animals for testing. Alternatively, individuals or mutual funds can invest in companies that have been screened by an ethical consulting service. A Boston firm, KLD Research & Analytics, provides such a screening service and has created the Domini Social Index (DSI), made up of 400 ethically screened companies. A similar service is available in Canada for Canadian stocks, the MJI, from Michael Jantzi Research; in the United Kingdom, the FTSE4Good Index has been created for companies listed on the London Stock Exchange. The performance of these indices compares well to those for non-screened stocks in each country. A current list of ethical mutual funds and an update on socially responsible investing (SRI) can be found at the websites of SocialFunds.com (http://www.socialfunds.com) in the United States and the Social Investment Organization (SIO) in Canada (http://www.socialinvestment.ca). Many consultants offer screening services to investors on a fee-for-service basis. The entire field of ethically screened investing has continued to grow.

These developments signal that business decisions are being judged against different standards than before, by groups that have billions of dollars at their disposal. For additional information, contact the Investor Responsibility Research Centre (IRRC) and similar websites.

Economic & Competitive Pressures

Although the public's expectations have been affected directly by the factors already discussed, there are a number of underlying or secondary factors that are also at work. For instance, in general, the pace of economic activity slowed during the late 1980s, early 1990s, and just before and after the millennium. This placed corporations and the individuals in them in the position of having to wrestle with "no growth" or shrinking volume scenarios instead of the expansion that had been the norm. In the 1990s, growing pressure from global competitors and the drive for improved, costly technology shrank profit margins. Absence of growth and shrinking margins led to downsizing to maintain overall profitability and desirability to capital markets. Whether to maintain their jobs, volume-incentive-based earnings, or their company, some people resorted to questionable ethical practices, including falsification of transactions and other records, and the exploitation of the environment or workers. The result has been part of the reason for triggering the cases of environmental or financial malfeasance.

The development of global markets has led to the manufacture and sourcing of products throughout the world. The accompanying restructuring has been viewed as enabling greater productivity and lower costs with lower rates of domestic employment. Therefore, the pressure on employed individuals to maintain their jobs may not abate as production increases. Nor, given greater competition, will greater volume necessarily increase profit, so the pressure on corporations will not abate to levels experienced in the past. In addition, corporations will be unable to rely on a cyclical return to profitability to restore the risk of unethical behavior to former levels. Consequently, it would appear that a return to former risk levels will depend on the institution of new regimes of ethical-behavior management and governance.

Financial Scandals: The Expectations Gap & the Credibility Gap

There is no doubt that the public has been surprised, stunned, dismayed, and devastated by financial fiascos. The list of recent classic examples would include: Enron, WorldCom, Adelphia, Tyco, HealthSouth, Parmalat, Royal Ahold, Barings Bank, Livent, and Bre-X, the U.S. subprime lending disaster as well as the slightly older U.S. Savings and Loan bankruptcies and bailout and the bankruptcies of several real estate companies.

As a result of these repeated shocks, the public has become cynical about the financial integrity of corporations, so much so that the term *expectations gap* has been coined to describe the difference between what the public thinks it is getting in audited financial statements and what it is actually getting. The public outrage over repeated financial fiascos has led, in both the United States and Canada, to tighter regulation, higher fines, and investigations into the integrity, independence, and role of the accounting and auditing profession, and more recently of executives and directors.

On a broader basis, continuing financial malfeasance has lead to a crisis of confidence over corporate reporting and governance. This lack of credibility has spread from the financial stewardship to encompass other spheres of corporate activity and has become known as the *credibility gap*. Audit committees and ethics committees, both peopled by a majority of outside directors; the widespread creation of corporate codes of conduct; and the increase of corporate reporting designed to promote the integrity of the corporation all testify to the importance being assigned to this crisis.

No longer is it presumed that "whatever company 'X' does is in the best interests of the country." Fiascos related to the environment or to dealings with employees, customers, shareholders, or creditors have put the onus on corporations to manage their affairs more ethically and to demonstrate that they have done so.

Devastated by the sequence of U.S. disasters in 2001 and 2002 involving Enron, Arthur Andersen, and WorldCom, public confidence evaporated in the business community, its financial reporting, and in the accounting profession. Capital markets were reeling. President Bush and other business leaders strove to restore lost confidence, but their efforts were largely in vain. Finally, in record time, the U.S. Congress and Senate passed the Sarbanes-Oxley Act of 2002 (SOX) on July 30. That act provides for the reform of both corporate governance and the accounting profession, first in the United States, then indirectly in Canada and around the world. Further details are provided in the next chapter.

Governance Failures & Risk Assessment

The Enron, Arthur Andersen, and WorldCom series of disasters made clear that current existing modes governing companies and reporting on their activities were not sufficient to protect investors' interests and, more broadly, the public interest in orderly markets and corporate activities.

Corporate directors have been expected to ensure that their corporations have been acting in the interests of investors within the range of activity deemed suitable by the societies in which they operated. But in the Enron, WorldCom, and other cases, the oversight by company directors failed to contain the greed of executives, managers, and other employees. These and other companies were out of control, and unacceptable practices resulted. To quote the U.S. Senate's report on the *Role of the Board of Directors in the Collapse of Enron*:

> (1) **Fiduciary Failure.** The Enron Board of Directors failed to safeguard Enron shareholders and contributed to the collapse of the seventh largest public company in the United States, by allowing Enron to engage in high risk accounting, inappropriate conflict of interest transactions, extensive undisclosed off-the-books activities, and excessive executive compensation. The Board witnessed numerous indications of questionable practices by Enron management over several years, but chose to ignore them to the detriment of Enron shareholders, employees and business associates.
>
> *Role of the Board of Directors in the Collapse of Enron,*
> U.S. Senate's Permanent Subcommittee on Investigations, 2002, 3.

Clearly, the public was fed up with directors, executives, and others enriching themselves at the public's expense. It was evident that directors and executives were not identifying, assessing, and managing ethics risks in the same manner or depth that they were for other business risks. But the Enron, Arthur Andersen, and WorldCom cases resulted in the bankruptcy of two of the world's largest companies and the disappearance of one of the world's most respected professional accounting firms within a year. This sudden reversal of fortunes, caused by the failure to govern ethics risks, changed the calculus of risk management profoundly. The probability of catastrophic failure caused by unmanaged ethics risks was undeniably real, and much higher than anyone expected.

Governance reform was perceived as necessary to protect the public interest. Where directors had been expected to assess and make sure that the risks faced by their corporation were properly managed, ethics risks were now seen to be a key aspect of the process. Governance reform to ensure that this would happen was overdue.

Increased Accountability Desired

The lack of trust in corporate processes and activities also spawned the desire for increased accountability on the part of investors and particularly by other stakeholders. Companies around the world have responded by publishing more information on their websites and free-standing reports on their corporate social responsibility (CSR) performance, including such subjects as environmental, health and safety, philanthropic, and other social impacts. Although some information in these reports is skewed toward management objectives, the advent of external verification and the reaction to misinformation are gradually improving the information content involved. The trend is definitely toward increased nonfinancial reporting to match the public's growing expectations.

Synergy Among Factors & Institutional Reinforcement

Linkages among the factors affecting public expectations for ethical performance have already been identified, but not the extent to which these linkages reinforce each other and add to the public's desire for action. Few days go by in which the daily newspapers, radio, and television do not feature a financial fiasco, a product safety issue, an environmental problem, or an article on gender equity or discrimination. In aggregate, the result is a cumulative heightening of the public's awareness of the need for controls on unethical corporate behavior. In addition, there are many examples emerging where business executives did not make the right decision and where ethical consumers or investors acted and were successful in making companies change their practices or improve their governance structures to ensure that future decision processes were more wholesome. The entire ethical consumer and SRI movement has been strengthened by the knowledge that acting on their concerns can make companies and society better, not poorer.

In turn, the public's awareness impacts on politicians, who react by preparing new laws or the tightening of regulations. In effect, the many issues reaching the public's consciousness result in institutional reinforcement and codification in the laws of the land. The multiplicity of ethical problems receiving exposure is focusing thought on the need for more ethical action, much like a snowball gathering speed as it goes downhill.

One of the most important examples of new legislation is the *U.S. Sentencing Guidelines of 1991.* As previously noted, it spawned a significant interest by directors and executives everywhere in North America in whether their companies were providing enough guidance to their personnel about proper behavior. The consequences for not doing so before had been minor since directors and senior officers had rarely been held personally accountable for the actions of their employees, and their companies had been able to escape significant fines.

A second example is the new antibribery regime spawned by Transparency International's influence on the Organization for Economic Cooperation and Development (OECD), some thirty of whose member countries have signed a protocol declaring that they will enact antibribery legislation similar to that of the U.S. Foreign Corrupt Practices Act, which bans bribery of foreign officials. The new antibribery regime is more advanced in that it seeks to facilitate extraterritorial legal action.

Perhaps the most significant example is the Sarbanes-Oxley Act (SOX) of 2002, which is driving the reform of corporate governance and professional accounting throughout the world. The rationale that generated SOX, its nature, and impact are the subject of Chapter 2.

The desire for global standards of corporate disclosure, auditing practice, and for uniform ethical behavior by professional accountants, has generated international accounting and auditing standards under the auspices of the International Accounting Standards Board (IASB) and the International Federation of Accountants (IFAC). Their creations, the International Financial Reporting Standards (IFRS) and the Code of Ethics for Professional Accountants, are the focal point for harmonization worldwide.

Since 2005, there has also been an increasing degree of interest by business leaders worldwide in the Principles for Business put forward by the Caux Round Table, as well as in Caux conferences and recommendations for ethical management practice. The Aspen Institute is a further example of an institution providing ethical leadership insights for corporate leaders. The willingness for corporate and academic leaders to become involved with such institutions is evidence of the interest and relevance of their work.

The movement toward higher levels of corporate accountability and ethical performance is no longer characterized only by leaders who are willing to go out on a limb: it has become mainstream and international.

Outcomes

Broadly speaking, public expectations have changed to exhibit less tolerance, heightened moral consciousness, and higher expectations of business behavior. In response to this heightening of expectations, a number of watchdogs and advisors have emerged to help or harry the public and business. Organizations such as Greenpeace, Pollution Probe, and Coalition for Environmentally Responsible Economies (CERES, formerly the Sierra Club) now maintain a watching brief on the business–environment interface. Consultants are available to advise corporations and so-called ethical investors on how to screen activities and investments for both profitability and ethical integrity. Mutual funds that specialize in ethical investments have sprung up to service the needs of small investors. Large investor activity has also become evident as many public-sector and not-for-profit pension funds have taken active interest in the governance of their investee corporations and have presented shareholder resolutions designed to cover their concerns. In the face of all of this interest, politicians have responded by increasing regulations and the fines and penalties (both personal and corporate) involved for malfeasance. The *credibility gap* has not favored business organizations. Lack of credibility has brought increasing regulation, international standards, as well as mainstream interest and profound changes in governance and management practices.

New Expectations for Business

New Mandate for Business

The changes in public expectations have triggered, in turn, an evolution in the mandate for business: the laissez-faire, profit-only world of Milton Friedman has given way to the view that business exists to serve society, not the other way around. For some, this may be stating the degree of change too strongly; but even they would concede that the relationship of business to society is one of interdependence where the long-run health of one determines that of the other.

In many forums, Milton Friedman made the following case:

> In a free-enterprise, private property system a corporate executive . . . has [the] responsibility to make as much money as possible while conforming to the basic rules of society, both . . . in law and in ethical custom. [This is] the appropriate way to determine the allocation of scarce resources to alternative uses.
>
> Friedman, 1970

Although there are many arguments for and against this position (see Mulligan 1986), there are three critical issues that deserve mention. They are (1) the deviation from a profit-only focus does not mean that profit will fall—in fact, profit may rise; (2) profit is now recognized as an incomplete measure of corporate performance and therefore an inaccurate measure for resource allocation; and (3) Friedman explicitly expected that performance would be within the law and ethical custom.

First, there is the myth that business could not afford to be ethical because too many opportunities would be given up for profit to be maximized; or that executives could not afford to divert their attention from profit or else profit would fall. In fact, research studies exist that show short-term profits increasing as well as decreasing when social objectives are taken into account by executives.[1] However, two long-term perspectives also strengthen the case that social and profit goals can mix profitably. The first is a study by Max Clarkson (1988), which ranked the social performance of sixty-plus companies on a modified Wartick and Cochran (1985) scale and found that above-average social performance is positively correlated with profits. The second is that the performance of some ethical mutual funds, such as the Parnassus Fund (U.S.) and the Investors Summa Fund (Canada), have surpassed that of the New York Stock Exchange as measured by the Standard & Poor's (S&P) Index, or the Toronto Stock Exchange Indices, respectively. A weighted index of 400 ethically screened U.S. stocks—the Domini Social Index—often outperforms the S&P 500. These perspectives are neither conclusive nor exhaustive, nor do they demonstrate causality. They should, however, give some comfort to executives, who hear the theoretical argument that the health of society and the business in it are interdependent, but who are wavering on the profitability of implementing a multiple-objective structure.

The second aspect of the Friedman argument that has eroded since it was first proposed is the accuracy with which profit guides the allocation of resources to their best use for society. In 1970, when Friedman began to articulate the profit-resource linkage, there was virtually no cost ascribed to the air and water used in the manufacturing process, nor was a significant cost ascribed to the disposal or treatment of wastes. Since the 1980s, the costs of these so-called externalities have skyrocketed and yet they are still not fully included in calculating the profit for the year for the polluting company under generally accepted accounting principles. Often, pollution costs are born by and charged against the profits of other companies, towns, or governments, so the original-company profit–maximum-resource-use-for-society linkage is far less direct than Friedman originally envisaged. As the cost associated with these and other externalities rises, the profit–resource use linkage promises to become less and less useful unless the framework of traditional profit computations is modified or supplemented. Perhaps environmental accounting, or schemes by which companies buy pollution credits, will yield some relief from this dilemma in the future.

Finally, Milton Friedman himself expressed the view that profit was to be sought within the laws and ethical customs of society. This is not appreciated by many who argue for profit-only in its strongest, laissez-faire, bare-knuckled form. Obviously, chaos would result if business was carried out in an absolutely-no-holds-barred environment. A minimum frame-work of rules is essential for the effective, low-cost working of our markets and the protection of all participants. Increased regulation is one response to outrageous behavior, or to the increasing ethical needs of society. What most profit-only advocates fail to see is that the alternative to increasing regulation by government is an increasing self-emphasis on better ethical governance and behavior. Interestingly, many U.S. states have already altered their corporate governance statutes to permit the consideration by directors of both shareholder and stakeholder interests.

Those who focus on profit-only often make short-term opportunistic decisions that jeopardize sustainable long-run profits. They often lose sight of the fact that sustained profit is the consequence of providing high-quality goods and services, within the law and ethical norms in an efficient and effective manner. It is far more effective to focus on providing goods and services

---

1. See, for example, the study by Curtis Verschoor, 1998.

required by society efficiently, effectively, legally, and ethically than to adopt the high-risk goal of making profit any way possible.

For these reasons, the profit-only mandate of corporations is evolving to one recognizing the interdependence of business and society. Future success will depend on the degree to which business can balance both profit and the interests of other stakeholders. This, in turn, will be impossible to manage unless new governance and reporting structures emerge. If ethical and economic objectives cannot be integrated or balanced successfully, and the interests of shareholders continue to unreasonably dominate those of stakeholders, the tension between business and society's stakeholders will continue to grow. Fortunately, the mandate for business is changing; so the focus is shifting from a narrow shareholder-oriented view of what business is achieving to include what and how a broader stakeholder-oriented set of achievements is achieved. *Judgments of the future success of corporations will be made within the broader stakeholder-oriented framework, including both what is achieved and how it is achieved.*

New Governance & Accountability Frameworks

Based on this analysis, successful corporations would be best served by governance and accountability mechanisms that focus on a different and broader set of fiduciary relationships than in the past. The allegiances of directors and executives must reflect stakeholder interests in terms of goals, processes, and outcomes. Governance objectives and processes must direct attention to these new perspectives, and modern accountability frameworks should include reports that focus on them. If not, the public's expectations will not be met, and regulations may be created to ensure such attention and focus.

Reinforced Fiduciary Role for Professional Accountants

The public's expectations for trustworthy reports on corporate performance cannot be met unless the professional accountants who prepare or audit those reports focus their primary loyalty on the public interest and adopt principles such as independence of judgment, objectivity, and integrity that protect the public interest. Loyalty to management and/or directors can be misguided because they have frequently proven to be so self-interested that they are untrustworthy. Directors who are supposed to govern management often rely extensively upon professional accountants to fulfill their fiduciary responsibilities. Consequently, the primary fiduciary responsibility of professional accountants should be to the public, or to the public interest. Otherwise, the expectations of stakeholders in society will not be met, and the credibility of corporations will erode, as will the credibility and reputation of the accounting profession.

This is not a new assignment. However, as shown in the Enron, Arthur Andersen, and WorldCom cases, professional accountants have, on occasion, lost track of whom they should ultimately be responsible to. Failure to understand this expectation, and the underpinning values of independence, integrity, and objective judgment and reporting, caused the collapse of the entire Arthur Andersen firm.

In addition, these corporate failures have brought the realization that loyalty to the public means more than just loyalty to current investors. Future investors rely on financial reports, and their interests need to be protected as well as those of other stakeholders in the corporation's broadened fiduciary model.

Reform of the accounting profession is underway in order to reinforce these expectations of the public. The impetus for recent reform, while begun with SOX, the SEC and the PCAOB in the United States, has shifted to harmonization with the global standards worked out under the auspices of the IASB and IFAC. As discussed in later chapters, these global standards have returned professional accountants to a focus on serving the public interest.

Responses & Developments

Emerging Governance & Stakeholder Accountability Models

The reaction by business to the evolution from a profit-only mandate to one recognizing the interdependence of business and society became more readily observable as the 1990s progressed. In addition, several other important trends developed as a result of economic and competitive pressures that had and continue to have an effect on the ethics of business, and therefore on the professional accountant. These trends included:

- expanding legal liability for corporate directors,
- management assertions to shareholders on the adequacy of internal controls, and
- a stated intention to manage risk and protect reputation,

even though significant changes were also occurring in how organizations operate, including:

- delayering, employee empowerment, and the use of electronic data interfaces, and
- increased reliance by management on non-financial performance indicators used on a real-time basis.

As a result of these trends and changes, corporations began to take a much greater interest in how ethical their activities were, and how to ensure that ethical problems did not arise. It became evident that the traditional command-and-control (top-down) approach was not sufficient, and that organizations needed to create an environment favorable to ethical behavior to foster it, not to impose it. Boards and management were becoming more interested in ethical issues in spite of the larger size, quicker pace, and complexity of business entities and dealings that were decreasing the ability to check and inspect the decisions of others. Consequently, it has become increasingly important that each employee have a personal code of behavior that is compatible with that of the employer. The pathway to these realizations took the following steps.

The initial corporate reaction to a more demanding ethical environment was the desire to know how ethical their activities have been, then to attempt to manage their employees' actions by developing a code of ethics/conduct. After implementing the code, the desire was to monitor activities in relation to it and to report on that behavior, first internally and then externally.

The desire to know about the appropriateness of their activities led many corporations to undertake an inventory of significant impacts on various aspects of society. Often organized by program and by stakeholder group, these listings could be used to identify specific issues, policies, products, or programs that were the most problematic and therefore needed earliest remedial attention.

It quickly became clear that the "inventory and fix" approach led to a "patched-up" system for governing employee behavior: one that was incomplete and did not offer ethical guidance on all or even most issues to be faced. Employees who had committed a malfeasance, whether voluntarily or not, could still frequently claim that "nobody told me not to do it." In order to reduce this vulnerability and provide adequate guidance, corporations began to develop and implement comprehensive codes of conduct/ethics.

Neither easy to develop nor universally accepted, codes usually had to be refined through a number of revisions. Implementation processes also had to be improved. Even today, some executives are uncertain of their role and how to play it most successfully to facilitate strong commitment by employees to the ethical principles involved. More detailed information on the role, nature, content, and monitoring of performance relative to codes is provided in Chapter 5. It is evident that codes of conduct will continue to be the touchstone for the ethical guidance of employees for the foreseeable future.

Although codes of conduct offer an essential framework for employee decision making and control, those corporations in highly vulnerable positions due to their products or productive processes found it in their interest to develop early warning information systems to facilitate fast remedial action in the event of a problem. For instance, Occidental Petroleum recognized its capacity to damage the environment and created a three-tier, notification-to-head-office requirement to provide timely information to senior management and experts in cleanup procedures. Depending on the seriousness of the environmental problem, a "significant matter" had to be reported by computer immediately, an "excursion" within twelve hours (the next business day in New York), or a "reportable incident" within the next reporting cycle (Friedman 1988). This type of notification system is essential to facilitate crisis management activities and to mobilize response resources on a worldwide basis in an effort to reduce the impact of the problem on the environment and the corporation.

Not content to encourage the use of ethics just through a code of conduct, leading-edge corporations sought ways to inculcate ethics into their corporate culture—the system of shared values that drive action—to foster specific consideration of ethical conduct in operating decisions, in strategic decision-making, and in crisis management practices. Mechanisms were developed to ensure that ethical principles were understood, reinforced, and not lost sight of. These include general training and training to instill decision frameworks designed to produce sound ethical decisions; compliance check-off lists; the encouragement of internal whistle-blowing to ombudspersons; mind-focusing scorecards and categorizations for operations and strategies; inclusion of ethical performance as a factor in the determination of remuneration and in continuing internal and external reports; the creation of specific ethical operating goals such as for equity employment levels; and the creation of whistle-blowing programs and executive positions like chief ethics or compliance officer, ombudsperson, vice president for environmental affairs, and of specific subcommittees of the board of directors to oversee the ethical performance of the corporation.

Although the commitment to these mechanisms grew during the 1980s and early 1990s, nothing galvanized the corporate community more than (1) the promulgation of the *U.S. Sentencing Guidelines* for environmental offenses on November 1, 1991, which led to widespread concern about "due diligence" procedures; and (2) the realization in the summer of 1992 that GE had been sued under the False Claims Act in the United States for $70 million by a whistle-blower too fearful of retribution to report internally to the company (Singer 1992, 19). The fact that the whistle-blower could receive up to 25 percent of the outcome was considered shocking, just as the size of the fines in the *U.S. Sentencing Guidelines* had been a year earlier. In combination, these events matured the realization that corporations ought to create an ethical operating environment in order to protect their interests and those of others with a stake in the activities of the corporation.

As a result of the *U.S. Sentencing Guidelines,* many U.S. directors and executives suddenly became very interested in the governance mechanism that was to convey appropriate guidance to their personnel. U.S.-owned, foreign subsidiaries were also involved, as were foreign-owned multinational companies operating in the United States. Consequently, and with the additional stiffening of penalties for environmental malfeasance in Canada, the governance structures of major companies that had been primarily focused on making a profit now began to include a serious focus on how that profit was made.

Early in 1994, Lynn Sharp Paine published a seminal article in the *Harvard Business Review* entitled "Managing for Integrity" in which she made the case for integrating ethics and management. It is reproduced as a reading at the end of the chapter. At about the same time, pronouncements from the Toronto Stock Exchange[2] (1994) and the Canadian Institute of

---

2. See paragraphs 4.3 and 4.4 on page 17 of the *Report of the Toronto Stock Exchange Committee on Corporate Governance in Canada,* December 1994.

Chartered Accountants[3] (1995) specified that directors were to provide the "social conscience" of their companies and that directors were responsible for developing and maintaining an ethical culture at their companies sufficient to support an adequate system of internal control. Without adequate ethical grounds for systems of internal control, the financial statements of the enterprise would be of varying accuracy, and the actions of employees might or might not correspond with what the directors and senior executives hoped. Many examples are available that attest to the fact that without adequate ethical underpinning, companies can get into difficulty.

Later, in 1996, the *Caremark National Case,*[4] which was decided in the Chancery Court of Delaware, added to directors' responsibilities the requirement of proactively seeking out ethical problems. Until this case was decided, directors could claim "hear no evil, see no evil" to avoid prosecution for some corporate wrongdoing, so there were times that directors "didn't want to hear about..." for their own protection. Unfortunately, that left the corporation rudderless. The bottom line is that the expectations for proper corporate governance have changed, and directors are responding—some more quickly than others.

Additionally during the 1990s, it became understood that management approaches must reflect accountability to stakeholders, not just shareholders. Companies have a wide range of stakeholders—employees, customers, shareholders, suppliers, lenders, environmentalists, governments, and so on—who have a stake in the activities or impacts of the corporation. Even though these stakeholders may not have a legal claim on the corporation, they can influence its fortunes in the short and long runs. Consequently, if a corporation wants to achieve its strategic objectives optimally, the interests of its stakeholders should be taken into account when management make decisions. The best way to do this is to build the recognition of stakeholder interests into the strategic planning exercise. Further insight into the principles of stakeholder management can be found at http://www.mgmt.utoronto.ca/~stake/ (The *Redefining the Corporation Project* website). Schematically, the emerging stakeholder accountability and governance frameworks are represented in Figures 1.1 and 1.2. It is now recognized that *although corporations are legally responsible to shareholders, they are strategically responsible to stakeholders.*

Management Based on Values, Reputation, & Risks

In order to incorporate the interests of stakeholders into the policies, strategies, and operations of their corporation, directors, executives, managers, and other employees must understand the nature of their stakeholders' interests and the values that underpin them. The reputation of the company and the degree of support garnered from stakeholders will depend on this understanding and on the ability of the company to manage the risks facing the company directly, as well as those impacting its stakeholders.

Numerous approaches have been developed for examining the interests of stakeholders, such as surveys, focus groups, and mapping according to stereotypes. These are developed more extensively in Chapter 5.

In addition, investigation is underway on the values that lie behind stakeholder interests so that a corporation's policies, strategies, and procedures can take them into account. These values differ somewhat depending on the stakeholder group, as well as regional differences. However, progress has been made toward a set of *hypernorms*—values that are respected by most groups or

---

3. See page 2, paragraph 8 of *Guidance for Directors—Governance Processes for Control,* December 1995, published by the Canadian Institute of Chartered Accountants, Toronto, Canada. See also pages 8 and 9 for a discussion of approving and monitoring the organization's ethical values.
4. For additional information on the *Caremark National Case,* see the case summary in the readings section of this chapter.

FIGURE 1.1

Map of Corporate Stakeholder Accountability

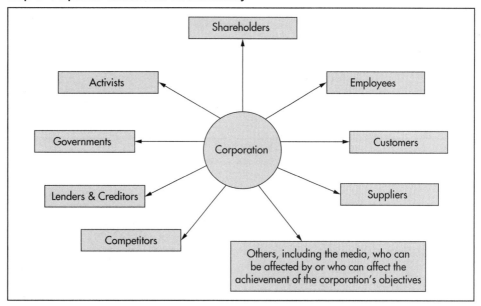

FIGURE 1.2

Corporate Governance Framework

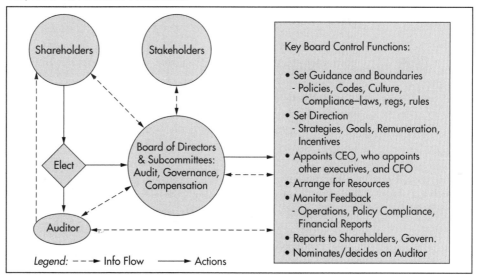

cultures around the world. According to researchers, the six values known to come closest to universal application around the world are those noted in Table 1.2.

The relevance of these six hypernorms is very significant to the future success of corporations. Consequently, they should be built into a corporation's code of conduct, policies, strategies, and activities in an attempt to make sure that the interests of many stakeholder groups are respected, and that the corporation's reputation will generate maximum support.

Reputation has also been a subject of considerable recent study. Not surprisingly, the factors seen as important determinants of reputation are closely aligned with the hypernorms

TABLE **1.2**

Hypernorms (Basic Values) Underlying Stakeholder Interests

A hypernorm is a value that is almost universally respected by stakeholder groups. Therefore, if a company's activities respect a hypernorm, the company is likely to be respected by stakeholder groups and will encourage stakeholder support for company activities.

Hypernorms involve the demonstration of the following basic values: Honesty, Fairness, Compassion, Integrity, Predictability, Responsibility

Source: R. Berenbeim, Director, Working Group on Global Ethics Principles, The Conference Board, Inc., 1999.

FIGURE **1.3**

Determinants of Reputation

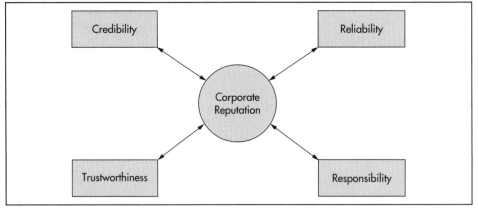

Source: Fombrun, p. 72.

previously identified. Charles Fombrun, of the Reputation Institute, has specified four determinants as identified in Figure 1.3.

Both management and auditors have become increasingly risk management oriented since the mid-1990s. Risk management techniques have been developing as directors, executives, and professional accountants recognize the value in identifying risks early and in planning to avoid or mitigate the unfortunate consequences inherent in the risks. Professional accountants have also shifted their audit approach to the examination of the risks facing a corporation, how the corporation has provided for these risks operationally, and how they have been accounted for in the records and financial reports.

An early study by Mercer Management Consulting identifies some of the risk events that were important in companies that experienced very large stock price drops between 1993 and 1998. Findings are shown in Table 1.3.

TABLE **1.3**

Risk Events Causing Drops of Over 25% Share Value, Percentage of *Fortune 1000* Companies, 1993–1998

Strategic (58%)	Customer demand shortfall (24%), Competitive pressure (12%), M & A Integration problems (7%), Misaligned products (6%), Others (9%)
Operational (31%)	Cost overruns (11%), Accounting irregularities (7%), Management ineffectiveness (7%), Supply chain pressures (6%)
Financial (6%)	Foreign, macro-economic, interest rates
Hazard and other (5%)	Lawsuits, natural disasters

Source: Mercer Management Consulting/Institute of Internal Auditors, 2001.

TABLE 1.4	**Important Risk Management Terms**

Risk is the chance of something happening that will have an impact on objectives.
Risk Management includes the culture, processes, and structures that are directed toward the effective management of potential opportunities and adverse effects.
Risk Management includes the systematic application of management policies, procedures, and practices to the tasks of establishing the context, identifying, analyzing, assessing, managing, monitoring, and communicating risk.

Source: *Managing Risk in the New Economy,* AICPA & CICA, 2001, p. 4.

Companies had not been looking systematically for such risks, but as the 1990s came to a conclusion, risk identification and assessment was becoming an important part of strategic and operational management processes, and the oversight of the risk management process was becoming an important part of directors' due diligence activities. Several studies have been published that provide insights on the subject, including those by the Institute of Internal Auditors (2001), the American Institute of Certified Public Accountants, and the Canadian Institute of Chartered Accountants (2001). Important risk management terms are reproduced in Table 1.4.

During late 2001 and into 2002, the financial world was rocked by the Enron, Arthur Andersen, and WorldCom scandals, and the resulting outrage triggered the creation of corporate governance reform through the enactment of the Sarbanes-Oxley Act of 2002 in the United States. This act and the resulting U.S. Securities and Exchange Commission (SEC) regulations have transformed corporate governance expectations significantly, including the requirement that directors are now expected to ensure that their corporation has, among many other governance mechanisms, an effective risk management process. Many jurisdictions around the world have responded by following suit.

Although most large corporations have put in place some form of risk management process, most do not specifically consider their ethics risks—*the risks of failing to meet the expectations of stakeholders*—in a broad and comprehensive way. However, since these ethics risks have proven to be so important to reputation and corporate sustainability in the Martha Stewart, Firestone tire recall, Enron, Arthur Andersen, WorldCom, and other similar cases, it would be a serious mistake not to include them in the risk management process. A representative list is provided in Table 1.5.

TABLE 1.5	**Ethics Risks—A Representative List**

STAKEHOLDER EXPECTATIONS NOT MET	ETHICS RISK
Shareholders	
Stealing, misuse of funds or assets	Honesty, integrity
Conflict of interests with officers	Predictability, responsibility
Performance level	Responsibility, honesty
Reporting transparency, accuracy	Honesty, integrity
Employees	
Safety	Fairness
Diversity	Fairness
Child and/or sweatshop labor	Compassion, fairness
Customers	
Safety	Fairness
Performance	Fairness, integrity
Environmentalists	
Pollution	Integrity, responsibility

In summary, particularly in view of the Enron, Arthur Andersen, WorldCom, and other cases, directors, executives, and professional accountants will find that meeting the expectations of stakeholders is increasingly important. This will involve delving into the values that determine a corporation's reputation, and managing those values so that potential risks are avoided and/or effectively mitigated. To ignore these ethics risks is to risk the fates evident in earlier corporate debacles.

Accountability

The rise of stakeholder interest and accountability, and the stunning financial debacles of Enron, Arthur Andersen, and WorldCom, has raised the desire for reports that are more relevant to the various interests of stakeholders, more transparent, and more accurate than in the past. In general, it is recognized that corporate reports frequently lack *integrity* because they do not cover some issues, nor is there always a clear, balanced presentation of how the interests of stakeholders will be affected. Sometimes issues will be mentioned, but in such an obtuse or unclear manner that the lack of *transparency* will cloud the understanding of the reader. *Accuracy*, or faithful representation, is, of course, fundamental to an understanding of the underlying facts.

The needed improvement in integrity, transparency, and accuracy has motivated the discussion among accountants about the nature of the guidelines they should use for preparation of financial reports—rules or principles. Enron's financial reports clearly lacked integrity, transparency, and accuracy, but they may have been in accord with a very narrow, rules-based interpretation of generally accepted accounting standards and legal definitions. Chapter 2 identifies how accounting rules and legal interpretations with regard to special purpose entities allowed Enron's board and executives to mislead the public, and allowed professional accountants to rationalize their participation in the process and even provide a clean audit certification of the misleading reports. The fact that the reports were probably technically compliant with the rules was taken as satisfactory, even though they did not show the whole story transparently or accurately, and many people were misled. The misuse of rules allowed fraud-intent Enron executives to take advantage of the reporting system. However, principles based on integrity, transparency, and accuracy are considered by many to provide more robust guidance than rules against such misuse.

The desire for relevancy has spawned a surge in reports that are principally nonfinancial in nature and are tailored to the needs of specific stakeholders. These stakeholder-oriented CSR reports, which are discussed more fully in Chapter 7, cover topics such as those identified in Table 1.6. They appear in hard copy and on corporate websites. Broadly applicable reporting frameworks are being developed to guide corporations by Global Reporting Initiative (GRI) for comprehensive reports, and by AccountAbility for sustainability reports.

Ethical Behavior & Developments in Business Ethics

In response to the changes previously described, there is a renewed interest in how philosophers defined ethical behavior, and the lessons that have been learned over the centuries. In addition, on a more applied level, several concepts and terms have been developed that facilitate an understanding of the evolution taking place in the accountability of business and in the making of ethical decisions.

TABLE 1.6	Stakeholder Report Topics	
Health and safety	Workplace responsibility
Sustainability	Environmental performance/impact
Philanthropy	Corporate social responsibility

| Philosophical Approaches to Ethical Behavior | Commerce and economics are as old as prehistoric times when business was based on trade and barter. The ethical theories concerning acceptable and unacceptable business behaviors are just as old, although their articulation, in a Western philosophical tradition, dates primarily from the Socratic era. Although these theories were developed at an earlier time, the logic underpinning them and the lessons involved are readily applicable to current business dilemmas, as the following examples indicate.

The Greek philosopher Aristotle argued that the goal of life is happiness, and happiness is achieved by leading a virtuous life in accordance with reason. Some of these virtues include integrity, honor, loyalty, courage, and forthrightness. In a business sense, this means that directors, executives, and accountants should demonstrate *integrity* in all their business dealings; they should *honor* the terms of contracts rather than look for loopholes; they should be *loyal* to their employees, customers, and suppliers; they should have the *courage* to be candid and transparent in their dealings with relevant stakeholders; and they should be *forthright* when providing explanations of good and bad business behavior.

The German philosopher Immanuel Kant held the position that people are ethical when they do not use other people opportunistically, and when they do not act in a hypocritical manner demanding a high level of conduct for everyone else, while making exceptions for themselves. Unfortunately, there are many instances of organizations that do not live up to this standard. Some treat employees, customers, and suppliers merely as a means, exploiting them for some short-term goal. Often businesses are rightly accused of hypocrisy when they fail to live up to their own internally generated codes of conduct.

The English philosopher John Stuart Mill argued that the goal of life is to maximize happiness and/or to minimize unhappiness or pain, and the goal of society is to maximize the net social benefits to all people. Degrees of happiness can be both physical and psychological. So, this theory implies that the goal of business is to contribute to increasing the physical and/or psychological benefits of society. This does not means that the goal of business is to maximize its profits; rather, the goal of business is to contribute to the overall good of society. Business does so by providing goods and services required by society.

The American philosopher John Rawls contends that society should be structured so that there is a fair distribution of rights and benefits, and that any inequalities should be to everyone's advantage. This implies that businesses act in an ethical manner when they do not have discriminatory prices and hiring systems. Nor should businesses provide goods and services to one segment of society at the expense of other segments of society. Pollution and exploiting developing countries so that developed nations can have an opulent lifestyle is not to everyone's advantage.

These are but four examples of Western philosophic approaches to business ethics. They are more fully explained in Chapter 3. Suffice to say that these theories set a high standard for acceptable business behavior. Studying these theories should help directors, executives, and accountants to better understand the ethical foundations of business and provide a basis for conducting business in a socially responsible manner.

| Business Ethics Concepts & Terms | Two developments are particularly useful in understanding business ethics, and how business and the professions can benefit from its application. They are the *stakeholder concept* and the concept of a *corporate social contract*.

As the ethical environment for business changed, observers and executives realized that many more people than just shareholders had an interest in the corporation or its activities. As previously noted, although some of these had no statutory claim on the corporation, they had a very real capacity to influence the corporation favorably or unfavorably. Moreover, as time went by, the claims of some of these interested parties became codified through statute or regulation.

It became evident that the interests of this set of people with a stake in the business or its impacts—who are affected by or can affect the achievement of the organization's objectives[5]—ought to be considered in corporate plans and decisions. For ease of reference, these people have come to be known as *stakeholders* and their interests as *stakeholders' rights*. Examples of stakeholder groups would include employees, customers, suppliers, lenders, creditors, borrowers, host communities, governments, environmentalists, and, of course, shareholders. A corporation's normal set of stakeholders was mapped in Figure 1.1.

The relationship between a corporation and its stakeholders has slowly but steadily broadened over the years. Initially, the corporation was established as a means of gathering large amounts of capital from shareholders. It was accountable only to those shareholders and its goal was to generate profits. Later, when larger factories appeared, times were such that child labor was prevalent and no cost was ascribed to environmental practices that today would not be condoned. As previously described, corporate accountability has broadened to go beyond just shareholders to embrace the reality of stakeholders, and the corporate mandate has evolved to respect stakeholders' interests and thereby engender their support. Profits are to be generated, but not at any cost to society and preferably in a way that supports society. This evolving relationship between corporations and society has come to be known, in concept, as the *corporate social contract*.

| **Approaches to Ethical Decision Making** | The evolving accountability to stakeholders within the newer versions of the corporate social contract have made it incumbent on executives to ensure that their decisions reflect the ethical values established for the corporation, and do not leave out of consideration any significant stakeholder's rights. This has led to the development of ethical decision-making approaches that combine both philosophical and practical techniques, such as *stakeholder impact analysis.*

The ethical principles developed by philosophers provide insights into the key dimensions of ethical reasoning. Decision makers should understand three basic philosophical approaches: *consequentialism, deontology, and virtue ethics.* Consequentialism requires that an ethical decision have good consequences; deontology holds that an ethical act depends upon the duty, rights, and justice involved; and virtue ethics considers an act ethical if it demonstrates the virtues expected by stakeholders of the participants. These approaches are expanded on in Chapter 4 and are incorporated into three practical ethical decision-making approaches.

All approaches begin with the identification of significant stakeholders, an investigation of their interests, and a ranking of those interests to ensure that the most important are given adequate attention during the remaining analysis, and more consideration at the decision stage. Chapter 4 provides insights into the saliency of the various stakeholder interests, which are very important to the making of ethical decisions.

The first practical analytical approach, known as the *Modified Five Question Approach*, involves challenging any proposed policy or action with five questions designed to rate the proposal on the following scales: profitability, legality, fairness, impact on the rights of each individual stakeholder, and on the environment specifically, as well as the demonstration of virtues expected by stakeholders. The questions are asked and options for action are discarded depending on the degree to which corporate ethical values and stakeholder interests are offended. Often, action options can be modified to be made more ethical as a result of these challenges (Tucker 1990).

The *Modified Moral Standards Approach*, originally developed by Professor Manuel Velasquez (1992), focuses on four dimensions of the impact of the proposed action: (1) whether

---

5. R. E. Freeman. *Strategic Management: A Stakeholder Approach.* Boston: Pitman, 1984.

it provides a net benefit to society; (2) whether it is fair to all stakeholders; (3) whether it is right; and (4) whether it demonstrates the virtues expected by stakeholders. Although there is some overlap with the first approach, Velasquez's focus is less company-centered and is therefore better suited to the evaluation of decisions in which the impact on stakeholders outside the corporation is likely to be very severe. Longer-term impacts are also more readily incorporated.

The last approach to stakeholder impact analysis to be presented in Chapter 4 is the *Modified Pastin Approach*, created by Professor Mark Pastin (1986), who extends the Moral Standards Approach by taking specific account of the culture within the corporation and of so-called commons problems. Pastin suggests that any proposed decision be evaluated in comparison to the company's ground rules (he calls this "ground rule ethics"); the net benefit it produces ("end-point ethics"); whether it impinges on any stakeholder's rights and requires rules to resolve the conflict ("rule ethics"); and, finally, whether it abuses rights apparently belonging to everyone ("problems of the commons"). The addition of the "virtues demonstrated" question (whether it demonstrates the virtues expected by stakeholders) produces a Modified Pastin approach that is quite practical and is best suited to decisions with impacts primarily on stakeholders directly attached to the corporation, such as employees or customers.

Chapters 4 and 7 provide frameworks for the management of issues using the stakeholder impact analysis.

The use of stakeholder impact analysis in management decision making and in the management of contentious issues will contribute significantly to the development of defensible positions that are necessary to the development and maintenance of stakeholder support for corporate activities.

The Ethics Environment for Professional Accountants

Role & Conduct

The aftermath of the Enron, Arthur Andersen, and WorldCom debacles will bring fundamental changes in the role and conduct of those professional accountants who have forgotten where their primary duty is owed. Professional accountants owe their primary loyalty to the public interest, not just to their own financial interests, company directors or management, or current shareholders at the expense of future shareholders. The reasons for these changes are made clear in Chapters 2, 3, 4, and 5, but just as in the case of corporate governance, cracks that had been apparent for some time in the governance framework for professional accountants became so serious that the public credibility of the profession was virtually destroyed. Reforms, through new regulations and supervisory structures, and internationally harmonized standards of disclosure and revised codes of conduct that rededicate the accounting profession to its original fiduciary roots, have become a necessary restorative that will influence professional accounting behavior around the world.

The need for additional changes in the role and conduct of professional accountants predates the recent debacles. Whether they are involved in the audit or assurance service functions, in management, in consulting, or as directors, professional accountants have been looked on historically as the arbiters of organizational accountability and experts in the science of decision making. Because we are witnessing a "sea change" in corporate accountability with a broadening beyond just shareholders to stakeholders, it is incumbent on accountants to understand this evolution and how it can impact upon their function. If they do not do so, substandard advice may be given, and the legal and nonlegal consequences for ethical shortfalls can be severe.

There is also a very real possibility that the *expectations gap* between what users of audits and financial statements thought they had been getting and what they are receiving will be exacerbated if accountants are seen to be out of step with emerging standards of ethical behavior. Studies have been undertaken, such as those by the Treadway Commission in the United States, the Macdonald Commission in Canada, and the Cadbury Report in the United Kingdom, which have called for recognition of new levels of ethical behavior in revisions to professional codes of conduct. Some professional codes were revised in response, but Enron and the other debacles have put the spotlight on further revisions. A thorough understanding of the reasons for these revisions and the underlying principles involved are essential for their proper application and the protection of professionals, the profession, and the public.

An appreciation of the sea change underway in the ethics environment for business is essential to an informed understanding of how professional accountants ought to interpret their profession's code as employees of corporations. Although the public expects all professional accountants to respect the professional values of objectivity, integrity, and confidentiality, which are designed to protect the fundamental rights of the public, an employee-accountant must respond to the direction of management and the needs of current shareholders. Trade-offs are difficult. In the future, there will be less escape from the glare of public scrutiny, and greater danger in greeting problems with a wink and a nod, or by sweeping them under the rug. Professional accountants will have to ensure that their ethical values are current and that they are prepared to act on them to best exercise their role and to maintain the credibility of, and support for, the profession.

Governance

Globalization and internationalization have come to the corporate world, the capital markets, and corporate accountability. Stakeholders are global in their reach, and events that were kept secret in far-off jungles are now shown worldwide each evening on CNN, BBC World News, or in revealing environmental protection or human rights documentaries. Corporations with dealings around the world are conscious that they are increasingly accountable for each of their operations and are looking for effective ways to manage, account for, and disclose activities around the world. These approaches are discussed in Chapter 5 and include the development and maintenance of ethics programs, ethical cultures, codes of conduct, and particularly ethical leadership.

In the accounting profession, the movement to a globally harmonized set of generally accepted accounting and auditing principles (GAAP and GAAS) to provide analytical efficiencies for the providers of capital to the world's markets and computational and audit efficiencies around the world. Consequently, there is a plan to gradually harmonize the set of GAAP developed by the International Accounting Standards Board (IASB) in London, England, and those developed by the U.S. Financial Accounting Standards Board (FASB) into a common set that will apply in all countries.

Concurrently, the International Federation of Accountants (IFAC) has developed an international Code of Ethics for Professional Accountants, and all IFAC-member countries have agreed to standardize their country's code on the same or similar basis to the new international code. The details of this international code are reviewed in Chapter 6.

The principles inherent in the new international code *will therefore become* the basis for future behavior and education of professional accountants. Difficult areas of professional behavior, such as the identification and management of conflicts of interest, will receive a fresh set of guidelines. These are also discussed in Chapter 6.

Globalization has also come to audit firms. They are developing global audit standards to serve their major clients, and supportive behavior standards to ensure their judgments are independent, objective, and accurate. The new rulings of the U.S. Securities and Exchange Commission, motivated by the Sarbanes-Oxley Act and the Enron, Arthur Andersen and

WorldCom fiascos, will inform these global standards. Consequently, the IFAC-SOX-SEC intention to reinforce the professional accountant's focus on the public interest will be extended worldwide even if disclosure and audit standards ultimately differ between publicly traded and privately held corporations.

Services Offered

In this recently redefined global environment, the offering of nonaudit services to audit clients, which was a contentious issue for Arthur Andersen in the Enron debacle, has been curtailed so that tighter conflict-of-interest expectations can be met. The advent and growth of multi-disciplinary firms in the late 1990s, which included professionals such as lawyers and engineers to provide a broader range of assurance and other services to their audit clients, has been curtailed by revised SEC and other standards and several major audit firms have sold off part of their consulting units. Professional accountants should be particularly alert to conflicts in which the values and codes of other professionals in their employ differ from those of the accounting profession. Chapters 5 and 6 provide insights into these conflicts of interest.

Managing Ethics Risks & Opportunities

The impact increasing expectations for business in general, and for directors, executives, and accountants in particular, has brought demands for governance reform, ethical decision making, and management that would benefit from leading-edge thinking on how to manage ethics risks and opportunities. Several important topics in this regard are discussed in Chapter 7.

Guidance is provided for the process of ethics risk identification, caution is advised against overreliance on external auditors for this purpose, and insights are offered for the management and reporting of ethics risks.

Next, effective strategies and mechanisms for influencing stakeholders are discussed with the view of developing and maintaining their support. Linkages are made between ethics risk management and traditional environmental scanning or issues management, and also to the field of business-government relations. Both of these can benefit significantly from a broadened, modern stakeholder accountability perspective.

Business and professional accounting inevitably depend on people—both as external, and perhaps more important, internal stakeholders such as employees. Understanding expectations for workplace ethics is extremely important to the success of all organizations and their executives. Employee rights are changing, as are expectations for privacy, dignity, fair treatment, health and safety, and exercising one's conscience. Development of trust, which depends on ethical values and is so important to communications, cooperation, the sharing of ideas, the excellence of innovation, and the exercise of modern leadership, is also a critical success factor. So important are these dimensions of workplace ethics that expert observers believe *the way employees view their own treatment by the company determines what the employees think about their company's ethics program.* A company cannot have an effective ethical corporate culture without laudable workplace ethics.

Most companies deal with different cultures in their hiring and management of personnel even if their operations are within one country. Most modern corporations, however, deal internationally and should understand how their impacts are regarded as well as the sensitivities they arouse. Handling these ethically is a growing expectation and will contribute significantly to the achievement of strategic objectives.

Part of the ethical puzzle for modern corporations to sort out is the giving and receiving of gifts, bribes, and facilitating payments. All of these create conflicts of interest, but they are expected in many cultures. Insights are provided, including comment on using moral imagination, into how to handle these challenges ethically, respect the interest of different cultures, and protect the corporation.

Corporate social responsibility (CSR) and telling the company's story through CSR reporting are important parts of strategic planning and the achievement of strategic objectives. Developing the kind of corporate citizenship the leaders and stakeholders of the company want is necessarily an extension of the ethical values that are fundamental to the organization's ethical culture. Exciting new frameworks are emerging that directors, executives, and professional accountants would be well advised to watch in order to take advantage of new opportunities as they arise. Reports on CSR programs and assurance thereon are growing rapidly.

Finally, businesspeople with experience know that crises are inevitable, and that crisis management approaches have been developed to ensure that corporations and executives do not suffer more damage to their prospects and reputation than necessary. In fact, if the ethical aspects of crises are properly managed, reputation can be enhanced. Incorporating ethics into crisis management can clearly turn a risk into an opportunity.

The next chapter, "Governance, Accounting, and Auditing Reform Post-Enron," examines the debacles that triggered the new era of governance and accountability for corporations and the accounting profession.

Questions

1. Why have concerns over pollution become so important for management and directors?

2. Why are we more concerned now than our parents were about fair treatment of employees?

3. What could professional accountants have done to prevent the development of the *credibility gap* and the *expectations gap*?

4. Why might ethical corporate behavior lead to higher profitability?

5. Why is it important for the clients of professional accountants to be ethical?

6. How can corporations ensure that their employees behave ethically?

7. Should executives and directors be sent to jail for the acts of their corporation's employees?

8. Why are the expectations of a corporation's stakeholders important to the reputation of the corporation and to its profitability?

9. How can a corporation show respect for its stakeholders?

10. How can conflicts between the interests of stakeholders be resolved by a corporation's management?

11. Why are philosophical approaches to ethical decision making relevant to modern corporations and professional accountants?

12. What are the common elements of the three practical approaches to ethical decision making that are briefly outlined in this chapter?

13. Is a professional accountant a businessperson pursuing profit or a fiduciary that is to act in the public interest?

14. Why is it important for a professional accountant to understand the ethical trends discussed in this chapter?

15. Why should a professional accountant be aware of the Ethics Code of the International Federation of Accountants?

16. Why is an ethical corporate culture important?

Reading Insights

The selection of readings that follows has been chosen to provide background material to enrich the understanding of the issues identified in this chapter. Lynn Sharp Paine's classic article provides the most compelling arguments for incorporating integrity into corporate decision making and operations, and provides insights into how to make this happen. The article by Andrew Singer reveals the significance of whistleblowing and the impact it may have on corporations. This impact is one of the catalysts that will lead companies to want to develop ethical corporate cultures in the future. The Caremark National law case dramatically altered directors' responsibilities for overseeing corporations to require them to search out ethical problems rather than wait until they were informed.

References

Achar, R., D. Nitkin, K. Otto, P. Pellizzari, and EthicScan Canada. *Shopping with a Conscience: The Informed Shopper's Guide to Retailers, Suppliers, and Service Providers in Canada.* Toronto: John Wiley & Sons, 1996.

American Institute of Certified Public Accountants (AICPA) and The Canadian Institute of Chartered Accountants (CICA), *Managing Risk in the New Economy,* 2001, p. 4.

Canadian Institute of Chartered Accountants. *Guidance for Directors—Governance Processes for Control.* Toronto, Canada, December 1995. See page 2, paragraph 8 and also pages 8 and 9 for a discussion of approving and monitoring the organization's ethical values.

Clarkson, Max. B. E. "Corporate Social Performance in Canada, 1976–86." *Research in Social Performance and Policy* 10, JAI Press, (1988): 241–265.

Domini Social Index, a market capitalized-weighted common stock index, consisting of 400 U.S. corporations that have passed multiple, broad-based social screens. Maintained by Kinder, Lydenberg, Domini & Co., Cambridge, MA.

Fombrun, C. J. *Reputation: Realizing Value from the Corporate Image.* Boston: Harvard Business School Press, 1996.

Freeman, R. E. *Strategic Management: A Stakeholder Approach.* Boston: Pitman, 1984.

Friedman, F. B. *Practical Guide to Environmental Management.* Environmental Law Institute, Washington, D.C., 1988, p. 34.

Friedman, M. "The Social Responsibility of Business to Increase Profits." *New York Times Magazine.* September 13, 1970.

The Institute of Internal Auditors Research Foundation. *Guidance for Directors—Governance Processes for Control,* Canadian Institute of Chartered Accountants, Toronto, Canada., December 1995. See page 2, paragraph 8 and also pages 8 & 9 for a discussion of approving and monitoring the organization's ethical values. *Enterprise Risk Management: Trends and Emerging Practices.* 2001.

Macdonald Commission, see *The Report of the Commission to Study the Public's Expectations of Audits,* Canadian Institute of Chartered Accountants, June 1988.

Mulligan, T. "A Critique of Milton Friedman's Essay 'The Social Responsibility of Business Is to Increase Its Profits.'" *Journal of Business Ethics,* 1986, 265–269.

Organization for Economic Cooperation and Development (OECD). http://www.oecd.org.

Paine, L. S. "Managing for Integrity." *Harvard Business Review,* March-April 1994, 106–117.

Pastin, M. *The Hard Problems of Management: Gaining the Ethics Edge.* San Francisco: Jossey-Bass, 1986.

Pellizzari, P. *Conscious Consumption: Corporate Social Responsibility and Canada's Grocery Giants.* Toronto: EthicScan Canada, 2002.

Placenti, F. M. "Caremark National Case." *The National Law Journal,* June 23, 1997, B5, B6.

Report of the Toronto Stock Exchange Committee on Corporate Governance in Canada. Toronto Stock Exchange, Toronto, December 1994, paragraphs 4.3 and 4.4, p. 17.

Sarbanes-Oxley Act of 2002. See www.thomsonedu.com/accounting/brooks.

Singer, A. W. "The Whistle-Blower: Patriot or Bounty Hunter." *Across The Board,* November 1992, 16–22.

Helson, J., K. Green, D. Nitkin, and A. Stein. *The Ethical Shopper's Guide to Canadian Supermarket Products.* Toronto: Broadview Press, 1992.

The Role of the Board of Directors in Enron's Collapse. U.S. Senate's Permanent Subcommittee on Investigations, July 8, 2002. See www.thomsonedu.com/accounting/brooks.

Treadway Commission, see the *Report of the National Commission on Fraudulent Public Reporting,* AICPA, 1987.

Tucker, G. "Ethical Analysis for Environmental Problem Solving." *Agenda for Action Conference Proceedings,* The Canadian Centre for Ethics and Corporate Policy, 1990, 53–57.

U.S. Sentencing Guidelines of 1991, November 1, 1991.

Velasquez, M. G. *Business Ethics: Concepts and Cases,* 3rd ed. Englewood Cliffs, NJ: Prentice Hall, 1992.

Verschoor, Curtis, C. "A Study of the Link between a Corporation's Financial Performance and Its Commitment to Ethics." *Journal of Business Ethics* 17, no. 13, (1998): 1509–16.

Wartick, S. L., and P. L. Cochran. "The Evolution of the Corporate Social Performance Model." *Academy of Management Review* 10, no. 4, (1985): 758–769.

Case Insights

The cases that follow are designed to stimulate an awareness of ethical issues currently facing business and accountants. Specifically, the scenarios covered are as follows:

- *China's Tainted Baby Milk Powder: Rumored Control of Online News* reveals the problems excessive pursuit of profit and of lax content and health regulation that caused deaths and illness of babies in China and pets in North America. In addition, the case identifies unexpected problems associated with rumored control of online news to manage reputation risks.

- *Should Porn be Sold by Cell Phone Companies?* addresses whether companies that supply goods and services to the public need to take ethical responsibility into account.

- *Virgin Mobile's Strip2Clothe Campaign: Exploitive and Risque?* asks whether the end justifies the means in a marketing sense. Is a marketing campaign unethical that aids the homeless, but is in questionable taste?

- *The Ethics of Bankruptcy: Jetsgo Corporation* explores how the CEO of Jetsgo misled his pilots and his passengers on the day before he voluntarily had his company declare bankruptcy.

- *Bausch & Lomb's Hazardous Contact Lens Cleaner* addresses the problems associated with a voluntary product recall.

- *Magnetic Toys Can Hurt* explains how a Mega Brands' product was potentially harmful to children if they swallowed powerful magnets contained in the toys. The product was only recalled after the company was pressured by the government and the public.

- *Martha Stewart's Lost Reputation* offers an opportunity to see how Martha lost her reputation and, with investors, a lot of money, based on allegations of selling a personal investment after receiving a tip from the CEO, who was a personal friend. What constitutes reputation? How do stakeholders fit into reputation and brand image development? What constitutes insider trading, and why is it a conflict-of-interest situation? Should insider trading be encouraged or banned? These are issues raised by the case.

- *The Union Carbide–Bhopal Case* is intended to raise the reader's awareness of ethical issues facing modern corporations. It presents the reader with an event that, while improbable, happens repeatedly in different scenarios, and offers the reader an opportunity to explore what they and others believe to be appropriate levels of corporate responsibility and ethical behavior.

- *Betaseron (A)* discusses the real dilemmas that were faced by a pharmaceutical management team when they faced difficult choices affecting customers' quality of life. The ethical implications of such decisions can be ignored, but not without cost.

- *Texaco in Ecuador* outlines the environmental difficulties Texaco faced in their oil operations in Ecuador. Even after leaving the country, Texaco was sued in U.S. courts by South Americans. Did Texaco act responsibly? Could this have been prevented?

- *Where Were the Accountants?* presents a brief series of scandals and ethical problems upon which management accountants, academic accountants, and auditors could have commented on in time to significantly mitigate the outcome. Why didn't they? Should they have?

- *Resign or Serve?* introduces the problem of balancing ethical trade-offs in a modern, creative economic world. How far should an auditor go to protect a fellow professional, the profession, or the public?

Ethics Case   *China's Tainted Baby Milk Powder: Rumored Control of Online News*

On July 16, 2008, it was announced that several Chinese producers of baby milk powder had been adding melamine, a chemical usually used in countertops, to increase the "richness" of their milk powder and to increase the protein count. Shockingly, the melamine-tainted milk powder was responsible for the deaths of four infants and the sickening of more than 6,200 more.[1] Milk

---

1. "Baidu Caught in Backlash Over Tainted Milk Powder," Sky Canaves, *WSJ.com*, September 19, 2008, downloaded November 18, 2008.

manufacturers had been using melamine as a low-cost way of "enriching" their product in both taste and protein count.

Melamine, a toxic chemical that makes countertops very durable, damages kidneys.[2] This fact came to world attention on March 16, 2007, when Menu Foods of Streetsville, Ontario, Canada, recalled dog and cat foods that it had mixed in Canada from Chinese ingredients that were found to include melamine.[3] Very quickly thereafter, pet owners claims and class action lawsuits threatened to put the company into bankruptcy until settlements where worked out.[4] A subsequent investigation by the U.S. Food and Drug Administration (FDA) led to the recall of pet food by major manufacturers, including Del Monte, Nestle Purina, Menu Foods, and many others.[5] On February 6, 2008, "the FDA announced that that two Chinese nationals and the businesses they operate, along with a U.S. company and its president and chief executive officer, were indicted by a federal grand jury for their roles in a scheme to import products purported to be wheat gluten into the United States that were contaminated with melamine."[6] It will be interesting to follow what penalties are ultimately paid by the Chinese manufacturers.

Although the story of melamine-tainted ingredients broke in mid-March 2007, the similarly tainted-milk powder link did not come to light in China until sixteen months later. Governmental follow-up has not been speedy even though unmarked bags of "protein powder" had probably been added to several other products, including baking powder and feed for chickens thus contaminating eggs and meat.[7] On October 8, 2008, the Chinese government stopped reporting updated figures of infant milk powder sufferers "because it is not an infectious disease, so it's not necessary to announce it to the public."[8] Knowledgeable members of the Chinese public, however, have been using the suitcases of their visiting relatives to import U.S.- and Canadian-made milk formula for their children.

It is also fascinating to consider another aspect of life in China—rumored control of online news. Although there is no proof of the rumors, which might have been started by competitors, the *Wall Street Journal*'s (WSJ) online service has reported that Baidu.com Inc., the company referred to as the "Google of China," is under attack for accepting payments to keep stories containing a specific milk manufacturing company's name from online searches about the tainted milk scandal even when the manufacturer was recalling the product. Local government officials also declined to confirm the milk manufacturer's problem during the same period.

Baidu.com "said it had been approached this week by several dairy producers but said that it 'flat out refused' to screen out unfavorable news and accused rivals of fanning the flames."[9] In a statement, it said: "Baidu respects the truth, and our search results reflect that commitment."

Currently, there is no evidence that Baidu .com did accept the screen-out payments as rumored, but it does face some challenges of its own making in trying to restore it reputation. For example, unlike Google that separates or distinguishes paid advertisements from nonpaid search results, Baidu.com integrated paid advertisements into its search listing until critics

2. See technical report prepared by the University of Guelph Laboratory Services at http://www.labservices.uoguelph.ca/urgent.cfm

3. Press Release: "Menu Foods Income Fund Announces Precautionary Dog and Cat Food Recall," Menu Foods website at http://www.menufoods.com/recall/Press_Recall_03162007.htm, downloaded on November 24, 2008.

4. "Menu Foods settling pet food suits," Dana Flavelle, thestar.com, April 2, 2008, downloaded on November 24, 2008, from http://www.thestar.com/Business/article/408926

5. See FDA website "Pet Food Recall (Melamine)/Tainted Animal Feed," at http://www.fda.gov/oc/opacom/hottopics/petfood.html, downloaded November 24, 2008

6. Ibid.

7. 2008 Chinese milk scandal webpage, Wikipedia, downloaded from http://en.wikipedia.org/wiki/2008_Chinese_milk_scandal#Source_of_contamination on November 24, 2008.

8. Ibid.

9. Op. cit., Baidu . . .

recently complained. In addition, companies could pay more and get a higher ranking for their ads. According to the *WSJ* article, a search for "mobile phone" generates a list where almost the entire first page consists of paid advertisements. Also, competitors fearing increased competition and new products from Baidu.com, which recently increased its market share to 64.4 percent, have begun to restrict Baidu's search software (spiders) from penetrating websites that the competitors control.

Baidu.com's profit growth had been strong, but for how long? Baidu.com, Inc. is traded on the U.S.'s NASDAQ Stock Market under the symbol BIDU. Since the rumors surfaced in late August/early September 2008, BIDU's share price has declined from $308 to almost $110 on November 20, 2008.

Questions

1. Given strong profit growth, has there been any damage to Baidu.com's reputation?

2. What would future reputational damage affect, and how could it be measured?

3. What steps could Baidu.com take to restore its reputation, and what challenges will it have to overcome?

4. Governments throughout the world have been slow to react publicly to serious problems such as SARS, mad cow disease, and now melamine contamination. Who benefits and who loses because of these delays?

5. In some cultures, a "culture of secrecy" or manipulation of the news is tolerated more than others. How can this be remedied by other governments, corporations, investors, and members of the public?

6. Many other companies with long supply chains, including subcontractors in far-off lands, have found themselves in difficulty. For example, in 1995 Nike was accused of employing child labor in Pakistan and Cambodia through its subcontractors and subsequently changed its policy and practices with respect to the minimum age of employees working in contract factories. However, it is very difficult to verify age when people do not have birth certificates or when they can be bought cheaply on the black market.

   a. Under such conditions, what are a firm's responsibilities with respect to checking that each stage in the supply chain is complying with company policy?

   b. Are there organizations that can help companies set standards and confirm adherence to them? If so, what are the organizations' mandates and website addresses?

   c. Should Menu Foods be held responsible for the melamine found in its products?

   d. Would your response be different if it was the lives of people that were at stake rather than the lives of animals?

   e. How and why does Nike disclose its policies and practices with regard to supply chain responsibility, and what are the major factors covered?

Ethics Case | *Should Porn be Sold by Cell Phone Companies?*

Telus Corp., the second largest wireless company in Canada, introduced an "adult content" service to their cell phone customers in 2007. Customers were charged $3-4 for downloads, and the company expected to make very large amounts of money based on observable internet trends.

Fairly quickly, however, Telus was under pressure from customers rather than the government to discontinue the service, even though the service was apparently legal. In response, Telus' company spokespeople argued that:

▌ the service consisted of photographs and videos featuring "full and partial nudity, but no sex"

▌ customers would be age verified very rigorously to prove they were adults, and

▌ the service was already universally available, although Telus was the first wireless carrier in north America to offer such a service.[1]

---

1. "Telus hangs up on mobile porn service", Virginia Galt, *The Globe and Mail*, February 21, 2007.

There were many complaints in the form of calls from cell phone users and the Roman Catholic Church threatening to discontinue their contracts with Telus. According to Archbishop Roussin, the service "takes the accessibility of pornographic material further into the public realm."[2]

At the same time, Telus was developing a community support program involving community investment boards and ambassadors in an effort to improve its reputation and acceptance. On its website at the time, Telus stated that:

> "At Telus, we aspire to be Canada's premier corporate citizen. We are committed to building a corporate culture of giving, and engaging the hearts and minds of our team members and retirees to improve the quality of life in our communities. We recognize that leading the way in corporate social responsibility is as important as our financial performance. We have made a commitment to our customers, shareholders and all stakeholders to stay ahead or our competitors in all aspects of business—economically, environmentally and socially. Corporate social responsibility remains an integral part of what we do–it defines our business practices and culture as we strive to achieve long-term sustainable growth."[3]

Ultimately, Telus withdrew the 'adult content' service.

Questions

1. If the porn service was legal, very profitable, and readily available elsewhere, was Telus right in shutting their service down. Why or why not?
2. Given such legal and profitable opportunities, should Telus abandon its corporate social responsibility initiative? Why or why not?

---

2. "BC Archbishop Considers Cancelling Telus Contract Over Porn Sales", Gudrun Schultz, LifeSiteNews.com, February 12, 2007.
3. Telus' website at **www.telus.com/** at the community investment page. The message has changed somewhat on the current website.

Ethics Case | *Virgin Mobile's Strip2Clothe Campaign: Exploitive, Risqué and Worthwhile?*

In July of 2008 Virgin Mobile USA began a 'Strip2Clothe' advertising campaign. There are millions of homeless teenagers in the US, and Virgin Mobile's website said "someone out there needs clothes more than you." Virgin Mobile invited teenagers to upload videos of themselves disrobing. For every uploaded striptease video, Virgin Mobile would donate a new piece of clothing. For every five times the video was viewed, an additional piece of clothing would be donated. Virgin Mobile said that they would screen all the videos. The strippers had to be 18 or older, and there was to be no full nudity. By July 12 there were 20 videos on the site that had generated 51,291 pieces of donated clothing.

The campaign sparked immediate criticism. Rebecca Lentz of The Catholic Charities of St. Paul and Minneapolis called the advertising campaign "distasteful and inappropriate and exploitative." Parents were concerned that their under 18 year-old children would strip, zip the video, and not reveal their real age. On Tuesday July 15, The National Network for Youth (NN4Y) said that it would decline to partner with Virgin Mobile. Some of the 150 charities represented by NN4Y objected to the campaign saying that it was inappropriate given that many homeless teenagers are sexually exploited. NN4Y said that any member organizations that wished to receive clothing donations through the Strip2Clothe campaign would have to contact Virgin Mobile directly.

In response to the public outcry, Virgin Mobile altered its campaign. On July 21 it launched 'Blank2Clothe' in which the company would accept any kind of talent video such as walking, juggling, singing, riding, and so on. All of the striptease videos were removed and the strippers were asked to send in new, fully clothed videos.

The arguments against the campaign were that: it targeted youth; many homeless teenagers are sexually exploited; the homeless normally need shelter and safety rather than clothes; and the campaign was in poor taste. But there were some supporters. Rick Koca, founder of StandUp For Kids in San Diego, said that the campaign wasn't hurting anyone and was raising public awareness. In the one week ending July 19 the controversy and the campaign had resulted in a further 15,000 clothing donations.

Questions

1. The Strip2Clothe campaign may have been in questionable taste, but it did raise tens of thousands of pieces of clothing for the homeless. Does the end justify the means?

2. Virgin Mobile has a history of using cut-edge advertisements. It poked fun at religion in its 2004 holiday commercial "Christmas-hanukwanzakah", and it had the company's founder, Sir Richard Branson, stand in a nude suit in New York's Times Square as part of a "Nothing to Hide" campaign. Are marketing tactics that are tasteless and risqué also unethical?

3. Some years before, the Benetton Group S.p.A. developed the United Colors of Benetton Campaign, originally to draw attention to prejudice against black people. The campaign broadened over time to include other prejudices and consist of a series of shocking pictures published in unexpected venues. For example, there were pictures of a nun kissing a priest, a bombed car in a street, a white dog kissing a black lamb, an AIDS activist on his death bed in front of a picture of a crucified Christ, and a white girl portrayed with an angelic halo and a black boy with hair like horns. Is the Virgin campaign substantively different that the Benetton campaign of 1992?

4. What rule would you put forward that would differentiate ethical from unethical advertising campaigns?

Sources

"Charities Can't Bare 'Strip2Clothe' Blitz," *McClatchy News Services,* July 14, 2008. http://www.bostonherald.com/news/national/midwest/view.bg?articleid=1106844&format=text

LaVallee, Andrew, "Virgin Mobile Pulls Back Racy Campaign," *The Wall Street Journal,* July 21, 2008. http://online.wsj.com/article/SB121660673649869421.html

Simons, Abby, "Homeless Youth Network Ditches 'Strip2Clothe' Campaign, *Minneapolis-St. Paul Star Tribune,* July 15, 2008. http://www.startribune.com/local/25489799.html

---

Ethics Case

The Ethics of Bankruptcy: Jetsgo Corporation

The discount airline Jetsgo Corporation began operations in June 2002. Within two-and-half years it grew to become Canada's third-largest airline, moving approximately 17,000 passengers per day on its fleet of 29 airplanes, 15 of which were company-owned Fokker F100s. With 1,200 employees, the company serviced 20 locations in Canada, a dozen in the Caribbean, and 10 in the United States.

Jetsgo was a private company owned by Michel Leblanc. Leblanc had lived his life around airplanes. His father owned a flight school; he learnt to fly at 16. In his twenties he was an aircraft salesman; in 1978 he co-owned an eleven airplane forest-spraying business. From 1985 to 1990 he was a partner in Intair a regional airline in Quebec. In 1991, he and a new partner started Royal Aviation Inc. which he sold in 2001 for $84 million in stock to Canada 3000. Although he was subsequently sued by Canada 3000 for providing inaccurate financial information, the case was never tried because Canada 3000 went into bankruptcy protection in November 2001.

In June 2002 he launched Jetsgo. On Friday March 11, 2005, just before the busy Spring-break travel week, Jetsgo entered bankruptcy protection stranding thousands of passengers who could not return home and annoying those who could not leave on their Spring-break holiday.

Throughout its short life, Jetsgo was plagued with both financial and maintenance problems. Leblanc kept operating costs low by:

| paying low wages;

| making pilots pay for their own training;

- leasing old aircraft;

- minimizing spare parts inventory by flying only two types of airplanes: the McDonald Douglas MD-83 and the Fokker F100; and

- promoting ticket sales through the Internet.

Despite these cost saving moves, the company still had financial and maintenance problems. From 2002 to 2005 it filed a total of 60 incident reports with Transportation Canada. These included:

- Three months after it began operations, a plane had to make an emergency landing in Toronto because of a hydraulic fuel leak.

- In January 2004, smoke filled the passenger cabin of one plane due to a hydraulic fuel leak.

- In April 2004, a plane made an emergency landing in Winnipeg because of a clogged engine oil filter.

- In December 2004, a plane heading to Mexico had to return to Toronto after flames were seen coming out of an engine.

- In January 2005, a plane, landing in poor weather, slid off the runway in Calgary hitting a runway sign before taking off again.

- In March 2005, a plane made an emergency landing in Columbia, S.C. because of incorrect oil pressure in an engine. It was the second such emergency landing for the plane due to oil pressures problems.

In November 2002, Transport Canada inspectors found 23 non-conformance items with the airline. In February 2005, Transportation Canada placed restrictions on Jetsgo, and on March 8 said that operations would be suspended on April 9 if the maintenance problems were not fixed. Three days later, on March 11, the company ceased operations.

The company also had financial and cash flow problems. In the first three months of 2005 it lost $22 million. It fell behind in its payment to NAV Canada, which operates Canada's air traffic control system. On March 7, 2005, Jetsgo had to write a certified check to NAV Canada for $1.25 million–a 'hostage payment' according to Leblanc–to forestall NAV Canada from seizing some of the company's planes. After it declared bankruptcy, Jetsgo was sued by NAV Canada for an additional $1.6 million for unpaid navigation services, and $5.5 million by the Greater Toronto Airport Authority for unpaid airport improvement fees, landing fees, terminal fees and parking fees. Eight of the company's leased aircraft were left in Toronto on March 11, while all of the company-owned Fokkers were flown to Quebec City and parked in a company-leased hangar.

Leblanc decided to close down operations commencing at midnight on Thursday March 10, but would not make a public announcement until Friday. Meanwhile, he left the online booking system open. Also, on Thursday, supervisors told 13 pilots to fly their Fokker airplanes to Quebec City for maintenance checks. Leblanc subsequently said that the 'white lie' told to the pilots was justified so that all the company-owned aircraft could be kept safely in Quebec City. Leblanc felt it was better to have all the planes in one place, where they could be guarded, rather than be left at various airports across the country. "It was a white lie, but a necessary lie. You can't tell them, or the job won't get done. Half of them would have refused. The objective would not have been fulfilled and we would have had airplanes all over the damn place today and the estate of Jetsgo would not be protected." The other two company-owned Fokkers were later moved to Quebec City.

The pilots and other employees were then phoned on Friday beginning at 12:30 a.m., waking many from their sleep, and told that the company was bankrupt and that they should stay away from the airports. Customers who arrived at the airports on Friday were abruptly told that operations had been shut down. Although he expressed regret that people's travel plans had been ruined, especially before the popular Spring break, and that there were many stranded passengers across North America, Leblanc was pleased that there was no unruly behavior. "Okay, on Friday morning, there were people who didn't fly," he said. "But did you see any airport riots? Did you see 2,000 people in the terminal punching Jetsgo employees? No." Afterwards, Leblanc blamed NAV Canada and unfair competition from WestJet Airlines for causing him to close down his airline.

The stranded passengers had to make alternative arrangements to get home; some had to buy tickets on other airlines. WestJet Airlines offered $35 standby fares to the stranded pilots, flight attendants, and maintenance personnel. Some travel agencies provided refunds to their clients, and the Royal Bank said that anyone who booked a ticket online using a Royal Bank Visa card would be reimbursed by the Bank. Nevertheless, critics have said that it was callous of Leblanc to have left the online reservation system open on Thursday when he knew that the reservations made that day would never be honored.

Questions

1. For many organizations, bankruptcy protection is just another operational and financial strategy. Discuss the ethical aspects of intentionally remaining silent, collecting money and then suddenly announcing that the company is bankrupt?

2. Do you accept that the little 'white lie' told to the pilots was justifiable?

3. Was it operationally wise for Jetsgo to keep the online reservation system open until the company officially declared bankruptcy? Was it an ethically correct or incorrect decision?

4. Should Leblanc have waited until the busy Spring-break holiday period was over to then close down operations?

Sources

CBC News, "Creditors seek to seize Jetsgo aircraft," March 23, 2005. http://origin.www.cbc.ca/money/story/2005/03/23/jetsgo-050323.html

CBC News, "Jetsgo's Michel Leblanc," September 5, 2006. http://www.cbc.ca/news/background/airlines/leblanc_michel.html

Cribb, Robert, Vallance-Jones, Fred and McMahon, Tamsin, "Jetsgo problems ignored," *Toronto Star,* June 16, 2006. http://www.thestar.com/News/article/144218

Jang, Brent, "Leblanc on sorrow, remorse and his little 'while lie': Admits he misled pilots to protect planes," *The Globe and Mail,* March 18, 2005. http://www.theglobeandmail.com/servlet/Page/document/v5/content/subscribe?user_URL=http://www.theglobeandmail.com%2Fservlet%2FArticleNews%2FTPStory%2FLAC%2F20050318%2FRJETSGO18%2FTPBusiness% 2F&ord=70437229&brand=theglobeandmail&force_login=true

---

Ethics Case   *Bausch & Lomb's Hazardous Contact Lens Cleaner*

On April 13, 2006, Bausch & Lomb's (B & L) CEO, Ron Zarrella, indicated that B & L would not be recalling their soft contact lens cleaner Renu with MoistureLoc. Drugstores in the U.S.A. were, however, removing the product from their shelves due to a concern over reported infections related to Fusarium keratitis, a fungus frequently found in drains and sinks. Zarrella went on to say that Renu kills the fungus that causes the infection, and he was considering how to rebuild the brand and mitigate the "ripple-effect" caused to other B & L products. Up to April 12th, B & L's shares had fallen by 7 percent due to these health concerns.

On May 31, 2006, B & L indicated that it was halting worldwide sales of Renu because tests showed that misuse could cause blindness due to Fusarium fungal infection. "B & L said it appeared common, if frowned-upon, lens care practices—like topping off solution in storage instead of replacing it—could leave a film on

lenses that shielded Fusarium from the sterilizing agent in MoistureLoc." The company also found unacceptable manufacturing practices in the company's Greenville, South Carolina factory, but said they did not relate to the infection problem.

When Zarrella was first questioned, he knew that there had been a number of incidents of infection in Hong Kong, which B & L had reported to the U.S. Centers for Disease Control and Prevention in December 2005, as well as other reports in the U.S.A. However, another product from the Greenville plant was also implicated. Although the incidence of infection were five times higher for Renu than for any other cleaner, the evidence was not enough to halt production and sales.

At the time, lens care contributed 20 percent of the company's revenue, which had amounted to $1.75 billion in the first nine months of 2006. When the recall was announced, the company's stock rose 12.7 percent, but was $10 below its early April level. Lawsuits subsequently occurred.

Questions

1. What lessons should be taken from B & L's Renu experience?
2. What should Zarrella have done, and when?

Sources

"Bausch & Lomb refuses to recall suspect lens cleaner", Juliann Walsh and Duncan Moore, The Toronto Star, April 13, 2006, C4.

"Bausch & Lomb halting lens cleaner sales worldwide", Barnaby J. Feder, International Herald Tribune, May 31, 2006.

Ethics Case | *Magnetic Toys Can Hurt*

Mega Brands has been selling Magnetix toys for many years. It also sells Mega Bloks, construction toys based on Spider-Man, Pirates of the Caribbean, as well as other products in over 100 countries. In 2006, Mega Brands had over $547 million in revenue, including over $100 from magnetic toys, but its share price fell approximately $27 to $20.30 in mid-July 2007. One reason for the fall was that a child, who had swallowed a magnet that had fallen out of a toy, had died in the late fall of 2005. The U.S. Consumer Products Safety Commission (CPSC) had issued a product recall in March 2006.

Subsequently, a number of lawsuits appeared involving other children who had suffered bowel complications. The symptoms resulting from a child swallowing a magnet are similar to those of a stomach ache, cold or flu, and so the problem is sometimes misdiagnosed. The consequences can be much worse if a child swallows more than one magnet, particularly if they are the super-powerful magnets like those in Magnetix toys. They are so strong that they do not pass through the child's digestive system; instead, the magnets rip through tissue as they are attracted to each other. Complex surgery is required for extraction and complications can continue afterward.

After refusing twice, Mega Brands engaged in two voluntary recalls at the request of the Commission in March 2006 and April 2007. Defective merchandise was still found on store shelves by CPSC investigators in April. Even then, at a hearing on June 18, 2007, Senator Robert Durban stated: "The company did everything in its power to derail the commission's effort to take the product off the shelf." In frustration, Senator Durban commented: "When a company is selling dangerous products in America and refuses to co-operate with the CPSC, we have few laws and few tools to use to protect consumers."

In addition, the company did not quickly comply with CPSC requests for information and violated the terms of one recall. Finally, on December 1, 2007, after failing to respond on time to a subpoena, data was submitted covering 1,500 complaint reports made to Mega Brands or to Rose Art Industries, the toy's manufacturer. Mega Brands asserted that they had to search through warehouses to gather the data, because they lacked an organized comprehensive reporting system.

A new product, supposedly improved, has been introduced with new labeling that indicates the suitable minimum age to be six instead of three.

Questions

1. If you were an executive of Mega Brands, what concerns would you express to the CEO about the Magnetix toy issues noted above?
2. If the CEO didn't pay any attention, what would you do?
3. Should the CPSC have more powers to deal with such hazards and companies? If so, what would they be? If not, why not?

Source

"Magnetic toys attract suits", Gretchen Morgenson, *Financial Post*, July 17, 2007 FP3

Martha Stewart's Lost Reputation

In June 2002, Martha Stewart began to wrestle with allegations that she had improperly used inside information to sell a stock investment to an unsuspecting investing public. That was when her personal friend Sam Waksal was defending himself against Securities and Exchange Commission (SEC) allegations that he had tipped off his family members so they could sell their shares of ImClone Systems Inc. (ImClone) just before other investors learned that ImClone's fortunes were about to take a dive. Observers presumed that Martha was also tipped off and, even though she proclaimed her innocence, the rumors would not go away.

On TV daily as the reigning guru of homemaking, Martha is the multi-millionaire proprietor, president and driving force of Martha Stewart Living Omnimedia Inc. (MSO), of which, on March 18, 2002, she owned 30,713,475 (62.6 percent[1]) of the class A, and 30,619,375 (100 percent) of the class B shares. On December 27, 2001, Martha's Class A and Class B shares were worth approximately $17 each, so on paper Martha's MSO class A shares alone were worth over $500 million. Class B shares are convertible into Class A shares on a one to one basis.

Martha's personal life became public. The world did not know that Martha Stewart had sold 3,928 shares of ImClone for $58 each on December 27, 2001[2] until it surfaced in June 2002.[3] The sale generated only $227,824 for Martha, and she avoided losing $45,673 when the stock price dropped the next day,[4] but it has caused her endless personal grief and humiliation, and the loss of reputation, as well

as a significant drop to $5.26 in the MSO share price.

What Happened?

Martha had made an investment in ImClone, a company that was trying to get the approval of the U.S. Food and Drug Administration (FDA) to bring to market an anti-colon cancer drug called Erbitux. Samuel Waksal, then the CEO of ImClone and a personal friend of Martha's, was apparently warned on or close to December 25, 2001 that the FDA was going to refuse[5] to review Erbitux.[6] According to SEC allegations, Sam relayed the information to his family so they could dump their ImClone shares on an unsuspecting public before the official announcement. Martha claims that she didn't get any inside information early from Sam, but regulators believe that she may have or from her broker or her broker's aide. The activities of several of Sam's friends, including Martha, are under investigation by the SEC.

Sam was arrested on June 12, 2002 and charged with "nine criminal counts of conspiracy, securities fraud and perjury, and then freed on $10 million bail."[7] In a related civil complaint, the SEC alleged that Sam "tried to sell ImClone stock and tipped family members before ImClone's official FDA announcement on Dec. 28."[8]

According to the SEC, two unidentified members of Sam's family sold about $10 million worth of ImClone stock in a two-day interval just before the announcement. Moreover, Sam also tried for two days to sell nearly 80,000 ImClone shares for about $5 million,

---

1. *Proxy Statement for 2002 Annual Meeting of Stockholders of Martha Stewart Living Omnimedia, Inc.,* held May 9, 2002, SEC Edgar Filing, at http://www.sec.gov/Archives/edgar/data/1091801/000095012302003236/y58395def14a.txt
2. "Martha scrutiny heats up: Shares of decorator's company end tough week as Martha Stewart's ImClone links prove troubling", *CNN/Money*, June 14, 2002.
3. "Martha Stewart Resigns From NYSE Board, *Reuters* per the *FOXNews.com*, October 5, 2002.
4. "Broker's aide pleads guilty in Martha Stewart matter", *Washington Post*, Oct. 2, 2002.
5. "ImClone ex-CEO takes the 5th: Sam Waksal declines to testify; His brother Harlan says his sales were not improper", *CNN/Money*, June 13, 2001.
6. Later it became known that the application for review had "multiple deficiencies" and provided insufficient information that the drug would work on its own. Ibid.
7. Ibid.
8. Ibid.

but two different brokers refused to process the trades.[9]

Martha has denied any wrongdoing. She was quoted as saying: "In placing my trade I had no improper information... My transaction was entirely lawful."[10] She admitted calling Sam after selling her shares, but claimed: "I did not reach Mr. Waksal, and he did not return my call."[11] She maintained that she had an agreement with her broker to sell her remaining ImClone shares "if the stock dropped below $60 per share."[12]

Martha's public, however, was skeptical. She was asked embarrassing questions when she appeared on TV for a cooking segment, and she declined to answer saying: "I am here to make my salad." Martha's interactions with her broker, Peter Bacanovic, and his assistant, Douglas Faneuil, are also being scrutinized. Merrill Lynch & Co. suspended Bacanovic (who was also Sam Waksal's broker[13]) and Faneuil, with pay, in late June. Later, since all phone calls to brokerages are taped and emails kept, it appeared to be damning when Bacanovic initially refused to provide his cell phone records to the House Energy and Commerce Commission for their investigation.[14] Moreover, on October 4, 2001, Faneuil "pleaded guilty to a charge that he accepted gifts from his superior in return for keeping quiet about circumstances surrounding Stewart's controversial stock sale."[15] Faneuil admitted that he received extra vacation time, including a free airline ticket from a Merrill Lynch employee in exchange for withholding information from SEC and FBI investigators.[16]

According to the *Washington Post* report of Faneuil's appearance in court:

On the morning of Dec. 27, Faneuil received a telephone call from a Waksal family member who asked to sell 39,472 shares for almost $2.5 million, according to court records. Waksal's accountant also called Faneuil in an unsuccessful attempt to sell a large bloc of shares, the records show.

Prosecutors allege that those orders "constituted material non-public information." But they alleged that Faneuil violated his duty to Merrill Lynch by calling a "tippee" to relate that Waksal family members were attempting to liquidate their holdings in ImClone.

That person then sold "all the Tippee's shares of ImClone stock, approximately 3,928 shares, yielding proceeds of approximately $228,000" the court papers said.[17]

One day later, on October 5th, it was announced that Martha resigned from her post as a director of the New York Stock Exchange—a post she held only four months—and the price of MSO shares declined more than 7 percent to $6.32 in afternoon trading.[18] From June 12th to October 12th, the share price of MSO had declined by approximately 61 percent.[19]

Martha's future took a further interesting turn on October 15th, when Sam Waksal pleaded guilty to six counts of his indictment, including: bank fraud, securities fraud, conspiracy to obstruct justice and perjury. But he did not agree to cooperate with prosecutors, and did not incriminate Martha.[20] Waksal's

---

9. Ibid.
10. "Martha scrutiny...," ibid.
11. Ibid.
12. Ibid.
13. "Aide to Martha Stewart's broker admits he withheld information from investigators", *CBCNEWS*, http://cbc.ca/news, Oct. 2, 2002
14. "Martha's Broker Under Microscope", *CBSNews.com*, July 9, 2001.
15. "Martha Stewart resigns...," ibid.
16. "Broker's aide pleads guilty... ," ibid.
17. "Broker's aide pleads guilty... ," ibid.
18. Ibid.
19. Assuming a value per share of $13.50 on June 12th, the decline to a low of $5.26 in early October amounted to a decline of 61 percent.
20. ImClone Founder Pleads Guilty", *CBSNews.com*, Oct. 15, 2002.

sentencing was postponed until 2003 so his lawyers could exchange information with U.S. District Judge William Pauley concerning Waksal's financial records.[21]

After October 15th, the price of MSO shares rose, perhaps as the prospect of Martha's going to jail appeared to become more remote, and/or people began to consider MSO to be more than just Martha and her reputation. The gain from the low point of the MSO share price in October to December 9, 2002 was about 40 percent.[22]

Martha still had a lot to think about, however. Apparently the SEC gave Martha notice in September of its intent to file civil securities fraud charges against her. Martha's lawyers responded and the SEC deliberated. Even if Martha were to get off with a fine, prosecutors could still bring a criminal case against her in the future. It is an interesting legal question, how, if Martha were to plead guilty to the civil charges, she could avoid criminal liability.[23]

On June 4, 2003, Stewart was indicted on charges of obstructing justice and securities fraud. She then quit as Chairman and CEO of her company, but stayed on the Board and served as Chief Creative Officer. She appeared in court on January 20, 2004 and watched the proceedings throughout her trial. In addition to the testimony of Mr. Faneuil, Stewart's personal friend Mariana Pasternak testified that Stewart told her Waksal was trying to dump his shares shortly after selling her Imclone stock.[24] Ultimately, the jury did not believe the counterclaim by Peter Bacanovic, Stewart's broker, that he and Martha had a prior agreement to sell Imclone if it went

2000–2002 Stock Chart of Martha Stewart Living Omnimedia Inc.

Reprinted courtesy of StatPro Canada, Inc.

below $60. Although Judge Cedarbaum dismissed the charge of securities fraud for insider trading, on March 5, 2004, the jury found Stewart guilty on one charge of conspiracy, one of obstruction of justice and two of making false statements to investigators.[25] The announcement caused the share price of her company to sink by $2.77 to $11.26 on the NYSE.[26]

Martha immediately posted the following on her website:

> I am obviously distressed by the jury's verdict, but I continue to take comfort in knowing that I have done nothing wrong and that I have the enduring support of my family and friends. I will appeal the verdict and continue to fight to clear my name. I believe in the fairness of the judicial system and remain confident that I will ultimately prevail.[27]

---

21. Ultimately, on June 10, 2003, Waksal was "sentenced to 87 months in prison for insider trading, bank fraud, perjury and obstruction of justice. He also was ordered to pay more than US$4 million in fines and restitution for illegally tipping off his daughter in December 2001, that shares in the company he founded were about to fall sharply." "Waksal Jailed for 7 Years," Peter Morton, *Financial Post*, June 11, 2003, FP3.

22. "Market betting Martha won't go to jail: Shares up 40 percent in 6 weeks", *Financial Post*, Dec. 10, 2001, IN1, 3.

23. "SEC Knocking On Martha's Door", *CBSNEWS.com*, Oct. 22, 2002.

24. "TIMELINE: Martha Stewart", CNNMONEY, downloaded March 5, 2004.

25. "Martha Stewart found guilty on all charges; vows to appeal," CBC.CA News, downloaded March 5, 2005.

26. Ibid.

27. "Martha Stewart: I will appeal," CNN.com, downloaded March 5. 2004.

Martha was subsequently sentenced to 5 months in prison and 5 months of home detention—a lower than maximum sentence under the U.S. Sentencing Guidelines—and she did appeal. Although she could have remained free during the appeal, on September 15, 2004 she asked for her sentence to start[28] so she could be at home in time for the spring planting season. Martha's appeal cited "prosecutorial misconduct, extraneous influences on the jury and erroneous evidentiary rulings and jury instructions" but on January 6, 2006, her conviction was upheld.[29]

Impact on Reputation

Martha may still disagree with the verdict. But there is little doubt that the allegations and her convictions had a major impact on Martha personally, and on the fortunes of MSO and the other shareholders that had faith in her and her company. Assuming a value per share of $13.50 on June 12th, the decline to a low of $5.26 in early October 2003 represents a loss of market capitalization (i.e. reputation capital as defined by Charles Fombrun[30]) of approximately $250 million or 61 percent. The value of MSO's shares did return to close at $35.51 on February 7, 2005,[31] but fell off to under $20 in early 2006. According to a New York brand-rating company, Brand-Keys, the Martha Stewart brand reached a peak of 120 (the baseline is 100) in May 2002, and sank to a low of 63 in March 2004.[32]

What will the future hold? Martha has returned to TV with a version of *The Apprentice* as well as her usual homemaking and design shows, and her products and magazines continue to be sold. Will Martha regain her earlier distinction? Would she do it again to avoid losing $45,673?

Questions

1. What was the basis of Martha Stewart's reputation?
2. Why did MSO's stock price decline due to Martha Stewart's loss of reputation?
3. Who is Martha Stewart's target market?
4. What qualities were associated with the Martha Stewart brand, before the controversy? Which of these were affected by the accusations of insider trading, and how? How would you find out for sure?
5. What level of sales and profits would MSO have reached if Martha's reputation had not been harmed? Refer to the SEC or MSO websites for information on financial trends.
6. What range would the stock price have been in at the end of 2002 based on your estimates?
7. Martha's overall net worth was huge relative to her investment in ImClone. Assuming she did not have inside information, was there any way she could have avoided the appearance of having it?
8. How could Martha have handled this crisis better?
9. Why is insider trading considered harmful? Should insider trading be banned if it assists in moving a stock price to new a equilibrium quickly, so that noninsiders are trading at appropriate prices sooner?
10. If you wished to sell an investment in a company where one of your friends is an insider, or even a significant employee, should you call your friend to advise him you are about to sell? Why, or why not?

Source: L.J. Brooks, Jan. 2003/Rev. Jan. 2006

28. "Martha to Judge: Jail Me Now," Drew Hassselback, *Financial Post*, September 16, 2004, FP1.
29. "Conviction stands, court tells celebrity homemaker Stewart," Larry Neumeister, *Toronto Star*, January 7, 2006, D3.
30. *Reputation: Realizing Value from the Corporate Image*, Charles J. Fombrun, Harvard Business School Press, 1996.
31. "Martha's comeback may be brief," Michael Santoli, *Financial Post*, February 8, 2005, IN3.
32. "Omnimedia eyes life without Martha," Peter Morton, *Financial Post*, March 9, 2004, FP1, FP4.

Bhopal-Union Carbide[1]

On April 24, 1985, Warren M. Anderson, the sixty-three-year-old chairman of Union Carbide Corporation, had to make a disappointing announcement to angry stockholders at their annual meeting in Danbury, Connecticut. Anderson, who had been jailed briefly by the government of India on charges of "negligence and criminal corporate liability," had been devoting all his attention to the company's mushrooming problems. His announcement concerned the complete breakdown of negotiations with officials in the Indian government: they had rejected as inadequate an estimated $200 million in compensation for the deaths of 2,000 people and the injuries of 200,000 others, which had been caused in December 1984 by a poisonous leak of methyl isocyanate gas from a Union Carbide pesticide plant located in Bhopal, India.[2] In the wake of more than $35 billion in suits filed against the company's liability coverage, reported to total only about $200 million, the company's stock tumbled. Angry stockholders filed suit, charging that they had suffered losses of more than $1 billion because the company's managers had failed to warn them of the risks at the Indian plant. Analysts predicted the company would be forced into bankruptcy. Ironically, the Union Carbide plant in Bhopal had been losing money for several years and Anderson had considered closing it.

The deadly methyl isocyanate gas that leaked from the Union Carbide plant is a volatile and highly toxic chemical used to make pesticides. It is 500 times more poisonous than cyanide, and it reacts explosively with almost any substance, including water. Late on the night of December 2, 1984, the methyl isocyanate stored in a tank at the Bhopal factory started boiling violently when water or some other agent accidentally entered the tank. A cooling unit that should have switched on automatically had been disabled for at least a year. Shakil Qureshi, a manager on duty at the time, and Suman Dey, the senior operator on duty, both distrusted the initial readings on their gauges in the control room. "Instruments often didn't work," Qureshi said later. "They got corroded, and crystals would form on them."

By 11:30 p.m. the plant workers' eyes were burning. But the workers remained unconcerned because, as they later reported, minor leaks were common at the plant and were often first detected in this way. Many of the illiterate workers were unaware of the deadly properties of the chemical. Not until 12:40 a.m., as workers began choking on the fumes, did they realize something was drastically wrong. Five minutes later, emergency valves on the storage tank exploded and white toxic gas began shooting out of a pipestack and drifting toward the shantytowns downwind from the plant. An alarm sounded as manager Dey shouted into the factory loudspeaker that a massive leak had erupted and the workers should flee the area. Meanwhile, Qureshi ordered company fire trucks to spray the escaping gas with water to neutralize the chemical. But water pressure was too low to reach the top of the 120-foot-high pipestack. Dey then rushed to turn on a vent scrubber that should have neutralized the escaping gas with caustic soda. Unfortunately, the scrubber had been shut down for maintenance fifteen days earlier. As white clouds continued to pour out of the pipestack, Qureshi shouted to workers to turn on a nearby flare tower to burn off the gas. The flare, however, would not go on because its pipes had corroded and were still being repaired.

Panicked workers poured out of the plant, and the lethal cloud settled over the neighboring shantytowns of Jaipraksh and Chola.

1. This case has been adapted from Velasquesz, Manuel, *Business Ethics: Concepts and Cases,* 3/e, © 1992, pp. 3–5. Reprinted by permission of Prentice-Hall, Inc., Englewood Cliffs, N.J.
2. All material concerning Union Carbide and the Bhopal plant, including all quotations and all allegations, is drawn directly from the following sources: *New York Times:* December 9, 1984, p. 1E; December 16, 1984, pp. 1, 8; January 28, 1985, pp. 6, 7; January 30, 1985, p. 6; April 25, 1985, p. 34; *San Jose Mercury News:* December 6, 1984, p. 16A; December 12, 1984, pp. 1, 1H; December 13, 1984, p. 1; *Time:* December 17, 1985, pp. 22–31.

Hundreds died in their beds, choking helplessly in violent spasms as their burning lungs filled with fluid. Thousands were blinded by the caustic gas, and thousands of others suffered burns and lesions in their nasal and bronchial passages. When it was over, at least 2,000 lay dead and 200,000 were injured. The majority of the dead were squatters who had illegally built huts next to the factory. Surviving residents of the slums, most of them illiterate, declared afterward that they had built their shacks there because they did not understand the danger and thought the factory made healthy "medicine for plants."

Union Carbide managers from the United States built the Bhopal plant in 1969 with the blessing of the Indian government, which was anxious to increase production of the pesticides it desperately needed to raise food for India's huge population. Over the next fifteen years, pesticides enabled India to cut its annual grain losses from 25 percent to 15 percent, a saving of 15 million tons of grain, or enough to feed 70 million people for a full year. Indian officials willingly accepted the technology, skills, and equipment that Union Carbide provided, and Indian workers were thankful for the company jobs, without which they would have had to beg or starve, as India has no welfare system. In return, India offered the company cheap labor, low taxes, and few laws requiring expensive environmental equipment or costly workplace protections. In comparison with other factories in India, the Union Carbide plant was considered a model, law-abiding citizen with a good safety record. Said a government official: "They never refused to install what we asked."

At the time of the disaster, the pesticide plant in Bhopal was operated by Union Carbide India Ltd., a subsidiary of the Union Carbide Corporation of Danbury, Connecticut, which had a controlling interest of 50.9 percent in the Indian company. The board of directors of Union Carbide India Ltd. included one top manager from the parent Union Carbide Corporation in the United States and four managers from another Union Carbide subsidiary, based in Hong Kong. Reports from the Indian company were regularly reviewed by the managers in Danbury, who had the authority to exercise financial and technical control over Union Carbide India Ltd. Although day-to-day details were left to the Indian managers, the American managers controlled budgets, set major policies, and issued technical directives for operating and maintaining the plant.

Before the tragedy, the Indian subsidiary had been doing poorly. In an effort to contain annual losses of $4 million from the unprofitable plant, local company managers had initiated several cost-cutting programs. Only a year before, the number of equipment operators on each shift had been reduced from twelve to five; morale dropped and many of the best operators quit and were replaced with workers whose education was below that required by company manuals. Although Warren Anderson and other Union Carbide Corporation (U.S.) managers insisted that responsibility for the plant's operations rested with the local Indian managers, they hastened to say that all cost-cutting measures had been justified.

Two years before the disaster, the American managers had sent three engineers from the United States to survey the plant and, as a result, had told the Indian managers to remedy ten major flaws in safety equipment and procedures. The Indian managers had written back that the problems were corrected. "We have no reason to believe that what was represented to us by Union Carbide India Ltd. did not in fact occur," said the U.S. managers. The U.S. managers had considered closing the failing plant a year earlier, but Indian city and state officials had asked that the company remain open to preserve the jobs of thousands of workers in the plant and in dependent local industries.

Questions

1. What are the ethical issues raised by this case?
2. Did the legal doctrine of "limited liability" apply to protect the shareholders of Union Carbide Corporation (U.S.)?
3. Were the Indian operations, which were being overseen by the managers of Union Carbide Corporation (U.S.), in compliance with legal or moral or ethical standards?

The Betaseron® Decision (A)

On July 23, 1993, the United States Food and Drug Administration (FDA) approved interferon beta-1b (brand name Betaseron®), making it the first treatment for multiple sclerosis to get FDA approval in twenty-five years. Betaseron was developed by Berlex Laboratories, a United States unit of Schering AG, the German pharmaceutical company. Berlex handled the clinical development, trials, and marketing of the drug, while Chiron, a biotechnology firm based in California, manufactured it. The groundbreaking approval of Betaseron represented not only a great opportunity for Berlex but also a difficult dilemma. Available supplies were insufficient to meet initial demand, and shortages were forecasted until 1996. With insufficient supplies and staggering development costs, how would Berlex allocate and price the drug?

The Challenge of Multiple Sclerosis

Multiple sclerosis (MS) is a disease of the central nervous system that interferes with the brain's ability to control such functions as seeing, walking, and talking. The nerve fibers within the brain and spinal cord are surrounded by myelin, a fatty substance that protects the nerve fibers in the same way that insulation protects electrical wires. When the myelin insulation becomes damaged, the ability of the central nervous system to transmit nerve impulses to and from the brain becomes impaired. With multiple sclerosis, there are *sclerosed* (i.e., scarred or hardened) areas in *multiple* parts of the brain and spinal cord when the immune system mistakenly attacks the myelin sheath.

The symptoms of MS depend to some extent on the location and size of the sclerosis. Symptoms include numbness, slurred speech, blurred vision, poor coordination, muscle weakness, bladder dysfunction, extreme fatigue, and paralysis. There is no way to know how the disease will progress for any individual because the nature of the course it takes can change over time. Some people will have a relatively benign course of MS, with only one or two mild attacks, nearly complete remission, and no permanent disability. Others will have a chronic, progressive course resulting in severe disability. A third group displays the most typical pattern, with periods of *exacerbations,* when the disease is active, and periods of *remission,* when the symptoms recede while generally leaving some damage. People with MS live with an exceptionally high degree of uncertainty because the course of their disease can change from one day to the next. Dramatic downturns as well as dramatic recoveries are not uncommon.

The Promise of Betaseron

Interferon beta is a protein that occurs naturally and regulates the body's immune system. Betaseron is composed of interferon beta-1b that has been genetically engineered and laboratory manufactured as a recombinant product. Although other interferons (i.e., alpha and gamma) had been tested, only beta interferon had been shown, through large-scale trials, to affect MS. Because it is an immunoregulatory agent, it was believed to combat the immune problems that make MS worse. However, the exact way in which it works was yet to be determined.

In clinical studies, Betaseron was shown to reduce the frequency and severity of exacerbations in ambulatory MS patients with a relapsing-remitting form of the disease. It did not reverse damage already done, nor did it completely prevent exacerbations from occurring. However, Betaseron could dramatically improve the quality of life for the person with MS; for example, people taking Betaseron were shown to have fewer and shorter hospitalizations. Betaseron represented the first and only drug to have an effect on the frequency of exacerbations.

Betaseron is administered subcutaneously (under the skin) every other day by self-injection. In order to derive the most benefits from the therapy, it was important that the MS patient maintain a regular schedule of the injections. Some flu-like side effects, as well as swelling and irritation around the injection, had been noted; however, they tended to decrease with time on treatment. In addition, one person who received Betaseron committed suicide, while three others attempted to kill themselves. Because MS often leads to depression, there was no way to know whether the administration of Betaseron was a factor. Lastly, Betaseron was not recommended for use during pregnancy.

The Betaseron Dilemma

In July of 1993, the FDA approval for Betaseron allowed physicians to prescribe the drug to MS patients who were ambulatory and had a relapsing-remitting course of MS. An estimated one-third of the 300,000 people with MS in the United States fell into that category, resulting in a potential client base of 100,000. However, the expedited FDA approval process took only one year instead of the customary three years taken to review new drug applications. As a result, Berlex was unprepared for its manufacture and distribution in the anticipated amount needed. Chiron Corporation had been making the drug in small quantities for experimental use and did not have the manufacturing facilities to handle the expected explosion in demand. Chiron estimated that it would have enough of the drug for about 12,000 to 20,000 people by the end of 1993. By the end of 1994, Chiron expected to be able to provide the drug to 40,000 patients. Depending on demand, it might take until about 1996 to provide the drug to all patients who requested it. Chiron's expanded manu-

facturing represented the only option for Berlex because the process required for another company to get FDA approval to manufacture the drug would take even longer.

In addition to availability, price was a concern because successes must fund the failures that precede them. Betaseron represented the results of years of expensive, risky research by highly trained scientists in modern research facilities. Furthermore, genetically engineered drugs were extremely expensive to manufacture. In the case of Betaseron, a human interferon gene was inserted into bacteria, resulting in a genetically engineered molecule. The stringent quality controls on the procedure take time and are expensive. As a result, the price of Betaseron was expected to be about $10,000 per year for each patient.

Betaseron brought great hope to people with MS and a great quandary to Berlex. How should Berlex handle the supply limitations, the distribution, and the price of this drug?

Source: By Ann K. Buchholtz, University of Georgia. This case was written from public sources, solely for the purpose of stimulating class discussion. All events are real. The author thanks Dr. Stephen Reingold, vice president, Research and Medical Programs of the National Multiple Sclerosis Society and Avery Rockwell, chapter services associate of the Greater Connecticut Chapter of the Multiple Sclerosis Society, and two anonymous reviewers for their helpful comments.

Ethics Case | *Texaco: The Ecuador Issue*[1]

In 1964, at the invitation of the Ecuadorian government, Texaco Inc. began operations through a subsidiary, TexPet, in the Amazon region of Ecuador. The purpose of the project was to "develop Ecuador's natural resources and encourage the *colonization* of the area."[2] TexPet was a minority owner of the project and its partner was Petroecuador, the government-owned oil company. Over the years from 1968 to 1992, the consortium extracted 1.4 billion barrels of oil from the Ecuadorian operations.

Ecuador benefited greatly during this period. Ecuador received approximately 98 percent of

all moneys generated by the consortium in the form of royalties, taxes, and revenues. Altogether, this amount represented more than 50 percent of Ecuador's gross national product during that period. TexPet's operations over the years provided jobs for 840 employees and approximately 2,000 contract workers, thereby benefiting almost 3,000 Ecuadorian families directly, in addition to the thousands of Ecuadorian nationals who supplied the company's needs for goods and services. Also, TexPet made substantial contributions to the Quito, Guayaquil, and Loja Polytechnics and

---

1. By Professor Timothy Rowley of the Rotman School of Management.
2. Sources: Texaco and other websites: http://www.texaco.com; see Ecuador pages.

other institutions of higher education. Oil is Ecuador's lifeblood—a $1 billion per year industry that accounts for 50 percent of the export earnings and 62 percent of its fiscal budget.

Unfortunately, problems also arose. Although Petroecuador acquired 100 percent of the ownership of the Transecuadorian pipeline in 1986, TexPet still accounted for 88 percent of all oil production and operated the pipeline in 1987 when it ruptured and was buried by a landslide. A spill of 16.8 million gallons (4.4 million barrels) occurred, which Texaco attributed to a major earthquake that devastated Ecuador.

Other spills apparently occurred as well. Although Texaco pulled out of the consortium in 1992 entirely (having retreated to be a silent minority partner in 1990), three lawsuits were filed against it in the United States—the Aquinda (November 1993), the Sequihua (August 1993), and the Jota (in 1994). The indigenous people who launched the lawsuits charged that, during two decades of oil drilling in the Amazon, Texaco dumped more than 3,000 gallons of crude oil a day—millions of gallons in total—into the environment. The indigenous people say their rivers, streams, and lakes are now contaminated, and the fish and wild game that once made up their food supply are now decimated. They asked in the lawsuit that Texaco compensate them and clean up their land and waters.

Maria Aquinda, for whom the suit is named, says that contaminated water from nearby oil wells drilled by the Texaco subsidiary caused her to suffer chronic stomach ailments and rashes and that she lost scores of pigs and chickens. Aquinda and 76 other Amazonian residents filed a $1.5 billion lawsuit in New York against Texaco. The class action suit, representing 30,000 people, further alleges that Texaco acted "with callous disregard for the health, well-being, and safety of the plaintiffs" and that "large-scale disposal of inadequately treated hazardous wastes and destruction of tropical rain forest habitats, caused harm to indigenous peoples and their property." According to the Ecuadorian environmental group Ecological Action, Texaco destroyed more than 1 million hectares of tropical forest, spilled 74 million liters of oil, and used obsolete technology that led to the dumping of 18 million liters of toxic

waste. Rainforest Action Network, a San Francisco-based organization, says effects include poor crop production in the affected areas, invasion of tribal lands, sexual assaults committed by oil workers, and loss of game animals (which would be food supply for the indigenous peoples).

Audits were conducted to address the impact of operations on the soil, water, and air and to assess compliance with environmental laws, regulations, and generally accepted operating practices. Two internationally recognized and independent consulting firms, AGRA Earth & Environmental Ltd. and Fugro-McClelland, conducted audits in Ecuador. Each independently concluded that TexPet acted responsibly and that there is no lasting or significant environmental impact from its former operations. Nonetheless, TexPet agreed to remedy the limited and localized impacts attributable to its operations. On May 4, 1995, Ecuador's Minister of Energy and Mines, the president of Petroecuador, and TexPet signed the *Contract for Implementing of Environmental Remedial Work and Release from Obligations, Liability, and Claims* following negotiations with Ecuadorian government officials representing the interests of indigenous groups in the Oriente. In this remediation effort, producing wells and pits formerly utilized by TexPet were closed, producing water systems were modified, cleared lands were replanted, and contaminated soil was remediated. All actions taken were inspected and certified by the Ecuadorian government. Additionally, TexPet funded social and health programs throughout the region of operations, such as medical dispensaries and sewage and potable water systems. That contract settled all claims by Petroecuador and the Republic of Ecuador against TexPet, Texaco, and their affiliates for all matters arising out of the consortium's operations.

In the summer of 1998, the $40 million remediation project was completed. On September 30, 1998, Ecuador's Minister of Energy and Mines, the president of Petroecuador, and the general manager of Petroproduccion signed the Final Release of Claims and Delivery of Equipment. This document finalized the Government of Ecuador's approval of TexPet's environmental remediation work and further stated that TexPet fully complied with all obligations established in the remediation agreement signed in 1995.

Meanwhile, in the United States, Texaco made the following arguments against the three lawsuits:

▌ Activities were in compliance with Ecuadorian laws, and international oil industry standards.

▌ Activities were undertaken by a largely Ecuadorian workforce—which Texaco believed would always act in the interest of its community/country.

▌ All investments/operations were approved and monitored by the Ecuadorian government and Petroecuador.

▌ All activities were conducted with the oversight and approval of the Ecuadorian government.

▌ Environmentally friendly measures were used, such as helicopters instead of roads.

▌ The health of Ecuadorians increased during the years Texaco was in Ecuador.

▌ Ninety-eight percent of the money generated stayed in Ecuador—50 percent of GDP during that period.

▌ Jobs were provided for 2,800.

▌ Money was provided for schools.

▌ Independent engineering firms found no lasting damage.

▌ A $40 million remediation program was started per an agreement with the Ecuadorian government.

▌ U.S. courts should not govern activities in a foreign country.

The three lawsuits were dismissed for similar reasons—the Sequihua in 1994, the Aquinda in 1996, and the Jota in 1997. The Aquinda lawsuit, for example, was launched in New York (where Texaco has its corporate headquarters) because Texaco no longer had business in Ecuador and could not be sued there. The case was dismissed by a New York court in November 1996 on the basis that it should be heard in Ecuador. Failing that, the Ecuadorian government should have been involved in the case as well, or that the case should have been filed against the government and the state-owned Petroecuador as well as Texaco. At that point, the Ecuadorian government did get involved and filed an appeal of the decision. This was the first time a foreign government had sued a U.S. oil company in the United States for environmental damage. In addition, in 1997, the plaintiffs in the Aquinda and Jota cases also appealed the district court's decisions.

On October 5, 1998, a U.S. court of appeals remanded both cases to the district court for further consideration as to whether they should proceed in Ecuador or the United States. Written submissions were filed on February 1, 1999. Texaco has long argued that the appropriate venue for these cases is Ecuador because the oil-producing operations took place in Ecuador under the control and supervision of Ecuador's government, and the Ecuadorian courts have heard similar cases against other companies. It is Texaco's position that U.S. courts should not govern the activities of a sovereign foreign nation, just as foreign courts should not govern the activities of the United States. In fact, Texaco claimed the Ambassador of Ecuador, the official representative of the government of Ecuador, noted in a letter to the district court that Ecuador would not waive its sovereign immunity.

Notwithstanding Texaco's arguments, the case was sent back to the court that threw it out, on the basis that the government of Ecuador does have the right to intervene. The question of whether the case can be tried in the United States or Ecuador under these circumstances will now be decided. Texaco claims that it has done enough to repair any damage and disputes the scientific validity of the claims—the Amazonians (or their supporters) seem to have the resources to continue fighting this suit in the U.S. courts.

Questions

1. Should Ecuadorians be able to sue Texaco in U.S. courts?

2. If an oil spill was caused by an act of God, an earthquake, should Texaco be held responsible?

3. Do you find Texaco's arguments against the lawsuits convincing? Why and why not?

Source: Texaco website: www.texaco.com; see Ecuador pages; various other websites.

Ethics Case

Where Were the Accountants?

"Sam, I'm really in trouble. I've always wanted to be an accountant. But here I am just about to apply to the accounting firms for a job after graduation from the university, and I'm not sure I want to be an accountant after all."

"Why, Norm? In all those accounting courses we took together, you worked super hard because you were really interested. What's your problem now?"

"Well, I've been reading the business newspapers, reports, and accounting journals lately, and things just don't add up. For instance, you know how we have always been told that accountants have expertise in measurement and disclosure, that they are supposed to prepare reports with integrity, and that they ought to root out fraud if they suspect it? Well, it doesn't look like they have been doing a good job. At least, they haven't been doing what I would have expected."

"Remember, Norm, we're still students with a lot to learn. Maybe you are missing something. What have you been reading about?"

"OK, Sam, here are a few stories for you to think about:

1. In this article, "Accountants and the S & L Crisis," which was in *Management Accounting* in February 1993, I found the argument that the $200 million fiasco was due to the regulators and to a downturn in the real estate market, not to accounting fraud . . . but I don't buy it entirely. According to this article, rising interest rates and fixed lending rates resulted in negative cash flow at the same time as a decline in value of the real estate market reduced the value underlying S & L loan assets. As a result, the net worth of many S & Ls fell, and regulators decided to change some accounting practices to make it appear that the S & Ls were still above the minimum capital requirements mandated to protect depositors' funds. Just look at this list of the seven accounting practices or problems that were cited:

    - write-off of losses on loans sold over the life of the loan rather than when the loss occurred,
    - use of government-issued *Net Worth Certificates* to be counted as S & L capital,
    - use of deals involving up-front money and near-term cash flow, which would bolster current earnings at the expense of later,
    - inadequate loan loss provisions due to poor loan monitoring,
    - write-off of goodwill created on the merger of sound S & Ls with bankrupt S & Ls over a forty-year period,
    - write-ups of owned property based on appraisal values, and
    - lack of market-based reporting to reflect economic reality.

    The problem, for me, is that many of these practices are not in accord with generally accepted accounting principles [GAAP] and yet the accountants went along—at least they didn't object or improve their practices enough to change the outcome. Why not? Where were the accountants?"

2. "I am also concerned about the expertise the accounting profession claims to have in terms of measurement and disclosure. For example, recently there have been many articles on the health costs created by smoking, yet there are no accountants involved. For instance, a May 1994 report by the Center on Addiction and Substance Abuse at Columbia University estimates that "in 1994 dollars, substance abuse will cost Medicare $20 billion in inpatient hospital costs alone" and that tobacco accounts for 80 percent of those hospitalizations. Over the next twenty years, substance abuse will cost the Medicare program $1 trillion. No wonder the trustees of the Medicare Trust Fund released a report on April 21 "predicting that the Fund would run out of money in seven years." These are important issues. Why do we have to wait for economists and special interest groups to make these calculations? Shouldn't accountants be able to make them and lend credibility and balance in the process? Wouldn't society benefit? Where were the accountants?

3. "What about the finding of fraud? Are auditors doing enough to prevent and catch fraudulent behavior? I know what our professors say: auditors can't be expected to catch everything; their job is not to search for fraud unless

suspicions are aroused during other activities; and their primary task is to audit the financial statements. But aren't the auditors just reacting to discovered problems, when they could be proactive? Couldn't they stress the importance of using codes of conduct and the encouragement of employees to bring forward their concerns over unethical acts? Why is proactive management appropriate in some other areas, such as ironing out personnel problems, but reactive behavior is appropriate when dealing with fraud? Reactive behavior will just close the barn door after the horse has been stolen. In the case of the Bank of Credit & Commerce International (BCCI), for example, at least $1.7 billion was missing."

"I guess I'm having second thoughts about becoming a professional accountant. Can you help me out, Sam?"

Question

1. What would you tell Norm?

Ethics Case   *To Resign or Serve?*

The Prairieland Bank was a medium-sized, Midwestern financial institution. The management had a good reputation for backing successful deals, but the CEO (and significant shareholder) had recently moved to San Francisco to be "close to the big-bank center of activity." He commuted into the Prairieland head office for two or three days each week to oversee major deals.

Lately the bank's profitability had decreased, and the management had begun to renegotiate many loans on which payments had fallen behind. By doing so, the bank was able to disclose them as current, rather than nonperforming, as the unpaid interest was simply added to the principal to arrive at the new principal amount. Discussions were also under way on changing some accounting policies to make them less conservative.

Ben Hunt, the audit partner on the Prairieland Bank account, was becoming concerned about the risk associated with giving an opinion on the fairness of the financial statements. During the early days of the audit, it became evident that the provision for doubtful loans was far too low, and he made an appointment to discuss the problem with the CEO and his vice president of finance. At the interview, Ben was told that the executives knew the provision was too low, but they didn't want to increase it because that would decrease their reported profits. Instead, they had approached a company that provided insurance to protect leased equipment, such as earth movers, against damage during the lease, and arranged for insurance against nonpayment on the maturity of their loans. As a result, they said, any defaults on their loans would be made up from the insurance company, so they didn't see any point to increasing the provision for loan losses or disclosing the insurance arrangement.

When he heard of this, Ben expressed concern to the Prairieland management, but they were adamant. Because Prairieland was such a large account, he sought the counsel of James London, the senior partner in his firm who was in charge of assessing such accounting treatments and the related risk to the auditing firm. James flew out to confer with Ben, and they decided that the best course of action was to visit the client and indicate their intent to resign, which they did.

After dinner, James was waiting at the airport for his plane home. By coincidence, he met Jack Lane, who held responsibilities similar to his own at one of the competing firms. Jack was returning home as well and was in good spirits. On the flight, Jack let it slip that he had just picked up an old client of James's firm, Prairieland Bank.

Questions

1. Which decision was right: to resign or to serve?

2. What should James do?

Readings

Managing for Organizational Integrity[1]

Lynn Sharp Paine

Many managers think of ethics as a question of personal scruples, a confidential matter between individuals and their consciences. These executives are quick to describe any wrongdoing as an isolated incident, the work of a rogue employee. The thought that the company could bear any responsibility for an individual's misdeeds never enters their minds. Ethics, after all, has nothing to do with management.

In fact, ethics has *everything* to do with management. Rarely do the character flaws of a lone actor fully explain corporate misconduct. More typically, unethical business practice involves the tacit, if not explicit, cooperation of others and reflects the values, attitudes, beliefs, language, and behavioral patterns that define an organization's operating culture. Ethics, then, is as much an organizational as a personal issue. Managers who fail to provide proper leadership and to institute systems that facilitate ethical conduct share responsibility with those who conceive, execute, and knowingly benefit from corporate misdeeds.

Managers must acknowledge their role in shaping organizational ethics and seize this opportunity to create a climate that can strengthen the relationships and reputations on which their companies' success depends. Executives who ignore ethics run the risk of personal and corporate liability in today's increasingly tough legal environment. In addition, they deprive their organizations of the benefits available under new federal guidelines for sentencing organizations convicted of wrongdoing. These sentencing guidelines recognize for the first time the organizational and managerial roots of unlawful conduct and base fines partly on the extent to which companies have taken steps to prevent that misconduct.

Prompted by the prospect of leniency, many companies are rushing to implement compliance-based ethics programs. Designed by corporate counsel, the goal of these programs is to prevent, detect, and punish legal violations. But organizational ethics means more than avoiding illegal practice; and providing employees with a rule book will do little to address the problems underlying unlawful conduct. To foster a climate that encourages exemplary behavior, corporations need a comprehensive approach that goes beyond the often punitive legal compliance stance.

An integrity-based approach to ethics management combines a concern for the law with an emphasis on managerial responsibility for ethical behavior. Though integrity strategies may vary in design and scope, all strive to define companies' guiding values, aspirations, and patterns of thought and conduct. When integrated into the day-to-day operations of an organization, such strategies can help prevent damaging ethical lapses while tapping into powerful human impulses for moral thought and action. Then an ethical framework becomes no longer a burdensome constraint within which companies must operate, but the governing ethos of an organization.

How Organizations Shape Individuals' Behavior

The once familiar picture of ethics as individualistic, unchanging, and impervious to organizational influences has not stood up to scrutiny in recent years. Sears Auto Centers' and Beech-Nut Nutrition Corporation's experiences illustrate the role organizations play in shaping individuals' behavior—and how even sound moral fiber can fray when stretched too thin.

In 1992, Sears, Roebuck & Company was inundated with complaints about its automotive service business. Consumers and attorneys general in more than 40 states had accused the company of misleading customers and selling them unnecessary parts and services, from brake jobs to front-end alignments. It would be a mistake, however, to see this situation

---

1. Reprinted by permission of *Harvard Business Review*. From "Managing for Organizational Integrity" by Lynn Sharp Paine (March–April 1994). Copyright © 1994 by the President and Fellows of Harvard College; all rights reserved.

exclusively in terms of any one individual's moral failings. Nor did management set out to defraud Sears customers. Instead, a number of organizational factors contributed to the problematic sales practices.

In the face of declining revenues, shrinking market share, and an increasingly competitive market for undercar services, Sears management attempted to spur the performance of its auto centers by introducing new goals and incentives for employees. The company increased minimum work quotas and introduced productivity incentives for mechanics. The automotive service advisers were given product-specific sales quotas—sell so many springs, shock absorbers, alignments, or brake jobs per shift—and paid a commission based on sales. According to advisers, failure to meet quotas could lead to a transfer or a reduction in work hours. Some employees spoke of the "pressure, pressure, pressure" to bring in sales.

Under this new set of organizational pressures and incentives, with few options for meeting their sales goals legitimately, some employees' judgment understandably suffered. Management's failure to clarify the line between unnecessary service and legitimate preventive maintenance, coupled with consumer ignorance, left employees to chart their own courses through a vast gray area, subject to a wide range of interpretations. Without active management support for ethical practice and mechanisms to detect and check questionable sales methods and poor work, it is not surprising that some employees may have reacted to contextual forces by resorting to exaggeration, carelessness, or even misrepresentation.

Shortly after the allegations against Sears became public, CEO Edward Brennan acknowledged management's responsibility for putting in place compensation and goal-setting systems that "created an environment in which mistakes did occur." Although the company denied any intent to deceive consumers, senior executives eliminated commissions for service advisers and discontinued sales quotas for specific parts. They also instituted a system of unannounced shopping audits and made plans to expand the internal monitoring of service. In settling the pending lawsuits, Sears offered coupons to customers who had bought certain auto services between 1990 and 1992. The total cost of the settlement, including potential customer refunds, was an estimated $60 million.

Contextual forces can also influence the behavior of top management, as a former CEO of Beech-Nut Nutrition Corporation discovered. In the early 1980s, only two years after joining the company, the CEO found evidence suggesting that the apple juice concentrate, supplied by the company's vendors for use in Beech-Nut's "100% pure" apple juice, contained nothing more than sugar water and chemicals. The CEO could have destroyed the bogus inventory and withdrawn the juice from grocers' shelves, but he was under extraordinary pressure to turn the ailing company around. Eliminating the inventory would have killed any hope of turning even the meager $700,000 profit promised to Beech-Nut's then parent, Nestlé.

A number of people in the corporation, it turned out, had doubted the purity of the juice for several years before the CEO arrived. But the 25 percent price advantage offered by the supplier of the bogus concentrate allowed the operations head to meet cost-control goals. Furthermore, the company lacked an effective quality-control system, and a conclusive lab test for juice purity did not yet exist. When a member of the research department voiced concerns about the juice to operating management, he was accused of not being a team player and of acting like "Chicken Little." His judgment, his supervisor wrote in an annual performance review, was "colored by naiveté and impractical ideals." No one else seemed to have considered the company's obligations to its customers or to have thought about the potential harm of disclosure. No one considered the fact that the sale of adultered or misbranded juice is a legal offense, putting the company and its top management at risk of criminal liability.

An FDA investigation taught Beech-Nut the hard way. In 1987, the company pleaded guilty to selling adultered and misbranded juice. Two years and two criminal trials later, the CEO pleaded guilty to ten counts of mislabeling. The total cost to the company—including fines, legal expenses, and lost sales—was an estimated $25 million.

Such errors of judgment rarely reflect an organizational culture and management philosophy that sets out to harm or deceive. More often, they reveal a culture that is insensitive or indifferent to ethical considerations or one that lacks effective organizational systems. By the same token, exemplary conduct usually reflects an organizational culture and philosophy that is infused with a sense of responsibility.

For example, Johnson & Johnson's handling of the Tylenol crisis is sometimes attributed to the singular personality of then-CEO James Burke. However, the decision to do a nationwide recall of Tylenol capsules in order to avoid further loss of life from product tampering was in reality not one decision but thousands of decisions made by individuals at all levels of the organization. The "Tylenol decision," then, is best understood not as an isolated incident, the achievement of a lone individual, but as the reflection of an organization's culture. Without a shared set of values and guiding principles deeply ingrained throughout the organization, it is doubtful that Johnson & Johnson's response would have been as rapid, cohesive, and ethically sound.

Many people resist acknowledging the influence of organizational factors on individual behavior—especially on misconduct—for fear of diluting people's sense of personal moral responsibility. But this fear is based on a false dichotomy between holding individual transgressors accountable and holding "the system" accountable. Acknowledging the importance of organizational context need not imply exculpating individual wrongdoers. To understand all is not to forgive all.

The Limits of a Legal Compliance Program

The consequences of an ethical lapse can be serious and far-reaching. Organizations can quickly become entangled in an all-consuming web of legal proceedings. The risk of litigation and liability has increased in the past decade as lawmakers have legislated new civil and criminal offenses, stepped up penalties, and improved support for law enforcement. Equally—if not more—important is the damage an ethical lapse can do to an organization's reputation and relationships. Both

Sears and Beech-Nut, for instance, struggled to regain consumer trust and market share long after legal proceedings had ended.

As more managers have become alerted to the importance of organizational ethics, many have asked their lawyers to develop corporate ethics programs to detect and prevent violations of the law. The *1991 Federal Sentencing Guidelines* offer a compelling rationale. Sanctions such as fines and probation for organizations convicted of wrongdoing can vary dramatically depending both on the degree of management cooperation in reporting and investigating corporate misdeeds and on whether or not the company has implemented a legal compliance program. (See the chart "Corporate Fines Under the Federal Sentencing Guidelines.")

Such programs tend to emphasize the prevention of unlawful conduct, primarily by increasing surveillance and control and by imposing penalties for wrongdoers. While plans vary, the basic framework is outlined in the sentencing guidelines. Managers must establish compliance standards and procedures; designate high-level personnel to oversee compliance; avoid delegating discretionary authority to those likely to act unlawfully; effectively communicate the company's standards and procedures through training or publications; take reasonable steps to achieve compliance through audits, monitoring processes, and a system for employees to report criminal misconduct without fear of retribution; consistently enforce standards through appropriate disciplinary measures; respond appropriately when offenses are detected; and, finally take reasonable steps to prevent the occurrence of similar offenses in the future.

There is no question of the necessity of a sound, well-articulated strategy for legal compliance in an organization. After all, employees can be frustrated and frightened by the complexity of today's legal environment. And even managers who claim to use the law as a guide to ethical behavior often lack more than a rudimentary understanding of complex legal issues.

Managers would be mistaken, however, to regard legal compliance as an adequate means for addressing the full range of ethical issues

Corporate Fines Under the Federal Sentencing Guidelines

What size fine is a corporation likely to pay if convicted of a crime? It depends on a number of factors, some of which are beyond a CEO's control, such as the existence of a prior record of similar misconduct. But it also depends on more controllable factors. The most important of these are reporting and accepting responsibility for the crime, cooperating with authorities, and having an effective program in place to prevent and detect unlawful behavior.

The following example, based on a case studied by the United States Sentencing Commission, shows how the *1991 Federal Sentencing Guidelines* have affected overall fine levels and how managers' actions influence organizational fines.

Acme Corporation was charged and convicted of mail fraud. The company systematically charged customers who damaged rented automobiles more than the actual cost of repairs. Acme also billed some customers for the cost of repairs to vehicles for which they were not responsible. Prior to the criminal adjudication, Acme paid $13.7 million in restitution to the customers who had been overcharged.

Deciding before the enactment of the sentencing guidelines, the judge in the criminal case imposed a fine of $6.85 million, roughly half of the pecuniary loss suffered by Acme's customers. Under the sentencing guidelines, however, the results could have been dramatically different. Acme could have been fined from 5 percent to 200 percent the loss suffered by customers, depending on whether or not it had an effective program to prevent and detect violations of law and on whether or not it reported the crime, cooperated with authorities, and accepted responsibility for the unlawful conduct. If a high-ranking official at Acme were found to have been involved, the maximum fine could have been as large as $54,800,000 or four times the loss to Acme customers. The following chart shows a possible range of fines for each situation:

WHAT FINE CAN ACME EXPECT?

	Maximum	Minimum
Program, reporting, cooperation, responsibility	$ 2,740,000	$ 685,000
Program only	10,960.000	5,480,000
No program, no reporting no cooperation, no responsibility	27,400,000	13,700,000
No program, no reporting no cooperation, no responsibility, involvement of high-level personnel	54,800,000	27,400,000

Based on Case No.: 88–266, United States Sentencing Commission, Supplementary Report on Sentencing Guidelines for Organizations.

---

that arise every day. "If it's legal, it's ethical," is a frequently heard slogan; but conduct that is lawful may be highly problematic from an ethical point of view. Consider the sale in some countries of hazardous products without appropriate warnings or the purchase of goods from suppliers who operate inhumane sweatshops in developing countries. Companies engaged in international business often discover that conduct that infringes on recognized standards of human rights and decency is legally permissible in some jurisdictions.

Legal clearance does not certify the absence of ethical problems in the United States either, as a 1991 case at Salomon Brothers illustrates. Four top-level executives failed to take appropriate action when learning of unlawful activities on the government trading desk. Company lawyers found no law obligating the executives to disclose the improprieties. Nevertheless, the executives' delay in disclosing and failure to reveal their prior knowledge prompted a serious crisis of confidence among employees, creditors, shareholders, and customers.

The executives were forced to resign, having lost the moral authority to lead. Their ethical lapse compounded the trading desk's legal offenses, and the company ended up suffering losses—including legal costs, increased funding costs, and lost business—estimated at nearly $1 billion.

A compliance approach to ethics also overemphasizes the threat of detection and punishment in order to channel behavior in lawful directions. The underlying model for this approach is deterrence theory, which envisions people as rational maximizers of self-interest, responsive to the personal costs and benefits of their choices, yet indifferent to the moral legitimacy of those choices. But a recent study reported in *Why People Obey the Law,* by Tom R. Tyler shows that obedience to the law is strongly influenced by a belief in its legitimacy and its moral correctness. People generally feel that they have a strong obligation to obey the law. Education about the legal standards and a supportive environment may be all that's required to insure compliance.

Discipline is, of course, a necessary part of any ethical system. Justified penalties for the infringement of legitimate norms are fair and appropriate. Some people do need the threat of sanctions. However, an overemphasis on potential sanctions can be superfluous and even counterproductive. Employees may rebel against programs that stress penalties, particularly if they are designed and imposed without employee involvement or if the standards are vague or unrealistic. Management may talk of mutual trust when unveiling a compliance plan, but employees often receive the message as a warning from on high. Indeed, the more skeptical among them may view compliance programs as nothing more than liability insurance for senior management. This is not an unreasonable conclusion, considering that compliance programs rarely address the root causes of misconduct.

Even in the best cases, legal compliance is unlikely to unleash much moral imagination or commitment. The law does not generally seek to inspire human excellence or distinction. It is no guide for exemplary behavior—or even good practice. Those managers who define ethics as legal compliance are implicitly endorsing a code of moral mediocrity for their organizations. As Richard Breeden, former chairman of the Securities and Exchange Commission, noted, "It is not an adequate ethical standard to aspire to get through the day without being indicted."

Integrity as a Governing Ethic

A strategy based on integrity holds organizations to a more robust standard. While compliance is rooted in avoiding legal sanctions, organizational integrity is based on the concept of self-governance in accordance with a set of guiding principles. From the perspective of integrity, the task of ethics management is to define and give life to an organization's guiding values, to create an environment that supports ethically sound behavior, and to instill a sense of shared accountability among employees. The need to obey the law is viewed as a positive aspect of organizational life, rather than an unwelcome constraint imposed by external authorities.

An integrity strategy is characterized by a conception of ethics as a driving force of an enterprise. Ethical values shape the search for opportunities, the design of organizational systems, and the decision-making process used by individuals and groups. They provide a common frame of reference and serve as a unifying force across different functions, lines of business, and employee groups. Organizational ethics help define what a company is and what it stands for.

Many integrity initiatives have structural features common to compliance-based initiatives: a code of conduct, training in relevant areas of law, mechanisms for reporting and investigating potential misconduct, and audits and controls to insure that laws and company standards are being met. In addition, if suitably designed, an integrity-based initiative can establish a foundation for seeking the legal benefits that are available under the sentencing guidelines, should criminal wrongdoing occur. (See the insert "The Hallmarks of an Effective Integrity Strategy," p. 51)

But an integrity strategy is broader, deeper, and more demanding than a legal compliance initiative. Broader in that it seeks to enable responsible conduct. Deeper in that it cuts to the ethos and operating systems of the organization and its members, their guiding values and patterns of thought and action. And more demanding in that it requires an active effort to define the responsibilities and aspirations that constitute an organization's ethical compass. Above all, organizational ethics is seen as the work of management. Corporate counsel may play a role in the design and implementation of integrity strategies, but managers at all levels

The Hallmarks of an Effective Integrity Strategy

There is no one right integrity strategy. Factors such as management personality, company history, culture, lines of business, and industry regulations must be taken into account when shaping an appropriate set of values and designing an implementation program. Still, several features are common to efforts that have achieved some success:

- *The guiding values and commitments make sense and are clearly communicated.* They reflect important organizational obligations and widely shared aspirations that appeal to the organization's members. Employees at all levels take them seriously, feel comfortable discussing them, and have a concrete understanding of their practical importance. This does not signal the absence of ambiguity and conflict but a willingness to seek solutions compatible with the framework of values.

- *Company leaders are personally committed, credible, and willing to take action on the values they espouse.* They are not mere mouthpieces. They are willing to scrutinize their own decisions. Consistency on the part of leadership is key. Waffling on values will lead to employee cynicism and a rejection of the program. At the same time, managers must assume responsibility for making tough calls when ethical obligations conflict.

- *The espoused values are integrated into the normal channels of management decision making and are reflected in the organization's critical activities:* the development of plans, the setting of goals, the search for opportunities, the allocation of resources, the gathering and communication of information, the measurement of performance, and the promotion and advancement of personnel.

- *The company's systems and structures support and reinforce its values.* Information systems, for example, are designed to provide timely and accurate information. Reporting relationships are structured to build-in checks and balances to promote objective judgment. Performance appraisal is sensitive to means as well as ends.

- *Managers throughout the company have the decision-making skills, knowledge, and competencies needed to make ethically sound decisions on a day-to-day basis.* Ethical thinking and awareness must be part of every manager's mental equipment. Ethics education is usually part of the process.

Success in creating a climate for responsible and ethically sound behavior requires continuing effort and a considerable investment of time and resources. A glossy code of conduct, a high-ranking ethics officer, a training program, an annual ethics audit—these trappings of an ethics program do not necessarily add up to a responsible, law-abiding organization whose espoused values match its actions. A formal ethics program can serve as a catalyst and a support system, but organizational integrity depends on the integration of the company's values into its driving systems.

and across all functions are involved in the process. (See the chart, "Strategies for Ethics Management," p. 52)

During the past decade, a number of companies have undertaken integrity initiatives. They vary according to the ethical values focused on and the implementation approaches used. Some companies focus on the core values of integrity that reflect basic social obligations, such as respect for the rights of others, honesty, fair dealing, and obedience to the law. Other companies emphasize aspirations—values that are ethically desirable but not necessarily morally obligatory—such as good service to customers, a commitment to diversity, and involvement in the community.

When it comes to implementation, some companies begin with behavior. Following Aristotle's view that one becomes courageous by acting as a courageous person, such companies develop codes of conduct specifying appropriate behavior, along with a system of incentives, audits, and controls. Other companies focus less on specific actions and more on developing attitudes, decision-making processes, and ways of thinking that reflect

STRATEGIES FOR ETHICS MANAGEMENT

Characteristics of Compliance Strategy		Characteristics of Integrity Strategy	
Ethos	Conformity with externally imposed standards	Ethos	Self-governance according to chosen standards
Objective	Prevent criminal misconduct	Objective	Enable responsible conduct
Leadership	Lawyer-driven	Leadership	Management-driven, with aid of lawyers, HR, others
Methods	Education, reduced discretion, auditing and controls, penalties	Methods	Education, leadership, accountability, organizational systems and decision processes, auditing and controls, penalties
Behavioral assumptions	Autonomous beings guided by material self-interest	Behavioral assumptions	Social beings guided by material self-interest, values, ideals, peers

Implementation of Compliance Strategy		Implementation of Integrity Strategy	
Standards	Criminal and regulatory law	Standards	Company values and aspirations; social obligations, including law
Staffing	Lawyers	Staffing	Executives and managers with lawyers, others
Activities	Develop compliance standards, train and communicate, handle reports of misconduct, conduct investigations, oversee compliance audits, enforce standards	Activities	Lead development of company values and standards, train and communicate, integrate into company systems, provide guidance and consultation, assess values performance, identify and resolve problems, oversee compliance activities
Education	Compliance standards and system	Education	Decision making and values compliance standards and system

their values. The assumption is that personal commitment and appropriate decision processes will lead to right action.

Martin Marietta, NovaCare, and Wetherill Associates have implemented and lived with quite different integrity strategies. In each case, management has found that the initiative has made important and often unexpected contributions to competitiveness, work environment, and key relationships on which the company depends.

Martin Marietta: Emphasizing Core Values

Martin Marietta Corporation, the U.S. aerospace and defense contractor, opted for an integrity-based ethics program in 1985. At the time, the defense industry was under attack for fraud and mismanagement, and Martin Marietta was under investigation for improper travel billings. Managers knew they needed a better form of self-governance but were skeptical that an ethics program could influence

behavior. "Back then people asked, 'Do you really need an ethics program to be ethical?'" recalls current President Thomas Young. "Ethics was something personal. Either you had it, or you didn't."

The corporate general counsel played a pivotal role in promoting the program, and legal compliance was a critical objective. But it was conceived of and implemented from the start as a companywide management initiative aimed at creating and maintaining a "do-it-right" climate. In its original conception, the program emphasized core values, such as honesty and fair play. Over time, it expanded to encompass quality and environmental responsibility as well.

Today the initiative consists of a code of conduct, an ethics training program, and procedures for reporting and investigating ethical concerns within the company. It also includes a system for disclosing violations of federal procurement law to the government. A corporate ethics office manages the program, and ethics representatives are stationed at major facilities. An ethics steering committee, made up of Martin Marietta's president, senior executives, and two rotating members selected from field operations, oversees the ethics office. The audit and ethics committee of the board of directors oversees the steering committee.

The ethics office is responsible for responding to questions and concerns from the company's employees. Its network of representatives serves as a sounding board, a source of guidance, and a channel for raising a range of issues, from allegations of wrongdoing to complaints about poor management, unfair supervision, and company policies and practices. Martin Marietta's ethics network, which accepts anonymous complaints, logged over 9,000 calls in 1991, when the company had about 60,000 employees. In 1992, it investigated 684 cases. The ethics office also works closely with the human resources, legal, audit, communications, and security functions to respond to employee concerns.

Shortly after establishing the program, the company began its first round of ethics training for the entire workforce, starting with the CEO and senior executives. Now in its third round, training for senior executives focuses on decision making, the challenges of balancing multiple responsibilities, and compliance with laws and regulations critical to the company. The incentive compensation plan for executives makes responsibility for promoting ethical conduct an explicit requirement for reward eligibility and requires that business and personal goals be achieved in accordance with the company's policy on ethics. Ethical conduct and support for the ethics program are also criteria in regular performance reviews.

Today top-level managers say the ethics program has helped the company avoid serious problems and become more responsive to its more than 90,000 employees. The ethics network, which tracks the number and types of cases and complaints, has served as an early warning system for poor management, quality and safety defects, racial and gender discrimination, environmental concerns, inaccurate and false records, and personnel grievances regarding salaries, promotions, and lay-offs. By providing an alternative channel for raising such concerns, Martin Marietta is able to take corrective action more quickly and with a lot less pain. In many cases, potentially embarrassing problems have been identified and dealt with before becoming a management crisis, a lawsuit, or a criminal investigation. Among employees who brought complaints in 1993, 75 percent were satisfied with the results.

Company executives are also convinced that program has helped reduce the incidence of misconduct. When allegations of misconduct do surface, the company says it deals with them openly. On several occasions, for instance, Martin Marietta has voluntarily disclosed and made restitution to the government for misconduct involving potential violations of federal procurement law. In addition, when an employee alleged that the company had retaliated against him for voicing said concerns about his plant on CBS news, top management commissioned an investigation by an outside law firm. Although failing to support the allegations, the investigation found that employees at the plant feared retaliation when raising health, safety, or environmental complaints. The company redoubled its efforts to identify and discipline those employees taking retaliatory action and stressed the desirability of an open work environment in its ethics training and company communications.

Although the ethics program helps Martin Marietta avoid certain types of litigation, it has occasionally led to other kinds of legal action. In a few cases, employees dismissed for violating the code of ethics sued Martin Marietta, arguing that the company had violated its own code by imposing unfair and excessive discipline.

Still, the company believes that its attention to ethics has been worth it. The ethics program has led to better relationships with the government, as well as to new business opportunities. Along with prices and technology, Martin Marietta's record of integrity, quality, and reliability of estimates plays a role in the awarding of defense contracts, which account for some 75 percent of the company's revenues. Executives believe that the reputation they've earned through their ethics program has helped them build trust with government auditors, as well. By opening up communications, the company has reduced the time spent on redundant audits.

The program has also helped change employees' perceptions and priorities. Some managers compare their new ways of thinking about ethics to the way they understand quality. They consider more carefully how situations will be perceived by others, the possible long-term, consequences of short-term thinking, and the need for continuous improvement. CEO Norman Augustine notes, "Ten years ago, people would have said that there were no ethical issues in business. Today employees think their number-one objective is to be thought of as decent people doing quality work."

Novacare: Building Shared Aspirations

NovaCare Inc., one of the largest providers of rehabilitation services to nursing homes and hospitals in the United States, has oriented its ethics effort toward building a common core of shared aspirations. But in 1988, when the company was called InSpeech, the only sentiment shared was mutual mistrust.

Senior executives built the company from a series of aggressive acquisitions over a brief period of time to take advantage of the expanding market for therapeutic services. However, in 1988, the viability of the company was in question. Turnover among its frontline employees—the clinicians and therapists who care for patients in nursing homes and hospitals—escalated to 57 percent per year. The company's inability to retain therapists caused customers to defect and the stock price to languish in an extended slump.

After months of soul-searching, InSpeech executives realized that the turnover rate was a symptom of a more basic problem: the lack of a common set of values and aspirations. There was, as one executive put it, a "huge disconnect" between the values of the therapists and clinicians and those of the managers who ran the company. The therapists and clinicians evaluated the company's success in terms of its delivery of high-quality health care. InSpeech management, led by executives with financial services and venture capital backgrounds,

measured the company's worth exclusively in terms of financial success. Management's single-minded emphasis on increasing hours of reimbursable care turned clinicians off. They took management's performance orientation for indifference to patient care and left the company in droves.

CEO John Foster recognized the need for a common frame of reference and a common language to unify the diverse groups. So he brought in consultants to conduct interviews and focus groups with the company's health care professionals, managers, and customers. Based on the results, an employee task force drafted a proposed vision statement for the company, and another 250 employees suggested revisions. Then Foster and several senior managers developed a succinct statement of the company's guiding purpose and fundamental beliefs that could be used as a framework for making decisions and setting goals, policies, and practices.

Unlike a code of conduct, which articulates specific behavioral standards, the statement of vision, purposes, and beliefs lays out in very simple terms the company's central purpose and core values. The purpose—meeting the rehabilitation needs of patients through clinical leadership—is supported by four key beliefs: respect for the individual, service to the customer, pursuit of excellence, and commitment to personal integrity. Each value is discussed with examples of how it is manifested in the day-to-day activities and policies of the company, such as how to measure the quality of care.

To support the newly defined values, the company changed its name to NovaCare and introduced a number of structural and operational changes. Field managers and clinicians were given greater decision-making authority, clinicians were provided with additional resources to assist in the delivery of effective therapy, and a new management structure integrated the various therapies offered by the company. The hiring of new corporate personnel with health care backgrounds reinforced the company's new clinical focus.

The introduction of the vision, purpose, and beliefs met with varied reactions from employees, ranging from cool skepticism to open enthusiasm. One employee remembered thinking the talk about values "much ado about nothing." Another recalled, "It was really wonderful. It gave us a goal that everyone aspired to, no matter what their place in the company." At first, some were baffled about how the vision, purpose, and beliefs were to be used. But, over time, managers became more adept at explaining and using them as a guide. When a customer tried to hire away a valued employee, for example, managers considered raiding the customer's company for employees. After reviewing the beliefs, the managers abandoned the idea.

NovaCare managers acknowledge and company surveys indicate that there is plenty of room for improvement. While the values are used as a firm reference point for decision making and evaluation in some areas of the company, they are still viewed with reservation in others. Some managers do not "walk the talk," employees complain. And recently acquired companies have yet to be fully integrated into the program. Nevertheless, many NovaCare employees say the values initiative played a critical role in the company's 1990 turnaround.

The values reorientation also helped the company deal with its most serious problem: turnover among health care providers. In 1990, the turnover rate stood at 32 percent, still above target but a significant improvement over the 1988 rate of 57 percent. By 1993, turnover had dropped to 27 percent. Moreover, recruiting new clinicians became easier. Barely able to hire 25 new clinicians each month in 1988, the company added 776 in 1990 and 2,546 in 1993. Indeed, one employee who left during the 1988 turmoil said that her decision to return in 1990 hinged on the company's adoption of the vision, purpose, and beliefs.

Wetherill Associates: Defining Right Action

Wetherill Associates, Inc.—a small, privately held supplier of electrical parts to the automotive market—has neither a conventional code of conduct nor a statement of values. Instead, WAI has a *Quality Assurance Manual*—a combination of philosophy text, conduct guide,

technical manual, and company profile—that describes the company's commitment to honesty and its guiding principle of right action.

WAI doesn't have a corporate ethics officer who reports to top management, because at WAI, the company's corporate ethics officer *is* top management. Marie Bothe, WAI's chief executive officer, sees her main function as keeping the 350-employee company on the path of right action and looking for opportunities to help the community. She delegates the "technical" aspects of the business—marketing, finance, personnel, operations—to other members of the organization.

Right action, the basis for all of WAI's decisions, is a well-developed approach that challenges most conventional management thinking. The company explicitly rejects the usual conceptual boundaries that separate morality and self-interest. Instead, they define right behavior as logically, expediently, and morally right. Managers teach employees to look at the needs of the customers, suppliers, and the community—in addition to those of the company and its employees—when making decisions.

WAI also has a unique approach to competition. One employee explains, "We are not 'in competition' with anybody. We just do what we have to do to serve the customer." Indeed, when occasionally unable to fill orders, WAI salespeople refer customers to competitors. Artificial incentives, such as sales contests, are never used to spur individual performance. Nor are sales results used in determining compensation. Instead, the focus is on teamwork and customer service. Managers tell all new recruits that absolute honesty, mutual courtesy, and respect are standard operating procedure.

Newcomers generally react positively to company philosophy, but not all are prepared for such a radical departure from the practices they have known elsewhere. Recalling her initial interview one recruit described her response to being told that lying was not allowed, "What do you mean? No lying? I'm a buyer. I lie for a living!" Today she is persuaded that the policy makes sound business sense. WAI is known for informing suppliers of overshipments as well as undershipments and for scrupulous honesty in the sale of parts, even when deception cannot be readily detected.

Since its entry into the distribution business 13 years ago, WAI has seen its revenues climb steadily from just under $1 million to nearly $98 million in 1993, and this in an industry with little growth. Once seen as an upstart beset by naysayers and industry skeptics, WAI is now credited with entering and professionalizing an industry in which kickbacks, bribes, and "gratuities" were commonplace. Employees—equal numbers of men and women ranging in age from 17 to 92—praise the work environment as both productive and supportive.

WAI's approach could be difficult to introduce in a larger, more traditional organization. WAI is a small company founded by 34 people who shared a belief in right action; its ethical values were naturally built into the organization from the start. Those values are so deeply ingrained in the company's culture and operating systems that they have been largely self-sustaining. Still, the company has developed its own training program and takes special care to hire people willing to support right action. Ethics and job skills are considered equally important in determining an individual's competence and suitability for employment. For WAI, the challenge will be to sustain its vision as the company grows and taps into markets overseas.

At WAI, as at Martin Marietta and Nova Care, a management-led commitment to ethical values has contributed to competitiveness, positive workforce morale, as well as solid sustainable relationships with the company's key constituencies. In the end, creating a climate that encourages exemplary conduct may be the best way to discourage damaging misconduct. Only in such an environment do rogues really act alone.

Source: Lynn Sharp Paine is a John G. McLean professor at the Harvard Business School, specializing in management ethics. Her current research focuses on leadership and organizational integrity in a global environment. Reprinted by permission of *Harvard Business Review*. From "Managing for Organizational Integrity" by Lynn Sharp Paine, March/April, 1994. Copyright © 1994 by the Harvard Business School Publishing Corporation; all rights reserved.

Readings | *The Whistle-blower: Patriot or Bounty Hunter?*

Andrew W. Singer
Across the Board, November 1992

The False Claims Act provides financial incentives for employees to report their companies' transgressions to the government. Does that debase their motives?

While serving in Vietnam, Emil Stache had the misfortune to stumble onto a booby-trapped Viet Cong bomb. The explosion killed several of his fellow soldiers, and Stache himself suffered severe shrapnel wounds to his left arm and shoulder. He later learned that the trap had been made from a defective U.S. bomb—one that never exploded.

Years later, Stache was manager of quality engineering and reliability at Teledyne Relays, a subsidiary of Teledyne, Inc. He suspected that Teledyne Relays falsified tests on the electromagnetic relays (electronic components used in missiles, planes, rockets and other military hardware) the company manufactured for the U.S. government.

Stache felt it his ethical duty to report the matter: He knew only too well the price of defective hardware. "It was the only thing he could do," explains his lawyer, John R. Phillips. "He complained about it. He got fired."

Stache brought a lawsuit against Teledyne Relays under the federal False Claims Act: he was later joined in the action by the Department of Justice. The suit claims that Teledyne Relays' failure to properly test the relay components defrauded the government of as much as $250 million. If found guilty, the Los Angeles–based company could be liable for as much as $750 million in damages, treble the amount that the government claims it was defrauded.

Who is Emil Stache? A patriot who just did his duty? That certainly is how Phillips and others see him. But if Stache's lawsuit succeeds, he stands to become a very rich patriot, indeed. According to provisions of the amended False Claims Act. Stache and his co-plaintiffs in the suit—another Teledyne Relays employee named Almon Muehlhausen and Taxpayers Against Fraud, a nonprofit organization founded by Phillips—could get 15 percent to 25 percent of any money recovered by the government. Stache himself theoretically could receive as much as $62 million.

(Contacted for comment on the case, Teledyne spokesperson Berkley Baker said, "We have no comment to make. It's in the legal system now.")

Creating Market Incentives

The amended False Claims Act grew out of public outrage in the mid-1980s over reports of fraud and abuse on the part of military contractors—of $600 toilet seats and country club memberships billed to the government. Congress decided to put some teeth into its efforts to reduce contracting fraud. In 1986, it passed the False Claims Act amendments, whose *qui tam* provisions allow employees who bring forward information about contractor fraud to share with the government in any financial recovery realized by their efforts. (*Qui tam* is Latin shorthand for, "He who sues for the king as well as himself.")

Those market incentives are now bearing fruit. In July, the government recovered $50 million in a case brought by a whistle-blower against a former division of Singer Co. And a week later, the government recovered the largest amount ever in such an action: a $59.5 million settlement with General Electric Co. (GE). That case, a scandal involving the sale of military-jet engines in Israel, was brought initially by the manager of a GE unit.

U.S. Rep. Howard L. Berman of California, a cosponsor of the 1986 amendment, expects recoveries from *qui tam* actions, most of which are against defense contractors, to reach $1 billion in the next two to three years. The Teledyne Relays suit looms as one of the largest

cases, but Phillips speaks of two others in the pipeline, one against Litton Industries Inc. and another that is under court seal, that could bring the government "staggering" amounts.

Undermining Voluntary Efforts?

Not surprisingly, many of the defense industry are aghast at the new False Claims Act—and, specifically, its *qui tam* provisions. The law has created "enormous concern in the defense industry," says Alan R. Yuspeh, a government-contracts attorney and partner in Howrey & Simon in Washington, D.C. Some fear that cases may proliferate and people with essentially technical disagreements may bring suits in the hope of reaping payoffs from an out-of-court settlement.

The *qui tam* provisions encourage "bounty hunting" and undermine voluntary ethics efforts, add critics. Why should an employee report wrongdoing to his company when he can hold out and earn millions from the government? And from the larger ethical perspective: Shouldn't people report fraud because it's the right thing to do, and not because they hope to reap a windfall profit?

"I think personally that the provision of bounties is misguided," said Gary Edwards, president of the Ethics Resource Center, a nonprofit education and consulting organization based in Washington, D.C. "It creates an incentive for individuals in companies that are trying to do a better job—not to report wrongdoing, but to gather data so as to participate in the reward."

"Encouraging tittle-tattles is destructive," declares Charles Barber, former chairman and CEO of Asarco, Inc., a *Fortune* 500 company that produces nonferrous metals. "The integrity of the organization has to be built another way," such as with corporate ombudsman offices. "You can't run a defense company if everyone is being watched."

"I deplore the way we have developed into such a litigious society in which everyone is jumping on the bandwagon to sue about anything that comes up," says Sanford N. McDonnell, chairman emeritus of McDonnell Douglas Corp., the nation's largest defense contractor.

"If We All Lived in an Ideal World..."

Phillips, who is generally credited with drafting the amended False Claims Act, responds: "If we all lived in an ideal world, where all did the right thing on principle, we would have no need for such a law. But we don't live in such a world." People who bring charges against their companies take great risks—to their jobs, their families and their careers, he says.

Most agree that the plight of the corporate whistle-blower has historically been a bleak one. A survey of 85 whistle-blowers by the Association of Mental Health Specialties (now Integrity International) in College Park, Md., in the late-1980s found that 82 percent experienced harassment after blowing the whistle, 60 percent got fired, 17 percent lost their homes, and 10 percent reported having attempted suicide. "You can't expect them to [report fraud] when there is nothing but risk and heartache down the road," says Phillips. Sharing in the recovery of damages is one way to right the balance.

Yuspeh, for one, isn't convinced. It is an "unsound piece of legislation. It almost invites disgruntled former employees who may have had some technical disagreement to go out and file a lawsuit." (It should be added that in recent years, large contractors have increasingly reported instances of wrongdoing or fraud to the government voluntarily, before evidence came to public light.)

Congressman Berman says the law works precisely as intended: By providing marketplace incentives, it encourages people to protect the government and the public from waste, fraud and abuse. "I'm not only happy with the law, I'm proud of it," he tells *Across the Board*.

Morally problematic"? "You mean like: If you have any information about a wanted criminal, we'll pay a reward?" asks Berman, rhetorically.

Those companies that commit fraud don't like the Act, suggests Berman, while those in compliance with the law aren't troubled by it. And he is skeptical of detractors who claim that these are merely technical disputes. "The test here is commission of fraud," he says.

Harks Back to the Civil War

The original False Claims Act dates back to the Civil War, where it was used to prosecute manufacturers who substituted sawdust for gunpowder in Union army supplies. Employees who exposed contractors who overcharged the government could, theoretically, earn 10 percent of the amount recovered. But under the old law, federal prosecutors who took over cases had the option of removing private plaintiffs, leaving whistle-blowers high and dry.

"Very few people were willing to do it under the old system," either through fear of losing their jobs, being black-balled within their industry, or shunned by their friends, says Phillips, a partner in the Los Angeles law firm of Hall & Phillips. It took a kind of heroic figure to blow the whistle, he says.

The amended False Claims Act aimed to fix some of those problems, "We tried to rebuild the law, to give it some teeth," explains Berman. "Where the government is not privy to information about fraud, the taxpayers are represented by private parties."

Even more important than the sheer amounts of money recovered, says Phillips, is the preventive effect of the statute on corporations. "The law has shaken up their internal practices. People who were previously inclined to go along with questionable practices are now doing the right thing," he says.

But companies say the statute undermines their voluntary ethics efforts. "I know their argument," replies Phillips. "But there's no basis to it. They're saying, 'We have a whole system set up. You should come to us first.' With fraud, he says, the government has an interest in being the first to know. The government is saying, 'We want information to come directly to us in cases of fraud.'"

"It will enhance corporate efforts, because companies can get socked with treble damages for fraud," says Berman. "Companies will become more vigilant."

Does he know of any contractors who support the amendments? "The goal of the act is not to please government contractors," snaps Berman. "The goal is to protect the government and the public."

Portrait of a Whistleblower

Corporate whistleblowers have traditionally been treated as malcontents, troublemakers, and misfits. And many have paid a steep price for their actions.

A 1987 survey of 87 whistleblowers by Dr. Donald Soeken, president of Integrity International in College Park, Md., noted: "All but one respondent reported experiencing retaliation which they attributed to their whistle-blowing. And that one individual merely indicated that 'nothing could be proved.'"

Soeken, who was a government whistle-blower himself, compares the whistleblower to a cross between a bloodhound and a bulldog. "He will track it down [i.e., the wrong-doing] and stand his ground. . . . His conscience is very strong, unwavering. He's the first one to feel guilty when something happens.

That certainly applies to Richard Walker, a whistleblower in the era *before* the amended False Claims Act. A scientist with a Ph.D. in physics, Walker worked for 27 years at American Telephone & Telegraph Co.'s (AT&T) prestigious Bell Laboratories.

In 1971, as head of a team of scientists working on a high-level military project for the U.S. Navy, he discovered serious errors in Bell Labs' computer projections. He informed his superior of the errors, and said they had better report them to the Navy. When his boss refused, Walker took matters into his own hands.

He decided to give a corporate seminar within Bell Labs, which was his prerogative as a manager. Walker spent an hour exposing the errors he had found and explaining how the company had overestimated the effectiveness of the project. "The way to avoid corruption is to get it out in the open," he told *Ethikos* in a 1987 interview, recalling his thinking at the time.

The immediate response within the company to his seminar seemed positive. "I thought, in view of his feedback, that I had gotten through to these people," said Walker.

He was mistaken, Several months later, Walker's boss wrote a letter to a high Bell Labs officer questioning Walker's technical competence. "On the basis of that criticism, I was moved out of that area and put into a totally inappropriate assignment. It was just a way of getting rid of me."

There was a succession of increasingly demeaning and meaningless assignments. He spent three-and-a-half years in a marine-cable engineering department, followed by a super-visory appointment at a "planning" center in which "for three-and-a-half years, they wouldn't tell me what my responsibilities were."

In 1979, Bell Labs fired Walker for allegedly not taking an active interest in his assigned work. In 1982, Walker brought suit against AT&T, charging that he had been fired without good cause. Walker devoted himself full time to his case. He had an entire room in his apartment set aside to store depositions and other evidence relevant to his case. He spent $50,000 of his own money pressing the litiga-tion. During this time, his wife divorced him and he was forced to sell the house he designed in affluent Mendham, N.J., where he raised his four children.

On March 23, 1987, *Walker vs. Bell* came to trial. Eight days later, the New Jersey judge dismissed the case that Walker had brought.

According to AT&T, justice was served. "Dr. Walker had ample opportunity to prove his allegations before the court, and the court rejected those allegations as being totally unfounded," the AT&T attorney who tried the case commented.

Walker took the defeat hard. Despite the advice of people like Soeken and others, he refused to let the matter rest. For years he tried to interest journalists, government officials and employee-rights organizations in this case. He barraged AT&T officers and directors with let-ters seeking redress for the wrong he felt he had suffered. All to no avail.

Eventually, Walker moved back to his home state of Michigan, where he remarried and is now working to establish a retreat for whistleblowers.

Walker may have been ahead of his time. New Jersey has since passed legislation to protect whistleblowers. AT&T now has an excessive network of corporate ombudsman to handle cases like his. And the amended False Claims Act has since been enacted.

John Phillips, an attorney who has represented other whistleblowers and a principal author of the amended False Claims Act says that one key effect of the amended Act is that it no longer requires a "heroic" figure to blow the whistle. The Act could also bring forth a higher order of whistleblower, he suggests. In the past,

whistleblowers "were not always the most stable people," noted Phillips in a 1989 interview with *Ethikos*. Many, he said, had a "need to confess" or to "point the finger at someone."

The people whom Phillips sees coming forward now to report wrongdoing by government contractors are still idealistic in some ways, but in many ways they are "far more credible, substantial, senior people than whistleblowers, from the pre-[False Claims Act] amendment era."—**A.W.S.**

The GE Case

The case involving General Electric's aircraft-engine division is one of the more interesting False Claims Act actions to arise. Employees in the division conspired with an Israeli general, Rami Dotan, to submit fraudulent claims for work done for the Israeli Air Force. General Electric eventually pleaded guilty to four federal criminal-fraud charges. It agreed to pay the Justice Department $9.5 million in fines for the criminal charges and $59.5 million for the civil case brought under the False Claims Act.

The Justice Department said the company's employees helped divert as much as $40 million to Dotan and others, money that ultimately came from the U.S. government. The scheme became known through a lawsuit filed by Chester Walsh, who served as general manager of the aircraft-engine division's Israeli unit from 1984 to 1988.

What irks General Electric is that Walsh reported the matter first to the government instead of the company, despite the fact that Walsh, like others at GE, signed an ethics statement each year affirming that he would report wrongdoing to the company if and when it was discovered.

"The man involved decided not to report wrongdoing," says Bruce Bunch, a GE spokesman. "He took no steps to stop it. "He participated in it, and all the time he signed our written statement each year that he would report any improprieties to management." It is General Electric's position that Walsh gathered information from 1986 to 1990 and then filed his lawsuit, from which he hoped to gain personally. Walsh could receive 25 percent of the nearly $60 million recovered by the government as a result of the civil suit. (A hearing that will determine the exact amount is set to begin in November in Cincinnati.)

If he had reported the corruption immediately, the case would have come to light, continues Bunch. "We had an ombudsman telephone number at the corporate office, outside of the business loop. Additionally, he could have called the Department of Defense ombudsman."

False Claims Suits Growing

How does the government view the False Claims Act? "It is hardly a secret that the Act is critical to the government's anti-fraud effort," Stuart Gerson, assistant attorney general, acknowledged last year. Gerson added, however, that the statute's *qui tam* provisions, which allow private citizens to bring actions on behalf of the government, have been controversial, affecting as they do "the climate of government contracting and the dynamics of a corporation's relationship with its employees."

As of April 1, six years since the amendments passed, 407 *qui tam* suits had been filed. The government took over 66 of these cases; it is currently litigating 29 cases and has settled or obtained judgments in 37 others. The total recoveries of $147 million from *qui tam* suits under the Act comprise about 13.5 percent of the government's total fraud recoveries for the six-year period. Individuals who brought suits had won $14.5 million as of April, but 75 cases were still under investigation. (The dollar amount doesn't include the large recoveries in July from the General Electric Co. case reported in the main story.)

The number of *qui tam* suits has grown steadily since 1986, notes Gerson, and it is expected to rise further. Thirty-three were filed in all of fiscal-year 1987, for example, while 78 were filed in the first eight months of fiscal-year 1991 alone. Cases involving the Department of Defense are by far the most numerous, but now actions being taken in other areas, including health care, agriculture, and the Department of Housing and Urban Development.

"In short, as attention is focused on the whistleblower suits, and significant recoveries have been reported, this form of action is proliferating," said Gerson.

However, some government officials recently have expressed second thoughts about the potentially large awards to individual whistleblowers. In the GE fraud case, Gerson said he had reservations about just how much credit and money the whistleblower and his lawyers should receive. It remains to be seen whether attempts will be made to curb such awards.—**A.W.S.**

A case of bounty hunting? "That clearly appears to be what happened here," says Bunch.

Phillips, who represents Walsh, claims that General Electric has smeared his client. "They claim Walsh is a money grubber. That's their party line." (GE Chairman John F. Welch, Jr. had been quoted in the *Corporate Crime Reporter,* a weekly legal publication, labeling Walsh as "a money-grubbing guy who sat back and waited in the weeds so the damages would mount." Bunch declines to comment on the accuracy of that quote.) Phillips tells a different story: "It was his dream job. It was very painful for him to do this."

Walsh feared for his job and even his life, Phillips says. He worried that anything he told GE would get back to Dotan, whom Phillips characterizes as a ruthless, violence-prone individual. His superiors at the aircraft-engine division were all aware of the arrangement with Dotan, Walsh believed, "He says that Dotan had people removed from their jobs at GE. The idea that he would go back and write a letter to Cincinnati [where the aircraft-engine division is based] about what he had seen was simply not credible," says Phillips.

As proof that Walsh's suspicions were well-founded, Phillips points to the fact that Dotan is now serving 13 years in prison in Israel. The general was charged by the Israeli government with kickbacks, theft, fraud, obstruction of justice and conspiring to kidnap and harm a fellow Israeli Ministry of Defense official.

Couldn't Walsh have gone to General Electric's corporate ombudsman, who is based in Fairfield, Conn., and is presumably outside the aircraft-engine division loop? "He doesn't know who's on the other end," answers Phillips. For all Walsh knew, Phillips says, the ombudsman might just get on the phone with Cincinnati to find out what was going on.

But couldn't he have called anonymously? "It's an 800 number. They can find out where it came from. There was no way he could protect his anonymity." Or so Walsh believed, Phillips says.

"The idea that people will call up blindly some number is ludicrous," Phillips says. "I don't think people have confidence in the GE program." (Subsequent to this interview, The *Wall Street Journal* ran a front-page story on the company headlined: "GE's Drive to Purge Fraud Is Hampered by Workers' Mistrust," which appeared to support many of Phillips' assertions.)

"A Detrimental Effect"

Whatever the whys and wherefores of the GE case, it seems clear that the *qui tam* provisions are causing havoc among those in charge of compliance at some defense companies. "Pandemonium" was how the ombudsman at one large defense company characterized the provisions and the large suits now being filed.

"I've heard from some company representatives who believe the availability of the *qui tam* rewards have had a detrimental effect, that they have caused people not to use their internal systems," says the Ethics Resource Center's Edwards.

"No company can be happy with *qui tam* procedures," says John Impert, director of corporate ethics policy and assistant general counsel at The Boeing Co., even though his company has been virtually untouched by the False Claims Act. "It provides incentives to employees to take an adverse position. This is illustrated graphically in the GE case."

It's important that people report matters of ethical concern, says McDonnell of McDonnell Douglas, "But I don't think they should receive remuneration for that," he says.

Won't this help eliminate the steep price whistle-blowers have paid for coming forward?" "I'm sure it will stimulate more action, more people coming forward, but I'd rather see it come from individuals who take it to the company ombudsman, and report it without attribution," says McDonnell.

Deputizing Citizens

Attorney Yuspeh and others are fundamentally at odds with the notion that individuals should bring lawsuits on the part of the U.S. government. "The role of initiating [lawsuits] on the part of the government is a role for the officer of the U.S. government. I have a big problem with individuals who have a personal profit motive, who have inside information, and who may be disgruntled because of downsizing, having the power of the government to advance a personal agenda."

Yuspeh notes that plaintiffs' lawyers tend to profit from the amended False Claims Act and its controversial *qui tam* provisions: "There's a lot of money for them to make." He would prefer an arrangement where informants would get some money from the government, but would not bring suit themselves. "At least the government is then deciding whether to bring a suit." This would also cut out the plaintiffs' legal fees.

"The problem with *qui tam* suits is that someone who would otherwise do this as part of their normal duties might now wait until they are no longer employed, or until they have an opportunity to enrich themselves," says LeRoy J. Haugh, who is vice president for procurement and finance of the Aerospace Industries Association, an organization based in Washington, D.C.

"Our biggest concern with *qui tam* proceedings is that someone who wants to bring a suit is at no risk at all," Haugh says. "If they can get a lawyer to handle it on a contingency basis and they win, they stand to win a great deal of money. And if they lose, they haven't lost anything, except the lawyer's time."

Answers Congressman Berman: "The situation here is that no one gets anything unless fraud is committed. Lawyer's won't take cases if they're not legitimate."

Still, Haugh says, the negative publicity generated from such suits—even if the company accused of wrongdoing is eventually found to be not guilty—"often overshadows efforts over the last seven or eight years on the part of many companies to comply with Defense Industry Initiative guidelines [a set of voluntary guidelines developed by the nation's largest defense contractors to promote ethical business conduct] and to put into place adequate checks and balances."

Importance of Building Trust

"I'm not saying that every suit that is brought is a frivolous suit," says Yuspeh, who served as coordinator of the Defense Industry Initiative (DII) steering committee. (He makes clear that he is speaking only for himself in making these comments, not the DII companies.) "Clearly some cases are meritorious. But it makes more sense to have officials of the U.S. government handle them."

Ethics Resource Center's Edwards doesn't quarrel with the notion that whistle-blowers have historically been treated very badly. But he points out that today they have protection under the law against retaliation, and that many excellent voluntary corporate programs have been initiated since the amendments were passed. Many companies today have ethics hotlines, ombudsman offices, extensive ethics-training programs and ethics committees. "Maybe several years ago it was necessary to entice them to blow the whistle," he says. But that isn't the case in many major American corporations today. "A well-developed ethics program should obviate the need for that," he adds.

Even Phillips concedes that voluntary corporate ethics efforts could be effective. "But you've got to convince people that the corporation wants you to do this, and that the corporation will reward you," he says.

Phillips may have hit on something there. Or to put the problem in quasi-dialectical terms: If the *thesis* back in the 1980s was egregious defense-industry waste and abuse, and the *antithesis* was the punitive (at least, from the industry perspective) bounty-hunting provisions of the False Claims Act, the *synthesis* could well be voluntary corporate ethics efforts that enjoy the full confidence of employees—and that really work.

"It takes time, no doubt about it," says McDonnell, referring to building trust within a company. "You can't just mandate it. It has to be built up by actual cases, and it's difficult to advertise it, because that [confidentiality] is the sort of thing you're trying to protect. But when it's done right, it gets the desired result."

Readings | *Law Case Summary: Caremark National Inc.*

L. J. Brooks

Late in 1996, the Chancery Court of the State of Delaware—a very influential court in corporate matters—handed down a decision that changed the expectations of directors for monitoring the affairs of the organizations they direct. The change held in the Caremark National Inc. case was to require directors to monitor organizational activities even when there is no cause for suspicion of wrongdoing.

Until the Caremark decision, the guiding case was the Delaware Supreme Court's 1963 decision in *Graham v. Allis-Chalmers Manufacturing Co.* In *Allis-Chalmers,* a case involving director's liability for violations of U.S. antitrust laws, the court had found that, "absent cause for suspicion," a board of directors had no legal duty to create a system for monitoring of or compliance with organizational activities. This allowed directors to argue an "ostrich" defense in the event of wrongdoing to the effect that they had "seen no evil nor heard no evil" and had made their decisions in good faith and to the best of their ability. As a result, the fiduciary duties of directors and the duty of care were somewhat circumscribed from the level of responsibility that some stakeholders felt reasonable.

The Chancery Court took the view, in the Caremark Case, a derivative lawsuit to one involving kickbacks to health care providers in violation of the Federal Anti-Referral Payments Law, that the directors could be liable for recovery of some of the company's $250 million in fines from its directors for breach of their duty of care by failing to take good faith measures to prevent or remedy the violations. The court noted, since employee actions could prevent a corporation from achieving its strategic goals, "that a director's obligation includes a duty to assure in good faith that [an] information reporting system, which the Board concludes is adequate, exists and that failure to do so under some circumstances may, in theory at least, render a director liable for losses caused by non-compliance with applicable legal standards." Moreover, due to the issuance of the *U.S. Sentencing Guidelines* on November 1, 1991, and their subsequent integration into expectations, directors must now consider the "due diligence defense" criteria that those guidelines have spawned when advancing their "good faith" defense. This means that the Chancery Court no longer considers a corporate compliance and monitoring program to be optional.

For further information, the reader is referred to an article by Frank M. Placenti in *The National Law Journal* on Monday June 23, 1997 (pages B5, B6). Further insights are possible if higher courts modify the Chancery Court's Caremark decision, but, until then, directors are well-advised to be ethically proactive in the development of strategic plans and operating policies and in the monitoring of performance.

Source: Across the Board, November 1992, pp. 16–22.

Reprinted with permission.

2

ENRON EVENTS MOTIVATE GOVERNANCE & ETHICS REFORM

Purpose of the Chapter

Enron and the subsequent Arthur Andersen and WorldCom fiascoes triggered a "sea change" of new expectations for governance and the accounting profession in United States, Canada, and around the world. These fiascoes created such a serious crisis of credibility in the corporate accounting, reporting, and governance processes that U.S. politicians created new frameworks of accountability and governance within the Sarbanes-Oxley Act to restore sufficient confidence to allow capital markets to return to normal functioning. In essence, the fiascoes accelerated and then the Sarbanes-Oxley Act crystallized heightened expectations for ethical behavior by businesspeople and members of the accounting profession. Subsequent events have reinforced the need for organizations to conduct their affairs within these new ethical expectations.

Understanding the issues, principles, and practices involved in these new expectations is essential to the anticipation and consideration of what will be appropriate future governance and behavior for corporations and professional accountants. Faced with applying a stream of new guidelines and regulations, including many spawned by the Sarbanes-Oxley Act, businesspeople and professional accountants will find their task facilitated by understanding their essence—the ethical underpinnings—of the new initiatives.

Governance & Accountability Reform

Overview & Timeline of Events and Developments

Multiple huge shocks generated a crisis of investor confidence in corporate and professional ethics that underpin North American capital market values and the trust that allows modern commerce. President Bush and leaders around the world were calling for answers and solutions to ensure compliance with fair values that the public could support and the public interest demanded. Ultimately, corporate governance and the accounting profession were shown to need reform to restore the trust and credibility needed for financial markets to work effectively.

In mid-October 2001, vaunted giant Enron restated manipulated earnings, and on December 2 filed for bankruptcy, destroying billions in value—especially of retirement investment—in the process. Amid stories of huge sham and fraudulent off-statement transactions, it became clear that senior executives enriched themselves beyond belief, while the board of directors and Arthur Andersen, the auditor, apparently were unaware or worse. Frequently, Enron executives claimed bad memories, ignorance, or the Fifth Amendment in front of Senate and congressional committees. Government and the SEC seemed at a loss to deal with the situation.

FIGURE 2.1   **Governance Reform Timeline**

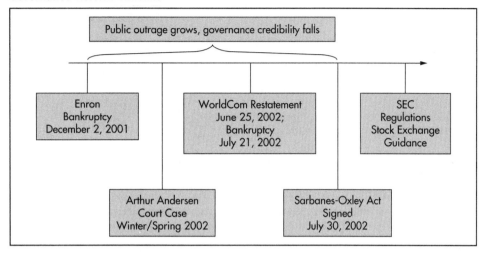

Stories also began to surface about a blatant, self-interested, and apparently in-your-face shredding of Enron audit documents by Arthur Andersen that ultimately produced charges on March 7, 2002, and, after protracted jury deliberations, an obstruction of justice conviction on June 15, 2002. Throughout the period from October 2001 to June 2002, Arthur Andersen's client base and practice disintegrated. A firm of 85,000 worldwide was essentially gone. In the United States, 24,000 employees lost their jobs because of the decisions of probably less than 100 colleagues.

Finally, on June 25, when Senate and Congress hearings were well along and some governance changes were starting to be considered, came the incredible specter of giant WorldCom also applying for bankruptcy protection. When it became known that executives had again manipulated profits through accounting shenanigans and the CEO had essentially loaned himself over $400 million without the apparent oversight of the board, the Congress and Senate were galvanized by growing public outrage to produce the Sarbanes-Oxley Act (SOX) on July 30, 2002.

SOX provides frameworks for reform of the corporate governance system based on integrity and accountability, and for the accounting profession based on independence and fiduciary duty to the public interest. The provisions of SOX will be observed by U.S. SEC registrants, and probably by the world's largest corporations that want access to U.S. capital markets and their auditors.

The worlds of corporate governance, governance of the accounting profession, and of business ethics have entered a time warp on fast-forward. Understanding what happened and why, and what the impact will be on corporations, the accounting profession, and upon business ethics will assist in interpreting and planning for future developments. See Figure 2.1.

The Enron Debacle

Background

With hindsight, most observers agree that Enron's problems were caused by a failure of the board of directors to exercise adequate oversight. This allowed the misuse of special purpose entities (SPEs), a form of partnership, to manipulate financial reports, mislead investors, and self-remunerate the perpetrators. Arthur Andersen, Enron's audit firm, has essentially disintegrated,

2.2 **Enron Stock Chart, Weekly Prices, 1997–2002**

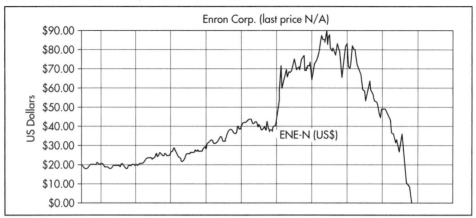

Reprinted courtesy of StatPro Canada, Inc.

and the accounting profession, as well as corporate governance, will be forever altered. All of this was not apparent until almost the end of the story.

Throughout the late 1990s, Enron's stock rose slowly on the New York Stock Exchange, within a trading range from $20 to $40. Within a few months of the start of the new millennium, as shown in Figure 2.2, Enron's stock price leapt to $70, based on the overall buoyancy of the stock markets in general, the favorable assessment accorded the company by analysts, and Enron's own reports of earnings and prospects.

During 2000, Enron's stock traded in a range of $60 to $90, peaked in August at $90.56, and closed the year close to $80. In 2001, however, the trend was precipitously downward until an Enron share was virtually worthless. Rumors of Enron's demise had been circulating for months when, on December 2, 2001, the company filed for protection from creditors under Chapter 11 of the *U.S. Securities Act*. On April 2, 2002, a share of Enron stock was worth only 24 cents on the over-the-counter market.

How and why did this occur? Who was to blame? What were the repercussions to be? Investors were scandalized, pensioners lost their life savings, the public was outraged, and the credibility of the financial markets and of the corporate world was shaken. How could the alleged financial manipulations have occurred under the watchful eyes of Enron's auditor, Arthur Andersen, and a blue-ribbon board of directors? Amid allegations that Enron alumni had infiltrated the U.S. government and its agencies, the ability and resolve of the Securities and Exchange Commission (SEC) and of the U.S. Justice Department were questioned.

Officials and politicians hurriedly looked for answers that would restore that credibility and the trust that had been lost. So great was the concern that President Bush himself pledged that the guilty would be punished aggressively by government agencies. Bush called for governance reforms and offered a ten-point plan for legislative action.[1]

After considerable delay and outcry, Enron's audit firm, Arthur Andersen LLP (AA), the fifth largest audit firm in the United States and one of the largest in the world, was charged on March 7, 2002, with obstruction of justice for shredding documents allegedly important to the government's investigation. As a condition of the charge, the SEC placed restrictions on AA to serve its SEC-registered clients, thus jeopardizing the ability of AA to continue as a firm. Ultimately, it disintegrated and was taken over piecemeal by competitors. A separate section is included later in this chapter that contains a full discussion of the troubles of Arthur Andersen,

1. Speech of March 7, 2002.

and how probably less than 100 AA people were responsible for the disaster that ruined a once-revered firm that employed 85,000 worldwide. In addition, the self-regulatory framework that the profession had enjoyed in the United States was further eroded.

Not surprisingly, the desire to know why the Enron disaster occurred spawned many investigations, including the following that are available for review and download from **www.cengage.com/accounting/brooks**.

- *The Powers Report* by a specially formed subcommittee of Enron's Board—February 1, 2002 (Powers)
- *The Role of the Board of Directors in Enron's Collapse* by the U.S. Senate's Permanent Subcommittee on Investigations—July 8, 2002 (Senate)
- *The Accounting Treatment of Prepays* by Robert Roach, Counsel and Chief Investigator, U.S. Senate's Permanent Subcommittee on Investigations—July 27, 2002 (Roach)

In addition, new governance initiatives continued to be issued and become relevant throughout the Enron fiasco period, including:

- The Joint Toronto Stock Exchange/Canadian Institute of Chartered Accountants Report on Governance
- The New York Stock Exchange Blue Ribbon Task Force Report and Regulations
- NASDAQ Governance Regulations
- Toronto Stock Exchange Regulations
- U.S. Securities and Exchange Commission Guidance
- Ontario Securities Commission Guidance

What Happened? Who Was to Blame?

The Powers Report | The Powers Report was prepared by a three-person subcommittee of the Enron board chaired by William Powers, Jr., who joined the board in September 2001 and resigned in February 2002. The Powers subcommittee was appointed on October 26, 2002, with the mandate to investigate related-party transactions that had surprised the board and resulted in several restatements of issued financial statements and reports. In the Powers Report's own words:

> On October 16, 2001, Enron announced that it was taking a $544 million after-tax charge against earnings related to transactions with LJM2 Co-Investment, L.P. ("LJM2"), a partnership created and managed by Fastow. It also announced a reduction of shareholders' equity of $1.2 billion related to transactions with that same entity.
>
> Less than one month later, Enron announced that it was restating its financial statements for the period from 1997 through 2001 because of accounting errors relating to transactions with a different Fastow partnership, LJM Cayman, L.P. ("LJM1"), and an additional related-party entity, Chewco Investments, L.P. ("Chewco"). Chewco was managed by an Enron Global Finance employee, Kopper, who reported to Fastow.
>
> The LJM1- and Chewco-related restatement, like the earlier charge against earnings and reduction of shareholders' equity, was very large. It reduced Enron's reported net income by $28 million in 1997 (of $105 million total), by $133 million in 1998 (of $703 million total), by $248 million in 1999 (of

$893 million total), and by $99 million in 2000 (of $979 million total). The restatement reduced reported shareholders' equity by $258 million in 1997, by $391 million in 1998, by $710 million in 1999, and by $754 million in 2000. It increased reported debt by $711 million in 1997, by $561 million in 1998, by $685 million in 1999, and by $628 million in 2000. Enron also revealed, for the first time, that it had learned that Fastow received more than $30 million from LJM1 and LJM2. These announcements destroyed market confidence and investors' trust in Enron. Less than one month later, Enron filed for bankruptcy.[2]

After investigation, the Powers Report presented the following in its Summary of Findings:

| Employees enriched themselves by millions without proper approvals—Fastow by $30 million, Kopper by at least $10 million, two others by at least hundreds of thousands of dollars.

| Partnerships—Chewco, LJM1, and LJM2 were established and used to enter into transactions that (1) could not be arranged with independent entities, (2) were designed "to accomplish favorable financial statement results, not to achieve *bona fide* economic objectives or to transfer risk,"[3] and (3) did not conform to U.S. accounting rules that could have enabled the hiding of assets and liabilities (debt).

| Other transactions were improperly entered into hedge or offset almost $1 billion in losses on Enron's merchant investments and thus improperly keep reported profit approximately $1 billion higher between the third quarters of 2000 and 2001. Only Enron had assets at risk in these transactions.[4]

| The original accounting treatments for the Chewco and LJM1 transactions were wrong, as were many others, in spite of extensive involvement and advice from Arthur Andersen. AA was paid $5.7 million above their audit fees for the Chewco and LJM1 advice.

| Much of the need for restatement arose because of the failure to satisfy two conditions required for special purpose entities (SPEs) to be independent from Enron. They are: "(1) an owner independent of the company must make a substantive equity investment of at least 3% of the SPE's assets, and that 3% must remain at risk throughout the transaction; and (2) the independent owner must exercise control of the SPE."[5] If these conditions had been satisfied, according to US accounting rules, Enron could have recorded gains and losses on transactions with the SPE, and the assets and liabilities of the SPE would not have been included in Enron's balance sheet, even though Enron and the SPE were closely related.

| **The Senate Subcommittee Report** | The Senate Permanent Subcommittee on Investigations released its *Report on the Role of the Board of Directors in the Collapse of Enron,* on July 8, 2002.

Based upon the evidence before it, including over one million pages of subpoenaed documents, interviews of thirteen Enron Board members, and the Subcommittee hearing on May 7, 2002, the U.S. Senate Permanent

---

2. Powers Report, 2, 3.
3. Ibid., 4.
4. Ibid., 4.
5. Ibid., 5.

Subcommittee on Investigations makes the following findings with respect to the role of the Enron Board of Directors in Enron's collapse and bankruptcy.

1. **Fiduciary Failure.** The Enron Board of Directors failed to safeguard Enron shareholders and contributed to the collapse of the seventh largest public company in the United States, by allowing Enron to engage in high risk accounting, inappropriate conflict of interest transactions, extensive undisclosed off-the-books activities, and excessive executive compensation. The Board witnessed numerous indications of questionable practices by Enron management over several years, but chose to ignore them to the detriment of Enron shareholders, employees and business associates.

2. **High Risk Accounting.** The Enron Board of Directors knowingly allowed Enron to engage in high risk accounting practices.

3. **Inappropriate Conflicts of Interest.** Despite clear conflicts of interest, the Enron Board of Directors approved an unprecedented arrangement allowing Enron's Chief Financial Officer to establish and operate the LJM private equity funds which transacted business with Enron and profited at Enron's expense. The Board exercised inadequate oversight of LJM transaction and compensation controls and failed to protect Enron shareholders from unfair dealing.

4. **Extensive Undisclosed Off-the-Books Activity.** The Enron Board of Directors knowingly allowed Enron to conduct billions of dollars in off-the-books activity to make its financial condition appear better than it was and failed to ensure adequate public disclosure of material off-the-books liabilities that contributed to Enron's collapse.

5. **Excessive Compensation.** The Enron Board of Directors approved excessive compensation for company executives, failed to monitor the cumulative cash drain caused by Enron's 2000 annual bonus and performance unit plans, and failed to monitor or halt abuse by Board Chairman and Chief Executive Officer Kenneth Lay of a company-financed, multi-million dollar, personal credit line.

6. **Lack of Independence.** The independence of the Enron Board of Directors was compromised by financial ties between the company and certain Board members. The Board also failed to ensure the independence of the company's auditor, allowing Andersen to provide internal audit and consulting services while serving as Enron's outside auditor.[6]

These findings lead the Senate Subcommittee to make recommendations for (1) strengthening the oversight of directors, and (2) strengthening the independence of directors, the audit committee, and auditors of publicly traded companies.[7]

Failure of the Directors to Oversee or Govern Enron Adequately

What Are Directors Expected to Do? | According to the Senate Subcommittee, the governance model should function as follows:

> **Fiduciary Obligations of Boards of Directors.** In the United States, the Board of Directors sits at the apex of a company's governing structure. A typical Board's duties include reviewing the company's overall business strategy; selecting and compensating the company's senior executives; evaluating the company's outside

---

6. Senate Subcommittee Report, 3.
7. Ibid., 4.

auditor; overseeing the company's financial statements; and monitoring overall company performance. According to the Business Roundtable, the Board's "paramount duty" is to safeguard the interests of the company's shareholders.[8]

Directors operate under state laws that impose fiduciary duties on them to act in good faith, with reasonable care, and in the best interest of the corporation and its shareholders. Courts generally discuss three types of fiduciary obligations. As one court put it:

> Three broad duties stem from the fiduciary status of corporate directors: namely, the duties of obedience, loyalty, and due care. The duty of obedience requires a director to avoid committing ... acts beyond the scope of the powers of a corporation as defined by its charter or the laws of the state of incorporation.... The duty of loyalty dictates that a director must act in good faith and must not allow his personal interest to prevail over the interests of the corporation.... [T]he duty of care requires a director to be diligent and prudent in managing the corporation's affairs.[9]
>
> In most states, directors also operate under a legal doctrine called the "business judgment rule," which generally provides directors with broad discretion, absent evidence of fraud, gross negligence or other misconduct, to make good faith business decisions. Most states permit corporations to indemnify their directors from liabilities associated with civil, criminal or administrative proceedings against the company. In addition, most U.S. publicly traded corporations, including Enron, purchase directors' liability insurance that pays for a director's legal expenses and other costs in the event of such proceedings.
>
> Among the most important of Board duties is the responsibility the Board shares with the company's management and auditors to ensure that the financial statements provided by the company to its shareholders and the investing public fairly present the financial condition of the company. This responsibility requires more than ensuring the company's technical compliance with generally accepted accounting principles. According to the Second Circuit Court of Appeals, this technical compliance may be evidence that a company is acting in good faith, but it is not necessarily conclusive. The "critical test," the Court said, is "whether the financial statements as a whole fairly present the financial position" of the company.[10]

Within this governance framework, Enron's directors were responsible for oversight of Enron's lines of business and strategies for financing them. One of the lines of business—the online energy trading business—required access to large lines of credit to ensure settlement of trading positions at the end of each day. At the same time, the nature of this business caused large earnings fluctuations from quarter to quarter, which made it a challenge to maintain a low credit rating, and therefore access to low-cost financing. Other lines of business, such as optical fiber networks (that were mostly not in use), represented cash drains as well. Therefore, according to the Senate Subcommittee:

> In order to ensure an investment-grade credit rating, Enron began to emphasize increasing its cash flow, lowering its debt, and smoothing its earnings on its financial statements to meet the criteria set by credit rating agencies like Moody's and Standard & Poor's.

---

8. *Statement of Corporate Governance,* The Business Roundtable, (September 1997), at 3.

9. *Gearheart Industries v. Smith International,* 741 F.2d 707, 719 (5th Cir.1984).

10. *U.S. v. Simon,* 425 F.2d 796, 805-6 (2nd Cir. 1969), quoting, in part, the trial judge. See also 15 USC 77s and 78m ("Every user ... shall ... keep books, records, and accounts, which, in reasonable detail, accurately and fairly reflect the transactions and disposition of the assets of the issuer.")

Enron developed a number of new strategies to accomplish its financial statement objectives. They included developing energy contracts Enron called "prepays" in which Enron was paid a large sum in advance to deliver natural gas or other energy products over a period of years; designing hedges to reduce the risk of long-term energy delivery contracts; and pooling energy contracts and securitizing them through bonds or other financial instruments sold to investors. Another high profile strategy, referred to as making the company "asset light," was aimed at shedding, or increasing immediate returns on, the company's capital-intensive energy projects like power plants that had traditionally been associated with low returns and persistent debt on the company's books. The goal was either to sell these assets outright or to sell interests in them to investors, and record the income as earnings which top Enron officials called "monetizing" or "syndicating" the assets. A presentation made to the Finance Committee in October 2000 summarized this strategy as follows.[11] It stated that Enron's "[e]nergy and communications investments typically do not generate significant cashflow and earnings for 1-3 years." It stated that Enron had "[l]imited cash flow to service additional debt" and "[l]imited earnings to cover dilution of additional equity." It concluded that "Enron must syndicate" or share its investment costs "in order to grow."

One of the problems with Enron's new strategies, however, was finding counterparties willing to invest in Enron assets or share the significant risks associated with long-term energy production facilities and delivery contracts.[12] The October 2000 presentation to the Finance Committee showed that one solution Enron had devised was to sell or syndicate its assets, not to independent third parties, but to "unconsolidated affiliates"—businesses like Whitewing, LJM, JEDI, the Hawaii125-0 Trust and others that were not included in Enron's financial statements but were so closely associated with the company that Enron considered their assets to be part of Enron's own holdings. The October 2000 presentation, for example, informed the Finance Committee that Enron had a total of $60 billion in assets, of which about $27 billion, or nearly 50 percent, were lodged with Enron's "unconsolidated affiliates."

All of the Board members interviewed by the Subcommittee were well aware of and supported Enron's intense focus on its credit rating, cash flow, and debt burden. All were familiar with the company's "asset light" strategy and actions taken by Enron to move billions of dollars in assets off its balance sheet to separate but affiliated companies. All knew that, to accomplish its objectives, Enron had been relying increasingly on complicated transactions with convoluted financing and accounting structures, including transactions with multiple special purpose entities, hedges, derivatives, swaps, forward contracts, prepaid contracts, and other forms of structured finance. While there is no empirical data on the extent to which U.S. public companies use these devices, it appears that few companies outside of investment banks use them as extensively as Enron. At Enron, they became dominant; at its peak, the company apparently had between $15 and $20 billion involved in hundreds of structured finance transactions.[13]

---

11. Hearing Exhibit 39, "Private Equity Strategy," Finance Committee presentation, October 2000.
12. As part of its asset light strategy, during the summer of 2000, Enron worked on a transaction called "Project Summer" to sell $6 billion of its international assets to a single purchaser in the Middle East. Enron's directors indicated during their interviews that this deal fell through when the purchaser's key decision maker became ill. Enron then pursued the asset sales on a piecemeal basis, using Whitewing, LJM, and others.
13. Senate Subcommittee Report, 7, 8.

| **How Was Enron's Board Organized, and How Did It Function?** | In 2001, Enron's board of directors had 15 members, several of whom had 20 years or more experience on the board of Enron or its predecessor companies. Many of Enron's directors served on the boards of other companies as well. At the hearing, John Duncan, former chairman of the Executive Committee, described his fellow board members as well-educated, "experienced, successful businessmen and women," and "experts in areas of finance and accounting."[14] The subcommittee interviews found the directors to have a wealth of sophisticated business and investment experience and considerable expertise in accounting, derivatives, and structured finance.

Enron board members uniformly described internal board relations as harmonious. They said that board votes were generally unanimous and could recall only two instances over the course of many years involving dissenting votes. The directors also described a good working relationship with Enron management. Several had close personal relationships with Board Chairman and Chief Executive Officer (CEO) Kenneth L. Lay. All indicated they had possessed great respect for senior Enron officers, trusting the integrity and competence of Mr. Lay; President and Chief Operating Officer (and later CEO) Jeffrey K. Skilling; Chief Financial Officer Andrew S. Fastow; Chief Accounting Officer Richard A. Causey; Chief Risk Officer Richard Buy; and the Treasurer Jeffrey McMahon and later Ben Glisan. Mr. Lay served as chairman of the board from 1986 until he resigned in 2002. Mr. Skilling was a board member from 1997 until August 2001, when he resigned from Enron.

The Enron Board was organized into five committees:

1. The **Executive Committee** met on an as-needed basis to handle urgent business matters between scheduled Board meetings. Its members in 2001 were Mr. Duncan, the Chairman; Mr. Lay, Mr. Skilling, Mr. Belfer, Dr. LeMaistre, and Mr. Winokur.

2. The **Finance Committee** was responsible for approving major transactions, which, in 2001, met or exceeded $75 million in value. It also reviewed transactions valued between $25 million and $75 million; oversaw Enron's risk management efforts; and provided guidance on the company's financial decisions and policies. Its members in 2001 were Mr. Winokur, the Chairman; Mr. Belfer, Mr. Blake, Mr. Chan, Mr. Pereira, and Mr. Savage.

3. The **Audit and Compliance Committee** reviewed Enron's accounting and compliance programs, approved Enron's financial statements and reports, and was the primary liaison with Andersen. Its members in 2001 were Dr. Jaedicke, the Chairman; Mr. Chan, Dr. Gramm, Dr. Mendelsohn, Mr. Pereira, and Lord Wakeham. Dr. Jaedicke and Lord Wakeham had formal accounting training and professional experience. Dr. Mendelsohn was the only Committee member who appeared to have limited familiarity with complex accounting principles.

4. The **Compensation Committee** established and monitored Enron's compensation policies and plans for directors, officers and employees. Its members in 2001 were Dr. LeMaistre, the Chairman; Mr. Blake, Mr. Duncan, Dr. Jaedicke, and Mr. Savage.

5. The **Nominating Committee** nominated individuals to serve as Directors. Its members in 2001 were Lord Wakeham, the Chairman; Dr. Gramm, Dr. Mendelsohn, and Mr. Meyer.

The board normally held five regular meetings during the year, with additional special meetings as needed. Board meetings usually lasted two days, with the first day devoted to committee meetings and a board dinner and the second day devoted to a meeting of the full board. Committee meetings generally lasted between one and two hours and were arranged to

---

14. *Hearing Record* at 34.

allow board members, who typically sat on three committees, to attend all assigned committee meetings. Full board meetings also generally lasted between one and two hours. Special board meetings, as well as meetings of the Executive Committee, were typically conducted by telephone conference.

Committee chairmen typically spoke with Enron management by telephone prior to committee meetings to develop the proposed committee meeting agenda. Board members said that Enron management provided them with these agendas as well as extensive background and briefing materials prior to Board meetings including, in the case of Finance Committee members, numerous deal approval sheets ("DASHs") for approval of major transactions. Board members varied in how much time they spent reading the materials and preparing for board meetings, with the reported preparation time for each meeting varying between two hours and two days. On some occasions, Enron provided a private plane to transport board members from various locations to a board meeting, and board members discussed company issues during the flight. Enron also organized occasional trips abroad, which some board members attended to view company assets and operations.

During the committee meetings, Enron management generally provided presentations on company performance, internal controls, new business ventures, specific transactions, or other topics of interest. The Finance Committee generally heard from Mr. Fastow, Mr. Causey, Mr. Buy, Mr. McMahon, and occasionally Mr. Glisan. The Audit Committee generally heard from Mr. Causey, Mr. Buy, and Andersen personnel. The Compensation Committee generally heard from the company's top compensation official, Mary Joyce, and from the company's compensation consultant, Towers Perrin. On occasion, the committees heard from other senior Enron officers as well. At the full board meetings, board members typically received presentations from each committee chairman summarizing the committee's work and recommendations, as well as from Enron management and, occasionally, Andersen or the company's chief outside legal counsel, Vinson & Elkins. Mr. Lay and Mr. Skilling usually attended Executive, Finance, and Audit Committee meetings, as well as the full board meetings. Mr. Lay attended many Compensation Committee meetings as well. The subcommittee interviews indicated that, altogether, board members appeared to have routine contact with less than a dozen senior officers at Enron. The board did not have a practice of meeting without Enron management present.

Regular presentations on Enron's financial statements, accounting practices, and audit results were provided by Andersen to the Audit Committee. The Audit Committee chairman would then report on the presentation to the full board. On most occasions, three Andersen senior partners from Andersen's Houston office attended Audit Committee meetings. They were D. Stephen Goddard, head of the Houston office; David Duncan, head of the Andersen "engagement team" that provided auditing, consulting and other services to Enron; and Thomas H. Bauer, another senior member of the Enron engagement team. Before becoming head of the Houston office, Mr. Goddard had led the Enron engagement team for Andersen. Mr. Duncan became the "worldwide engagement partner" for Enron in 1997, and from that point on typically made the Andersen presentations to the Audit Committee. The Audit Committee offered Andersen personnel an opportunity to present information to them without management present.

Minutes summarizing Committee and Board meetings were kept by the corporate secretary, who often took handwritten notes on committee and board presentations during the board's deliberations and afterward developed and circulated draft minutes to Enron management, board members, and legal counsel. The draft minutes were formally presented to and approved by committee and board members at subsequent meetings. Outside of the formal committee and board meetings, the Enron directors described very little interaction or communication either among Board members or between Board members and Enron or Andersen personnel, until the company began experiencing severe problems in October 2001. From October until the company's bankruptcy on December 2, 2001, the board held numerous special meetings, at times on almost a daily basis.

Enron board members were compensated with cash, restricted stock, phantom stock units, and stock options.[15] The total cash and equity compensation of Enron board members in 2000 was valued by Enron at about $350,000 or more than twice the national average for board compensation at a U.S. publicly traded corporation.[16,17]

Enron's Questionable Transactions

An understanding of the nature of Enron's questionable transactions is fundamental to understanding why Enron failed. What follows is a very abbreviated overview of the essence of the major important transactions with the SPEs, including: Chewco, LJM1, LJM2, and the Raptors. A much more detailed, but still abbreviated, summary of these transactions is included in the *Enron's Questionable Transactions Case* at the end of this chapter.

Enron had been using specially created companies called special purpose entities (SPEs) for joint ventures, partnerships, and the syndication of assets for some time. But a series of happenstance events lead to the realization by Enron personnel that SPEs could be used unethically and illegally to:

- Overstate revenue and profits

- Raise cash and hide the related debt or obligations to repay

- Offset losses in Enron's stock investments in other companies

- Circumvent accounting rules for valuation of Enron's treasury shares

- Improperly enrich several participating executives

- Manipulate Enron's stock price thus misleading investors and enriching Enron executives who held stock options

In November 1997, Enron created an SPE called Chewco to raise funds or attract an investor to take over the interest of Enron's joint venture investment partner, CalPERS,[18] in an SPE called Joint Energy Development Investment Partnership (JEDI). Using Chewco, Enron had bought out CalPERS interest in JEDI with Enron-guaranteed bridge financing, and tried to find another investor.

Enron's objective was to find another investor, called a counterparty, that would:

- Be independent of Enron

- Invest at least 3 percent of the assets at risk

- Serve as the controlling shareholder in making decisions for Chewco

Enron wanted a 3-percent, independent, controlling investor because U.S. accounting rules would allow Chewco to be considered an independent company, and any transactions

---

15. See Hearing Exhibits 35a and 35b on Enron board member compensation, prepared by the subcommittee based on information in Enron filings with the Securities and Exchange Commission. Phantom stock units at Enron were deferred cash payments whose amounts were linked to the value of Enron stock.

16. See "Director Compensation; Purposes, Principles, and Best Practices," *Report of the Blue Ribbon Commission of the National Association of Corporate Directors* (2001), page V (average total board compensation at top 200 U.S. public corporations in 2000 was $138,747).

17. *Senate Subcommittee Report,* 8-11.

18. The California Public Employees' Retirement System.

between Enron and Chewco would be considered at arm's length. This would allow "profit" made on asset sales from Enron to Chewco to be included in Enron's profit even though Enron would own up to 97 percent of Chewco.

Unfortunately, Enron was unable to find an independent investor willing to invest the required 3 percent before its December 31, 1997, year end. Because there was no outside investor in the JEDI-Chewco chain, Enron was considered to be dealing with itself, and U.S. accounting rules required that Enron's financial statements be restated to remove any profits made on transactions between Enron and JEDI. Otherwise, Enron would be able to report profit on deals with itself, which, of course, would undermine the integrity of Enron's audited financial statements because there would be no external, independent validation of transfer prices. *Enron could set the prices to make whatever profit it desired and manipulate its financial statements at will.*

That, in fact, was exactly what happened. When no outside investor was found, Enron's CFO, Andrew Fastow, proposed that he be appointed to serve as Chewco's outside investor. Enron's lawyers pointed out that such involvement by a high-ranking Enron officer would need to be disclosed publicly, and one of Fastow's financial staff—a fact not shared with the board—Michael Kopper, who continued to be an Enron employee, was appointed as Chewco's 3-percent, independent, controlling investor, and the chicanery began.

Enron was able to "sell" (transfer really) assets to Chewco at a manipulatively high profit. *This allowed Enron to show profits on these asset sales and draw cash into Enron accounts without showing in Enron's financial statements that the cash stemmed from Chewco borrowings and would have to be repaid. Enron's obligations were understated—they were "hidden" and not disclosed to investors.*

Duplicity is also evident in the way that Chewco's funding was arranged. CalPERS' interest in JEDI was valued at $383 million; of that amount, Kopper and/or outside investors needed to be seen to provide 3 percent, or $11.5 million. The $383 million was arranged as follows:

$240.0	Barclays Bank PLC—Enron would later guarantee this
132.0	JEDI to Chewco under a revolving credit agreement
0.1	Kopper and his friend Dodson ($125,000)
11.4	Barclays Bank PLC "loaned"[19] to Dodson/Kopper companies
$383.5	

These financing arrangements are diagramed in Figure 2.3.

Essentially, Enron as majority owner put no cash into the SPE. A bank provided virtually all of the cash, and in reality the so-called 3-percent, independent, controlling investor had very little invested—not even close to the required 3-percent threshold. Nonetheless, Chewco was considered to qualify for treatment as an arm's-length entity for accounting purposes by Enron and its auditors, Arthur Andersen. Enron's board, and presumably Arthur Andersen, were kept in the dark.

A number of other issues in regard to Chewco transactions were noted in the Powers Report, including:

- Excessive management fees were paid to Kopper for little work.[20]

- Excessive valuations were used upon winding-up thus transferring $10.5 million to Kopper.

- Kopper sought and received $2.6 million as indemnification from tax liability on the $10.5 million.

- Unsecured, nonrecourse loans totaling $15 million were made to Kopper and not recovered.

- Enron advance-booked revenues from Chewco.

---

19. "Loaned" through shell companies, and for "certificates" that would generate a yield.
20. Fastow's wife did most of the work.

FIGURE 2.3

Chewco Financing, in Millions

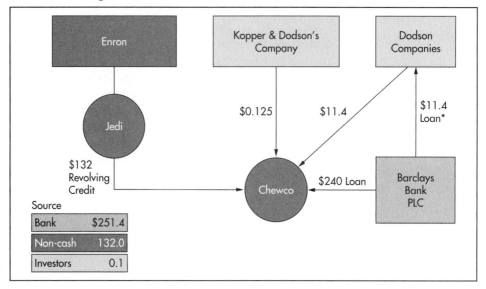

This pattern of financing—no or low Enron cash invested, banks providing most of the funding, Enron employees masquerading as 3-percent, independent, controlling investors—continued in other SPEs. Some of these SPEs, such as the LJM partnerships, were used to create buyers for Enron assets over which Enron could keep control, but convert fixed assets into cash for growth at inflated prices, thus overstating cash and profits. Other SPEs, such as LJM1 and LJM2, provided illusionary hedge arrangements to protect Enron against losses in its merchant[21] investment portfolio, thereby falsely protecting Enron's reported profits.

In March 1998, Enron invested in Rhythms NetCommunications, Inc. (Rhythms), a business Internet service provider. Between March 1998 and May 1999, Enron's investment of $10 million in Rhythms stock soared to approximately $300 million. Enron recorded the increase in value as profit by increasing the value of its investment on its books. But Jeffrey K. Skilling, Enron's CEO, realized that the mark-to-market accounting procedure used would require continuous updating, and the change could have a significant negative affect on Enron's profits due to the volatility of Rhythms stock price. He also correctly foresaw that Rhythms stock price could plummet when the Internet bubble burst due to overcapacity.

LJM1 (LJM Cayman LP), was created to hedge against future volatility and losses on Enron's investment in Rhythms. If Rhythms stock price fell, Enron would have to record a loss in its investment. However, LJM1 was expected to pay Enron to offset the loss, so no net reduction would appear in overall Enron profit. As with Chewco, the company was funded with cash from other investors and banks based partly on promises of large guaranteed returns and yields. Enron invested its own shares, but no cash.

In fact, LJM1 did have to pay cash to Enron as the price of Rhythms stock fell. This created a loss for LJM1 and reduced its equity. Moreover, at the same time as LJM1's cash was being paid to Enron, the market value of Enron's shares was also declining, thus reducing LJM1's equity even further. Ultimately, LJM1's effective equity eroded, as did the equity of the SPE (Swap Sub) Enron created as a 3-percent investment conduit. Swap Sub's equity actually became negative.

---

21. A merchant investment is an investment in a company's shares that are held for speculative purposes, not for control purposes.

These erosions of cash and equity exposed the fact that the economic underpinning of the hedge of Rhythms stock was based on Enron's shares—in effect, Enron's profit was being hedged by Enron's own shares. Ultimately, hedging yourself against loss provides no economic security against loss at all. Enron's shareholders had been misled by $95 million profit in 1999 and $8 million in 2000. These were the restatements announced in November 2001, just before Enron's bankruptcy on December 2, 2001.

Unfortunately for Enron, there were other flaws in the creation of LJM1 that ultimately rendered the arrangement useless, but by that time investors had been mislead for many years. For example, there was no 3-percent, independent, controlling investor—Andrew Fastow sought special approval from Enron's chairman to suspend the conflict of interest provisions of Enron's *Code of Conduct* to become the sole managing/general partner of LJM1 and Swap Sub; and Swap Sub's equity became negative and could not qualify for the 3-percent test unless Enron advanced more shares, which it did. Ultimately, as Enron's stock price fell, Fastow decided the whole arrangement was not sustainable, and it was wound up on March 22, 2000. Once again, the wind-up arrangements were not properly valued; $70 million more than required was transferred from Enron, and LJM1 was also allowed to retain Enron shares worth $251 million.

Enron's shareholders were also misled by Enron's recording of profit on the treasury shares used to capitalize the LJM1 arrangement. Enron provided the initial capital for LJM1 arrangements in the form of Enron's own treasury stock, for which it received a promissory note. Enron recorded this transfer of shares at the existing market value, which was higher than the original value in its treasury, and therefore recorded a profit on the transaction. Since no cash had changed hands, the price of transfer was not validated, and accounting rules should not have allowed the recording of any profit.

Initially, the LJM1 arrangements were thought to be so successful at generating profits on treasury shares, hedging against investment losses, and generating cash, that LJM2 Co-Investment LP (LJM2) was created in October 1999 to provide hedges for further Enron merchant investments in Enron's investment portfolio. LJM2 in turn created four SPEs, called "Raptors," to carry out this strategy using similar methods of capitalization based on its own Treasury stock or options thereon.

For a while, the Raptors looked like they would work. In October 2000, Fastow reported to LJM2 investors that the Raptors had brought returns of 193, 278, 2,500, and 125 percent, which was far in excess of the 30 percent annualized return described to the finance committee in May 2000. Of course, as we know now, Enron retained the economic risks.

Although nontransparent arrangements were used again, the flaws found in the LJM1 arrangements ultimately became apparent in the LJM2 arrangements, including:

I Enron was hedging itself, so no external economic hedges were created.

I Enron's falling stock price ultimately eroded the underlying equity and creditworthiness involved, and Enron had to advance more treasury shares or options to buy them at preferential rates[22] or use them in "costless collar"[23] arrangements, all of which were further dilutive to Enron earnings per share.

---

22. Raptors III and IV were not fully utilized and/or used to shore up the equity of Raptors I and II.
23. A "costless collar" is a two-step arrangement wherein Enron offered to contain LJM2's risk of Enron's stock price falling below a lower limit using its own Treasury shares, while at the same time making an offsetting arrangement for LJM2 to pay Enron if Enron's share price were to rise above a threshold. Since the arrangements offset one another in risk premium, and Treasury stock was to be used, the transaction was considered to be an equity transaction which did not affect the income statement of Enron. See page 110 of the Powers Report.

2.1

Enron's Key Special Purpose Entities (SPEs)

SPE SCHEME	PURPOSE	IMPACT
Chewco/JEDI	Syndicated investment	Off balance sheet liabilities hidden ($628 million), Revenues recognized early, Profits on own shares
LJM	Provided market for assets	Artificial profits, Off balance sheet liabilities hidden, Equity overstated ($1.2 billion)
LJM1/Rhythms	Investment "hedge"	Unrecognized losses ($508 million)
LJM2/Raptors	Investment "hedge"	Unrecognized losses ($544 million)

▌ Profits were improperly recorded on treasury shares used or sheltered by nonexistent hedges.

▌ Enron officers and their helpers benefited.

In August 2001, matters became critical. Declining Enron share values, and the resulting reduction in Raptor creditworthiness, called for the delivery of so many Enron shares that the resulting dilution of Enron's earnings per share was realized to be too great to be sustainable. In September 2001, accountants at Arthur Andersen and Enron realized that the profits generated by recording Enron shares used for financing at market values was incorrect because no cash was received, and shareholders' equity was overstated by at least $1 billion.

The overall affect of the Raptors was to misleadingly inflate Enron's earnings during the middle period of 2000 to the end of the third quarter of 2001 (September 30) by $1,077 million, not including a September Raptor winding-up charge of $710 million.

On December 2, 2001, Enron became the largest bankruptcy in the world, leaving investors ruined, stunned, and outraged—and quite skeptical of the credibility of the corporate governance and accountability process.

By that time, the Enron SPEs and related financial dealings had misled investors greatly. Almost 50 percent of the reported profits driving Enron stock up so dramatically were false. Table 2.1 summarizes the impacts of Enron's questionable transactions through key Enron SPEs.

▌ Enron Culture, Conflicts of Interest & Whistle-blowers

How could the employees of Enron, Arthur Andersen, and Vinson & Elkins stand by when the returns to the Enron SPEs were so incredibly high at 193, 278, 2,500, and 125 percent? The returns to individuals involved were also spectacular even though they were already being paid by Enron, as Table 2.2 shows.

Many Enron employees knew about the lack of integrity of the SPE dealings, but few came forward, and the ears of the board did not hear their stories. Perhaps more would have come forward, or made a more determined effort to contact the board, if conditions within Enron were different.

Enron's culture was lacking in integrity to a surprising degree. For example, it is reported that a sham energy trading floor was created to mislead a group of stock analysts. The floor was complete with computers, desks, chairs, and traders. What employee would have thought that

2.2

Payments to Fastow & Helpers

	INVESTMENT	RETURN, IN MILLIONS	OTHER, IN MILLIONS
A. Fastow	$25,000	$ 4.5 in 2 mo.	$30 + stock options
M. Kopper	125,000	10.0 incl. Dodson	$2 in fees
B. Glisan	5,800	1.0	
K. Mordaunt	5,800	1.0	

TABLE 2.3	**Enron Whistle-Blowers**			

Enron Whistle-Blowers

	BLEW TO	ACTION	SUBSEQUENTLY
Cliff Baxter, Vice Chair	Lay	None	Exercised $32 million in stock options, just agreed to testify to Congress, found shot dead in his car—an apparent suicide—on Jan. 25, 2002
McMahon, Treasurer	Fastow	None	Reassigned, later returned as CEO
Kaminski, Risk Mgr.	Fastow	None	Continued
Sherron Watkins	Lay	None	Discussed with Skilling and asked Vinson & Elkins to review

such an elaborate hoax could be created without the knowledge of the senior executives? And who would come forward with other tales of wrongdoing knowing that the senior officials encouraged or acquiesced to such outrageous behavior? A further example of major malfeasance is the reciprocal wash trading engaged in with other energy companies during the California energy crisis during the summer of 2000, which was designed to inflate demand and Enron revenues without generating any profits since there was no substantive transaction. An Enron employee would have to be an ethical hero to come forward to report ethical problems when Enron's culture and senior officers were apparently willing to go along with, or even lead in, the wrongdoing.

Some employees did come forward, however. Not surprisingly, they made little impact on the minds and actions of senior Enron management, and none on Enron's directors. As Table 2.3 shows, some came to Andrew Fastow and others to Kenneth Lay. Fastow was clearly making himself wealthy and was not about to turn himself in, or change his ways. Lay consulted Enron's lawyers about Sherron Watkins's initially anonymous letter, but they had been paid as consultants to set up the SPE strategy and were not likely to report that they had made a mistake. Whether Lay did this purposely or not will probably never be known. In any event, the board of directors failed to pick up on many red flags, and apparently remained blissfully in the dark until too late. The board trusted Lay and Fastow to serve their interests and those of the shareholders, and the shareholders, pensioners, and employees paid the price.

The Sherron Watkins letter, sent on August 15, 2001, and that is available, along with her Senate Subcommittee testimony of February 14, 2002, at **www.cengage.com/accounting/ brooks**, is discussed at some length in the Powers Report beginning on page 172. Sherron was a competent professional accountant who had worked for Arthur Andersen for many years before joining Enron. She complained that the aggressive accounting being practiced by Enron would implode, and it did. When Lay apparently did not change things because of her letter and their meetings, she was quite prepared to testify before investigating committees. If only a very few knowledgeable board members had heard her concerns, perhaps action could have been taken earlier. Sherron is a highly principled woman who knew what could happen and feared the worst. She realized the stakes were so high that she ultimately put her concerns for her own self-interest aside and came forward. Initially, however, she sent her letter anonymously—an indication of her concern about the reception and treatment she expected.

One of the unexplained Enron conundrums is why the following men who occupied senior positions at Enron, all of whom had continuous interaction with board members, apparently did not come forward with concerns:

- Richard Causey, Chief Accounting Officer
- Richard Buy, Chief Risk Officer
- Ben Glisan, Treasurer and senior accountant

Why weren't they loyal agents of Enron? Perhaps they were just too anxious to keep Andrew Fastow happy. Perhaps their lack of loyalty had something to do with the desire to please

2.4

Enron Stock Proceeds, October 1998 to November 2001, Over $30 Million

Lou Pai	Chairman, Enron Accelerator	$353.7 million
Ken Lay	Chairman	101.3
Rebecca Mark-Jusbasche	Director	79.5
Ken Harrison	Director, Portland General Electrics	75.2
Kenneth Rice	Chairman, Enron Broadband	72.8
Jeffrey Skilling	Director (former CEO)	66.9
Mark Frevert	Vice Chairman	50.3
Stanley Horton	Global Chairman	45.5
Joseph Sutton	Vice Chairman	40.1
J. Clifford Baxter	Vice Chairman	35.2
Joseph Hirco	CEO, Enron Broadband	35.2
Andrew Fastow	Chief Financial Officer	30.5

Source: © 2002 *Washington Post.* Reprinted with permission.

Fastow and Lay, who had a significant influence over Enron's stock option incentive plan. It was a particularly lucrative plan, as Table 2.4 shows.

Startlingly, many boards of directors took the view that *stock options were of no cost to the issuing companies* because they were not recorded on the financial statements when earmarked for the recipient.[24] Prevailing practice in the United States was to record stock options only when and if exercised, and then only at the exercise price, not at market price. The chairman of Enron's compensation committee implied this during his Senate Subcommittee testimony on the subject of Lay's overall compensation of $141 million for 2001, the stock option portion of which was approximately $130 million.[25]

Arthur Andersen's Role

Arthur Andersen (AA) was, as Enron's auditor, supposed to be a professional fiduciary looking out for the interests of Enron's shareholders and their representatives, Enron's board of directors. That they did not do so—because they missed or ignored huge manipulations—and then were caught shredding Enron audit documents, added significantly to the outrage felt by investors, pensioners, media, and politicians. *Confidence in financial markets, in corporate governance and financial statements that underlay investor decisions, and in the audit profession eroded dramatically.*

Ultimately, AA's ability to audit SEC registrant companies was suspended by the SEC because of repeated difficulties, such as were found with the Enron audit, in the audits of Sunbeam, Waste Management, Inc., and, later, WorldCom. Clients left for other firms. AA was found shredding Enron audit working papers, and found guilty of obstructing justice as a result. Partners and staff left to join other firms. Essentially, a firm of 24,000 employees in the United States and 85,000 worldwide vaporized in less than a year. Details of AA's deficiencies are outlined more fully in the accompanying case, *Arthur Andersen's Troubles.* The once-proud firm that defined the standard for integrity occupied the following roles with regard to Enron:

- Auditor
- Consultant on accounting and other matters, including SPE transactions

---

24. In 2004, Warren Buffet championed a change in treatment by encouraging many companies to record stock options as compensation expense when granted rather than wait exercised.

25. Testimony of Charles Lemaistre on May 7, 2002, at http://www.senate.gov/~gov_affairs/050702lemaistre.htm

- Internal auditor, since this function was contracted out by Enron to AA
- Advisor on tax matters
- Advisor, reviewer of financial disclosure

For the year 2000, AA is said to have received fees of approximately $52 million: $25 million for audit work and $27 million for other services. There is little doubt that Enron was one of AA's largest clients, and was growing. AA's internal culture was reportedly driven by the desire for revenue, so Enron was one of AA's prize possessions.

Given these facts, AA and its personnel were confronted by several conflicts of interest, which may have impinged on and weakened their resolve to act in their fiduciary relationship as auditors, including:

- Auditing their own work as SPE consultants, leading to a lack of objectivity
- Self-interest versus the public's interest, leading to wishing not to upset Enron management and thus:
  - Losing a very large, prestigious audit and a huge audit fee
  - Partners not liked by Enron were removed from the audit
  - Noncompliance with company policies and codes was not brought to the attention of the board
  - AA's internal debates over Enron's questionable accounting treatments and business risks were not aired with the audit committee to ensure that the members were knowledgeable
- Public disclosures were not satisfactory to inform investors
- Audit staff wishing to leave AA and join Enron.

Of course, AA's shortcomings may be due, in part, to:

- A lack of competence, such as displayed in the Rhythms decisions
- A failure of AA's internal policies whereby the concerns of a Quality Control or Practice Standards partner could be and were overruled by the audit partner in charge of the Enron account. AA was the only one of the Big 5 accounting firms to have this flaw, and it left the entire firm vulnerable to the decision of the person with the most to lose by saying no to a client
- Lack of information caused by Enron staff not providing critical information, or failure on the part of AA personnel to ferret it out
- A misunderstanding of the fiduciary role required by auditors

Regardless of the causes, AA did not live up to the expectations of the public, the board, current shareholders, the accounting profession, and regulators. Ultimately, AA was indicted and convicted in 2002 for the obstruction of justice because personnel in several cities shredded Enron audit papers. AA claimed these were not important, but this lacked credibility and could not be substantiated since the shredding had taken place. The impact of this conviction was that AA's ability to audit companies that were SEC registrants (required for share listing and trading on the New York Stock Exchange or NASDAQ) was initially in doubt, and finally withdrawn. The reputation and ability of the firm to function was eroded. AA personnel joined other accounting firms in the United States and around the world. AA was finished as a firm, and the Big 5 firms became the Big 4.

FIGURE 2.4

Enron's Governance & Control Structure was Short-Circuited

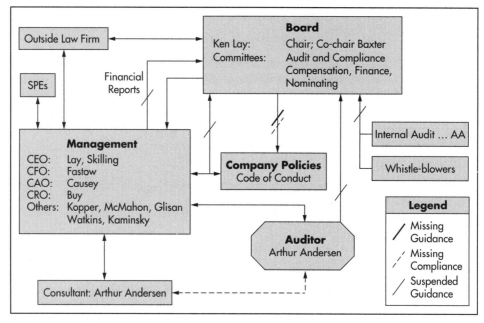

The fact that AA's conviction was overruled by the U.S. Supreme Court in 2005 because of faulty jury instructions came too late to change the course of history.[26] The accounting profession was altered forever in the United States, and received a "wake up" call in other parts of the world.[27] Independence, objectivity, fiduciary duty, and the primacy of the public interest came into sharper focus.

Enron's Governance & Control System was Short-Circuited

In view of the conflicts of interest of Fastow and his helpers, of the rest of the senior management team, of Enron's lawyers, and particularly those of Arthur Andersen, it is quite clear that Enron's directors were unable to rely on the information they were receiving, or on Enron's company policies being followed. Enron's management was out of control. This was the directors' own fault. They failed to understand their role included a challenge and compliance cycle, and trusted too much when there were many red flags warning that questions should have been pressed. Figure 2.4 shows the elements of Enron's system that were short-circuited and therefore not reliable for the governance of Enron in the shareholders best interests.

Banks Were Willing Accomplices in Enron SPES & "Prepays"

Many of the schemes used by Fastow to mislead investors and strip money out of Enron relied upon the participation of large financial institutions like Barclays Bank in the Rhythms hedge transaction. Many bank personnel knew that the deals they were being called to finance were not serving a wholesome economic purpose. They knew that bank funds were being passed through to finance Enron in off-balance sheet schemes that would mislead investors. *Enron's banks were*

---

26. "Supreme Court overrules jury—but too late to save Andersen," Barry McKenna, *Globe & Mail*, Report on Business, June 1, 2005, B1, B11.

27. In Canada, for example, a Canadian Public Accountability Board (CPAB) was created.

knowledgeable accomplices—aiding and abetting—in the schemes to defraud Enron's investors, and have since faced sanctions and lawsuits from the SEC, the State of New York and others.

The Senate Investigations Committee has undertaken a review of some of these arrangements, known as "prepays," to see if there is evidence that the banks knew that the transactions involved had no economic substance.[28] The report of investigator Roach identified two banks, JPMorgan Chase (twelve deals worth $3.7 billion) and Citigroup (fourteen deals worth $4.8 billion), as the primary sources of Enron "prepay" funding, and concludes that "the parties involved in the Enron prepays were aware of the entire structure and its accounting purpose."[29]

Enron's "prepays" were mechanisms for Enron to record prepayments for future energy delivery as current operating earnings and cash flow rather than as cash flow from financing operations. The *Roach Report* states:

> Under the Enron prepay structure, a participating bank would send cash (the money destined for Enron) to the third party, in exchange for the future delivery of a fixed amount of a commodity. The third party, in turn, would enter into an identical arrangement with Enron, and effectively serve as a pass through for the bank funding to get to Enron. Enron would repay the funding in a fixed amount of the commodities, which would pass through the third party en route to the bank. Up to this point this appears to be a "real" trade because all three parties bear the risk that the price of the underlying commodity will change. This is called price risk and it is an essential element in a true trading transaction.
>
> But, Enron prepays also entailed a transaction known as a "swap" in order to mitigate price risk. Under a swap agreement, Enron exchanged (with the bank) the floating price of the commodity for the fixed price of the commodity. The net effect is to cancel out any price risk to all parties in the trade.... the third party was not independent and the terms of the prepay were predetermined based on Enron's decision as to how much operating cash flow it needed to report ...[30]

The linked structure used by Enron did not comply with AA's internal criteria that were established "to distinguish true trading activity from loans."[31] An AA June 1999 audit memo found by Roach clearly shows that AA recognized the problem and how it needed to be rectified. The *Roach Report* does not state whether the AA memo was followed by Enron.

An additional complication has arisen. One bank that has reinsured their loans to Enron is finding that the reinsurors are refusing to pay up, arguing that the banks knew that the underlying transactions were a sham. Therefore, they argue that the reinsurance arrangements were not made in good faith, that risks were beyond the norm, and therefore that the reinsurance for subsequent loss is void.[32]

Table 2.5 presents the huge lawsuit settlement payments that Enron's accomplice banks agreed to up to December 31, 2005.

Direct lawsuits for complicity, and the possibility that reinsurance will be declared void, have had a sobering effect on the participation of banks in such schemes in the future. Banks are screening partners and deals much more carefully and are less ready to participate in arrangements that may look legal, but are probably unethical. *This is one of the most significant outcomes of the Enron debacle.*

---

28. See the testimony of Senior Investigator Roach on July 23, 2002.
29. *Roach Report,* Appendix A, A-8.
30. Ibid., A-8.
31. *Roach Report,* Appendix A, A-7.
32. The Royal Bank of Canada sued Rabobank, a reinsuror, seeking to recover a $500 million loan, but ended up settling—in a confidential agreement—for a lesser amount that produced an after-tax reduction in net income of $74 million. See Feb. 16, 2004 news release by The Royal Bank of Canada.

TABLE 2.5

Enron's Accomplice Banks' Lawsuit Settlements to December 31, 2005

	$	COMMENT
Merrill Lynch	80m	March 2003 Fine imposed by the SEC. Four of the Bank's executives were found guilty of fraud and conspiracy, facing sentences of up to 15 years in prison (Daniel Bayly, Robert Furst, William Fuhs, and James Brown).
JP Morgan Chase	2.2bn	August 2005. First Enron-related U.S. Bank settlement. The bank denied wrongdoing.
	135m	August 2003. Fine imposed by the SEC. JP Morgan's Q2/Q3 profits were $1.83bn.
Citigroup	1.7bn	June 2005. Citigroup did not admit liability, and said money already set aside for legal costs would cover the payment.
	120m	August 2003. Fine imposed by the SEC. Citigroup's Q2/Q3 profits were $4.3bn.
Canadian Imperial Bank of Commerce	2.8bn	June 2005. More than annual profit yr 2005.
	80m	December 2003. Fine imposed by the SEC. Two CIBC executives also will pay fines totaling $600,000.
Toronto Dominion Bank	130m	August 2005
Royal Bank of Canada	25m	August 2005
Royal Bank of Scotland	42m	August 2005

Source: SEC files, newspaper articles, and Enron's website at http://www.enron.com/corp/pressroom/releases/2005/ene2005.html for Mega-claims settlements.

Enron's Tax Avoidance

Enron's banks were not the only willing accomplices in the company's questionable transactions. Several accounting firms, investment bankers, and law firms allegedly provided highly questionable advice on twelve large structured transactions that sheltered over $2 billion in tax from 1995 until its bankruptcy on December 2, 2001. Although these transactions may barely adhere to the letter of the law, they have been branded as unethical by members of the Senate Committee on Finance.

According to the Senate Committee's *Report*,[33] Enron's management discovered that tax transactions could not only save tax, but could be used to generate financial statement earnings. Thereafter, Enron's tax department was looked on as a "profit center."[34]

Generally, four strategies were used in the structured transactions:

- Duplication of a single economic loss (i.e., deduction of the same loss twice)
- Shifting of tax basis from a nondepreciable asset (nontaxable) to a depreciable asset (taxable) with little or no outlay
- Generation of tax deductions for the repayment of principal (which is highly questionable)
- Generation of fees for serving as an accommodation party for another taxpayer[35]

Enron recorded the credits arising from the first two strategies as financial income.

Unfortunately, the Senate's analysis of Enron's structured transactions (summarized on Table 3 of the Senate *Report*) revealed "*a pattern of behavior showing that Enron deliberately engaged in transactions that had little or no business purpose in order to obtain favorable tax and*

---

33. *Report of the Investigation of Enron Corporation and Related Entities Regarding Federal Tax and Compensation Issues, and Policy Recommendations, Volume 1: Report,* U.S. Senate Committee on Finance, February 2003, released 2/22/03, http://www.house.gov/jct/s-3-03-vol1.pdf.
34. Ibid., 8.
35. Ibid., 8.

accounting treatment."[36] Although a proper business purpose is a fundamental prerequisite for such tax benefits, according to the Senate *Report,* "Enron represented the business purpose of the transaction, and Enron's counsel did not bother to look beyond the representation."[37] Most proposed transactions received a "'Should' comply with technical tax law requirements" assurance opinion from advisers or counsel.[38]

Moreover, the Senate *Report* indicates that the transactions were exceedingly complicated, thus precluding a meaningful review by tax auditors. This complexity was engineered with the advice of a small pool of sophisticated outside advisers. Sometimes these advisers counseled Enron directly, and sometimes each other. The following tax advisers' names appeared as promoters and/or primary tax opinion providers on the twelve structured transactions:

Arthur Andersen	4 times	
Bankers Trust	5 "	
Vinson Elkins	3 "	
Deloitte Touche	2 "	
Akin, Gump, Strauss, . . .	2 "	
6 others	1 "	incl. Chase Manhattan, Deutsche Bank, Ernst Young

The Senate *Report* comments[39] that:

A critical component of many of Enron's transactions was the involvement of an accommodation party such as an Enron employee or the party promoting the transaction. Enron's activities show that, in general, when transactions can be structured by parties that have the shared goal of obtaining favorable tax treatment, the tax rules do not function as intended and may produce undesirable results.

Enron's aggressive interpretation of business purpose, the cooperation of accommodation parties, the protections provided by tax opinions, the complex design of transactions, advantages over IRS—all were factors that contributed to Enron's ability to engage in tax-motivated transactions. Until the costs of participating in tax-motivated transactions are substantially increased, corporations such as Enron will continue to engage in transactions that violate the letter or the spirit of the law.

Time will tell whether the exposure generated by the Senate *Report* proposed, or the proposed tightening of loopholes and increases in sanctions and penalties, will change the practice of these and other tax advisers permanently in the future. Their actions may be legal, but in the case of Enron, not considered ethical because they offended the public interest. The short-term evidence—bad press, lawsuits and settlements from Deloitte & Touche and Ernst & Young, and the transition of tax advice from aggressive tax opportunism to a more responsible, conservative nature—suggest that a change is underway.

Enron Prosecutors and Prosecutions

Enron executives have faced criminal, civil, and administrative proceedings, leading to jail terms, fines, and agreements not to act in the future as directors or officers of companies whose shares are

---

36. Ibid., 16.
37. Ibid., 16.
38. Ibid., 16.
39. Senate *Report,* 16.

publicly traded. Prosecutions—often been initiated by the SEC—have led to increased expectations of performance and for prosecutorial aggressiveness where miscreant executives are suspected. Eliot Spitzer, then the respected Attorney General for New York, and Patrick J. Fitzgerald, U.S. Attorney for the Northern District of Illinois, emerged as the iconic attack-dog-like public prosecutors who went after corporate criminals with gusto. It is suspected that Spitzer, in particular, was intent on going after miscreant celebrities and senior executives quickly to set an example for others, particularly where the SEC was slow to act. Both Spitzer and Fitzgerald utilized the practice of offering lower-penalty deals to less senior executives—particularly to CFOs—in return for information and testimony that can be used against more senior executives. Table 2.6 shows the status of key Enron prosecutions.

| The Aftermath

The aftermath for Arthur Andersen and the accounting profession are dealt with in the previous sections and in the accompanying case, *Arthur Andersen's Troubles*.

The Senate Investigations Committee deliberations were previously noted with regard to the role of Enron's management and directors. Their report appeared on July 8, 2002. Prior to this, the Enron bankruptcy and the Senate Hearings had raised the awareness of the public, politicians, and regulators to governance failures and their impact. As noted in the earlier discussion of the governance timeline, many groups had brought forward changes in governance structures.

TABLE 2.6

Enron Key Executive Indictments—to December 31, 2005

	INDICTED BY	FOR	PLEA/COOPERATE ✔	RESULT
Ken Lay, Chair, Chair and CEO	Jul 2004, 2 trials: 1 jury, 1 judge	Conspiracy, fraud & false statements	Not guilty Not guilty	Guilty in both trials, but died before sentencing, so verdicts vacated
Jeffrey Skilling, CEO	Feb 2004	Conspiracy, fraud, false statements, insider trading	Not guilty	24 yr, 4 month sentence Restitution $45 million
Andrew Fastow, CFO	Jan 2004	Securities fraud	Plea agreement (guilty) ✔	10 yr sentence, later reduced to 6 yrs, forfeit $23.8 mil
Lea Fastow, Assistant Treasurer	May 2004	Tax fraud	Plea agreement (guilty) ✔	1 yr sentence
Richard Causey, CAO	Dec 2005	Securities fraud	Plea agreement (guilty) ✔	7 yr sentence Forfeit $1.25 million
Michael Kopper	Aug 2002	Fraud and money laundering	Plea agreement (guilty) ✔	37 month sentence Forfeit $12 million
Mark Koenig, Investor Relations	Aug 2004	Securities fraud	Plea agreement (guilty)	18 month sentence Forfeit $1.49 million
Ben Glisan, Treasurer	Dec 2002 Sep 2003	Fraud Fraud	Denied wrongdoing, later ✔	5 yr sentence, ✔ later brought favors, forfeit $625,000.
Kenneth Rice, CEO Broadband Services	Apr 2005	Securities fraud	Plea agreement (guilty) ✔	10 yr sentence Forfeit $29.4 million
Kevin Hannon	Sep 2005	Securities fraud	Guilty	5 yr sentence Forfeit $250,000
Timothy Despain Assistant Treasurer	Apr 2004	Securities fraud	Plea agreement (guilty) ✔	5 yr sentence, released on $100,000 bail
Enron Board of Directors (18 members)	Jan 2005	Breach of Fiduciary Duty		Settlement $168 million; $155 million covered by insurance

Source: SEC Files, newspaper articles, see also http://www.chron.com/news/specials/enron/   ✔ = Cooperates with prosecutors

Enron Reference Information

TABLE 2.7

Selected Enron Financial Statement Details

	2000	1999	1998
Summary Income Statement (millions)			
Revenues	$101,789	$40,112	$31,260
Operating income	1,953	802	1,378
IBIT	2,482	1,995	1,582
Net income before Cumulative Accounting Changes	979	1,024	703
Net Income	979	893	703
EPS (in dollars)- basic	1.22	1.17	1.07
- diluted	1.12	1.10	1.01
Detail of IBIT (millions)			
Transport & distribution			
Trans. Services	$ 391	$ 380	$ 351
Portland General	341	305	286
Wholesale Services	2,260	1,317	968
Retail Energy Services	165	(68)	(119)
Broadband Services	(60)		
Exploration & prod.	–	65	128
Corporate and other	(615)	(4)	(32)
IBIT	2,482	1,995	1,582
Summary Balance Sheet (billions)			
Current assets	$ 30.4	$ 7.3	
Investments, other	23.4	15.4	
Property, plant, equip, net	11.7	10.7	
Total Assets	65.5	33.4	
Current liabilities	28.4	6.8	
Long-term debt	8.6	7.2	
Deferred credits and other	13.8	6.5	
Shareholders' Equity	11.5	9.6	
Total Liabilities & Shareholders' Equity	65.5	33.4	

On June 26, 2002, WorldCom announced that it had discovered a $4.3 billion manipulation of earnings. The resulting outrage galvanized the construction and passage of the Sarbanes-Oxley Act on July 30, 2002, which provided the blueprint for a new framework for governance to be developed in the United States and which will inform developments around the world. Not surprisingly, the key concepts included accountability, transparency, independence, objectivity, fiduciary duty, and the primacy of the public interest.

As Enron executives and accomplices are indicted, settled with, or convicted, and as the SEC and other regulators respond to the Sarbanes-Oxley Act, the long-run changes in corporate governance and practice and the accounting profession continue to emerge.

| Downloadable Enron Case Source Document Files

 To assist readers of this case, the following downloadable files are available at **www.cengage.com/accounting/brooks**.

| The Powers Report

| The Senate's Permanent Subcommittee on Investigations Report on The Role of the Board of Directors in the Collapse of Enron

| Senate Subcommittee Testimony of Robert Roach, Appendices

| Sarbanes-Oxley Act of 2002

Governance & Accountability Changes up to WorldCom

Even before the Enron scandal appeared and resulted in a filing for bankruptcy protection on December 2, 2001, there had been some recognition that governance and accounting changes were desirable. After Enron, there was turmoil and growing outrage over the cavalier way that Enron executives claimed ignorance, bad memories, or pleaded the Fifth Amendment. Arthur Andersen representatives did not help in their testimony, and there was a growing concern that no one was being brought to justice. There seemed to be no accountability, or little will on the part of justice officials to get tough with the culprits that had caused so much anxiety and loss, and had enriched themselves so handsomely in the process.

Even though there were some attempts to strengthen corporate governance and accountability before Enron, it is almost impossible to convey the growing sense of investor and public outrage throughout December 2001 and into the early summer of 2002. President Bush promised further reforms to restore confidence in the financial markets, but failed to slow the market slide. Then, on June 25, 2002, came the shocking news that the giant corporation, WorldCom, was also in financial difficulty. This progression of disasters galvanized two U.S. lawmakers, Paul Sarbanes and Michael Oxley, to merge their efforts and bring forward the landmark governance reform legislation known as the Sarbanes-Oxley Act of 2002.

Table 2.8 is a partial list of key guideline and regulatory changes that had been brought into being before and after the Enron fiasco, and before the WorldCom bankruptcy announcement on July 21, 2002.

WorldCom: The Final Catalyst

WorldCom, Inc., the second largest U.S. telecommunications giant and almost 70 percent larger than Enron in assets, announced on June 25, 2002, that it had overstated cash flow by $3.8 billion.[40] Then WorldCom applied for bankruptcy protection on July 21, 2002, and subsequently eclipsed Enron as the world's largest bankruptcy. This came as a staggering blow to the credibility of capital markets.

It occurred in the middle of the furor caused by:

I The Enron bankruptcy on December 2, 2001, and the related Congress and Senate hearings and Fifth Amendment testimony by Enron executives

I The depression of the stock markets

I The pleas by business leaders and President Bush for restoration of credibility and trust to corporate governance, reporting, and the financial markets

I Responsive introduction of governance guidelines by stock exchanges and the Securities and Exchange Commission

I Debate by the U.S. Congress and Senate of separate bills to improve governance and accountability

I Arthur Andersen's conviction for obstruction of justice on June 15, 2002

WorldCom failed because of bad business judgments that were hidden from investors by accounting manipulations and executive skullduggery, which are explained more fully in the case, *WorldCom: The Final Catalyst,* located at the end of the chapter. Arthur Andersen LLP was WorldCom's auditor.

---

40. Simon Romero and Alex Berenson, "WorldCom says it hid expenses, inflating cash flow $3.8 billion," *New York Times,* June 26, 2002.

TABLE	2.8	Key Changes in Governance Guidelines and Regulations

ANNOUNCED	SOURCE OF CHANGE
1994	*The Dey Report, "Where were the Directors?"* Toronto Stock Exchange To review corporate governance and make recommendations for best practice.
1999	*Five Years to the Dey,* Report on Corporate Governance, Toronto Stock Exchange and The Institute of Corporate Directors To survey and analyze governance procedures at TSE companies.
May 2000	*The Combined Code: Principles of Good Governance and Principles of Best Practice* Based on the Hempel (1998), the Cadbury (1992) and Greenbury Reports (1995), used by companies listed on the London Stock Exchange.
2000	*Guidance for Directors on the Combined Code,* The Turnbull Report. See Combined Code purpose.
Nov. 21, 2001	*The Saucier Report, "Beyond Compliance: Building a Governance Culture,"* Joint Committee on Corporate Governance, CICA/TSE To review the current state of corporate governance in Canada, compare Canadian and international best practices, and make recommendations for changes that will ensure Canadian corporate governance is among the best in the world.
Apr. 26, 2002	*Toronto Stock Exchange (TSX) Guidelines,* Amended Revisions effective Dec.31, 2002 to adopt some Saucier Report recommendations.
Apr. 4, 2002	SEC Blue Ribbon Committee Discussions
2002 Various	Business Roundtable—various statements
June 6, 2002	*NYSE Corporate Governance Listing Requirements,* Effective Aug. 2002, after SEC approval A review at the request of Harvey Pitt, SEC Chairman, to enhance the accountability, integrity, and transparency of companies listed on the NYSE.
June 28, 2002	SEC Order effective Aug, 14, 2002 CEO and CFO to certify 8-K, quarterly and annual financial reports.
July 9, 2002	President George Bush's Proposals Speech

Notes: A synthesis of the 2002 proposals of the SEC, NYSE, and NASDAQ is available at www.torys.com as publication No. 2002–16T. More recent regulations are also reviewed. Visit **www.cengage.com/accounting/brooks** for links to key governance organizations' Websites.

WorldCom's accounting manipulations involved very basic, easy-to spot types of fraud.[41] Overstatements of cash flow and income were created because one of WorldCom's major expenses, line costs, or "fees paid to third party telecommunication network providers for the right to access the third parties' networks,"[42] were accounted for improperly. Essentially, line costs that should have been expensed, thus lowering reporting income, were offset by capital transfers or charged against capital accounts, thus placing their impact on the balance sheet rather than the income statement. In addition, WorldCom created excess reserves or provisions for future expenses, which they later released or reduced, thereby adding to profits. The manipulation of profit through reserves or provisions is known as "cookie jar" accounting.

The aggregate overstatement of income quickly rose to more than $9 billion[43] by September 19, 2002, for the following reasons:

▎ $3.85 billion for improperly capitalized expenses, announced June 25, 2002[44]

▎ $3.83 billion for more improperly capitalized expenses in 1999, 2000, 2001, and the first quarter of 2002, announced on August 8, 2002[45]

---

41. Bruce Myerson, "A WorldCom primer," the Associated Press, June 26, 2001.
42. *Complaint: SEC v. WorldCom, Inc.,* U.S. Securities and Exchange Commission, June 26, 2002, para. 5, www.sec.gov/litigation/complaints/complr17588.htm.
43. "WorldCom to reveal more bogus accounting," the Associated Press, September 19, 2002; David E. Royella and "WorldCom faces two new charges, misstatement grows," David E. Royella, *Financial Post,* November 6, 2002, FP4.
44. WorldCom Inc., Form 8-K, *Current Report Pursuant to Section 13 or 15(D) of the Securities Exchange Act of 1934,* August 14, 2002, para. 2, www.sec.gov/archives/edgar/.
45. Ibid., para. 3.

> $2.0 billion for manipulations of profit through previously established reserves, dating back to 1999

Ultimately, the WorldCom fraud totaled $11 billion.

Key senior personnel involved in the manipulations at WorldCom included: Bernard J. Ebbers, CEO; Scott D. Sullivan, CFO; Buford Yates Jr., Director of General Accounting; David F. Myers, Controller; Betty L. Vinson, Director of Management Reporting, from January 2002; and Troy M. Normand, Director of Legal Entity Accounting, from January 2002. Their motivation and mechanism for these manipulations is evident from the SEC's description of what happened at the end of each quarter, after the draft quarterly statements were reviewed. Steps were taken by top management to hide WorldCom's problems and boost or protect the company's stock price in order to profit from stock options, maintain collateral requirements for personal loans, and keep their jobs. These steps were required, in part, to offset the downward pressure on WorldCom's share price caused by U.S. and European regulators' rejection of WorldCom's US $115 billion bid for Sprint Communications.[46] Ebbers' company had been using takeovers rather than organic growth to prop up earnings, and the financial markets began to realize this would be increasingly difficult.

According to the SEC:

> Specifically, after reviewing the consolidated financial statements for the third quarter of 2000, WorldCom senior management determined that WorldCom had failed to meet analysts' expectations. WorldCom's senior management then instructed Myers, and his subordinates, including Yates, VINSON and NORMAND, to make improper and false entries in WorldCom's general ledger reducing its line cost expense accounts, and reducing—in amounts corresponding to the improper and false line cost expense amounts—various reserve accounts. . . .
> There was no documentation supporting these entries, and no proper business rationale for them, and they were not in conformity with GAAP.[47]

Manipulations followed the same pattern for the fourth quarter of 2000, but a change in technique was required for the first quarter of 2001 for fear of discovery by the auditors. Senior management instructed that line cost expenses be fraudulently reclassified:

> . . . to a variety of capital asset accounts without any supporting documentation or proper business rationale and in a manner that did not conform with GAAP. . . .
> . . . In particular, . . . NORMAND telephoned WorldCom's Director of Property Accounting (the "DPA") and instructed him to adjust the schedules he maintained for certain Property, Plant & Equipment capital expenditure accounts (the "PP&E Roll-Forward") by increasing certain capital accounts for "prepaid capacity"[48]

In future periods, the increase of certain accounts for "prepaid capacity" remained the manipulation of choice.

It should be noted that Ebbers was not an accountant. He was, however, ably assisted in these manipulations by Scott Sullivan, his chief financial officer, and David Myers, his controller. Both Sullivan and Myers had worked for Arthur Andersen before joining WorldCom.

---

46. "Ebbers became symbol of scandals," *Financial Post,* July 14, 2005, FP1, FP3.
47. *Complaint: SEC v. Betty L. Vinson, and Troy M. Normand,* U.S. Securities and Exchange Commission, modified October 31, 2002, www.sec.gov/litigation/complaints/comp17783.htm.
48. Ibid., para. 4, 5, and 6.

Other fascinating revelations offer a glimpse behind the scenes at WorldCom:

1. WorldCom also announced that it might write off $50.6 billion in goodwill or other intangible assets when restating for the accounting errors noted above. Apparently WorldCom acquisition decisions had been faulty.

2. Investigation revealed that Bernard Ebbers had been loaned $408.2 million. He was supposed to use the loans to buy WorldCom stock or for margin calls as the stock price fell. Instead, he used it partly for the purchase of the largest cattle ranch in Canada, construction of a new home, personal expenses of a family member, and loans to family and friends.[49]

3. "When ... asked whether he was afraid of Ebbers, he (Sullivan) said: "At times, at times I wasn't. He can be very intimidating."[50]

Former Attorney-General Richard Thornburgh[51] was appointed by the U.S. Justice Department to investigate the collapse and bankruptcy of WorldCom. In his *Report to the U.S. Bankruptcy Court* in Manhattan on November 5, 2002, he said:

> One person, Bernard Ebbers, appears to have dominated the company's growth, as well as the agenda, discussions and decisions of the board of directors,...
>
> A picture is clearly emerging of a company that had a number of troubling and serious issues..." relating to "culture, internal controls, management, integrity, disclosure and financial statements.
>
> While Mr. Ebbers received more than US $77 million in cash and benefits from the company, shareholders lost in excess of US $140 billion in value.[52]

The WorldCom saga continued as the company's new management tried to restore trust in its activities. As part of this effort, the company changed its name to MCI. "On August 26, 2003, Richard Breeden, the Corporate Monitor appointed by the U.S. District Court for the Southern District of New York, issued a report outlining the steps the Company will take to re-build itself into model of strong corporate governance, ethics and integrity ... (to) foster MCI's new company culture of 'integrity in everything we do.'"[53] The company moved deliberately to reestablish the trust and integrity it requires to compete effectively for resources, capital, and personnel in the future.

The SEC has filed complaints, which are on its website against the company, and its executives. The court has granted the injunctive relief the SEC sought. The executives have been enjoined from further such fraudulent actions, and subsequently banned by the SEC from practicing before it, and some have been banned by the court from acting as officers or directors in the future.

WorldCom, as a company, consented to a judgment imposing everything the Commission wanted, including extensive reviews and provision of:

❘ Governance systems, policies, plans, and practices.

❘ Internal accounting control structure and policies.

---

49. Royella, "WorldCom faces two new charges."
50. "Ex-WorldCom CFO implicates Ebbers," *Toronto Star,* February 8, 2005, D9.
 51. Richard Thornburgh issued two reports on WorldCom problems. These can be found at **www.cengage.com/accounting/brooks**.
52. Don Stancavish, "WorldCom dominated by Ebbers," Bloomberg News, in *Financial Post,* November 5, 2002, FP13.
53. MCI website, "Governance: Restoring the Trust," http://global.mci.com/about/governance/restoringtrust/, (accessed January 3, 2006).

Training and education to minimize future securities' laws violations.

Civil fines.[54]

Ebbers and Sullivan were each indicted on nine charges: one count of conspiracy, one count of securities fraud, and seven counts of false regulatory findings.[55] Sullivan pled guilty on the same day he was indicted, and later cooperated with prosecutors and testified against Bernie Ebbers "in the hopes of receiving a lighter sentence."[56]

Early in 2002, Ebbers stood up in church to address the congregation saying: "I just want you to know that you're not going to church with a crook."[57] Ebbers took the stand and argued "that he didn't know anything about WorldCom's shady accounting, that he left much of the minutiae of running the company to underlings."[58] But after eight days of deliberations, on March 15, 2005, a federal jury in Manhattan didn't buy his "aw shucks," "hands-off," or "ostrich-in-the-sand" defense. They believed Sullivan, who told the jury that Ebbers repeatedly told Sullivan to "'hit his numbers'—a command . . . to falsify the books to meet Wall Street expectations."[59]

On July 13, 2005, Ebbers was sentenced to twenty-five years in a federal prison.[60] Once a billionaire, he also lost his house, property, yacht, and fortune. At sixty-three years of age, in January 2006, Ebbers appealed his sentence. Sullivan's reduced sentence was for five years in a federal prison, forfeiture of his house, ill-gotten gains, and a fine.

Investors lost over $180 million in WorldCom's collapse,[61] and they lost more in other companies as well as confidence in credibility of the financial markets, governance mechanisms, and financial statements continued to deteriorate.

Governance Reform—The Sarbanes-Oxley Act of 2002

The announcement by WorldCom of their massive accounting earnings manipulation fraud struck the capital markets, media, and politicians like a lightening bolt. Senator Paul Sarbanes, a Democrat, was trying to push forward a bill of governance and accounting reforms through the U.S. Senate. Congressman Michael Oxley, a Republican, was trying to do the same through the U.S. House of Representatives. Opposition was stiff to both bills, but immediately after the WorldCom announcement, the two men joined forces and the Sarbanes-Oxley Act of 2002 was passed through both the Congress and the Senate and became law on July 30, 2002. It was an amazing galvanization and an unexpected but hoped for outcome.

Sarbanes-Oxley Act (SOX): New Governance for Corporations & the Accounting Profession

SOX is the most far-reaching U.S. security law enacted since the *Securities Act of 1933* and the *Securities Exchange Act of 1934*, which spawned the Securities and Exchange Commission (SEC)

---

54. *SEC Litigation Release No. 17883*/ December 6, 2002, http://www.sec.gov/litigation/litreleases/ lr17883.htm.

55. "Jury convicts Ebbers on all counts in fraud case," MSNBC, March 15, 2005, http:// www.msnbc.msn.com/id/7139448/.

56. Crawford, "Ex-WorldCom CEO Ebbers guilty."

57. "Ebbers became symbol of scandals," *Financial Post,* July 14, 2005, FP1, FP3.

58. Crawford, "Ex-WorldCom CEO Ebbers guilty."

59. "Jury convicts Ebbers on all counts in fraud case."

60. "Ebbers became symbol of scandals."

61. Ibid., "Ebbers became symbol of scandals." Also Richard J. Newman estimated investor losses to as much as $200 million in "Time for payback," in Stern in the News, NYU Stern, at http://w4.stern.nyu .edu/news/news/2003/october/1027usnews.htm.

in 1934 to administer the acts. Many of the provisions of SOX required SEC action for implementation, and future studies to access the best path for future guidance.

SOX has created an international regulatory framework for corporations seeking access to the U.S. capital markets and their auditors. SOX sets new standards for governance that will apply to all SEC registrant companies—those listed on U.S. stock exchanges—including those large foreign companies that are listed on the U.S. exchanges. Over 200 of Canada's largest companies, and many other large international enterprises, will therefore have to comply with any new rules.

Also, SOX establishes a new framework for the U.S. accounting profession that replaces self-regulation by the profession with a Public Company Accounting Oversight Board (PCAOB). The PCAOB will oversee all accounting firms—U.S. and foreign—that audit SEC registrants, as well as the accounting and disclosure rules those companies follow.

Prior financial disasters, including the Enron, Arthur Andersen, and WorldCom governance debacles, raised the awareness in the United States, Canada, Australia, and the United Kingdom that the governance frameworks had to be improved. Specifically, in order to deal with the governance credibility crisis and restore confidence in the current corporate capital markets system, action was needed to meet public expectations in regard to the following matters:

- Clarification of the roles, responsibilities, and accountabilities of the board of directors, its subcommittees, of the directors themselves, and of the auditors.

- Reduction of the conflicts of interest influencing the directors, executives, and auditors so that they would exercise loyalty, independent judgment, and objectivity in the best interest of the shareholders or the company; or in the case of the auditor, in the public interest.

- Ensure that the directors were sufficiently informed on corporate plans and activities, the adequacy of company policies and internal controls to ensure compliance, and actual compliance, including whistle-blowers concerns.

- Ensure that directors possess adequate financial competence and other expertise where required.

- Ensure that financial reports were accurate, complete, understandable and transparent.

- Ensure that accounting standards are adequate to protect investor's interests.

- Ensure that the regulation and oversight of auditors of public companies, as well as their appointment and operating parameters, are adequate and appropriate to serve the public interest.

The developments proposed in SOX to remedy these problem areas are discussed next within the context of the new governance frameworks for corporations and for the auditing profession, as well as other matters. A .PDF version of SOX is available at **www.cengage.com/ accounting/brooks** together with a summary of certain SOX provisions relevant to oversight of the accounting profession. For reference, SOX is organized as indicated in Table 2.9.

New SOX Corporate Governance Framework

The new SOX framework takes the perspective that honest and full accountability to shareholders, and therefore to the public, is of paramount importance. Such accountability is identified as a prime responsibility of corporate directors to ensure and senior corporate officers to deliver, and that they are free from bias in doing so. In addition, since the accuracy and integrity of such an accountability regime depends upon the independent scrutiny of auditors, directors are charged with ensuring that, through the audit subcommittee of the board, the auditors are

2.9 **Organization of the Sarbanes-Oxley Act of 2002**

SECTIONS	TITLE	
1, 2, 3		Short Title, Definitions, Table of Contents
101–109	I	Public Company Oversight Board
201–209	II	Auditor Independence
301–308	III	Corporate Responsibility
301		Public Company Audit Committees (including whistle-blower encouragement) Corporate Responsibility for Financial Statements (including CEO and CFO certification)
401–409	IV	Enhanced Financial Disclosures
404		Management Assessment of Internal Controls
406		Code of Ethics for Senior Financial Officers
501	V	Analyst Conflicts of Interest
601–604	VI	Commission Resources and Authority
701–705	VII	Studies and Reports
801–807	VIII	Corporate Criminal Fraud Accountability
901–906	IX	White Collar Crime Penalty Enhancements
1001	X	Corporate Tax Returns
1001–1007	XI	Corporate Fraud and Accountability

free from conflicts of interest, have access to and report to the board, and so on. These matters are provided for in SOX through the introduction of specific provisions related to:

I Clarification of the responsibility of directors and officers for public accountability and its integrity.

I Enhanced conflict of interest provisions designed to ensure sufficient directors are independent from management.

I Clarification of the role, responsibility and membership of audit subcommittees of the board, so that:

- The audit subcommittee:

  - Is "directly responsible for the appointment, compensation, and oversight of any public accounting firm employed by that issuer . . ."[62] including the resolution of any disputes with management.
  - Must establish procedures to receive and address complaints regarding accounting, auditing, and internal controls, including establishing procedures to allow employees to submit anonymous complaints.[63]
  - Must approve any nonaudit services to be provided by the auditors.

- Only independent[64] directors can serve on the audit subcommittee,

  - All must be financially competent.
  - One must be, and be identified to be, a financial expert.[65]

---

62. SOX, Section 301 (2), p. 33.
63. Ibid., Section 301(4), p. 34.
64. SOX, Section 310 (3), p. 33 states that independence requires that "a member of an audit committee may not, other than in his capacity as a member of the audit committee, the board of directors, or any other board committee—(i) accept any consulting, advisory, or other compensatory fee from the issuer; or (ii) be an affiliated person of the issuer or any subsidiary thereof."
65. A "financial expert" is defined in SOX, SEC 407 (b), p. 47, as a person who has "(1) an understanding of GAAP and financial statements, (2) experience in (A) the preparation or auditing of financial statements of generally comparable issuers, and (B) the application of such principles in connection with the accounting for estimates, accruals and reserves; and (3) experience with internal accounting controls; and (4) an understanding of audit committee functions."

❙ Auditors report to the audit subcommittee, and are to be met without management present, and vice versa.

❙ The subcommittee must be given adequate budget and time to complete its work, including the right to hire and consult outside experts.

❙ Additional disclosures:

- To allow scrutiny of transactions between principal stockholders and management.
- To report upon the corporation's internal controls, including the management's responsibility for establishing, maintaining, and assessing their effectiveness.
- Accelerated reporting of corporate disclosures and stock trades.

❙ *Management assessment and signed certification by the CEO and CFO* to the board and SEC of the integrity of:

- Quarterly and annual financial reports, and SEC forms.
- Systems of internal control underlying and ensuring that integrity.[66]

❙ Requirement for a code of ethics and compliance thereto for senior financial officers.

❙ The illegality of exercising any undue influence on the conduct of audits.

❙ Proper action by insiders for stock trading and dealing with stock analysts.

❙ Sanctions for wrongdoing, including forfeiture of bonuses and profits, officer and director bars from service, and penalties.

❙ New SOX Framework for the U.S. Accounting Profession

Auditors, as noted previously, will be more responsive to the audit subcommittee of the board, who will arrange their appointment, reappointment, fees, and settle disputes; and they will be much less responsive to senior management who often played a dominant role in these matters. In this regard, auditors will be working with financially competent, independent directors whose interests should be more directed than they may have been toward clear, comprehensive public reports.

Auditors must report directly to audit committees on the following matters:

❙ All critical accounting policies and practices to be used.

❙ All alternative treatments of financial information under GAAP that have been discussed with management.

❙ The ramifications of the use of the alternative treatments and disclosures and the treatment preferred by the auditor.

❙ All other material written communications between the auditor and management, including any management letter and schedule of unadjusted differences.

❙ Their review of and attestation on management's assessment of the company's internal controls, including:

- "... whether the internal control structure and procedures include maintenance of records that accurately and fairly reflect the company's transactions and disposition of assets;

---

66. This is known as Section 404 review compliance work.

- whether there is reasonable assurance that the transactions are recorded as necessary to permit the preparation of financial statements in accordance with GAAP and made in accordance with proper authorization by management and directors; and

- a description of material weaknesses in internal controls found on the basis of testing done and material noncompliance."[67]

In addition, SOX establishes a Public Company Accounting Oversight Board (PCAOB) that will:

▌ Consist of five members (only two of which can be CPAs) with five-year staggered terms.

▌ Inspect, discipline, and write rules governing accounting firms that audit public companies.

▌ Establish auditing and attestation standards, including quality control and independence standards for the audit of public companies.

▌ Maintain a register of foreign firms that audit SEC registrants, and who will be subject to PCAOB regulations and discipline.

In order to stop auditors from auditing results of their own nonaudit services, auditors are prohibited from offering the nonaudit services listed here, and may offer other nonaudit services such as tax services to SEC registrants only if permitted by the client's Audit Subcommittee:

▌ "... bookkeeping and other services related to the accounting records or financial statements of the client;

▌ financial information system design and implementation;

▌ appraisal or valuation services;

▌ fairness opinions, or contribution-in-kind reports;

▌ actuarial services;

▌ internal audit outsourcing services;

▌ management functions or human resources;

▌ broker or dealer, investment adviser, or investment banking services;

▌ legal services and expert services unrelated to the audit; and any other service the PCAOB determines by regulation is not permissible."[68]

Finally, an audit partner cannot serve as the engagement partner or the concurring partner for over five concurrent years.

▌ New SOX Frameworks for Other Matters

SOX has provisions covering/requiring the need for a code of conduct for attorneys serving registrants, the treatment of analyst conflicts of interest, and penalties for fraud and white collar crime. In addition, SOX required the following studies to chart the best course ahead:

▌ U.S. General Accounting Office (GAO)—problems associated with the consolidation of major accounting firms

▌ Comptroller General—mandatory rotation of audit firms

---

67. The Sarbanes-Oxley Act, *Financial Reporting Release,* PricewaterhouseCoopers, August 2002, 3.
68. Ibid., 4.

❚ SEC—adoption of "principles-based" accounting system; role and function of credit rating agencies; actions of violators and violations; enforcement actions; possible complicit earnings manipulation activities of investment banks and financial advisers

Finally, SOX states that it is a crime to knowingly destroy, alter, or falsify records needed in federal investigations and bankruptcy proceedings, with such crime to be punishable by a fine and/or imprisonment of up to twenty years.[69]

❚ Implementation by the SEC

The SEC was charged with introducing new regulations or changes in its regulations to implement the proposed SOX frameworks within defined time frames, subject to research studies where appropriate.

It should be noted, however, that although the proposed SOX frameworks push governance and accountability reform a long way, the SEC might push the reforms even further. One such case is the proposed SEC rule for lawyers that discover a violation. Lawyers would have to report any material violation of securities laws, or fiduciary duty, or similar material violation found to their client's chief legal counsel or to the CEO. If there is no appropriate response the attorney must report to the audit committee, the board, or a committee of outside directors. If this "up-the-ladder" reporting does not generate an appropriate response, and the violation would likely result in substantial injury to the financial interest or property of the issuer or of investors, the outside attorney would have to make a "noisy exit," which would involve withdrawal from representation of the issuer, notification to the SEC of the withdrawal, and repudiation of any submission to the SEC that the lawyer believes is tainted.

Law firms have argued that the proposed rule goes further than the SOX intended and proposes to make them into whistle-blowers, and that the noisy withdrawal provision is inconsistent with fundamental rights, such as attorney-client privilege and confidentiality. Time will tell whether outside lawyers have responsibilities worthy of noisy exit disclosure to those outside the SEC and client.[70]

Impact on Governance, Accountability & Reporting, & Management Practice

The SOX governance framework will focus the attention of directors and management on issues that are of critical importance to the proper governance and reporting process. In particular, the following developments will bring positive and long overdue changes:

❚ Specific focus on improved accountability and reporting to public shareholders, and related internal control and whistle-blower systems, and upon the related certification by CEO and CFO—where false certification will be considered a *criminal* offense.

❚ Strengthening of the role of the audit committee, the full independence of serving directors, information flow, and the ability of auditors to report on and engage the committee in meaningful discussion.

❚ Clarification of roles, responsibilities, and competencies of directors and board subcommittees.

---

69. SOX, Section 802 (a), p. 57.
70. "SEC aims to make lawyers whistle-blowers," Torys LLP, December 19, 2002, www.torys.com. The SEC subsequently circulated an exposure draft and then a re-exposure draft of proposed rules regarding the noisy exit but, as of late 2008, had not put forward binding regulations.

▌ Definition of and emphasis on avoiding conflict of interest situations, as well as codes of conduct for the CFO and others.

▌ Increased penalties for wrongdoing.

However, finding enough financial experts to serve as directors, and as identified directors on audit committees, will be a challenge. Time requirements and legal risk have escalated, forcing the reduction of the number of boards on which one can sit, and much higher board fees and special fees for sitting on audit committees. Training in director competencies is growing and will become the norm.

It is unlikely that smaller companies and foreign companies will voluntarily fully adopt the new governance regime due to its time-consuming nature and cost. This may create a two-tier governance system that may not favor some investors. Some corporations will resign their SEC registration and remove themselves from the U.S. capital markets, as Porsche has already done.

In the end, if the SOX governance system had been in place, would the Enron, World-Com, and other financial disasters have been avoided? Certainly the probability of avoidance would have been much higher.

Impact on the Accounting Profession & Auditing Practice

The U.S. accounting profession has lost its relatively unfettered ability to offer nonaudit service to clients based solely on the judgment and self-regulation of accountants. Nonaudit services offered have been circumcised, and because they must usually be provided by firms not performing the company's audit, are less efficient or more costly to provide to audit clients.

Audit service fee margins increased dramatically as a result of the extremely large demands for Section 404 compliance work assisting with the review of the integrity of corporate internal controls and the accuracy of financial statements. The surge in demand precipitated a shortage of qualified audit personnel. There was such an outcry against the cost of compliance with Section 404—estimated at $7.8 million in 2004 for each of the Fortune 1000 companies[71]—that the SEC responded by indicating that it never intended that the work should be absolutely exhaustive, but based on judgment.[72] This produced some relief from the paranoia of some CEOs and CFOs worried about jail terms, and from lawyers and auditors who were advising an ultraconservative approach. Nonetheless, the cost of Section 404 work has been enormous. Is the cost worth the extra protection? According to one informed observer, Lynn Turner,[73] who is a former chief accountant at the SEC, the aggregate cost of the Section 404 compliance work for all U.S. registrants is less (which he estimated at $5 billion) than the amount lost by Enron investors alone ($90 billion). The benefit–cost relationship is even more extremely favorable if losses from any other corporate scandals are avoided in the future. Ongoing annual costs of Section 404 compliance should fall as systems are put in place, improved, and documented. Better internal control systems should also moderate increased annual audit costs that appear to have risen up to 16 percent in the two years following the Enron debacle.[74]

---

71. *Sarbanes-Oxley Section 404 Costs and Remediation of Deficiencies: Estimates from a Sample of Fortune 1000 Companies,* Charles River Associates, Washington, April 2005, 2.
72. *Commission Statement on Implementation of Internal Control Reporting Requirements, 2005-74,* U.S. Securities and Exchange Commission, Washington, D.C., May 16, 2005.
73. Remarks by Lynn Turner on August 9, 2004, at the 2004 Annual Meeting of the American Accounting Association.
74. Ibid.

In U.S. and foreign jurisdictions, some smaller professional accounting firms have foregone auditing SEC or stock market registrants because they wish to maintain the nature and margins of their current integrated practices. This may mean that a two-tier system of auditors develops throughout the world—one for the large corporations and another for the small. A two-tier system for GAAP for big or small corporations may also become more attractive.

The full impact of SOX continues to unfold, but the strengthening of accountability, and of independence standards and the relationship of the auditor to the audit subcommittee, will help the auditor serve the public interest.

Impact on Business Ethics Trends

The Enron, Arthur Andersen, and WorldCom cases have produced much greater awareness of ethical issues and trends that were under way, including conflicts of interest and the control of self-interest, fiduciary duty of directors to shareholders/company and of auditors to the public interest, and the general good business sense of developing an ethical culture. That ethical culture should be based on honesty, fairness, compassion, integrity, predictability, and responsibility, and focused on the development of trust and the respect for stakeholder interests. In fact, U.S. and foreign corporations that have good governance and accountability do embrace these, and have indicated that they have already been doing, in substance, what SOX recommends.

The infamous corporate debacles have also produced a new awareness that ethics and reputation are linked much more directly than earlier thought to be the case. Moreover, as in most product liability cases, the fine for Arthur Andersen of $500,000 (or the largest earlier fine of $7 million) proved to be insignificant compared to the loss of future revenue. Most important, the concept of franchise risk[75] has taken on an entirely new reality since Arthur Andersen, a firm of vaunted reputation and 85,000 employees, essentially disappeared in less than one year, and two of the world's most highly regarded corporations are in bankruptcy proceedings. Comprehensive risk management must include ethics risks and higher estimates for franchise risk.

Modern strategic, risk-oriented audit approaches will have to incorporate ethics risks and higher estimates for franchise risk as well. Corporate internal control systems should include ethics risk monitoring, and new systems should be developed to do so.

Professional accountants tended to subjugate fiduciary values to revenue generation considerations until AA's debacle. Professional accounting bodies and firms have subsequently stressed that quality and the public interest should dominate the profit-oriented business concerns of the professionals or their firms. The switch from professional self-regulation in the United States could be beneficial if applied successfully around the world, but a two- or multi-tier regime emerge might emerge that could leave the public interest at risk?

Finally, the need for business and professional ethics education, which illustrates through cases like Enron, Arthur Andersen, and WorldCom how important ethics are to corporate and to professional accounting firm culture and performance, has never been more evident.

Beyond the First Five Years

The Enron, Arthur Andersen, and WorldCom fiascoes came to a head in July 2002 when they necessitated the passing of the Sarbanes-Oxley Act that mandated and/or triggered governance reform for large corporations around the world. With the passage of time, questions have been raised over many issues including: what has changed, and how much; whether investors are better

---

75. The risk of losing the franchise to operate.

protected; whether directors and executives bear more legal risk than they should; whether corporations no longer take on risky opportunities appropriately; and whether the extra cost of meeting new governance regulations and expectations are too large relative to the benefits they provide. Studies are now appearing [see **www.cengage.com/accounting/brooks**] that shed light on these matters with the benefit of the increasing perspective that time in-use provides. Some of the SOX provisions, related regulations and interpretations have been diminished in their application, but expectations for good governance have not. However, SOX provided a crystallization of these expectations that continues to inform investors, courts, directors, executives, and accountants on appropriate behavior—and is still creating new ripple effects in the form of new challenges to be faced.

The original impact of SOX has been reduced in several ways. For example, the requirement for CEOs and CFOs to certify financial statements were accurate and that internal controls designed to ensure that accuracy were in place and effective, originally generated extremely extensive review and audit work by audit firms to document existing internal controls and to verify their efficacy. The exhaustive extent and resulting huge cost of the review and audit work was determined largely by fear on the part of CEOs and CFOs for the large fines and/or jail terms involved if they made an erroneous certification of accuracy, or the internal controls were not effective. Fortunately, however, in 2007 the PCAOB[76] and the SEC[77] issued a clarification that reasonable judgment in the form of a top-down, risk-based approach to the evaluation of internal control was to be exercised as to the extent of the review and assurance work, rather than a 100-percent examination.

In addition, in June 2006, "U.S. District Court Judge James Robart held that financial statement certifications ... are not in and of themselves evidence of the intent to deceive the investing public. ... Corporate officers make mistakes. ... Securities fraud, however, requires more than a mistake—it requires a misstatement that was either intentional or deliberately reckless."[78] In other words, "scienter" or intent must be proven, not just assumed.

Both of these developments meant that the cost of early SOX review and audit work was excessive relative to what was actually expected. Moreover, the internal controls improvement stimulated by the CEO and CFO interest, and the review and audit work, gave rise to more accurate financial reports and fewer financial fiascoes. As a result, early studies of the net costs and benefits of the SOX reforms were probably artificially negative, and did not reflect the lower levels of ongoing audit costs, or of fiascoes avoided, or the benefit of the return of confidence and credibility in capital markets. In summary, while there is no doubt that review and audit costs rose as a result of SOX, in the longer run there is probably a net benefit over cost. Early estimates appear to bear this out. Investors are now thought to have lost an estimated $20 billion after recoveries in the Enron bankruptcy *alone*, whereas total early SOX review and audit costs are estimated are $5 billion with continuing audit costs estimated to rise by approximately 3 percent.

Contemplating a complete reversal of SOX-spawned reforms is therefore probably pointless, whereas piecemeal remission is likely. For example, in February 2007 under its new chairman Christopher Cox, the SEC put forward a brief to the U.S. Supreme Court "urging the adoption of a legal standard that would make it harder for shareholders to prevail in fraud

---

76. Public Company Accounting Oversight Board Auditing Standard No. 5 (PCAOB Release No. 2007-005), An Audit of Internal Control Over Financial Reporting That Is Integrated with An Audit of Financial Statements, May 24, 2007.
77. SEC Release 33-8810/34-55929) *Management's Report on Internal Control Over Financial Reporting,* June 27, 2007.
78. "CEOs Breathe Easier," Sandra Rubin, *National Post,* June 14, 2006, FP9.

lawsuits against publicly-traded companies and their executives. At the same time, the agency's chief accountant, Conrad Hewitt former managing partner of Ernst & Young, told a conference that it was considering ways to protect large accounting firms from large damage awards in cases brought by investors in companies. ... Cox ... said ... that both efforts were in the best interests of investors because they were aimed at preventing the accounting industry from further consolidation and limiting what he called 'fraudulent lawsuits' including some that he said had been filed by 'professional plaintiffs.'"[79] Hewitt indicated that five European countries had adopted ways to limit auditor liability including monetary caps, and limits based on the size of the client corporation or of the fee charged.

Another aspect of the SOX reforms that affects the accounting profession is the establishment of agencies such as the U.S. Public Company Accounting Oversight Board (PCAOB) or the Canadian Public Accountability Board (CPAB) that were intended to oversee or audit the auditors. Their impact on public accounting has been significant and growing, even if the criticism of big firms or lawsuits against them have been lower than some observers would prefer. The fact that there is now an independent, external body that is monitoring the professional firms, and it has the potential to harm the reputation of assurance firms as well as their pocket books has had a significant affect on the internal quality control mechanisms of those firms which should bode well for the future.

It is apparent that, although controversy exists about the efficiency of the SOX-triggered governance reforms, corporate directors are a more independent, expert group, whose roles are better defined, and whose attention to governance matters is much more wholesomely investor-oriented than prior to 2002. CEOs and CFOs are now much more concerned with financial accuracy and related systems. Professional accountants are more aware of their professionalism and the need to serve the public interest rather than the CEO and CFO who, in the past, had paid them. Expectations are higher, performance is better, and we have not had as serious corporate chicanery as that experienced before SOX took effect. Refinements in SOX-triggered machinery are to be expected—wholesale changes are not.

---

79. "SEC Seeks to Ease Post-Enron Reforms," Stephen LaBaton, *The New York Times* as reprinted in the *Financial Post*, February 14, 2007, FP15.

Questions

1. What were the common aspects that were necessary for the Enron and WorldCom debacles to occur?

2. What actions by directors, executives, and professional accountants could have prevented the Enron and WorldCom debacles?

3. Was the enactment of the Sarbanes-Oxley Act (SOX) necessary? Why or why not?

4. What are the three most important improvements in the governance structure that could result from SOX?

5. What were the common elements in Arthur Andersen's approach that appeared to allow the disasters at Enron, WorldCom, Waste Management, and Sunbeam?

6. What is wrong with Enron's banks financing transactions they knew were without economic substance?

7. How should boards of directors change incentive remuneration schemes for executives to lessen the risk of motivating executives to risk manipulations to enrich themselves?

8. What lessons should be learned from reviewing the events described in this chapter?

Case Insights

The cases that follow—Enron, Arthur Andersen, and WorldCom, Waste Management, and Sunbeam— have become icons in the history of governance and accountability. Taken together, they reflect the greed of fraud-intent management, the failure of conflicted governance systems and the integrity of the corporate reporting systems, and the misunderstanding of the fiduciary duties of directors and professional accountants. The seeds of Arthur Andersen's downfall are evident throughout. The first three cases are more detailed accounts of material summarized in Chapter 2.

- *Enron's Questionable Transactions*—a detailed account of the questionable transactions underlying the massive fraud made possible by flaws in corporate and professional accounting governance.

- *Arthur Andersen's Troubles*—the story of the once revered, but systemically flawed, auditor of all these companies that forgot to whom fiduciary duty was owed.

- *WorldCom: The Final Catalyst*—the timely and massive fraud that triggered meaningful reform of corporate and professional accounting governance.

- *Waste Management, Inc.*—one of Arthur Andersen's early audit failures where the accounting manipulations of management and a dominated corporate governance system led to bankruptcy.

- *Sunbeam Corporation*—Arthur Andersen failed to stop Chainsaw Al Dunlap, who hoodwinked his board and intimidated his accounting staff into manipulating financial reports.

Principal References

Available at **www.cengage.com/accounting/brooks**

Sarbanes-Oxley Act of 2002.

SEC Reports, Press Releases, and Complaints, regarding Enron, Arthur Andersen, and WorldCom.

Testimony of Robert Roach, Appendices, U.S. Senate Permanent Subcommittee on Investigations.

The Powers Report, 2001.

The Role of the Board of Directors in the Collapse of Enron, The U.S. Senate's Permanent Subcommittee on Investigations Report, 2002.

Ethics Case

Enron's Questionable Transactions

An understanding of the nature of Enron's questionable transactions is fundamental to understanding why Enron failed. What follows is a summary of the essence of the major important transactions with the SPEs, including Chewco, LJM1, LJM2, and the Raptors. This summary extends the comments presented in Chapter 2, beginning on page 66.

Chewco Transactions

Chewco Investments LP[1] was created in November 1997 to buy the 50 percent interest owned by CalPERS, the California Public Employees' Retirement System, in a joint venture investment partnership called Joint

Energy Development Investment Limited Partnership (JEDI). JEDI had operated since 1993 as a nonconsolidated SPE. Enron wanted to create a larger unit with capital of $1 billion, and CalPERS asked to be bought out. Chewco was created as a vehicle to attract a replacement for CalPERS and to buy out CalPERS' interest in JEDI.

Originally, Andrew Fastow proposed that he be appointed to manage Chewco temporarily until an outside investor, or counterparty, could be found. According to the Powers Report, Enron lawyers advised against this since his senior officer status would have required proxy disclosure. Instead, Michael Kopper, who worked at Enron for Fastow, a

---

1. Chewco was named for "Chewbacca," the *Star Wars* character.

fact known only to Jeffrey K. Skilling on the board of directors,[2] was appointed.

Enron planned to guarantee loans for bridge financing to buy out CalPERS' interest in JEDI, which had been valued at $383 million. The intention was to replace the bridge financing with the investment of an outside investor, but none was found. Enron's financial year end passed on December 31, 1997; without an independent, controlling outside investor with at least 3 percent of the capital at risk, $11.5 million in this case (3 percent of $383 million), the activities of both JEDI and Chewco had to be consolidated into Enron's financial statements and on a retroactive basis. Whether through negligence or inability to find a proper counterparty, the accounts of Enron had to be restated to include the dealings of JEDI.

"In November and December of 1997, Enron and Kopper created a new capital structure for Chewco, which had three elements:

| $240 million unsecured subordinated loan to Chewco from Barclays Bank PLC, which Enron would guarantee;

| $132 million advance from JEDI to Chewco under a revolving credit agreement; and

| $11.5 million in equity (representing approximately 3% of total capital) from Chewco's general and limited partners.[3]

These financing arrangements are diagrammed in Figure 1.

Essentially, Enron—as majority owner—put no cash into the SPE. A bank provided virtually all of the cash, and in reality the so-called 3 percent independent, controlling investor had very little invested—not even close to the required 3 percent threshold. Nonetheless, Chewco was considered to qualify for treatment as an arm's-length entity for accounting purposes by Enron and its auditors, Arthur Andersen. Enron's board, and presumably Arthur Andersen, was kept in the dark.

Kopper invested approximately $115,000 in Chewco's general partner and approximately $10,000 in its limited partner before transferring his limited partnership interest to William Dodson [Kopper's domestic partner]."[4] The rest of the $11.5 million—$11.4, to be exact—was loaned by Barclays Bank to

FIGURE 1

Chewco Financing, in Millions

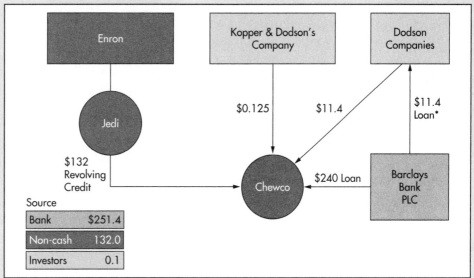

Source	
Bank	$251.4
Non-cash	132.0
Investors	0.1

---

2. Powers Report, 41.
3. Powers Report, 49.
4. Powers Report, 49.

Kopper/Dodson, although the original wording was unusual in that it implied that the monies were for "certificates" that would generate a "yield."[5]

Ultimately, Kopper and Dodson created a series of limited partnerships (LLPs) and limited companies (LLCs) through which to operate their interests, but Kopper was *de facto* the managing general partner of Chewco. This meant there was no outside investor with 3 percent of equity at risk. Moreover, Barclays asked that $6.6 million be reserved against the $11.4, and the $6.6 million was pledged/deposited with them, so that the resulting net of $4.8 million did not satisfy the 3 percent rule for nonconsolidation. According to the Powers Report, the existence of the $6.6 million reserve was well known at Enron.[6] However, in Congressional Committee testimony, the CEO of Arthur Andersen stated that they had reviewed and approved the financial arrangement as qualifying under the 3 percent rule, and received $80,000 for this advice.[7] The $6.6 million reserve was created as part of a transfer of $16.6 million from JEDI through Chewco to two of the limited partnerships controlled by Kopper and Dodson, namely Big River Funding LLC and Little River Funding LLC.

The entire complicated structure created for the Chewco financing transaction can be viewed on page 51 of the Powers Report.

The Powers Report goes on to detail several subsequent transactions that took place before Enron unraveled in late 2001 that appear not to have been in the best interests of Enron, including:

▌ Management and other fees paid through to Kopper amounted to $2 million for essentially little work, some of which was done by Fastow's wife; most of the rest of the work was on time that Kopper was being paid as an Enron employee.

▌ The fee for Enron guaranteeing the Barclays loan was under that called for by the market risk assumed.

When it was decided to liquidate JEDI, the buyout of Chewco's interest was valued at a premium of $1 million by Jeffrey McMahon (then senior vice president, finance and treasurer of Enron). He told Fastow, who undertook to negotiate with Kopper, and came back indicating that Skilling had approved a $10 million payment.[8] Fastow denied this to the Powers committee but declined to comment on a handwritten note from Kopper that confirmed Fastow's participation. Ultimately, a premium of $10.5 million was paid. This represented a return of 360 percent.

▌ Kopper demanded later and received $2.6 million in September 2001 as an indemnification against the tax consequences of the $10.5 million premium. Enron's in-house counsel had originally declined this request, but was overruled by Fastow, who told them that Skilling had approved.

▌ Upon closing the repurchase of JEDI, Chewco was not required to repay the $15 million it had loaned on an unsecured and nonrecourse basis to Kopper and Dodson for them to invest in Osprey trust certificates. Osprey was a limited partner in Whitewing Associates, another related company that will be discussed later.

▌ The Powers Report also noted that from December 1997, Enron began to incorrectly pre-book revenue for services not yet provided in regard to the Barclays guarantee fee and the JEDI management fee arrangement that Chewco assumed, in the amounts of $10 million and $25.7 million, respectively.

When Enron's affairs began to unravel in public, the board started an investigation that led to the bankruptcy filing on December 2, 2001. The Powers Report states:

In late October 2001, the Enron Board (responding to media reports) requested a briefing by Management on Chewco. Glisan [Ben F. Glisan, Jr., the Enron "transaction support" employee with principal responsibility

---

5. Ibid., 50.
6. Ibid., 52.
7. Ibid., 53.
8. Powers Report, 61.

for accounting matters in the Chewco transaction, signed many of the documents on Enron's behalf] was responsible for presenting the briefing at a Board meeting on short notice. Following the briefing, Enron accounting and legal personnel (as well as Vinson & Elkins) undertook to review documents relating to Chewco. This review identified the documents relating to the funding of the Big River and Little River reserve accounts in December 1997 through the $16.6 million distribution from JEDI.

Enron brought those documents to the attention of Andersen, and consulted with Andersen concerning the accounting implications of the funded reserve accounts. After being shown the documents by Enron and discussing the accounting issues with Enron personnel, Andersen provided the notice of "possible illegal acts" that Andersen's CEO highlighted in his Congressional testimony on December 12, 2001.

Enron's accounting personnel and Andersen both concluded that, in light of the funded reserve accounts, Chewco lacked sufficient outside equity at risk and should have been consolidated in November 1997. In addition, because JEDI's nonconsolidation depended on Chewco's status, Enron and Andersen concluded that JEDI also should have been consolidated in November 1997. In a Current Report on Form 8-K filed on November 8, 2001, Enron announced that it would restate its prior period financials to reflect the consolidation of those entities as of November 1997.[9]

LJM Partnerships and The Raptors: LJM1

On June 28, 1999, the Enron board approved Fastow's proposal that he invest $1 million and become the sole managing/general partner of LJM1 (LJM Cayman LP), which would raise funds from outside investors that could be used to hedge the possible loss of market value of Enron's investment in Rhythms NetConnections, Inc. (Rhythms for short). Fastow said that he would receive fees, that the Enron Code of Conduct would require special action (suspension of the code) by the chairman, and that his participation "would not adversely affect the interests of Enron."[10] The Powers Report continues: "LJM1 was formed in June 1999. Fastow became the sole and managing member of LJM Partners, LLC, which was the general partner of LJM Partners, L.P. This, in turn, was the general partner of LJM1. Fastow raised $15 million from two limited partners, ERNB Ltd. . . . and Campsie Ltd." A diagram of the financing of LJM1 can be found on page 70 of the Powers Report.

LJM1 ultimately "entered into three transactions with Enron: (1) the effort to hedge Enron's position in Rhythms NetConnections stock, (2) the purchase of a portion of Enron's interest in a Brazilian power project (Cuiaba), and (3) a purchase of certificates of an SPE called 'Osprey Trust.'"[11]

The Rhythms hedge transaction is significant because it introduces the basic form for future hedge transactions. Per the Powers Report on page 77:

> In March 1998, Enron invested $10 million in the stock of Rhythms NetConnections, Inc. ("Rhythms"), a privately-held internet service provider for businesses using digital subscriber line technology, by purchasing 5.4 million shares of stock at $1.85 per share. On April 7, 1999, Rhythms went public at $21 per share. By the close of the trading day, the stock price reached $69. By May 1999, Enron's investment in Rhythms was worth approximately $300 million, but Enron was prohibited (by a lock-up agreement) from selling its shares before the end of 1999. Because Enron accounted for the investment as part of its merchant portfolio, it marked the Rhythms position to market, meaning that increases and decreases in the value of Rhythms stock were reflected on Enron's income statement.

Skilling was concerned about mitigating the volatility caused by these mark-to-market

---

9. Powers Report, 66, 67.
10. Ibid., 69.
11. Ibid., 70.

increases and decreases, and Fastow and Glisan devised a hedging transaction to do so. The arrangement also resulted in Enron recognizing the appreciation in value of Enron's own stock—a recognition that GAAP does not normally permit except under strict conditions where cash is received for the stock confirming the market value. Their proposal was to capitalize an SPE with Enron stock, and have the SPE hedge the value of the Rhythms investment so that the SPE would pay Enron if the Rhythms investment decreased. This payment would be shown as revenue by Enron and offset the loss in the Rhythms investment on Enron's books.

Ultimately, $95 million in lost Rhythms' value was offset and Enron's income was higher as a result. In addition, Enron recorded profit on the Enron shares transferred. Unfortunately, LJM1 did not qualify as having 3 percent invested by an independent, controlling general partner (because Fastow was not independent), and the Enron stock was paid for by a promissory note, not cash. Moreover, it became clear that the creditworthiness of the SPE depended upon the Enron shares transferred, and since the value of Enron shares declined in 2000 and 2001, that creditworthiness was eroded below the level required to pay Enron its offsets. Enron, it became obvious, was attempting to hedge itself—largely a game of smoke and mirrors in the absence of outside investment to absorb the economic risk. In spite of these problems, Arthur Andersen and Enron's law firm, Vinson & Elkins, indicated that the hedge was reasonable, and that it could go ahead as Fastow and Glisan intended. Ultimately, however, on reexamination by Arthur Andersen, it was determined (in October 2001) that the financial statements for 1999–2001 had to be restated. In November, Enron announced that "it would restate prior period financial statements to reflect the consolidation retroactive to

1999, which would have the effect of decreasing Enron's net income by $95 million in 1999 and $8 million in 2000."[12]

The Powers Report describes the Rhythms transaction beginning on page 79, with a diagram on page 81 and a discussion of the hedge beginning on page 82. It is noted on page 83 that the equity of the SPE used for the transaction (Swap Sub, of which LJM1 owned part) was negative and thus the transaction could not have qualified for the 3 percent nonconsolidation rule. This sprung from the fact that: "At its formation on June 30, 1999, Swap Sub had negative equity because its liability (the Rhythms put, valued at $104 million) greatly exceeded its assets ($3.75 million in cash plus $80 million in restricted Enron stock).[13] This was what Arthur Andersen found upon reexamination in October 2001. Arthur Andersen's CEO said:

> In evaluating the 3 percent residual equity level required to qualify for non-consolidation, there were some complex issues concerning the valuation of various assets and liabilities. When we reviewed this transaction again in October 2001, we determined that our team's initial judgment that the 3 percent test was met was in error. We promptly told Enron to correct it.[14]

Within two weeks after the transaction closed on June 30, 1999, it was realized that the volatility of earnings had not improved to the degree desired,[15] and four more derivative actions were entered into to make the hedge act more like a swap. These did not cure the problem sufficiently, and due to the continuing concern for the erosion of creditworthiness, the decision was made to liquidate the hedge. In February or March 2000, Vince Kaminski estimated that there was a 68 percent probability that the structure would default, and he claims he relayed this to the accounting group.[16]

---

12. Powers Report, 84.
13. Powers Report, 83.
14. Ibid., 84.
15. Ibid., 85. See Footnote 30 of the Powers Report. Because the put provided one-sided protection, Enron was exposed to income statement volatility when Rhythms' price increased and subsequently decreased. In addition, Enron was subject to income statement volatility from the time value component of the put option.
16. Ibid., 87.

In early March 2000, negotiations to unwind Swap Sub were begun between Causey and Fastow with Fastow giving the impression that he had no personal interest in the outcome—which he was just negotiating for the limited partners of LJM1. On March 8, 2000, Enron gave Swap Sub a put on 3.1 million shares of Enron at $71.31 per share, which was $4.12 over the closing price, thus conveying approximately $12.8 million in value to Swap Sub. Perhaps this was by mistake. Subsequently, Fastow proposed that Swap Sub receive $30 million from Enron for the unwind, and this was agreed to. The unwind was completed per an agreement dated March 22, 2000, which was not subjected to an independent fairness examination, nor was the board advised, nor DASH sheets executed. Arthur Andersen reviewed the deal, but said nothing. Not until later was it realized that the value ascribed to the shares reacquired by Enron was as unrestricted shares, and no discounting was employed to reflect that they were restricted. *As a result, an estimated $70 million more than what was required was transferred to Swap Sub, and ultimately to Fastow and his associates.*[17] *In addition, LJM1 was allowed to retain 3.6 million post-split Enron shares related to the original transaction, which, on April 28, 2000, had an undiscounted value of $251 million at closing price.*[18]

Many of Enron's employees were involved in these transactions, but none were approved to benefit as required by the Enron Code of Conduct, and the board apparently did not know of their involvement. However, the employees benefited mightily, as is detailed later.

In May, as noted earlier, McMahon expressed his reservations about Enron accounting and deals to Fastow and was reassigned. Glisan became the new treasurer of Enron.

LJM Partnerships and The Raptors: LJM2

In October 1999, Fastow proposed a second LJM partnership, LJM2 Co-Investment LP (LJM2), where he would serve as a general

partner through intermediaries to encourage up to $200 million of outside investment that could be used to purchase assets that Enron wanted to syndicate. This, Fastow said, would provide Enron the funds needed to grow quickly and at less cost than by other means. This was not done blindly, as the following shows:

> The minutes and our interviews reflect that the Finance Committee discussed this proposal, including the conflict of interest presented by Fastow's dual roles as CFO of Enron and general partner of LJM2. Fastow proposed as a control that all transactions between Enron and LJM2 be subject to the approval of both Causey, Enron's Chief Accounting Officer, and Buy, Enron's Chief Risk Officer. In addition, the Audit and Compliance Committee would annually review all transactions completed in the prior year. Based on this discussion, the Committee voted to recommend to the Board that the Board find that Fastow's participation in LJM2 would not adversely affect the best interests of Enron.[19]

Later, the board reviewed the discussion, and gave their approval. LJM2 was formed in October 1999, and its general partner was LJM2 Capital Management, LP. Limited solicitation developed approximately fifty limited partners raising $394 million including the contributions of the general partner. Again, Fastow arranged a series of intermediaries as follows: "The general partner, LJM2 Capital Management, LP, itself had a general partner and two limited partners. The general partner was LJM2 Capital Management, LLC, of which Fastow was the managing member. The limited partners were Fastow and, at some point after the creation of LJM2, an entity named Big Doe LLC. Kopper was the managing member of Big Doe. (In July 2001, Kopper resigned from Enron and purchased Fastow's interest in LJM2.)"[20]

A diagram of this structure is on page 74 of the Powers Report. Subsequently, a management agreement was executed between Enron

---

17. Ibid., 91.
18. Ibid., 91.
19. Powers Report, 71.
20. Ibid., 73.

and LJM2 that specified which full-time Enron employees were to work on LJM2 matters.

Once again, the issue arises of whether LJM2 qualified for nonconsolidation. A series of transactions were entered into that created profit on Enron's earnings statement based upon the assumption that LJM2 was not to be consolidated under the 3 percent rule. Fastow was not a completely independent third party who possessed the risks and rewards of ownership. However, he could be removed by a 75 percent (and later 66 percent) vote of the limited partners. Were these restrictions enough? Initially Arthur Andersen and Enron's lawyers, Vinson & Elkins, thought so, but the Powers Committee was not so certain.[21]

LJM2 and The Raptors

In aggregate, the Raptors, which were Rhythms-like hedging arrangements for several of Enron's other merchant investments, had a huge impact on Enron's financial results. Unfortunately, three of the four were modeled after the ill-fated Rhythms, and they had the same shortcomings, so that their impact had to be reversed when their lack of creditworthiness was exposed. They acted as dampeners of the accounting volatility related to earnings, but they were not useful hedges of economic risk. The termination of the Raptor arrangements in the third quarter of 2001 was one of the mighty blows that undermined investor confidence in Enron.

The following table (Table 1) showing the impact of the Raptors appears on page 133 of the Powers Report. The Report also discloses that shareholders' equity was overstated by $1.2 billion due to improper accounting for Enron stock transferred as stock sold in the following excerpt:

The transactions between Enron and LJM2 that had the greatest impact on Enron's financial statements involved four SPEs known as the "Raptors." Expanding on the concepts underlying the Rhythms transaction (described earlier), Enron sought to use the "embedded" value of its own equity to counteract declines in the value of certain of its merchant investments. Enron used the extremely complex Raptor structured finance vehicles to avoid reflecting losses in the value of some merchant investments in its income statement. Enron did this by entering into derivative transactions with the Raptors that functioned as "accounting" hedges. If the value of the merchant investment declined, the value of the corresponding hedge would increase by an equal amount. Consequently, the decline—which was recorded each quarter on Enron's income statement—would be offset by an increase of income from the hedge.

As with the Rhythms hedge, these transactions were not true economic hedges. Had Enron hedged its merchant investments with a creditworthy, independent outside party, it may have been able successfully to transfer the economic risk of a decline in the investments. But it did not do this. Instead, Enron and LJM2 created counterparties for these accounting hedges—the Raptors—but Enron still bore virtually all of the economic risk. In effect, Enron was hedging risk with itself.

TABLE 1

Impact of the Raptors on Earnings, in Millions

QUARTER	REPORTED EARNINGS	EARNINGS WITHOUT RAPTORS	RAPTORS' CONTRIBUTION TO EARNINGS
3Q 2000	$364	$295	$69
4Q 2000	286	(176)	462
1Q 2001	536	281	255
2Q 2001	530	490	40
3Q 2001	(210)	(461)	251
TOTAL	$1506	$429	$1,077

*Third quarter 2001 figures exclude the $710 million pre-tax charge to earnings related to the termination of the Raptors.

---

21. Powers Report, 76.

TABLE 2

Enron's Raptors—Selected Details

NAME	APPROVED IN 2001	DIAGRAM ON	CAPITAL (MIL) FROM LJM2	REQUIRED (MIL) LJM2 RETURN	EXPECTED (MIL) HEDGE CAP. USED
Raptor I Talon	May	101	$30	$41	$500
Raptor II Timberwolf	June 2		$30	$41	$513
Raptor III Porcupine	Not	116	$30	$39.5	Only TNPC
Raptor IV Bobcat	Aug. 7		$30	$41	Nil

In three of the four Raptors, the vehicle's financial ability to hedge was created by Enron's transferring its own stock (or contracts to receive Enron stock) to the entity, at a discount to the market price. This "accounting" hedge would work, and the Raptors would be able to "pay" Enron on the hedge, as long as Enron's stock price remained strong and especially if it increased.... When the value of many of Enron's merchant investments fell in late 2000 and early 2001, the Raptors' hedging obligations to Enron grew. At the same time, however, the value of Enron's stock declined, decreasing the ability of the Raptors to meet those obligations. These two factors combined to create the very real possibility that Enron would have to record at the end of first quarter 2001 a $500 million impairment of the Raptors' obligations to it. Without bringing this issue to the attention of the Board, and with the design and effect of avoiding a massive credit reserve, Enron Management restructured the vehicles in the first quarter of 2001. In the third quarter of 2001, however, as the merchant investments and Enron's stock price continued to decline, Enron finally terminated the vehicles. In doing so, it incurred the after-tax charge of $544 million ($710 million pre-tax) that Enron disclosed on October 16, 2001 in its initial third quarter earnings release.

Enron also reported that same day that it would reduce shareholder equity by $1.2 billion. One billion of that $1.2 billion involved the correction of accounting errors relating to Enron's prior issuance of Enron common stock (and stock contracts) to the Raptors in the second quarter of 2000 and the first quarter of 2001; the other $200 million related to termination of the Raptors.[22]

Details of these activities are available in the Powers Report on pages 98–133. The following table is provided for reference purposes.

Raptors I and II were capitalized in almost identical manners. For Raptor I (Talon), in April 2000, LJM2 contributed $30 million cash. Enron contributed (through a wholly owned subsidiary) $1,000 cash, a $50 million promissory note, and Enron shares, or rights to shares, worth $537 million, which could not be sold, pledged, or hedged for three years. The value of the shares was therefore discounted by 35 percent, which agreed with a fairness evaluation by PricewaterhouseCoopers (PwC). Enron received a promissory note from Talon in the amount of $400 million.

An interesting arrangement apparently was not reflected in the setup documents seen by the board, but was understood by those working on the deal, namely that Talon could not write any derivatives until LJM2 received at least its capital back plus $11 million ($41 million) or 11 percent annualized return. If this return was not received in six months, Enron could be forced to buy back its shares at their unrestricted value. Enron was to get any return after the $41 million was paid.

These arrangements were very generous to LJM2. In addition, however, $41 million in profit was created for Talon by Enron purchasing from Talon a put option that would require Talon to purchase Enron shares in six months at a $41 million premium. This was

---

22. Powers Report, 97, 98.

strange and generous because Enron was betting its own stock would go down, and the terms of the put did not reflect the lack of creditworthiness of Talon.[23]

The option was settled early, on August 3, 2000, by Causey on behalf of Enron and Fastow, and since Enron stock had gone up, only $4 million of the $41 million was returned to Enron. Talon paid $41 million to LJM2, which earned 193 percent, plus Enron paid its accounting fees and a management fee of $250,000 per year. Talon was free to start hedging, which it did.

Unfortunately, the capacity of Talon to hedge Enron's merchant investments was limited by Talon's ability to pay Enron in the value of the merchant investment(s) declined. This ability, or creditworthiness, depended in turn upon Talon's assets, which included some cash but mostly shares of Enron. As the market price of those Enron shares declined in the fall of 2000, the possibility that Talon could not pay—thus forcing Enron to record losses— grew so large that Enron sought to shore up Talon's creditworthiness by using a "costless collar" arrangement. The Powers Report describes the arrangement as follows:

> To protect Talon against a possible decline in Enron stock price—which would decrease the value of Talon's principal asset, and thereby decrease its credit capacity on October 30, 2000, Enron entered into a "costless collar" on the approximately 7.6 million Enron shares and stock contracts in Talon. The "collar" provided that, if Enron stock fell below $81, Enron would pay Talon the amount of any loss. If Enron stock increased above $116 per share, Talon would pay Enron the amount of any gain. If the stock price was between the floor and ceiling, neither party was obligated to the other. This protected Talon's credit capacity against possible future declines in Enron stock.[24]

Unfortunately, the protection was only designed to protect within a narrow range, and

Enron's stock was destined to fall below the $81 level. Based on Talon's revised contract, its creditworthiness would only protect Enron for about another $10 per share fall below the $81 level. If Enron's share price was to fall below $71, Talon could not pay off and Enron would have to record net losses on its merchant investments.

In addition, the "costless collar" dealt with Talon's Enron shares as if they were not restricted, thus not honoring the 35 percent discount for the three-year restriction period that underlay the original fairness valuation and setup calculations. To make the "costless collar" arrangements legal, Causey signed a waiver of the three-year restrictions (worth $187 million), thus conveying even more value to Talon than was originally expected.[25]

Before there were any hedge transactions between Talon (Raptor I) and Enron, Fastow told Enron's Executive Committee that "there had been tremendous utilization by the business units of Raptor I,"[26] and asked for the establishment of Raptor II on June 22, 2000. The presentation requesting the establishment of Raptor IV was made on August 7, 2000, by Ben Glisan, who "noted that Raptor I was almost completely utilized and that Raptor II would not be available for utilization until later in the year."[27] This deferred availability of Raptor II reflects the need to repay LJM2 its $41 million similar to the Raptor I arrangements before hedging could start.

The arrangements to capitalize Raptors II and IV were indeed similar to that used for Raptor I, as the Powers Report states:

> Just as it had done with Talon in Raptor I, Enron paid Raptor II's SPE, "Timberwolf," and Raptor IV's SPE, "Bobcat," $41 million each for share-settled put options. As in Raptor I, the put options were settled early, and each of the entities then distributed approximately $41 million to LJM2. Although these distributions meant that both Timberwolf and Bobcat were available

---

23. Powers Report, 103, 104.
24. Ibid., 110.
25. Powers Report, 111.
26. Ibid., 112.
27. Ibid., 112.

to engage in derivative transactions with Enron, Enron engaged in derivative transactions only with Timberwolf. These transactions, entered into as of September 22, 2000 and December 28, 2000, had a total notional value of $513 million.[28]

Raptor II did enter into merchant investment hedge transactions with Enron. Raptor IV never did because, due to the continued erosion of both merchant investment values and Enron share prices, on March 26, 2001, Raptor IV's creditworthiness had to be combined with that of the other Raptors to shore up the entire Raptor program. However, prior to the creation of a combined Raptor credit pool, for the same reasons as noted for Raptor I, Enron arranged "costless collars" for Raptors II and IV on November 27, 2000, and January 24, 2001, respectively. Again, the impact of the collars was limited, and the restricted share shares values factored into the setup transfer valuations was waived.

Raptor III was different from the other Raptors because it was intended to hedge only the merchant investment in The New Power Company (TNCP), and it did not hold Enron shares or rights to Enron shares as assets. Instead, Enron provided it warrants or rights to purchase TNCP shares at a very low value, which essentially amounted to the same thing as holding shares. This avoided seeking board approval to use Enron shares, and avoided the dilutive effect on Enron's EPS (earnings per share) that using such shares would have produced.

On September 27, 2000, Enron (through a subsidiary named "Pronghorn") and LJM2 created the Raptor III SPE "Porcupine" as shown in the diagram on page 116 of the Powers Report. Once again, Enron's contribution followed the earlier Raptor framework except for the substitution of TNCP shares/ rights, and LJM2 contributed $30 million. This left the Raptor III hedge in the position of having to pay Enron for declines in the value of TNCP from assets largely consisting of TNCP shares or rights. If the shares of TNCP declined, the need to pay would rise and the means to pay decreased. This "doubling" of

the importance of TNCP meant that the risk of default was higher than for other Raptors, and certainly more sensitive to declines in the share values of Enron's TNCP merchant investment. Arthur Andersen and Enron's lawyers Vinson & Elkins both received fees for pre-clearing the Raptor III arrangements. Enron's board did not appear to have approved the creation of Raptor III, and no DASH sheets were prepared. LJM2's return was set at the $39.5 million or 30 percent per year, and LJM2 received the $39.5 million in one week—yielding a return of 2,500 percent.

By mid-December 2000, the assets of Raptors I and III had declined, and their liabilities increased so much that both had negative equity and therefore did not have the ability to pay off Enron in regard to the hedges undertaken. Unless something was done quickly, Enron would have had to reflect significant losses on the year-end statement for 2000 due to this lack of creditworthiness. Therefore, according to the Powers Report,

> ... Enron's accountants, working with Andersen, decided to use the "excess" credit capacity in Raptors II and IV to shore up the credit capacity in Raptors I and III. A 45-day cross-guarantee agreement, dated December 22, 2000, essentially merged the credit capacity of all four Raptors. The effect was that Enron would not, for year end, record a credit reserve loss unless there was negative credit capacity on a combined basis. Enron paid LJM2 $50,000 to enter into this agreement, even though the cross-guarantee had no effect on LJM2's economic interests. We have seen no evidence that Enron's Board was informed of either the credit capacity problem or the solution selected to resolve that problem. Enron did not record a reserve for the year ending December 31, 2000.[29]

It is noteworthy that the Powers Report goes on to say in a footnote that:

> At the time, Andersen agreed with Enron's view that the 45-day cross-guarantee among

---

28. Ibid., 113, 114.
29. Powers Report, 120.

the Raptors to avoid a credit reserve loss was permissible from an accounting perspective. The workpapers that Andersen made available included a memorandum dated December 28, 2000, by Andersen's local audit team, which states that it consulted two partners in Andersen's Chicago office on the 45-day cross-guarantee. The workpapers also include an amended version of the December 28, 2000 memorandum, dated October 12, 2001, stating that the partners in the Chicago office advised that the 45-day cross-guarantee was not a permissible means to avoid a credit reserve loss.[30]

In early 2001, Enron's stock price continued to decline as did its merchant investments. As a result the cross-guarantee proved to be insufficient and a more permanent solution was sought. On March 26, 2001, the Raptor arrangements were restructured by a cross-collateralization of the Raptors, and by the infusion of more Enron shares. Essentially, Enron assigned its interest in hedge payments from any Raptor to any other Raptor that could not pay for its hedge commitments. Consequently, Enron was protected by the creditworthiness of all the Raptors taken together. However, the credit problems of Raptors I and III were too great for Raptors II and IV to carry, and (1) in return for notes receivable totaling $260 million, Enron had to agree to advance Raptors II and IV up to 18 million Enron shares that could not be sold, pledged or hedged for four years (necessitating a 23 percent discount); (2) to increase credit capacity, Enron sold 12 million shares of Enron's stock to Raptors II and IV in exchange for notes receivable totaling $568 million; and (3) Enron hedged any restricted shares held by the Raptors. This last hedging, however, overtook the 23 percent discount calculations for the notes receivable, a fact that was brought forward to the auditors and Enron's accountants by Kaminski. "Restructuring the Raptors allowed Enron to avoid reflecting the $504 million credit reserve loss in its first quarter

financial statements. Instead, it recorded only a $36.6 million credit reserve loss."[31]

Ultimately, in the late summer of 2001, the continuing decline of Enron and TNCP share values caused a further large deficiency of Raptor creditworthiness. In addition:

> The collaring arrangements Enron had with the Raptors aggravated the situation, because Enron now faced the prospect of having to deliver so many shares of its stock to the Raptors that its reported earnings per share would be diluted significantly.

> At the same time, an unrelated, but extraordinarily serious, Raptor accounting problem emerged. In August 2001, Andersen and Enron accountants realized that the accounting treatment for the Enron stock and stock contracts contributed to Raptors I, II and IV was wrong. Enron had accounted for the Enron shares sold in April 2000 to Talon (Raptor I), in exchange for a $172 million promissory note, as an increase to "notes receivable" and to "shareholders' equity." This increased shareholders' equity by $172 million in Enron's second, third and fourth quarter 2000 financial reports. Enron made similar entries when it sold Enron stock contracts in March 2001 to Timberwolf and Bobcat (Raptors II and IV) for notes totaling $828 million. This accounting treatment increased shareholders' equity by a total of $1 billion in Enron's first and second quarter 2001 financial reports. Enron accountants told us that Andersen was aware of, and approved, the accounting treatment for the Enron stock contracts sold to the Raptors in the first quarter of 2001. Andersen did not permit us to interview any of the Andersen personnel involved.

> In September 2001, Andersen and Enron concluded that the prior accounting entries were wrong, and the proper accounting for these transactions would have been to show the notes receivable as a reduction to shareholders' equity. This would have had no net effect on Enron's equity balance.

---

30. Ibid., 120.
31. Powers Report, 125.

Enron decided to correct these mistaken entries in its third quarter 2001 financial statements. At the time, Enron accounting personnel and Andersen concluded (using a qualitative analysis) that the error was not material and a restatement was not necessary. But when Enron announced on November 8, 2001 that it would restate its prior financials (for other reasons), it included the reduction of shareholders' equity. The correction of the error in Enron's third quarter financial statements resulted in a reduction of $1 billion ($172 million plus $828 million) to its previously overstated equity balance.

In mid-September, with the quarter-end approaching, Causey met with Lay (who had just recently reassumed the position of CEO because of Skilling's resignation) and Greg Whalley (Enron's COO) to discuss problems with the Raptors. Causey presented a series of options, including leaving the vehicles in place as they were, transactions to ameliorate the situation, and terminating the Raptors. Lay and Whalley directed Causey to terminate the Raptors. Enron did so on September 28, 2001, paying LJM2 approximately $35 million. This purchase price apparently was the result of a private negotiation between Fastow (who had sold his interest in LJM2 to Kopper in July), on behalf of Enron, and Kopper, on behalf of LJM2. This apparently reflected a calculation that LJM2's residual interest in the Raptors was $61 million. Enron accounted for the buy-out of the Raptors under typical business combination accounting, in which the assets and liabilities of the acquired entity are recorded at their fair value, and any excess cost typically is recorded as goodwill.

However, Andersen told Enron to record the excess as a charge to income. As of September 28, 2001, Enron calculated that the Raptors' combined assets were approximately $2.5 billion, and their combined liabilities were approximately $3.2 billion. The difference between the Raptors' assets and liabilities, plus the $35 million payment to LJM2, resulted in a charge of approximately $710 million ($544 million after taxes) reflected in Enron's third quarter 2001 financial statements.

It is unclear whether the accounting treatment of the termination was correct. Enron's transactions with the Raptors had resulted in the recognition of earnings of $532 million during 2000, and $545 million during the first nine months of 2001, for a total of almost $1.1 billion. After taking the unwind charge of $710 million, Enron had still recognized pre-tax earnings from its transactions with the Raptors of $367 million. Thus, it may have been more appropriate for Enron to have reversed the full $1.1 billion of previously recorded pre-tax earnings when it bought back the Raptors.[32]

Unbelievably, Fastow reported to the LJM2 investors in October 2000 that the Raptors had brought returns of 193 percent, 278 percent, 2,500 percent, and 125 percent, which were far in excess of the 30 percent annualized returns described to the Finance Committee in May 2000. Moreover, since Enron retained the economic risks involved, these returns are evidently for something else. The Powers Report concludes by identifying seven accounting issues raised by the Raptors that are alleged to be questionable.[33]

Questions

Answers should be based on the case as presented, and relevant sections of Chapter 2.

1. Which segment of its operations got Enron into difficulties?

2. How were profits made in that segment of operations (i.e., what was the business model)?

3. Did Enron's directors understand how profits were being made in this segment? Why or why not?

4. Enron's directors realized that Enron's conflict of interests policy would be violated by Fastow's proposed SPE management and

32. Powers Report, 125–128.
33. Ibid., 129–132.

operating arrangements because they proposed alternative oversight measures. What was wrong with their alternatives?

5. Ken Lay was the chair of the board and the CEO for much of the time. How did this probably contribute to the lack of proper governance?

6. What aspects of the Enron governance system failed to work properly, and why?

7. Why didn't more whistle-blowers come forward, and why didn't some make a significant difference? How could whistle-blowers have been encouraged?

8. What should the internal auditors have done that might have assisted the directors?

9. Identify conflicts of interests in:

   • SPE activities

   • Arthur Andersen's activities

   • Executive activities

10. How much time should a director of Enron have been spending on Enron matters each month? How many large company boards should a director serve on?

11. How would you characterize Enron's corporate culture? How did it contribute to the disaster?

Ethics Case

Arthur Andersen's Troubles

Once the largest professional services firm in the world, and arguably the most respected, Arthur Andersen LLP (AA) has disappeared. The Big 5 accounting firms are now the Big 4. Why did this happen? How did it happen? What are the lessons to be learned?

Arthur Andersen, a twenty-eight-year-old Northwestern University accounting professor, co-founded the firm in 1913. Tales of his integrity are legendary, and the culture of the firm was very much in his image. For example, "Just months after [Andersen] set up shop in Chicago, the president of a local railroad insisted that he approve a transaction that would have inflated earnings. Andersen told the executive there was "not enough money in the City of Chicago" to make him do it."[1] In 1954, consulting services began with the installation of the first mainframe computer at General Electric to automate its payroll systems. By 1978, AA became the largest professional services firm in the world with revenues of $546 million, and by 1984 consulting brought in more profit than auditing. In 1989, the consulting operation, wanting more control and a larger share of profit, became a separate part of a Swiss partnership from the audit operation. In 2000, following an arbitrator's ruling that a break fee of $1 billion be paid, Andersen Consulting split completely and changed its name to

Accenture. AA, the audit practice, continued to offer a limited set of related services, such as tax advice.[2]

Changing Personalities and Culture

Throughout most of its history, AA stood for integrity and technical competence. The firm invested heavily in training programs and a training facility in St. Charles, a small town south of Chicago, and developed it until it had over 3,000 residence beds and outstanding computer and classroom facilities. AA personnel from all over the world were brought to St. Charles for training sessions on an ongoing basis. Even after the consulting and audit operations split, both continued to use the facility.

Ironically, AA was the first firm to recognize the need for professional accountants to study business and professional accounting formally. In the late 1980s, AA undertook a number of programs to stimulate that formal education, including the development of ethics cases, the creation of an approach to the resolution of professional ethical problems, and the hosting of groups of 100 accounting academics to get them started in the area. Most had no formal ethics training and were uncertain how to begin ethics teaching, or even if they should. It is likely that AA's farsighted policies are responsible for the genesis of much of the professional ethics education and research in accounting that is going on today.

---

1. "Fall from Grace," *Business Week*, August 12, 2002, 54.
2. Ibid., see table on page 53.

TABLE

TABLE 1

Arthur Andersen's Problem Audits

CLIENT	PROBLEM MISSED, DATE	LOSSES TO SHAREHOLDERS	JOB LOSSES	AA FINE
WorldCom	$4.3 billion overstatement of earnings announced on June 25, 2002	$179.3 billion	17,000	N.A.
Enron	Inflation of income, assets, etc., bankrupt Dec. 2, 2001	$66.4 billion	6,100	$.5 million (for shredding)
Global Crossing	Candidate for bankruptcy	$26.6 billion	8,700	
Waste Management*	Overstatement of income by $1.1 billion, 1992–1996	$20.5 billion	11,000	$7 million
Sunbeam*	Overstatement of 1997 income by $71.1 million, then bankruptcy	$4.4 billion	1,700	
Baptist Foundation of Arizona	Books cooked, largest nonprofit bankruptcy ever	$570 million	165	

*Cases are at the end of the chapter
Source: "Fall from Grace," *Business Week*, August 12, 2002, 54.

What happened to the AA culture that focused on integrity and technical competence? What changed that would account for AA's involvement in the following major financial scandals as the audit firm that failed to discover the underlying problems?

Some observers have argued that a change in AA's culture was responsible. Over the period when the consulting practice was surpassing the audit practice as the most profitable aspect of the firm, a natural competitiveness grew up between the two rivals. The generation of revenue became more and more desirable, and the key to merit and promotion decisions. The retention of audit clients took on an increasingly greater significance as part of this program, and since clients were so large, auditors tended to become identified with them. Many audit personnel even looked forward to joining their clients. In any event, the loss of a major client would sideline the career of the auditors involved at least temporarily, if not permanently. For many reasons, taking a stand against the management of a major client required a keen understanding of the auditor's role, the backing of senior partners in your firm, and courage.

The pressure for profit was felt throughout the rest of the audit profession, not just at Arthur Andersen. Audit techniques were modified to require higher levels of analysis, and lower investment of time. Judgment sampling gave way to statistical sampling, and then to strategic risk auditing. While each was considered better than its predecessor, the trend was toward tighter time budgets, and the focus of the audit broadened to include to development of value-added nonaudit outcomes, suggestions, or services for clients. Such nonaudit services could include advice on the structuring of transactions for desired disclosure outcomes and other work on which the auditor would later have to give an audit opinion.

According to discussions in the business and professional press, many audit professionals did not see the conflicts of interest involved as a problem. The conflict between maximizing audit profit for the firm and providing adequate audit quality so that the investing public would be protected was considered to be manageable so that no one would be harmed. The conflict between auditing in the public interest with integrity and objectivity that could lead to the need to roundly criticize mistakes that your firm or you had made in earlier advice was considered not to present a worry. In addition, the conflict between the growing complexity of transactions, particularly those involving derivative financial instruments, hedges, swaps, and so on, and the desire to restrain audit time in the interest of profit was thought to be within the capacity of auditors and firms to resolve. The growing conflict for auditors between serving the interests of the management team that was often instrumental in making the appointment of auditors, and the interests of shareholders was recognized but did not draw reinforcing statements from firms or professional accounting bodies. Some professional accountants did not understand whether they should be serving the interests of current shareholders or future shareholders, or what serving the public interest had to do with serving their client. They did not understand the difference between a profession and a business.

Ethical behavior in an organization is guided by the ethical culture of that organization, by any relevant professional norms and codes, and particularly by the "tone at the top"[3] and the example set by the top executives. Also, presumably the selection of the CEO is based partly on the choice of the values that an organization should be led toward. Joe Berardino was elected AA's CEO on January 10, 2001, but he had been partner-in-charge of the AA's U.S. audit practice for almost three years before. He was the leader whose values drove the firm from 1998 onward, and probably continued those of his predecessor. What were his values? Barbara Ley Toffler, a former Andersen partner during this period and before, has provided the following insight:

> When Berardino would get up at a partners meeting, all that was ever reported in terms of success was dollars. Quality wasn't discussed. Content wasn't discussed. Everything was measured in terms of the buck.... Joe was blind to the conflict. He was the most aggressive pursuer of revenue that I ever met.[4]

Arthur Andersen's Internal Control Flaw

Given this "tone at the top," it is reasonable to assume that AA partners were going to be motivated by revenue generation. But if too many risks are taken in the pursuit of revenue, the probability of a series of audit problems leading to increasingly unfavorable consequences becomes greater. That is exactly what happened. Unfortunately, the leaders of AA failed to recognize the cumulative degree to which the public, the politicians, and the SEC were angered by the progression of AA audit failures.

If they had recognized the precarious position they were in, the AA leadership might have corrected the flaw in the AA internal control that allowed the Enron audit failures to happen. *AA was the only one of the Big 5 to allow the partner in charge of the audit to override a ruling of the quality control partner.* This meant that at AA, the most sensitive decisions were taken by the person who was most concerned with the potential loss of revenue from the client in question, and who was most likely to be subject to the influence of the client. In all of the other Big 5 firms, the most sensitive decisions are taken by the person whose primary interest is the compliance with GAAP, the protection of the public interest, and the reputation of the firm.

On April 2, 2002, the U.S. House Energy and Commerce Committee[5] released a memo dated December 18, 1999, from Carl Bass, a partner in AA's Professional Services Group in Chicago, to David Duncan, the AA partner in charge of the Enron account. That memo asked for an accounting change (believed to be in regard to SPE transactions) that would have resulted in a $30–$50 million charge to Enron's earnings. In February 2000, Bass emailed Duncan to object to the setting up of an LJM partnership because he indicated that "this whole deal looks like there is no substance."[6] On March 4, 2001, Bass wrote that "then-chief financial officer Andrew Fastow's role as manager of special partnerships compromised deals Enron made with the entities."[7] Duncan overruled Bass on the first issue, and Bass was removed from Enron audit oversight on March 17, 2001, less than two weeks after he questioned Fastow's role in Enron's SPEs. In any other Big 5 firm, Duncan would not have been able to overrule a quality control partner on his own. History might

---

3. "This is a concept emerging in new governance standards that boards of directors are to monitor.
4. "Fall from Grace," 55, 56.
5. "Andersen under fire over memos: Carl Bass Documents," *Financial Post,* April 4, 2002, FP1, FP10.
6. "Andersen partner warned on Enron in '99: Questioned Partnerships," *Financial Post,* April 3, 2002, FP9.
7. "Andersen under fire," FP1.

have been different if a quality-focused internal control procedure had been in place at AA, rather than one that was revenue focused.

Arthur Andersen's Apparent Enron Mistakes

The previously presented "Enron Debacle" discussion covers in detail many of the questionable accounting transactions, legal structures, and related disclosures that AA reviewed as auditors of and consultants to Enron. Without repeating these in detail, it is possible to provide the following summary of significant issues that AA could be questioned about in court proceedings:

| AA apparently approved as auditors and consultants (and collected fees for the consulting advice) the structure of many Special Purpose Entities (SPE) that were used to generate false profits, hide losses, keep financing off Enron's consolidated financial statements, and failed to meet the required outsider 3 percent equity-at-risk, and decision control criteria for nonconsolidation.

| AA failed to recognize the Generally Accepted Accounting Principle (GAAP) that prohibits the recording of shares issued as an increase in shareholders equity unless they are issued for cash (not for notes receivable).

| AA did not advise Enron's audit committee that Andrew Fastow, Enron's CFO, and his helpers were involved in significant conflict of interest situations without adequate alternative means of managing these conflicts.

| AA did not advise the Enron Audit Committee that Enron's policies and internal control were not adequate to protect the shareholders interests even though AA had assumed Enron's internal audit function.

| Many transactions between Enron and the SPEs were not in the interest of Enron shareholders since:

- Enron profits and cash flow were manipulated and grossly inflated, misleading investors and falsely boosting management bonus arrangements.

- Extraordinarily overgenerous deals, fees, and liquidation arrangements were made by Fastow, or under his influence, with SPEs owned by Fastow, his family, and Kopper, who was also an employee of Enron.

| AA apparently did not adequately consider the advice of its quality control partner, Carl Bass.

| AA apparently did not find significant audit evidence, or did not act upon evidence found, related to the:

- Erroneous valuation of shares or share rights transferred to SPEs.

- Side deals between Enron and banks removing the banks' risk from transactions such as the:
  - Chewco SPE Rhythms hedge.
  - Numerous prepay deals for energy futures even though AA made a presentation to Enron on the GAAP and AA requirements that precluded such arrangements.[8]

Why Did Arthur Andersen Make These Apparent Mistakes?

The term "apparent" is used because AA's side of the story has not been heard. The so-called mistakes may have logical, reasonable explanations, and may be supportable by other accounting and auditing experts. That stated, these apparent mistakes may have been made for several reasons, including:

| Incompetence, as displayed and admitted in the Rhythms case

| Judgment errors as to the significance of each of the audit findings, or of the aggregate impact in any fiscal year

| Lack of information caused by Enron staff not providing critical information, or failure on the part of AA personnel to ferret it out

| Time pressures related to revenue generation and budget pressures that prevented adequate audit work and the full consideration of complex SPE and prepay financial arrangements

---

8. Testimony of Robert Roach to the Senate Permanent Subcommittee on Investigations, July 23, 2002, Appendix A, A-6.

▌ A desire not to confront Enron management or advise the Enron board in order not to upset management, and particularly Fastow, Skilling, and Lay

▌ A failure of AA's internal policies whereby the concerns of a quality control or practice standards partner can and was overruled by the audit partner in charge of the Enron account. AA was the only one of the Big 5 accounting firms to have this flaw, and it left the entire firm vulnerable to the decision of the person with the most to lose by saying no to a client

▌ A misunderstanding of the fiduciary role required by auditors

Because AA has now disintegrated, it is unlikely that the cause of specific audit deficiencies will ever be known. However, it is reasonable to assume that all of the causes listed played some part in the apparent mistakes that were made.

A review of additional cases of failure where Arthur Andersen was the auditor, such as the Waste Management and Sunbeam failures that appear at the end of the chapter, reveal that AA's behavior was strikingly similar to that in the Enron debacle. In each case, AA appears to have been so interested in revenue generation that they were willing not to take a hard line with their clients. AA personnel apparently believed that there was no serious risk of default and that, over time, accounting problems could be worked out. At the very least, AA's risk-assessment process was seriously flawed. Also, when AA's client had a combined chairman of the board and CEO who intimidated or was willingly helped by his CFO, neither additional professional accountants working for the corporations nor other nonaccounting personnel who knew of the accounting manipulations raised their concerns sufficiently with AA or the Audit Committee of their board of directors to stimulate corrective action. This lack of courage and understanding of the need and means to stimulate action left AA, the board, and the public vulnerable.

Shredding Enron Audit Documents: Obstruction of Justice

The final disintegration of AA was not caused directly by the Enron audit deficiencies, but by a related decision to shred Enron audit documents, and the conviction on the charge of obstruction of justice that resulted. This charge, filed on March 7, 2002, raised the prospect that if AA were convicted, the Securities and Exchange Commission (SEC) would withdraw AA's certification to audit SEC registrant companies.[9] That would preclude those large public companies that needed to be registered with the SEC to have their shares traded on U.S. stock exchanges (the NYSE and NASDAQ) or raise significant amounts of capital in the United States.

Since these clients represented the bulk of AA's U.S. and foreign accounting practices, if convicted AA would be effectively reduced to insignificance unless a waiver could be arranged from the SEC. The SEC, however, was very angry about the Enron audit deficiencies, particularly in view of the earlier similar cases involving the AA audits of Waste Management and Sunbeam. In regard to the Waste Management debacle, "The commission argued that not only did Andersen knowingly and recklessly issue materially false and misleading statements, it failed to enforce its own guidelines to bring the company in line with minimally accepted accounting standards."[10] As a condition of the $7 million fine paid in June 2001 settling AA's Waste Management audit deficiencies, AA had agreed to rectify its audit inadequacies, and the SEC believed that AA had not honored this undertaking. Consequently, since AA's behavior in the Enron debacle was so similar, the SEC provided only a temporary and conditional waiver,[11] pending the outcome of the trial.

The conviction was announced on Saturday, June 15, 2002, but many large clients had already transferred their work to other large audit firms. Some boards of directors and CEOs thought that AA's reputation was so damaged by

---

9. AA could also face probation for up to five years and a $500,000 fine as well as fines for up to twice any gains or damages the court determines were caused by the firm's action.
10. "'Back time' may catch Andersen," *Toronto Star,* March 21, 2002, D11.
11. "SEC Announces Actions for Issuers in Light of Indictment of Arthur Andersen LLP," SEC Release 2002-37.

the Enron fiasco that they no longer wanted to be associated with AA, or that such an association might weaken their company's ability to attract financing at the lowest rates. The outrage of the public was so intense that other boards could not face the lack of credibility that continuing with AA would have produced with their shareholders. Still other boards realized that if AA were convicted, there would be a stampede to other firms, and their company might not be able to make a smooth transition to another SEC-certified audit firm if they waited to switch. By the time the conviction was announced, only a small percentage of AA's largest clients remained. Even though AA's chances of acquittal upon appeal were considered by some observers to be good, AA was a shell of its former self and was essentially finished as a firm in the United States, and ultimately around the world.

The chain of events that led to the shredding of some of AA's Enron audit documents begins before Enron decided to announce a $618 million restatement of earnings and a $1.2 billion reduction of equity on October 16, 2001. An SEC investigation was launched into Enron's accounting on October 17, and AA was advised on October 19. However, AA had advised Enron that such an announcement was necessary to correct its accounting for SPEs and, on October 9 as the eight-page indictment states, "retained an experienced New York law firm to handle further Enron-related litigation."[12] Eleven days later, the subject of shredding was discussed as part of an emergency conference call to AA partners, and shredding began three days after that.[13]

Shredding was undertaken in AA's Houston office, as well as in London, Chicago and Portland. "... according to the U.S. government, ... the destruction was 'wholesale', with workers putting in overtime in order to get the

job done." "Tonnes of paper relating to the Enron audit were promptly shredded as part of the orchestrated document destruction. The shredder at the Andersen office at the Enron building was used virtually constantly and to handle the overload, dozens of large trunks filled with Enron documents were sent to Andersen's Houston office to be shredded."[14]

At the trial, AA argued differently. AA's lawyer attempted to clarify the purpose of Chicago-based AA lawyer Nancy Temple's email of October 10 to Michael Odom of AA's Houston office. In that email she wrote that "it might be useful to consider reminding the (Enron audit) team that it would be helpful to make sure that we have complied with the policy[15] which calls for destruction of extraneous and redundant material."[16] This lack of relevance, of course, was difficult to prove after the documents in question had been destroyed. Essentially, AA contended that "the order to follow the document retention policy was an innocent effort to organize papers, e-mails and computer files and eliminate extraneous material."[17]

David Duncan, however, testified against AA. He had been fired from AA (where he had been the partner in charge of the Enron audit) on January 15, one day after he met with the U.S. Justice Department. He said: "I obstructed justice ... I instructed people on the (Enron audit) team to follow the document retention policy, which I knew would result in the destruction of documents."[18]

The jury deliberated for many days, emerged, and was sent back for additional deliberations. Ultimately, AA was declared guilty. Although AA planned to appeal, it agreed to cease all audits of public companies by the end of August. Ironically, AA's conviction turned upon the jury's view that the shredding was part of a broad conspiracy, and that rested on testimony that was re-read to the

12. *Grand Jury Indictment on the Charge of Obstruction of Justice, United States of America against Arthur Andersen, LLP,* filed in the United Sates District Court Southern District of Texas on March 7, 2002, 5.

13. Op. cit., "Back time" D11.

14. Ibid., D11.

15. "Auditor evidence attacked," *Toronto Star,* May 22, 2002, E12.

16. Ibid., E12.

17. Ibid., E12.

18. "Andersen partner admits wrongdoing," *Toronto Star,* May 14, 2002, D3.

jury, indicating that an AA memo (or memos) was altered. The acts of shredding alone were not enough for conviction. The jury was reported as concluding that:

> Duncan eventually pleaded guilty to one count of obstruction and testified on the government's behalf, but jurors said afterwards that they didn't believe his testimony. Instead, the jury agreed that Andersen in-house attorney Nancy Temple had acted corruptly in order to impede the SEC's pending investigation. Speaking to reporters, juror Jack Gallo said that one of Temple's memos was critical in helping the jury reach its verdict. The memo, from last October, was a response to an email from Duncan about Enron's third quarter earnings statement. Enron wanted to describe a massive earnings loss as "non-recurring," but Duncan advised Enron against using that phrase. Temple's memo advised Duncan to delete any language that might suggest that Andersen disagreed with Enron, and further advised Duncan to remove her own name from his correspondence, since she did not want to be called as a witness in any future litigation stemming from Enron's earnings announcements.[19]

On October 16, 2002, AA was fined the maximum of $500,000 and placed on five years' probation. AA appealed out of principle, even though only 1,000 employees remained. Interestingly, on May 31, 2005, the U.S. Supreme Court overturned the conviction on the grounds that the "jury instructions failed to convey the requisite consciousness of wrongdoing"[20]—that AA personnel needed to think they were doing wrong rather than right to be convicted. The U.S. government must decide whether to retry the case. Unfortunately, the Supreme Court's ruling came too late for AA.

Lingering Questions

Within a few months, arrangements had been made for the AA units around the world to join other firms, but not before many staff had left, and not all those remaining were hired by the new employers. A firm of 85,000 people worldwide, including 24,000 in the United States, was virtually gone.

Was this an appropriate outcome? Perhaps only 100 AA people were responsible for the Enron tragedy, but 85,000 paid a price. Will the reduced selection of large accounting firms, the Big 4, be able to serve the public interest better than the Big 5? What if another Big 4 firm has difficulty. Will we have the Big 3, or are we now facing the Final Four? Will fate await other individual AA partners and personnel beyond David Duncan, or by the AICPA through the exercise of its code of conduct? Will a similar tragedy occur again?

Emerging Research

These questions, and others, have stimulated the accounting research community to investigate them. Conferences are being held, and research articles are appearing.

One of the early studies, by Paul R. Chaney and Kirk L. Philipich entitled "Shredded Reputation: The Cost of Audit Failure,"[21] provided insights into the impact of AA's problems on its other corporate clients and their investors. On January 10, 2002, AA admitted shredding Enron's documents, and in the ensuing three days the stock prices of most of AA's 284 other large clients that were part of the Standard & Poor's 1,500 Index fell. Over that time, these stocks dropped an average of 2.05 percent and lost more than $37 million in market value. This was the largest movement observed for the four critical information events tested. The other events were November 8, 2001, when Enron announced its restatements, December 12, 2001, when AA's CEO admitted AA made an error, and February 3, 2002, the day following the release of the Powers Report, when AA hired former Federal Reserve Chairman Paul Volcker to chair an independent oversight board to shore up AA's credibility. Volcker later resigned

---

19. Greg Farrell, "Arthur Andersen convicted of obstruction of justice," *USA TODAY*, June 15, 2002.
20. Barry McKenna, "Supreme Court overrules jury—but too late to save Andersen," *Globe & Mail*, Report on Business, June 1, 2005, B1, B11.
21. Paul R. Chaney and Kirk L. Philipich, "Shredded reputation: The cost of audit failure," *Journal of Accounting Research*, Vol. 40 No. 4, September 2002, 1235–1240.

when it became evident that AA was unwilling to embrace significant changes.

Additional research studies have examined many aspects of the conduct of the directors, executives, lawyers, and accountants involved in the Enron, Arthur Andersen, and WorldCom tragedies. In addition, the roles of regulators, of directors, and of professional independence have come under scrutiny. These studies are to be found in many academic and professional journals as well as the popular business press. In particular, useful articles can be found in the *Journal of Business Ethics, Business Ethics Quarterly, Journal of Accounting Research, Contemporary Accounting Research, Journal of Research in Accounting Ethics*, and *Business Week*.

Questions

1. What did Arthur Andersen contribute to the Enron disaster?

2. Which Arthur Andersen decisions were faulty?

3. What was the prime motivation behind the decisions of Arthur Andersen's audit partners on the Enron, WorldCom, Waste Management, and Sunbeam audits: the public interest or something else? Cite examples that reveal this motivation.

4. Why should an auditor make decisions in the public interest rather than in the interest of management or current shareholders?

5. Why didn't the Arthur Andersen partners responsible for quality control stop the flawed decisions of the audit partners?

6. Should all of Arthur Andersen have suffered for the actions or inactions of fewer than 100 people? Which of Arthur Andersen's personnel should have been prosecuted?

7. Under what circumstances should audit firms shred or destroy audit working papers?

8. Answer the "Lingering Questions" on page 120.

Ethics Case

WorldCom: The Final Catalyst

This case presents, with additional information, the WorldCom saga included in Chapter 2. Questions specific to WorldCom activities are located at the end of the case.

Worldcom Lights the Fire

WorldCom, Inc., the second largest U.S. telecommunications giant and almost 70 percent larger than Enron in assets, announced on June 25, 2002, that it had overstated its cash flow by $3.8 billion.[1] This came as a staggering blow to the credibility of capital markets. It occurred in the middle of the furor caused by:

▎ The Enron bankruptcy on December 2, 2001, and the related Congress and Senate hearings and Fifth Amendment testimony by Enron executives

▎ The depression of the stock markets

▎ The pleas by business leaders and President Bush for restoration of credibility and trust to

corporate governance, reporting, and the financial markets

▎ Responsive introduction of governance guidelines by stock exchanges and the Securities and Exchange Commission

▎ Debate by the U.S. Congress and Senate of separate bills to improve governance and accountability

▎ The conviction of Arthur Andersen, auditor of both Enron and WorldCom, for obstruction of justice on June 15, 2002

WorldCom's Accounting Manipulations

WorldCom's accounting manipulations involved very basic, easy-to-spot types of fraud.[2] Overstatements of cash flow and income were created because one of WorldCom's major expenses, line costs, or "fees paid to third party telecommunication network providers for the

---

1. Simon Romero and Alex Berenson, "WorldCom says it hid expenses, inflating cash flow $3.8 billion," *New York Times*, June 26, 2002.
2. Bruce Myerson, "A WorldCom primer," the Associated Press, June 26, 2001.

right to access the third parties networks,"[3] were accounted for improperly. Essentially, line costs that should have been expensed, thus lowering reporting income, were offset by capital transfers or charged against capital accounts, thus placing their impact on the balance sheet rather than the income statement. In addition, WorldCom created excess reserves or provisions for future expenses, which they later released or reduced, thereby adding to profits. The manipulation of profit through reserves or provisions is known as "cookie jar" accounting.

The aggregate overstatement of income quickly rose to more than $9 billion[4] by September 19, 2002, for the following reasons:

| $3.85 billion for improperly capitalized expenses, announced June 25, 2002[5]

| $3.83 billion for more improperly capitalized expenses in 1999, 2000, 2001, and the first quarter of 2002, announced on August 8, 2002[6]

| $2.0 billion for manipulations of profit through previously established reserves, dating back to 1999

Ultimately, the WorldCom fraud totaled $11 billion.

Key senior personnel involved in the manipulations at WorldCom included:

| Bernard J. Ebbers, CEO

| Scott D. Sullivan, CFO

| Buford Yates Jr., Director of General Accounting

| David F. Myers, Controller

| Betty L. Vinson, Director of Management Reporting, from January 2002

| Troy M. Normand, Director of Legal Entity Accounting, from January 2002

According to SEC's complaint against Vinson and Normand:[7]

4. WorldCom fraudulently manipulated its financial results in a number of respects, including by improperly reducing its operating expenses in at least two ways. First, WorldCom improperly released certain reserves held against operating expenses. Second, WorldCom improperly recharacterized certain operating costs as capital assets. Neither practice was in conformity with generally accepted accounting principles ("GAAP"). Neither practice was disclosed to WorldCom's investors, despite the fact that both practices constituted changes from WorldCom's previous accounting practices. Both practices artificially and materially inflated the income WorldCom reported to the public in its financial statements from 1999 through the first quarter of 2002.

5. Many of the improper accounting entries related to WorldCom's expenses for accessing the networks of other telecommunications companies ("line costs"), which were among WorldCom's major operating expenses. From at least the third quarter of 2000 through the first quarter of 2002, in a scheme directed and approved by senior management, and participated in by VINSON, NORMAND and others, including Yates and Myers, WorldCom concealed the true magnitude of its line costs. By improperly reducing reserves held against line costs, and then—after effectively exhausting its reserves—by recharacterizing certain line costs as capital assets, WorldCom falsely portrayed itself as a profitable business when it was not, and concealed the large losses it suffered. WorldCom's fraudulent accounting

3. Complaint: *SEC v. WorldCom, Inc.,* U.S. Securities and Exchange Commission, June 26, 2002, para. 5, www.sec.gov/litigation/complaints/complr17588.htm.

4. "WorldCom to reveal more bogus accounting," Associated Press, September 19, 2002; David E. Royella, "WorldCom faces two new charges, misstatement grows," *Financial Post,* November 6, 2002, FP4.

5. WorldCom Inc., *Form 8-K, Current Report Pursuant To Section 13 Or 15(D) Of The Securities Exchange Act Of 1934,* August 14, 2002, para. 2, www.sec.gov/archives/edgar/.

6. Ibid., para. 3.

7. *Complaint: SEC v. Betty L. Vinson, and Troy M. Normand,* U.S. Securities and Exchange Commission, modified October 31, 2002, para. 4, 5, 6, www.sec.gov/litigation/complaints/comp17783.htm.

practices with respect to line costs were designed to and did falsely and fraudulently inflate its income to correspond with estimates by Wall Street analysts and to support the price of WorldCom's common stock and other securities.

6. More specifically, in the third and fourth quarters of 2000, at the direction and with the knowledge of WorldCom's senior management, VINSON, NORMAND and others, by making and causing to be made entries in WorldCom's books which improperly decreased certain reserves to reduce WorldCom's line costs, caused WorldCom to overstate pretax earnings by $828 million and at least $407 million respectively. Then, after WorldCom had drawn down WorldCom's reserves so far that the reserves could not be drawn down further without taking what senior management believed was an unacceptable risk of discovery, VINSON, NORMAND and others, again at the direction and with the knowledge of senior management, made and caused to be made entries in World-Com's books which improperly capitalized certain line costs for the next five quarters, from the first quarter 2001 through the first quarter 2002. This accounting gimmick resulted in an overstatement of World-Com's pretax earnings by approximately $3.8 billion for those five quarters.

The motivation and mechanism for these manipulations is evident from the SEC's description of what happened at the end of each quarter, after the draft quarterly statements were reviewed. Steps were taken by top management to hide WorldCom's problems and boost or protect the company's stock price in order to profit from stock options, maintain collateral requirements for personal loans, and keep their jobs. These steps were required, in part, to offset the downward pressure on WorldCom's share price caused by U.S. and European regulators' rejection of WorldCom's US $115 billion bid for Sprint

Communications.[8] Ebbers' company had been using takeovers rather than organic growth to prop up earnings, and the financial markets began to realize this would be increasingly difficult.

According to the SEC:

27. In or around October 2000, at the direction and with the knowledge of WorldCom senior management, VINSON, NORMAND and others, including Yates and Myers, caused the making of certain improper entries in the company's general ledger for the third quarter of 2000. Specifically, after reviewing the consolidated financial statements for the third quarter of 2000, WorldCom senior management determined that WorldCom had failed to meet analysts' expectations. WorldCom's senior management then instructed Myers, and his subordinates, including Yates, VINSON and NORMAND, to make improper and false entries in WorldCom's general ledger reducing its line cost expense accounts, and reducing—in amounts corresponding to the improper and false line cost expense amounts—various reserve accounts. After receiving instructions through Yates, VINSON and NORMAND ensured that these entries were made. There was no documentation supporting these entries, and no proper business rationale for them, and they were not in conformity with GAAP. These entries had the effect of reducing third quarter 2000 line costs by approximately $828 million, thereby increasing World-Com's publicly reported pretax income by that amount for the third quarter of 2000.[9]

Manipulations followed the same pattern for the fourth quarter of 2000, but a change was required for the first quarter of 2001 for fear of discovery.

29. In or around April 2001, after reviewing the preliminary consolidated financial statements for the first quarter of 2001, WorldCom's senior management determined that WorldCom had again failed to

8. "Ebbers became symbol of scandals" *Financial Post*, July 14, 2005, FP1, FP3.
9. *Complaint: SEC v. Betty L. Vinson, and Troy M. Normand*, U.S. Securities and Exchange Commission, modified October 31, 2002, www.sec.gov/litigation/complaints/comp17783.htm

meet analysts' expectations. Because World-Com's senior management determined that the company could not continue to draw down its reserve accounts to offset line costs without taking what they believed to be unacceptable risks of discovery by the company's auditors, WorldCom changed its method of fraudulently inflating its income. WorldCom's senior management then instructed Myers, and his subordinates, including Yates, VINSON and NORMAND, to make entries in World-Com's general ledger for the first quarter of 2001 which fraudulently reclassified line cost expenses to a variety of capital asset accounts without any supporting documentation or proper business rationale and in a manner that did not conform with GAAP.

30. Specifically, in or around April 2001, at the direction and with the knowledge of World Com's senior management, defendants VINSON, NORMAND and others, including Yates and Myers, fraudulently reduced first quarter 2001 line cost expenses by approximately $771 million and correspondingly increased capital asset accounts, thereby fraudulently increasing publicly reported pretax income for the first quarter of 2001 by the same amount. In particular, in or about April 2001, NORMAND telephoned WorldCom's Director of Property Accounting (the "DPA") and instructed him to adjust the schedules he maintained for certain Property, Plant & Equipment capital expenditure accounts (the "PP&E Roll-Forward") by increasing certain capital accounts for "prepaid capacity." NORMAND advised the DPA that these entries had been ordered by WorldCom's senior management. Correspondingly, a subordinate of NORMAND made journal entries in WorldCom's general ledger, transferring approximately $771 million from certain line cost expense accounts to certain PP&E capital expenditure accounts.[10]

In future periods, the increase of certain accounts for "prepaid capacity" remained the manipulation of choice.

WorldCom's Other Revelations

It should be noted that Ebbers was not an accountant—he began as a milkman and bouncer, and became a basketball coach and then a Best Western Hotel owner before he entered the Telcom business,[11] where his sixty acquisitions and style earned him the nickname "the Telcom Cowboy." However, he was ably assisted in these manipulations by Scott Sullivan, his Chief Financial Officer, and David Myers, his Controller. Both Sullivan and Myers had worked for Arthur Andersen before joining WorldCom.

Other spectacular revelations offer a glimpse behind the scenes at WorldCom. The company, which applied for bankruptcy protection in July 21, 2002, also announced that it might write off $50.6 billion in goodwill or other intangible assets when restating for the accounting errors previously noted. Apparently other WorldCom decisions had been faulty.

The revelations were not yet complete. Investigation revealed that Bernard Ebbers, the CEO, had been loaned $408.2 million. He was supposed to use the loans to buy WorldCom stock or for margin calls as the stock price fell. Instead, he used it partly for the purchase of the largest cattle ranch in Canada, construction of a new home, personal expenses of a family member, and loans to family and friends.[12]

Finally, it is noteworthy that:

"At the time of its scandal, WorldCom did not possess a code of ethics. According to WorldCom's Board of Director's Investigative Report, the only mention of "ethics" was contained in a section in WorldCom's Employee Handbook that simply stated that "... fraud and dishonesty would not be tolerated" (WorldCom 2003, p. 289). When a draft version of a formal code was

---

10. *Complaint: SEC v. Betty L. Vinson, and Troy M. Normand,* U.S. Securities and Exchange Commission, modified October 31, 2002, www.sec.gov/litigation/complaints/comp17783.htm.
11. Krysten Crawford, "Ex-WorldCom CEO Ebbers guilty," *CNN*/Money, March 15, 2005, http://money.cnn.com/2005/03/15/news/newsmakers/ebbers/?cnn=yes
12. Royella, "WorldCom faces two new charges," FP4.

presented to Bernie Ebbers ... for his approval before the fraud was discovered in 2001, his response was reportedly that the code of ethics was a "... colossal waste of time" (WorldCom 2003, 289)."[13]

Why Did They Do it?

According to U.S. Attorney General John Ashcroft:

the alleged Sullivan-Myers scheme was designed to conceal five straight quarterly net losses and create the illusion that the company was profitable.[14]

In view of Ebbers' $408.2 million in loans, which were largely to buy or pay margin calls on WorldCom stock and which were secured by WorldCom stock, he would be loathe to see further deterioration of the WorldCom stock price. In short, he could not afford the price decline that would follow from lower World-Com earnings.

In addition, according to the WorldCom's *2002 Annual Meeting Proxy Statement,*[15] at December 31, 2001, Ebbers had been allocated exercisable stock options on 8,616.365 shares and Sullivan on 2,811,927. In order to capitalize on the options, Ebbers and Sullivan (and other senior employees) needed the stock price to rise. A rising or at least stable stock price was also essential if WorldCom stock was to be used to acquire more companies.

Finally, if the reported results became losses rather than profits, the tenure of senior management would have been shortened significantly. In that event, the personal loans outstanding would be called and stock option gravy train would stop. In 2000, Ebbers and Sullivan had each received retention bonuses of $10 million so they would stay for two years after

September 2000. In 1999, Ebbers received a performance bonus allocation of $11,539,387, but he accepted only $7,500,000 of the award.[16]

An Expert's Insights

Former Attorney General Richard Thornburgh was appointed by the U.S. Justice Department to investigate the collapse and bankruptcy of WorldCom. In his *Report to the U.S. Bankruptcy Court* in Manhattan on November 5, 2002, he said:

One person, Bernard Ebbers, appears to have dominated the company's growth, as well as the agenda, discussions and decisions of the board of directors, ...

A picture is clearly emerging of a company that had a number of troubling and serious issues ... [relating to] culture, internal controls, management, integrity, disclosure and financial statements.

While Mr. Ebbers received more than US $77 million in cash and benefits from the company, shareholders lost in excess of US $140 billion in value.[17]

The Continuing Saga

The WorldCom saga continues as the company's new management try to restore trust it its activities. As part of this effort, the company changed its name to MCI. "On August 26, 2003, Richard Breeden, the Corporate Monitor appointed by the U.S. District Court for the Southern District of New York, issued a report outlining the steps the Company will take to rebuild itself into a model of strong corporate governance, ethics and integrity ... (to) foster MCI's new company culture of 'integrity in everything we do.'"[18] The company is moving deliberately to reestablish the trust and integrity

13. Mark S. Schwartz, "Effective Corporate Codes of Ethics: Perceptions of Code Users," *Journal of Business Ethics,* 55:323–343, 2004, p. 324, and WorldCom 2003, *Report of the Investigation by the Special Investigative Committee of the Board of Directors"* June 9, 2003.

14. "WorldCom accounting fraud rises to $7 billion," *The Baltimore Sun,* August 9, 2002.

15. WorldCom's *2002 Annual Meeting Proxy Statement,* SEC Edgar File, April 22, 2002, www.sec.gov/Archives/edgar/data/723527/000091205702015985/0000912057-02-015985.txt.

16. Ibid.

17. Don Stancavish, "WorldCom dominated by Ebbers," Bloomberg News, in *Financial Post,* November 5, 2002, FP13.

18. *MCI* website, *Governance: Restoring the Trust,* http://global.mci.com/about/governance/restoringtrust/, (accessed January 3, 2006).

it requires to compete effectively for resources, capital, and personnel in the future.

The SEC has filed complaints, which are on its website, against the company and its executives. The court has granted the injunctive relief the SEC sought. The executives have been enjoined from further such fraudulent actions, and subsequently banned by the SEC from practicing before it, and some have been banned by the court from acting as officers or directors in the future.

WorldCom, as a company, consented to a judgment:

> ... imposing the full injunctive relief sought by the Commission; ordering an extensive review of the company's corporate governance systems, policies, plans, and practices; ordering a review of WorldCom's internal accounting control structure and policies; ordering that WorldCom provide reasonable training and education to certain officers and employees to minimize the possibility of future violations of the federal securities laws; and providing that civil money penalties, if any, will be decided by the Court at a later date.[19]

Bernie Ebbers and Scott Sullivan were each indicted on nine charges: one count of conspiracy, one count of securities fraud, and seven counts of false regulatory findings.[20] Sullivan pleaded guilty on the same day he was indicted and later cooperated with prosecutors and testified against Bernie Ebbers "in the hopes of receiving a lighter sentence."[21]

Early in 2002, Ebbers stood up in church to address the congregation saying: "I just want you to know that you're not going to church with a crook."[22] Ebbers took the stand and argued "that he didn't know anything about WorldCom's shady accounting, that he left much of the minutiae of running the company to underlings."[23] But after eight days of deliberations, on March 15, 2005, a federal jury in Manhattan didn't buy his "aw shucks," "hands-off," or "ostrich-in-the-sand" defense.

The jury believed Sullivan, who told the jury that Ebbers repeatedly told him to "'hit his numbers'—a command . . . to falsify the books to meet Wall Street expectations."[24] They did not buy Ebbers' "I know what I don't know" argument, "especially after the prosecutor portrayed a man who obsessed over detail and went ballistic over a US $18,000 cost overrun in a US $3-billion budget item while failing to pick up on the bookkeeping claim that telephone line costs often fluctuated—fraudulently—by up to US $900-million a month. At other times, he replaced bottled water with tap water at WorldCom's offices, saying employees would not know the difference."[25]

On July 13, 2005, Ebbers was sentenced to twenty-five years in a federal prison.[26] Once a billionaire, he also lost his house, property, yacht, and fortune. At 63 years of age, he is appealing his sentence. Sullivan's reduced sentence was for five years in a federal prison, forfeiture of his house, ill-gotten gains, and a fine.

Investors lost over $180 million in WorldCom's collapse,[27] and more in other companies as the confidence in credibility of the financial markets, governance mechanisms and financial statements continued to deteriorate.

Questions

1. Describe the mechanisms that WorldCom's management used to transfer profit from other time periods to inflate the current period.

19. *SEC Litigation Release No. 17883*/ December 6, 2002, http://www.sec.gov/litigation/litreleases/lr17883.htm.
20. "Jury convicts Ebbers on all counts in fraud case," *MSNBC,* March 15, 2005, http://www.msnbc.msn.com/id/7139448/.
21. Crawford, "Ex-WorldCom CEO Ebbers guilty."
22. "Ebbers became symbol of scandals," FP1, FP3.
23. Crawford, "Ex-WorldCom CEO Ebbers guilty."
24. "Jury Convicts Ebbers on all counts in fraud case."
25. "Ebbers became symbol of scandals."
26. Ibid.
27. Ibid.

2. Why did Arthur Andersen go along with each of these mechanisms?

3. How should WorldCom's board of directors have prevented the manipulations that management used?

4. Bernie Ebbers was not an accountant, so he needed the cooperation of accountants to make his manipulations work. Why did WorldCom's accountants go along?

5. Why would a board of directors approve giving its Chair and CEO loans of over $408 million?

6. How can a board ensure that whistle-blowers will come forward to tell them about questionable activities?

Ethics Case

Waste Management, Inc.

Waste Management, Inc. (WMI), founded by cousins Dean Buntrock and Wayne Huizenga, first came to public attention in 1971 when the founders began to buy up many small family-owned waste haulers in a successful effort to consolidate the waste disposal industry in the United States. By 1990, as a result of strong growth through acquisitions and operations, WMI had become the largest waste management company in the United States. Wayne Huizenga left WMI in 1984 to found his Blockbuster empire.[1]

Unfortunately, real growth was bolstered by "aggressive accounting policies" and, when profitability and real growth slowed in the early 1990s,[2] Dean Buntrock and his associates began to manipulate the company's financial reports to keep to its appearance of success.[3] Without this successful appearance, the company's stock price would have fallen, making WMI stock far less useful in acquiring additional haulers, as well as making executive stock options worth far less.

Ultimately, the lack of real growth came to light, management was changed, and investigations began. In February 1998, WMI announced the restatement of its 1992–1996 reported earnings, acknowledging that profits had been overstated by $3.54 billion pre-tax. The impact on WMI's share price was not favorable, and although steep declines did not emerge until the second half of 1998, the stock's growth trend was broken.

The U.S. Securities and Exchange Commission investigated and laid charges citing massive fraud against former WMI officials; Arthur Andersen, WMI's auditor; and several of Arthur Andersen's partners. Significant fines and sanctions were applied. Arthur Andersen paid a fine of $7 million, and key partners were fined and banned from practicing before the SEC. In order to settle two class action lawsuits with irate shareholders, WMI paid $677 million, with Arthur Andersen contributing $95 million. WMI refused to pay pensions and severance to the senior officers implicated in the scandal.

Arthur Andersen was the company's auditor throughout this period, and the firm was well aware of WMI's accounting practices. Why didn't they stand up to their client? What could they have done? What should they have done? Did this experience change their approach to risk management?

Waste Management Stock Chart, Weekly Prices, 1998–2003

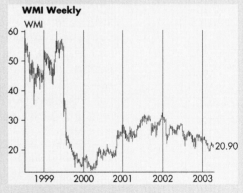

Reprinted courtesy of StatPro Canada, Inc.

---

1. "Can waste management climb out of the muck?" *Business Week,* March 23, 1998.

2. Ibid. The decline was due to a surplus of dump space and declining prices, and a slowing of stock-based acquisitions due to low attractiveness of company stock.

3. Actually, the use of aggressive or liberal accounting policies and questionable disclosure probably began prior to 1992. "Burying trash in big holes—on the balance sheet," *Business Week,* May 11, 1992.

Discovery

Dean Buntrock retired as CEO in June 1996, but continued as the chairman of WMI's board of directors. He appointed his longtime second-in-command Phillip B. Rooney, the company's president and chief operating officer, as CEO, but Rooney resigned in February 1997 due to pressure from unhappy WMI shareholders, and Buntrock was pressed back into service. In July 1997, Buntrock turned over his chairman's title to Ronald T. Lemay, who was formerly an executive at Sprint Corp. However, on October 29, after only three months, Lemay resigned and went back to Sprint. A former Chrysler vice chairman, newly named director and turn-around expert, Robert S. Miller, was appointed interim chairman and CEO. According to Miller, LeMay got "a whiff of the accounting problems" and "He left because it was deep enough and he hadn't hit bottom yet."[4]

Nonetheless, LeMay had initiated an investigation into the accounting manipulations that subsequently became the starting point for recognizing the 1992–1996 financial reports needed restatement to correct numerous overstatements, and the point of departure for the ensuing SEC investigation. According to the SEC's information release of March 26, 2002, the defendants, WMI's senior officers (Buntrock; Rooney; James E. Koenig, executive vice president and CFO; Thomas C. Hau, vice president, corporate controller, and chief accounting officer; Herbert Getz, senior vice president general counsel, and secretary; and Bruce D. Tobecksen, vice president of finance), aided by Arthur Andersen and its partners, "perpetrated a massive financial fraud lasting more than five years."[5] The information release goes on to state that in its related complaint the SEC alleges the following:

> Defendants fraudulently manipulated the Company's financial results to meet predetermined earnings targets.

The Company's revenues and profits were not growing fast enough to meet these targets, so defendants instead resorted to improperly eliminating and deferring current period expenses to inflate earnings. They employed a multitude of improper accounting practices to achieve this objective. Among other things, defendants:

| avoided depreciation expenses on their garbage trucks by both assigning unsupported and inflated salvage values and extending their useful lives,

| assigned arbitrary salvage values to other assets that previously had no salvage value,

| failed to record expenses for decreases in the value of landfills as they were filled with waste,

| refused to record expenses necessary to write off the costs of unsuccessful and abandoned landfill development projects,

| established inflated environmental reserves (liabilities) in connection with acquisitions so that the excess reserves could be used to avoid recording unrelated operating expenses,

| improperly capitalized a variety of expenses, and

| failed to establish sufficient reserves (liabilities) to pay for income taxes and other expenses.[6]

The Impact

These manipulations gave rise to the following aggregated amounts over the period from 1992 to 1996, as indicated by the cumulative restatement announced in early 1998, as reported in the SEC complaint:

The Restatement—Then the Largest in Corporate History

> 293. The accounting review started in mid-July by Buntrock's successor continued through the end of the year, with the same

---

4. "Where it hurts: An accounting scandal endangers big payout for a retired CEO—Waste Management's board withholds $40 million from Buntrock, others—Alma mater loses $3 Million," Jeff Bailey, *The Wall Street Journal,* May 19, 1999.

5. "Waste Management, Inc. Founder and Five Other Former Top Officers Sued for Massive Earnings Management Fraud," Litigation Release No. 17435/ March 26, 2002, Accounting and Auditing Enforcement Release No. 1532, U.S. Securities and Exchange Commission (see **www.cengage.com/ accounting/brooks**.).

6. Ibid.

CUMULATIVE RESTATEMENTS OF PRE-TAX INCOME (THROUGH 12/31/96)	(IN MILLIONS)
Vehicle, equipment, and container depreciation expense	$509
Capitalized interest	192
Environmental and closure/post-closure liabilities	173
Purchase accounting related to remediation reserves	128
Asset impairment losses	214
Software impairment reversal	(85)
Other	301
Pre-tax subtotal	**$1,432**
Restatements of Pre-Tax Income (1/1/97 through 9/30/97)	$250
Income Tax Expense Restatement (through 9/30/97)	$190
Total Restated items	**$1,872**

long-time Company controllers conducting the review. AA continued as the Company's auditor, but a new engagement team was assembled to audit the Company's restated financial statements. The audit committee oversaw the work on the Restatement and engaged another big 5 accounting firm to shadow the audit work of AA and advise the committee regarding the various accounting issues.

294. The details of the massive Restatement finally came in early 1998. In February 1998, Waste Management announced that it was restating its financial statements for the period 1992 through 1996 and the first three quarters of 1997. At the time, the Restatement was the largest in history. In the Restatement, the Company admitted that, through the first three quarters of 1997, it had materially overstated its reported pre-tax earnings by approximately $1.7 billion and understated certain elements

of its tax expense by $190 million. See table below.

295. Additionally, contemporaneous to the Restatement, the Company also recorded approximately $1.7 billion in impairment losses and other charges. The total amount of the Restatement and fourth quarter charges was approximately $3.6 billion.[7]

The WMI restatement acknowledged that its reported net after-tax income had been misstated by the following amounts in each of the years from 1992 to 1996 inclusive, as reported in the SEC complaint:

14. In the Restatement, the Company acknowledged that its original financial statements had misstated its net after-tax income as in the table below.

The Company acknowledged that, in total, it had overstated its net after-tax income by over $1 billion.[8]

YEAR	ORIGINALLY REPORTED (THOUSANDS)	AS RESTATED (THOUSANDS)	PERCENT OVERSTATED
1992	$850,036	$739,686	15
1993	$452,776	$288,707	57
1994	$784,381	$627,508	25
1995	$603,899	$340,097	78
1996	$192,085	$(39,307)	100+
Q1–Q3 1997	$417,600	$236,700	76

7. *Complaint: SEC v. Dean Buntrock, Phillip B. Rooney, James E. Koenig, Thomas C. Hau, Herbert A. Getz, and Bruce D. Tobecksen,* No. 02C 2180, U.S. Securities and Exchange Commission, March 26, 2002, 64–65 (see **www.cengage.com/accounting/brooks**.)

8. Ibid., 4–5.

Who Did It, and Why?

The complaint goes on to explain each defendant's participation in the fraud, essentially indicating that Buntrock masterminded the fraud, and that the other defendants actively participated in and/or knew or recklessly disregarded facts indicating that WMI's financial statements or disclosures contained material misstatements and omissions. In the process, the . . .

defendants received the following estimated ill-gotten gains, from their bonuses, retirement benefits, trading and charitable giving alone:

	Ill-gotten Gains
Buntrock	$16,917,761
Rooney	$9,286,124
Koenig	$951,005
Hau	$640,100
Getz	$472,500
Tobecksen	$403,779[9]

For these wrongdoings, the SEC made the following claims against all or some of the defendants: securities fraud, filing false periodic reports, falsification of books and records, and lying to auditors.[10] In summary, the SEC sought:

a final judgment as to each defendant that permanently enjoins him, orders the disgorgement of ill-gotten gains plus prejudgment interest, imposes civil penalties as a lesson to him and to others, and prohibits him from serving as an officer or director of a public company.[11]

Arthur Andersen's Role

The SEC's Litigation Release does not mince words about the role of Arthur Andersen's partners. It states:

Defendants were aided in their fraud by the Company's long-time auditor Arthur Andersen LLP ("Andersen"), which repeatedly issued unqualified audit reports on the Company's materially false and misleading

annual financial statements. At the outset of the fraud, management capped Andersen's audit fees and advised the Andersen engagement partner that the firm could earn additional fees through "special work." Andersen nevertheless identified the Company's improper accounting practices and quantified much of the impact of those practices on the Company's financial statements. Andersen annually presented Company management with what it called Proposed Adjusting Journal Entries ("PAJEs") to correct errors that understated expenses and overstated earnings in the Company's financial statements.

Management consistently refused to make the adjustments called for by the PAJEs. Instead, defendants secretly entered into an agreement with Andersen fraudulently to write off the accumulated errors over periods of up to ten years and to change the underlying accounting practices, but to do so only in future periods. That signed, four-page agreement, known as the Summary of Action Steps (attached to the Commission's complaint), identified improper accounting practices that went to the core of the company's operations and prescribed thirty-two "must do" steps for the company to follow to change those practices. The Action Steps thus constituted an agreement between the company and its outside auditor to cover up past frauds by committing additional frauds in the future.

Defendants could not even comply with the Action Steps agreement. Writing off the errors and changing the underlying accounting practices as prescribed in the agreement would have prevented the company from meeting earnings targets and defendants from enriching themselves.[12]

In a separate announcement[13] of settlements reached on June 19, 2001, the SEC

---

9. Ibid., 5.

10. Ibid., 79–81.

11. Ibid., 6.

12. SEC Litigation Release No. 17435, 3.

13. "Arthur Andersen . . . and Partners Settle . . . ," Litigation Release No. 17039/ June 19, 2001, Accounting and Auditing Enforcement Release No. 1410/ June 19, 2001, U.S. Securities and Exchange Commission (see **www.cengage.com/accounting/brooks**).

detailed its findings against Arthur Andersen and the following of its partners:

❚ Robert E. Allgyer, partner responsible for the audit, who was "known as the 'rainmaker' inside Andersen for his skill at winning business by pitching consulting, tax and other non-audit services."[14]

❚ Edward G. Maier, the risk management partner for Andersen's Chicago office.

❚ Walter Cercavschi, the concurring partner on the WMI audit.

❚ Robert Kutsenda, then Central Region audit practice director for Andersen.

The SEC findings as detailed beginning on page 3 of the June 19 Litigation Release, or in the longer Administrative Proceedings of the same date,[15] provide an interesting year-by-year expansion of the summary noted above. In addition, the Litigation Release makes the following salient points:

❚ As reported to the audit committee, between 1991 and 1997, Andersen billed Waste Management corporate headquarters approximately $7.5 million in audit fees. Over this seven-year period, while Andersen's corporate audit fees remained capped, Andersen also billed Waste Management corporate headquarters $11.8 million in other fees, much of which related to tax, attest work unrelated to financial statement audits or reviews, regulatory issues, and consulting services.

❚ A related entity, Andersen Consulting, also billed Waste Management corporate headquarters approximately $6 million in additional nonaudit fees. Of the $6 million in Andersen Consulting fees, $3.7 million related to a Strategic Review that analyzed the overall business structure of the Company and ultimately made recommendations on implementing a new operating model designed to "increase shareholder value."

Allgyer was a member of the Steering Committee that oversaw the Strategic Review, and Andersen Consulting billed his time for these services to the Company. In setting Allgyer's compensation, Andersen took into account, among other things, the Firm's billings to the Company for audit and nonaudit services.

❚ As the Commission stated in its Order as to Andersen,

• [u]nless the auditor stands up to management as soon as it knows that management is unwilling to correct material misstatements, the auditor ultimately will find itself in an untenable position: it either must continue issuing unqualified audit reports on materially misstated financial statements and hope that its conduct will not be discovered or it must force a restatement or qualify its report and thereby subject itself to the liability that likely will result from the exposure of its role in the prior issuance of the materially misstated financial statements.

❚ The Commission in this case found that

• Andersen failed to stand up to management to prevent the issuance of materially misstated financial statements. Instead, Andersen allowed the Company to establish—and then continue for many years—a series of improper accounting practices. As a result, Andersen found itself in 1998 in the position of auditing the Restatement and issuing an unqualified audit report in which it acknowledged that the prior financial statements on which it had issued unqualified audit reports were materially misstated.

❚ The Commission ultimately found in its Order as to Andersen that

• the circumstances of this case, including the positions within the Firm of the partners who were consulted by the engagement team, the gravity and duration of the

14. David Ward and Loren Steffy, "How Andersen went wrong," *Bloomberg Markets,* May 2002.
15. "Order Instituting Public Administrative Proceedings, Making Findings and Imposing Remedial Sanctions Pursuant to the Commission's Rules of Practice," *Securities Exchange Act of 1934,* Release No. 44444/June 19, 2001, Accounting and Auditing Enforcement Release No. 1405/June 19, 2001, Administrative Proceeding File No. 3-10513, Securities and Exchange Commission (see **www.cengage .com/accounting/brooks**.).

misconduct, and the nature and magnitude of the misstatements mandate that the Firm be held responsible for the acts of its partners in causing the Firm to issue false and misleading audit reports in the Firm's name.

The Commission's Complaint alleges and the Commission's Order found that Andersen knew or was reckless in not knowing that the unqualified audit reports that it issued for the years 1993 through 1996 were materially false and misleading because the audits were not conducted in accordance with GAAS and the financial statements did not conform to GAAP. The Complaint further alleges that Andersen violated section 10(b) of the Exchange Act and rule 10b-5 thereunder. The Commission's Order as to Andersen finds that Andersen engaged in improper professional conduct within the meaning of rule 102(e)(1)(ii) of the Commission's *Rules of Practice*.[16]

As a result of the Commission's complaint, and without admitting or denying the allegations or findings in the Commission's complaint and orders, Arthur Andersen and the partners consented to the actions in the accompanying table.

Surprisingly, Arthur Andersen was not fired as WMI's auditor until 2001. According to audit committee members, Arthur Andersen was kept on to help with the accounting probe. "If you want to find where the bones are buried, ... 'you've got to use the dog.'"[17]

Other Impacts

Arthur Andersen and Waste Management, Inc., have been sued in numerous class actions by irate shareholders. To date they have paid out the following amounts:

Regarding the restatement of earnings: $220 million (Andersen $75 mil.)[18]

Securities violations: $457 million (Andersen $20 mil.)[19]

Not surprisingly, the confidence that shareholders were willing to place in WMI management

---

SEC SANCTIONS RELATED TO IMPROPER AUDIT PRACTICES WITH REGARD TO THE AUDITS FOR 1992–1997 OF WASTE MANAGEMENT, INC.

	Permanent Injunction Enjoining From Future Violations of Sections or Rules of the Securities Exchange Act	Civil Penalty (Fine)	Censure under Rule 102(e) for improper professional conduct Denial of right to appear or practice before the SEC as an accountant, with the right to request reinstatement after . . .
Arthur Andersen	Section 10(b) [1934] Rule 10b-5 [1934]	$7 million	Censure
Robert Allgyer	Section 10(b) [1934] Rule 10b-5 [1934] Section 17(a) [1933]	$50,000	Censure Denial, 5 years
Edward Maier	Section 10(b) [1934] Rule 10b-5 [1934] Section 17(a) [1933]	$40,000	Censure Denial, 3 years
Walter Cercavschi	Section 10(b) [1934] Rule 10b-5 [1934] Section 17(a) [1933]	$30,000	Censure Denial, 3 years
Robert Kutsenda	—	—	Censure Denial, 1 year

---

16. "Arthur Andersen ... and Partners Settle."

17. "Where It Hurts."

18. Ibid.

19. Calmetta Coleman, "Waste Management to pay $457 million to settle shareholder class-action lawsuit," *The Wall Street Journal*, November 8, 2001.

and future earnings announcements was severely eroded.

On a personal level, Mr. Buntrock and other senior executives discovered in May 1999 that the approximately $40 million due them for pension and deferred compensation was withheld by the WMI board until the accounting investigation was completed. This followed the precedent set in the case of the former Sunbeam CEO, Albert J. Dunlap, who expected $5.5 million. Cendant Corp., however, which found its pretax profits were overstated by $500 million, paid retiring CEO, Walter A. Forbes, the full $35 million in severance due in July 1998.[20] Now that the precedent appears to have shifted, the question arises as to whether executives found to have knowingly or unknowingly, but negligently, contributed to a financial scandal should be forced to pay towards class action settlements reached.

Questions

1. Why didn't Arthur Andersen stand up to WMI management?
2. What aspects of their risk management model did the Arthur Andersen partners incorrectly consider?
3. To whom should Arthur Andersen have complained if WMI management was acting improperly?
4. Did the WMI board and audit committee do their jobs?
5. Were the fines levied high enough?
6. Should you use the same "dog" to discover the "bones" in an accounting scandal?

---

20. "Where It Hurts."

Ethics Case | *Sunbeam Corporation and Chainsaw Al*

In July 1996, Albert J. Dunlap was hired as CEO and Chairman by Sunbeam's board of directors to revive the company from a period of lagging sales and profits, and make it an attractive acquisition target. "Chainsaw Al," as he was known for his staff- and cost-cutting style as a turn-around expert, had a reputation for results that immediately propelled the price of Sunbeam stock upward by 60 percent to $18.63.[1] By 1997, he planned to eliminate half of Sunbeam's 6,000 employees and 87 percent of its products.[2] "According to Sunbeam managers, it . . . resulted in near-total chaos."[3] However, 1997 reported sales rose by $184 million or 18.7 percent.[4]

In March 1998, Sunbeam paid $2.5 billion to buy the companies manufacturing Coleman stoves, Mr. Coffee coffee makers, and First Alert smoke detectors. Dunlap was rewarded with a $2 million annual salary and stock options worth millions.[5] Sunbeam's stock peaked at $52.

Unfortunately, "Chainsaw" had used manipulative accounting techniques to inflate Sunbeam's financial results. When properly restated, for example, Sunbeam's reported net income for 1997 was reduced from $109.4 million to $38.3 million.[6]

In early 1998, the lack of real success in the selling of Sunbeam's products could no longer

---

1. "Chainsaw Al: He anointed himself America's best CEO. But Al Dunlap drove Sunbeam into the ground," *Business Week,* October 18, 1999.
2. Ibid.
3. Ibid.
4. *Sunbeam Corporation's 1997 Annual Report,* SEC 10-K Filing, March 2, 1998 (see **www.cengage.com/accounting/brooks**).
5. *Sunbeam 1999 Annual Meeting Proxy Statement,* SEC Edgar Filing, May 14, 1999 (see **www.cengage.com/accounting/brooks**).
6. "Andersen's other headache: Sunbeam," *BusinessWeek,* January 29, 2002.

FIGURE 1

Stock Price Movement During the Stewardship of Mr. Dunlap

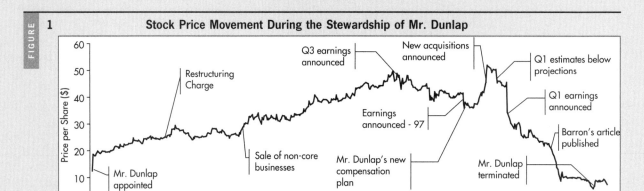

Reprinted with permission of Shyam V. Sunder, from Working Paper Series ACC-99-07 Sunbeam, Inc, Stern School of Business, NYU.

be easily masked and the manipulations had to offset the lowered sales and be larger than earlier manipulations in order to create an attractive percentage gain in sales and profits. Moreover, since some of the manipulations used in 1996 and 1997 had recorded future sales too early, there were even fewer sales to count in 1998, and using the same manipulative techniques at ever larger levels raised issues of credibility.

Interestingly, at least two people were not fooled: Deidra DenDanto, a 26-year-old, recently hired member of Sunbeam's internal audit staff, and Andrew Shore, a stock analyst at Paine Weber, Inc.[7] Deidra challenged the manipulative practices from the start, but got little support from her superiors. She finally resigned on April 3 after sending a letter to the board of directors.[8] Shore became wary of the high inventory and accounts receivable levels Dunlap was creating as early as the second quarter of 1997.

On April 3, 1998, Sunbeam had to announce that revenue and orders would be 5 percent lower than expected. Chainsaw Al did not put forward a credible front during the conference call. In addition, Andrew Shore had just found that two senior officers had left—Rich Goudis, chief of investor relations,

resigned on April 3,[9] and Donald Uzzi, executive vice president for worldwide consumer products, had been fired earlier[10]—and Shore had downgraded his rating of the company's shares. The company's share price fell by almost 25 percent to $34.375.[11]

The accounting manipulations used were unraveling, and stories began to appear in the press. The most damaging appeared in *Barron's,* and an impromptu board meeting was held on June 9 during which Dunlap, Russell A. Kersh, the CFO; and Robert J. Gluck, the controller, refuted the charges.[12] Kersh did, however, reveal that it would be tough to make 1998 projections. At the end of the meeting, Dunlap demanded the board's support or he (and Kersh) would leave the company. The directors were stunned and incredulous. They did some checking with other executives including David C. Fannin, Sunbeam's executive vice president and chief counsel. They met again with Fannin on June 13 and Chainsaw Al was fired by phone later that day along with the CFO.[13] He asked for, but was given no explanation. Sunbeam then announced that its prior financial statements could not be relied upon. In the same month, the Securities and Exchange

7. "Chainsaw Al."
8. Ibid.
9. Ibid.
10. "How Al Dunlap self-destructed," *BusinessWeek,* July 6, 1998.
11. Ibid.
12. Ibid.
13. Ibid.

Commission began their investigation into Sunbeam's accounting practices.

A new management team was hired, but the fundamental weaknesses of Sunbeam products in their markets were tough to remedy. In November 1998, Sunbeam issued restated financial statements for the fourth quarter of 1996, all quarters of 1997, and the first quarter of 1998. As a result, Sunbeam's stock price declined to approximately $7 from $52 in March, eight months earlier.

On February 5, 2001, Sunbeam filed for protection while reorganizing under Chapter 11 of the *U.S. Bankruptcy Code*.[14]

On May 15, 2001, the SEC charged Dunlap, former CFO Russell A. Kersh, controller Robert J. Gluck, and vice presidents Donald R. Uzzi and Lee B. Griffin, as well as Arthur Andersen LLP partner Phillip Harlow, with fraud. The SEC also announced the settlement of similar charges against Sunbeam's former counsel, David Fannin.[15]

SEC Findings

The SEC based its fraud charges on the following summary of its findings:

> From the last quarter of 1996 until June 1998, Sunbeam Corporation's senior management created the illusion of a successful restructuring of Sunbeam in order to inflate its stock price and thus improve its value as an acquisition target. To this end, management employed numerous improper earnings management techniques to falsify the Company's results and conceal its deteriorating financial condition. Specifically, senior management created $35 million in improper restructuring reserves and other "cookie jar" reserves as part of a year-end 1996 restructuring, which were reversed into income the following year. Also in

> 1997, Sunbeam's management engaged in guaranteed sales, improper "bill and hold" sales, and other fraudulent practices. At year-end 1997, at least $62 million of Sunbeam's reported income of $189 million came from accounting fraud. The undisclosed or inadequately disclosed acceleration of sales through "channel-stuffing" also materially distorted the Company's reported results of operations and contributed to the inaccurate picture of a successful turnaround.

> When these measures did not lead to a sale of the Company by year-end 1997, senior management took increasingly desperate measures to conceal Sunbeam's mounting financial problems, meanwhile attempting to finance the acquisition of three other companies in part through the public sale of debt securities. Management engaged in additional accelerated sales and sales for which revenue was improperly recognized, deleted certain corporate records to conceal pending returns of merchandise, and misrepresented the Company's performance and future prospects in press releases and in meetings with analysts and lenders.

> In June 1998, negative statements in the press about the Company's sales practices prompted Sunbeam's Board of Directors to begin an internal investigation. This resulted in the termination of certain members of senior management, including Sunbeam's chief executive officer and chief financial officer, and, eventually, in an extensive restatement of the Company's financial statements from the fourth quarter of 1996 through the first quarter of 1998. As a result, Sunbeam's restated 1997 income was approximately one-half of the amount previously reported.[16]

14. "Order Instituting Public Administrative Proceedings, Pursuant to Section 8A of the *Securities Act of 1933* and Section 21A of the *Securities Exchange Act of 1934,* Making Findings, and Imposing a Cease-And-Desist Order", *Securities Act of 1933* Release No. 7976/May 15, 2001, *Securities Exchange Act of 1934* Release No. 44305/May 15, 2001, Accounting and Auditing Enforcement Release No. 1393/May 15, 2001, Administrative Proceeding File No. 3-10481, Securities and Exchange Commission, May 15, 2001, (SEC Litigation Release) (see **www.cengage.com/accounting/brooks**).

15. "SEC sues former CEO, CFO, other top officers of Sunbeam Corporation in massive fraud," SEC News Headline Report 2001-49, May 15, 2001 (see **www.cengage.com/accounting/brooks**).

16. SEC Litigation Release, op. cit.

The details[17] of the manipulative techniques that were uncovered by the SEC are of particular interest, as follows:

▎ Overstatement of 1996 restructuring charges, thus creating inflated or "cookie jar" reserves to be reversed later to bolster future profits. This overstatement of restructuring charges by a newly installed management team is known as the "big bath" approach because of the attribution of large losses to ousted management, leaving it clean for the new group. At least $35 million of the total restructuring charge of $337.6 million was improperly created, including:

- $18.7 million of overstated restructuring costs not in conformity with generally accepted accounting principles (GAAP).

- $6 million overstatement of a $12 million reserve against a future environmental litigation/remediation (this litigation was settled late in 1997 for $3 million).

- $2.1 million overstatement of inventory loss by erroneously considering some good inventory as bad, and then selling it at inflated margins in 1997.

- $2.3 million overstatement of 1996 advertising expenses for service to be rendered in 1997.

- Overstatement of part of the $21.8 million reserve for cooperative advertising for local retailers.

These "cookie jar" reserves were drawn down through-out 1997, having an effect on reported figures. (See table.)

▎ Nondisclosure of unusual or "infrequent" sales:

- $19.6 million of deeply discounted products (a one-time sale) were sold in the first quarter of 1997 without disclosure, thus conveying to investors a false picture of sustainable sales.

▎ Recording of accelerated and false sales, through:

- Contingent sales
  - In March 1997, Sunbeam booked as a sale $1.5 million revenue from an arrangement where a wholesaler held barbeque grills over the quarter end but could return all unsold grills for credit after the quarter end with Sunbeam paying all costs of shipment and storage. No risks of ownership were assumed by the wholesaler.

▎ "Early-buy incentives," including offering excessive discounts and other incentives to induce customers to place orders before they would otherwise have done so. This practice was not disclosed so investors were unaware of lowered margins and future sales would be jeopardized.

▎ "Bill and hold" sales began to be used in the second quarter of 1997. If customers would order goods before they needed them, Sunbeam offered to hold the goods in Sunbeam's warehouse until they requested later delivery. Sunbeam would pay all storage, shipment, and insurance expense. Unsold goods could be returned for full credit. The SEC considered these transactions "little more than projected orders disguised as sales."

QUARTER OF 1997	COOKIE JAR RESERVE	IMPROVEMENT OF INCOME
Q1	$4.3 million - non-GAAP	13%
	$2.1 million – inventory	6%
	$330,000 – advertising expense	
Q2	$8.2 million – non-GAAP	
	$5.6 million – coop advertising	
Q3	$2.9 million – non-GAAP	
	$663,000 – advertising expense	
Q4	$1.5 million – non-GAAP	
	$9.0 million – litigation	

17. Ibid.

The preceding three techniques would be considered "channel-stuffing"—the over-loading of distribution channels by inducing or forcing the channel members (i.e., wholesalers, distributors, retailers, etc.) to acquire goods before they would otherwise order them. This practice causes the goods ordered prematurely to clog up the channel and delay further orders until the backlog is sold. For example, according to an internal Sunbeam memo, by May 1998, "Wal-Mart Stores, ... which prefers four weeks inventory, was loaded with 23.6 weeks of Sunbeam appliances."[18] Obviously there will be a delay before a company can attain normal sales levels—unless the channel is stuffed to a greater degree.

Recording of rebates from suppliers for purchases in later periods as income in the period the rebate was received or negotiated. $2.75 million was falsely recorded in the second quarter of 1997 as early sales instead of reductions in the cost of goods sold in later periods. An additional $1.9 million was recorded in the third quarter.

Purported sale of spare parts inventory to a company that had serviced Sunbeam products for a fixed fee per unit. $11 million in revenue and $5 million in income was recorded. However, Arthur Andersen, Sunbeam's auditor, found that Sunbeam had guaranteed a five percent profit margin to the "customer" on resale of the inventory, and a fee for service of an indeterminate value, and indicated that Sunbeam's revenue recognition was improper. Sunbeam reserved $3 million against the value of the transaction, but refused to reverse it. Arthur Andersen regarded the restated net transaction as not material and therefore did not qualify their opinion for it.

Improper deletion from Sunbeam's computer system of all product return authorizations in the first quarter of 1998. Although Sunbeam had to honor their agreements, many returns were delayed past the quarter end so that the company's reserve for returns appeared to be adequate when, in fact, it was understated and income correspondingly overstated. At the end of 1997, Sunbeam reduced its reserve from $6.5 million to $2.5 million without reasonable justification. At the end of January 1998, Sunbeam further reduced it by another $1 million when, in fact, there was approximately $18 million in impending returns and the company's established approach should have called for a reserve of $4.5 million.

Extending the first quarter of 1998 from March 29 to March 31 to capture more sales in the quarter.

The SEC further claims that no acquisitor had surfaced for Sunbeam, and the financial picture was so grave in early 1998 that Chainsaw Al negotiated the purchase of three companies—Coleman, First Alert, and Signature Brands—with the view of creating another restructuring or "cookie jar" reserve. The 1998 manipulations described above, and others, were intended to maintain the illusion of favorable momentum to facilitate the placement of $700 million of zero coupon bonds and raise a sufficient revolving line of credit ($1.7 billion) to complete the purchases. Sunbeam completed the acquisition on March 30, 1998, but never disclosed that the increase in gross sales for the two extended days, March 30 and 31, amounted to $38 million.

While Sunbeam executives were manipulating the company's financial reports, they were also making a continuous stream of misleading statements to financial analysts, the SEC, and to the investing public. These are detailed in the SEC's Litigation Release.

The SEC's claim, in summary, was that these manipulations accounted for an overstatement of Sunbeam's income by 50 percent during 1997, and that this fraudulent misrepresentation was significant to the decisions of the investing public.

How Did They Do It?

According to published reports, soon after Chainsaw Al was hired, he recruited Russell Kersh, with whom he had worked before, to be his CFO. Then he gave huge stock options to 250 of the 300 top officers at Sunbeam—so significant that many would have had to forego

---

18. "Chainsaw Al."

gains of $1 million or more if they resigned before the three-year vesting period. This potential gain was obviously why these senior executives endured Dunlap's intimidating performance review sessions, which were referred to as "Hair Spray Days" due to the stream of air from Dunlap's mouth that blew back the executive's hair. "It was like a dog barking for hours, ... He just yelled, ranted and raved. He was condescending, belligerent, and disrespectful."[19]

Dunlap's cost-cutting measures resulted in the firing of so many people that normal functions could not be carried out. At one stage, the Sunbeam computer system broke down during an upgrade and couldn't be fixed for months due to lack of technicians that had been fired. During this period Sunbeam reportedly lost track of shipments, could not bill customers properly, and could not collect accounts receivable.[20]

Making the projected quarterly numbers was always a difficult exercise. "But in the fourth quarter [of 1997], however, no amount of game playing or beating up on people could produce the numbers Dunlap had promised investors. So he turned to his longtime ally and CFO, Russell Kersh, who had been with him through his stints at Lily Cup and Scott Paper. In the often esoteric interpretations that are made in accounting, Kersh was rarely conservative or bashful about his creative competence during his tenure as Sunbeam's CFO. In a self-congratulatory tone, he would point to his chest and boast to fellow executives that he was 'the biggest profit center' the company had. Dunlap knew it as well. At meetings, executives recalled, Dunlap would say: 'If it weren't for Russ and the accounting team, we'd be nowhere.' Several executives heard Dunlap shout at subordinates: 'Make the goddamn number. And Russ, you cover it with your ditty bag.' "[21]

"To investors who made millions by following him, Dunlap was, if not a god, certainly a savior. He parachuted into poorly performing companies and made tough decisions that quickly brought shareholders sizable profits. 'We're all seduced by the possibility of big wins,' says Paine Webber Inc. analyst Andrew Shore."[22]

Arthur Andersen's Role

With all this going on, it is reasonable to ask how Arthur Andersen staff members could not have known about the poor internal controls on sales, accounts receivable, and inventory associated with the computer system breakdown. Did they not review internal audit reports? If their audit procedures were more strategic or analytical than procedural, why did they not identify the abnormal growth of inventory and accounts receivable that Andrew Shore did? Perhaps the auditors did not exercise sufficient professional skepticism[23] in recognizing the abnormality or, if they recognized it, in exploring the explanations received from Sunbeam's management.

Deidra DenDanto, one of Sunbeam's internal auditors and formerly of Arthur Andersen, knew of the accounting manipulations. Why didn't Arthur Andersen? Perhaps Arthur Andersen recognized many of the problems discussed above (as the SEC claims), but regarded them as not material. In one instance the SEC notes that the auditor may have regarded a partially adjusted matter (the recording as revenue of the purported sale of Sunbeam's spare parts inventory) as not material in relation to Sunbeam's reported figures, but implies that this was too simplistic an analysis. The comparisons necessary for a proper assessment of materiality should be based on the client's adjusted figures, and on many more factors than most would expect.[24]

Whether Arthur Andersen knew about Sunbeam's problems, and how much they

19. "Chainsaw Al."
20. Ibid.
21. Ibid.
22. "How Al Dunlap self-destructed."
23. See "Auditor skepticism and revenue transactions," Jimmy W. Martin, *The CPA Journal,* New York, August 2002.
24. See FASB, Concepts Statement No. 2, p. 125, and SEC Staff Accounting Bulletin: No. 99—Materiality, August 12, 1999, p. 4.

knew, will probably never be known with certainty. In their defense against the SEC claims, Andersen claimed that "revisions found in the restatement were purely the result of changes in approach mandated by Sunbeam's new management."[25] Lawyers and Sunbeam executives regarded this position as "Andersen doing anything to evade blame."[26]

Board of Director's Role

Given this defense, however, it is possible that Andersen did not review all accounting, internal control, and other concerns with the audit committee of the board or the board of directors itself or, if it did, Andersen may not have branded them as material.[27] One reason for this could be that Chainsaw Al was both the CEO and chair of the board, so open discussion and questioning of management may not have been encouraged. Another reason could be that Andersen wanted to protect its audit and nonaudit fees.

Nonetheless, the board of directors is not supposed to accept what the external auditors say without any probing or discussion. If issues were raised, questions about the nature of the transactions and the auditors' judgments about materiality should have been posed by board members. These might have surfaced information on the company's practices or the auditor's judgments that required further investigation.

In addition, the board is expected to ensure that the company has proper policies and internal controls so that the policies are followed. This area is the specific mandate of the controller and internal audit group. Although Deidra Den-Danto had made numerous reports about her concerns, these do not appear to have reached the board, except perhaps too late in March or early April 1998. Perhaps a whistle-blowing program reporting to the audit committee might have

assisted the Sunbeam board. The board seems to have been out of touch with the reality of Sunbeam's operations.

One matter the board did not handle properly was the investigation of Chainsaw Al's resume and background before it hired him. Apparently, there were several years missing from his resume, thus hiding a period "a quarter century ago [when] he was also fired from Nitec Paper Corp. amid similar allegations; in both cases, amazingly high profits were reported and used to justify huge payouts to Dunlap, only to have auditors later conclude that profits were fictitious."[28] Dunlap denied any wrongdoing.

Results of the SEC Charges

In April 2001, Arthur Andersen agreed to pay Sunbeam shareholders $110 million to settle a class action lawsuit.[29]

On September 4, 2002, the SEC announced[30] that, without admitting or denying the SEC's allegations, Dunlap and Kersh consented to the entry of judgments before the court:

> (1) permanently enjoining each of them from violating the antifraud, reporting, books and records, and internal controls provisions of the federal securities laws; (2) permanently barring each of them from serving as officers or directors of any public company, and (3) requiring Dunlap to pay a civil penalty of $500,000 and Kersh to pay a civil penalty of $200,000.

The Release further notes that:

> Dunlap paid $15,000,000 and Kersh $250,000 out of their own funds to settle a related class action. Neither Dunlap nor Kersh sold Sunbeam stock or received performance-based bonuses during the relevant period.

---

25. "Andersen's other headache: Sunbeam."
26. Ibid.
27. Ibid.; SEC Litigation Release.
28. "The incomplete resume: A special report; An executive's missing years: Papering over past problems," Floyd Norris, New York Times, July 16, 2001.
29. "Andersen's other headache: Sunbeam."
30. "Former Top Officers of Sunbeam Corp. Settle SEC Charges ...", SEC Litigation Release No. 17710/September 4, 2002, Accounting and Auditing Enforcement Release No. 1623/September 4, 2002.

The Commission's action against three other former officers of Sunbeam, Robert J. Gluck, Donald R. Uzzi and Lee B. Griffith, and against Phillip Harlow, the audit partner on the Arthur Andersen engagements to audit Sunbeam's 1996, 1997 and 1998 year-end financial statements, remains pending. Trial is scheduled for January 2003.

Questions

1. Explain how Chainsaw Al used "cookie jar" reserves to inflate Sunbeam's profit.

2. Can "bill and hold" practices ever be considered sales that should be recorded in the period in which the goods are initially "held"?

3. Why didn't Sunbeam's board of directors catch on to the manipulations?

4. How should a board make sure that it gets the information it needs to monitor management actions and accounting policies?

5. If you are a professional accountant who reports an ethical problem to your superior who does nothing, what more should you do?

6. What problems can you identify with Arthur Andersen's work as auditor of Sunbeam?

7. How should a board assess the performance of their company's auditors?

8. While it is attractive to have a CEO who is a strong person with a high profile, how should a board manage or keep track of such a person without demotivating them?

9. Can a board effectively monitor a CEO who is also the chair of the board?

Ethical Behavior

| Introduction

Part 1 provided an understanding of ethical concerns and expectations that directors, executives, and professionals are facing that are shaping the future. Both traditional stakeholder concerns and the Sarbanes-Oxley Act acceleration provided by the Enron, Arthur Andersen, and WorldCom debacles are responsible for redefining the accountability and governance frameworks for organizations and particularly the accounting profession. The downside for organizations that fail to understand and provide for the shift is becoming significant. Directors, executives, and professionals involved will face serious consequences because they will be seen as not fulfilling their newly defined expectations as a fiduciary for due diligence expectations. As a result, organizations and professions are endeavoring to ensure that their personnel understand the ethical behavior expected of them.

Philosophers have been dedicated to the study of ethical behavior for millennia, and Chapter 3 presents important contributions from several to provide a background from which directors, executives, and professional accountants can reason ethically. Based on this background, Chapter 4 presents several practical approaches to ethical decision making—really the core of ethical behavior—that facilitate the development of strategy as well as day-to-day decisions business people must face.

3

ETHICAL BEHAVIOR—PHILOSOPHERS' CONTRIBUTIONS

Purpose of the Chapter

Philosophers have been dedicated to the study of ethical behavior for millennia. The ideas, concepts, and principles they have developed have long been recognized as important touchstones for the assessment of corporate and personal activities. Currently, it is understood that the ethicality of the strategies and actions of corporations and individuals cannot be left to chance. Consequently, directors, executives, and professional accountants need an awareness of expected ethical parameters, and need to build these into the culture of their organizations. Given the diverse nature of individuals now making up our corporations and the global challenges they face, it is no longer defensible to leave the principles of ethical behavior up to the individuals involved. Organizations must choose to employ individuals who are ethically aware, and must provide them with an understanding of which ethical principles drive action. The philosopher's contributions discussed in Chapter 3 and made practical in Chapter 4 provide a helpful basic background to enable directors, executives, and professional accountants to make ethical plans and decisions. To ignore the wisdom in Chapters 3 and 4 would be irresponsible, and would leave important gaps of ethical understanding and vulnerability.

Ethics is a branch of philosophy that investigates normative judgments about what behavior is right or what ought to be done. The need for ethics arises from the desire to avoid real-life problems. It does not address issues of what you should or should not believe; those are contained in religious codes. Instead, ethics deals with the principles that guide human behavior. It is the study of norms and values concerning ideas of right and wrong, good and bad, as well as what we ought to do and what we should eschew doing. The ethical theories described in this chapter will not provide boilerplate solutions to practical problems. Instead, the theories and frameworks provide guidance to assist decision makers in determining acceptable and unacceptable business behavior and actions.

Decisions spring from beliefs about what norms, values, and achievements are expected, and what the rewards and sanctions are for certain actions. Ethical dilemmas arise when norms and values are in conflict, and there are alternative courses of action available. This means that the decision maker must make a choice. Unlike many other business decisions that have clear decision-making criteria, with ethical dilemmas there are no objective standards. Therefore, we need to use subjective moral codes. The ethical theories described in this chapter explain how to understand, implement, and act in accordance with moral codes concerning appropriate business behavior.

Although the fundamental principles and ideals of all of the ethical theories described in this chapter have application to business, each theory is not without its critics. So we need to demonstrate tolerance as we work though the strengths and weaknesses of the theories. Remember, they provide guidance about factors to consider, not decision tools that will always yield the same answer. It is still up to the decision maker to consider the issues, make the final decision, act accordingly, and live with the consequences.

Ethics & Moral Codes

The *Encyclopedia of Philosophy* defines ethics in three ways:

(1) a general pattern or "way of life,"
(2) a set of rules of conduct or "moral code," and
(3) inquiry *about* ways of life and rules of conduct.

In the first sense we speak of Buddhist or Christian ethics; in the second, we speak of professional ethics and unethical behavior. In the third sense, ethics is a branch of philosophy that is frequently given the special name of metaethics.[1]

This book is interested in the second sense of ethics, as it relates to moral codes concerning human conduct and behavior in a business setting. We will not address religious beliefs about how humans should live their lives, and the proper way of achieving the various goals of a religious life. Nor are we interested in metaethics, the theory about ethics. Instead, we are interested in studying the moral codes that relate to business behavior.

Morality and moral codes are defined in the *Encyclopedia of Philosophy* as containing four characteristics:

(1) beliefs about the nature of man;
(2) beliefs about ideals, about what is good or desirable or worthy of pursuit for its own sake;
(3) rules laying down what ought to be done and what ought not to be done; and
(4) motives that incline us to choose the right or the wrong course.[2]

Each of these four aspects will be explored using the four major ethical theories that apply to people making ethical decisions in a business environment: utilitarianism, deontology, justice and fairness, and virtue ethics.[3]

Each of the theories places a different emphasis on these four characteristics. For example, utilitarianism stresses the importance of rules in pursuing what is good or desirable, whereas deontology examines the motives of the ethical decision maker. Virtue ethics tends to examine humans in a more holistic fashion looking at the nature of humanity. Although each theory emphasizes different aspects of moral codes, they all have many common features, especially a concern of what should and should not be done. But, as Rawls notes, no theory is complete and so we must be tolerant of their various weaknesses and deficiencies. "The real question at any given time is which of the views [theories] already proposed is the best approximation overall [of what we should do]."[4] The goal is to be able to use these theories to help in our ethical decision making.

Most people, most of the time, know the difference between right and wrong. Ethical dilemmas rarely involve choosing between these two stark alternatives. Instead, ethical dilemmas normally arise because there is no entirely right option. Instead, there are compelling reasons for each of the alternatives, so it is up to the individual to decide which alternative to choose. An ethical decision maker should not choose what others have chosen simply to be consistent with

---

1. *The Encyclopedia of Philosophy*, ed. Paul Edwards, Macmillan Publishing Co., Inc., New York, 1967, Vol. 3, p. 81–82.
2. Ibid., Vol. 7, p. 150.
3. These four were identified in the AACSB Ethics Education Committee Report (2004) as essential for business students and accountants to understand. The Association to Advance Collegiate Schools of Business (AACSB) accredits business schools and programs worldwide. See http://www.aacsb.edu. The Ethics Education Report is available at http://www.aacsb.edu/resource_centers/EthicsEdu/eetf.asp.
4. Rawls, John. *A Theory of Justice*, Harvard University Press, Cambridge, 1971, p. 52.

other people, to follow the crowd. Instead, to act as an ethical person means that you are capable of taking a stand on an important and difficult problem of human life and be able to explain and justify your stance. You must be able to clearly articulate and defend why you selected that course of action, using ethical theories and reasons.

As indicated in Figure 3.1, the ethical theories that are explained in this chapter provide guidance in making ethical decisions. Although there are many other ethical theories, these are the ones that are particularly useful in making ethical decisions in a business context. But we are not naïve. We are aware that sometimes we don't do what we decide we should do. Even though you shouldn't have that chocolate éclair because you are on a diet, sometimes you eat it anyway. In business, there are many constraints that influence whether or not a decision maker actually does the right thing. These mitigating factors can be broadly grouped into organizational constraints and personal characteristics. Organizational constraints include reward systems, organizational culture, and the tone at the top of the firm. People will do what they are paid to do, and if the reward system encourages questionable behaviors or discourages ethical discussion of a proposed course of action, then employees will not factor ethics into their decision-making process. The values of the organization influence employee behavior, as well as the behavior of senior managers. If employees see that the firm tacitly encourages misleading customers, and that the board of directors flaunts the corporate code of conduct, then junior employees will think that ethics, and doing the right thing, are unimportant in business. These organizational constraints are discussed in more detail in the discussion of corporate culture in Chapter 5.

Personal characteristics that influence actually doing what the individual knows is correct include a misguided understanding of business, an overcommitment to the firm and ethical immaturity. Some employees mistakenly think that the goal of business is only to make a profit. As long as the business succeeds, the techniques (i.e., means) used are erroneously thought to be irrelevant. Later in this chapter, we will discuss the principle of the end justifies the means. An overcommitment to the firm can also cloud ethical judgment. John De Lorean, the founder of the De Lorean Motor Car Company, was so committed to his firm that he attempted to illegally sell

FIGURE 3.1   **The Ethical Reasoning Process**

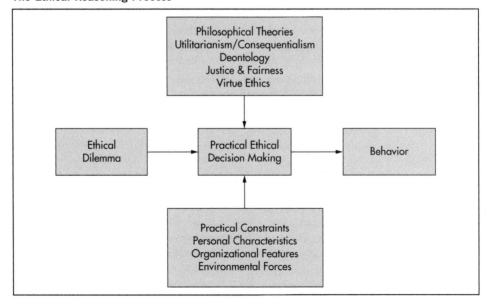

cocaine in order to obtain the cash necessary to keep his company afloat.[5] There are numerous other acts of misguided loyalty to the firm. However, the most important personal constraint may very well be ethical immaturity. Like physical maturity, ethical maturity comes with age and experience. It is easy to speculate what you would do in a hypothetical situation. Many of the cases in this book present hypothetical problems for you to solve. The choices that you make will help to develop and reinforce your judgment, values, and moral code.[6] But you won't really know what you will actually do until you are confronted with an actual problem and have to make a decision.

Usually, there is no single right answer in resolving ethical problems. Nor is the decision simply a matter of a leap of faith. Instead, it requires careful and thoughtful analysis. Then, once the decision is made and the course of action is decided on, the decision maker must actually take action or decide not to act. Frameworks are provided in this chapter and the next to help you to make an ethical decision. What you actually do is up to you, and you will have to live with the consequences.

Ethics & Business

Archie Carroll astutely observes that you can only talk meaningfully about business ethics if the business is economically viable.[7] If it is not profitable, then it goes out of business and the question of what is appropriate and inappropriate business behavior is moot. Consequently, a primary goal of a for-profit firm is to remain in business. It does this by providing goods and services that are required by society in an efficient and effective manner. This is a fundamental goal of business, but it is not the only goal, and should not be pursued at any cost. Profit is the consequence of doing business well. But business must also adhere to the applicable laws and regulations as a bare minimum. Applicable laws provide the base level of acceptable business behavior. Importing cocaine may be profitable but it is illegal. The third and fourth responsibilities of business, according to Carroll, are to be ethical and socially responsible. Business operates within society and these are the other norms of society. By contrast, some people will argue that being economically viable and obeying the law are the only two responsibilities of business, and that ethics has nothing to do with business. Why, then, should business people be ethical?

Three of the most common explanations for why individuals should be ethical are grounded on views about religion, our relationship with others, and our perception of ourselves. As was mentioned, one definition of ethics is that it has to do with a pattern of how we should live our lives based on religious principles. In the Jewish-Christian tradition this would include following the laws of "do unto others as you would have them do unto you," "do not bear false witness," and "love your neighbor as yourself." Similar laws are proscribed by other religions. For many people, it is respect for such laws and religious codes that govern behavior. We should be ethical because that is God's law.

Others believe that ethics has nothing to do with religion per se. Instead, it has to do with our regard for other people, demonstrated through love, sympathy, beneficence, and the like. We are social animals who live in society with other people. We naturally develop strong emotional attachment to other people, which we often show through acts of love and self-sacrifice. Through

---

5. Levin, Hillel. *Grand Delusions: The Cosmic Career of John De Lorean*, New York, Viking Press, 1983.
6. For further discussion of the development of judgment (e.g., Kohlberg's Six Stages of Moral Reasoning), values, and moral codes, see Chapters 5 and 6.
7. Carroll, Archie. "The Pyramid of Corporate Social Responsibility: Toward the Moral Management of Organizational Stakeholders," *Business Horizons*, Vol. 34 (1991), 39–48.

our interactions, we become sympathetic to their emotions and feelings. We reproduce in ourselves the pleasures, pains, and satisfactions that we recognize are being felt by others based on our own experiences of pleasure, pain, and satisfaction. Ethics represents our sympathetic identification with others and is often manifest in acts of beneficence, friendship, and love.

Still others believe that we behave ethically because of enlightened self-interest. This last view is compelling for many businesspeople. The first characteristic of morality, as defined earlier, has to do with beliefs about the nature of people. A fundamental aspect of human nature is that we are self-interested. Although we live with others in society, each of us is living our unique individual life. Our thinking takes the following pattern. It is my life. As such, factors that influence me are important to me. I am interested in factors that will have an impact on my life. I am interested in myself. However, there is a difference between self-interest and selfishness. Selfishness only concerns the individual, and places the individual's needs and concerns above those of others. Self-interest, by contrast, is an interest *concerning* the self, not an interest *in* the self. Self-interest is not narrowly defined as only being about me. Instead, it is an interest in all matters that relate to me, my family, my friends, and the society in which I live. Self-interest has an intimate connection with economic behavior.

Self-Interest & Economics

In the movie *Wall Street*, the principal character Gordon Gekko, played by Michael Douglas, argues, in his presentation to the board of directors of Teldar Paper, that business is grounded on greed. "The point is, ladies and gentlemen, that greed, for lack of a better word, is good. Greed is right, greed works. Greed clarifies, cuts through, and captures the essence of the evolutionary spirit. Greed, in all its forms; greed for life, for money, for love, knowledge has marked the upward surge of mankind." The better word that Gordon Gekko is looking for is self-interest, rather than greed. It is self-interest, not greed that moves the economy. In social and economic theory self-interest works and is good; selfishness, avarice, and greed do not. In case after case, unbalanced greed has created vulnerabilities and has proved to be a highly risky strategy for the individuals and corporations that pursue it—usually ending in disaster.

The concept of self-interest has a long tradition in English empirical philosophy to explain both social harmony and economic cooperation. **Thomas Hobbes (1588–1679)** argued that self-interest motivates people to form peaceful civil societies. Writing after the English civil war (1642–1651), he was analyzing factors that contributed to a stable society and those that lead to a state of war. He began with the observation that people have multiple natural desires, a fundamental one is self-preservation. People are also driven by their short-term interests. Some may want a present good and are willing to acquire it by any means. But this can lead to war and conflict as people compete for the same things. When people are driven by their base desires, by unbridled self-interest, anarchy occurs. There is no economic prosperity, no social infrastructures, and no civilized social order. Peace, by contrast, is probably in everyone's best long-term interests. It avoids the uncertainties and dangers of what Hobbes calls a state of nature, where life is "solitary, poore, nasty, brutish, and short."[8] But peace means accepting rules that limit individual freedom. People will no longer be able to pursue their personal goals when that would have a negative affect on other people.

From this perspective, civil society can be seen as a voluntary contract among individuals in which some individual freedoms and rights are given up in exchange for peace and self-preservation. This is enlightened self-interest. The desire for personal security means that

---

8. Hobbes, Thomas. *Leviathan*, edited with an introduction by C. B. Macpherson, Penguin Books, Middlesex, 1968, p. 186.

individuals voluntarily limit their person freedoms in order to secure social harmony. As such, society can be seen as a Leviathan, a commonwealth that guarantees peace and security to its citizens. Although this may have some negative short-term consequences, most will realize that voluntarily refraining from exploiting others will ensure their personal security. For Hobbes, self-interest leads to cooperation and the formation of a civil society.

Following in this tradition, **Adam Smith (1723–1790)** argued that self-interest leads to economic cooperation. In his opus, *An Inquiry into the Nature and Causes of the Wealth of Nations*, he observes that both buyers and sellers are interested in satisfying their individual needs and desires. Buyers want to derive the most relative satisfaction or utility from their consumer purchases. Sellers want to earn the maximum profit they can from the transaction. In a perfect market, buyers and sellers negotiate to Pareto-optimum equilibrium, what Smith calls the natural price. If the seller sets the price too high, no one will buy the product. If the price is too low, consumers will be more than willing to buy the product. As the demand for the product increases, either the seller will increase the price, or new sellers will enter the market in an attempt to satisfy consumer demands for the product. If the price then rises too high, the buyers will leave the market. This is what is meant by a free market; both buyers and sellers can freely and without compulsion enter and exit the marketplace. As a result, competition among vendors and consumers push prices to the point at which markets clear, at which all the goods available for sale sell at prices that consumers are willing to pay for those products and vendors are willing to accept for their products.

Profits occur when goods and services are provided in an efficient and effective manner. Smith uses the example of a pin factory. Ten men working independently can produce less than twenty pins per day. However, these same ten men, working cooperatively with each man doing one part of the pin-making process, can produce almost 48,000 pins per day. Utilizing the available labor, in an efficient and effective manner, results in the maximum number of pins of a uniform quality being produced in a given amount of time. Higher production through a cooperative division of labor is in everyone's best interests.

The invisible hand of the marketplace results in a Pareto-optimum position where it is impossible to improve anyone's condition without worsening the condition of someone else. This means that society as a whole is better off. Self-interested individuals unintentionally increase the wealth of their nation. "He generally, indeed, neither intends to promote the publick interest, nor knows how much he is promoting it. By preferring the support of domestick to that of foreign industry, he intends only his own security; and by directing that industry in such a manner as its produce may be of the greatest value, he intends only his own gain, and he is in this, as in many other cases, lead by an invisible hand to promote an end which was no part of his intention."[9]

Smith is often, mistakenly, seen as the advocate of unfettered capitalism. This is not the case. He did advocate minimal governmental interference in the marketplace. The government should only be responsible for establishing and paying for the infrastructures of society, including such things as the transportation system, public education and the justice system. Business should be able to handle all other matters. However, it is important to note that selfishness, avarice and greed are not part of Smith's model. Smith was both an economist and an ethicist. He held the chair in moral philosophy at the University of Glasgow. In 1790 he published his *Theory of Moral Sentiments*, a treatise in which he developed an ethics based on sympathy. Sympathy is our feeling the passions of others. It is being affected by the sentiments of other people with a corresponding feeling within us. Because we identify with the emotions of others we strive to establish good

9. Smith, Adam. *An Inquiry into the Nature and Causes of the Wealth of Nations*, edited with an introduction and notes by Kathryn Sutherland, Oxford University Press, Oxford, 1993, p. 291–292.

relations with other people. We desire their approbation and shun their disapprobation. This provides the basis for benevolent acts and social justice. *For Smith, individuals do not act out of narrow selfishness, but rather out of sympathy for both oneself and for others. In other words, ethical behavior is grounded on the sentiment of sympathy, which in turn constrains unbridled self-interest.*

How does this relate to his economic theory? The key features of Smith's economic model are, first, that the economy is a cooperative social activity. Firms provide goods and services that are required by society. Sellers and buyers work toward a common objective, satisfying their needs at mutually agreeable prices. These are not atomistic transactions, but rather are socially constructed events. Business is a social activity, and society operates on ethical principles. Second, markets are competitive, not adversarial. Trade is dependent on fair play, honoring contracts, and mutual cooperation. Healthy competition ensures the highest quality goods and services are provided at the lowest prices. Competition also means that firms strive to operate as efficiently and effectively as possible, in order to maximize their long-term profits. Finally, ethics constrains economic opportunism. Ethics keeps narrow selfishness and unbridled greed in check. According to Smith, individuals follow ethical guidelines for the good of society. By analogy, they should also follow ethical guidelines for the good of the economy. So, in answer to Gordon Gekko, it is self-interest, not greed, that moves the marketplace, and self-interest has the unintended consequence of improving the social welfare of everyone.

Smith's insight is that self-interest leads to economic cooperation. Self-interest is the motivation for a division of labor, and a cooperative division of labor means that more and better products can be provided to society in an efficient and effective manner. The marketplace will price these products based on consumer needs, their availability, their quality, and other qualitative aspects of the product. The profits that ensue to the vendor are a result of providing goods and services. So, the goal of the marketplace is not for a firm to make a profit. Rather, the purpose is for firms to provide goods and services in an efficient and effective manner; i.e., by being profitable. Profit is the means, not the end. In a competitive environment, the wants and desires of both buyers and sellers are satisfied through self-interested contracting. Cooperative contracting results in the buying and selling of goods and services at Pareto-optimum prices. Such a system promotes the economic well-being of all and the nation as a whole.

Ethics, Business & The Law

Business, ethics, and the law can be seen as three intersecting circles in a Venn diagram as per Figure 3.2. Area 1 represents aspects of business activity that are not covered by the law or ethics. For example, in North America, assets are presented on the left side of the balance sheet, whereas

FIGURE 3.2 **Intersection of Business, Law & Ethics**

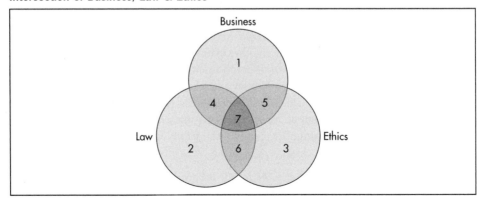

liabilities and owners' equity are on the right. This convention has nothing to do with ethics or the law, and the presentation of assets, liabilities and owners' equity on British balance sheets is different. In Area 2 are laws that have nothing to do with ethics or business. Driving on the right-hand side of the road is a convenience law, so that people don't bump into one another. In Australia and the United Kingdom, the law is reversed. Area 3 represents ethical prohibitions that do not concern business and are not illegal. Lying or cheating on a spouse would be an example of this.

There are many overlaps among the law, ethics, and business. Area 4 represents the myriad of rules and regulations that firms must follow; laws that are passed by governments, regulator agencies, professional associations, and the like. There are also many overlaps between the law and ethics (Area 5), a primary one being the prohibition against killing. Area 6 is the focus of this book, the overlap between business activity and ethical norms. This is also the area where some deny that there is an overlap. Their argument is that Area 4 exists, but that as long as firms do not violate the law, they are behaving ethically. That is, the law and ethics are one and the same when it comes to business. The main message of this book is that ethics should guide behavior beyond the law. The law is usually the minimum standard of acceptable behavior, but sometimes laws conflict (as in different countries) or are out of date, or do not exist in one locale, but should. In such cases, ethics requires performance beyond the bare legal minimum.

Area 7, the intersection of law, ethics, and business, normally only becomes a problem if the law says one thing, whereas ethics says the opposite. In Nazi Germany during World War II, the law was prejudicial against Jews. What should an ethical business person do when (1) the law encourages the exploitation of Jews, (2) the law is beneficial to the business person since the Jewish employees do not have to be paid, and yet, (3) the business man knows the exploitation of these people is wrong? The story of *Schindler's List* vividly portrays the ethical dilemma when law, business and ethics intersect but are incompatible.

The remainder of this chapter outlines some of the major ethical theories that are used by business people to help resolve ethical dilemmas. This is not an exhaustive list, but it does cover the major philosophies that are used in the area of business ethics.

Major Ethical Theories Useful in Resolving Ethical Dilemmas

Teleology: Utilitarianism & Consequentialism—Impact Analysis

Teleology has a long history among English empirical philosophies. **John Locke (1632–1704)**, **Jeremy Bentham (1748–1832)**, **James Mill (1773–1836)**, and his son **John Stuart Mill (1806–1873)** all examined ethics from a teleological perspective. Teleology is derived from the Greek word *telos*, which means ends, consequences, and results; and so, *teleological theories study ethical behavior in terms of the results or consequences of ethical decisions.* Teleology resonates with many results-oriented business people because it focuses on the impact of decision-making. It evaluates decisions as good or bad, acceptable or unacceptable, in terms of the consequences of the decision.

Investors judge an investment as good or bad, worthwhile or not, based on its expected return. If the actual return is below the investor's expectation, then it is deemed to be a bad investment decision; if the return is greater than expected, it is considered a good or worthwhile investment decision. Ethical decision making follows a similar pattern. In the same way that the goodness and badness of an investment is assessed on the basis of the results of the financial decision, ethical goodness or badness is based on the consequences of the ethical decision. Ethical decisions are right or wrong as they lead to either positive or negative results. Ethically good decisions result in positive outcomes, whereas ethically bad decisions lead to either less positive outcomes or negative consequences. However, the consequences of an ethical decision are not themselves ethical. The consequence is simply what happens.

The ethicality of the decision maker and the decision are determined on the basis of the nonethical comparative value of the action or consequence. If the decision brings about a positive result, such as helping an individual to achieve self-realization, then the decision is said to be an ethically correct one. Other positive nonethical results would include such things as happiness, enjoyment, health, beauty, and knowledge, whereas negative nonethical results would include unhappiness, misery, illness, ugliness, and ignorance. In other words, judgments about right and wrong, or ethical correctness are based solely on whether or not good or bad happens.

Teleology has its clearest articulation in utilitarianism, most noticeable in the writings of Bentham and J. S. Mill. In *Utilitarianism* Mill wrote: "The creed which accepts as the foundation of morals, Utility, or the Greatest Happiness Principle, holds that actions are right in proportion as they tend to promote happiness, wrong as they tend to produce the reverse of happiness. By happiness is intended pleasure, and the absence of pain; by unhappiness, pain, and the privation of pleasure."[10]

Utilitarianism defines good and evil in terms of the nonethical consequences of pleasure and pain. The ethically correct action is the one that will produce the greatest amount of pleasure or the least amount of pain. This is a very simple theory. The goal of life is to be happy and all those things that promote happiness are ethically good as they tend to produce pleasure or alleviate pain and suffering. For utilitarians, pleasure and pain may be both physical and mental. The alleviation of stress, anguish, and mental suffering are as important as reducing physical pain and discomfort. For example, the stress level of an employee may increase when her supervisor asks her to complete an assignment but then provides her with little information, insufficient time to produce the report, and makes unrealistic demands in terms of the quality of the report. The increased stress does not contribute to her general happiness or to the pleasure of completing the assignment. For a utilitarian, they only things worth having are pleasurable experiences, and these experiences are good simply because they are pleasurable. However, in this case, completing the assignment is neither pleasurable nor, from the employee's perspective, good. It does not contribute to her utility or to her general happiness.

Mill was quick to point out that pleasure and pain have both quantitative and qualitative aspects. Bentham developed a calculus of pleasure and pain based on intensity, duration, certainty, propinquity, fecundity, purity, and extent[11] Mill added that the nature of the pleasure or pain is also important. Some pleasures are more desirable than others and worth the effort of achieving. An athlete, for example, trains daily to compete in the Olympics. The training may be very painful, but the athlete keeps his eye on the prize, winning the gold medal. The qualitative pleasure of standing on the podium exceeds the quantitatively grueling road to becoming an Olympic champion.

Hedonism focuses on the individual, and seeks the greatest amount of personal pleasure or happiness. **Epicurus (341–270 B.C.)** argued that the goal of life is secure and lasting pleasure, a life in which pains are accepted only if they lead to greater pleasures, and pleasures are rejected if they lead to greater pains. Utilitarianism, by contrast, measures pleasure and pain not at the individual level but, rather, at the level of society. The pleasure of the decision maker as well as everyone who could possibly be affected by the decision, need to be considered. But additional weight should not be given to the decision maker. The "happiness that forms the utilitarian standard of what is right in conduct, is not the agent's own happiness, but that of all concerned.

---

10. Mill, John Stuart. *Utilitarianism*, edited by Roger Crisp, Oxford University Press, Oxford, 1998, p. 55.
11. Bentham, Jeremy. *An Introduction to the Principles of Morals and Legislation*, in *The Utilitarians*, **Graden City,** Dolphin Books, 1961, p. 37–40.

As between his own happiness and that of the others, utilitarianism requires him to be as strictly impartial as a disinterested and benevolent spectator."[12] A CEO who talks the board of directors into giving the CEO a $100-million bonus may derive great happiness from the bonus, but if he does not consider the effects that the bonus might have on all the other employees in his firm, his peer group of other executives, and society as a whole, then he is ignoring the ethical aspects of his decision.

When using utilitarianism, the decision maker must take a broad perspective concerning who, in society, might be affected by the decision. Failure to do so can be extremely costly to a firm. Consider the case of Shell UK and the decommissioning of the Brent Spar oil rig. The Brent Spar was an oil storage and tanker loading platform located in the North Sea. Built in 1976, it became obsolete in 1991. Shell decided that the best alternative for economic and environmental reasons was to sink the platform in the Atlantic Ocean. They applied for and received permission from the British government to do so. However, Shell failed to consider the impact that this decisions would have on other stakeholders, including society as a whole. Beginning in February 1995 Greenpeace launched a concerted campaign to halt the sinking of the platform. Although Greenpeace greatly exaggerated the environmental impact of sinking the platform, their campaign was costly to Shell; there were boycotts of Shell products in Europe, and damage to some stations in Germany. In June 1995, Shell agreed not to sink the platform, and the platform was moored in Norway until it was reconstructed as part of a ferry terminal in 1999. The entire episode was very costly to Shell and occurred, in part, because the company failed to realize that the decommissioning decision had important consequences for other stakeholders, beyond Shell UK and the British government. (See the case "The Brent Spar Decommissioning Disaster" at the end of Chapter 7 for a more detailed analysis.)

The key aspects to utilitarianism are, first, that ethicality is assessed on the basis of non-ethical consequences. Next, ethical decisions should be oriented towards increasing happiness and/or reducing pain, where happiness and pain can be either physical or psychological. Furthermore, happiness and pain relate to all of society and not just to the personal happiness or pain of the decision-maker. Finally, the ethical decision maker must be impartial and not give extra weight to personal feelings when calculating the overall net probable consequences of a decision.

| **Act & Rule Utilitarianism** | Over time, utilitarianism has evolved along two main lines, called act utilitarianism and rule utilitarianism. The former, sometimes referred to as *consequentialism,*[13] *deems an action to be ethically good or correct if it will probably produce a greater balance of good over evil.* An action is ethically bad or incorrect if it will probably produce the opposite. Rule utilitarianism, on the other hand, says that we should follow the rule that will probably produce a greater balance of good over evil and avoid the rule that will probably produce the reverse.

The presumption is that it is possible, in principle, to calculate the net pleasure or pain associated with a decision. For Mill "the truths of arithmetic are applicable to the valuation of happiness, as of all other measurable quantities."[14] Returns on investments can be measured; so too happiness. This means that the decision maker must calculate, for each alternative course of action, the corresponding amount of pleasure for each person who will probably be affected by the decision. Similarly, the amount of displeasure or pain for each person under each of the

---

12. Mill, op.cit., p. 64.
13. Consequentialism is the version of utilitarianism that the AACSB advocate as being useful for business decisions. See the next chapter for the reasons why.
14. Mill, op. cit., p. 105.

alternatives needs to be measured. The two sums are then netted and the ethically correct action is the one that produces the greatest net positive balance or the least negative balance of pleasure over pain. Furthermore, in the same way that an investor is indifferent between two investments that each has the same level of risk and return, two alternatives would each be ethically correct if they both have the same net arithmetic score and each of these scores is higher than the scores of any of the other alternatives that are available to the decision maker.

Rule utilitarianism is somewhat simpler. It recognizes that human decision making is often guided by rules. For example, most people believe that it is better to tell the truth than to lie. Although exceptions are acknowledged, truth telling is the standard of normal ethical human behavior. So, the guiding principle for a rule utilitarian is: follow the rule that tends to produce the greatest amount of pleasure over pain for the greatest number of people who will probably be affected by the action. Truth-telling normally produces the greatest pleasure for most people most of the time. Similarly, accurate, reliable financial statements are extremely useful to investors and creditors in making investment and credit decisions. False financial statements are not useful since they lead to incorrect financial decisions. The rule "financial statements should fairly reflect the financial position of the firm" should produce the greater amount of happiness for investors than the alternative rule "financial statements should be falsified." Truth-telling and candor normally produces the best consequences and so these are the principles that should be followed.

| **Means & Ends** | Before identifying some of the problems with utilitarianism, we must understand what the theory is not. The principle—promote the greatest amount of happiness for the largest number of people—does not imply that the end justifies the means. The latter is a political theory not an ethical principle. The foremost proponent of this political philosophy was **Niccolò Machiavelli (1469–1527)**, who wrote the *Prince* for Lorenzo Medici as a primer on how to maintain political power. In it he advised that "in the actions of men, and especially of princes, from which there is no appeal, the end justifies the means."[15] The state, as sovereign power can do whatever it wishes, and the prince, as ruler of the state, can use any political strategy in order to maintain power. Machiavelli was quite clear that duplicity, subterfuge and deception are acceptable means for a prince to maintain control over the populous and his rivals. A "prince, and especially a new prince, cannot observe all those things which are considered good in men, being often obligated, in order to maintain the state, to act against faith, against charity, against humanity, and against religion."[16] Clearly, this is a political theory, and a questionable one at that; but it is not an ethical theory.

Unfortunately, "the end justifies the means" is often taken out of context, and incorrectly used as an ethical theory. In the movie *Swordfish*, Gabriel, played by John Travolta, poses the following to Stanley, played by Hugh Jackman: "Here's a scenario. You have the power to cure all the world's diseases but the price for this is that you must kill a single innocent child, could you kill that child, Stanley?" The decision that is called for is unethical because it offends the significant rights of one or more individuals; but by phrasing the question this way, Gabriel is trying to give ethical justification to a political statement. He is attempting to lead Stanley into saying that the action is justified because more are saved with the sacrifice of one. This may be an extreme example, but the decisions of CEOs often have profound impacts on the lives of other people. Toxic waste, hazardous products and working conditions, pollution, and other environmental problems are

15. Machiavelli, Niccolò. *The Prince and the Discourses*, with an introduction by Max Lerner, The Modern Library, New York, 1950, p. 66.
16. Ibid., 65.

often defended on the basis that the end justifies the means. This principle is also used to defend cheating by university students, abuses of power by some CEOs, and the betrayal of their corporate responsibilities by some boards of directors.

However, a rule-utilitarian would say that there are some classes of actions that are manifestly right and wrong regardless of their consequences as either good or bad. Pollution and hazardous products do not increase the overall long-term well-being of society. The killings of innocent children, the extraction of excessive perquisites by opportunistic CEOs, and boards that ignore their firm's corporate codes of conduct are never ethically correct behaviors, regardless of the consequences. Each of these actions is wrong because these sorts of actions have an obvious negative effect on the general happiness of society as a whole.

The political principle—the end justifies the means—is not an ethical theory. First, it incorrectly assumes that means and ends are ethically equivalent, and second it incorrectly assumes that there is only one means to achieving the end. Take the case of two executives who collude to falsify a set of financial statements. The one because she will receive a bonus based on the firm's reported net income. The other executive conducts the fraud in order to forestall bankruptcy believing that if the firm continues in business then the staff will have employment, customers will be able to purchase the firm's products, and suppliers will still be able to make sales to the firm. Their means are both the same, they perpetrate a financial statement fraud. But their ends are different: the former is from pure economic selfishness; the other is from a misguided sense of loyalty to the firm's various stakeholders. Most would view these two individuals as dissimilar despite the similar means to obtaining their different ends. The two motivations or ends—economic selfishness and misguided altruism—and the one means—fraud—are not ethically equivalent. Most would view the means as wrong, have antipathy for the one executive and perhaps some sympathy for the latter executive.

More important, the end justifies the means often implies that either there is only one means to achieving the end or that if there are a variety of means to achieving the end, then all the means are ethically equivalent. But this is not the case. There are many ways of traveling across the country, but the costs vary with the mode of transportation. They are not equivalent. Similarly, there are various ways of temporally forestalling bankruptcy, one of which is to perpetrate a financial statement fraud. But there are other alternatives, including refinancing. Although refinancing and fraud may lead to the same end, the two means are ethically quite different. The one is ethically correct and the other is not. It is the job of the manager to be able to see this difference, and then to use her/his moral imagination to identify an alternative means to achieving the same end.

Some people misuse utilitarianism by saying that the end justifies the means. But this is an inappropriate application of an ethical theory. For a utilitarian, the end never justifies the means. Instead, the moral agent must consider the consequences of the decision in terms of producing happiness, or in terms of the rule that if followed will probably produce the most happiness for all. The overall appeal of utilitarianism is that it appears to be quite simple whereas the full consideration of all consequences is challenging if a comprehensive result is desired. It uses a simple standard: the goal of ethical behavior is to promote happiness. It is also forward looking; it concentrates on the future happiness of those who will be affected by the decision. It also acknowledges the uncertainty of the future, and so it focuses on probable consequences. Finally, the theory is expansive and unselfish; the best ethical alternative is the one that promotes the greatest pleasure for all concerned. This may be why the theory resonates with business people. Managers are accustomed to making decisions under conditions of uncertainty, assessing the probable consequences to identifiable stakeholders and then choosing the alternative that probably will have the best net results for all concerned parties. However, the theory is not without its problems.

| **Weaknesses in Utilitarianism** | Utilitarianism presupposes that such things as happiness, utility, pleasure, pain, and anguish can be quantified. Accountants are very good at measuring economic transactions, because money is a uniform standard of measurement. Almost all economic transactions can be measured in a currency, for examples, euros, and everyone knows what one euro will purchase. However, there is no common unit of measurement for happiness, nor is one person's happiness the equivalent of another person's happiness, whereas one euro means the same to both. And money is an inadequate proxy for happiness. Not only does money not buy happiness, it cannot capture the degree of happiness felt when sitting on the shores of a favorite lake watching the sunset on a warm summer evening or the pleasure in seeing the smile on the face of a mother holding her newborn.

Another problem concerns the distribution and intensity of happiness. The utilitarian principle is to produce as much happiness as is possible and to distribute that happiness to as many as is possible. Raphael uses the example of alms giving.[17] You can give $50 each to two old-age pensioners, who can then buy two warm sweaters. Or, you can give 100 pensioners enough money for a cup of coffee each. The intensity of the happiness is surely greater for the two pensioners who receive warm sweaters. But more people are positively affected by distributing $1 so that each pensioner can all buy a cup of coffee. Which alternative should you choose? The utilitarian principle is too vague to be useful in this instance. Should a CEO increase wages by 0.05 percent across the board, which would make all the employees slightly better off and presumably a bit happier, or should the CEO double the salaries of the top management team, thereby greatly increasing the general happiness of seven vice presidents? Assuming the net arithmetic happiness of both options is the same (regardless of how the happiness and unhappiness of the employees is measured), are both options equivalent? Is there not the perception of injustice in the latter? Utilitarianism can often appear to be as cold and unfeeling as Machiavelli's advice on the use of naked political power.

Another measurement problem concerns scope. How many people are to be included? Only those who are alive? If not, then for how many future generations? Consider the problems of global warming and pollution. The short-term happiness of current generations may come at the pain of future generations. If future generations are to be included, then the overall amount of happiness must increase greatly to accommodate enough happiness being available to be allocated to both this and subsequent generations. Furthermore, is the timing of the happiness important? Assuming that the net scores are the same regardless of the ordering, is happiness today and pain tomorrow the same as pain today and happiness tomorrow? Are we willing to have exorbitant fuel costs today and the associated economic pain so that there will be adequate fuel supplies for future generations?

This point is clearly illustrated by Al Gore in his book and video, *An Inconvenient Truth*, in which he identifies how pollution is leading to global warming, and that we are reaching a point where rejuvenation of our environment may not be possible. This conclusion is the same as that developed by a United Nations study[18] in the late 1980s.

Minority rights may be violated under utilitarianism. In a democracy, the will of the majority rules on Election Day. People are comfortable with this because those who lose in one election always have the chance of having their party come into power in the next election. It is not as simple with ethical decision making. Consider the following example. There are two options available that will affect only four people. The one action will create two units of

---

17. Raphael, D. D. *Moral Philosophy*, Oxford University Press, Oxford, 1981, p. 47.
18. The Brundtland Report, *Our Common Future*, United Nations World Commission on Environment and Development, NY, 1987.

happiness for each of the four people. The other alternative will create three units of happiness for three people and no happiness nor unhappiness for the fourth person. The second alternative generates more happiness (nine units) versus eight units under option one. However, under the second alternative one individual receives no happiness. In this case, unlike the election example, there is no possibility of waiting for a subsequent opportunity for another distribution of happiness in which that person might share. Is it fair, that one individual does not get to share in any happiness? Ethical decision making under utilitarianism may be perceived as unfairly benefiting some stakeholder groups at the expense of other stakeholder groups.

Utilitarianism ignores motivation and focuses only on consequences. This leaves many people unsatisfied. Consider the previous example of the two executives who fraudulently issue a set of financial statements. The motivation of the two executives is quite different. Many would consider that they have different degrees of ethical culpability, with the bonus-based executive acting worse than the misguided altruist. However, utilitarianism would judge both as equally ethically remiss because the consequence of their decision is the same, a financial statement fraud. This is an example of the saying: "The road to hell is paved with good intentions." Utilitarianism by itself is insufficient to produce a comprehensive ethical decision. To overcome this problem, an alternative ethical theory, deontology, assesses ethicality on the motivation of the decision-maker rather than on the consequences of the decision.

Deontological Ethics—Motivation for Behavior

Deontology[19] evaluates the ethicality of behavior based on the motivation of the decision-maker, and according to a deontologist an action can be ethically correct even if it does not produce a net balance of good over evil for the decision maker or for society as a whole. This makes it a useful complement to utilitarianism because an action that satisfies both theories can be said to have a good chance of being ethical.

Immanuel Kant (1724–1804) provided the clearest articulation of this theory in his treatise *Groundwork of the Metaphysics of Morals.* For Kant, the only unqualified good is a good will, the will to follow what reason dictates regardless of the consequences to oneself. He also argued that all our moral concepts are derived from reason rather than from experience. A good will manifests itself when it acts for the sake of duty, where duty implies a recognition and adherence to a law or precept. It says "in this situation I ought to do such and such," or "in this situation I should refrain from doing such and such." The assertions that this is what I ought to do, or that this is what I ought not to do are absolutely binding and permit no exceptions. This sense of acting out of a sense of duty is unique to mankind. Everything in nature acts according to the laws of nature, but only humans can act according to the idea of a law, that is, in accordance with rational principles.

For Kant, duty is the standard by which ethical behavior is judged. Moral worth exists only when a person acts from a sense of duty. You are acting correctly when you follow your ethical duties and obligations, not because they might lead to good consequences, and not because they might increase your pleasure or happiness, but rather you do them for duty's sake. It is the motive of duty that gives moral worth to the action. Other actions may be based on self-interest or on a consideration for others. When you deal honestly with your customers because you want their repeat business, you are acting out of self-interest rather than from duty. Acting in this way may be praiseworthy but it lacks moral worth. According to deontologists, it is only when you act out a sense of duty that you are acting ethically.

---

19. Derived from the Greek word *deon*, meaning duty or obligation, deontology has to do with one's ethical duties and responsibilities.

Kant developed two laws for assessing ethicality. The first is the *Categorical Imperative.* "I ought never to act except in such a way that I can also will that my maxim should become a universal law."[20] This is the supreme principle of morality. It demands that you should only act in a manner such that you would be prepared to have anyone else who is in a similar situation act in a similar way. It is an imperative because it must be obeyed, and is categorical because it is unconditional and absolute. It must be followed even if obedience is contrary to what you would prefer to do. A rational principle or moral law is being laid down for everyone to follow, including you.

There are two aspects to this categorical imperative. First, Kant assumes that a law entails an obligation, and this implies that an ethical law entails an ethical obligation. So, any ethical action that an individual is obligated to perform must be in accordance with an ethical law or maxim. This means that all ethical decisions and behavior can be explained in terms of ethical maxims, that is, in terms of laws that must be obeyed. The second part of the imperative is that an action is ethically correct if and only if the maxim that corresponds to the action can be consistently universalized. You must be willing to have your maxim be followed by anyone else who is in a similar kind of situation, even if you would be adversely affected personally because that other individual followed and obeyed your maxim. You are not allowed to make yourself an exception to the rule.

Kant uses the example of breaking promises. Assume that you want to break a promise. If you do so, then you are making that a maxim that can be followed by other people. But if others follow that maxim then you may be taken advantage of when they break their promises to you. So, it would be illogical to say that everyone else should keep their promises except for you. You cannot say that it is acceptable for you to lie to your investors about the quality of your firm's financial statements, while also saying that it is unacceptable for other's to falsify their financial statements because you might lose your investment if you unwittingly rely on their false financial reports.

Kant's second rule is a *Practical Imperative* for dealing with other people. "Act in a way that you always treat humanity, whether in your own person or in the person of any other, never simply as a means, but always at the same time as an end."[21] For Kant, laws have universal application, and so the moral law applies without distinction to everybody. This means that everyone must be treated equally under the moral law. In the same way that you are an end, an individual with moral worth, so also is everyone else. They, too, must be treated as ends in themselves, as individuals of moral worth. Hence, you cannot use them in a way that ignores their moral worth in the same way that you cannot ignore your personal moral worthiness.

The practical imperative does not suggest that you cannot use people, but simply that if you treat them as means then you must simultaneously treat then as ends. For example, a professional accountant employs accounting students. The hourly billing rate that is charged to clients for the students' work is considerably more than the rate being paid to the students. The professional accountant reaps the benefits of the students' labor, and they are a means to the accountant's financial prosperity. Is this an unethical relationship?

An old-time master-slave relationship treated the slave as a means and not as an end. The slave is considered to have no moral worth, no desires and unable to make choices. On the other hand, a healthy employer-employee relationship treats the employee with respect and dignity as both a means and an end. It recognizes that the employee has the power to make choices and decisions, including ethical ones, and that these decisions have the potential to

---

20. Kant, Immanuel. *Groundwork of the Metaphysic of Morals,* translated with an introduction by H. J. Paton, Harper, New York, Torchbooks, 1964, p. 17.
21. Ibid., pp. 66–67.

influence the employee, as well as others, such as the client, the client's personnel and the employer.

Everyone is entitled to pursue their own personal goals as long as they do not violate the practical imperative. This is the *Kantian Principle*. Treating others as ends acknowledges that we are all part of society, part of a moral community. In the same way that I am to act positively toward my own ends, I also have a duty to act positively toward their ends. So, I treat my employees as ends when I help them fulfill their desires (to learn accounting and have employment) while accepting that they are as able as I to make ethical decisions that may have an impact on society, on our moral community.

| **Weaknesses in Deontology** | Just like other ethical theories, deontology has its problems and weaknesses. A fundamental problem is that the categorical imperative does not provide clear guidelines for deciding what is right and wrong when two or moral laws conflict and only one can be followed. Which moral law takes precedent? In this regard, utilitarianism may be a better theory, since it can evaluate alternatives based on their consequences. Unfortunately, with deontology, consequences are irrelevant. The only thing that matters is the intention of the decision-maker and the decision maker's adherence to obey the categorical imperative while treating people as ends rather than as a means to an end.

The categorical imperative sets a very high standard. For many, it is a hard ethic to follow. There is no shortage of examples in which people are not treated with respect and dignity, where they are seen as merely tools in the production cycle to be used and then discarded after their usefulness is gone. Firms have suffered customer boycotts for using sweatshop labor, or underage workers, or failing to provide a living wage, or for outsourcing to repressive regimes. Kathie Lee Gifford's clothing line sold by Wal-Mart suffered serious consequences in 1996 when it was revealed that her products were manufactured in sweatshops. So also did Nike. To live up to the Kantian ideal means acknowledging that we are all part of a moral community that places duty above happiness and economic well-being. Business might very well be better off if more managers follow their ethical duties, and follow them simply because they are their ethical duties. However, following one's duty may result in adverse consequences, such as an unjust allocation of resources. As such, many argue that instead of focusing on consequences and intentions or motivations, ethics should instead be grounded in the principles of justice and fairness.

| Justice & Fairness—Examining the Balance

The English philosopher **David Hume (1711–1776)** argued that the need for justice occurs for two reasons: people are not always beneficent and there are scarce resources. In keeping with the English empiricist tradition, Hume believed that society was formed through self-interest. Since we are not self-sufficient, we need to cooperate with others for our mutual survival and prosperity (i.e., to engender the support of our stakeholders). However, given a limited number of resources, and the fact that some can benefit at the expense of others, there needs to be a mechanism for fairly allocating the benefits and burdens of society. Justice is that mechanism. It presupposes that people have legitimate claims on scarce resources and that they can explain or justify their claims. This, then, is the meaning of justice, to render or allocate benefits and burdens based on rational reasons. There are also two aspects to justice, procedural justice (the process for determining the allocation) and distributive justice (the actual allocations).

| **Procedural Justice** | Procedural justice concerns how justice is administered. Key aspects of a just legal system are that the procedures are fair and transparent. This means that everyone is treated equally before the law and that rules are impartially applied. Preference is not given to one person based on physical characteristics (ethnicity, gender, height, or hair

color) nor on social or economic status (the law is applied in the same way to both the rich and poor). There should be a consistent application of the law both within the legal jurisdiction and over time. Also, justice is to be assessed based on the facts of the case. This means that the information used to assess the various claims needs to be relevant, reliable, and validly obtained. Finally, there must be the right of appeal; the one who looses the claim should be able to ask a higher authority to review the case in order that any potential miscarriage is corrected. Both the assessment of the information used for the allocation, and the ability to appeal, depend upon the transparency of the process. These are the characteristic of blind justice where all are treated fairly before the law. Both sides present their claims and reasons, and the judge decides.

How does this apply to business ethics? In a business setting, procedural justice is not normally an important issue. Most organization's have standard operating procedures that are clearly understood by all employees. The procedures may be right or wrong, but, because they are the standards, they are normally consistently applied. As such, most employees are willing to present their case to an ombudsperson or senior official or even a subcommittee of the board of directors and let that person or committee then rule on the matter. Once a decision is taken, or a new policy is established, most employees are willing to adhere to it because they feel that their alternative position was given a fair hearing. (See the case "Team Player Problems" at the end of Chapter 6 for a dilemma concerning procedural justice.)

Distributive Justice

Aristotle (384–322 B.C.) may very well have been the first to argue that equals should be treated equally, and unequals should be treated unequally in proportion to their relevant differences. "This, then, is what the just is—the proportional; the unjust is what violates the proportion."[22] The presumption is that everyone is equal. However, if someone wants to argue that two people are not equal, then the burden of proof is on demonstrating that, in this situation, they are unequal based on relevant criteria. An example would be if a prospective employee was confined to a wheel chair, but otherwise able to perform normal duties. Would it be unethical (unfair) not to hire the worker, or would it be more ethical to provide wheelchair access to the work station?. Another example is equal pay for equal work. After years of blatant discrimination, pay equity legislation has now guaranteed that both men and women are paid the same wage for the same job.

By contrast, if they are not really equal then they should not be treated equally. Pay differentials are just if they are based on real differences, such as training and experience, education, and differing levels of responsibility. A new lawyer is not paid as much as the more experienced senior partner of the firm. Although they both have the same formal law school training, the older partner has a deeper well of experience to draw on, and so should be able to make quicker, better, and more accurate decisions than the less experienced junior.

Under distributive justice there are three main criteria for determining the just distribution: need, arithmetic equality, and merit. The taxation systems in most developed countries are based on need. The rich, who can afford to pay, are taxed so that funds can be distributed to the less fortunate in society. From those who have to those who have not. Distributive justice based on need is not common within a business setting. However, it would be logical for a company's budget process to be based on fair allocations of scarce resources in order not to risk the demotivation of the executives and employees in the disenfranchised units. Another instance

22. Aristotle. *The Nicomachean Ethics*, translated with an introduction by David Ross, revised by J. L. Ackrill and J. O. Urmson, Oxford University Press, Oxford, 1925, p. 114.

would involve the consideration of what might be a fair profit to leave in the country where it is earned, rather than use transfer pricing techniques to redistribute it to a tax haven to minimize overall enterprise tax paid.

Another distribution method is based on arithmetic equality. For example, in order to ensure an equal distribution of a cake, have the person who cuts the cake get the last piece. Assuming that everyone is just as eager to share in the cake, and that everyone would prefer to get a larger than a smaller piece, then the person cutting will make sure that all pieces are of an equal size so that the first piece is no different than the last, the one that goes to the cake cutter. Unequal distributions are deemed to be unjust.

In a business setting, the principle of arithmetic equality can be considered violated when a firm has two classes of shares that have equal rights to dividends (cash flow rights) but unequal voting rights (control rights), and therefore unequal rights to control the destiny of their cash flow rights. Many companies in Germany, Canada, Italy, Korea, and Brazil have dual class shares for which cash flow rights do not equal control rights. In Canada, for example, the Class A shares normally may have ten votes each and the Class B shares have only one vote each. In this way, a shareholder can have, say, 54 percent of the control rights through ownership of the Class A shares, while having only 14 percent of the cash flow rights based on the total number of Class A and Class B shares outstanding. Such a Class A shareholder is called a minority controlling shareholder, and may unjustly take advantage of the other shareholders. The minority (controlling) shareholder can always out vote any objection of the majority shareholders. (For an example of an opportunistic minority controlling shareholder see the case "Lord Conrad Black's Fiduciary Duty?" at the end of Chapter 5.)

Another distribution method is based on merit. This means that if one individual contributes more to a project then that individual should receive a greater proportion of the benefits from the project. Shareholders who own more shares are entitled to receive more dividends in proportion to their larger share holdings. Merit pay is another example. Employees who contribute more to the financial prosperity of the firm should share in that prosperity, often in the form of a bonus. Bonuses based on financial performance are quite common. Unfortunately, such merit based plans can also encourage directors, executives, and employees to artificially increase net income in order to receive a bonus. Bernie Ebbers needed to hide operating losses suffered by WorldCom so that his company's stock price would remain high to forestall having to pay margin calls on his WorldCom shares that were secured by those same WorldCom shares. (See the case "WorldCom: The Final Catalyst" at the end of Chapter 2.)

In terms of distributed justice, perceptions are critical. For example, if an employee feels that he is being underpaid then he might begin to shirk his duties and not put in his full effort. The perception that an employee is not receiving his just deserts may have adverse consequences for the firm. People who steal company assets will often justify their illegal behavior on the basis that they deserve the money that they defraud from their employers. (See Chapter 4 for a discussion of the rationalizations used by people to justify unethical behavior.) Employees might feel that they have been unjustly treated when favoritism is shown. When the brother-in-law of the owner of the company is made a vice president even thought he lacks the requisite qualifications, employees often feel that the appointment was unfair or unjust. Transfer pricing may also be perceived to be unfair. One divisional manager, for example, may not consider it fair that she has to pay a high internal price for an overhead item, when the same item can be bought outside the corporate entity at a lower cost. She may be loath to have her highly profitable division subsidize an overhead division that generates no revenue for the firm. Although this internal redistribution of profits may be just, the manager may not consider it fair, especially if she has a merit-pay bonus based on the reported net income of her division.

· | Justice as Fairness | One of the problems with distribute justice is that the allocations may not be fair. The American philosopher **John Rawls (1921–2002)** addressed this issue by developing a theory of justice as fairness. In *A Theory of Justice*, he presents an argument grounded in the classical position of self-interest and self-reliance. No one can ever get all the things one wants because there are other people who will prevent this from happening for they, too, may want the same things. Therefore, there is a need for everyone to cooperate because that is in everyone's best interest. As such, society can be seen as a cooperative arrangement for mutual benefit; it is a venture that balances conflicts of interests with identity of interests. There is an identity of interests since cooperation makes for a better life for everyone. However, human nature, being that each person would prefer to receive a larger share of the benefits and a small share of the burdens, creates a conflict of interest on how the benefits and burdens of society should be allocated. The principles that determine a fair allocation among the members of society are the principles of justice. "The concept of justice I take to be defined, then, by the role of its principles in assigning rights and duties and in defining the appropriate division of social advantages."[23]

Using the philosophical device of a hypothetical social contract Rawls asks: What principles of justice would free and rational people choose under a veil of ignorance? The veil of ignorance means that the people setting these principles do not know in advance their place in society (class, social status, economic and political situation, gender, ethnicity, or which generation they belong to), their primary goods (rights, liberties, powers, and opportunities), nor their natural goods (health, vigor, intelligence, imagination, and the like). "It is a state of affairs in which the parties are equally represented as moral persons and the outcome is not conditioned by arbitrary contingencies or the relative balance of social forces."[24] Justice as fairness means that whatever principles they agree to in this initial state would be considered fair by all. Otherwise, there would be no agreement on the terms of the social contract.

Rawls believes that in this hypothetical initial state people would agree on two principles: that there should be equality in the assignment of basic rights and duties; and that social and economic inequalities should be of benefit to the least advantaged members of society (the *Difference Principle*) and that access to these inequalities should be open to all (*fair equality of opportunity*). "First: each person is to have an equal right to the most extensive basic liberty compatible with a similar liberty for others. Second: social and economic inequalities are to be arranged so that they are both (a) reasonably expected to be to everyone's advantage, and (b) attached to positions and offices open to all."[25]

The *Difference Principle* recognizes that natural endowments are undeserved. Some people live in areas that have many natural resources; others are born into rich and privileged families; some are endowed with natural gifts or talents that are in high demand. No one person deserves or merits more than another simply because of these accidents of birth. That would be unjust. On the other hand, it is just for these people to use their natural gifts, talents and advantages not only for their own benefit, but also for the benefit of the less endowed. Under the principle of justice as fairness, what is right and fair is that everyone should benefit from social and economic inequalities.

For Rawls, the diffusion of benefits should be to everyone's benefit, and offices and positions within a firm should be open to everyone if they have the requisite talents and skill set. Started as a boutique manufacturer of ice cream in Vermont in 1978, Ben & Jerry's Homemade,

---

23. Rawls, John., Op. cit., 1971, p. 10.
24. Ibid., p. 120.
25. Ibid., p. 60.

Inc. found a niche in superpremium ice cream market in the 1980s. The company's founders, Ben Cohen and Jerry Greenfield, developed a managerial philosophy that embodies much of Rawls' Difference Principle. The company only used socially responsible suppliers, and 7.5 percent of pretax profits were distributed annually to projects of social change. They also imposed a five-to-one salary ratio, which was raised to seven-to-one in 1990. This meant that the highest paid employee could only receive a salary that was five times (later, seven times) greater than the lowest paid employee. There was also a salary floor; no employee's salary could fall below a fixed amount. It was initially set at $20,000 when the average *per capita* income in Vermont was $17,000. These corporate policies are an embodiment of the Difference Principle. Inequalities are acknowledged and recognized, but they are also used for the betterment of all, in this case for suppliers and employees living in Vermont. Positions of increasing responsibility within the firm are open to all. Compare Ben & Jerry's salary ratio with the huge salaries paid to most chief executive officers. In 2005 the average CEO in the United States was paid 262 times the average worker. Rawls would say that such discrepancy is justice only if paying an executive 262 times more helps the lowest paid employee within the firm. If not, then the high executive salary is unjust. "Thus it seems probable that if the privileges and powers of legislators and judges, say, improve the situation of the less favored, they improve that of citizens generally."[26] This means that remuneration structures as well as the privileges and powers of current CEOs should be designed to improve the welfare of all employees within the organization, and should be of benefit to society as a whole.

How do firms demonstrate justice as fairness? Consider the pharmaceutical company Merck & Co. and river blindness. River blindness (onchocerciasis) is a disease that is carried by parasitic worms that live in many rivers in Africa. The parasites can cause serve discomfort, often resulting in blindness. In 1978, Merck & Co. accidentally discovered a drug, mectizan, which cures river blindness. They offered the drug for sale to various African nations, but these impoverished counties said that they could not afford the drug. So, Merck & Co. said that they could have the drug for free. But these countries responded that they did not have a distribution system for getting the drug to the affected people often because they lived in remote areas. So, Merck & Co. set up their own distribution system for getting the drug to the people who needed it. Cynics might argue that Merck & Co. was distributing this as a lost leader to either generate goodwill or to promote the sale of its other pharmaceutical products. However, the people who were receiving mectizan are destitute; they will never be able to purchase any pharmaceuticals regardless of the manufacturer. So, Merck & Co. was now paying for producing and distributing a product that was generating no revenue for the firm, and would probably result in no additional sales of any of their other products. Was this a wise business decision? It may not have been economically prudent, but it was certainly just. They were helping some of the least advantaged. This is justice as fairness.

Rawls argues against utilitarianism since it may calculate and therefore deem unfair situations to be acceptable. He gives the example that a slave-owner might argue that, given the structure of his society, slavery is a necessary institution since the net pain to the slave might not outweigh the utility derived from the slave-owner from owing the slave. But slavery is wrong, not because it is unjust, but because it is unfair. It is not a situation where, under a veil of ignorance, both parties would agree that the practice is acceptable and to the benefit of the slave, the least advantaged person in the social contract. Multinationals operating in third world countries need to bear this in mind. Is the wage that they are paying fair? Is the wage to the benefit of everyone in society, including those who are not employed by the multinational? Is the wage

---

26. Ibid., p. 82.

structure a system that both parties would agree to if they were in the initial state? If not, the wage is not fair or just.

| **Virtue Ethics—Examining the Virtue Expected** | Virtue ethics draws its inspiration from the Greek philosopher **Aristotle (384–322 B.C.)**. In *The Nicomachean Ethics,* he explored the nature of a good life. He thought that the goal of life is happiness. This is not happiness in a hedonistic sense. Instead, happiness, for Aristotle, is an activity of the soul. We fulfill our goal of being happy by living a virtuous life, a life in accordance with reason. Now, virtue is a character of the soul that is demonstrated only in voluntary actions, that is, in acts that are freely chosen after deliberation. So, we become virtuous by regularly performing virtuous acts. But Aristotle also felt that there is a need for ethical education so that people will know what acts are virtuous.

Aristotle thought that we can understand and identify virtues by arranging human characteristics in triads, with the two extremes being vices and the middle one being a virtue. For Aristotle, courage is the mean between cowardice and rashness; temperance is between self-indulgence and insensibility. The other virtues of pride, ambition, good temper, friendliness, truthfulness, ready wit, shame, and justice can similarly be seen as the middle way between two vices. Virtue is the golden mean. This is not an arithmetic mean, but rather a path between extreme positions that would vary depending on the circumstances. You need to use your reason to identify the mean in each ethical situation and you become better at doing this with experience, by acting virtuously. Practice makes perfect.

Virtue ethics focuses on the moral character of the decision maker rather than the consequences of the action (utilitarianism) or the motivation of the decision maker (deontology). It adopts a more holistic approach to understanding human ethical behavior. It recognizes that there are many aspects to our personalities. Each of us has a variety of character traits that are developed as we mature emotionally and ethically. Once these character traits are formed they tend to remain fairly stable. Our personalities are many faceted and our behavior is reasonably consistent. Although we all have numerous, and often similar, virtues we demonstrate them in varying degrees, despite similar situations.

By focusing on the whole person, who has a unique combination of virtues, this theory avoids false dichotomies. It denies that the consequences of actions are either right or wrong, or that the motivation of the decision maker was either good or bad. In a business setting, virtue ethics eschews the notion that executives wear two hats; one hat representing personal values, and the other corporate values, believing that an executive can only wear one hat at a time. In 1988 two executives at Beech-Nut Nutrition Corporation were convicted of selling millions of bottles of apple juice that they knew contained little or no apples. Neils Hoyvald and John Lavery argued that they were being loyal corporate executives, making decisions that were necessary for the survival of the firm. Their crime, they contended, was at worst an error in judgment. At the same time as they were orchestrating a cynical and reckless fraud against babies, who were the consumers of their bogus apple juice, they were model citizens with impeccable records. The lawyer for Hoyvald described him as "a person we would be proud to have in our family." How many executives erroneously see themselves as wearing two hats; one for corporate values and the other for personal values? They forget it is the same head under each of the hats. Virtue ethics denies false dichotomies such as: it is either business or ethics; you can do good or be profitable; check your personal values at the door when you show up for work. The advantage of virtue ethics is that it takes a broader view recognizing that the decision maker has a variety of character traits.

| **Weaknesses with Virtue Ethics** | There are two interrelated problems with virtue ethics. What are the virtues that business people should have, and how is virtue demonstrated in

the workplace? A key virtue in business is integrity. Nearly one-third of the CFOs polled by Robert Half Management Resources[27] said that integrity was the most important quality for a business leader to possess. Integrity involves being honest and upstanding. For a firm, it means that the firm's actions are consistent with its principles. It is demonstrated by not compromising on core values even when there is strong pressure to do so. Consider the case of fund-raising by nonprofit organizations. Most organizations in the not-for-profit sector have very clear objectives: universities teach and conduct research; a hospice provides solace to the dying; a choir society trains children to sing. The driving force for many nonprofits is their core values as described in the organization's mission statement. A nonprofit demonstrates integrity by not accepting donations from individuals and organizations that have values that are opposed to the core values of the nonprofit. For example: a Cancer Society does not usually accept money from tobacco companies; Mothers Against Drunk Driving declined a donation from Anheuser-Bush, the brewery. Although they often need the funds, many nonprofits are not willing to compromise their core values and principles for money. (Also see the article "Managing for Organizational Integrity" at the end of Chapter 1.)

In 1982 the pharmaceutical company, Johnson & Johnson, withdrew Tylenol from the market, after a number of people in the Chicago area, who had taken Extra Strength Tylenol died. At the time of the crisis, Tylenol had 37 percent of the analgesic market, which contributed 7.4 percent to the company's gross revenues and 17 to 18 percent of its net income. Five bottles had been tampered, and the capsules injected with cyanide by a still unknown person. An internal investigation revealed that the problem had not occurred in the manufacturing process; the FBI, who was investigating the deaths, recommended that the product not be withdrawn because Johnson & Johnson was not at fault in the poisoning; and legal counsel advised against withdrawing the product lest it indicate culpability on the part of the firm. At the time, product recalls were extremely rare events. Nevertheless, the CEO James Burke withdrew the product because it violated the firm's mission statement. Written by Robert Woods Johnson in the 1940's, the credo of Johnson & Johnson is that the company's responsibilities are to the medical community, its customers and suppliers, its employees, the communities in which its people work, and to its stockholders. For Burke this was an easy decision. The company had to maintain the safety of its customers; Tylenol was an unsafe product; therefore, it had to be recalled. But, this was not an individual decision based on the values of a single executive. The decision was in keeping with the firm's values and organizational culture. How many other company's could demonstrate this level of integrity by voluntarily removing a profitable product and causing the stock price to fall simply because it violates the company's core values?

At the individual level, what are the important virtues that business people should have? Bertrand Russell thought that Aristotle's list was applicable to the respectable middle-aged since it lacked ardor and enthusiasm and seemed to be grounded on the principles of prudence and moderation. He may be right. The list may also represent the values of middle-class accountants. A recent attempt by Libby and Thorne to identify the virtues that public accountants hold dear came up with an Aristotelian-type list that included honesty, sincerity, truthfulness, reliability,

---

27. Robert Half Management Resources, "Honesty Still the Best Policy: CFO Survey Finds Integrity Most Desired Leadership Quality." May 31, 2007. Retrieved July 14, 2008 from http://www .roberthalfmr.com/portal/site/rhmr-us/template.PAGE/menuitem.31317bed3c331817 d775a81002f3dfa0/?javax.portlet.tpst=fa75a8924eee72a957946a5202f3dfa0&javax.portlet.prp_ fa75a8924eee72a957946a5202f3dfa0_releaseId=1856&javax.portlet.prp_fa75a8924eee72a 957946a5202f3dfa0_request_type=RenderPressRelease&javax.portlet.begCacheTok=com.vignette .cachetoken&javax.portlet.endCacheTok=com.vignette.cachetoken

dependability and trustworthiness.[28] However, the problem with virtue ethics is that we are unable to compile an exhaustive list of virtues. Furthermore, virtues may be situation specific. A public accountant may need courage when telling a CFO that her accounting policy does not result in the fair presentation of her company's financial statements. A CEO requires candor and truthfulness when explaining a potential downsizing to company employees and those who live in the community who will be adversely affected by a plant closing.

Many items on the list may be self-contradictory in certain circumstances. Should you tell the truth or be compassionate when dealing with a dying relative? Assume that you know that, as a result of adverse economic factors, your employer is going to lay off three employees at the end of next week. One of those employees tells you that she has just bought a new condominium and that although it is expensive, she can afford the mortgage payments because she has this good job. Do you tell her that she should not sign the agreement because she will be laid off next week (compassion) or do you remain silent because your boss told you the names of the employees in confidence (not betraying a trust)?

Moral Imagination

Business students are trained to become business managers, and business managers are expected to be able to make hard decisions. Managers are to be creative and innovate in the solutions that they come up with to solve practical business problems. They should be no less creative when it comes to ethical problems. Managers should use their moral imagination to determine win-win ethical alternatives. That is, decisions need to be good for the individual, good for the firm, and good for society.

This chapter has provided a background on the theoretical foundations to make ethical decisions. Chapter 4 will provide an ethical decision-making framework. Together these two chapters should help in allowing you to be creative and imaginative in solving and resolving ethical problems and dilemmas.

An Illustration of Ethical Decision Making[29]

Dealing with Disappointed Apple iPhone Customers

On September 5, 2007, Steve Jobs, the CEO of Apple Inc, announced that the spectacularly successful iPhone would be reduced in price by $200 from $599, its introductory price of roughly two months earlier.[30] Needless to say, he received hundreds of e-mails from irate customers. Two days later, he offered early customers who paid the full price a $100 credit good at Apple's retail and online stores. Was this decision to mitigate the $200 price decrease, and the manner of doing so, appropriate from an ethical perspective?

| **iPhone Analysis** | The ethicality of this iPhone marketing decision can be analyzed using different ethical theories, and interestingly, the conclusions are not the same. Ethical theories help to frame a question, and they help in highlighting aspects of the case that might be

---

28. Libby, Theresa and Thorne, Linda, "Auditors' Virtue: A Qualitative Analysis and Categorization", *Business Ethics Quarterly*, Vol. 14, No. 3, 2004.

29. Also see the Raiborn, Massoud, Morris, and Pier article "Ethics of Options Repricing and Backdating: Banishing Greed from Corporate Governance and Management" included as a Reading Insight at the end of this chapter. It provides an analysis of the issue of backdating stock options using the ethical theories outlined in this chapter. The Raiborn et al. article is also summarized and used in the Ethics Case "The Ethics of Repricing Stock Options" included at the end of this chapter.

30. David Ho, "Apple CEO apologizes to customers," *The Toronto Star*, September 7, 2007, B4.

overlooked if the case is analyzed in purely economic terms. The theories can also help in explaining and defending the option you ultimately choose. But, in the end, you must have the courage of your convictions and make a choice.

| **Utilitarianism** | Utilitarianism argues that the best ethical alternative is the one that will produce the greatest amount of net pleasure to the widest audience of relevant stakeholders. In this case, pleasure can be measured in terms of customer satisfaction. Presumably, the customers who bought the iPhone at both the higher and lower prices are satisfied with the product and so there is no product dissatisfaction. The only dissatisfaction is the affect among the customers who paid $599. They were upset that they paid $200 more than the current customers who were purchasing the identical product at $399. Steve Jobs received over a hundred emails in the two days after the price was dropped.

Does the dissatisfaction of the $599 group outweigh the satisfaction of the $399 group? Presumably, there are a larger number of customers purchasing the iPhone at the lower price, and so, all other things being equal, there will be a greater number of satisfied customers at the $399 price than the number of dissatisfied customers at the $599 price. So, the conclusion would be to do nothing.

However, utilitarianism requires that you examine the consequences to all stakeholders. The dissatisfied customers voiced their displeasure to Steve Jobs through their emails to him. This presumably lowered his feeling of satisfaction that he had a lot of happy Apple customers. These dissatisfied customers might also take their anger out at the sales representatives at the Apple stores. More important, they may show their dissatisfaction by not purchasing any additional Apple products. To mitigate this, Steve Jobs should offer rebates to the $599 customers that are equal to their level of dissatisfaction. That is, the rebates should be sufficient enough to ensure that these customers return to buy other Apple products rather than take their business to the competition.

| **Deontology** | Deontology looks at the motivation of the decision-maker rather than the consequences of the decision. Are you willing to make it a universal rule, that whenever prices fall all previous customers should be subsidized? The iPhone was launched in June 2007 at a price of $599 per unit. Customers willingly paid $599 for the product. Nevertheless, two months later, on September 5, the price was dropped to $399. Presumably, the costs of production had not decreased during the summer, and so, the $200 price reduction was because the iPhone was initially overpriced, even though customers were purchasing the product at $599 per unit.

Thus, the deontological question becomes: should rebates be given whenever products are incorrectly priced too high and the price is shortly thereafter lowered and the price reduction is not a result of product efficiencies? That is, is it ethically correct to compensate those who have been overcharged? It would appear that Apple thinks so, and as result the company was willing to give an in-store rebate to anyone who bought the iPhone at the higher price. If the company did not offer a rebate, then it would be treating its initial customers merely as a means of generating abnormal rents (i.e., profits). From a deontological perspective, a rebate should be offered because otherwise you are treating the first group of customers opportunistically, as a means to the company's end.

However, by offering a rebate, has the company set a bad precedent for itself? Every time the price of a product falls should all the customers who paid the higher price receive a rebate? Technological advances are so rapid that the manufacturing costs of electronics are constantly decreasing. As a consequence, the price of electronics tends to decrease over time. The iPhone version 2.0, launched in June 2008 one year after the original iPhone, has more features than the original phone and is priced at $199 per unit. Should all those who paid $399 for the original iPhone be given a rebate, too?

It is clear that the 2008 model is different from the original 2007 model. But what if the differences were not readily apparent to the consumer? Assume that the selling price decreases because of production efficiencies. Are you prepared to make a rebate every time the current price falls because the current costs of production have decreased? This may be the perception of Apple customers if the company begins to pay rebates.

Remember, from a deontological perspective the consequences are unimportant. What is important is that the decision was made for the right reasons. The fact that customers cannot differentiate between overcharging and production efficiencies is irrelevant. The only relevant aspect is that the decision maker knows the difference between overcharging and production efficiencies, and that the decision maker makes a rebate in the former case but not in the latter. The fact that the presence or absence of a rebate may influence future sales is irrelevant.

| **Justice & Fairness** | Distributive justice argues that equals should be treated equally and unequals should be treated unequal in relationship to their relevant inequalities and differences. Are all customers equal? This would depend on your timeframe. If you assume that there will be no repeat business from any customer, then they are not equal. A fair price is defined as one that a willing buyer and willing seller would accept in a noncoercive arm's length transaction. Assuming there was no undue sales pressure, then the customers who bought the iPhone at $599 thought that that was a fair price. The ones who bought the iPhone at $399, also, presumably, considered that to be a fair price. So, both groups were willing to pay fair value for the product at the time of purchase. There is no ethical reason to reverse those transactions. There were both at fair, albeit different, prices.

By contrast, if a business is attempting to establish an ongoing relationship with its customers, who will be buying numerous products over a long period of time, then all customers are equal. As such they need to be treated equally. This means that a business does not want to alienate any of its customer base and so it will offer a rebate to make everyone equal.

Rawls argues that social and economic inequalities are just if these inequalities are to everyone's benefit. This means that a price differentiation is just if it relates to production cost differences. Assume that the cash flow from the $599 sales were used to fund production efficiencies that permitted the company to maintain the same profit margin while reducing the price of the product to $399. If this had been the case, then the price inequality is to everyone's advantage. The higher price permitted the lower price to occur. However, the actual price decrease occurred two months after the launch of the product. Presumably, there were no production changes during the summer. So, this price differentiation is not to everyone's advantage and as such would not be considered just.

| **Virtue Ethics** | Virtue ethics focuses on the moral character of the decision maker. What values does Steve Jobs want his company to project? The website of Apple Inc. has separate web pages concerning responsible supplier management and Apple's commitment to the environment. The company projects an image of high quality with high ethical standards. The last thing this company wants is criticism that it is not behaving responsibly.

Two days after the price of the iPhone was dropped to $399 Steve Jobs publicly apologized for the pricing error and offered a $100 in-store rebate to those customers who had paid $599 for the product. What values is Steve Jobs demonstrating by making a public apology? By admitting his pricing error and atoning for the error by offering a rebate he is demonstrating rectitude. By being honest and straightforward in his apology, he is taking personal responsibility for the mistake.

On the other hand, you might say that he is not demonstrating integrity because he is recanting under pressure. This was not a free decision. He was reacting to public pressure. He had received hundreds of e-mails from irate customers. Furthermore, he waited two days before succumbing to the pressure. Instead, he should have demonstrated courage by not offering a rebate. He could have said that the $599 was a fair price at that time, and that $399 is a fair price at this time. No one was coerced into buying the product at either price.

| **Moral Imagination or Marketing Ploy?** | Moral imagination means coming up with a creative and innovate solution to an ethical dilemma. The price of the iPhone was dropped to $399 in order to better market the product during the holiday season. Was offering a $100 rebate an example of moral imagination, or was it simply another marketing ploy?

Both sets of customers paid fair value for their iPhones, which implies that no rebate should be offered. But, if a rebate should be offered, then presumably it should be for $200, thereby making the sales price to both sets of customers equal. So, the two options are to either provide no rebate or a $200 rebate. However, Apple chose a third alternative, not to give a rebate but instead to give a partial credit. The $599 customers were given a $100 in-store credit towards future purchases. Such a credit costs Apple far less than a cash rebate of $100. Furthermore, the $100 is half of the price decrease. So, if the $599 price was incorrectly set too high, and Jobs was truly contrite about his pricing error, then why did he not offer a full cash rebate of $200?

An argument can be made that Steve Jobs was willing to admit his pricing mistake, but he was not willing to suffer the full financial consequences of his error. By adopting this compromise position, he managed to deflect customer criticism without having to make an actual cash settlement. Cynics may say that this third option was mostly motivated by marketing concerns and very little by ethical concerns. That it was a marketing ploy to appease irate customers, and that Apple is appearing to be ethically responsible without having to bear the full economic consequences of its decision.

In conclusion, a decision maker would be wise to consider how consumers, employees, and others will react to a proposed decision. Will it fulfill their ethical expectations of what is right or wrong? Ethical theories can provide useful perspectives that should be weighed when arriving at an overall conclusion about the ethicality of the decision.

Questions

1. How would you respond when someone makes a decision that adversely affects you while saying, "it's nothing personal it's just business"? Is business impersonal?

2. Is someone who makes an ethical decision based on enlightened self-interest worthy of more or less praise than someone who makes a similar decision based solely on economic considerations?

3. Because happiness is extremely subjective, how do you objectively measure and assess happiness? Do you agree with J. S. Mill that arithmetic can be used to calculate happiness? Is money a good proxy for happiness?

4. Is there any categorical imperative that you can think of that would have universal application? Isn't there an exception to every rule?

5. Assume that Firm A is a publicly-traded company that puts its financial statements on the web. This information can be accessed and read by anyone, even those who do not own shares of Firm A. This a free-rider situation, where an investor can use Firm A as a means to making an investment decision about another company. Is this ethical? Does free-riding treat another as a means and not also as an end?

6. How does a business executive demonstrate virtue when dealing with a disgruntled shareholder at the annual meeting?

7. Commuters who have more than one passenger in the car are permitted to drive in a special lane on the highway while all the other motorists have to contend with stop-and-go traffic. Does this have anything to do with ethics? If so, then assess this situation using each of the following ethical theories: utilitarianism, deontology, justice, fairness, and virtue ethics.

Case Insights

- *Apple iPhone—Dealing with Disappointed Customers* is an illustrative application of the problem Apple Corporation encountered when it suddenly and dramatically decreased the price of its iPhone within months of introducing the product. The customers who bought the iPhone at the earlier and higher price were not pleased.

- *Terrorist Payments* presents the dilemma a CEO faces when a terrorist group "offers" to protect the company's South American personnel and operations. Should the company continue to make the payments even if they are immaterial in amount?

- *Disclosure of Non-Business-Related Crimes: Cesar Correia* tells the story of two entrepreneurs who start a business and then lose customers when the customers learn that one of the entrepreneurs has a criminal past. If the crime does not relate to business should it be disclosed? Does the other entrepreneur have the right to know about his partner's criminal past?

- *The Ethics of Repricing and Backdating of Employee Stock Options* addresses several issues concerning employee stock options. Do they actually motivate employees? Do they encourage earnings management? Is manipulating the timing of the granting of stock options in the best interest of the shareholders?

Reading Insights

Using four different ethical theories, Raiborn, Massoud, Morris, and Pier, analyze the ethics of repricing and backdating employee stock options.

References

Aristotle, *The Nicomachean Ethics*, translated with an introduction by David Ross, revised by J. L. Ackrill and J. O. Urmson, Oxford University Press, 1925.

Bentham, Jeremy. *An Introduction to the Principles of Morals and Legislation*, in *The Utilitarians*, Dolphin Books, 1961.

Carroll, Archie. "The Pyramid of Corporate Social Responsibility: Towards the Moral Management of Organizational Stakeholders," *Business Horizons*, Vol. 42, (1991), p. 39–48.

Encyclopedia of Philosophy, ed. Paul Edwards, Macmillan Publishing Co., Inc., 1967.

Frankena, William K. *Ethics*, Prentice Hall, 1963.

Gore, Al. *An Inconvenient Truth: The Planetary Emergency of Global Warming and What We Can Do About It*, Rodale, 2006.

Hobbes, Thomas. *Leviathan*, edited with an introduction by C. B. Macpherson, Penguin Books, 1968.

Hume, David. *A Treatise of Human Nature*, edited with an introduction by Ernest C. Mossner, Penguin Books, 1969.

Kant, Immanuel. *Groundwork of the Metaphysics of Morals*, translated with an introduction by H. J. Paton, Harper Torchbooks, 1964.

Libby, Theresa and Thorne, Linda. "Auditors' Virtue: A Qualitative Analysis and Categorization," *Business Ethics Quarterly*, Vol. 14, No. 3, 2004.

Levin, Hillel. *Grand Delusions: The Cosmic Career of John De Lorean.* Viking Press, 1983.

Machiavelli, Niccolò. *The Prince and the Discourses*, with an introduction by Max Lerner, The Modern Library, 1950.

Mackie, J. L. *Ethics: Inventing Right and Wrong*, Penguin Books, 1977.

MacIntyre, Alasdair. *After Virtue*, University of Notre Dame Press, 1981.

Mill, John Stuart. *Utilitarianism*, edited by Roger Crisp, Oxford University Press, 1998.

Raphael, D. D. *Moral Philosophy*, Oxford University Press, 1981.

Rawls, John. *A Theory of Justice*, Harvard University Press, 1971.

Russell, Bertrand. *A History of Western Philosophy*, Simon and Schuster, 1945.

Smith, Adam. *An Inquiry into the Nature and Causes of the Wealth of Nations*, edited with an introduction and notes by Kathryn Sutherland, Oxford University Press, 1993.

Smith, Adam. *The Theory of Moral Sentiments*, Regency Publishing, Inc., 1997.

Ethics Case

Terrorist Payments

Alex McAdams, the recently retired CEO of Athletic Shoes, was honored to be asked to join the Board of Consolidated Mines International Inc. Alex continues to sit on the Board of Athletic Shoes, as well as the Board of Pharma-Advantage, another publicly traded company on the New York Stock Exchange. However, CMI, as it is known, is a major step up for Alex.

CMI was formed as the United Mines Company in the 1870s, by an American railway magnate, and in 1985 it became Consolidated Mines International Inc. It operates mines in Central America and northern South America. In 2004, its revenues were approximately $4.5 billion and it employed about 25,000 people worldwide.

In deciding whether to accept the board seat, Alex conducted his own due diligence. As a result, there were two issues that he wanted to raise with Cameron Derry, the CEO of CMI. One concerned the allegations of questionable business practices. The other concerned the political instability in several of the Latin American countries in which the CMI mines are located. Today Alex was meeting with Cameron at the Long Bar Lounge.

During lunch Cameron candidly talked about the history of the company and the bad press that it often received. "In the 1920s we were accused of bribing government officials and using our political connections to have unions outlawed. In the 1950s we were accused of participating in the overthrow of a Latin American government. In the 1990s there were charges that we were exploiting our employees, polluting the environment, and facilitating the importation of cocaine into the U.S. But, none of these allegations has ever been proven in a court of law," said Cameron. "And we've even successfully sued one newspaper chain that published a series of these unproven stories about us.

"As for the political environment, Alex, you're right. There is no effective government in many of the countries in which we operate. In fact it is often the paramilitary that are in control of the countryside where we have our mines. These are very unsavory organizations, Alex. They have their own death squads. They have been involved in the massacre, assignation, kidnapping, and torture of tens of thousands of Latin Americans, most of them peasants and workers, as well as trade unionists and left-wing political figures."

"Do they interfere with CMI's operations?" asked Alex.

"No, and that's because we've been paying them off. It's now 2007 and we've been paying them since 1997. To date we've given them about $1.7 million in total. Don't look so shocked, Alex. Occasionally, we have to do business with some very unsavory characters. And the United Peoples Liberation Front that controls much of the region around our mines is probably the worst of the lot. They are involved in disappearances, murder, rape, and drug trafficking. The payments we make to them are for our protection. If we don't make these payments it could result in harm to our personnel and property."

"That's extortion!"

"We don't call it that. We list these payments as being for 'security services', but we have no invoices to support the payments, and beginning in 2002 we began making direct cash payments to them.

"But, we now have an additional problem. The United States government has declared the United Peoples Liberation Front to be a terrorist organization, and our outside legal counsel has advised us to stop making the payments. But if we stop I'm afraid of what might happen to our employees. I don't want to support drug trafficking and terrorism, but I need our mines to stay open.

"I'm telling you this, Alex, because if you join the Board, the first item on next month's agenda is these payments. I want the Board to approve that we continue to make these payments in order to ensure the safety of our Latin American employees and operations."

Questions

1. Should Alex join the Board of directors of Consolidated Mines International Inc.?

2. If Alex joins the Board, should he vote in favor of continuing to make the payments to the United Peoples Liberation Front?

3. What other options are available to Alex?

Ethics Case

The Case of Cesar Correia

In 1984, when he was eighteen years old, Cesar Correia murdered his father, killing him with a baseball bat. Cesar then dumped the body in the Assiniboine River. The body was eventually found, and Cesar confessed to the crime. He pleaded guilty to manslaughter and was sentenced to prison for five years.

Background His father, Joachim, was abusive to Cesar, to Cesar's brother, and to Cesar's mother. The judge said that Joachim was a cruel and abusive man whose home "was a living hell". The judge said, "I have no difficulty in concluding it instilled in the heart and mind of the accused a sense of devastation, desperation and frustration, which was consumed in a burning hatred for his father." Cesar argued that he was protecting his mother and younger brother.

The Murder Cesar and his father got into an argument while working on the family car. Cesar went and got a baseball and clubbed his father from behind, hitting him three or four times. He then got a smaller bat and hit him once or twice more. Cesar then wrapped the body in a blanket and put it and his bicycle in the family car. He drove to the Assiniboine River were he dumped the body in the river, leaving the car, and returning home on the bicycle. Both Cesar and his mother claimed that they did not know what happened to Joachim. Cesar helped in the search for his missing father. A few weeks later, the body was found by some children and Cesar quickly confessed to the police when questioned by them. He was initially charged with murder, but later pleaded guilty to manslaughter.

Afterwards While at prison he completed his university education, graduating from the University of Manitoba in 1989, with a Bachelor of Science degree in computer sciences and statistics. After he was released from jail, he moved to Toronto and began working in the information technology industry.

In Canada, people can apply for a pardon five years after the expiration of their sentence. They must have completed their sentence and demonstrated that they are law-abiding citizens. In 1996, twelve years after the murder and conviction, Cesar applied for and received a pardon which expunged his criminal record.

Infolink Technologies Ltd. In 1999 Cesar formed an information dissemination company, Infolink Technologies Ltd., with George Theodore. Infolink, of which Cesar was president, traded on the Toronto Stock Exchange until 2007 when it went private. The Ontario Securities Commission, that oversees the Toronto Stock Exchange, requires that all directors and officers of public companies disclose any criminal convictions and "any other penalties or sanctions imposed by a court or regulatory body that would likely be considered important to a reasonable investor in making an investment decision."

The Lawsuit In 2003 George resigned from the company and then sued Cesar for lost profits on two transactions. George contended that two customers backed out of deals when they found out about Cesar's conviction.

Questions

1. Ignoring any legal issues, was Cesar ethically obligated to inform his partner, George, of his criminal past?

2. Did George have a right to know about Cesar's criminal past?

| Ethics Case | *The Ethics of Repricing and Backdating Employee Stock Options* |

Employee stock options allow company executives to buy shares of their company at a specified price during a specified time period. They are given to executives as a form of noncash compensation. The option or "strike price" is normally equal to the market price of the stock on the day that the option is granted to the employee. The stock option is intended to motivate the executive to increase the stock price of the firm. If the stock rises, the investor is pleased. If the stock rises, the executive exercises the option, buys the stock from the company at the strike price and then immediately sells those shares on the stock exchange at the current (higher) market price to obtain a capital gain. This is considered to be a win-win situation. Both the investor and the employee gain from the increase in the market price of the company's stock.

However, sometimes the stock price falls and the current price is less than the strike price. Such stock options are referred to as "underwater" or "out of the money." In such cases, companies will sometimes reprice the stock options to a price that is less than the current market price, or cancel the underwater options and issue new options that are priced at the new current market price. Both repricing and backdating of stock options have effectively been curtailed as a result of Sarbanes-Oxley disclosure requirements. As a result two new strategies are available. One is to "spring-load" the options by issuing them to employees just before good news is announced to investors. The other is to "bullet-dodge" by delaying the granting of stock options until after bad news has been released.

An analysis of the ethics of repricing, backdating, spring-loading, and bullet-dodging is contained in the article "Ethics of Options Repricing and Backdating: Banishing Greed from Corporate Governance and Management," reprinted at the end of the chapter. In their article that was published in the October 2007 issue of *The CPA Journal*, Raiborn, Massoud, Morris, and Pier present four ethical arguments.

The *theory of justice* says that equals should be treated equally, and unequals treated unequally in proportion to their inequalities. All investors are equal, and executive investors should be treated no differently from all other investors in the company. As such, preferential treatment through the backdating of stock options is inappropriate and unethical. Spring-loading and bullet-dodging are grounded on management's inside knowledge of good and bad news that will have an impact on the company's stock price. Their inside knowledge discriminates against all the other shareholders who do not know the good or bad news.

Utilitarianism or consequentialism argues that the ethically correct decision must be of benefit to most shareholders in the long-term. Backdating stock options benefits the executive at the expense of the other shareholders. It is not in the best interest of the majority of the shareholders of the company. Spring-loading and bullet-dodging are only in the short-term interests of a minority of the shareholders (i.e., executive shareholders) and not in the best long-term interested of all the other (majority) shareholders.

From a *deontological* perspective, backdating and repricing are akin to lies because the intention is to manipulate and deceive the other shareholders. Deontology does not accept that the end justifies the means. Furthermore, it does not allow exceptions to a rule. Spring-loading and back-dating treat one category of shareholders (management) differently than the other category of shareholders (all the current and future shareholders). As such it is unlikely that everyone in society would accept as a universal rule that management should be given preferential treatment.

It is difficult to say that manipulating stock options, through any of these four tactics, is the sign of a virtuous person. *Virtue ethics* does not accept discrimination and prudential treatment of insiders as the mark of an ethical businessperson.

The conclusion of the article by Raiborn et al. is that the repricing of stock options may be legal but it is certainly unethical. Their concluding paragraph reads:

> Stock options were designed as a way to provide pay for performance, not to reward poor performance by backwards-looking repricing or backdating. Such activities undermine the incentive justification for use of stock option plans. Executives deserve compensation packages that provide both short-run benefits and a long-run motivation to increase organizational value for all stakeholders. Compensation methods that cause the tone at the top to be perceived as a cacophony of greed should be banished from the orchestra.

Questions

1. Do you think that stock options actually motivate employees to work for the long-term good of the company?

2. Do you think that stock options inadvertently encourage managers to engage in questionable accounting activities, such as earnings management, to artificially increase the company's net income and thereby the value of the executives stock options?

3. Do you agree or disagree with the four ethical arguments summarized above and contained in more detail in the article by Raiborn, Massoud, Morris, and Pier? Explain why.

4. Should a board of directors approve repricing or backdating stock options for outstanding executives whose current stock options are underwater due to uncontrollable economic factors, and who might be lured away unless some incentives to stay are created? What other incentives might work?

Reading | *Ethics of Options Repricing and Backdating: Banishing Greed from Corporate Governance and Management*

Cecily Raiborn, Marcos Massoud, Roselyn Morris, and Chuck Pier

OCTOBER 2007— Just when it seemed that America's corporate scandals had tapered off and public trust in executives was beginning to rebound, the media revealed two techniques that corporations were using to enhance management pay packages: the repricing and the backdating of stock options. Stock options have been used as a means of paying top-level employees since approximately 1957; they became extremely popular in the early 1980s for employees in the high-tech start-up companies of Silicon Valley.

Stock Options

Stock options allow employees to purchase a particular number of common shares of company stock at a specified price over a specified time period. The option or "strike" price was commonly set at the market price at the date of the option grant. Tying the option price to the market price benefited both the issuing company and the employee at the grant date: The company did not have to record any compensation expense for accounting purposes upon issuance; the employee did not receive a taxable benefit upon issuance and needed to pay taxes only when the exercised options were sold in the future. In the wake of FASB's issuance of Statement of Financial Accounting Standards (SFAS) 123(R), *Share-Based Payment*, all stock options must be recognized as compensation expense based on the option's fair value on the grant date. Even options with a strike price set at or below the stock's fair-market value on the grant date carry some value, and compensation expense must be estimated by the use of an option-pricing model.

Options were commonly issued to supplement the amount of executive non–performance-based cash compensation above the tax-allowed $1 million deductibility level, to provide executives with an "owner perspective," or to incentivize executives to work for (or remain at) an organization that was currently cash poor but had strong future prospects.

Essentially, stock options were designed to reward current performance with a future benefit when executives neither needed nor desired additional current cash. Because stock options could be cashed in and the shares subsequently sold, there always existed a motivation for executives with options to quickly boost the stock price, through fair means or foul. As some recent corporate scandals show, foul often meant manipulating financial statements to increase net income and, concurrently, stock prices. In addition to financial statement shenanigans, net income could also be increased by firing workers and closing plants—tactics well known to Al Dunlap, especially during his tenure as Sunbeam's chairman of the board. In other words, it is possible for executives to engineer opportunities for their stock options to rise in value.

Repricing Stock Options

When stock prices rise above a given option price, the expectation is that the managers who received such options will exercise them and become larger shareholders in the corporation. Such holdings should motivate executives to have a greater interest in making the entity ever more profitable, because personal and corporate performance objectives are aligned. The bull market of the 1990s brought substantial value to stock options, but when the market began a downturn, investor value dropped substantially. Although investor value dropped with share prices, the average CEO total compensation in American companies was higher in 2002 than in 1999 ("Leaders: Running Out of Options; Pay for Performance," *The Economist*, December 11, 2004). In other words, executive-owners continued to benefit from huge pay packages while investor-owners suffered from the downturn in the value of their stock portfolios. At least some decrease in portfolio values was a direct result of the market's reaction to the financial scandals created by the executive-owners of corporations.

As stock prices declined, the value of executives' stock options also fell. In many cases, the market price fell below the option price, meaning the option is "underwater" or "out of the money," making the original compensation benefit worthless.

One solution that some companies adopted was to reprice previously granted stock options to a price below the current market price. Disclosure of repricings for stock options held by "named executive officers" (generally the CEO and the other four most highly compensated executives) is required under Regulation S-K Item 402(i). In 2000, FASB Interpretation (FIN) 44, *Accounting for Certain Transactions Involving Stock Compensation*, determined that such repricings would require variable accounting treatment from the modification date. (Instead of repricing the options specifically, a company may also engage in "synthetic" or "6&1" repricing, which has no current income statement effect. In this technique, the company cancels the underwater options and replaces them with new options six months and one day later; the new options are set at the then-current market price.)

This variable accounting treatment would create a negative income statement impact equal to the number of repriced shares multiplied by the difference between the original option price and the year-end market price; the treatment would continue for each year until the options were exercised, forfeited, or cancelled. Therefore, the more the stock's market price rises after the repricing, the greater the reduction in future earnings. The executive benefits from the reduction in option price, but the company and the other non–stock-option-holding investors face a lowered net income, which, in turn, could generate a lower share price. Repricings effectively reward executives for corporate difficulties, rather than hold them accountable. In addition, if the company has to acquire treasury stock in the future to satisfy option holders upon exercise, the market activity could create an even higher price and greater gains to the exercising employee. Such gains would benefit all stockholders but could make potential new investors less able to acquire the higher-priced stock.

It is important to note that a company does not have to reprice all outstanding options, but "may tailor [its] repricings to include or exclude certain options and/or groups of employees or optionees" (P. Garth Gartrell, "Stock Options and Equity Compensation after the 'Crash,'" *Journal of Deferred Compensation*, Fall 2001). If options for high-level executives were repriced while those of lower-level employees were not (or were not repriced to the same degree), one might view such discriminatory treatment as unethical, given that the executives should be held responsible for the downturn in earnings that presumably precipitated the downturn in stock price.

Boards of directors have defended the repricing of executive stock options by stating that it helps retain executives who are essential to company performance. The authors believe that the issue that must be addressed in the face of this logic is how essential such executives actually are if they were the people in charge during the market decline. There is some evidence that the performance and retention rationales behind repricing are flawed. First, results from one study spanning five decades showed "no evidence of a systematic relationship between equity and firm performance" (Catherine M. Daily and Dan R. Dalton, "The Problem with Equity Compensation," *Journal of Business Strategy*, July/August 2002). Second, three separate studies indicated that "over the two-year period after repricing, CEO turnover [was] approximately twice as high for repricing firms compared to a matched group of firms that did not reprice" (Dan R. Dalton and Catherine M. Dalton, "On the Decision to Reprice Stock Options: Almost Never," Journal of Business Strategy, vol. 26, no. 3, 2005).

Backdating Stock Options

As discussed earlier, when stock options are issued, the strike price is typically set to equal the market price at the option date to avoid recording compensation expense and the incurring taxable income to the recipient. The results of a study by Erik Lie ("On the Timing of CEO Stock Option Awards," *Management Science*, May 2005) suggested that many stock option awards made during the period 1992 to 2002 were actually "timed retroactively"— dated to coincide with a low price, which then rose after the grant date. In 2006, Charles Forelle and James Bandler ("The Perfect Payday," *Wall Street Journal*, March 18, 2006) reported that all six of the option packages granted to Affiliated Computer Services Inc.'s

CEO Jeffrey Rich from 1995 to 2002 were dated at the bottom of a steep drop in stock price, with the odds of such an occurrence "around one in a billion." The SEC decided to look into the issue of backdating option prices, and by mid-2007 more than 140 companies were under investigation. The companies involved range from the low-tech to the high-tech, from the start-up to the well-established. Some companies came forth voluntarily; some were subpoenaed. Many are conducting their own internal investigations. It seems that the practice of backdating has been prevalent but hidden for quite a while.

Prior to 2002, a company was not required to report its issuance of stock options until after the close of the fiscal year, providing ample time to backdate options. Section 403 of the Sarbanes-Oxley Act (SOX) tightened the reporting requirements for the issuance of executive stock options; companies now must report options on Form 4 within two days of their issuance. This requirement should significantly reduce the opportunity for backdating, if companies comply with the new regulation. However, a recent study found that, from September to November 2002 (SOX was enacted in July 2002), one-fifth of companies were still not meeting the two-day requirement (Randall Heron and Erik Lie, "Does Backdating Explain the Stock Price Pattern Around Executive Stock Option Grants?" *Journal of Financial Economics*, February 2007). One would hope that such delays have been resolved since that study was conducted.

Another troublesome issue has arisen in companies' response to backdated stock options. According to Charles Forelle ("Executives Get Bonuses as Firms Reprice Options," *Wall Street Journal*, January 20–21, 2006), some companies (such as KLA-Tencor Corp.) that engaged in backdating have opted to adjust the executive options to reflect the price actually existing on the grant award dates, but have provided the executive with a cash "bonus" for the amount lost from repricing. Such a tactic could be seen as an extra reward to the executive, who obtains cash even if the stock prices fall from the bad publicity resulting from backdating: a win-win situation for the executive and a lose-lose situation for other shareholders.

Rather than accepting executive greed or poor organizational ethics as the crux of the problem, blame is now being partially placed on the same 1993 tax law that caused a surge in stock options by limiting the deductibility of executives' non-performance-based cash compensation to $1 million. According to SEC Chairman Christopher Cox (who was a member of Congress when the 1993 law was enacted) and Public Company Accounting Oversight Board (PCAOB) Chairman Mark Olson, this law "unintentionally sparked a trend ... for companies to get more creative with incentives for their executives" (Marie Leone and Sarah Johnson, "Backdating Blamed on 1993 Tax Rule," CFO, September 6, 2006, http://www.cfo.com). Some U.S. senators are now contending that the law should be repealed, that companies should be allowed to pay executives any amount, fully deductible for tax purposes.

It is obvious to the authors that the law did, in fact, prompt many companies to use stock options as a form of noncash compensation, but to infer that this justifies the backdating of options seems a huge leap of logic. Whether all cash compensation of CEOs should be tax deductible is an issue that should be addressed on its independent merits, or lack thereof, with a clear eye toward acknowledging the massive discrepancy that exists between worker pay and executive compensation in the United States. According to a *BusinessWeek* survey of large U.S. corporations, CEO pay rose from 107 times that of an average worker in 1990 to 431 times that of an average worker in 2004, with a multiple of 525 in 2000 (United for a Fair Economy, *The Growing Divide: Inequality and the Roots of Economic Insecurity*, February 2006; http://www.faireconomy.org/econ/workshops/workshop_pdfs/GD_Charts1.9.pdf#search=%22%20CEO%20pay%22). These relationships do not seem to indicate that the backdating of stock options was somehow necessary to provide a "reasonable" wage for CEOs!

The problem with options backdating is not just the improper benefit provided to the executives receiving the options, but also the detriment caused to other investors and to the organization's reputation. One study showed that backdating stock options added approximately $600,000 to the average executive's pay at 48 companies between 2000 and 2004, but the market value decline in those companies since the investigations into the practice began has been approximately $500 million, or more than $10 per share, on average (Eric Dash, "Report Estimates the Costs of a Stock Options Scandal," *New York Times*, September 6, 2006). In addition, companies are now facing potentially massive restatements that could reduce reported income, which would likely trigger further downturns in stock value. Shareholder and pension-fund lawsuits have been launched against some companies and are on the horizon for others. During 2006, despite a large decline in the total number of class-action lawsuits involving securities issues from the previous year, 20 suits related to options backdating were filed against companies (Nathan Koppel, "Legal Bear: Stock Class-Actions Fall," *Wall Street Journal*, January 2, 2007). Companies providing corporate directors and officers (D&O) insurance are also asking questions, attempting to determine whether premiums are sufficient or, in the event of illegal activities, whether coverage is in effect.

Spring-Loading and Bullet-Dodging

Because the SOX disclosure requirements make it essentially impossible to backdate stock options, some companies have turned to two other tactics to increase executive pay: spring-loading and bullet-dodging. Spring-loading refers to the practice of issuing options shortly before announcing good news to investors; bullet-dodging refers to delaying an option grant until after bad news has been reported. Some people are criticizing these techniques as being a form of insider trading or trading in the company stock by using non-public information that, if known by the general investing public, would significantly influence the company's stock price. SEC Commissioner Paul Atkins ("Remarks Before the International Corporate Governance Network 11th Annual Conference," July 6, 2006; http://www.sec.gov/news/speech/2006/spch070606psa.htm) disagreed that these tactics are equivalent to insider trading, in part because corporate boards always have "inside information" but cannot predict how the news will affect the investing public. Atkins believes that opportune timing of options grants merely provides the best benefit to the grantee at the least cost to the corporation.

Potentially, however, the issue could be viewed as an extension of Regulation Fair Disclosure, issued by the SEC in August 2000. Regulation FD's stated purpose is to curb selective disclosures by corporate boards and executives of material, nonpublic information to favor research analysts or portfolio managers before giving the information to the general public. Technically, the timing of options grants does not fall under Regulation FD; however, a case could be made that the end results are similar: Someone or some group benefits to the exclusion of others. In the case of selective disclosures, certain analysts and their clients benefit; in the case of option timing, certain inside executives benefit.

Using Indexing to Determine Option Price

Many people might argue that backdating and repricing have occurred because companies thought it was unfair to penalize executives for recent downturns in stock prices that were due to macroeconomic pressures and industry fluctuations beyond the control of CEOs. While backdating and repricing present questionable behaviors by corporate compensation committees, an alternative methodology—indexing stock options—might be viewed as more fair and effective in rewarding the highest-performing executives. In such a process, the board of directors would select a group of companies, such as industry rivals, to serve as a benchmarking peer group. The option-issuing company indexes or ties the exercise price to the benchmark group. In theory, economic and industry factors should affect similar companies in similar fashion. Thus, if share prices for the benchmark group rise by an average of 10% in a given year, then the option-issuing company's shares should rise comparably. If instead the company's shares rise 15%, then an assumption can be made that the executives provided a positive 5% controllable organizational impact and, as such, deserve additional performance-based pay. Indexed options cannot be exercised at a

profit unless the issuing company's stock price either outperforms, or falls less steeply than, its peer comparison companies. Schering-Plough began using performance-based indexed options as part (20%) of the stock-option compensation granted to its senior executives in 2005. Other companies using indexed stock options include Level 3 Communications, Chiron, Capital One, RCN Corp., Perceptron, and Nuvelo. Many other companies voted on adopting the use of indexed options in 2006, but few of those measures were approved.

Despite the inherent fairness in the indexing concept, many major U.S. companies oppose it. The authors believe this is so primarily because it would make one organization's compensation plan less attractive than those offered by competitors. A second possibility is that indexing could create more pressure to "do anything necessary" to outperform the index group and, potentially, lead to more corporate frauds. Consider the monetary benefits that would have been awarded to Enron executives had the company's performance been tied to any industry group! On the positive side, indexing would eliminate the situation in which CEOs are granted millions of dollars of options in a rapidly rising stock market when the companies led by those CEOs performed worse than competitors. Indexing would also stop the practice of repricing stock options.

Ethical Issues

Given the impetus for a positive "tone at the top," as well as the massive difference in pay between the upper and lower levels of employees in an organization, compensation committees should investigate how the stock option issue is judged from other, acceptable ethical frameworks. Such perspectives can serve as the basis for asking important questions when compensation packages are being awarded.

It was noted above that repricing options differently for different groups of grantees may be viewed as unethical. Using virtue ethics to gauge this tactic, the authors examined both the action and the reasons for taking a particular action as follows: If repricing is motivated by self-interest and by the company's interest in retaining the executive, then the action is unethical because the remaining stakeholders of the organization are not being considered or are being deceived by the process. The justice theory of ethics requires equals to be treated the same way but allows unequals to be treated differently; executives could be viewed as equals and all others could be viewed as unequals. As such, differential repricing between the two groups would be considered ethical and appropriate. Consider, however, that the Organization for Economic Cooperation and Development (OECD) and the International Corporate Governance Network (ICGN) state that boards should treat all shareholders of a corporation "equitably" and make certain "that the rights of all investors ... are protected" ("ICGN Statement on Global Corporate Governance Principles: OECD Principles as Amplified, Section II— The Equitable Treatment of Shareholders," http://www.icgn.org/organisation/documents/cgp/cgp_statement_cg_principles_jul1999.php). The international business community, in the form of the OECD and ICGN, provides no indication that executives should be viewed any differently from other shareholders. In remuneration guidelines adopted in July 2006, the ICGN stated that repricing stock options without shareholder approval should be considered "inappropriate" and that in "no circumstances should boards or management be allowed to back date grants to achieve a more favorable strike price (in the case of options)" (ICGN Remuneration Guidelines, http://icgn.org/organisation/documents/erc/guidelines_july2006.pdf).

Assessing options repricing and backdating from an ethical theory of rights perspective requires determining who is entitled (or has the right) to what. Investors and creditors who have provided funds to an organization have the right to receive accurate, reliable, and transparent financial statements. Optionsbackdating and repricing either ignore or do not consider that right of those investors and creditors, and, as such, these techniques would be seen as unethical. Any corporate officers who are CPAs must remember that the accounting profession's ethics place the public interest (investors and creditors) ahead of all other interests. Engaging in options backdating and repricing as a corporate employee, or an external auditor, with knowledge that such actions have taken place, would be unethical from a professional perspective.

Options backdating and repricing can also be viewed from a utilitarian perspective. The decision of whether the actions are ethical would be made by weighing the benefits to management as individuals and the perceived benefits to the company and its shareholders (via increases in share price) against the costs of the action and the long-term negative effects on investors and creditors of false and misleading financial information. From an ethical perspective, an individual who rationalizes an unethical action designed to increase the decision maker's wealth by claiming that the action benefits the company and its stakeholders has fallen victim to the rationalization part of the fraud triangle discussed in Statement on Auditing Standards (SAS) 99, *Consideration of Fraud in a Financial Statement Audit.*

The Kantian theory of ethics (named for the 18th-century German ethicist Immanuel Kant) directs one to act only as if the action were to become universal law. From this perspective, if stock option backdating and repricing were intended to manipulate or deceive any stakeholders, then the action would be considered a lie and could not be justified by Kantian ethics; the ends do not justify the means.

The issues of spring-loading and bullet-dodging can also be viewed from these three ethical standpoints. If one accepts the fiduciary responsibility of management to all organizational shareholders, then selectively timing the distribution of options places executives in a better position than other shareholders and, as such, discriminates against nonexecutive owners. The ethical theory of utilitarianism is violated by spring-loading and bullet-dodging because there are more market participants who are not executives than there are those who are executives. These two tactics also violate Kantianism: It is highly unlikely that the populace would agree that treating one category of market participants (executives) differently from another category (all other investors and potential investors) would be appropriate. In addition, if spring-loading and bullet-dodging are analyzed from the perspective of Aristotle's moral theory (i.e., an action is ethical if it is what a "virtuous" person would do under the circumstances), it is difficult to conclude that people of high virtue would knowingly engage in such a form of discrimination. Thus, although these two activities are undoubtedly legal, they are without question unethical—and the investing public has had its fill of the lack of business ethics!

New Reporting Requirements for Options

The manner in which stock options are recorded and reported has been a controversial subject since the 1972 issuance of Accounting Principles Board (APB) Opinion 25, *Accounting for Stock Issued to Employees.* More recent guidance, such as SFAS 123, *Accounting for Stock-Based Compensation*; SFAS 148, *Accounting for Stock-Based Compensation: Transition and Disclosure* (2002); and SFAS 123(R), *Share-Based Payment* (2004), has not settled the controversy.

SEC rules [conforming with SFAS 123(R)] now require that the entirety of each executive officer's compensation be shown in a single amount and that the policies and goals of the compensation programs be made in "plain English." Tabular compensation presentations must include the following:

▌ The SFAS 123(R) grant date and the fair value of the option on the grant date by officer;

▌ The closing market price on the grant date if that price is higher than the option exercise price; and

▌ The date that the board of directors (or compensation committee of the board) actually granted the options, if that date differs from the grant date.

According to SEC Chairman Christopher Cox (testimony given concerning options backdating, U.S. Senate Committee on Banking, Housing and Urban Affairs, September 6, 2006; http://www.sec.gov/news/testimony/2006/ts090606cc.htm), reports to investors must also describe "whether, and if so how, a company has

engaged (or might engage in the future) in backdating or any of the many variations on that theme concerning the timing and pricing of options. For example, if a company has a plan to issue option grants in coordination with the release of material nonpublic information, that [information] will now be clearly described." Thus, if the new SOX section 403 disclosure rules are adhered to completely, it is unclear how future backdating activities could occur. But if such activities do transpire, they are significantly more likely to occur with knowledge by and complicity of the board's compensation and audit committees.

The First to Fall

The first company to actually pay a fine in connection with backdating charges was Brocade Communications Systems Inc. Formal charges were announced in July 2006 and the company agreed to pay a $7 million penalty to settle the allegations on May 31, 2007. (In April 2007, Apple Inc.'s former CFO, Fred Anderson, agreed to pay a fine of $150,000 and to repay option gains of about $3.5 million, but the company itself had not been sued by the SEC.) In January 2005, Brocade announced earnings restatements for fiscal years 1999–2004; those restatements reduced the company's net earnings by $279 million.

In June 2007, a criminal trial commenced against Brocade's former CEO, Gregory Reyes, who was charged with 10 felony counts of securities fraud, including defrauding shareholders by changing stock options dates and falsifying and forging related documents to hide such activities. At that time, Reyes was the first executive to stand trial, although executives at other companies had been charged with crimes related to backdating. (Interestingly, Reyes never backdated any options to himself, only for employees he wanted to retain at the company.) Reyes' lawyer took the position that the CEO had no intent to defraud: The accounting rules were too complex to be understood by Reyes and many others. The trial lasted until early August 2007, and, after six days of deliberation, the jury found Reyes guilty of all charges— apparently not buying the "byzantine accounting" argument.

Balancing Ethics and Incentives

Companies that have been found to backdate options must restate the financial statements. SEC Staff Accounting Bulletin (SAB) 99 specifically addressed this issue by requiring that an error involving an increase in management compensation be restated regardless of the amount. The company's taxable income could also be affected if restatements require the recognition of additional compensation expense. In turn, the option recipients may find themselves subject to an IRS tax audit, because additional corporate recognition of compensation expense would entail the recognition of income by the recipients. The use of stock option pricing models required by SFAS 123(R) could create future ethical and technical problems if those models are based on inaccurate assumptions or variables as input to the valuation process. The PCAOB was concerned enough about stock option auditing to issue guidance on this subject in *Staff Questions and Answers—Auditing the Fair Value of Share Options Granted to Employees* (October 2006; http://www.pcaob.org/Standards/Staff_Questions_and_Answers/2006/Stock_Options.pdf).

So much interest and concern over stock option backdating and repricing, evinced by so many individuals and organizations, bodes poorly for the legitimacy of the potential motives for such actions. Such actions cannot withstand examination under any ethical test and should raise concern among investors, creditors, executives, and boards of directors. Based on the outcome of the Brocade case, such concerns have permeated the minds of potential jurors and thus the wider public.

Stock options were designed as a way to provide pay for performance, not to reward poor performance by backwards-looking repricing or backdating. Such activities undermine the incentive justification for use of stock option plans. Executives deserve compensation packages that provide both short-run benefits and a long-run motivation to increase organizational value for all stakeholders. Compensation methods that cause the tone at the top to be perceived as a cacophony of greed should be banished from the orchestra.

Sources

Cecily Raiborn, PhD, CPA, CMA, is the McCoy Endowed Chair in Accounting at Texas State University, San Marcos, Texas.

Marcos Massoud, PhD, CPA, is the Robert A. Day Distinguished Professor of Accounting at the Peter F. Drucker Graduate School of Management of Claremont McKenna College, Claremont, Calif.

Roselyn Morris, PhD, CPA, is a professor of accounting, and **Chuck Pier, PhD**, is an assistant professor of accounting, both at Texas State University, San Marcos, Texas.

4

PRACTICAL ETHICAL DECISION MAKING

Purpose of the Chapter

When a businessperson or professional accountant faces an ethical problem, the first recourse for guidance should be to corporate and professional codes of conduct. These *often* do not apply specifically to the problem faced and require interpretation to fit the circumstances. When this is required, the decision maker should be able to use the principles, approaches, and frameworks discussed in this chapter to make practical defensible ethical decisions.

Introduction

When the broad principles or specific rules embodied in codes of conduct do not specifically apply to the particular problem a professional accountant is facing, the decision maker can be guided by general ethical principles to arrive at a defensible ethical decision. What are these general ethical principles and how should they be applied? Building on the philosophers' contributions discussed in Chapter 3, this chapter explores these ethical principles and develops a practical, comprehensive decision framework based on how a proposed action would impact upon the stakeholders to the decision. The chapter concludes by proposing a comprehensive framework for making ethical decisions.

Motivating Developments

The Enron, Arthur Andersen, and WorldCom scandals gave rise to public outrage, the collapse of capital markets, and ultimately the Sarbanes-Oxley Act of 2002, which brought about widespread governance reform. Subsequent corporate scandals involving Adelphia, Tyco, Health-South, and others served to further heighten public awareness that corporate executives can make better decisions, and should do so to preserve the profitability and viability of their corporations. Ensuing court cases as well as related fines, imprisonments, and settlements have underscored the need for those decisions to reduce vulnerability to legal actions as well.

The court of public opinion has also been harsh to companies and individuals who have behaved unethically. Loss of reputation due to unethical and/or illegal acts has proven to be revenue and profit reducing, damaging to share prices, and career ending for many executives even before the acts are fully investigated and responsibility for them is fully proven.

These developments have been so important that corporate executives and directors now must give increased attention to corporate governance and the guidance it provides, in addition to their own role. Additionally, business schools that want worldwide accreditation by the Association to Advance Collegiate Schools of Business (AACSB)[1] are to incorporate ethics education into their policies, practices, and curricula. Specifically, according to the AACSB's

---

1. Association to Advance Collegiate Schools of Business (AACSB) accredits business schools and programs worldwide. See www.aacsb.edu.

Ethics Education Task Force,[2] business school curricula should deal with several ethical matters, including corporate social responsibility, governance, ethical corporate culture, and ethical decision making (AACSB, 2004).

In 2003, the International Federation of Accountants (IFAC) also pronounced upon the ethics education required for ethics education of professional accountants. Their International Education Standards for Accountants (IES 1-6, 2003) provides, in IES 4, the details of the professional values, ethics, and attitudes required for professional accountants to understand and discharge their duties under the IFAC Code of Ethics for Professional Accountants.[3]

The lesson is clear. It is no longer enough to make decisions and take actions that are legal—actions must also be ethically defensible.

Ethical Decision-Making Framework (EDM)

In response to the need for ethically defensible decisions, this chapter presents a practical, comprehensive, multifaceted framework for ethical decision making. This framework incorporates traditional requirements for profitability and legality, as well as requirements shown to be philosophically important and those recently demanded by stakeholders. It is designed to enhance ethical reasoning by providing:

I Insights into the identification and analysis of key issues to be considered and questions or challenges to be raised

I Approaches to combining and applying decision-relevant factors into practical action

A decision or action is considered ethical or "right" if it conforms to certain standards. Philosophers have been studying which standards are important for millennia, and business ethicists have recently been building on their work. Both groups have found that one standard alone is insufficient to ensure an ethical decision. Consequently, the EDM framework proposes that decisions or actions be compared against four standards for a comprehensive assessment of ethical behavior.

The EDM framework assesses the ethicality of a decision or action by examining the:

I Consequences or well-offness created in terms of net benefit or cost;

I Rights and duties affected;

I Fairness involved;

I Motivation or virtues expected.

The first three of these considerations—*consequentialism, deontology,* and *justice*—are examined by focusing on the impacts of a decision on shareholders and other affected stakeholders, an approach known as *stakeholder impact analysis.* The fourth consideration—the *motivation* of the decision maker—is an approach known as *virtue ethics.* It provides insights likely to be helpful when assessing current and future governance problems as part of a normal risk management exercise. *All four considerations must be examined thoroughly and appropriate ethical values must be applied in the decision and its implementation if a decision or action is to be defensible ethically.*

Practical EDM—the overriding focus of this chapter—is based on concepts developed by philosophers, which are discussed in Chapter 3, and which are reviewed later in this chapter. Developing an understanding of the decision-making approaches philosophers pioneered is essential. Table 4.1 provides a cross-reference of EDM considerations and relevant philosophical theories.

---

2. The AACSB's Ethics Education Task Force is at http://www.aacsb.edu/resource_centers/EthicsEdu/eetf.asp.

3. IES 1-6, including IES 4, is reproduced on the BPA website for further reference.

TABLE 4.1

EDM Considerations: Philosophical Underpinnings

EDM CONSIDERATIONS	PHILOSOPHICAL THEORIES
Well-offness or well-being	Consequentialism, utilitarianism, theology[4]
Respect for the rights of stakeholders	Deontology (rights and duties)[5]
Fairness among stakeholders	Kant's Categorical Imperative,[6] justice as impartiality[7]
Expectations for character traits, virtues	Virtue[8]
Specific EDM Issues	
Different behavior in different cultures (bribery)	Relativism,[9] subjectivism[10]
Conflicts of interest, and limits to self-interested behavior	Deontology, subjectivism, egoism[11]

 For reference purposes, a list of definitions is provided at **www.cengage.com/accounting/brooks**.

Philosophical Approaches—An Overview: Consequentialism (Utilitarianism), Deontology & Virtue Ethics

Philosophers have long been focused on making the best decision from a societal as well as individual perspective, but the salience of their philosophies has not been well-appreciated or understood in business and the professions. This is about to change.

Stimulated to improve ethics education and EDM by the Enron, Arthur Andersen, and WorldCom scandals, and the ensuing governance reform, the AACSB Ethics Education Task Force (2004) has called for business students to be familiar with three philosophical approaches to ethical decision making: *consequentialism (utilitarianism), deontology,* and *virtue ethics.* Each of the three approaches contributes differently to a useful and defensible approach for ethical decision making in business or personal life. However, because some philosophical principles and theories conflict with others and appear to clash with acceptable business practice, particularly in some cultures around the world, it is best to use a multifaceted set of considerations drawn from all three approaches to determine the ethicality of actions, and guide choices to be made.

The basic question that interests philosophers is: What makes a decision or action or person more or less good or ethical? Each of the three philosophical approaches to ethical decision making—consequentialism, deontology, and virtue ethics—focuses on a different conception of a right action. These will be reviewed in turn. Bear in mind, however, since philosophers have been studying what makes an act good or morally right for thousands of years, it is not possible to provide a complete understanding of philosophical concepts in a few pages. The following brief understanding of underlying philosophical approaches is intended to enable the use of the practical decision techniques developed later in this chapter. (For a more detailed explanation and analysis of these philosophical theories, see Chapter 3.) Readings are cited to facilitate further study of philosophical concepts.

---

4. See John Stuart Mill (1861/1988).
5. See, for example, http://en.wikipedia.org/wiki/Deontology, or http://www.molloy.edu/academic/philosophy/sophia/kant/deontology.htm.
6. See Immanuel Kant (1964) and Stumpf (1988, particularly Chapter 15).
7. See Rawls (1971).
8. See Aristotle (1925) and Cafaro (1998) at http://www.bu.edu/wcp/Papers/TEth/TEthCafa.htm.
9. See, for example, http://plato.stanford.edu/entries/relativism/.
10. See, for example, http://academics.vmi.edu/psy_dr/subjectivism.htm
11. See, for example, http://www.iep.utm.edu/e/egoism.htm or http://plato.stanford.edu/entries/egoism/

Consequentialism, Utilitarianism, or Teleology

Consequentialists are intent on maximizing the utility produced by a decision. For them, the rightness of an act depends on its consequences. This approach is essential to a good ethical decision and an understanding of it will be part of AACSB-accredited business school education in the future. According to the AACSB,

> The consequentialist approach requires students to analyze a decision in terms of the harms and benefits to multiple stakeholders and to arrive at a decision that produces the greatest good for the greatest number.[12]

Consequentialism holds that an act is morally right if and only if that act maximizes the net good.[13] In other words, an act and therefore a decision is ethical if its favorable consequences outweigh its negative consequences. Moreover, some believe that only the act that maximizes the net benefit of favorable minus negative consequences is morally right or ethical. Philosophers also debate:

I Which consequences should be counted;

I How they should be counted;

I Who deserves to be included in the set of affected stakeholders that should be considered.

For example, should the consequences to be considered be actual rather than foreseen, foreseeable, intended, or likely? Should the consequences to be considered depend on the values involved, such as the impact on life, health, pleasure, pain, privacy rights, or property rights; and with what weighting? How should the overall assessment be developed?

I Based only on the best consequences instead of:

- attributing value to only satisfactory outcomes,

- on all of the outcomes or just parts thereof.

I Based on total net good rather than average per person.

I Based on the impacts on all persons or just a select set.

I Based on the assumption that all consequences are considered of equal impact or that some are more important.

I Should the impact of the act on the decision maker or agent involved be considered?

An excellent overview of these variations and useful references can be found in the work of Walter Sinnott-Armstrong (2003).

Classic *utilitarianism*—concerned with overall utility—embraces all of these variants, and therefore it is only of partial usefulness in making ethical decisions in a business, professional, or organizational context. *Consequentialism*, however, refers to a subset of these variants that may be defined to avoid problematic measurements or other issues, or in order to make the process more relevant to the act, decision, or context involved. Because utilitarianism and consequentialism focus on the results or "ends" of an action, they are sometimes referred to as *teleological*.[14] In the development of the practical EDM approaches that follow, this chapter will adopt a consequentialist approach involving the impact analysis of decisions and actions upon a comprehensive set of stakeholders and their interests, based upon foreseeable likely impacts, which are

---

12. AACSB, 2004, 12.
13. Alternatively, an ethical choice could be the one that minimizes the net negative impact of choices where one *must* be made.
14. *Teleos* in Greek means "end," and the study of "ends" is known as teleology.

value weighted in importance. The total net benefit of alternative decisions and actions is considered to identify the best and/or most defensible choices.

Deontology

Deontology[15] is different from consequentialism in that deontologists focus on the obligations or duties motivating a decision or actions rather than on the consequences of the action.

Deontological ethics takes the position that rightness depends on the respect shown for duty, and the rights and fairness that those duties reflect. Consequently:

> A deontological approach raises issues related to duties, rights, and justice considerations and teaches students to use moral standards, principles, and rules as a guide to making the best ethical decision.[16]

Deontological reasoning is largely based on the thinking of Immanuel Kant (1964). He argued that a rational person making a decision about what would be good to do, would consider what action would be good for all members of society to do. Such an act would improve the well-being of the decision maker and the well-being of society as well.

Kant began to search for an overriding principle that would guide all action—an imperative that everyone should follow without exception, which could therefore be considered universal or categorical. His search led to what is known as Kant's Categorical Imperative, which is a dominant principle or rule for deontologists. Kant's principle indicates that there is a duty or imperative to:

> Always act in such a way that you can also will that the maxim of your action should become a universal law.[17]

This means that "if you cannot will[18] that everyone follow the same decision rule, your rule is not a moral one." (Kay, 1997)

As a universal principle, everyone should follow it. Suppose a person is considering whether to lie or tell the truth. Kant would argue that lying would not be a good rule because others following the same rule would lie to you—an eventuality you would not want. Honesty would, however, qualify as a good rule. Similarly, impartiality would also qualify rather than favoritism. Moreover, the Golden Rule—do unto others as you would have them do unto you—would readily[19] qualify as a universal principle.

Using the same approach could yield a universal respect for human rights and for fair treatment for all. This can be best achieved by adopting the position that one must fulfill obligations or duties that respect moral or human rights and legal or contract[20] rights. Furthermore, it can only be achieved if individuals act with "enlightened self-interest" rather than pure self-interest. Under enlightened self-interest, the interests of individuals are taken into account in decisions—they are not simply ignored or overridden. Individuals are considered "ends" rather than used as "means" to achieve an end or objective.

---

15. *Deon* in Greek means obligation.
16. AACSB, 2004, p. 12.
17. Charles D. Kay, "Notes on Deontology", 1997, http://www.webs.wofford.edu/kayed/ethics/deon.htm.
18. "Will" can be taken to mean "wish, want, desire, or intend."
19. Kant foresaw, however, that an individual might "will" bad consequences on others such as by willing euthanasia on everyone. He sought to avoid such ill will affects by further specifying that individuals be always considered "ends" rather than "means," and that an individual's freedom and their ability to choose freely should be respected.
20. Legal and contract rights are those protected by law, regulation, and/or contract.

The concepts of fair treatment and impartiality are fundamental to the development of the concepts of distributive, retributive, or compensatory justice. John Rawls developed a set of principles of justice involving expectations for equal civil liberty, maximization of benefits to the least advantaged, and the provision of fair opportunities (Rawls, 1971). His approach utilized the concept of a "veil of ignorance" to simulate conditions of uncertainty to enable decision makers to evaluate the impact of their actions on themselves. Decision makers were to decide on the best action without knowing if they would be the ones benefiting or losing by it.

Action based on duty, rights, and justice considerations are particularly important to professionals, directors, and executives who are expected to fulfill the obligations of a fiduciary. These would include actions that maintain the trust of a client of someone reliant on the more-knowledgeable, expert professional to act in the client's best interest with regard to matters of considerable value. The professional accountant, for example, has a duty to act in the client's best interest provided such action does not contravene the law and/or the codes and guidelines of related professional and regulatory bodies, such as generally accepted accounting principles (GAAP), generally accepted auditing standards (GAAS), Securities and Exchange Commission (SEC), and securities commission regulations. Directors and executives must observe governance laws in order to protect shareholders and other stakeholders as noted in Chapter 5. These duties must supersede self-interest, bias, and favoritism.

Unfortunately, utilitarianism and consequentialism focus on utility and may lead to decisions or acts that ignore, downplay, or circumscribe the justice or fairness of a decision, and its respect for the duties owed to and rights expected by those involved. However, *augmenting the consequentialist approach with a deontological analysis specifically including fair treatment will guard against the situation where the desire for what some consider to be beneficial consequences (or ends) will be allowed to justify the use of illegal or unethical actions (means) to achieve those ends.* For example, a deontological analysis could avoid endangering the health of workers and/or the public in order to minimize the costs of hazardous waste disposal. From a philosophical perspective, as well as from the perspective of damaged investors, workers, and other stakeholders who have suffered from recent financial scandals, unfettered pursuit of self-interest and short-term profit has led to illegal and unethical acts that are regrettable.

For society, protecting some individual rights—to life and health—is usually more important than maximizing the net benefit to all. However, occasionally, such as in times of war or dire emergency, a choice justified by consequential analysis is considered ethically preferential to a choice justified by deontological considerations.

Virtue Ethics

Consequentialism emphasizes the consequences of actions, and deontology uses duties, rights and principles as guides to correct moral behavior; whereas virtue ethics is concerned with the motivating aspects of moral character demonstrated by decision makers. Responsibility—especially culpability or blameworthiness—in both morality and law, has two dimensions: the *actus reus* (guilty act) and the *mens rea* (guilty mind).[21] Consequentialism, which examines the former, is said to be "act centered" rather than "agent centered," as deontology and virtue ethics are.

According to the AACSB,

> Virtue ethics focuses on the character or integrity of the moral actor and looks to moral communities, such as professional communities, to help identify ethical issues and guide ethical action.[22]

---

21. Jack T. Stevenson, in personal correspondence, December 2005.
22. AACSB, 2004, p. 12.

Aristotle's central question was: What is the good life and how can I live it (Cafaro, 1998)? The answer evolved to mean that flourishing, excellence, and happiness were criteria for the good life, but there was a continuing debate over whether the focus should be our communities' interests, or our own, or both. Moreover, excellence was said to involve "intellectual, moral and physical excellence, the excellence of human beings and their creations and achievements . . .," which again could be taken individually or in regard to broader communities. The focus of modern[23] virtue ethics is, however, on character virtues that lead to "enlightened self-interest"; it is not just focused on self-serving fulfillment.

Virtues are those character traits that dispose a person to act ethically and thereby make that person a morally good human being. For Aristotle, a virtue allowed a person to make reasonable decisions. Prudence was his key virtue in determining the proper choice between extremes. His other three important or Cardinal virtues were courage, temperance, and justice. For Christian philosophers, these virtues were not sufficient,[24] and they added the theological or Christian virtues of faith, hope, and charity. Other dispositions that are often cited as virtues include: honesty, integrity, enlightened self-interest, compassion, fairness, impartiality, generosity, humility, and modesty.

Virtues need to be cultivated over time so that they become imbedded and are therefore a consistent reference point. "If you possess a virtue, it is part of your character, a trait or disposition that you typically show in action. It is not just something that you are *able* to exhibit, but something that you usually or *dependably* exhibit."[25]

For virtue ethicists, possessing a virtue is a matter of degree. For example, being honest can mean that one tells the truth. But a person's honesty can be considered stronger or of a higher order if she/he deals only with honest people or causes, works for honest companies, has honest friends, raises her/his children to be honest, and so on. Similarly, the reason a person acts virtuously is important. For example, an honest act undertaken to gain a greedy end result is considered to be less virtuous than one taken because it is believed to be the right thing to do to improve society and/or to discharge a duty to another person or organization. A further problem in reaching the fullest levels of virtue is lack of moral or practical wisdom, such as is evident in some acts of overgenerosity, or too much compassion or courage, which can sometimes be harmful.

Although the lack of a "right" reason for virtuous action may seem academic, without such a reason some businesspeople or professionals are prone to act for greedy self-interest rather than modern enlightened self-interest, and are likely to commit unethical and/or unethical acts. They represent higher risks of ultimate deception and malpractice because they lack a basic commitment to virtue or professionalism unless it suits their own purpose. Conversely, overvirtuosity may result in emotional acts by executives or employees before seeking and receiving full information, or in taking too much risk, or in harming others unnecessarily. Both the lack of virtue and the lack of what Aristotle would call "prudence" constitute ethics risks to good governance.

There are a number of reservations about the strength of virtue ethics as an approach to EDM. For example, virtue ethics has to do with the process of decision making incorporating moral sensitivity, perception, imagination, and judgment, and some claim that this does not lead to easily useful EDM principles. Other criticisms are relevant, however, including that:

| The interpretation of a virtue is culture-sensitive,

---

23. Note that Aristotle's early formulations referred more to personal happiness and pleasure than to enlightened self-interest.
24. To ensure a union with God upon death.
25. Jack T. Stevenson, in personal correspondence, December 2005.

| As is the interpretation of what is justifiable or right.

| One's perception of what is right is to some degree influenced by ego or self-interest.

A fuller discussion of virtue ethics and the points raised may be found in Chapter 3, and in the work of Rosalind Hursthouse (2003) and Nafsika Athanassoulis (2004), as well as through the readings noted at **www.cengage.com/accounting/brooks**.

Sniff Tests & Common Rules of Thumb— Preliminary Tests of the Ethicality of a Decision

The philosophical approaches provide the basis for useful practical decision approaches and aids, although most executives and professional accountants are unaware of how and why this is so. Directors, executives, and professional accountants have, however, developed tests and rules of thumb that can be used to assess the ethicality of decisions on a preliminary basis. If these preliminary tests give rise to concerns, a more thorough analysis should be performed using the stakeholder impact analysis techniques discussed later in this chapter.

It is often appropriate for managers and other employees to be asked to check a proposed decision in a quick, preliminary manner to see if an additional full-blown ethical analysis is required. These quick tests are often referred to as sniff tests. Commonly applied sniff tests are noted in Table 4.2.

If any of these quick tests are negative, employees are asked to seek out an ethics officer for consultation, or perform a full-blown analysis of the proposed action. This analysis should be retained, and perhaps reviewed by the ethics officer. A reading on "Sniff Tests" is attached at the end of this chapter.[26]

Many executives have developed their own rules of thumb for deciding whether an action is ethical or not. For example, Carroll[27] identifies the first six rules in Table 4.3 as important, according to practicing managers.

Unfortunately, although these sniff tests and rules of thumb are based on ethical principles and are often very useful, *they rarely, by themselves, represent a comprehensive examination of the decision* and therefore leave the individuals and corporation involved vulnerable to making an unethical decision. For this reason, the more comprehensive techniques of stakeholder impact analysis should be employed whenever a proposed decision is questionable or likely to have significant consequences.

TABLE 4.2

Sniff Tests for Ethical Decision Making

Would I be comfortable if this action or decision were to appear on the front page of a national newspaper tomorrow morning?

Will I be proud of this decision?

Will my mother be proud of this decision?

Is this action or decision in accord with the corporation's mission and code?

Does this feel right to me?

---

26. Leonard J. Brooks, "Sniff Tests," *Corporate Ethics Monitor*, Vol.7, No. 5 (1995), p. 65.
27. A. B. Carroll, "Principles of Business Ethics: Their Role in Decision Making and Initial Consensus," *Management Decision*, Vol. 28, No. 8 (1990), pp. 20–24; see Figure 3.

4.3 **Rules of Thumb for Ethical Decision Making**

Golden Rule:	Do unto others as you would have them do unto you.
Disclosure Rule:	If you are comfortable with an action or decision after asking yourself whether you would mind if all your associates, friends, and family were aware of it, then you should act or decide.
The Intuition Ethic:	Do what your "gut feeling" tells you to do.
The Categorical Imperative:	You should not adopt principles of action unless they can, without inconsistency, be adopted by everyone else.
The Professional Ethic:	Do only what can be explained before a committee of your professional peers.
The Utilitarian Principle:	Do "the greatest good for the greatest number."
The Virtue Principle:	Do what demonstrated the virtues expected.

Source: Principle Source: A.B. Carroll, "Principles of Business Ethics: Their Role in Decision Making and Initial Consensus," *Management Decision*, 28:8 (1990): 20–24, see Figure 3.

Figure 4.1 is provided to link philosophers' principles and the criteria assessed by practical sniff tests, rules of thumb, and stakeholder impact analysis. Comparison of the sniff tests and rules of thumb noted above with the elements of Figure 4.1 will reveal that they usually focus on a fraction of the full set of criteria rather than a comprehensive set as does stakeholder impact analysis.

Stakeholder Impact Analysis—Comprehensive Tool for Assessing Decisions and Actions

Overview

Since John Stuart Mill developed the concept of *utilitarianism* in 1861, an accepted approach to the assessment of a decision and the resulting action has been to evaluate the end results or consequences of the action. To most businesspeople, this evaluation has traditionally been based on the decision's impact on the interests of the company's owners or shareholders. Usually these impacts have been measured in terms of the profit or loss involved, because profit has been the measure of well-offness that shareholders have wanted to maximize.

4.1 **Ethical Decision-Making Approaches and Criteria**

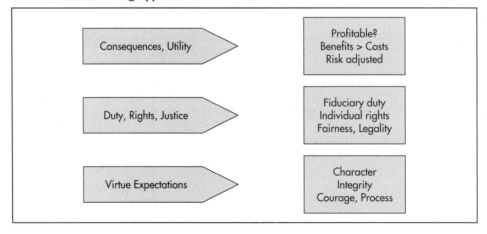

Source: AACSB EETF Report, June 2004.

This traditional view of corporate accountability has recently been
First, the assumption that *all* shareholders want to maximize *only* short-term
represent too narrow a focus. Second, the rights and claims of many nonshareholder
as employees, consumers/clients, suppliers, lenders, environmentalists, host communitie
governments that have a stake or interest in the outcome of the decision, or in the company itself,
are being accorded status in corporate decision making. Modern corporations are now
accountable to shareholders and to nonshareholder groups, both of which form the set of
stakeholders[28] to which a company responds (see Figure 4.2). It has become evident that a
company cannot reach its full potential, and may even perish, if it loses the support of one of a
select set of its stakeholders known as *primary stakeholders*. These ideas on stakeholders and their
emerging role are fully developed in Chapter 1.

The assumption of a monolithic shareholder group interested only in short-term profit is
undergoing modification because modern corporations are finding their shareholders are also
made up of persons and institutional investors who are interested in longer-term time horizons
and in how ethically business is conducted. The latter, who are referred to as *ethical investors*,
apply two screens to investments: do the investee companies make a profit in excess of appropriate hurdle rates, and do they earn that profit in an ethical manner? Because of the size of the
shareholdings of the mutual and pension funds, and other institutional investors involved,
corporate directors and executives have found that the wishes of ethical investors can be ignored
only at their peril. Ethical investors have developed informal and formal networks through which
they inform themselves about corporate activity, decide how to vote proxies, and how to
approach boards of directors to get them to pay attention to their concerns in such areas as
environmental protection, excessive executive compensation, and human rights activities in
specific countries, such as South Africa.

FIGURE **4.2**   **Map of Corporate Stakeholder Accountability**

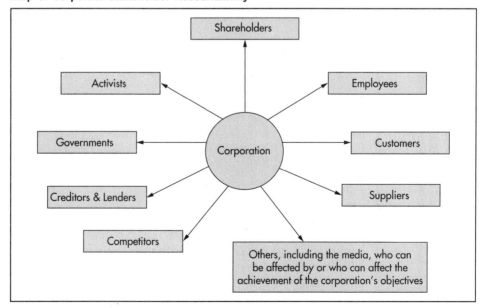

---

28. A stakeholder is anyone who is affected by or can affect the objectives of the organization (Freeman,
1984, p. 25).

Ethical investors and many other investors, as well as stakeholder groups, tend to be unwilling to squeeze the last ounce of profit out of the current year if it means damaging the environment or the rights of other stakeholders. They believe in managing the corporation on a broader basis than short-term profit only. *Usually, the maximization of profit in a longer than one-year time frame requires harmonious relationships with most stakeholder groups and their interests.* A negative public relations experience can be a significant and embarrassing price to pay for a decision-making process that fails to take the wishes of stakeholder groups into account. Whether or not special interest groups are also shareholders, their capacity to make corporations accountable through the media is evident and growing. The farsighted executive and director will want these concerns taken into account before offended stakeholders have to remind them. *Corporations are finding that in the past they have been legally and pragmatically accountable to shareholders, but they are also becoming increasingly accountable to stakeholders.*

Fundamental Interests of Stakeholders

Taking the concerns or interests of stakeholders into account when making decisions, by considering the potential impact of decisions on each stakeholder, is therefore a wise practice if executives want to maintain stakeholder support. However, the multiplicity of stakeholders and stakeholder groups makes this a complex task. To simplify the process, it is desirable to identify and consider a set of commonly held or fundamental stakeholder interests to be used to focus analyses and decision making on ethical dimensions, such as the following:

1. Their interest(s) should be better off as a result of the decision.
2. The decision should result in a fair distribution of benefits and burdens.
3. The decision *should* not offend any of the rights of any stakeholder, including the decision maker, and
4. The resulting behavior should demonstrate duties owed as virtuously as expected.

The first springs from consequentialism, the second, third, and fourth from deontology and virtue ethics.

To some extent, these fundamental interests have to be tempered by the realities facing decision makers. For example, although a proposed decision should maximize the betterment of all stakeholders, trade-offs often have to be made between stakeholders' interests. Consequently, the incurrence of pollution control costs may be counter to the interests of short-term profits that are of interest to some current shareholders and managers. Similarly, there are times when all stakeholders will find a decision acceptable even though one or more of them, or the groups they represent, may be worse off as a result. In recognition of the requirement for trade-offs and for the understanding that a decision can advance the well-offness of all stakeholders as a group, even if some individuals are personally worse off, this fundamental interest should be modified to focus on the *well-offness* of stakeholders rather than only on their betterment. *This modification represents a shift from utilitarianism to consequentialism.*

Once the focus on betterment is relaxed to shift to well-offness, the need to analyze the impact of a decision in terms of all four fundamental interests becomes apparent. It is possible, for example, to find that a proposed decision may produce an overall benefit, but the distribution of the burden of producing that decision may be so debilitating to the interests of one or more stakeholder groups that it may be considered grossly unfair. Alternatively, a decision may result in an overall net benefit and be fair, but may offend the rights of a stakeholder and therefore be considered not right. For example, deciding not to recall a marginally flawed product may be cost effective, but would not be considered to be "right" if users could be seriously injured. Similarly, a decision that does not demonstrate the character, integrity or courage expected will be considered ethically suspect by stakeholders. Consequently, *a proposed decision can be declared unethical if it fails to provide a net benefit*[29]*, or is unfair, or offends the rights of a stakeholder including reasonable expectations for virtuous behavior* (see Table 4.4). Testing a proposed decision against only one principle is definitely shortsighted, and usually results in a faulty diagnosis.

Measurement of Quantifiable Impacts

Profit | Profit is fundamental to the interests of shareholders and is essential to the survival and health of our corporations. In inflationary times, profit is essential simply to replace inventory at the higher prices required. Fortunately, the measurement of profit is well developed and needs few comments about its use in ethical decision making. It is true, however, that profit is a short-term measure, and that several important impacts are not captured in the determination of profit. Both of these conditions can be rectified in the following sections.

Items Not Included in Profit: Measurable Directly | There are impacts of corporate decisions and activities that are not included in the determination of the profit of the company that caused the impact. For example, when a company pollutes, the cost of cleanup is usually absorbed by individuals, companies, or municipalities that are downstream or downwind. These costs are referred to as *externalities,* and their impact can often be measured directly by the costs of cleanup incurred by others.

In order to see a complete picture of the impacts of a decision, the profit or loss from a transaction should be modified by the externalities it creates. Frequently, corporations that ignore their externalities over time will find that they have underestimated the true cost of the decision when fines and cleanup costs are incurred, or bad publicity emerges.

Items Not Included in Profit: Not Measurable Directly | Other externalities exist where the cost is included in the determination of the company's profit, but where the benefit is enjoyed by persons outside of the company. A donation or scholarship are examples of this kind of externality, and obviously it would be attractive to include an estimate of the benefits involved in the overall evaluation of the proposed decision. The problem is that neither the benefit nor the cost of some negative impacts, such as the loss of health suffered by people absorbing pollution, can be measured directly, but they should be included in an overall assessment.

Although it is impossible to measure these externalities directly, it is possible to measure these impacts indirectly through the use of *surrogates* or mirror image alternatives. In the case of the scholarship, a surrogate for the benefit could be the increase in earnings gained by the recipient. The value of the loss of health could be estimated as the income lost plus the cost of medical treatment plus the loss of productivity in the workplace involved as measured by the cost of fill-in workers.

The accuracy of these estimates will depend on the closeness of the mirror image measure. It is likely, however, that the estimates arrived at will understate the impact involved; in the previous

TABLE 4.4	**Fundamental Interests of Stakeholders**	
	Well-offness	The proposed decision should result in more benefits than costs.
	Fairness	The distribution of benefits and burdens should be fair.
	Right	The proposed decision should not offend the rights of the stakeholders and the decision maker.
	Virtuosity	The proposed decision should demonstrate virtues reasonably expected.

All four interests must be satisfied for a decision to be considered ethical.

---

29. Unless it is a choice of the least worst of a net negative set of options.

example, no estimate was made for the intellectual gain of the education permitted by the scholarship or the pain and suffering involved as a result of the loss of health. Nevertheless, it is far better to make use of estimates that are generally accurate, rather than make decisions on the basis of direct measures that measure precisely only a fraction of the impact of a proposed decision.

The measurement and use of surrogates to estimate external impacts of corporate decisions is discussed further in the article by Brooks (1979), which appears as a reading at the end of this chapter.

| Bringing the Future to the Present | The technique for bringing future impacts of a decision into an analysis is not difficult. It is handled in a parallel manner to capital budgeting analysis, where future values are discounted at an interest rate that reflects the expected interest rates in future years. This approach is demonstrated as part of *cost–benefit analysis* (CBA) in Brooks (1979). Using the net present value approach of capital budgeting analysis, the benefits and costs of a proposed action can be assessed as follows:

Net Present Value = Present Value of Benefits − Present Value of Costs of Proposed Action

where benefits include revenues and good externalities, and costs include costs plus bad externalities.

Frequently, executives who have learned the hard way to keep their focus on short-term profit will reject the idea of including externalities in their analyses. However, *what is being advocated here is not that they abandon short-term profit as a yardstick, but that they also consider impacts that are now externalities that have an excellent chance of affecting the company's bottom line in the future.* It is likely, for example, that pollution costs will be turned into fines and/or cleanup will be required. Moreover, the advantages bestowed through donations will strengthen society and allow the corporation to reach its full potential in the future. What cost–benefit analysis allows a decision maker to do is to bring these future benefits and costs into the present for a fuller analysis of a proposed decision. For example, Table 2 of the Cost–Benefit Analysis reading (Brooks, 1979) could be reformatted as Table 4.5 to give the decision maker a clearer view of present and possible future impacts on profit.

TABLE 4.5

Cost-Benefit Analysis: Short- and Long-Term Profit Impact

	POLLUTION CONTROL EQUIPMENT IMPACT ON PROFIT			UNIVERSITY ADMISSION SCHOLAR-SHIPS IMPACT ON PROFIT		
	SHORT-TERM	LONG-TERM	TOTAL	SHORT-TERM	LONG-TERM	TOTAL
Benefits (Present Valued at 10 percent)		$500,000	$500,000			
Reduction in worker health costs	$200,000		$200,000			
Increase in worker productivity						
Improvement in level of earnings of scholarship recipients					$600,000	$600,000
Total benefits	$200,000	$500,000	$700,000		$600,000	$600,000
Costs (Present valued at 10 percent)						
Pollution equipment	$350,000		$350,000			
Scholarships paid				$400,000		$400,000
Total costs	$350,000		$350,000	$400,000		$400,000
Net benefit-costs	($150,000)	$500,000	$350,000	($400,000)	$600,000	$200,000

| **Dealing with Uncertain Outcomes** | Just as in capital budgeting analysis, there are estimates that are uncertain. However, a full range of techniques has been developed to factor this uncertainty into the analysis of proposed decisions. For example, the analysis can be based on best estimates, on three possibilities (most optimistic, pessimistic, and best estimate), or on expected values developed from a computer simulation. All of these are *expected values,* which are combinations of a value and a probability of its occurrence. This is normally expressed as follows:

$$\text{Expected Value of an Outcome} = \text{Value of the Outcome} \times \text{Probability of that Outcome Occurring}$$

The advantage of this expected value formulation is that the cost–benefit analysis framework can be modified to include the risk associated with outcomes to be included. This new approach is referred to as *risk–benefit analysis* (RBA), and it can be applied where risky outcomes are prevalent in the following framework:

$$\text{Risk-Adjusted or Expected Value of Net Benefits} = \text{Expected Present Value of Future Benefits} - \text{Expected Present Value of Future Costs}$$

| **Identifying Stakeholders & Ranking Their Interests** | The measurement of profit, augmented by externalities discounted to the present and factored by riskiness of outcome, is more useful in assessing proposed decisions than profit alone. However, the usefulness of a stakeholder impact analysis depends on the full identification of all stakeholders and their interests, and on a full appreciation of the significance of the impacts on the position of each.

There are occasions, for instance, when the simple adding up of benefits and costs does not fully reflect the importance of a stakeholder or of the impact involved, such as when the capacity of a stakeholder to withstand the impact is low. For example, if a stakeholder is poor, he will not be able to buy remedial treatment, or alternatively his reserves may be so low that other family members—perhaps children—will suffer. On the other hand, a scholarship to a poor recipient could create a benefit for that person and others of significantly greater impact than to a person who is well off. In these situations, the values included in the CBA or RBA can be weighted, or the net present values created can be ranked according to the impact created on the stakeholders involved. The ranking of stakeholders and the impacts on them based on their situational capacity to withstand is also used when nonmeasurable impacts are being considered.

Relative financial strength does not provide the only rationale for ranking the interests of stakeholders. In fact, several more compelling reasons exist, including the impact of the proposed action on the life or health of a stakeholder, or on some aspect of our flora, fauna, or environment that is near a threshold of endangerment or extinction. Usually, the public takes a very dim view of companies that put profits ahead of life, health, or the preservation of our habitat. In addition, making these issues a high priority will often trigger a rethinking of an offending action so as to improve it by removing its offensiveness.

The illustrative *Castle Manufacturing Inc.* case solution provided at the end of this chapter extends the concept of ranking stakeholders to correlate legal rights, financial and psychological capacity to withstand the impact, and the resulting probable public impact of the action. It is interesting that an item may not be "material" to a lay investor in an accounting sense, but may be quite significant to stakeholders. In the long run, such sensitivity to corporate decisions may rebound on the shareholders through the bottom line. In time, the *accounting concept of materiality* as we know it may be inadequate and need to be expanded.

Two research thrusts can prove quite useful in identifying and understanding stakeholder groups and their interactions. Mitchell, Agle, and Wood (1997) suggest that stakeholders and their interests be evaluated on three dimensions: *legitimacy* or legal and/or moral right to influence the organization; *power* to influence the organization through the media, government, or other means; and perceived and real *urgency* of the issues arising. Such an analysis forces the consideration of impacts thought to be very damaging (particularly to external stakeholders) to the fore, so that if an executive decides to go ahead with a suboptimal plan, at least the potential downside will be known. The three sets of claims are identified in Figure 4.3.

Logic suggests that claims where the three circles overlap in Figure 4.3 (i.e., legitimate and/or viewed as legitimate, urgent, and are held by the powerful) will always be the most important. However, this is not necessarily the case. Other urgent stakeholder claims can become the most important if they garner more support of the powerful and those with legitimate claims, and are ultimately seen to have legitimacy.

Many executives forget that an organization's stakeholders change over time, as does the power they wield depending on the urgency they feel about issues brought to their attention. In real life, stakeholders without legitimacy or power will try to influence those with clout, and they succeed. Another researcher, Tim Rowley (1997), has suggested that a set of stakeholders be considered as a *dynamic network*, and that projections be made about who in the network will influence whom, to forecast which issues and interests will become more important. These concepts are developed in the illustrative case *Bribery or Opportunity in China*, located at the end of the chapter.

| Summary | The previously discussed approaches to the measurement of impacts of proposed decisions are summarized in Table 4.6.

FIGURE 4.3   **Stakeholder Identification and Interests**

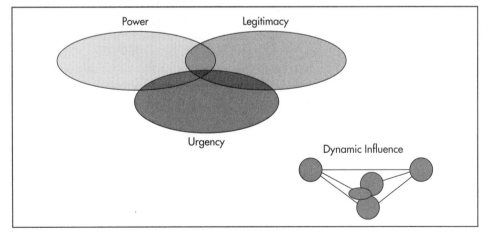

Sources: Mitchell, Agle, and Wood, 1997; Rowley, 1997.

TABLE 4.6   **Approaches to The Measurement of Quantifiable Impacts of Proposed Decisions***

A.   Profit or loss only
B.   A. plus externalities (i.e., Cost-Benefit Analysis/CBA)
C.   B. plus probabilities of outcomes (i.e., Risk-Benefit Analysis/RBA)
D.   CBA or RBA plus ranking of stakeholders

*Optimal decisions usually result from the most thorough approach.

Assessment of Nonquantifiable Impacts

Fairness Among Stakeholders | Although the expectation of fair treatment is a right that individuals and groups can properly expect to receive, it is treated here on its own because of its importance to ethical decision making. The concern for fair treatment has been evident in society's recent preoccupation with such issues as discrimination against women and other matters of hiring, promotion, and pay. Consequently, a decision will be considered unethical unless it is seen to be fair to all stakeholders.

Fairness is not an absolute concept. It is evidenced by a relatively even distribution of the benefits and burdens springing from a decision. For example, it is possible that a decision to increase taxes may weigh more heavily on high-income earners but be seen as relatively fair in terms of their capacity to pay those taxes. Reasonability and perspective are required to judge fairness accurately.

Rights of Stakeholders | A decision will only be considered ethical if its impacts do not offend the rights of the stakeholders impacted upon, and the rights of the person(s) making the decision. This latter point can be seen in the case of a decision being made by executives who subscribe to values that make them offended by child labor or by low standards of worker safety in developing countries. The executives making the decision are stakeholders to it in their own right.

An individual stakeholder or a stakeholder group in North America[30] may generally expect to enjoy the rights listed in Table 4.7.

Some of these rights have been accorded protection under laws and legal regulations, while others are enforced through common law or through public sanction of offenders. For example, employees and consumers are protected under statute for health and safety, whereas dignity and privacy tend to be subject to common law, and the exercise of conscience is subject to public sanction.

In many cases, even where protection is afforded through statute, considerable judgment is required to know when an individual's rights are being violated. Drug testing in the form of urinalysis, for example, appears to be warranted when the health of the worker and fellow workers is at stake, but the degree of jeopardy has to be severe. Airline pilots are considered worthy of urinalysis but, at the moment, drivers of transport trucks are not. There are many reasons for this, including the lack of accuracy and timeliness of the tests, and the stigma that attaches to a false accusation. However, it appears to be reasonable to test a truck driver's reflexes and hand-eye coordination using computer games just prior to his/her shift, so evidently the stigma of failing a computer game related closely to the task to be performed is acceptable in today's society. This complex interplay of statute, regulation, common law, and judgment based on values makes it advisable to give any apparent infringement of a stakeholder's rights very careful scrutiny.

TABLE 4.7	Stakeholder Rights

- Life
- Health and safety
- Fair treatment
- Exercise of conscience
- Dignity and privacy
- Freedom of speech

---

30. The importance attached to these rights varies somewhat in different cultures around the world.

Stakeholder Impact Analysis: Traditional Decision-Making Approaches

Several approaches have been developed that utilize stakeholder impact analysis to provide guidance about the ethicality of proposed actions to decision makers. Discussions of three traditional approaches follow. Choosing the most useful approach depends on whether decision impacts are short rather than long run, involve externalities and/or probabilities, or take place within a corporate setting. The approaches may be blended into a tailored hybrid approach to best cope with a specific situation.

It is imperative to recognize, however, that whereas each approach deals with the deontological considerations of impacts on rights, fairness, and the duties expected, none specifically incorporate a thorough review of the motivation for the decisions involved, or the virtues or character traits expected in the modern stakeholder accountability era. A comprehensive ethical analysis must therefore go beyond the traditional Tucker, Velasquez, and Pastin models to incorporate an assessment of the motivation, virtues, and character traits exhibited in comparison with those expected by stakeholders.

Traditional 5-Question Approach

The 5-question approach, or 5-box approach, as Graham Tucker has called it, in a reading at the end of this chapter, involves the examination or challenge of a proposed decision through the five questions in Table 4.8. The proposed decision is to be challenged by asking all of the questions. If a negative response is forthcoming (or more than one) when all five questions are asked, the decision maker can attempt to revise the proposed action to remove the negative and/or offset it. If the revision process is successful, the proposal will be ethical. If not, the proposal should be abandoned as unethical. Even if no negative response is forthcoming when the questions are first asked, an effort should be made to improve the proposed action using the five questions as a guide.

The order of asking the questions is not important, but all of the first four questions must be asked to ensure that the decision maker is not overlooking an important area of impact. Some ethical problems are not as susceptible to examination by the 5-question approach as to the other approaches described in following sections. For instance, the first question focuses on profit, which is a substantially less comprehensive measurement tool than cost–benefit analysis and/or risk–benefit analysis, with or without the ranking of stakeholders depending on their ability to withstand the impact of the decision. As it stands, however, the 5-question framework is a useful approach to the orderly consideration of problems without many externalities and where a specific focus is desired by the decision-process designer. For an expanded treatment of this approach, refer to the reading at the end of the chapter by Graham Tucker (1990).

Keep in mind that *the traditional 5-question approach does not specifically incorporate a thorough review of the motivation for the decisions involved, or the virtues or character traits expected.*

TABLE 4.8 **Traditional 5-Question Approach to Ethical Decision Making**

The following five questions are asked about a proposed decision:

IS THE DECISION	STAKEHOLDER INTEREST EXAMINED
1. profitable?	Shareholders'—usually short-term
2. legal?	Society at large—legally enforceable rights
3. fair?	Fairness for all
4. right?	Other rights of all
5. going to further sustainable development?	Specific rights

Question 5 is an optional question designed to focus the decision-making process on a particular issue of relevance to the organization(s) or decision maker involved.

Traditional Moral Standards Approach

The moral standards approach to stakeholder impact analysis builds directly on three of the fundamental interests of stakeholders that are identified in Table 4.4. It is somewhat more general in focus than the 5-question approach, and leads the decision maker to a more broadly based analysis of net benefit rather than just profitability as a first challenge of proposed decisions. As a result, it offers a framework that is more suited to the consideration of decisions that have significant impacts outside the corporation than the 5-question framework.

The three standards making up the moral standards approach are listed in Table 4.9. Questions that sprang from each standard and that ought to be applied to each decision are also offered.

As shown in Table 4.9, the satisfaction of the utilitarian principle is examined through a question that focuses on cost–benefit analysis or risk–benefit analysis rather than just profit. Consequently, the full range of options discussed in Table 4.6 can be employed as befits the need.

In addition, as explained in Velasquez (1992), the examination of how the proposed decision respects individual rights looks at the impact of the decision on each stakeholder's rights as noted in Table 4.7, as well as at the process involved. For example, has deception or manipulation been used, or some type of force such as coercion, or has there been some other limit placed on information made available to the individuals impacted on or on their freedom to choose a response or limit their redress? If so, their rights have not been respected. One of the interesting questions raised in this connection is whether notification of the intent to undertake an action implies the consent of those individuals impacted on. Usually, notification does not imply consent unless the notification provides full information, allows time for consideration, and reasonable options are at hand to avoid the impact.

The question focusing on distributive justice, or fairness, is handled in the same way as in the 5-question approach. For a full treatment of the moral standards approach, see *Business Ethics: Concepts and Cases* by Manuel G. Velasquez, (1992). As noted earlier, *the traditional Moral Standards Approach does not specifically incorporate a thorough review of the motivation for the decisions involved, or the virtues or character traits expected.*

Traditional Pastin Approach

In his book, *The Hard Problems of Management: Gaining the Ethical Edge*, Mark Pastin (1986) presents his ideas on the appropriate approach to ethical analysis, which involves examining the four key aspects of ethics noted in Table 4.10.

Pastin uses the concept of *ground rule ethics* to capture the idea that individuals and organizations have ground rules or fundamental values that govern their behavior or their desired behavior. If a decision is seen to offend these values, it is likely that disenchantment or retaliation will occur. Unfortunately, this could lead to the dismissal of an employee who acts without a good understanding of the ethical ground rules of the employer organization involved. In order to understand the prevailing ground rules, to correctly gauge the organization's commitment to

---

TABLE 4.9

Traditional Moral Standards Approach to Ethical Decision Making*

MORAL STANDARD	QUESTION OF PROPOSED DECISION
Utilitarian:	
Maximize net benefit to society as a whole	Does the action maximize social benefits and minimize social injuries?
Individual rights:	
Respect and protect	Is the action consistent with each person's rights?
Justice:	
Fair distribution of benefits and burdens	Will the action lead to a just distribution of benefits and burdens?

*All three moral standards must be applied; none is a sufficient test by itself.

4.10   **Pastin's Approach to Stakeholder Impact Analysis**

KEY ASPECT	PURPOSE FOR EXAMINATION
Ground rule ethics	To illuminate an organization's and/or an individual's rules and values
End-point ethics	To determine the greatest net good for all concerned
Rule ethics	To determine what boundaries a person or organization should take into account according to ethical principles
Social contract ethics	To determine how to move the boundaries to remove concerns or conflicts

proposals and to protect the decision maker, Pastin suggests that an examination of past decisions or actions be made. He calls this approach *reverse engineering* a decision, because an attempt is made to take past decisions apart to see how and why they were made. Pastin suggests that individuals are often guarded (voluntarily or involuntarily) about expressing their values, and that reverse engineering offers a way to see, through past actions, what their values are.

In his concept of *end-point ethics*, Pastin suggests employing the full extent of the treatments summarized in Table 4.6. The application of these techniques to the Ford Pinto Case (which appears at the end of this chapter) should illuminate the concept of utilitarianism and illustrate the pitfalls of focusing an analysis on only short-term profit.

The concept of *rule ethics* is used to indicate the value of rules that spring from the application of valid ethical principles to an ethical dilemma. In this case, the valid ethical principles involve the respect for and protection of the rights of individuals as are discussed in Table 4.7, and derivative principles such as the golden rule of "Do unto others as you would have them do unto you." The establishment of rules based on respect for individual rights can prove helpful when an interpretation is particularly difficult, or when senior executives want to remove ambiguity about what they believe should be done in certain situations. For example, Pastin suggests that rules, formulated by senior executives to assist their employees, can divide possible actions into those that are obligatory, prohibited, or permissible. Similarly, rules can be crafted so as to make them categorical (i.e., no exceptions allowed) or prima facie (exceptions are allowed in certain circumstances), or to trigger consultation with senior executives. As such, rule ethics represent Pastin's examination of the impact of proposed decisions on the rights of the individuals involved.

The concept of fairness is incorporated by Pastin into his idea of *social contract ethics*. Here he suggests that formulating the proposed decision into an imaginary contract would be helpful because it would allow the decision maker to change places with the stakeholder to be impacted upon. As a result, the decision maker could see if the impact was fair enough to enter freely into the contract. If the decision maker found that he or she was not prepared to enter into the contract with the roles reversed, then the terms (or boundaries) of the contract should be changed in the interests of fairness. This technique of role reversal can prove to be quite helpful, particularly in the case of strong-willed executives who are often surrounded by "yes" men or women. In the case of a real contract, this approach can be useful in projecting how proposed actions will affect the contract, or whether a contract change (such as in a union contract) will be resisted.

Like the other two approaches to stakeholder analysis, the traditional Pastin Approach *does not specifically incorporate a thorough review of the motivation for the decisions involved, or the virtues or character traits expected.*

Extending & Blending the Traditional Approaches

From time to time, an ethical problem will arise that does not fit perfectly into one of the approaches described. For instance, the issues raised by an ethical problem may be examined by the 5-question approach, except that there are significant long-term impacts or externalities that call for cost–benefit analysis rather than profitability as a first-level question. Fortunately, cost–benefit analysis can be substituted or added to the approach to enrich it. Similarly, the concept of ground rule ethics can be grafted onto a non-Pastin approach, if needed in a decision that deals with an in-company setting. Care should be taken when extending and blending the approaches, however, to ensure that each of the areas of well-offness, fairness, and impact on individual rights are examined in a comprehensive analysis—otherwise the final decision may be faulty.

Integrating Philosophical & Stakeholder Impact Analysis Approaches

The philosophical approaches—consequentialism, deontology, and virtue ethics—that were developed early in this chapter and in Chapter 3 underlay, and should be kept in mind to inform and enrich, the analysis when using the three stakeholder impact approaches. In turn, the stakeholder impact analysis approach used should provide an understanding of the facts, rights, duties, and fairness involved in the decision or act that are essential to a proper ethical analysis of the motivations, virtues, and character traits expected. Consequently, in an effective, comprehensive analysis of the ethicality of a decision or proposed action, the traditional philosophical approaches should augment the stakeholder models, and vice versa, as shown in Figure 4.4.

Modifying the Traditional Stakeholder Impact Analysis Approaches: Assessing Motivation, Expected Virtues, & Character Traits

Why Consider Motivation and Behavioral Expectations?

As previously noted, *a comprehensive ethical analysis must go beyond the traditional Tucker, Velasquez, and Pastin Approaches to incorporate an assessment of the motivation, virtues, and character traits involved in comparison with those expected by stakeholders.*

FIGURE 4.4 **Ethical Decision-Making Approaches**

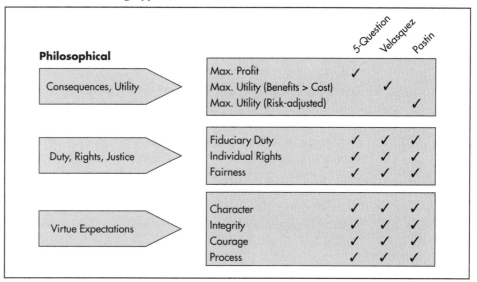

		5-Question	Velasquez	Pastin
Philosophical				
Consequences, Utility	Max. Profit	✓		
	Max. Utility (Benefits > Cost)		✓	
	Max. Utility (Risk-adjusted)			✓
Duty, Rights, Justice	Fiduciary Duty	✓	✓	✓
	Individual Rights	✓	✓	✓
	Fairness	✓	✓	✓
Virtue Expectations	Character	✓	✓	✓
	Integrity	✓	✓	✓
	Courage	✓	✓	✓
	Process	✓	✓	✓

Source: AACSB EETF Report, June 2004.

Unfortunately, as recent scandals indicate, in the past decision makers have not recognized the importance of stakeholder's expectations of virtue. If they had, the decisions made by corporate executives and by accountants and lawyers involved in the Enron, Arthur Andersen, WorldCom, Tyco, Adephia, and others might have avoided the personal and organizational tragedies that occurred. Some executives were motivated by greed rather than by enlightened self-interest focused on the good of all. Others went along with unethical decisions because they did not recognize that they were expected to behave differently and had a duty to do so. Some reasoned that because everyone else was doing something similar, how could it be wrong? *The point is that they forgot to consider sufficiently the virtues (and duties) they were expected to demonstrate.* Where a fiduciary duty was owed to future shareholders and other stakeholders, the virtues expected—character traits such as integrity, professionalism, courage, and so on—were not taken into account sufficiently. *In retrospect, it would have been wise to include the assessment of virtue ethics expectations as a separate step in any EDM process to strengthen governance and risk management systems and guard against unethical, short-sighted decisions.*

It is also evident that employees who continually make decisions for the wrong reasons—even if the right consequences result—can represent a high governance risk. Many examples exist where executives motivated solely by greed have slipped into unethical practices, and others have been misled by faulty incentive systems. Sears Auto Center managers were selling repair services that customers did not need to raise their personal commission remuneration, and ultimately caused the company to lose reputation and future revenue.[31] Many of the recent financial scandals were caused by executives who sought to manipulate company profits to support or inflate the company's share price in order to boost their own stock option gains. *Motivation based too narrowly on self-interest can result in unethical decisions when proper self-guidance and/or external monitoring is lacking.* Because external monitoring is unlikely to capture all decisions before implementation, it is important for all employees to clearly understand the broad motivation that will lead to their own and their organization's best interest from a stakeholder perspective. Consequently, decision makers should take motivations and behavior expected by stakeholders into account specifically in any comprehensive EDM approach, and organizations should require accountability by employees for those expectations through governance mechanisms.

Ethical Assessment of Motivation & Behavior

During the earlier discussion of virtue ethics, several aspects of ethical behavior were identified as being indicative of *mens rea* (a guilty mind), which is one of the two dimensions of responsibility, culpability, or blameworthiness. Although some of the virtues named by philosophers may not resonate with modern stakeholders, those listed in Table 4.11 do play a role in framing current expectations for ethical business behavior. If personal or corporate behavior does not meet these expectations, there will probably be a negative impact on reputation and the ability to reach strategic objectives on a sustained basis in the medium and long term.

The stakeholder impact assessment process will offer an opportunity to assess the motivations that underlie the proposed decision or action. Although it is unlikely that an observer will be able to know with precision the real motivations that go through a decision maker's mind, it is quite possible to project the perceptions that stakeholders will have of the action. In the minds of stakeholders, perceptions will determine reputational impacts whether those perceptions are correct or not. Moreover, it is possible to infer from remuneration and other motivational systems in place whether the decision maker's motivation is likely to be ethical or not.

---

31. See Sears Auto Centers cases at http://harvardbusinessonline.hbsp.harvard.edu/b02/en/common/ item_detail.jhtml?id=394009

TABLE 4.11	Motivation, Virtue, Character Traits, & Process Expectations

Motivations expected:
    Self-control rather than greed
    Fairness or justice considerations
    Kindness, caring, compassion, and benevolence
Virtues expected:
    Dutiful loyalty
    Integrity and transparency
    Sincerity rather than duplicity
Character traits expected:
    Courage to do the right thing per personal and/or professional standards
    Trustworthiness
    Objectivity, impartiality
    Honesty, truthfulness
    Selflessness rather than selfishness
    Balanced choices between extremes
Processes that reflect the motivations, virtues, and character traits expected

In order to ensure a comprehensive EDM approach, in addition to projecting perceptions and evaluating motivational systems, the decisions or actions should be challenged by asking questions about each of the items listed in Table 4.11. For example,

> Does the decision or action involve and exhibit the integrity, fairness, and courage expected?

Alternatively,

> Does the decision or action involve and exhibit the motivation, virtues, and character expected?

The objective of these techniques should be to construct a profile about the motivations, virtues, character traits, and processes involved with and exhibited by the decision or action that can be compared to those expected. *The resulting virtue ethics gap analysis is an essential consideration in a comprehensive EDM analysis—see Table 4.12—designed to produce ethically defensible decisions and actions, and improve governance processes.*

In conclusion, in order to ensure a comprehensive EDM analysis, assessments of the motivation, virtues expected and character traits expected, must be added to the traditional approaches thereby producing a *Modified 5-Question or Tucker Analysis, a Modified Moral Standards Approach, a Modified Pastin Approach, or a hybrid combination of those modified approaches.*

TABLE 4.12	A Comprehensive Approach to EDM

CONSIDERATION	DESCRIPTION
Well-offness or *Consequentialism*	The proposed decision should result in more benefits than costs.
Rights, duty or *Deontology*	The proposed decision should not offend the rights of the stakeholders, including the decision maker.
Fairness or *Justice*	The distribution of benefits and burdens should be fair.
Virtue expectations or *Virtue Ethics*	The motivation for the decision should reflect stakeholders' expectations of virtue.

All four considerations must be satisfied for a decision to be considered ethical.

Other Ethical Decision-Making Issues

Commons Problems

The term *commons problem* refers to the inadvertent or knowing overuse of jointly owned assets or resources. The concept first arose when villagers in old England overgrazed their livestock on land that was owned in common, or jointly with everyone else in the village, and the term *commons* was used to identify this type of pasture.

The problem of overgrazing could not be stopped because everyone had a right to use the pasture and thus could not be prevented from doing so. Only when the majority of villagers agreed to regulate the commons did the overgrazing stop. Sometimes, when they could not agree, outside authority was called on to settle the matter. Outdated though these issues seem, the problem of the commons is still with us in modern times. For example, pollution represents the misuse of the environment, a commons we all share. Similarly, if everyone in a business attempts to draw on capital funds, or an expense budget, or a service department, the result will be akin to overgrazing.

The lesson to be learned from this is that frequently the decision maker, who is not sensitized to the problem of the commons, will not attribute a high enough value to the use of an asset or resource, and therefore make the wrong decision. Awareness of the problem should correct this and improve decision making. If an executive is confronted by the overuse of an asset or resource, they will do well to employ the solutions applied in olden times.

Developing a More Ethical Action

Iterative improvement is one of the advantages of using the proposed EDM framework. Using the set of philosophical approaches, the 5-question approach, the moral standards, Pastin, or commons approaches allows the unethical aspects of a decision to be identified, and then iteratively modified to improve the overall impact of the decision. For example, if a decision is expected to be unfair to a particular stakeholder group, perhaps the decision can be altered by increasing the compensation to that group, or by eliminating or replacing the offending words, image, or specific action. At the end of every EDM approach, there should be a specific search for a win-win outcome. This process involves the exercise of *moral imagination*.

Occasionally, directors, executives, or professional accountants will suffer from *decision paralysis* as a result of the complexities of analysis or the inability to determine the maximal choice for reasons of uncertainty, time constraints, or other causes. Herbert Simon[32] proposed the concept of *satisficing* to solve this problem. He argued that one "should not let perfection be the enemy of the good"—iterative improvement until no further progress can be made should yield a solution that should be considered good enough and even optimal at that point in time.

Common Ethical Decision Making Pitfalls

Avoiding common ethical decision-making pitfalls is imperative. Experience has shown that unaware decision makers repeatedly make the following mistakes:

> *Conforming to an unethical corporate culture.* There are many examples where corporate cultures that are not based on ethical values have influenced or motivated executives and employees to make unethical decisions. As noted in Chapters 2 and 5, the *unethical cultures* at Enron, WorldCom, Arthur Andersen, Tyco, Adephia, and others led executives and employees to make tragically wrong decisions. In many instances an *absence of ethical*

---

32. Herbert Simon coined the term satisficing in 1957. See http://en.wikipedia.org/wiki/Satisficing

leadership—the wrong "tone at the top"—was responsible. In others, companies were silent or *insufficiently clear on core values*, or these were misinterpreted, to allow unethical and illegal actions. On other occasions, *unethical reward systems* motivated employees to manipulate financial results or focus on activities not in the organization's best interest. Frequently, decision makers have been subject to *unreasonable pressures* to meet unrealistic expectations or deadlines, and have made decisions that bring short-term relief at a significant cost to longer term performance or objectives. Sometimes, employees simply *lack sufficient awareness of ethical issues and expectations* to be able to appreciate the need for ethical actions, and the companies screening, monitoring, training and reinforcement programs are inadequate to prevent unethical decisions.

| *Misinterpreting public expectations.* Many executives erroneously think unethical actions to be acceptable because:

- "It's a dog eat dog world out there," or

- "Everyone's doing it," or

- "If I don't do it someone else will," or

- "I'm off the hook because my boss ordered me to do it," or

- It's a story or practice mentioned in the popular press, media, or movies.

In today's world, these justifications for unethical decisions are very suspect. Each action contemplated must be rigorously considered against the ethical standards discussed in Chapters 3 and 4.

| *Focusing on short-term profit and shareholder only impacts.* Often, the most significant impacts (for nonshareholder stakeholders) of a proposed action are those that surface in the future and those that befall nonshareholder stakeholders first. Only after these groups react do shareholders bear the cost for misdeeds. The remedy for this myopia is to ensure an adequate time horizon for the analysis, and to take into account externalities on a cost–benefit basis even though the impact measured is felt initially by a nonshareholder group.

| *Focusing only on legalities.* Many managers are only concerned with whether an action is legal. They argue, "If it's legal, it's ethical." Unfortunately, many find their corporation unnecessarily subject to consumer boycotts, employee slowdowns, increasing government regulation to cover loopholes, and fines. Some don't care because they are only intending to stay at this corporation for a short while. The fact is that laws and regulations lag behind what society wants, but reaction does come and sometimes well before new laws and regulations are promulgated. One reason is that corporations lobby against such rule changes. Just because a proposed action is legal does not make it ethical.

| *Limits to fairness.* Sometimes decision makers are biased or want to be fair only to groups they like. Unfortunately for them, they do not have the ability to control public opinion and usually end up paying for their oversight. Many executives have been put off by activist organizations such as Greenpeace, but have learned that environmental issues are ignored at their peril. A full review of fairness to all stakeholders is the only way to ensure an ethical decision.

| *Limits to rights canvassed.* Bias is not restricted to fairness. Decision makers should canvass the impact on all rights for all stakeholder groups. Also, decision makers should be encouraged to take their own values into account when making a decision. Courts in North America no longer react favorably to the defense that, "I was ordered to do it by my boss." Employees are expected to use their own judgment, and many jurisdictions

have set up protective whistle-blowing and "right to refuse" statutes to encourage employees to do so. Often, managers that force unfortunate actions on subordinates are really not speaking in the best interests of shareholders anyway.

| *Conflicts of interest.* Bias based on prejudice is not the only reason for faulty assessments of proposed actions. Judgment can be clouded by conflicting interests—the decision maker's personal interest versus the corporation's best interest, or the interests of a group the decision maker is partial to versus the corporation's best interest can both account for erroneous assessments and decisions. Sometimes employees get caught on what is called a *slippery slope* where they begin with a minor decision which conflicts with the interest of their employer, which is followed by another and another of growing significance; and it becomes extremely difficult to correct or admit to their earlier decisions Often, an employee will be caught by doing a minor favor, which leads to a greater favor, and so on, but when the employee wants to stop granting further favors, they are told that they cannot stop or their boss will hear of their earlier actions; and they are caught on a slippery slope.

| *Interconnectedness of stakeholders.* Often decision makers fail to anticipate that what they do to one group will redound to trigger action by another. For example, despoiling the environment in a far-off country can cause negative reactions by domestic customers and capital markets.

| *Failure to identify all stakeholder groups.* The need to identify all stakeholder groups and interests before assessing the impacts on each is self-evident. However, this is a step that is repeatedly taken for granted, with the result that important issues go unnoticed. A useful approach to assist with this problem is to speculate on the downside that might happen from the proposed action, and try to assess how the media will react. This often leads to the identification of the most vulnerable stakeholder groups.

| *Failure to rank the specific interests of stakeholders.* The common tendency is to treat all stakeholder interests as equal in importance. However, those that are urgent usually become the most important. Ignoring this is truly shortsighted, and may result in a suboptimal and unethical decision.

| *Leaving out well-offness, fairness, or rights.* As previously pointed out, a comprehensive ethical decision cannot be made if one of these three aspects is overlooked. Repeatedly, however, decision makers short-circuit their assessments and suffer the consequences.

| *Failure to consider the motivation for the decision.* For many years, businesspeople and professionals weren't concerned about the motivation for an action, as long as the consequences were acceptable. Unfortunately, many decision makers lost sight of the need to increase overall net benefits for all (or as many as possible), and made decisions that benefited themselves, or only a select few, in the short run and disadvantaged others in the longer run. These shortsighted, purely self-interested decision makers represent high governance risks for organizations.

| *Failure to consider the virtues that are expected to be demonstrated.* Board members, executives, and professional accountants are expected to act in good faith and discharge the duties of a fiduciary for people relying on them. Ignoring the virtues expected of them can lead to dishonesty, lack of integrity in the preparation of reports, failure to act on behalf of stakeholders, and failure to discharge courage in confronting others who are involved in unethical acts, or in whistle-blowing when needed. Professional accountants who ignore virtues expected of them are prone to forget that they are expected to protect the public interest.

A Comprehensive Ethical Decision-Making Framework

A comprehensive EDM approach should include all four of the considerations outlined in Table 4.12. But this can be achieved within a philosophical analysis, a stakeholder impact analysis, or a hybrid analysis. Which one should a decision maker choose?

The best EDM approach will depend upon the nature of the proposed action or ethical dilemma and the stakeholders involved. For example, a problem involving short-term impacts and no externalities may be best suited to a modified 5-question analysis. A problem with longer-term impacts and/or externalities is probably better suited to a modified moral standards approach, or modified Pastin approach. A problem with significance for society rather than a corporation would likely be best analyzed using a philosophical approach, or the modified moral standards approach. Whatever the EDM approach used, the decision maker must consider all of the fundamental issues raised in Table 4.4 and articulated in Table 4.12.

Summary of Steps for an Ethical Decision

The approaches and issues previously discussed can be used independently or in hybrid combination to assist in producing an ethical decision. Experience has shown that completing the following three steps provides a sound basis for challenging a proposed decision.

1. *Identify* the facts and all stakeholder groups and interests likely to be affected.
2. *Rank* the stakeholders and their interests, identifying the most important and weighting them more than other issues in the analysis.
3. *Assess the impact* of the proposed action on each stakeholder group interests with regard to their well-offness, fairness of treatment, and other rights, including virtue expectations, using a comprehensive framework of questions, and making sure that the common pitfalls discussed later do not enter into the analysis.

It may be helpful to organize an ethical decision analysis using the seven steps outlined by the American Accounting Association (1993) as follows:

1. Determine the facts—what, who, where, when, and how.
2. Define the ethical issue(s).
3. Identify major principles, rules, and values.
4. Specify the alternatives.
5. Compare values and alternatives, and see if a clear decision emerges.
6. Assess the consequences.
7. Make your decision.

Steps toward an ethical decision are summarized in Figure 4.5.

Conclusion

Stakeholder impact analysis offers a formal way of bringing into a decision the needs of an organization and its individual constituents (society). Trade-offs are difficult and can benefit from such advances in technique. It is important not to lose sight of the fact that the concepts of stakeholder impact analysis that are reviewed in this chapter need to be applied not as single techniques but together as a set. Only then will a comprehensive analysis be achieved and an ethical decision made. Depending on the nature of the decision to be faced, and the range of stakeholders to be affected, a proper analysis could be based on consequentialism, deontology,

4.5   **Steps Toward an Ethical Decision**

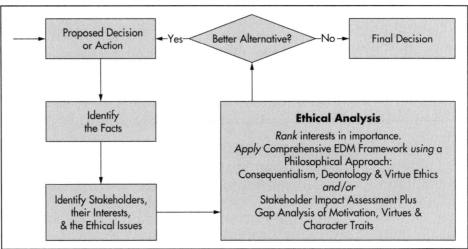

and virtue ethics as a set, or within one of the modified 5-question, moral standards, or Pastin approaches, taking into account the possible existence of commons problems that might arise. Any comprehensive EDM approach must include not only an examination of the impacts of the decision or action, but also a gap analysis of the motivations, virtues, and character traits involved.

A professional accountant can use stakeholder analysis in making decisions about accounting, auditing, and practice matters, and should be ready to prepare or assist in such analyses for employers or clients just as is currently the case in other areas. Although many hard-numbers-oriented executives and accountants will be wary of becoming involved with the "soft" subjective analysis that typifies stakeholder and virtue expectations analysis, they should bear in mind that the world is changing to put a much higher value on nonnumerical information. They should beware of placing too much weight on numerical analysis lest they fall into the trap of the economist, who, as Oscar Wilde put it: "knew the price of everything and the value of nothing."

Directors, executives, and accountants should also understand that the techniques discussed in this chapter offer a means of better understanding the interplay between their organization and/or profession and its potential supporters. The assessment of impacts on stakeholders when combined with the ranking of each stakeholder's ability to withstand the action will lead to the better achievement of strategic objectives based on satisfied stakeholders. Operating successfully in an increasingly demanding global network of stakeholders will require that future actions are not only legal, but also ethically defensible.

Questions

1. Why should directors, executives, and accountants understand consequentialism, deontology, and virtue ethics?

2. Before the recent financial scandals and governance reforms, few corporate leaders were selected for their "virtues" other than their ability to make profits. Has this changed, and if so, why?

3. Is it wise for a decision maker to take into account more than profit when making decisions that have a significant social impact? Why?

4. If a framework for ethical decision-making is to be employed, why is it essential to incorporate all four considerations of well-offness, fairness, individual rights and duties, and virtues expected?

5. Is the modified 5-question approach to ethical decision-making superior to the modified versions of the moral standards or Pastin approach?

6. Under what circumstances would it be best to use each of the following frameworks: the philosophical set of consequentialism, deontology, and virtue ethics; the modified 5-question; modified moral standards; and the modified Pastin approach?

7. How would you convince a CEO not to treat the environment as a cost-free commons?

8. How can a decision to downsize be made as ethical as possible by treating everyone equally?

9. From a virtue ethics perspective, why would it be logical to put in place a manufacturing process beyond legal requirements?

10. List the companies that have faced ethical tragedies due the following failings in their ethical culture:
    a. Lack of ethical leadership.
    b. Lack of clarity about important values.
    c. Lack of ethical awareness and expectations by employees.
    d. Lack of monitoring of ethicality of actions.
    e. Unethical reward systems.
    f. Unreasonable pressures for unrealistic performance.

11. Give an example of behavior that might be unethical even though "everyone is doing it".

Reading Insights

The two readings that are provided for this chapter are intended to offer the reader further elaboration on cost–benefit analysis and the 5-question approach to ethical decision-making.

References

AACSB International (Association to Advance Collegiate Schools of Business). *Ethics Education in Business Schools: Report of the Ethics Education Task Force*, St. Louis, MO, 2004, http://www.aacsb.edu/resource_centers/EthicsEdu/eetf.asp.

American Accounting Association. *Ethics in the Accounting Curriculum: Cases & Readings*, updated edition. Sarasota, FL: American Accounting Association, 1993. See Introduction by William May.

Aristotle. *The Nicomachean Ethics*, translated with an introduction by David Ross, revised by J. L. Ackrill and J. O. Urmson, Oxford University Press, 1925.

Athanassoulis, Nafsika. "Virtue Ethics," *The Internet Encyclopedia of Philosophy*, 2004, http://www.iep.utm.edu/v/virtue.htm.

Brooks, L. J. "Cost–Benefit Analysis," *CAmagazine*, October 1979, 53–57.

Brooks, L.J. "Sniff Tests," *Corporate Ethics Monitor*, 7:5 (1995): 65.

Cafaro, Philip. "Virtue Ethics (Not Too) Simplified," paper presented at the Twentieth World Congress of Philosophy, in Boston, MA, from August 10–15, 1998, see http://www.bu.edu/wcp/Papers/TEth/TEthCafa.htm.

Carroll, A.B. "Principles of Business Ethics: Their Role in Decision making and Initial Consensus," *Management Decision*, 28:8 (1990): 20–24.

Freeman, R. Edward. *Strategic Management: A Stakeholder Approach*, Boston, MA: Pitman, 1984.

Hursthouse, Rosalind. "Virtue Ethics," *The Stanford Encyclopedia of Philosophy*, Fall 2003 Edition, Edward N. Zalta, ed., http://plato.stanford.edu/archives/fall2003/entries/ethics-virtue/.

International Federation of Accountants. *International Standards for the Education of Professional Accountants* (IES 1-6) including *IES 4: Professional Values, Skills and Attitudes*, New York, NY, 2003; IES 4: 59–65.

Kant, Immanuel. *Groundwork of the Metaphysics of Morals*, translated with an introduction by H. J. Paton, Harper Torchbooks, 1964.

Kay, Charles D. "Notes on Deontology," 1997, http://www.webs.wofford.edu/kayed/ethics/deon.htm.

Mill, John S. *Utilitarianism*, edited with introduction by Roger Crisp, New York: Oxford University Press, 1998. First published in 1861.

Mitchell, R. K., Agle, B. R., and Wood, D. J. "Toward a Theory of Stakeholder Identification and Salience: Defining the Principle of Who and What Really Counts," *Academy of Management Review*, 22, no. 4 (1997): 853–886.

Pastin, M. *The Hard Problems of Management: Gaining the Ethics Edge*. San Francisco: Jossey-Bass 1986.

Rawls, John. *A Theory of Justice*. Cambridge, MA: Harvard University Press, 1971.

Rowley, T. "Moving Beyond Dyadic Ties: A Network Theory of Stakeholder Influences," *Academy of Management Review*, 22, no. 4 (1997): 887–910.

Roty, Amelie Oksenberg (ed). *Essays on Aristotle's Ethics*. Berkeley, CA: University of California Press, 1980.

Sinnott-Armstrong, Walter. "Consequentialism," *Stanford Encyclopedia of Philosophy*, 2003, http://plato.stanford.edu/archives/fall2003/entries/consequentialism/.

Stumpf, Samuel Enoch. *Socrates to Sartre: A History of Philosophy*. New York: McGraw-Hill, 1988.

Tucker, G. "Ethical Analysis for Environmental Problem Solving," *Agenda for Action Conference Proceedings*, The Canadian Centre for Ethics & Corporate Policy, 1990, 53–57.

Velasquez, M. G. *Business Ethics: Concepts and Cases*, Englewood Cliffs, NJ.: Prentice-Hall, 1992.

Case and Illustrative Application Insights

Illustrative Applications

- *Dealing with Disappointed Apple iPhone Customers Case*—a comprehensive ethical analysis of the decision Apple made to re-price the iPhone soon after its introduction—an extension of the illustration from Chapter 3.

- *Bribery or Opportunity in China*—a real-life example of how a young executive faced the realities of business abroad, and how he came to an innovation solution.

- *Proposed Audit Adjustment?*—describes the thinking involved in proposing an adjustment to year-end audited financial statements.

- *When Does an "Aggressive Accounting" Choice Become Fraudulent?*—indicates how the fundamental interests of stakeholders described in Table 4.4 ought to generate issues to be considered in a stakeholder impact analysis on the topic of accounting choices.

Cases

- *Vioxx Decisions—Were They Ethical?*—provides an opportunity for students to research a serious dilemma that is currently in the news and develop a comprehensive, practical ethical analysis of the decisions faced by Merck, the manufacturer, which now faces over 9,000 lawsuits and 18,000 plaintiffs. Students will also consider how the current dilemma could have been avoided.

- *Just Do It—Make the Numbers!* CFOs are often influenced, ordered or coerced to bend the rules to make financial results better and often equal to prior projections released to the public. It's not an easy decision when your demanding boss is standing over you. What should a professional accountant consider before doing so?

- *Smokers Are Good for the Economy—Really* presents an argument that is counterintuitive in that cigarette smoking can be good. Does this actuarial/economics–based argument take into account all that a comprehensive ethical analysis should?

- *The Ford Pinto* case is a classic that shows in stark relief the danger of ignoring the social impacts of a decision in favor of maximizing short-run profit. The original cost–benefit analysis was quite faulty, and our appreciation of safety has changed a lot since the Pinto was created, but the same problems continue to recur.

- *Kardell Paper* involves the possible pollution of a river with potentially life-threatening consequences. In addition to dealing with uncertainty, the reader learns to appreciate issues such as whistle-blowing, representative corporate governance at the board level, and due diligence requirements on the part of executives and board members.

An Illustration of Comprehensive Ethical Decision Making

Dealing with Disappointed Apple iPhone Customers Case

On September 5, 2007, Steve Jobs, the CEO of Apple Inc, announced that the spectacularly successful iPhone would be reduced in price by $200 from $599, its introductory price of roughly two months earlier.[1] Needless to say, he received hundreds of e-mails from irate customers. Two days later, he offered early customers who paid full price a $100 credit good at Apple's retail and online stores. Was this decision to mitigate the $200 price decrease, and the manner of doing so, appropriate from an ethical perspective?

If Apple management had used a *sniff test* before the decision, they might have come to the conclusion that their mothers wouldn't have been proud of or comfortable with it. Similarly, they might have discovered that the price reduction may have offended the Apple Code of Conduct for treatment of customers.

If Apple had considered the *stakeholder impacts* that the decision involved, they would have realized that, while past consumers would be most affected, the reputation of Apple would also be tarnished, and that could affect future consumers who they were trying to encourage. In addition, Apple employees—many of whom had been attracted by the strong Apple reputation for providing innovative solution of high quality—would question the company's motives, which could weaken their loyalty and commitment.

If Apple personnel had applied *traditional philosophers' ethical tests*, they would have found the following:

Consequentialism
From a profit perspective, Apple was expecting to more than offset the $200 per unit drop in margin with a gain in volume of sales. For the iPhone alone, this may have been correct, but Apple has many products that are to be bought by other customers who could be affected negatively and who would see the decision as an opportunistic price decrease from an extraordinarily high starting price. Gouging behavior could be suspected, which would undermine Apple's wholesome value proposition and non-iPhone sales would suffer as a result. Overall, management might not be certain of making a combined net profit on sales of iPhones and other products.

Duty, Rights, and Justice Issues
Apple executives have a duty to make profits, as long as doing so doesn't violate any laws. In this case, early customers of the iPhone might have a legally enforceable right to sue for unfair practices, but individual actions would be far less likely than a class action. While the outcome is a matter of speculation, the prospect of further bad press that tarnishes Apple's image is of considerable concern due to the ripple affects noted above. The impact of unfairness of the price reduction could be magnified significantly by bad press. It is unlikely, although the early purchasers had the notoriety of having the newest technology available, that Apple management would have thought the $200 price reduction was fair if they had been personally affected.

Virtues Expected
In the minds of Apple's customers and employees, Jobs has an image of

---

1. David Ho, "Apple CEO apologizes to customers," *The Toronto Star*, September 7, 2007, B4.

a far-sighted technical genius who has been driven to provide great value for his stakeholders, and this image has been transferred to Apple itself. For many stakeholders, the $200 price decrease doesn't match up to the expectations they have come to expect of Jobs or of Apple.

Apple might also have used the questions developed in the modified *Tucker Framework* to test the proposed $200 price decrease. If so, the answers could have been as follows:

1. Is it profitable?—outcome is not clear as discussed earlier

2. Is it legal?—probably, unless a consumer protection act is offended

3. Is it fair?—not according to some customers and employees

4. Is it right?—no, according to some executives, employees, and potential customers

5. Does it demonstrate the expected virtues?—no, as discussed earlier

6. Optional question: Is it sustainable (environmentally or over time)? The environmental impact issue is not involved in this decision, but the medium and longer-term impacts are likely to be negative and may be

significant. It would be unwise to repeat such a decision, or to ignore the possible future negative impacts to reputation.

On balance, Apple should consider the $200 price decrease to be unfair and unwise without some mitigation for early purchasers of the iPhone. Is the credit of $100 adequate, and its restricted use appropriate? Another analysis could be run, and a sound solution arrived at in an iterative fashion, applying moral imagination where possible. In this case it is probable that judgment will have to be applied. Time will tell. In any event, Jobs could have avoided the initial negative press and damage to his and Apple's reputation, if Apple had used the ethical decision making tools to analyze the decision before putting it into action.

It should be noted that, although price discounts of the type described in this case are not uncommon, and are not generally regarded as serious ethical problems, they have an ethical aspect that can be assessed using the ethical decision making approaches discussed in this chapter. They certainly represent risks that could weaken the reputation of executives and the company involved.

Source: Reprinted with permission from: *Ethics & Governance: Developing & Maintaining An Ethical Corporate Culture*, L.J. Brooks & David Selley, Canadian Centre for Ethics & Corporate Policy, Toronto, Canada, 2008.

Illustrative Application of Stakeholder Impact Analysis

Bribery or Opportunity in China Case

Note: Names have been changed

John Low, a North American born of Chinese descent, was given the opportunity of his lifetime. He was asked to go to China and set up a manufacturing subsidiary in a medium-sized city in the middle of the country. He had arrived in the city and had attempted to set up a new building and manufacturing facility which would employ thirty people, but had run into many delays in dealings with the local authorities. Ultimately, John met with the three senior officials and asked what the problem was. They indicated that things would go a lot faster if John's company was to make them a payment of

$100,000 each. This, they said, was quite reasonable in view of what other companies had been paying.

John was in a quandary. When he had been sent to China, his boss had told him that under no circumstances were any bribes to be paid. It was against company policy and it would not be tolerated. On the other hand, John was expected to get his job done, and his boss had told him that unless he did so, another manager would be sent to take over John's position. John knew that his budget contained a provision for payments to agents, but the total allowed was only

$150,000. He knew that if the facility was delayed, every month of delay would cost his company a contribution of approximately $25,000. John told the senior officials repeatedly that there was no way his company would pay them, but they were insistent.

Questions

1. Should John pay the bribes?
2. Is there something else he could do instead?

Illustrative Solution

The first step in a stakeholder impact analysis is to identify all stakeholder groups affected by

the proposed action and their interests. At the end of the identification process, the stakeholders and their interests are to be ranked in importance. These two steps can be facilitated by means of a tabular analysis as shown below.

In this situation, with the proposed action being to pay the bribes or not, there aren't many externalities, but there are legalities and company ground rules. Consequently, John could use a hybrid ethical decision framework based upon the 5-question, but with the use of net benefit in addition to profit and ground rule ethics. The questions or challenges for the proposed action are therefore as shown in the table on the top of next page, with responses noted.

Analysis of Stakeholders and Their Interests

STAKEHOLDER	INTEREST	LEGITIMACY/LEGAL INFLUENCE	POWER TO AFFECT CO.	URGENCY OF CLAIM	PRIMARY OR SECONDARY	RANK IN IMPORTANCE: 1 IS HIGHEST, 3 IS LOWEST
John	Potential success or dismissal, unless a new idea can be found. Prob. of discovery estimated at 60%	Yes	Yes	High	Primary	1
Local employees	Delay in job, or no job	No	Not yet	Low	Secondary for now	3
John's boss	John's success is his own, but he runs the risk of sanction if John is found to have bribed	Yes	Yes	High, but less than John's	Primary	2
Other managers elsewhere	Company policy will be eroded, so observance will be difficult, since employees will know of breach	Yes	Yes	Medium	Primary	2
Shareholders	Financial success earlier, but costs of bribes will raise costs, and will be called for in many situations. Possible fines and bad publicity if caught, and *Foreign Corrupt Practices Act* or similar applies, so profits down, Prob. 40%	Yes	Yes	High	Primary	1
Chinese officials	$300,000 richer if not caught, then? Prob. 10 %	Yes	Yes	Medium/high	Primary	1
Directors and senior executives	Directors same as shareholders. Exec. no bonuses and could be dismissed	Yes	Yes	High, but less than John's	Primary	1
Elderly Chinese in town (leaders in society)	No benefit until local employment starts, or other benefit created	No	Yes, very influential	Low	Appears secondary, but could be primary	1
Chinese government	Bribes raise cost of doing business in China	Yes	Yes, but distant	Low	Secondary for now	3
John's family	Unknown if he has any					Not Applic.

Challenges to Proposed Action: Payment of Bribes

QUESTION OR CHALLENGE	RESPONSE
1. Is it profitable?	Maybe for company. $25K per month × 40% prob. of being caught—cost of fines and additional bribes elsewhere. John, probably not, as prob. of being caught is 60%.
2. Is it legal?	Not really, but maybe if creative arrangement with an agent is successful and/or this is considered a facilitating payment, not a bribe.
3. Is it fair?	Not to John, or his boss, or top management, to China, or to elderly Chinese.
4. Is it right? Generally?	Everyone is doing it, so maybe.
Per company ground rules?	Not per company ground rules and code.
Per John?	Not known.
5. Does it provide the highest net benefit for all?	Maybe, unless a better idea is found.

Based on this analysis, John found several responses that were negative or not clearly positive, indicating an unethical—and in this case illegal—decision. Yet, he had to bribe or admit failure unless he could find an ethical alternative.

John also asked himself whether the decision to bribe would involve and exhibit the motivations, virtues, and character traits expected. His answers appear in the table below.

Bribery was not in accord with expected motivations, virtues or character traits, so John began to look for other alternatives. He began to consider the primary stakeholders to the company's long-run success in the area. He realized that the company's relationship with the Chinese elderly was going to be of high long-run significance because the elderly are very influential in Chinese culture. What could he do to satisfy the elderly and perhaps bring the local officials on-side as well? At the same time he did not want to offend his company's ground rules which were to observe the code and not to bribe.

He had noticed that there wasn't really a good place for the elderly to gather, like his own parents had back home. In the end, he asked his boss if his company ever supported community centers, and the answer was yes. The company's donations budget would provide the funds and company officials were quite interested in paying for a senior citizens' center and park in the Chinese town as part of the company's good corporate citizen program of supporting the communities that they operated in. John proposed this to the senior Chinese officials who wanted the bribes, indicating that his company would not make such payments directly to anyone. The officials, however, would get credit by association with the park and center and would, of course, serve on the Board of Directors of the Center when it was finished.

John's plant was ready in record time, and he was awarded a citation by his company's CEO who was also the person in charge of the company's ethics program. It seemed apparent that he had found a solution that provided the highest net benefit to all—a true win-win-win arrangement—that matched well to expected motivations, virtues, and character traits.

Expected Motivations, Virtues, & Character Traits

QUESTION: DOES THE DECISION OR ACTION (TO BRIBE) INVOLVE OR EXHIBIT THE EXPECTED:	RESPONSE
Motivations	Possibly, but higher levels of self-control, fairness, and/or caring may be possible with other alternatives.
Virtues	No. John would be breaching his CEO/company's expectations. Dutiful loyalty, integrity, and sincerity would be below expectations. Duplicity would be required, rather than transparency, to appear to comply with company codes and Chinese law.
Character Traits	No. It is doubtful that John would be considered trustworthy, honest, or truthful if he bribes and is found out.

<table>
<tr><td>

Illustrative
Application of
Stakeholder
Impact
Analysis

</td></tr>
</table>

Proposed Audit Adjustment Case—Castle Manufacturing Inc.

Larry Plant, the Chief Financial Officer of Castle Manufacturing Inc., was involved in a lengthy discussion with Joyce Tang of the company's auditing firm, Bennett & Sange at the conclusion of the audit fieldwork.

"Look Joyce, we just can't afford to show that much profit this year. If we do record the $1.5 million after-tax adjustment you propose, our profit will be 20 percent higher than we had two years ago and 5 percent higher than we reported last year. On the other hand, without the adjustment, we would be close to last year's level. We are just about to enter negotiations with our labor unions, and we have been complaining about our ability to compete. If we show that much profit improvement, they will ask for a huge raise in rates. Our company will become non-competitive due to higher labor rates than our offshore competition. Do you really want that to happen?"

"But Larry, you really earned the profit. You can't just ignore it!"

"No, I'm not suggesting that, Joyce. But virtually all of the goods making up the profit adjustment were in transit at our year end—so let's just record them as next year's sales and profits."

"But, Larry, they were all sold FOB your plant, so title passed to the buyer when they were shipped."

"I know that, Joyce, but that was an unusual move by our overzealous sales staff, who were trying to look good and get a high commission on year-end numbers. Anyway, the customer hadn't inspected them yet. Just this once, Joyce, let's put it into next year. It's not really a significant amount for our shareholders, but it will trigger a much bigger problem for them if the unions get a hold of the higher profit numbers. As you know, about 40 percent of our shares were willed to the United Charities Appeal here in town, and they could sure benefit by higher profits and dividends in the future. I bet the difference in their dividends could be up to $400,000 per year over the life of the next five-year contract."

Question

1. What should Joyce do?

Illustrative Solution

Several approaches to ethical decision making are presented in the chapter: the philosophical, or those to be used with an assessment of the motivations, virtues, and character traits—the 5-question approach, the moral standards approach, and the Pastin approach. In this illustrative solution, the 5-question framework will be used, with expansions, where necessary, drawn from other approaches.

The 5-question approach calls for the identification of the stakeholders impacted by the decision and then poses five questions or challenges to assess whether these impacts are ethical or not. If some aspect of the decision is considered not to be ethical, the proposed decision/action may be altered to mitigate or remove the unethical element.

In this case, the auditor has proposed that a $1.5 million adjustment be made to increase the profitability of the client Castle Manufacturing Inc. The CFO is resisting, proposing instead that the impact on profit be put into the next year so as to gain a bargaining advantage over the company's unions, who will use the profit figures to negotiate a new five-year agreement. Joyce Tang, the auditor, must decide whether the proposal to shift the adjustment to the next year is ethical: if not, she must convince the CFO to record the adjustment or qualify her audit report. It is not immediately apparent whether the adjustment is material or not: if it was, the correct action would be to qualify the audit report if the CFO were to hold fast to his proposal.

Identification of Stakeholders and Their Interests

The CFO's proposal would impact on the following stakeholders:

STAKEHOLDERS	INTERESTS
Directly Impacted:	
Current shareholders wishing to sell their shares in the short run	They would want the adjustment recorded in the current year to boost profit and share values.
Current shareholders wishing to hold on to their shares	They would want the adjustment deferred to minimize the labor settlement and maximize future profits and dividends.
Future shareholders	They would want an accurate assessment of profitability to properly assess whether or not to buy into the company. If profits are depressed, they might not buy in, so the increased future profits may not be relevant.
Employees	They would want profits accurately stated to provide a higher basis for negotiation assuming this would not jeopardize the long-run viability of the enterprise.
Company management	Depending on their bonus arrangements and their altruism, they would want short or longer-term recognition of the adjustment.
Directors	They would want the long-run profit improvement, provided they would not be sued for sanctioning something illegal.
Creditors, suppliers, and lenders	If the labor negotiations result in higher profitability and liquidity, these stakeholders would want the adjustment deferred.
Governments and regulators	They would want profits accurately stated because this would result in higher taxes and fewer potential complaints from other stakeholders (e.g., unions).
Joyce and her audit firm	They would want to minimize the chance of legal and professional challenges arising from the audit that would result in fines and/ or loss of reputation, but they also would wish to continue auditing a healthy client.
Indirectly Impacted:	
Recipients of the funds generated by the United Charities Appeal	They would want the adjustment deferred.
Altruistic management of the United Charities Appeal	They would want the adjustment properly dealt with, which would probably mean that they would side with the employees.
Host communities	They would want the highest labor rate settlement possible without jeopardizing the long-run health of the enterprise.
The auditing profession	It would want to avoid loss of reputation for the profession.

Ranking of Stakeholder's Interests

The stakeholders' interests in the decision identified above can be ranked as to their importance on "possessing legal rights," "ability to withstand both financially and psychologically" (a rank of "1" is worst), and "probable public reaction on behalf of" scales, as follows:

STAKEHOLDERS IMPACTED	POSSESS LEGAL RIGHTS	RANK OF ABILITY TO WITHSTAND	PROBABLE PUBLIC REACTION FOR
Current shareholders—wishing to sell	Yes—first	3	Low
Current shareholders—wishing to hold	Yes—tie	3	Low
Future shareholders	Yes	3	Low
Employees:	No—none	2	Strong
- if contract is GAAP based	Yes	2	Strong
- if financial statement is used in negotiation	Yes—poss.	2	Strong
Company management—dependent on contract	Yes or no	3	Low
Directors	Yes	2	Low
Creditors, suppliers	No	4	Low
Lenders—dependent on contract	No or yes	4	Low
Governments and regulators	Yes	4	Moderate
Joyce and her audit firm	Yes	2	Strong
Recipients of charity funds	No	1	Strong
Altruistic management of charity	No	3 or 2	Strong
Host communities	No	4	Moderate
Auditing profession	No	3	Strong

It is evident from these rankings that the strength of legal rights does not correspond to the rankings of a stakeholder's ability to withstand the decision or to the probable public reaction on behalf of each stakeholder if the decision to defer the adjustment becomes public. Moreover, the legal rights of stakeholders with differing interests are equal. The "probable public reaction" scale, which corresponds strongly to the "ability to withstand" scale, offers a good idea of how politicians, governments, and regulators will react. Consequently, decision makers would be unwise to focus only on the legality of stakeholder positions.

Of course, the likelihood of the deferment becoming public has to be estimated. Unfortunately, most decision makers overlook the possibility of an altruistic or disgruntled whistle-blower making the disclosure public or, alternatively, revealing it to the union bargaining team. As a result, the valid probability of revelation is usually far higher than the decision maker's assessment.

Application of the 5-Question Approach

Question 1: Profitability

There is no doubt that the deferment of an upward adjustment of $1.5 million to profit will decrease profit this year and increase it the next. In addition, there is some possibility, if the decision doesn't become public or known to the union, that the company's profits over the life of the contract will rise substantially if total dividends will rise by $1.0 million per year ($400,000/40 percent). However, if the decision becomes known, the union may retaliate and bargain harder, lawsuits may be launched against the company, the executives, and the auditors, and governments may levy tax penalties and fines. Consequently, the outcome on the profitability question is uncertain for the company and therefore for its shareholders and their dependants (and for the auditor, for that matter).

Question 2: Legality

Given that the decision to defer the adjustment is in the gray area of Generally Accepted Accounting Principles (GAAP) (it is not clearly material—although it is suspiciously significant—nor is it contravening usual company practice, the customers have not inspected the goods at year end, and it is a conservative treatment), it might be declared reasonable in a court of law. However, the legal process, which usually covers the company, its management and directors, and the auditor as being joint and severally liable, will involve legal fees, expert witness testimony, commitment of time (which soaks up billable time), and the potential of having to pursue other co-defendants for restitution if they are found to be culpable rather than the auditor. Of course, the auditor could mitigate these legal consequences be qualifying her report, but that would obviate the exercise and could create ill will with the CFO and possibly the rest of the management and directors. Because the legal interests do not coincide, and a lawsuit is likely if the deferment is known, the decision maker may not be able to take comfort from the fact that the deferment is probably within the boundaries of GAAP and therefore legal.

Question 3: Fairness

While the decision to defer the $1.5 million adjustment may not be considered material to an investor making the decision to invest or divest, it may be very significant to the employees and their union, and to the charity and its dependents. Consequently, not to disclose the $1.5 million this year may be unfair to these interest groups. If the decision becomes public, this unfair treatment may result in lawsuits and may bring the company, its auditors, and the auditing profession into disrepute with the public. The claim would be that these parties were not acting in the public interest; that the auditors failed to lend credibility to the financial statements and thereby failed to protect the public.

Question 4: Impact on Rights

To the extent that the proposed decision impacted negatively on the rights of stakeholders, in terms of life, health, privacy, dignity, etc. (i.e. rights other than fairness and legal rights which are canvassed in questions 2 and 3), the decision would be considered unethical. In this case, there are no lives at stake, but conceivably the health and well-being of the

SUGGESTED FORMAT PROJECTED	SHORT-TERM PROFIT	FIVE-YEAR PROFIT	COST–BENEFIT ANALYSIS	RISK–BENEFIT ANALYSIS
Revenues/cost savings/benefits				
Costs/opportunity costs				
Net profit/net benefits				

employees and particularly the ultimate recipients of the charity are at stake. The extent of this infringement would be revealed by further investigation. Given the information in the case, the degree of infringement of stakeholder rights is unclear.

Question 5: Does it contribute favorably to sustainable development and/or survivability?

From the environmental perspective, the deferment decision appears to have nothing to do with the company's impact on sustainable development. Also, there is probably no impact on the ability of the company to survive because the $1.5 million adjustment appears to be only 5 percent of the after-tax profit before the adjustment. However, it is unlikely that the deferment could be repeated year after year without offending GAAP.

Summary of Findings of 5-Question Approach

This analysis has shown that the proposed deferment is probably legal but may not be profitable, fair, or respectful of stakeholder's rights. Certainly the examination of just a one-year time frame would have proven to be misleading. Further analysis appears needed to reach a conclusive decision on many issues, and even then reflection will be needed to weigh the trade-offs between interests.

Extensions of the 5-Question Approach

The stakeholder impact challenges inherent in the 5-question approach, the moral standards approach, and Pastin's approach can be grouped into three areas: well-offness, fairness, and rights.

On the dimension of well-offness, it is evident that looking only at the profitability of the decision focuses discussion of the interests of shareholders rather than stakeholders. The way to broaden the focus is to prepare an analysis over a longer rather than shorter time frame so some of the externalities are included; to use cost–benefit analysis to bring in intangibles, such as the loss of quality of life; and to use risk–benefit analysis to include probabilities of occurrences. These enhancements have been included intuitively in the previous analysis but could be sharpened with further investigation and presented formally to the decision maker to assist in their decision, perhaps in the format above.

This presentation would allow the decision maker to see what the short-term and longer-term impact on profits was, and what the overall net benefits were likely to be for all stakeholders. Frequently, the benefits and costs accruing to stakeholders ultimately accrue to shareholders, so this presentation will allow a decision maker to project what may result from the decision. In this case, we do not have enough information to develop estimates for the costs and benefits associated with the positions of many stakeholders.

With regard to fairness, the concept of ranking stakeholders on several dimensions has already been employed. If the fairness of an impact is ever in doubt, one way to assess it is to put yourself in the position of the stakeholder being assessed. If you would be willing to change places with the other party, then the decision is probably fair. If not, the decision may be made fair by altering or reengineering its impact in some way.

The consideration of impacts on stakeholder rights can be enhanced beyond the level employed in this analysis by a heightened awareness of commons problems. Sometimes rights shared with others are taken for granted, but they should not be. The environment is one example of this, but there may be others on which specific decisions impact.

Expected Motivations, Virtues, and Character Traits

QUESTION: DOES THE DECISION OR ACTION INVOLVE OR EXHIBIT THE EXPECTED:	RESPONSE
Motivations	Possibly not. As a professional accountant, Joyce is supposed to use her unbiased, fair judgment to protect the public interest by following GAAP and her professional accounting code. This protects future shareholders from harmful actions that would benefit existing shareholders.
Virtues	If Joyce's action of lowering profit by $1.5 million becomes known, future shareholders, some current shareholders, and the employees will consider it unethical because Joyce will appear: - to be disloyal to her profession and those shareholders, - to be lacking in integrity and the desire to support transparency, and - duplicitous.
Character Traits	The disenchanted stakeholders will take the view that Joyce is untrustworthy, partial to some stakeholders, and lacking the courage to stand up for the rights of all stakeholders.

Assessment of Motivations, Virtues, and Character Traits Expected

All of the stakeholder impact assessment approaches, or any hybrid approach, should be augmented by an assessment of motivations, virtues, and character traits involved in and exhibited by the decision or action compared to what is expected. In this case, for Joyce Tang, the decision maker, this assessment would be as follows.

In this decision, there doesn't appear to be much room for re-engineering to make its impact more ethical, so it must be faced as it is.

Conclusion

Although the proposed decision appears to hold some promise of profitability, and could be within GAAP and legal, it does not appear to be fair or right to several stakeholders. *Although the proposed action's impact may not be material for* *investors, it is significant to several stakeholders.* The proposed action does not match expectations for ethical motivations, virtues, or character traits. Consequently, it is somewhat unethical and may result in significant negative reaction for the directors, auditor, and auditing profession. These matters and their consequences should be fully explained to the Audit Committee of the Board of Directors. In the post-Sarbanes-Oxley regime, the Audit Committee should be informed by the auditor of such disputes with management and what the auditor's opinion was. If the Audit Committee agrees with management (whose mandate includes the preparation of the financial statements) to exclude the $1.5 million profit, the full board should be advised and the auditor should consult within her firm to arrive at a consensus position on whether or not to qualify the audit report. In this way, the decision can be shared among those who would be held responsible.

Illustrative Application of Stakeholder Impact Analysis

When Does An "Aggressive Accounting" Choice Become Fraudulent?

Fraudulent choices of accounting treatment are those which contain such an element of deception that a reasonably informed and careful investor or other financial report user would be misled to his or her detriment as a result. For instance, revenue or expenses may be misstated to improperly increase current profit (thus diminishing future profits) to raise share prices or increase management bonuses. This would put future shareholders at a disadvantage as they would be buying shares at inflated prices while the company's assets would be reduced by the bonus money paid out.

There are, however, times when generally accepted accounting principles (GAAP) allow a choice among alternative treatments where some are more aggressive than others which are considered conservative usually because of their tendency not to inflate current profits. For instance, a company's management may choose different approaches to depreciate its fixed assets which would give rise to different depreciation charges against profit. Similarly, a range of choices is available for accounting for goodwill, or the recognition of warrantee expense, or the recognition of revenue from construction contracts. If these accounting choices are made without consideration of all possible accounting practices, current and future shareholders may not be properly served. However, unless there is an effective ethical framework for deciding which of these choices to make, accounting choices may become too aggressive and fraudulent.

The following ethical framework and issues may be helpful in making choices that are aggressive but not fraudulent.

FUNDAMENTAL STAKEHOLDER INTEREST	ISSUES TO BE CONSIDERED
Well-offness	Are current and future shareholders' interests reported clearly and accurately, and as the related economic reality warrants?
Fairness	Are the interests of current shareholders, future shareholders, management or other stakeholders unfairly disadvantaged with the benefit being transferred to another stakeholder?

Right(s)	Are the rights of stakeholders observed, including adherence to:
	• Professional fiduciary focus on duty to the public
	• Professional standards–objectivity, accuracy, integrity, competency, fair presentation
	• GAAP
	• Securities Commissions guidelines for:
	  • Full, true and plain disclosure
	  • Specific disclosures
	• Company policies such as for clarity and completeness?

Virtue Expectation	Motivations, Virtues, Character Traits (see Table 5.9)

Ethics Case

Vioxx Decisions—Were They Ethical? [1]

On September 30, 2004, Merck voluntarily withdrew its rheumatoid arthritis drug (Vioxx) from the market, due to severe adverse effects observed in many of its users (Exhibit 1). As a result, Merck's share price fell $11.48 (27%) in one day, translating to a market-cap loss of $25.6 billion. On August 19, 2005, the day a Texas jury found Merck liable for the death of a Vioxx user, the company's market cap fell another $5 billion. During this trial it became apparent that Merck had been profiting from Vioxx during the time it knew Vioxx had serious adverse effects.

Merck had obtained approval from the US Food and Drug Administration (FDA) for its drug Vioxx on May 20, 1999. By 2003 Vioxx was available in more than 80 countries and sales had soared to over $2.5 billion per year. Concurrently, increasing evidence (including data from Merck's own studies) suggested that

---

1. This case is based upon an assignment submitted by Rahbar Rahimpour, one of the author's Executive MBA students at the Rotman School of Management. Mr. Rahbar gave permission for this use.

those taking Vioxx were at an increased risk of cardiac arrest and stroke. Yet the drug remained on the market until September 2004.

The impact of the withdrawal on Merck's shareholders, management, patients, FDA and other stakeholders was dramatic. Public confidence and trust in Merck and other pharmaceutical companies were eroded. Currently, there are more than 9600 lawsuits from more than 18,200 plaintiffs pending against Merck. The company recently announced that it is setting $970 million aside to deal with these lawsuits, although some estimates are that Vioxx could cost Merck more than $20–$25 billion.

The FDA has been following the Vioxx case with interest, and has created a website page to provide information and updates at http://www.fda.gov/cder/drug/infopage/COX2/default.htm. Significant information is contained in the FDA's Public Health Advisory on Vioxx as its manufacturer voluntarily withdraws the product (FDA News (9/30/2004) that is reproduced below as Exhibit 1) and in the FDA Vioxx Questions and Answers (9/30/2004) webpage at http://www.fda.gov/cder/drug/infopage/vioxx/vioxxQA.htm. Two journal references are also provided.

Questions

1. Utilizing the information provided and available from web sources, use the ethical decision making techniques discussed in the chapter to form an opinion about whether Merck's decisions regarding Vioxx were ethical? Show your analysis.

2. In order to protect the public more fully, what should the FDA do given the Vioxx lessons?

References

Comparison of upper gastrointestinal toxicity of rofecoxib and naproxen in patients with rheumatoid arthritis. VIGOR Study Group, *New England Journal of Medicine,* Nov 2000 23;343 (21):1520–8, 2 p following 1528.

Cardiovascular events associated with rofecoxib in a colorectal adenoma chemoprevention trial. *New England Journal of Medicine,* Mar 2005 17;352(11):1092–102. Epub 2005 Feb 15.

EXHIBIT 1

Letter from the FDA Acknowledging Merck's Voluntary Withdrawal of Vioxx.

FDA Home Page | Search FDA Site | FDA A-Z Index | Contact FDA

FDA News

FOR IMMEDIATE RELEASE
P04-95
September 30, 2004

Media Inquiries: 301-827-6242
Consumer Inquiries: 888-INFO-FDA

FDA Issues Public Health Advisory on Vioxx as its Manufacturer Voluntarily Withdraws the Product

The Food and Drug Administration (FDA) today acknowledged the voluntary withdrawal from the market of Vioxx (chemical name rofecoxib), a non-steroidal anti-inflammatory drug (NSAID) manufactured by Merck & Co. FDA today also issued a Public Health Advisory to inform patients of this action and to advise them to consult with a physician about alternative medications.

Merck is withdrawing Vioxx from the market after the data safety monitoring board overseeing a long-term study of the drug recommended that the study be halted because of an increased risk of serious cardiovascular events, including heart attacks and strokes, among study patients taking Vioxx compared to patients receiving placebo. The study was being done in patients at risk of developing recurrent colon polyps.

"Merck did the right thing by promptly reporting these findings to FDA and voluntarily withdrawing the product from the market," said Acting FDA Commissioner Dr. Lester M. Crawford. "Although the risk that an individual patient would have a heart attack or stroke related to Vioxx is very small, the study that was halted suggests that, overall, patients taking the drug chronically face twice the risk of a heart attack compared to patients receiving a placebo."

Dr. Crawford added that FDA will closely monitor other drugs in this class for similar side effects. "All of the NSAID drugs have risks when taken chronically, especially of gastrointestinal bleeding, but also liver and kidney toxicity. They should only be used continuously under the supervision of a physician."

FDA approved Vioxx in 1999 for the reduction of pain and inflammation caused by osteoarthritis, as well as for acute pain in adults and for the treatment of menstrual pain. It was the second of a new kind of NSAID (Cox-2 selective) approved by FDA. Subsequently, FDA approved Vioxx to treat the signs and symptoms of rheumatoid arthritis in adults and children.

At the time that Vioxx and other Cox-2 selective NSAIDs were approved, it was hoped that they would have a lower risk of gastrointestinal ulcers and bleeding than other NSAIDs (such as ibuprofen and naproxen). Vioxx is the only NSAID demonstrated to have a lower rate of these side effects.

Merck contacted FDA on September 27, 2004, to request a meeting and to advise the agency that the long-term study of Vioxx in patients at increased risk of colon polyps had been halted. Merck and FDA officials met the next day, September 28, and during that meeting the company informed FDA of its decision to remove Vioxx from the market voluntarily.

In June 2000, Merck submitted to FDA a safety study called VIGOR (Vioxx Gastrointestinal Outcomes Research) that found an increased risk of serious cardiovascular events, including heart attacks and strokes, in patients taking Vioxx compared to patients taking naproxen. After reviewing the results of the VIGOR study and other available data from controlled clinical trials, FDA consulted with its Arthritis Advisory Committee in February 2001 regarding the clinical interpretation of this new safety information. In April 2002, FDA implemented labeling changes to reflect the findings from the VIGOR study. The labeling changes included information about the increase in risk of cardiovascular events, including heart attack and stroke.

Recently other studies in patients taking Vioxx have also suggested an increased risk of cardiovascular events. FDA was in the process of carefully reviewing these results, to determine whether further labeling changes were warranted, when Merck informed the agency of the results of the new trial and its decision to withdraw Vioxx from the market.

Additional information about this withdrawal of Vioxx, as well as questions and answers for patients, is available online at http://www.fda.gov/cder/drug/infopage/vioxx/default.htm.

Ethics Case | *Just Make the Numbers!*

The discussion between Don Chambers, the CEO, and Ron Smith, the CFO, was getting heated. Sales and margins were below expectations, and the stock market analysts had been behaving like sharks when other companies' published quarterly or annual financial results failed to reach analysts' expectations. Executives of companies whose performance numbers failed to meet the levels projected by the executives or the analysts were being savaged. Finally, in frustration, Don exclaimed:

"We must make our quarterly numbers! Find a way, change some assumptions, capitalize some line expenses—just do it! You know things will turn around next year."

And he stormed out of Ron's office.

Question

1. What should Ron consider when making his decision?

Ethics Case

Smokers Are Good for the Economy—Really[1]

Antismoking advocates cheered in the summer of 1997 when the U.S. tobacco industry agreed to pay out more than US$368.5 billion to settle lawsuits brought by forty states seeking compensation for cigarette-related Medicaid costs. Mississippi Attorney General Mike Moore, who helped organize the states' legal campaign, called the pact "the most historic public health achievement in history." But were the states right to do what they did?

The fundamental premise of lawsuits, and other anti-tobacco initiatives, is that smokers—and, hence, tobacco companies—place an added tax on all of us by heaping extra costs onto public health care systems. The argument is that those, and other social costs, outweigh the billions in duty and tax revenue that our governments collect from cigarette distribution.

But a basic actuarial analysis of that premise suggests that quite the opposite is true. As ghoulish as it may sound, smokers save the rest of us money because they die sooner and consume far less in health care and in benefits such as pensions. The extra costs they do generate are far outweighed by the subsidies they pay each time they plunk down their money for a pack of cigarettes.

First of all, let's look at life expectancy consistently over the past decade. In 1994 testimony before the U.S. Senate Finance Committee, the U.S. Office of Technology Assessment showed that the average smoker dies fifteen years earlier than a nonsmoker, so smokers cost society less in health care bills than nonsmokers because they die about a decade earlier. The longer a person lives, the more it costs to treat him or her, especially since the vast majority of health care costs occur in the last few years of life.

One of the paradoxes of modern medicine is that advances in treatments that extend lives have actually increased lifetime health care costs.

People who would have died from an acute illness during their working life in the past are now enjoying lengthy retirements, and suffering various debilitating diseases that require high-cost medical intervention. According to an expert, former Colorado governor Richard Lamm, who is now director of the Center for Public Policy and Contemporary Issues at the University of Denver, the average nonsmoker is treated for seven major illnesses during his or her lifetime. The average smoker survives only two major illnesses.

So how much more do nonsmokers add to the national health care bill than smokers? One of the best studies is by Duke University economist Kip Viscusi,[2] who conducted an exhaustive comparative analysis in 1994 for a conference on tax policy hosted by the National Bureau of Economic Research in Washington, DC.

Viscusi concluded that smokers, in essence, subsidize the health care costs of nonsmokers. Using government statistics, Viscusi calculated the medical costs of tobacco by adding up things like the percentage of patient days for lung cancer treatment in hospitals that can be attributed to smoking and burn injuries and deaths from fires started by mislaid cigarettes. Viscusi then took into account other costs—by dying younger, smokers deprive society of income tax. Viscusi even added a charge for costs related to second-hand smoke. Viscusi then calculated how much tobacco saves society. Because they receive considerably fewer payments from government and employer pension plans and other retirement benefits, and consume fewer drug benefits, nursing home and hospital dollars, he estimates that the average American smoker saves society on each pack of cigarettes sold in the United States, leaving a net surplus of 31 cents over the costs attributable to smoking (see 3 percent

1. This case was taken substantially, with permission, from an article written by John Woolsey, a prominent actuary who has been involved in the study of the costs of health care. The article, "Society's Windfall Profit from Smokers," was published in the *Ottawa Citizen* on August 4, 1998.
2. Viscusi, W. Kip. "Cigarette Taxation and the Social Consequences of Smoking." *Tax Policy and the Economy*, (1995): 51–101.

discount column, in the chart below). Adding the 80 cents per package in taxes that American smokers pay brings the total surplus to $1.11 for every pack of smokes.

Other experts have argued that there is a loss of productivity to society because smokers take more sick days than nonsmokers. But is this cost borne by the economy as a whole, or by individual smokers whose absences mean that they will not reach their full earnings potential due to missed job promotions and merit pay? The bottom line in all this is that an actuarial approach shows that the facts do not support current political claims about the cost of smoking. Smokers actually leave the economy better off and should be encouraged, not discouraged through taxes, restrictions, and lawsuits.

Questions

1. What can an ethical analysis add to Viscusi's actuarial analysis?

2. Would an ethical analysis change the conclusion reached? Why?

External Insurance Costs Per Pack of Cigarettes

	1993 COST ESTIMATE DISCOUNT RATE			1993 COST ESTIMATE WITH TAR ADJUSTMENT DISCOUNT RATE		
	0%	3%	5%	0%	3%	5%
Costs						
Medical care <65	0.288	0.326	0.357	0.330	0.373	0.410
Medical care ≥65	0.375	0.172	0.093	0.384	0.177	0.096
Total medical care	0.663	0.498	0.451	0.715	0.550	0.505
Sick leave	0.003	0.012	0.019	0.000	0.013	0.020
Group life insurance	0.222	0.126	0.084	0.241	0.136	0.091
Nursing home care	20.584	20.221	20.074	20.599	20.226	20.076
Retirement pension	22.660	21.099	20.337	22.886	21.193	20.365
Fires	0.014	0.016	0.018	0.014	0.016	0.018
Taxes on earnings	0.771	0.351	0.107	0.883	0.402	0.122
Total net costs	21.571	20.317	0.268	21.633	20.302	0.315

Source: Viscusi, W. Kip. "Cigarette Taxation and the Social Consequences of Smoking," *Tax Policy and the Economy*, National Bureau of Economic Research (1995): 74.

Ethics Case   *Ford Pinto**

In order to meet strong competition from Volkswagen as well as other foreign domestic subcompacts, Lee Iacocca, then president of Ford Motor Co., decided to introduce a new vehicle by 1970, to be known as the Pinto. The overall objective was to produce a car at or below 2,000 pounds with a price tag of $2,000 or less. Although preproduction design and testing normally requires about three-and-a-half years and the arrangement of actual production somewhat longer, design was started in 1968 and production commenced in 1970.

---

*More comprehensive cases on the Pinto problem can be found in Donaldson, T., & Gin, A. R. *Case Studies in Business Ethics*. Englewood Cliffs, NJ: Prentice-Hall , 1990, pp. 174–83 (original case by W. M. Hoffman); and Valasquez, M. G. *Business Ethics: Concepts and Cases*. Englewood Cliffs, NJ: Prentice-Hall , 1988, pp. 119–23.

The Pinto project was overseen by Robert Alexander, vice president of car engineering, and was approved by Ford's Product Planning Committee, consisting of Iacocca, Alexander, and Ford's group vice president of car engineering, Harold MacDonald. The engineers throughout Ford who worked on the project "signed off" to their immediate supervisors, who did likewise in turn to their superiors, and so on to Alexander and MacDonald and, finally, Iacocca.

Many reports were passed up the chain of command during the design and approval process, including several outlining the results of crash tests, and a proposal to remedy the tendency for the car to burst into flames when rear-ended at 21 miles per hour. This tendency was caused by the placement of the car's gas tank between the rear axle and the rear bumper such that a rear-end collision was likely to drive the gas tank forward to rupture on the bolts for the rear axle differential housing. The ruptured tank would then spew gas into the passenger compartment to be ignited immediately by sparks or a hot exhaust.

The remedies available to Ford included mounting the gas tank above the rear axle, which would cut down on trunk space, or installing a rubber bladder in the gas tank. Ford experimented with the installation of rubber bladders but apparently decided they were not cost-effective. Later, as part of a successful lobby effort against government regulations for mandatory crash tests (crash tests were delayed eight years, until 1977), Ford's cost–benefit analysis came to light in a company study entitled "Fatalities Associated with Crash-Induced Fuel Leakage and Fires." As the details previously outlined show, the costs of installing the rubber bladder vastly exceeded the benefits.

Ford took the $200,000 figure for the cost of a death from a study of the National Highway Traffic Safety Administration, which used the estimates in the table on the previous page.

Questions

1. Was the decision not to install the rubber bladder appropriate? Use the 5-question framework to support your analysis.

2. What faults can you identify in Ford's cost–benefit analysis?

3. Should Ford have given its Pinto customers the option to have the rubber bladder installed during production for, say, $20?

FATALITY PAYMENT COMPONENT	1971 COSTS
Future productivity Losses	
Direct	$132,000
Indirect	41,300
Medical costs	
Hospital	700
Other	425
Property damage	1,500
Insurance Administration	4,700
Legal and court	3,000
Employer losses	1,000
Victim's pain and suffering	10,000
Funeral	900
Assets (lost consumption)	5,000
Miscellaneous	200
Total per fatality:	**$200,725**

Ford's Cost–Benefit Analysis

	EACH	TOTAL
Benefits: Savings		
180 burn deaths	$200,000	$36,000,000
180 serious burn injuries	$67,000	12,060,000
2,100 burned vehicles		1,470,000
		$49,530,000
Costs:		
11 million cars	$11	$121,000,000
1.5 million light trucks	$11	16,500,000
		$137,500,000

The Kardell Paper Co.*

Background

The Kardell paper mill was established at the turn of the century on the Cherokee River in southeastern Ontario by the Kardell family. By 1985, the Kardell Paper Co. had outgrown its original mill and had encompassed several facilities in different locations, generating total revenues of $1.7 billion per year. The original mill continued to function and was the firm's largest profit center. The Kardell family no longer owned shares in the firm, which had become a publicly traded company whose shares were widely held.

Kardell Paper Co. was a firm with a record of reporting good profits and had a policy of paying generous bonuses to the chief executive officer and other senior executives.

Kardell's original mill was located near Riverside, a community of 22,000. Riverside was largely dependent on the mill, which employed 500 people. The plant, while somewhat outdated, was still reasonably efficient and profitable. It was not designed with environmental protection in mind, and the waste water that discharged into the Cherokee River was screened only to remove the level of contaminants required by provincial regulation. There were other industrial plants upstream from the Kardell plant.

The residential community of Riverside, five miles downstream from the plant, was home to many of the Kardell plant's management, including Jack Green, a young engineer with two children, ages one and four.

Jack, who was assistant production manager at the Kardell plant, was sensitive to environmental issues and made a point of keeping up on the latest paper mill technology. Jack monitored activity at the plant's laboratory, which in 1985 employed a summer student to conduct tests on water quality in the Cherokee River immediately downstream from the plant.

These tests were taken across the entire width of the river. The tests conducted nearest the plant's discharge pipe showed high readings of an industrial chemical called sonox.

Farther away from the plant, and on the opposite shore of the river, the water showed only small trace amounts of sonox. Sonox was used in the manufacture of a line of bleached kraft paper that Kardell had begun to make at its plant in recent years.

The Issue

The student researcher discovered that the plant lab was not including the high readings of sonox in its monthly reports to management, so the student showed the complete records to Jack. In the summer of 1985, Jack made a report to the CEO with a recommendation that in-depth studies be conducted into the situation and its implications for public health and long-term effects on the ecology.

In recommending that Kardell carry out an "environmental audit" of its operations, Jack pointed out that local doctors in Riverside had been expressing concern over what appeared to be an unusually high rate of miscarriages and respiratory disorders in the community. Jack told the CEO there were data suggesting a possible link between health problems and sonox, but no definite proof. Medical research into sonox's possible effects on humans was continuing.

In bringing his concerns to the CEO's attention, Jack offered as a possible solution the option of Kardell adopting a new processing technology which used recycling techniques for waste water. This technology, already employed by a handful of plants in Europe, enabled a plant to operate in a "closed cycle" that not only protected the environment but reclaimed waste material, which was then sold to chemical producers. Thus, in the long term the new process was cost-effective. In the short run, however, refitting the existing Kardell plant to incorporate the new technology would cost about $70 million, and, during the retrofit, the plant would have to operate at reduced capacity levels for about a year and possibly be closed down altogether for an additional year to make the change-over.

---

*The Kardell case was prepared by David Olive, Graham H. Tucker, Tim J. Leech, and David Sparling.

The Response

Kardell's traditional response to environmental concerns was reactive. The company took its cues from the regulatory climate. That is, the provincial environment ministry would apply control orders on the plant as new limits on emissions of various compounds came into effect, and Kardell would then comply with these orders.

In raising his concerns in 1985, Jack pointed out that the Ministry of Environment, responding to the serious nature of concerns raised by the sonox issue, was considering internal proposals from its staff that additional research be done into the sources and implications of sonox. Given the early stage of work in this area, Jack could offer no indication of when, if ever, the Ministry would enact new regulations to do with sonox. He argued, however, that the ground rules might change, as they had with previous compounds, and that Kardell should give some thought to the worst-case scenario of how the sonox issue could turn out down the road.

Kardell's CEO was sympathetic to the concerns raised by Jack, a valued employee of the company who had proved himself in the past by identifying many cost-efficiency measures. The CEO felt obliged, however, to match Jack's concerns about sonox against the substantial cost of refitting the plant. The CEO felt there simply was not enough data upon which to base such an important decision, and he was wary of any external force that attempted to influence the company's affairs. The CEO told Jack, "We simply can't let these 'greens' tell us how to run our business."

While the CEO did not feel it would be appropriate for Kardell to adopt the recommendations in Jack's report, the CEO did take the step of presenting the report to the board of directors, for discussion in the fall of 1985.

Kardell's board of directors represented a cross-section of interest groups. Everyone on the board felt a responsibility toward the shareholders, but, in addition, some members of the board also paid special attention to community and labor concerns. The board was composed of the CEO and president of the firm, along with several "outside" directors: two local businesspeople from Riverside, a representative of the paperworkers' union at the plant, a mutual fund manager whose firm held a large block of Kardell shares on behalf of the fund's investors, an economist, a Riverside city councillor, and the corporation's legal counsel.

Each member of the board spoke to Jack's report from his or her perspective. The Riverside representatives—the city councillor and the two businesspeople—wanted assurances that the community was not in any danger. But they also said, in the absence of any firm proof of danger, that they were satisfied Kardell probably was not a source of harmful emissions.

The lawyer pointed out that legally Kardell was in the clear: it was properly observing all existing regulations on emission levels; in any case, there was no clear indication that the Kardell mill was the only source of sonox emissions into the Cherokee River. While acknowledging the health concerns that had recently arisen over sonox, the lawyer thought it prudent to wait for the government to establish an acceptable limit for sonox emissions. Besides, the lawyer added, while liability actions had been initiated against two or three other mills producing sonox, these claims had been denied through successful defense actions in court on the grounds of lack of clear evidence of a significant health hazard.

The labor representative expressed concern about any compound that might affect the health of Kardell employees living in the area. But the labor official also had to think about the short-term consideration of job loss at the plant and the fact that, with the plant shut down, there were few other employment opportunities in the area to fill the gap. The board representatives from Riverside pointed out that, obviously, the local economy would be severely affected by the shutdown to refit the plant. And the mutual fund manager agreed with the CEO that, at least in the short term, Kardell's profitability and share price would suffer from a decision to undertake a costly overhaul of the facility.

The Decision

After much debate, the board decided to defer consideration of Jack's proposals pending the results of government research into this issue. It also asked Jack to continue monitoring the regulatory climate so that the plant would always be in basic compliance with provincial emission standards.

During the next two years, Jack presented similar warnings to the board regarding sonox and continued to meet with the same response. As a precautionary measure, he kept copies of his reports in his own files so there could never be any question of the timing or substance of his warnings to the board. During this same period, an above-average incidence of miscarriages, birth defects, and respiratory ailments was reported in the Riverside area.

Questions

1. Who are the stakeholders involved, and what are their interests?

2. Which stakeholders and interests are the most important? Why?

3. What was wrong with the quality of the board of directors' debate?

4. What is the downside if the right decision is not made—consider economic factors and also what Jack might do?

Source: *Agenda for Action Conference Proceedings*, the Canadian Center for Ethics & Corporate Policy, 1990, pp. 20–21. Reprinted with the permission of the Canadian Center for Ethics & Corporate Policy.

Readings   *Cost–Benefit Analysis*

Leonard J. Brooks, Jr., CA
CAmagazine, October 1979

Corporate management has become increasingly aware that business decisions often have an impact that cannot be easily measured by traditional accounting analysis. Governments and special interest groups have been quick to point out that many costs resulting from business decisions are not reflected in (or are external to) corporate accounts. Pollution damage costs, for instance, must be borne by neighbors, not by the companies causing the problems. Understandably, then, corporate executives are searching for analytical techniques that will take account of such external costs and benefits when they are deliberating company policy, resource allocation (to pollution controls, for example), desirability of potentially harmful projects and other programs that will have an impact on the general public. Inevitably, they are looking to their accountants to develop the required cost–benefit analyses to supplement usual rate of return projections.

There are many reasons why management will continue to voluntarily ask for and use cost–benefit analyses. The best managers usually try to reduce uncertainty in their decision making as much as possible, and knowing in advance the costs and benefits of an action could forestall inciting an unpleasant reaction by an angry populace. Furthermore, data developed using cost–benefit techniques can serve as an excellent predictor of cash costs that will show up later in the traditional accounts. Also, the social choices governing the implementation of government programs and regulations are often based on cost–benefit analyses. It may even be that organizations, both profit and non-profit, will someday be forced to justify their social existence in terms of cost–benefit analyses. Already, about 90% of the *Fortune 500* companies make social responsibility disclosures in their annual reports.[1]

There are already many indications that the use of cost–benefit analysis may become mandatory. For example, governments are about to require summaries of social costs and benefits before allowing new chemical plants to be built. A growing number of public-spirited shareholders are demanding increased disclosure of corporate contributions to society. An

---

1. *Social Responsibility Disclosure: 1977 Survey of Fortune 500 Annual Reports* (Cleveland: Ernst & Ernst , 1977).

TABLE 1

Uses of Cost–Benefit Analysis

PRIVATE SECTOR ORGANIZATIONS
- Support for government subsidy; grant or tariff.
- Estimate of impact of pollution on society.
- Valuation of employee time spent on public activities.
- Evaluation and allocation of resources to public projects or causes.
- Monitor mechanism for net corporate social contribution to society for the year and to date.
- Individuals.
- Support for damage claims arising from loss of life, eyes, limbs, etc.
- Valuation of leisure time.

PUBLIC SECTOR ORGANIZATIONS
Evaluation of social program alternatives leading to allocation of resources for:
- Health programs.
- Education programs.
- Recreation facilities.
- Conservation projects (flood control dams, reservoirs).
- Transportation improvement projects (airports, subways, tunnels, etc.).
- Formulation of regulations for pollution control.

increasingly burdened electorate is challenging government largesse and is insisting on documented justification of new or further spending programs. Thus, in view of such pressures, accountants would be well-advised to become more familiar with the techniques and potential problems of cost–benefit analysis.

Cost–benefit analysis (CBA) can be used to (a) determine whether projects should be undertaken, and (b) to monitor the performance of a company or project. Table 1 provides a partial list of the areas where CBA is now being used in both the private and public sectors of our economy. The format for presentation of these impacts, their scope and other factors will be discussed later; first, it is useful to see how CBA differs from traditional accounting analyses in terms of scope and focus.

Shortfalls of Traditional Accounting Data

In comparison with cost–benefit analysis, traditional accounting analysis falls short on four counts:

1. It focuses on past actions, which are not as relevant as future actions for decision making.

2. It does not take into account external factors.

3. It considers some resources to be free, or to have no cost.

4. Its focus is far more narrow, relating almost always to shareholders' interests, rather than stakeholders' (or society's) interests.

The first shortfall, decision-time orientation, will not be news to most readers. The classic cartoon portraying the manager as an airline pilot flying a plane while looking backwards epitomizes the situation of decision makers using only historical financial reports in their deliberations. Fortunately, CBA looks ahead at what might happen so that decisions can be tempered by foresight.

Not taking external factors into account, the second shortfall, is more serious. In the case of pollution, the cost of clean-up or health damage is rarely shown in the accounts of the corporation responsible, since it is not borne by the company but by someone else. Yet such costs are undeniably real, and to omit them from the net profit figure significantly weakens it as a measure of the polluter's "contribution to society." To be fair, we should point out that the reverse (i.e., costs borne by a company and benefits reaped by society; company-funded scholarships, for example) also exists and should be taken into a corporation's analysis of costs and benefits.

The third type of shortfall noted in traditional accounting analysis is the consideration of many resources as being free. This usually occurs where no market mechanism exists to exact payment for resource use. Air and water are the most ready examples of "free" resources, but governments are already moving to regulate their use to protect the interests of other members of society, both present and future. Consequently, capital investment decisions should from now on reflect the potential costs of air and water regulation.

The fourth shortfall, the narrow focus of accounting analysis, is a result of the traditional desire to reflect the impact of corporate actions on the interest of shareholders. But corporations affect, and are responsible to, many other groups in society as well, and these are becoming more vocal in corporate affairs. These groups (employees, neighbors, customers, suppliers, bankers, etc.) are usually referred to as stakeholders, and stakeholder interest has been the focus of a number of recently developed accounting systems.[2]

Currently, however, there is considerable debate over the scope of these new hybrid accounting systems. In 1972, Linowes proposed that a "net social corporate contribution to society" be calculated; curiously, however, he limited the calculations to voluntary expenditures, and did not include, for example, costs involuntarily incurred to comply with government regulations.[3] Abt in 1977, proposed that the cost–benefit analysis leading to the determination of corporate net social equity include both voluntary and involuntary expenditures and be integrated into traditional financial statements.[4] The AICPA agreed that an integrated system would be ideal but, because of costs and the fact that CBA is still in an early stage of development, it has opted for a less sophisticated approach focusing on the organization's impact on, in turn: the environment, human resources, suppliers, etc.[5]

Indeed, although others have suggested even more complex approaches to organizational worth,[6] the long-term answer probably lies in a modification of the Abt Associates, Inc. traditional accounting model plus cost–benefit analysis.[7] But, as the AICPA found, the cost for a moderately large company to set up a system of accounts to duplicate the Abt model, before costing the data assembly each year, could be as much as $300,000—a price too high for most industries to contemplate at this time.[8] In addition, reports generated by this system will be of questionable value until industry standards of comparison are available and the knowledgeability of traditional financial report readers has been improved. Finally, time is required to thoroughly determine the interrelationships of the various comprehensive models.

Obviously, then, costs and other practical considerations will probably mean that the incorporation into financial reports of the disclosure of significant corporate impacts on society will happen gradually, taking into account one area at a time. Yet there should be no illusion that this type of one-dimensional analysis is all that is needed. As a part measure, however, it will make information available to relevant stakeholder groups and allow governments to provide, for instance, pollution standards by which corporate performance can be measured. And, regardless of whether CBAs are used to facilitate decisions or to monitor corporate performance, the basic techniques should be understood.

2. R. Estes, *Corporate Social Accounting* (New York, NY: John Wiley & Sons, 1976).
3. D. Linowes, "An Approach to Socio-Economic Accounting, *The Conference Board Record,* Vol. IX, No. 11 (November 1972).
4. C. C. Abt, *The Social Audit for Management* (New York: AMACOM, 1977).
5. Committee on Social Measurement, *The Measurement of Corporate Social Performance* (New York: The American Institute of Certified Public Accountants, 1977).
6. In L. J. Brooks, *Canadian Corporate Social Performance* (Hamilton, Ontario, Canada: The Society of Management Accountants of Canada), 1986, Chapter 3.
7. Abt. *Op. cit.*
8. *Ibid.* pp. 112–113.

Techniques of Cost–Benefit Analysis

Instead of the normal captions "revenue," "expense" and "net profit," CBA terminology would be "benefits," "costs" and "excess of benefits over costs." The CBA concepts of benefits and costs are broader than revenues and expenses, because they take into account future and hitherto external values. Projects should be undertaken if benefits exceed costs or the benefits/cost ratio is greater than one. Usually, the larger the benefit/cost ratio, the more attractive the project; but occasionally, if a company has only limited funds to invest, small projects that are attractive from a benefit point of view must be bypassed in favor of larger projects that produce higher absolute levels of benefit. In other words, if only part of the resources available to be invested will be absorbed by the project(s) with the highest benefit/cost ratio, it is preferable to choose a project with a slightly lower benefit/cost ratio which uses more of the resource base and contributes overall benefits.

To illustrate, an unsophisticated yet typical CBA is set out in Table 2. The values used are hypothetical but readily attainable by means we'll discuss later.

The general framework for CBA is identical to the discounted cash flow approach used in capital budgeting analysis. For example, the present value of net costs or net benefits may be derived from the sum of the future values discounted at an appropriate discount rate, or

present value of net costs or net benefits

$$= \frac{B_1 - C_1}{(1 + r)^1} + \frac{B_2 - C_2}{(1 + r)^2} + \frac{B_3 - C_3}{(1 + r)^3} + \ldots\ldots\infty$$

$$= \sum_{n=1}^{\infty} \frac{B_n - C_n}{(1 + r)^n}$$

where:

B is the benefit for the year, accruing at the end of the year.

C is the cost for the year.

r is the discount rate per annum reflecting the opportunity cost for capital invested in projects of comparable risk.

1, 2, 3, . . . n specifies the period/year with n the final period.

TABLE 2

JM Co. Ltd. Cost–Benefit Analysis of Social Impact Proposals: March 1979

	POLLUTION CONTROL EQUIPMENT PROTECTING WORKERS IN PLANT	UNIVERSITY ADMISSION SCHOLARSHIPS
Benefits (Present Valued at 10%)		
Reduction in worker health costs borne by society	$500,000	
Increase in worker productivity	200,000	
Improvements in level of earnings of scholarship recipients		$600,000
	700,000	600,000
Costs (Present Valued at 10%)		
Pollution equipment	350,000	
Scholarships paid		400,000
	$350,000	$200,000
Benefit/cost ratio	2/1	3/2
Decision		
(1) if only one project can be funded	X	
(2) if all projects with a positive benefit/cost/ratio can be funded	X	X
Time horizon: 10 years from March 1979		

While there may be some difference of opinion over the validity of considering increased earnings of scholarship recipients as the "benefit" of these payments, such a measure is, on balance, conservative and facilitates a numeric comparison with the project costs and thus results in a more informed decision.

The Discount Rate

Monies used to finance projects are necessarily withheld from other uses such as private investment or personal consumption. Therefore, the cost of such financing is properly measured by computing the cost of the opportunity foregone, whether that is the lost after-tax marginal rate of return on other investments or the price consumers would be willing to pay not to forego deferring their consumption. Since such alternative costs are not practically available, the results of CBA studies are usually discounted at a weighted average marginal rate based on the projected sources of financing to be employed. The weighted average marginal cost of capital approach has prevailed in practice even though economists have noted that, in some instances, the use of a single discount rate may not produce valid integrations of present and future consumption foregone.[9]

In the case of a corporation, the discount rate is usually its average weighted after-tax cost of capital, plus a risk factor depending on the nature of the project's cash flows, less whatever the amount with which the company wishes to subsidize projects with heavy social orientation. A similar approach should be followed for non-profit organizations. For government agencies, however, it has been argued that their size and taxing mandate produces a relatively risk-free cost of capital which, if they used it, would be lower than the cost to firms in the private sector. Over time, the use of the lower governmental rate would result in an increasingly larger rate of investment by the public sector in comparison with that of the private, and the balance of activity would shift further toward the former. To counteract this tendency, the governments of Canada and Britain use a 10% discount rate on most projects.[10]

Measurement of Costs and Benefits

Although there are problems in choosing the appropriate discount rate, they are minor in comparison with the difficulties of identifying and measuring the annual future costs and benefits themselves.

Whenever possible, direct measurement is preferable. For example, when assessing the costs resulting from air pollution caused by a generating station, we can measure the saving (benefit) from the use of coal or natural gas instead of oil. The costs could also be partially measured by a direct survey estimate of the increase in local health costs attributable to respiratory problems and to the increased house maintenance costs due to smoke damage.[11]

Unfortunately, many costs and benefits cannot be determined directly, and surrogate or indirect means must be used to estimate the values involved, although, admittedly, it is virtually impossible to capture all of the relevant characteristics in the surrogate value. For instance, and continuing our pollution example, it is impossible to measure directly the aesthetic values that will be lost in the cloud of smoke and smell that will enfold the community if coal is used as a fuel. An indirect or surrogate value could be estimated for this aesthetic loss, however, by surveying the local residents to see how much they would be willing to pay to have the problem improved or removed. From this survey a type of demand curve for smoke and smell abatement could be fashioned and aesthetic values estimated.[12] The cost of a pollution control project could then be compared with the curve to see if the overall demand is large enough to justify going ahead.

9. M. S. Feldstein, "The Inadequacy of Weighted Discount Rates," in *Cost–Benefit Analysis,* ed. R. Layard (Harmondsworth, Middlesex, U.K.: Penguin Books, Ltd. , 1973), pp. 311–322.

10. D. B. Brooks, *Conservation of Minerals and of the Environment* (Ottawa: Canada Department of Energy Mines and Resources , 1974).

11. M. O. Alexander and J. L. Livingstone, "What Are the Real Costs and Benefits of Producing "Clean Electric Power?" *Public Utilities Fortnightly* (August 30, 1973).

12. Estes, *Op. cit.,* pp. 111–114.

Another approach to determining the cost of pollution is to calculate the full cost of health damage incurred based on the value of the time lost by patients while ill. For patients who would not have been working for wages if well, the appropriate approach would be to identify the most lucrative opportunity lost by being ill; and, once this is done, the value loss, or opportunity cost, can be estimated by (for instance) estimating the cost of task delay or of paying someone else to complete the task. If a patient loses wages while ill, then this would be one measure of the opportunity cost of time lost.

A further example of surrogate measurement is the evaluation of the net benefit derived from a company-sponsored training program (total cost $60,000) for 50 personnel. Unable to measure the benefit directly, we make the assumption that the benefit will be reflected by increased earnings (say $5,000 per annum) over the expected 20-year average working life of each employee. Hence the net benefit of the courses would be $2,068,500 (calculated as $50 \times \$5,000\ a_{20}\ 10\%$ [i.e., a 20-year annuity at 10% rate of discount: less $60,000)] before tax.

Additional CBA approaches are outlined in Table 3.[13]

Shortcomings of Cost–Benefit Analysis

Some accountants will argue that CBA is too subjective and too removed from their traditional pursuits to be worth studying. But this argument overlooks:

▌ The longevity of CBA, which has been used since before 1844.[14]

▌ The prominence of CBA in governmental decision making.

▌ The apparent likelihood that CBA techniques will be employed in the private sector to provide a focus for decisions on corporate programs that will have an impact on society.

Accountants have traditionally assumed a central role in providing data for decisions in the private sector and, if this position is to be maintained, it is in the accountant's best interest to be familiar with CBA techniques and their shortcomings. Furthermore, since accountants are often directly involved with (or indirectly subject to) CBA decisions in the public sector, they will be unable to make decisions properly, to advise less-skilled decision makers, or to challenge specific CBA proposals effectively,

---

TABLE 3 — **Different Methods of Evaluating the Benefits of a Recreation Facility**

Calculation of:
1. Gross expenditure by users on travel, equipment, etc.;
2. Market value of fish caught (production or output value);
3. Production cost of project (input value);
4. Market value of recreation services produced × number of users.

Survey of:
1. Users' willingness to pay for use;
1. Users' (and other interested parties') willingness to pay to prevent deprival of use or enjoyment.

---

13. J. L. Knetsch and R. K. Davis, "Comparisons of Method for Recreation Evaluation," in *Water Research,* ed. A. V. Kneese and S. C. Smith (Baltimore: The John Hopkins Press for Resources for the Future, Inc., 1966).

14. J. Dupuit, "On the Measurement of Utility of Public Works" (translated from the French published in 1844). *International Economic Papers,* Vol. 2 (London: Macmillan & Co. Ltd.), 1952.

unless they are aware of the relevant CBA techniques and their shortcomings. The reasoning behind our stressing the importance of informed advice will become more apparent when the variety and seriousness of CBA shortcomings are understood. The shortcomings can be grouped into three categories:

| Choices available to the preparer.

| Constraints to be considered by the preparer and user.

| Issues not resolvable by CBA.

The Choices Available

The choices are many and, if too inaccurate, would bias a CBA to the point where unwise decisions would result. There are methods by which bias and unreasonableness can be mitigated, but first the decision maker must understand the potential problems.

When beginning a CBA, the preparer must make certain assumptions such as the rate of discount (r%) and the time horizon over which costs and benefits will be taken into account. Obviously, the choice of a long time horizon might favor some projects, even though the uncertainties of estimation are too great to warrant the inclusion of costs and benefits to be incurred 20–25 years from now. If too high a discount rate is chosen, distant costs and benefits will have less impact on the CBA than they should and, even if no longer-term costs and benefits exist, decision makers might reject proposals when their existing opportunities for investment are far less than r%.

Since it is essential that an accurate opportunity cost be estimated for the monies to be used to finance each CBA project, is the 10% test rate used by Canadian and British governments appropriate? For instance, if 10% is too low, there will be a tendency for the public sector to accept more projects than the private sector would. On the other hand, since private sector capital budgeting decisions do not incorporate all the costs or external factors that public sector CBAs do (thereby inflating projected rates of return), maybe the 10% test rate is acceptable. Surely accountants should have a thorough understanding of this fundamental issue.

Which costs and benefits to include or exclude is another basic choice to be made, one

that reflects the special interests of the group making the CBA decision. If the decision makers are an upstream town council, they may be unwilling to include in their analysis the cost incurred by a downstream town to clean up pollution put into the river by the upstream municipality. If, in the same situation, all filtration costs were borne by the province (a larger political jurisdiction to which both towns belong), then the costs of clean-up would be recognized. In other words, decision makers can be led astray if the boundaries of the CBA analysis are not broad enough.

Bias can enter CBA through unfortunate choices of surrogates and of the methods used to assess people's values. Surrogates are rarely mirror images of what one is attempting to measure. Table 3 indicates a wide range of alternatives available to evaluate a park or other recreation facility. Some alternatives listed are more conservative than others, so decision makers should examine surrogates closely to avoid being misled. It should also be kept in mind that the surrogates chosen will most often focus on output or production values, rather than on consumption values. For instance, when evaluating the time of an unemployed person, the conventional CBA approach focusses on his or her production opportunity loss (nil since he/she is unemployed) and he is not asked how much his inactivity or leisure is worth.

Having listed some of the pitfalls, it is comforting to note that a wary review, looking for each item mentioned, can be aided greatly by sensitivity analysis. The discount rate, the time horizon and the choice of surrogate can be varied to see if the CBA outcome changes and in what way. Since CBA is a technique used most frequently to rank several possible projects, it is not essential that a project be valued exactly, but rather that it may be ranked better or worse than other alternatives.

Constraints

With respect to the constraints that must be considered by CBA preparers and users, it is imperative that projects be mutually exclusive; or, if a joint project is under consideration, that the CBA analysis include all aspects of the project. Furthermore, accepted projects must meet legal requirements and be amenable to administration. Occasionally, budgetary constraints are removed and decision makers are told to spend their predetermined budget without regard to the opportunity cost (r%) of the money spent. In this case, however, only analyses using an appropriate discount rate will ultimately be defensible.

Unresolvable Issues

The CBA decision maker must realize that many issues can never be fully resolved by CBA techniques. CBA doesn't take into account issues of equity, such as the advisability of penalizing one group to the advantage of another. Moral issues are likewise excluded or abstractly incorporated. For instance, the $600,000 spent earlier on scholarships might feed 50,000 children in southeast Asia. Similarly, the loss of an eye, limb or human life is valued by the discounted earnings stream foregone, whereas, fortunately, society is willing to pay large amounts to maintain the lives of leukemia victims and provide dialysis equipment for kidney patients whose future incomes may be nil. Even value judgments on issues of less importance than human life may not be handled to everyone's satisfaction. Beauty is in the eye of each beholder and to impute an aesthetic judgment for a whole group based on the average of several individual opinions may not provide an accurate picture. On the other hand, decision makers' judgments often depend on external factors and are therefore enhanced by quantitative CBA analysis, however rough and imperfect.

CBA Is Here to Stay

Society in general, public organizations, private corporations and individuals are increasingly looking beyond traditional accounting analysis for broader impact measurements. Traditional accounting will remain valuable, but, in advanced societies, organizations must be aware and take account of their external impacts as well. Governments are already making social choices for all of us based on cost– benefit analysis. Accountants, therefore, would be well advised to increase their understanding of cost–benefit analysis and its pitfalls, or else lose their place at the right hand of decision makers.

> Leonard J. Brooks, Jr., MBA, CA, is an associate professor in the Department of Political Economy at the University of Toronto and the discipline representative for commerce at the university's Erindale College in Mississauga. He is also a former audit manager with Touche Ross & Co. in Toronto.
>
> Reprinted with permission, from the October 1979 issue of *CAmagazine,* published by the Canadian Institute of Chartered Accountants, Toronto, Canada.

Readings | *Ethical Analysis for Environmental Problem Solving*

Graham Tucker
Canadian Centre for Ethics & Corporate Policy, 1990

Introduction

Today, no company can claim to be "ethical" unless it is demonstrating a concern for the environment. The focus of this conference is on the tools of ethical analysis and problem solving that can provide a practical framework for action.

Before finalizing a business decision, an executive should ask a series of questions designed to ensure the best possible choice is made both for the shareholders as well as other stakeholders. These questions ought to be asked in the following order to canvass the values shown:

1. Is it profitable? (market values)

2. Is it legal? (legal values)

3. Is it fair? (social values)

4. Is it right? (personal values)

5. Is it sustainable development? (environmental values)

These questions have been built into the "five-box" framework for ethical analysis which is shown in Figure 1.

Figure 1 Questions

The focus on values is critical to the proper analysis of business decisions because morality, which is becoming more and more critical to the health of corporations and society, cannot be legislated. It depends on the value system of corporate leaders and employees. Moreover, the tough choices required among alternatives often defy quantification and must be based on the values of the decision-maker.

Nowadays, it is not safe to judge a prospective action just on its contribution to profits, because the action may not be legal. Even if it is profitable and legal, society will penalize the company if the action is not also perceived to be fair and right. Recently, as the fragility of our global environment has become clear, society has begun to demand that corporate actions fit into the sustainable development of our economy.

The application of the "five-box" framework for analysis will be developed in the analysis of the Kardell Paper Co. case, after a discussion of some terms used in ethical analysis and the outlining of a framework for ethical problem solving.

Some Important Distinctions

It's important that we make important distinctions (a) between management and leadership and (b) between being legal and being ethical. Lack of clear distinction in these areas causes a lot of confused thinking in business ethics.

When managers are successful, usually it is because they are high-energy, hard-driving individuals who know how to play by the rules of the game. They efficiently and single-mindedly strive to achieve the goals of the organization. But they may or may not be leaders.

Robert Greenleaf, author of the book *Servant Leadership,* defines leaders as "those who better see the path ahead and are prepared to take the risks and show the way." The characteristic which sets leaders apart from managers is their intuitive insight and the foresight which enables them to go out ahead and show the way. Why would anyone accept the leadership

---

FIGURE 1   **A Framework for Ethical Analysis—Changing Ground Rules and a Sustainable Future**

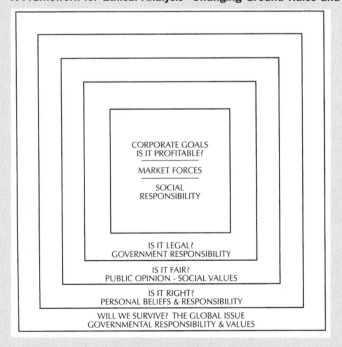

CORPORATE GOALS
IS IT PROFITABLE?

MARKET FORCES

SOCIAL RESPONSIBILITY

IS IT LEGAL?
GOVERNMENT RESPONSIBILITY

IS IT FAIR?
PUBLIC OPINION - SOCIAL VALUES

IS IT RIGHT?
PERSONAL BELIEFS & RESPONSIBILITY

WILL WE SURVIVE? THE GLOBAL ISSUE
GOVERNMENTAL RESPONSIBILITY & VALUES

of another, except that the other sees more clearly where it's best to go? The manager, by contrast, tends to be part of the bureaucracy that wants to preserve the status quo. The managerial role determines the values. Managers do what's expected of them. That role often overrides the managers' personal values.

Role responsibility can be very powerful. The management of Johns-Manville knew for years that its product asbestos was linked by scientists to lung cancer in its employees. Similar situations existed with the Ford Pinto and the Dalkon Shield.

Managers often feel powerless to act outside of their prescribed role; they feel that they don't have the authority to buck the system. The corporate authority may be sanctioning the unethical behavior. It takes the moral authority of a leader to change the system, and this is often notably lacking in both politics and business.

Robert Greenleaf points out that the failure of businesspeople to use foresight and take creative action before a crisis arises is tantamount to *ethical failure,* because managers in these cases lack courage to act when there is still some freedom to change course. Many managers opt for short-term profit at the expense of long-term viability. On that basis there are probably a lot of people walking around with an air of innocence which they would not have if society were able to pin the label "unethical" on them for their failure to foresee crises and to act constructively when there was freedom to act.

Similarly, it is important that we distinguish between being legal and being ethical. The law is frequently quite distinct from morality. It is mainly concerned with the minimum regulation required for public order, whereas ethics attempts to achieve what is "best" for both the individual and society. Thus it's possible to be operating within the law and yet be unethical. The legal limits for a certain pollutant may have been established before it was discovered to be unsafe at that level. The company may be operating legally. Yet by knowingly endangering the health of workers or the community, the company is acting in an unethical manner.

Many corporate codes of ethics express a commitment to keeping the letter of the law, but that may not protect them from censure when the new data becomes public knowledge. Obviously we have to have laws and regulations to avoid the chaos of a lawless society. However, the ethical crunch that is being experienced by the business world today is that the communications revolution is putting more information in the hands of the public. It used to be possible to exercise power and control by withholding or concealing information. If you don't know that asbestos dust is giving you lung cancer you can't do anything about it. The public now finds out very quickly what is going on, and it is demanding ethical conduct because this affects its well-being.

We have recently witnessed dramatic changes in Eastern Europe, as shared information has empowered previously powerless people to rise up and take control of their own destiny in seeking a better life. Precisely the same power is at work in our society, changing the rules of the game for business. Five years ago, the concern for the environment ranked sixth in the value system of the Canadian public. Today it ranks number one. This in turn is empowering government to enact much tougher regulations. Those companies that are either too entrenched in the old rules or lack the foresight to see the long-term consequences of what is now perceived by the public to be unethical behavior will fail. Whereas those companies which use a combination of ethical foresight and good business, and have the courage to make the changes required, will survive and prosper.

Legislation may provide a level playing field, but legislation alone cannot solve the problem. Similarly, strong corporate statements about environmental values also are useless if business does not have the ethical will to comply with them. The health of our environment depends more than anything else upon corporate moral leadership, which reflects the personal values of executives and employees. And this is where we move from theory to the realm of applied ethics, which is concerned with the practical outcome of business decisions.

Value Judgments

The name of the game is making value judgments in the light of our personal values. I want to say a few words about values so that we can have a common language in this conference.

Values are the criteria by which we make our judgments or choices, and establish our goals and priorities. For most of us, there is a bit of a gap between our ideal personal values and our actual or operative values, and we need to be honest about what our values really are.

The situation is complicated for us today as social values are changing, and this is redefining ethical standards. The ground rules are changing.

Studies have shown the following characteristics resulting from people having clear or unclear values:

UNCLEAR VALUES	CLEAR VALUES
Apathetic	Know who they are
Flighty	Know what they want
Inconsistent	Positive
Drifter	Purposeful
Role player	Enthusiastic
Indecisive	Decisive

Both individually and corporately, it is to our advantage to develop a clear set of values, because confused values will result in confused ethical decisions.

Ethical analysis usually uncovers value conflicts which occur below the surface of our thinking. They can't be settled by rational argument. Only as we listen respectfully to each other's value perspective is it possible to find a reasonable accommodation of the difference. This is why stakeholder analysis is so important.

Rule Ethics

This brings us to the two-basic ethical concepts we will apply in our case study today. The first is rule ethics.

Rule ethics states that you make your decisions about right or wrong on the basis of valid ethical principles, norms or ground rules. In other words, we ask, "Will this proposed action be violating civil law, or company policy in the code of ethics?" This is a good place to start, but as mentioned before, it may not produce ethical decisions. The decisions that result may be legal—but if the ground rules have changed, they may not be ethical.

The next level of rule ethics consists of the rules or principles that come out of our moral traditions, which in our society are mainly the Judeo-Christian moral norms such as "Thou shalt not kill, steal, lie, cheat or oppress."

The underlying question in rule ethics is, Whose rules are you following? It used to be that the corporation had its own rules, which related only to market forces, and it was not felt to be necessary to consider the values of society. That is, "What's good for General Motors is good for the rest of us." Cynically, the Golden Rule has become, "He who has the gold makes the rules."

Utilitarianism, or End-Point Ethics

John Stuart Mill said that, "To determine whether an action is right or wrong, one must concentrate on its likely consequences—the end point or end result. What is the greatest benefit for the greatest number?"

This led to cost–benefit analysis: does the benefit justify the cost? And to risk–benefit analysis: does not benefit justify the business risk?

In other words, you begin with rule ethics, in which the stakeholders test a decision by asking:

Is it legal?

Is it fair?

Is it right?

Is it environmentally sound?

Then you move to the end-point ethics, which seeks the greatest benefit for the greatest number—and this, finally, forces us to make some trade-offs to achieve the greatest good.

So far, we have been considering the process of ethical analysis. However, there is a tendency to think that having analyzed the problem we have solved it. Unless we take it to the next step of rational problem solving, nothing much is going to happen.

The process I am going to introduce is ethically neutral. The thing that makes it ethical is the particular values and ground rules you apply in the process. If the ethical analysis has been done thoroughly, you will have already sorted out the values that you will apply at the various decision points in the problem-solving process.

Creative problem solving involves lateral thinking, or second-order thinking.

First-order thinking is the obvious course of action that first occurs to the mind of the manager or executive.

Second-order thinking involves "reframing" the problem and considering it from a different perspective.

For example, if you look at a business problem from the perspective of each of the five boxes on the chart, you might generate some creative alternatives which might not come to mind if only the corporate box is considered. It will take courage for every business enterprise to make the ethical shift for a sustainable future, but some can and *are* leading the way.

Graham H. Tucker was the founder and former director of the King-Bay Chaplaincy in Toronto, and former executive director of the Canadian Centre for Ethics & Corporate Policy. Rev. Tucker was the author of *The Faith-Work Connection.*

Source: Tucker, G. "Ethical Analysis for Environmental Problem Solving," *Agenda for Action Conference Proceedings,* The Canadian Centre for Ethics & Corporate Policy, 1990, 53–57. Reprinted with the permission of the Canadian Centre for Ethics & Corporate Policy.

A FRAMEWORK FOR ETHICAL PROBLEM SOLVING

Consider the following issues while employing the eight steps listed below:

1. **Establish objectivity.**
   Who is doing the analysis and what interests do they represent? What are the ground rules of the company and of the decision-making group?

2. **Scan the situation; identify the problem.**
   Separate out the "core problem" from the subproblems. Whose problem is it? Why is it a problem?

3. **Analyze the problem.**
   Use the "five-box," or "five-question" framework . . . to analyze the situation. What are the operative ground rules or values from the perspective of corporation's existing rules, as well as the legal, public, personal and environmental implications? Who makes the decision? Who are the stakeholders? What are their ground rules? Is it fair to all concerned?

4. **Determine the cause of the problem.**
   Why and how are the rules being broken? Are the rules being broken Prima facie or Categorical? Is there any justification? Specify the cause.

5. **Establish the objective.**
   Describe the desirable outcome, or end-point. Is it achievable? How would you measure it? What is the time frame?

6. **Explore the options.**
   Brainstorm possible solutions. Create alternative courses of action.

7. **Decide on the best solution.**
   Who will be affected by each option? Evaluate the impacts from each option on each group of stakeholders. Which option maximizes the benefits and minimizes the burden? Will it pass the five-box ethics test?

8. **Plan and implement the solution.**

Ethical Governance, Accountability & Management

Introduction

Part 3 builds on the issues, concepts, and frameworks developed earlier to offer guidance on how to incorporate ethical thinking and behavior into the accountability and governance frameworks, strategies and activities of corporations and of professional accounting, and on how to manage specific ethical challenges. The necessity for good ethical thinking and behavior sprang from the ethical concerns and expectations, as well as the governance reform requirements, explored in Part 1. Part 2 provided knowledge of philosophical and practical approaches to making sound, defensible, ethical decisions when employees are uncertain because codes are unclear or do not specifically apply.

Chapter 5 examines how ethics can best be incorporated into modern corporate accountability and governance mechanisms that respond to stakeholder expectations and avoid threats to good governance. An effective guidance program requires an ethical culture—strongly supported by top management, a code of conduct, trust, ethics risk management, whistle-blower mechanism, reinforcement, and compliance. Threats to good governance, such as conflicts of interest and poor risk management, are also discussed.

Chapter 6 goes on to discuss the role and responsibilities of professional accountants in the new accountability and governance framework. Their role, both as external auditors and as employees of corporations, is a key component in the credibility of corporations and their reports. The future prestige of the accounting profession depends on embracing the fiduciary role that public expectations demand.

5

CORPORATE ETHICAL GOVERNANCE & ACCOUNTABILITY

Purpose of the Chapter

Businesses, directors, executives, and professional accountants are facing increasingly demanding expectations from shareholders and other stakeholders for what organizations are doing and how they are doing it. At the same time, the environments that organizations operate in are increasingly complex, as are their ethical challenges. Organizational governance and accountability mechanisms are therefore under considerable strain, and improvement is highly desirable.

Trial-and-error decision making involves too high a risk of unfortunate consequences for the reputation and achievement of strategic objectives of the organization, the profession, the employees, and the professional accountants. Consequently, the leaders of the organization or the accounting profession and firms are expected to put in place governance programs that provide adequate ethical guidance and accountability programs that satisfy expectations. Even though the introduction of ethical governance and accountability programs is voluntary, and some organizations will never do so, those directors, executives, and professional accountants who wish to reduce the risks involved in ethical malfeasance and enjoy the benefits of continuing stakeholder support will.

Directors, executives, and professional accountants all have essential roles to play in the emerging framework for ethical governance and accountability. They are all serving mostly the same set of expectations, but have different levels of duty and responsibility. This chapter deals with both the common and distinct aspects related to each role. First, the emerging framework is developed, and then common threats to good governance are discussed, followed by matters related to the corporation and those relating to professional accountants.

Modern Governance & Accountability Framework— To Shareholders & Other Stakeholders

New Expectations—New Framework To Restore Credibility

Chapter 1 explained the concerns that organizations, and particularly corporations, are facing with regard to what they are doing and how they are doing it. Even before the Enron, Arthur Andersen, and WorldCom debacles, the public was pressing corporations over misleading financial reports and scandals; protection of the environment, worker, customer, and human rights; instances of bribery, undue influence, and incredible greed; and failure to govern within the bounds expected by stakeholders and to be accountable to them.

Stakeholders found that they could have significant impacts on a corporation's consumer markets, capital markets, and on the support offered the corporation by other stakeholder groups, such as employees and lenders. A corporation's reputation could be significantly affected by irate stakeholders. Directors and executives watching boycotts, reduced revenue and profit streams, or turn-downs by outstanding recruits or employees, found that the support of stakeholders was essential to the optimal achievement of medium- and long-term corporate objectives. Some directors and executives wanted that support, and with the help of academics and others, a new governance and accountability framework was developed, complete with new tools and techniques.

Then along came the Enron, Arthur Andersen, and WorldCom debacles. They showed the world the faults and vulnerabilities inherent in the old style shareholder-only governance and accountability model. The credibility of North American corporations, professional accountants, and capital markets was so severely eroded in the minds of the public that President Bush and business leaders had to call repeatedly for reforms. Finally, as Chapter 2 describes, the U.S. Congress and Senate were galvanized to rise above partisan politics to amalgamate two proposals and pass the Sarbanes-Oxley Act (SOX) of July 30, 2002, within one month and a few days of WorldCom's declaration of bankruptcy.

SOX has reformed the governance and accountability framework for corporations wishing to raise funds from the U.S. public and/or have their shares traded on U.S. stock markets. The framework laid out in SOX is being put in place by the Securities and Exchange Commission (SEC). It applies to SEC registrants and to the professional accountants and outside lawyers who serve them. This means, for example, that over 250 of Canada's largest companies whose securities are traded on U.S. markets have to comply, as do their professional accountants and outside lawyers. The SOX framework also applies to other foreign corporations, and their auditors and legal advisors. Over time, it will be the standard on which governance and accountability frameworks around the world are based.

Expectations from decades of stakeholder concerns and about the immediate need to restore credibility have given rise to the new framework of governance and accountability. SOX represented a response to an acceleration of stakeholder concerns brought on by the scandals that affected the lives of investors, and particularly pensioners, employees and their dependants, and many others. In the end, the shortfall in expected behavior was so egregious that only quick reform—a new framework—could restore the necessary trust in corporate governance and accountability.

Accountability to Shareholders or Stakeholders?

The growing capacity of nonshareholder stakeholders to influence the achievement of corporate objectives and their increasing sensitivity made it very attractive for corporations to encourage stakeholder support. The Enron, Arthur Andersen, and WorldCom scandals showed that corporate activities designed to favor *current* executives, directors, and some shareholders were not necessarily in the interest of future shareholders or current shareholders who wished for long-term success, such as pensioners-investors, employees, lenders, and other stakeholders. So damaging were the actions intended to benefit executives, directors, and investors in the short term that the credibility of the entire corporate governance and accountability process was jeopardized.

The SOX reforms were designed to refocus the governance model on responsibility of directors on their fiduciary duty beyond their own self-interest to that of shareholders as a whole and to the public interest. To quote the Senate Subcommittee[1] that investigated the Enron fiasco:

---

1. *Report on The Role of The Board of Directors in the Collapse of Enron,* U.S. Senate Permanent Subcommittee on Investigations, July 8, 2002.

Fiduciary Obligations of Boards of Directors. In the United States, the Board of Directors sits at the apex of a company's governing structure. A typical Board's duties include reviewing the company's overall business strategy; selecting and compensating the company's senior executives; evaluating the company's outside auditor; overseeing the company's financial statements; and monitoring overall company performance. According to the Business Roundtable, the Board's 'paramount duty' is to safeguard the interests of the company's shareholders.[2]

Directors operate under state laws that impose fiduciary duties on them to act in good faith, with reasonable care, and in the best interest of the corporation and its shareholders. Courts generally discuss three types of fiduciary obligations. As one court put it:

> Three broad duties stem from the fiduciary status of corporate directors: namely, the duties of obedience, loyalty, and due care. The duty of obedience requires a director to avoid committing . . . acts beyond the scope of the powers of a corporation as defined by its charter or the laws of the state of incorporation. . . . The duty of loyalty dictates that a director must act in good faith and must not allow his personal interest to prevail over the interests of the corporation. . . . [T]he duty of care requires a director to be diligent and prudent in managing the corporation's affairs.[3]

Given the recent corporate scandals and the documented capacity of stakeholders to influence the achievement of corporate objectives, it would be well within the directors' duty to safeguard the interests of shareholders, and prudent to take into account the interests of stakeholders when creating their governance structure.

Because stakeholder interests can potentially conflict with some shareholder interests, many states have formally modified the statutes by which corporations are created to allow directors to take stakeholder interests into account when appropriate. Directors will have to examine the trade-offs between shareholders and stakeholders and choose one or the other, or a blended solution.[4] Fortunately, a longer-term shareholder perspective frequently coincides with stakeholder interests.

---

2. *Statement of Corporate Governance,* The Business Roundtable (September 1997) at 3.

3. *Gearheart Industries v. Smith International,* 741 F.2d 707, 719 (5th Cir. 1984).

4. This is not the case in some jurisdictions. A recent Supreme Court of Canada decision placed the interest of shareholders ahead of the interest of bondholders. BCE Inc. was involved in a $52 billion takeover. The bondholders went to court arguing that the takeover would unreasonably increase the debt load of the company thereby making their bonds riskier. In a unanimous decision the Supreme Court reversed a lower court ruling that threatened to stop the largest leveraged buyout in Canadian history on the basis that the board of directors had failed to adequately consider the rights of the bondholders. In reversing the lower court decision, the Supreme Court implied that bondholders are only entitled to receive what is in the bondholder agreement. According to Poonam Puri, "It seems as through the court is saying that in this context of the sale of the company, the directors have a clear duty to maximize value for the shareholders, and they don't have to consider the interest, rights or expectations of creditors beyond those that have been negotiated." In the case of the BCE takeover, the directors have chosen to support the interest of shareholders over all other stakeholders, and this decision has the approval of the courts. (See Silcoff and Tait, *Financial Post,* June 20, 2008. http://www.financialpost.com/story.html?id=602600.) Interestingly, the deal later failed because it failed to meet a key condition of viability in that the increased debt load was forecast by KPMG to be too heavy for BCE to carry. (See Theresa Tedesco, "BCE deal dead, telecom giant seeks compensation," Canwest News Service at www.canada.com, December 11, 2008. http://www.canada.com/topics/news/story.html?id=1061692.)

Based on the reality of stakeholder pressures and the desire to encourage stakeholder support, corporations realize that they are strategically accountable to stakeholders (if not legally in all jurisdictions) and are governing themselves to minimize the risks and maximize the opportunities inherent in the stakeholder accountability framework. De facto, corporations are increasingly realizing that they are accountable to all of the stakeholders shown in Figure 5.1.

Governance for Broad Stakeholder Accountability

Governance Process Based on Stakeholder Interests | Once a corporation's directors and/or executives realize that *the corporation is accountable legally to shareholders, and strategically to additional stakeholders* who can significantly affect the achievement of its objectives, it becomes logical and desirable that they govern the corporation with the interests of all important stakeholders in mind. Shareholders are, in fact, a stakeholder group—and probably the most important on a continuing basis—but they are no longer the only stakeholder group whose interests should influence corporate actions.

In order to minimize harmful stakeholder reactions, and optimize opportunities in the future, corporations should assess how their actions impact upon the interests of their important stakeholder groups. This has been the underlying focus for environmental scanning and issues management for decades. What has changed is that *stakeholder impact analysis* has recently become significantly more developed as have the tools employed in examining, ranking, and assessing stakeholder interests—to the point that incorporating them into the governance process is now both feasible and desirable.

A schematic of the stakeholder accountability oriented governance process is shown in Figure 5.2.

In a *stakeholder-accountability oriented governance process* (SAOG), the board of directors must take all stakeholder interests into account and make sure that they are built into the company's vision, mission, strategy, policies, codes, practices, compliance mechanisms, and feedback arrangements. If this is not done, the company's actions may fail to take important interests into account, and the company may lose the support of one or more stakeholder groups.

FIGURE 5.1   **Map of Corporate Stakeholder Accountability**

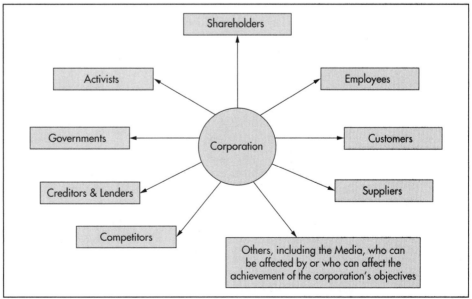

5.2   **Stakeholder Accountability Oriented Governance Process**

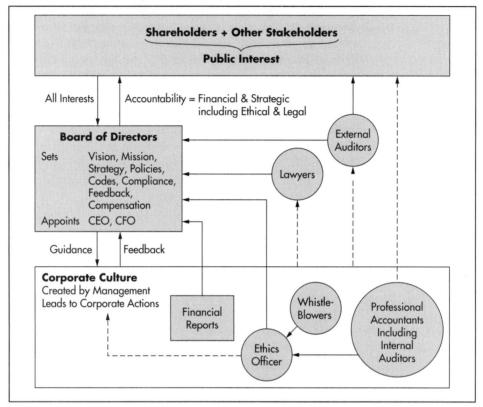

For example, not enough emphasis on customer value or safety, or too much on short-term profit, may cost the support of customers. The Ethics Case: *Ford/Firestone Tire Recall* illustrates such a problem.

Appropriate guidance reinforced by feedback mechanisms must be given to management, and reinforced by an ethical corporate culture, or else management can honestly say that no one told them what boundaries they should be operating within. This guidance will influence the preparation of financial reports and other sources of feedback, and also the behavior exhibited in dealings with customers, employees, and other stakeholders.

The board of directors may be advised by several agents if the behavior of management is questionable. Shareholders usually elect the external auditors to provide an expert opinion on whether the financial statements prepared by management present fairly the results of operations and financial position of the company and are in accordance with generally accepted accounting principles (GAAP). As Chapter 2 pointed out, Enron and other scandals have rededicated the audit profession to protecting the public interest when applying GAAP, not the interests of the senior management or current directors. External auditors are required to meet with the Audit Committee of the board and discuss the financial statements, as well as their work and opinions, and the state of the company's internal control measures.

In addition, a company's internal auditors' role is to assess whether its policies are comprehensive and are being observed. They should regularly report directly and in person, without management being present, to the Audit Committee, even though they may report on a day-to-day basis to the CEO or CFO.

Due to the SOX proposals, the company's lawyers will be expected to make the board of directors aware of problems if management does not respond appropriately when told of improprieties.[5]

Another element of modern SAOG systems should be an Ethics Officer (EO) or Ombudsperson who watches over the ethical culture and serves as the person to whom whistle-blowers report anonymously. The EO should report to the Audit Committee of the board and be the conduit through which a generic report of whistleblowers reaches the board. Similar to the internal auditors, the EO may report on a day-to-day basis to the CEO but should report regularly to the Audit Committee in person without other management being present. It should be noted that, while SOX regulations require the Audit Committee to establish a whistle-blower mechanism that brings them information on financial matters, the board also needs to monitor nonfinancial whistle-blower concerns because these often influence company reputation significantly, and thereby affect the company's ability to reach its strategic objectives effectively. From a governance perspective, it is extremely shortsighted not to establish a whistle-blower program providing information to the board of directors on both financial and nonfinancial matters.

Professional accountants in the company's employ are called on by their professional codes of conduct to serve the pubic interest. Consequently, they should report financial wrongdoing to the CFO, and if appropriate action is not taken, to the EO, CEO, and auditors. They are not allowed to be involved with misrepresentation and should therefore be ready to whistle-blow inside their corporation and, per the SOX reforms, specifically to the Audit Committee of the board.

| **Identifying Organizational Values—The Foundation of Behavior** | The new framework for accountability is based on responding to shareholder and other stakeholder interests, and the modern governance framework should direct corporate personnel to the integration of those interests into their strategies, planning, and decision making. Chapters 1 and 2 show that the public has expectations not only about what is done, but how it is accomplished. Consequently, discovering what those interests are, which are the most important, and where the risks are that should be managed is a necessary sequence that should precede the establishment of an organization's vision, mission, strategies, policies, and procedures.

This process is represented as a diagram in Figure 5.3. The specific measures used to identify, assess, and rank the stakeholder interests faced by a specific organization were discussed in Chapter 4.

In essence, what is required is an exploration of the stakeholder interests and expectations for the organization, so that respect for these can be built into the values that drive behavior. This will lessen the chance that personnel will be motivated to take decisions and actions that are not in the interests of stakeholders, but that are important to the achievement of company objectives.

This linkage between motivation and action is reflected in Figure 5.4. Individuals hold beliefs about what is right or improper. Those beliefs stem from many sources, but principally from the values that individuals hold. Some values were taught directly or through example by their parents, respected individuals, their bosses, friends, and so on, but other beliefs spring from the rules and motivational systems in place (or absent) at the organization. Beliefs motivate people to act.

The actions of individual personnel are understood collectively to be the "corporation's behavior." The corporation per se is inanimate. *People make things happen, so it is essential that their motivations are aligned with stakeholder expectations, which can only be reliably accomplished by*

---

5. This point is illustrated in the Ethics Case: *Terrorist Payments* in Chapter 3.

5.3

Stakeholder Interests Ranking, Risk Assessment & Usage

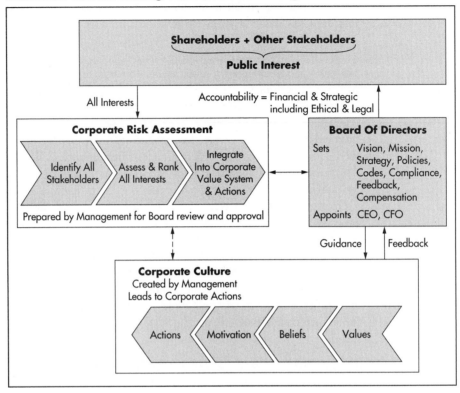

5.4

Aligning Values for Ethical Motivation & Action

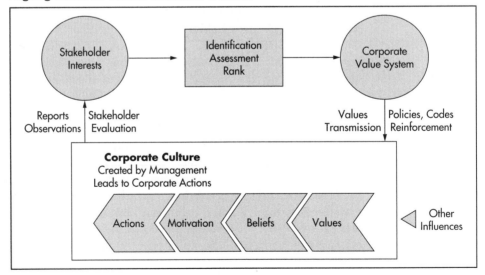

ensuring that the values underlying corporate motivational elements (i.e., corporate culture, codes, policies, etc.) are similarly aligned. Ensuring this alignment is a vital responsibility for directors, whether they are considering stock option bonus systems, penalties for malfeasance, or paper medals (awards) for outstanding exemplars.

The identification, assessment, and ranking of stakeholder interests should develop a comprehensive set of values for an organization. However, it should be recognized that values and their priority vary in different national, regional, or religious cultures. This presents increasing complexities as the number of different cultures that an organization deals with increases. Some cultures place a high importance on the rights of individuals. Others place primacy on duty to family, company, religious beliefs, and so on.

In the face of competing value systems for the motivation of personnel, corporations should consider which set of values most aligns with those of their shareholders, and of their most important stakeholders—perhaps those that can influence their largest consumer and capital markets. Modern media coverage is shrinking the world, so activities that take place on the other side of the world will be known—and quickly—by interested stakeholders everywhere. Greenpeace, CNN, and other organizations will see that pollution incidents, for example, are brought to everyone's attention quickly.[6]

Researchers are intent on providing answers to this multicultural diversity of values problem. They are working to identify a set of universal values or *hypernorms* that could be embedded in corporate values systems. Although their strict interpretation differs somewhat depending on the culture, six relatively universal respected values have been identified. These universal values are honesty, fairness, compassion, integrity, predictability, and responsibility (Table 5.1).

Directors should consider embedding these hypernorms in their corporate values systems in order to ensure that all important values are included, and that maximum acceptance and respect is assured in dealings with many cultures.

| Guidance Mechanisms—Ethical Culture & Code of Conduct

The values that a corporation's directors wish to instill in order to motivate the beliefs and actions of its personnel need to be conveyed to provide the required guidance. Usually, such guidance takes the form of a code of conduct that states the values selected, the principles that flow from those values, and any rules that are to be followed to ensure that appropriate values are respected. As noted in a later section, some research has been done into the improvement of the effectiveness of a code. For example, principles are more useful than just rules because principles facilitate interpretation when the precise circumstances encountered do not exactly fit the rule prescribed. A blend of principles and rules is often optimal.

TABLE 5.1   **Cultural Values & Hypernorms**

SPHERE/CULTURE	BASIS OF VALUE-SYSTEM
North American	Rights-based: rights, justice, utility
Sino-Confucian	Duty-based: obligation to family
Japan	Duty-based: obligation to company
Middle East	Duty-based: obligation to savior
Europe	Personal rights
South America	Duty-based: obligation to family, religious values
Impact Evident On:	Dealing with people . . . hiring, gender
	Bribery
	Motivation for doing business
	Short- or long-term time horizons
	Importance of quality-of-life issues
Hypernorm Values:	Honesty, Fairness, Compassion, Integrity, Predictability, Responsibility

---

6. See the Ethics Case: *The Brent Spar Decommissioning Disaster* in Chapter 7 for the dilemma faced by Shell UK when Greenpeace challenged the environmental impact of a management decision.

Unfortunately, a code on its own may be nothing more than "ethical art" that hangs on the wall but is rarely studied or followed. *Experience has revealed that, to be effective, a code must be reinforced by a comprehensive ethical culture.* Developing an ethical culture involves continually applying significant effort over several dimensions. A code should be the subject of a training session for new recruits on joining an organization, with yearly update sessions. Moreover, the ethical behavior expected must be referred to in speeches and newsletters by top management as often as they refer to their health and safety program, or their antipollution program, for example, or else it will be seen as less important by employees. If personnel never or rarely hear about ethical expectations, they will know that they are not a serious priority. Similarly, there should be an ethical behavior reporting mechanism linked to feedback, recognition, and promotion systems. Whistle-blowers are also part of a needed monitoring, risk management, and remediation system. More often than not, a corporation that has a code of conduct without supporting it in an ethical culture is simply engaging in window dressing—not in providing effective ethical guidance.

The development of effective codes of conduct, and of the necessary supportive ethical culture, is discussed later in this chapter.

Threats to Good Governance & Accountability

The assumption that personnel will automatically be motivated to behave as the owners wanted is no longer valid. People are motivated more by self-interest than in the past, and are likely to come from different cultures that emphasize different priorities of duty. As a result, there is greater need for clear guidance and for identifying and effectively managing threats to good governance and accountability. Discussion of three significant threats follows.

Misunderstanding Objectives & Fiduciary Duty

Even when different cultures are not an issue, personnel can misunderstand the organization's objectives and their own role and fiduciary duty. For example, many directors and employees of Enron evidently believed that the company's objectives were best served by actions that brought short-term profit:

- through ethical dishonesty—manipulation of energy markets in California, or sham displays of trading floors;
- that was illusory—SPE transactions;
- that benefited themselves at the expense of other stakeholders—payment of extraordinary fees and commissions to SPEs.

Frequently, employees are tempted to cut ethical corners, and they have done so because they believed that their top management wanted them to; they were ordered to do so; or they were encouraged to do so by misguided or manipulatable incentive programs. These actions occurred although the board of directors would have preferred (sometimes with hindsight) that they had not. Personnel simply misunderstood what was expected by the board because guidance was unclear, or they were led astray and did not understand that they were to report the problem for appropriate corrective action, or to whom or how.

Lack of proper guidance or reporting mechanisms may have been the result of directors and others not understanding their duty as a fiduciary. As noted earlier, directors owe shareholders and regulators several duties, including obedience, loyalty, and due care; safeguarding of assets; accurate, comprehensive, and transparent reports; and so on. Many directors have been looking out for their own interests, and they have spent little time protecting shareholders, other stakeholders, and the public interest from top management. Even where good guidance was in place, compliance mechanisms were nonexistent, rusty, or neglected because most directors concentrated on moving the company forward, not in protecting it from ethical downsides.

Fortunately, SOX has clarified much of this lack of understanding of fiduciary relationships for directors, executives, and also for professional accountants. Professional accountants at Arthur Andersen forgot they should have been serving the public interest when giving their opinion that Enron's financial statements were in accordance with generally accepted accounting principles (GAAP). Instead, by failing to contradict the initiatives of management, Arthur Andersen allowed unreported variations that prejudiced the interest of shareholders wanting to hold their stock and those wishing to buy in the future, as well as the interests of employees, long-term lenders, and others.

Fortunately, the ensuing investigation and SOX has clarified the primacy of the public interest as the foremost concern of professional accountants. This clarification is not only for external auditors but also for professional accountants employed by organizations. As employees, they owe a loyalty to their employer, but that does not supersede their duty to the public interest, their profession, or themselves. When acting as executives or managers, professional accountants must observe their professional code of conduct and, for example, cannot be associated with misrepresentations. These priorities of duty will be discussed more fully later.

Similarly, as discussed in Chapter 2, external lawyers who discover serious illegalities that are not rectified by management may be expected by the SEC to reveal these matters to the board through a "noisy departure" process. Amazingly, many law firms are arguing against the imposition of this process, asserting that such disclosure may not be in the company's interest. A silent departure would certainly favor the interests of management who know what is going on, rather than the directors, investors, and other stakeholders who do not.

Failure to Identify & Manage Ethics Risks

Recognition of the increasing complexity, volatility, and risk inherent in modern corporate interests and operations, particularly as their scope expands to different countries and cultures, has led to the requirement for risk identification, assessment, and management systems. In the late 1990s, it became a requirement that boards of directors ensure that their companies' risk management processes were effective,[7] and a number of studies were published illustrating how such a system might be developed and what types of risk might be targeted.[8]

However, *the systematic search for ethics risks—those where the expectations of stakeholders may not be met—has not been targeted* and should be, now that the need for stakeholder-oriented accountability and governance is emerging. Table 5.2 illustrates the aspects of risk that are usually investigated by corporate examiners.

Usually there is an examination designed to safeguard assets by internal auditors who will also ensure compliance with policies. External auditors examine the financial statements and see that internal controls are in place that will ensure accurate financial reports. But given the Enron, WorldCom, and other recent fiascos, *both types of auditor are now expected to spend more time searching for fraudulent activities—*those where there is intent to deceive.[9] External auditors have resisted being charged with full responsibility for this in the past, because fraud is very difficult to discover and the costs of doing so are much greater than boards of directors have been willing to authorize, and management has been willing to incur.

---

7. The Toronto Stock Exchange, for example, identified risk management as a matter requiring oversight by directors in 1995.
8. See, for example, AICPA/CICA, and the Institute for Internal Auditors publications on risk management identified in Chapter 1.
9. Per the following pronouncements, for example: CICA Handbook Section 5135 (2002); AICPA: SAS 99 (2002); International Auditing and Assurance Standards Board (IAASB) ISA 240 (2001, rev. 2004).

TABLE 5.2	Areas of Corporate Risk Assessment

Governance and objectives

Areas of impact
    Reputation
    Assets, revenues, costs
    Performance
    Stakeholders

Sources of risk
    Environmental
    Strategic
    Operational
    Informational

Specific hazards

Degree of control over risk—little, some, great deal

Documentation

In only a very few companies has there been a systematic annual process designed to focus the attention of directors, executives, and advisors on those areas where the company's actions may not meet the expectations of stakeholders. Dow Corning has had an "ethics audit process" but, based on the silicone breast implant episode,[10] its orientation has apparently been toward avoiding scientifically justified, legal liability rather than making sure the interests of customers and other stakeholders are met. The Tylenol recall is an example of where planning ahead for customer interests made Johnson & Johnson famous. Dow Corning, by contrast, resorted to bankruptcy protection, and their parent companies made a public plea that the legal liability did not reach upward to them. As usual in product liability cases, the fine paid by Dow Corning was small relative to the damage to reputation, ongoing business relationships, and the ongoing support of stakeholders.

All of Dow Corning's stakeholders would have benefited by a broader definition of ethics risk—one that identified where the expectations of stakeholders may not have been met. The Dow Corning audit process, which was also somewhat flawed, can be readily repaired to serve as one approach to the discovery of ethical risks. Other approaches could involve making an annual reflection routine part of annual ethics sign-off and/or training processes. Charging internal audit with responsibility for identification and assessment, and the ethics officer with ongoing responsibility for discovery, assessment, and reporting to the CEO and Audit Committee of the board, are logical steps to take as well. Reward recognition should be accorded to personnel who bring issues forward. Prevention is the most important aspect of crisis management, and ethics risks have a nasty way of becoming crises if not diagnosed early enough.

The principles of Ethics Risk Management are summarized in Table 5.3. The importance of maintaining the support of stakeholders is becoming more apparent and widely accepted, as Ethics Risk Management becomes a normal element of the due diligence requirements for a board of directors, and a significant part of management's responsibility.

TABLE 5.3	Ethics Risk Management Principles

Normal definitions of risk are too narrow for stakeholder-oriented accountability and governance.
An ethics risk exists where the expectations of a stakeholder may not be met.
Discovery and remediation are essential in order to avoid a crisis or the loss of support of stakeholders.
Assign responsibility, develop annual processes, board review.

10. See the Ethics Case: *Dow Corning Silicon Breast Implants*

Conflict of Interests

Conflict of interests has been a subject of extreme importance in recent scandals in which employees, agents, and professionals failed to exercise proper judgment on behalf of their principals. In the Enron fiasco, senior officers, lawyers, and professional accountants acted in their own self-interest rather than for the benefit of the shareholders of Enron. The conflict between the self-interest of the decision makers and the interest of the shareholders interfered with the judgment being applied, causing the interests of the shareholders to be subjugated to the self-interest of the decision makers. As a result, Enron declared bankruptcy, investors lost their savings, and capital markets lost credibility and fell into turmoil. Because of this, the governance frameworks for corporations and professional accounting have been changed forever.

Stated simply, a conflict of interests occurs when the independent judgment of a person is swayed, or might be swayed, from making decisions in the best interest of others who are relying on that judgment. An executive or employee is expected to make judgments in the best interest of the company. A director is legally expected to make judgments in the best interest of the company and its shareholders, and to do so strategically so that no harm and perhaps some benefit will come to other stakeholders and the public interest. A professional accountant is expected to make judgments that are in the public interest.

Decision makers usually have a priority of duties that they are expected to fulfill, and a conflict of interests confuses and distracts the decision maker from that duty, resulting in harm to those legitimate expectations which are not fulfilled. This situation is pictured in Figure 5.5, where a decision maker (D) "has a conflict of interest if, and only if, (1) D is in a relationship with another (P) requiring D to exercise judgment in P's behalf and (2) D has a special interest tending to interfere with the proper exercise of judgment in that relationship."[11]

A conflict of interest is *potential* if, and only if, D is not yet in a situation in which D must (or, at least, should) make that judgment. A conflict of interest is *actual* if, and only if, D is in a situation in which D must (or, at least should) make that judgment.[12] Sometimes the term *apparent* conflict of interest is used, but it is a misnomer because it refers to a situation where no

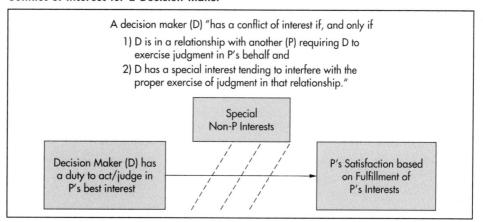

FIGURE 5.5

Conflict of Interest for a Decision Maker

A decision maker (D) "has a conflict of interest if, and only if

1) D is in a relationship with another (P) requiring D to exercise judgment in P's behalf and

2) D has a special interest tending to interfere with the proper exercise of judgment in that relationship."

Special Non-P Interests

Decision Maker (D) has a duty to act/judge in P's best interest

P's Satisfaction based on Fulfillment of P's Interests

---

11. *Conflict of Interest in the Professions,* edited by Michael Davis and Andrew Stark, Oxford University Press, 2001, 8. Note that D and P can be a person or a corporate body. Davis uses only P.

12. Ibid., 15.

conflict of interest exists, although as a result of lack of information someone other than D would be justified in concluding (however tentatively) that D does have one.[13] Figure 5.6 illustrates these concepts.

A special or conflicting interest could include "any interest, loyalty, concern, emotion, or other feature of a situation tending to make D's judgment (in that situation) less reliable that it would normally be, without rendering D incompetent. Financial interests and family connections are the most common sources of conflict of interest, but love, prior statements, gratitude, and other subjective tugs on judgment can also be interest (in this sense)."[14] Table 5.4 provides a list of causes of conflicting interests.

FIGURE 5.6   **Types of Conflict of Interest**

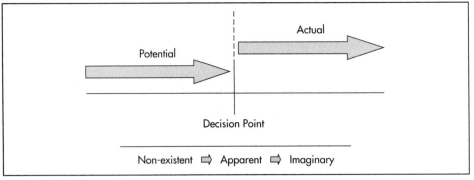

TABLE 5.4   **Causes of Conflicting Interests**

How might judgment be swayed . . .

- Any interest, influence, loyalty, concern, emotion, or other feature tending to make judgment less reliable than normal

Self-interest . . .

- Bribes, kickbacks—payments or property to decider, family, designees
- Gifts, free travel, favors,
- Special advantages—non market discounts on goods
- Special treatment—flattery, social involvement
- Dealings with family, relatives, or relations

Fraud . . .

- Misappropriation of funds or property
- Cheating on expense accounts
- Falsifying documents
- Stealing cash, assets, or resources
- Falsifying results to obtain bonuses, merit pay, or promotion

Misunderstanding . . .

- Confused signals or incentives
- Boss/everybody's doing it
- Cultural differences

Slippery slope . . .

- Where a small favor leads to ever larger demands

---

13. Ibid., 18.
14. Ibid., 9.

Concern over a conflict of interest stems from:

I the fact that people who are relying upon D's decision may be harmed if D does not respond or compensate;

I if D knows or should have known, but does not tell P, then D is perpetrating a deception;

I if D's judgment will be less reliable than it ordinarily is.

A conflict of interest is more than just bias, which can be measured for and adjusted. However, because of the unknown nature and therefore extent of the influences, *concern should be for any tendency toward bias.*[15]

I **Management to Avoid & Minimize Consequences** I To remedy the concerns over a conflict of interest, three general approaches should be considered: (1) avoidance, (2) disclosure to those stakeholders relying on the decision, and (3) management of the conflict of interest so that the benefits of the judgment made outweigh the costs.

Avoidance is the preferred approach if the appearance of having a conflict of interests can be avoided as well as the reality. The appearance of having a conflict can often be as harmful to the decision maker's reputation as having a real conflict because it is almost impossible to recover lost credibility and reputation without extreme effort and cost, and then only with luck. Consequently, for example, it is advisable to provide rules against giving or receiving kickbacks, because it is incredible to argue later that they really didn't matter.

Management of potential conflicts is a potentially useful approach if avoidance is not possible and the cost-benefit trade-off of management measures is favorable. The probability that reputation will be lost, and the related cost, must be taken into account in the trade-off analysis. The important aspects related to the management of conflicts of interest are identified in Table 5.5.

The first step in the process of managing to defend against these influences is to ensure that all employees are *aware* of their existence and consequences. This can be done through codes of conduct[16] and related training. One of the items that should be covered in the training is the "slippery slope" problem, in which an individual can be enticed into a relationship by a seemingly innocuous request for a small favor, then a larger one, and then find that they are told that unless they go along with a serious infraction, their past secrets will be revealed. The start of the slope is too gentle for some to notice, but the slope becomes steeper and more slippery very quickly.

The second step is to *create an understanding* of the reasons: why the employer cannot afford unmanaged conflict of interests situations; and why guidelines have been developed to prevent their occurrence, their exploration though counseling if recognized, their reporting if they have occurred, as well as penalties for their occurrence and nonreporting. Annual written confirmations of ethical behavior and adherence to the employer's code of conduct should

---

15. Ibid., 11, 12.

16. Codes of ethics and excellent guidance are available for professionals. For example, the International Federation of Accountants (IFAC) has developed a code of ethics to guide professional accountants that is analyzed in more detail in Chapter 6. It acknowledges that occasionally situations arise that threaten the accountant's ability to comply with the ethics code. These situations include self-interest, self-review, advocacy, familiarity and intimidation. The nature and significance of the threat is situation specific. Nevertheless, the IFAC code has outlined some broad principles or safeguards that may reduce or eliminate the threat. But, when all else fails, the public accountant should remove his/ herself from the situation. In other words, even if there is an adverse economic consequence from doing so, the public accountant must avoid the conflict by walking away.

TABLE 5.5	**Management of Conflicting Interests**

Steps to Be Taken

Ensure awareness through:
- Codes of conduct and
- Related initial and ongoing training

Create a program and an understanding of:
- Employer's concerns regarding conflict of interests
- Major issues:
  - Avoidance is preferable
  - Slippery slope
  - Management techniques:
    - Annual sign-off, confirmation review and compliance
    - Guidelines for gifts, behavior
    - Counseling, reporting, reinforcement
    - Chinese walls/firewalls, scrutiny

include reference to conflicts of interest encountered by the signatory, and those identified involving others.

Guidelines that can prove helpful are those that specify when it may be acceptable to give or accept a gift or preferential treatment. Useful questions to ask in this regard are shown in Table 5.6. They are intended to assess whether the offering is likely to sway the independent judgment of the professional. Obviously something worth a very modest amount, perhaps under $100, that is offered to a group of people as a publicity venture is much less of a problem than a large-value item offered to one person who has considerable influence over the fortunes of the giver.

Additional reinforcement of problems and good examples through publicity will also serve to keep the awareness and understanding fresh. Compliance systems must be in place to provide another type of reinforcement, with appropriate penalties for significant wrongdoings.

| Agency Theory, Ethics & Sears | Directors, executives, and professional accountants should appreciate that incentive systems that they use to motivate employees can provide appropriate or inappropriate reinforcement, depending on the way in which they are designed. In many ways, the stock option plans available to executives in the Enron, WorldCom, Waste Management, and Sunbeam cases were responsible for motivating them to the detriment of all stakeholders involved.

According to agency theorists, shareholders expect and hope managers, and in turn nonmanagerial employees, will behave in line with the goals set for the corporation. The

TABLE 5.6	**Guidelines for Acceptance of Gifts or Preferential Treatment**

1. Is it nominal or substantial?
2. What is the intended purpose?
3. What are the circumstances?
4. What is the position of sensitivity of the recipient?
5. What is the accepted practice?
6. What is the firm/company policy?
7. Is it legal?

principals or shareholders hope that their agents will be motivated to act as the principals wish. Incentive systems and punishment systems are created to try to influence the agents to stay on the right path. Clearly, as the public's expectations for corporate performance now include ethical standards, the reward and punishment systems set up should also reflect ethical dimensions, or shareholders are going to be disappointed. In fact, the corporation's strategic plans should include ethical dimensions to ensure that their agents, both inside and outside the corporation, are properly influenced and conflicts of interest are avoided. One recent case in point involves the incentive system put in place by Sears for the managers of their auto service stores. The managers' remuneration depended upon the volume of sales made by the store, but this lead to the selling of services that customers didn't need to boost the managers' earnings. A national scandal erupted, and Sears apologized for creating a misleading incentive system.

| **Chinese Walls/Firewalls** | An important system for preventing ethical malfeasance, the "Chinese wall" or "firewall" concept deserves further comment. This practice utilizes the analogy to an impervious wall to describe those measures and methods that would prevent the transmission of client information from one part of an organization or consortium to another. Such firewalls or Chinese walls are not tangible in a three-dimensional sense, but refer to a multidimensional set of measures such as:

| instructions to keep information confidential;

| instructions not to read, listen to, or act on specific types of information;

| educational programs and reinforcements by top management;

| monitoring and compliance sign-off procedures;

| scrutiny of insider or key-person trading of securities;

| physical barriers to information transmission, such as:

- separate computer- or physical-storage systems,
- segregation of duties to different employees,
- segregation of information in a different location or building, etc.,
- different lock systems;

| appointment of a Compliance Officer who would monitor the effectiveness of the wall;

| disciplinary sanctions for breach of the wall.

Chinese walls or firewalls have been a normal part of business and professional operations for many years. For example, when a client is involved in the preparation of a public offering of securities, those members of the offering team (lawyers, professional accountants, and underwriters) are expected not to divulge advance details of the underwriting to the other members of their respective firms, or to anyone else. The public issuance of securities, as presently known, would be impossible without the Chinese wall construct. Fortunately, even though in the final analysis a Chinese wall relies on the integrity of the personnel involved for its effectiveness, such arrangements are considered effective to protect the public interest and to safeguard the interest of current clients as well as former clients.

| **Forensic Experts & Evidence: The 20/60/20 Rule** | The time may come when a director, executive, or professional accountant must consider whether a conflict of interests has led to serious breach of duty, a fraudulent act, or a loss that must be recovered pursuant to an insurance policy. In such instances, an investigative and forensic expert may be called

on if existing company personnel would benefit from assistance. The expert will employ appropriate techniques based on an understanding of the situation.

Many managers may believe that their associates and employees would rarely engage in unethical behavior. However, forensic experts indicate that their experience suggests that the general population can be divided into three groups:

- 20% would never commit a fraud.
- 60% would commit a fraud if the chance of getting caught is considered low.
- 20% would seek to commit a fraud regardless of the circumstances.

Although some believe the percentages to be closer to 10/80/10, it is important to ask who would commit a fraud and what are the circumstances that could come into play in the decision?

| **The GONE Theory: Identifying Potentially Harmful Situations & Likely Perpetrators** | Forensic experts point out that in most instances of fraud or opportunistic behavior, they can begin to identify prospective perpetrators through the use of the GONE Theory. The acronym GONE stands for circumstances that account for motivation of illicit behavior, in which the letters represent:

- G—Greed.
- O—Opportunity to take advantage.
- N—Need for whatever is taken.
- E—Expectation of being caught is low.

The experts point out that identifying personnel who have or exhibit these characteristics can head off problems if adequate precautions are taken. These would include additional review and diligence on the part of supervisors, transfer to less vulnerable areas, signaling that extra review or audit procedures were in place, and so on. For example, if an employee exhibited signs of a lifestyle well beyond his or her means, then extra scrutiny might be warranted.

| **Duty Depends On a Person's Role** | Although this analysis of conflict of interests has focused on the individual, it should be noted that the analysis is similar for groups of individuals within a corporation, organization, or profession. But either as individuals or groups of individuals, it is often the roles taken on, and therefore the duties assumed and expected by those relying on the actions to be taken, that define the nature of conflicts of interest. For example, it is unlikely that a professional accountant auditing or judging financial statements can audit objectively her or his own work without bias, or maintain objectivity if asked to assume an advocacy role by a client. In order to ensure sufficient objectivity to maintain their duty to serve the public interest, professional accountants have developed standards designed to ensure independence.[17] These will be discussed in the next chapter.

---

17. See, for example, the International Federation of Accountants (IFAC) *Code of Ethics for Professional Accountants,* November 2001, or the *IFAC Code of Ethics for Professional Accountants,* International Federation for Accountants Ethics Committee, NY, NY, June 2005, http://www.ifac.org/Store/Category.tmpl?Category=Ethics&Cart=1215563035160178. Both versions of the IFAC are downloadable from **www.cengage.com/acounting/brooks**

Key Elements of Corporate Governance & Accountability

Developing, Implementing, & Managing an Ethical Corporate Culture

Directors, owners, and senior management are in the process of realizing that they and their employees need to understand that (1) their organizations would be wise to consider the interests of stakeholders, not just shareholders; and that (2) appropriate ethical values are to be considered when decisions are being made. *Because organizational, professional, and personal values provide the framework to decision making, it is vital that organizations create an environment or culture where appropriate shared values are created, understood, fostered and committed to by all concerned.* This cannot be reliably achieved by simply leaving ethics solely to the judgment of individuals in a workforce of divergent experiences and backgrounds to work out by trial and error. Nor can it be achieved simply by sending a letter urging employees to be on their best behavior, or by just publishing a code of conduct. In order to ensure commitment to the ethical principles or values considered appropriate for the organization, it must be evident to the members of the organization that top management is fully supportive and that such support is evident throughout the organization's governance systems.

Experts in organizational behavior who have been studying organizational culture, such as Edgar Schein, believe that developing the right shared values in an organization, and commitment to them, can lead to many benefits. He takes the view that the organization's culture is a cognitive framework, consisting of attitudes, values, behavioral norms, and expectations shared by organization members (Schein 1985). Wayne Reschke and Ray Aldag have brought together in a model (see Figure 5.7) those elements generally thought to comprise an organization's

5.7 Organizational Culture, Individual/Team Outcomes & Organizational Effectiveness

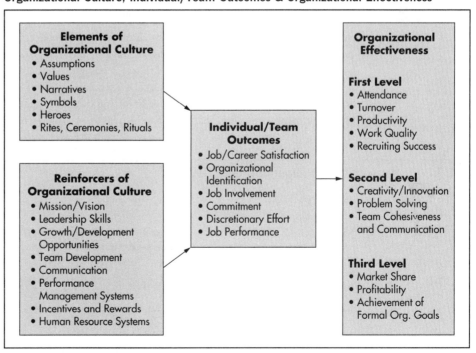

Source: A Model of the Impact of Organizational Culture on Individual/Team Outcomes and Organization Effectiveness, *The Business Case for Culture Change*, W. Reschke & R. Aldag, Center for Organizational Effectiveness, August 2000.

culture and the mechanisms available to reinforce that culture. They have identified aspects of individual, team, and organizational performance that might benefit from appropriate development of that culture. Others have developed ways of assessing and profiling an organization's culture[18] in order to improve the culture, provide motivation toward a goal, or assess cultures of merging organizations and manage the change to a new, shared culture. Usually the place to start assessments is with the organization's strategic core—its philosophy and mission, its vision, what it believes drives its value added, and how it treats its stakeholders. All of these elements and "reinforcers" of organizational culture will be increasingly more dependent on their ethical aspects, as will the resulting behavior. In order to ensure an effective understanding and ongoing commitment to the organization's ethical principles, many companies create an ethics program.

Perhaps the most important aspect of an ethics program designed to ensure an effective understanding and commitment to the organization's ethical principles is the choice of program orientation. According to researchers, there are five orientations for the design and operation of ethics programs. These are described in Table 5.7.

The researchers went on to evaluate the effectiveness of the impact of these orientations on several dimensions by administering over 10,000 surveys to randomly selected employees in six large American companies from a variety of industries. The seven dimensions on which the impact was evaluated were:

1. Unethical/illegal behavior.

2. Employee awareness of ethical issues that arise at work.

3. Looking for ethics/compliance advice within the company.

4. Delivering bad news to management.

5. Ethics/compliance violations are reported in the organization.

6. Better decision making in the company because of the ethics/compliance program.

7. Employee commitment to the organization.

According to their research, confirmed by consulting experience on the design of corporate ethics programs, *the most important factor in encouraging employee observance is that the employees perceive that the ethics program is values-based.* This produced significantly more positive outcomes on all seven dimensions. Compliance and external orientations also produced favorable outcomes on the seven dimensions, but not as positive as for the values-based approach. The external orientation outcomes were less than the compliance-based approach. A purely defensive, CYA approach, was considered "harmful", as it resulted in negative outcomes across all dimensions. It

---

TABLE 5.7

Ethics Program Orientation Types

ORIENTATION	PRIMARY FOCUS
Compliance-based	Preventing, detecting, and punishing violations of the law
Integrity or Values-based	Defines organizational values and encourages employee commitment
Satisfaction of external stakeholders	Improvement of image with and relationships with external stakeholders (customers, the community, suppliers)
Protect top management from blame	"CYA" or cover your ____
Combinations of the above	Values- and compliance-based, for example

Sources: Treviño, Weaver, Gibson and Toffler, 1999, 135–139; Paine, 1994, 111; Badaracco & Webb, 1995, 15.

---

18. See, for example, J. A. Chatman and K. A. Jehn, "Assessing the Relationship between Industry Characteristics and Organizational Culture: How Different Can You Be?" *Academy of Management Journal* 37 (1994): 522–33.

was suggested the combined approaches could be effective, such as if a values orientation were "backed up with accountability systems and discipline for violators" where "values can include concern for customers, suppliers, and the community as well as shareholders and internal stakeholders such as employees." (Treviño et al. 1999, 139)

The study also provides some useful insights into the important aspects of an ethical culture. These are included in Table 5.8. The findings presented in Table 5.8 can be particularly useful for a company that is assessing what it might do to institute a new ethics program or improve its current ethical culture. According to a study by Weaver, Treviño, and Cochran (1999b), formal ethics programs usually include the dimensions listed in Table 5.9.

The Sarbanes-Oxley Act and related changes in governance guidelines from stock exchanges and other sources have resulted in the expectation that respectable corporations will have at least the basic elements of an ethics program. Recently, the emphasis has shifted to making ethics programs effective.

KPMG Forensic Advisory's *Integrity Survey* 2005–2006 presents interesting data that is instructive, including data shown in Table 5.10 that was gleaned from over 4,000 survey responses from U.S. employees (KPMG 2005). The responses summarized above reveal that there is considerable room for improvement in the effectiveness of ethics programs. Further data in the KPMG study shows just how important the existence of an ethics program can be. Respondents were separated into "with program" and "without program" groups and their answers to further questions are summarized in Table 5.11. The table shows, for example, that CEOs and other top executives are considered to be setting the "right tone at the top" by 84% of respondents where an ethics program is present, but by only 29% without an ethics program—a

---

TABLE 5.8   **Ethical Culture: Important Aspects**

An ethical culture combines formal and informal elements to guide employee thought and action, including:

- Ethical leadership by executives and supervisors,*
- Reward systems incorporate ethical considerations,*
- Perceived fairness, fair treatment of employees,*
- Open discussion of ethics in the organization,*
- Authority structure that emphasizes an employee's accountability and responsibility to question his or her own actions, and an obligation to question authority when something seems wrong,*
- Organizational focus that communicates care for employees and the community, rather than self-interest,
- Official policies and procedures (code of ethics, practice, conduct),
- Supporting offices (e.g. ethics officer, ombudsperson),
- Supporting structures (e.g. telephone hotline, whistle-blower protection, code sign-off, training, etc.).

*Most influential factors as found by Treviño et al.

TABLE 5.9   **Ethical Programs' Usual Dimensions**

1. Formal ethics codes
2. Ethics committees developing policies, evaluating actions, investigating and adjudicating policy violations
3. Ethics communications systems
4. Ethics officers or ombudspersons coordinating policies, providing education, or investigating allegations
5. Ethics training programs to raise awareness and help employees respond to ethical problems
6. Disciplinary processes for unethical behavior

TABLE 5.10	Presence of Program Elements per KPMG *Integrity Survey* 2005–2006				
RESPONSE TO: MY ORGANIZATION . . .		FORMALLY	INFORMALLY	UNSURE	NOT AT ALL
Has a code of conduct that articulates the values and standards of the organization		77%	10%	10%	3%
Has a senior-level ethics compliance officer		51%	7%	32%	10%
Performs background investigations on prospective employees		60%	10%	23%	7%
Provides communication and training to employees on its code of conduct		69%	17%	8%	5%
Has a confidential and anonymous hotline that employees can use to report misconduct or seek advice		48%	6%	24%	22%
Audits and monitors employees and managers compliance with its code		44%	23%	24%	10%
Has policies to hold employees and managers accountable for code of conduct violations		65%	12%	17%	7%
Provides incentives for employees to uphold the code of conduct		23%	13%	28%	37%
Has policies to investigate and take corrective action if misconduct is alleged		65%	11%	18%	8%

Source: Reprinted from KPMG *Integrity Survey* 2005–2006, Copyright © 2006 KPMG LLP, with permission.

gain of 55%. In addition, it is apparent that *the existence of an ethics program improves perceptions and potentially the related behaviors on all dimensions.*[19]

Once an ethics program is established, the next step is to make it as effective as possible. In a general sense, higher effectiveness results from the comprehensiveness with which a program sets the corporation's culture and employs the reinforcers of culture that are identified in Figure 5.7. Based on a study of *Fortune 500* companies, Weaver et al. (1999b) argue that the degree to which a values or compliance orientation characterizes an ethics program's mode of control can be seen in the program's emphasis on encouraging shared values, supporting employee aspirations, communicating values, and building trust and confidence. They conclude that the dominant influence of the U.S. Sentencing Guidelines has been to orient top management commitment and corporate ethics programs toward compliance rather than integrity or values. This orientation—according to the earlier Treviño et al. (1999) study—will not provide the best adherence to desired ethics values. Hopefully, over time, top management will learn that a values orientation that involves encouraging shared values, supporting employee aspirations, communicating values, and building trust and confidence will produce significant benefits, and ethics programs will move in that direction.

---

19. Survey reprinted from KPMG *Integrity Survey* 2005–2006, Copyright © 2006 KPMG LLP, a U.S. limited liability partnership and a member firm of the KPMG network of independent member firms affiliated with KPMG International, a Swiss cooperative. All rights reserved. Printed in the U.S.A.

All information provided is of a general nature and is not intended to address the circumstances of any particular individual or entity. Although we endeavor to provide accurate and timely information, there can be no guarantee that such information is accurate as of the date it is received or that it will continue to be accurate in the future. No one should act upon such information without appropriate professional advice after a thorough examination of the facts of a particular situation.

For additional news and information, please access KPMG's global Web site on the Internet at **http://www.kpmg.com**.

TABLE 5.11	Ethics Programs Enhance Perceptions and Behaviors per KPMG *Integrity Survey* 2005–2006		
		WITH ETHICS PROGRAM	
PERCEPTION OR BEHAVIOR		**BETTER**	**OVERALL**
Observed—Misconduct in prior 12 months		6%	59%
• Violations of organizational values and principles in the prior 12 months		12%	43%
Preventing Misconduct—Feel pressures to do whatever it takes to meet targets		10%	50%
• Lack understanding of standards that apply to their jobs		9%	53%
• Believe policies and procedures are easy to bypass or override		16%	40%
• Believe rewards are based on results, not the means used to achieve them		16%	41%
Detecting Misconduct—Would feel comfortable reporting misconduct to a supervisor		40%	88%
• Would feel comfortable reporting misconduct to legal department		48%	73%
• Would feel comfortable reporting misconduct to internal audit		44%	63%
• Would feel comfortable reporting misconduct to board of directors		39%	59%
Responding to Misconduct—Believe appropriate action would be taken		43%	87%
• Believe they would be protected from retaliation		46%	75%
• Believe they would be satisfied with the outcome		44%	68%
• Believe they would be doing the right thing		27%	92%
Perceived Tone & Culture—CEO & other top execs set the right "tone at the top"		55%	84%
• Are approachable with ethical concerns		43%	76%
• Value ethics & integrity over short-term business goals		54%	82%
• Would respond appropriately if became aware of misconduct		50%	86%
Team Culture & Environment—People feel motivated to "Do the right thing"		39%	90%
• People feel comfortable raising and addressing ethics concerns		49%	85%
• People apply the right values to their decisions and behaviors		37%	90%
• People share a high commitment to integrity		41%	90%
• The opportunity to engage in misconduct is minimal		42%	80%
• The willingness to tolerate misconduct is minimal		49%	84%

Source: Reprinted from KPMG *Integrity Survey* 2005–2006, Copyright © 2006 KPMG LLP.

It is worth noting that current research suggests that the values-oriented ethics program can have other benefits in addition to those described above or noted in Table 5.11. In particular, *building trust within an organization* can have favorable impacts on employees' willingness to share information and ideas, thereby enhancing the innovation quotient of the enterprise and its ability to adapt and take advantage of its opportunities. This process is called *ethical renewal*. Properly cultivated trust can also create commitment to organizational goals and enhance productivity, all of which will raise the ability of the enterprise to profit and compete. This can all be fostered with appropriate attention in the design of the code of conduct (Brooks 2000). Others are also working on trust as is evidenced by entire special volumes of journals, such as the *Business Ethics Quarterly*, Vol. 8, No. 2, April 1998; and *Academy of Management Review*, Vol. 23, Issue 3, July 1998.

In the development of ethical cultures, most companies have embraced the concept of written ethical guidance, but they have fallen far short of embracing many of the supportive mechanisms that are important to the development and maintenance of a healthy ethical culture. Among the omissions of most concern are: lack of strong CEO involvement, lack of training, failure to renew employee commitment to the code annually, and the lack of communications and meetings dealing with ethics. From other sources, we find concerns raised about lack of formal program follow-through; failure to create a credible investigation follow-up and sanction process; employing "quick fix" approaches rather than building a long-term solution; training by people who don't have a commitment to live with the result—in other words, top management should be more prominent; and telephone answering by distant outsiders, which makes callers have difficulty believing that the company cares and is taking their calls seriously (Treviño et al. 1999). In addition, ironically, when the current evidence is compared to what they could be as control systems, ethical cultures were found to be suboptimal.

The discussion to this point has provided an understanding of why organizations—be they corporations, not-for-profit organizations, or professional firms—should develop an ethical culture, what shape that culture should take, and why. Table 5.12 puts these ideas together in an orderly sequence, with additional ideas found in later chapters that a manager, ethics officer, or professional accountant can use to develop and maintain an ethical corporate culture. Information obtained from the Ethics Officer Association and the Center for Business Ethics at Bentley College would be helpful in keeping abreast of current developments.

The design and introduction of an ethics program is well within the capacity of professional accountants because of their exposure to the nature, purpose, and workings of internal control systems that are essential underpinnings to credible financial statements and reporting. Professional accounting bodies have developed pronouncements and guidelines related to ethics programs and antifraud programs, such as the AICPA's Statement on Auditing Standards, No. 99,[20] which contains material on management antifraud programs and controls. The large professional

TABLE 5.12	Development & Maintenance of an Ethical Corporate Culture	
STEP		**PURPOSE**
Assign responsibility:		Successful initiatives usually involve:
Chairman or CEO		• top level accountability and adequate *budget*
Ethics officer		• champions, arbiters
Ethics committee		• monitoring, feedback, advice and cheerleading
Ethics Audit		To understand the organization's ethical practices, and its network of stakeholders and interests
Ethics risk assessment		To identify important ethics problems that could arise (Ch. 6)
Top management support		Absolutely vital to successful adherence
Develop consensus on key ethical values		Necessary to frame policies and procedures
Develop code of conduct, ethical decision-making criteria and protocols including sniff tests		Provide guidance for employees and all other stakeholders
Develop ethics program:		To successfully present and provide supporting mechanisms for the guidance process
Leaders involvement		
Launch		
Training		
Reinforcement policies:		
Compliance sign-off		
Measurements of performance		
Include in strategic objectives and managers objectives		
Include in monitoring and reward structures		
Communications programs		
Exemplar award system		
Ethics inquiry service		Information, investigation and whistle-blower protection
Crisis management		To ensure that ethics are part of survival reactions
Establish a review mechanism		

---

20. See www.aicpa.org/download/antifraud/SAS-99-Ehibit.pdf.

@ accounting bodies and many consulting firms have developed ethics and integrity services, and forensic or governance services which may be accessed at **www.cengage.com/acounting/brooks**.

Corporate Codes of Conduct

Purpose, Focus & Orientation | According to The Conference Board,

> The foundation of most corporate ethics programs is the company code or business conduct statement. Company business ethics principles statements stress two objectives: (1) improving employee capability for making decisions that are in accord with policy and legal requirements; and (2) giving concrete expression to the company's sense of mission and its view of the duties and responsibilities that corporate citizenship entails.[21]

An effective code is the embodiment of an organization's values. It represents the major organizational structure in which to implement ethical policy (see Patrick Murphy (1988) "Creating Ethical Corporate Structures" reprinted at the end of this chapter) and to signal and communicate behavioral expectations and culture, as well as to provide strategic and legal positioning for the organization. It is an essential part of a modern system of internal control. Unless employees are told in writing how they are expected to behave, managers, executives, and directors are vulnerable to charges that they failed to provide adequate guidance to their workers. If so, the company and its officers and directors can be fined heavily, and, in some jurisdictions, the officers and directors can go to jail. More important, it has been suggested that the fines and court costs involved in ethical dilemmas are usually smaller than the lost future profit margin because of the disenchantment of customers. Whistle-blowing outside the corporation may also be prevented by effective ethical codes because they can help to create an ethical culture in which employees believe doing what is right is expected, and bringing forward concerns over unethical behavior will not result in ethical martyrdom.

Codes can be drafted to fulfill different rationales and to provide different depths of coverage. Table 5.13 describes four common levels of coverage.

The rationales[22] for developing codes that were discovered by The Conference Board's survey were:

1. *Instrumental*—to make employees aware that "employee adherence to the company's ethical principles is critical to bottom-line success";

2. *Compliance*—to provide a "statement of do's and don'ts to govern employee conduct";

3. *Stakeholder Commitment*—to offer a discussion of what is expected behavior in stakeholder relationships;

TABLE 5.13	**Depths of Code Coverage**
Credo	Inspirational short statement on key values
Code of Ethics	Deals with ethics principles (short)
Code of Conduct	Deals with principles plus additional examples, etc.
Code of Practice	Detailed rules of practice

21. *Global Corporate Ethics Practices: A Developing Consensus,* The Conference Board, New York, 1999, 16.
22. Ibid., 24–27.

4. *Values/Mission*—to establish "certain ethics principles, modes of behavior, and habits of mind as essential to what it means to be an employee or representative of the company" (see Johnson & Johnson credo in the reading by Murphy at the end of this chapter);

5. *None or a composite* of the above.

In its survey of global ethics practices, The Conference Board found that these rationales were chosen with different frequencies depending on the country or region involved. In the United States, the dominant "instrumental" choice reflects the pressures from stakeholders and the legalistic environment faced. Potentially heavy sanctions have been created for misdeeds due to the advent of the U.S. Foreign Corrupt Practices Act and the U.S. Sentencing Guidelines. Elsewhere, except in Latin America, the values/mission approach was most popular. The choices of rationale, by region,[23] are noted in Table 5.14.

Corporate codes of conduct should encourage employees behavior at the higher levels of Kohlberg's (1981, 1984) stages of moral development. Kohlberg argues that people develop and move through six stages in their moral maturity. At the first stage people are ethical because they fear being punished if they are not; small children are normally at this stage. At the next stage, individuals are ethical because they realize that it is in their best interest to be so; an example would be children playing with one another's toys. At the third stage people acknowledge that ethical behavior is what others expect; people are ethical because of peer pressure. The fourth stage is where individuals accept obedience to moral and ethical laws. At the fifth stage individuals develop a concern for the social welfare of society, and at the final stage individuals develop a principled conscience, adhering to moral and social codes because they are the moral principles that guide society. Each stage has a broader perspective, than the one before, of the role, duties and obligations of the individual in society. Although few individuals may achieve the sixth stage, organizational structures should be established to encourage and facilitate individuals moving to higher levels of moral reasoning. Corporate codes of conduct can help.[24]

The research findings of Weaver et al. (1999b), Treviño et al. (1999), and others noted earlier indicate that a corporate code that adopts an integrity or values orientation will be more effective in engendering adherence to desired ethical standards than other alternatives. Most successful will be a code that is a combination that focuses on the important values that the corporation wants to apply in its stakeholder relationships, but where this is reinforced by sanctions inherent in the compliance approach. Such a composite orientation code would encourage shared values, support employee aspirations, communicate values, and build trust and confidence, while indicating that processes were in place to monitor and judge ethical performance. In this form, the composite orientation code would provide motivation to employees on all of Kohlberg's six stages of moral reasoning.

TABLE 5.14 Dominant Rationales for Codes by Region

	UNITED STATES	CANADA	EUROPE	LATIN AMERICA	JAPAN
Instrumental	64%	30%	—	50%	17%
Stakeholder	5	10	30	—	17
Legal Compliance	14	—	—	25	33
Values/Mission	14	40	60	25	33
None	2	20	10	—	—
N = 72					

Source: Global Corporate Ethics Practices: A Developing Consensus, The Conference Board, New York, 1999, 28.

---

23. Ibid., 28.
24. Kohlberg's six stages of moral development are more fully discussed in Chapter 6.

The form and nature in which guidance is given and action expected can also limit or foster optimal motivation for moral reasoning. Four alternatives are possible for the nature of the guidance provided. The alternative chosen will provide a signal to employees about the way the organization thinks about its control structure, ranging from an autocratic, imposed control structure on one end of the spectrum to self-imposed control on the other end. Table 5.15 identifies the four alternatives and the nature of control they signal.

In view of the findings of Abraham Maslow (1954) and Douglas McGregor (1960), and subsequently others who argued that an autocratic management style was less effective than a democratic or participative approach, it is likely that using only imposed control techniques could be similarly suboptimal. Maslow argued that autocratic management techniques involved influence attempts directed at the lower level of his hierarchy of human needs (physiological, safety), whereas a democratic or participative approach was directed at higher-level needs (affiliation, esteem, and self-actualization) and therefore was more likely to provide a sustainable and more engaging level of motivation. In a world that has since moved toward employee empowerment rather than imposed control (Simons 1995), a code that employs only imposed control is likely to be less effective than one that encourages self-control. A code that successfully encourages self-control would appeal to individuals on all of Kohlberg's six stages of moral reasoning, whereas the imposed control code would motivate for the lower four stages. In keeping with the reasoning in favor of a composite-oriented, values-based, and compliance-based code, consulting experience has shown that the most successful codes encourage self-control or empowerment, with absolute rules being introduced where necessary. These codes usually provide a set of principles with explanations or rationales being given for each. These principles and their rationales are to be used by employees to reason how to deal with the decisions they face, or to determine whom to contact if they need counsel.

| **Code Content & Scope** | Numerous readings are available that outline the topics that are covered in different codes, such as those by Clarkson and Deck (1992); White and Montgomery (1980); Mathews (1987); Berenbeim (1987); and Brooks (1989). Examples of different codes are available on the websites of major corporations.

The choice of orientation of the code and its topics depends somewhat on the scope of the code. Is the code intended to provide guidance to the company's own employees, its suppliers and vendors, and/or its joint venture partners? Geographic locale, union contracts, legal restrictions, competitive practices, and the degree of ownership and/or partner support inherent in the scope decision are critical to the orientation and choice of topics to be included. If a company cannot be comfortable about the guidance to be given, then it should consider whether the arrangement is too high a risk to be undertaken. For example, to do business in a repressive regime that does not respect human rights, or with a partner that does not do so, should give rise to consideration of noninvolvement.

In the late 1990s, Nike found that its suppliers used sweatshops and child labor, producing low-cost products; this triggered boycotts and necessitated the development of monitoring and

TABLE 5.15	**Code Guidance Alternatives & the Control/Motivation Signaled**	
	GUIDANCE PROVIDED	**CONTROL/MOTIVATION SIGNALED**
	Obey these rules	Imposed Control
	Seek advice before acting	
	Act on your best judgment, but disclose what you have done	
	Guiding principles that indicate "this is what we are and what we stand for"	Self-control

Sources: Clarkson & Deck, 1992, Clarkson, Deck & Leblanc, 1997.

reporting mechanisms. Recently, stakeholder activists have become much more aggressive in making companies accountable for the actions of suppliers and joint ventures. Four organizations are leading the development of supplier/workplace standards and codes of conduct—Social Accountability International (SAI) and Fair Labor Association (FLA), Maquila Solidarity, and the International Labor Office (ILO). SAI has developed the SA 8000, which is a standard designed to improve working conditions globally, and is engaged in the training of auditors for the certification of companies adhering to SA 8000. It is modeled after the ISO standards.

Table 5.16 presents a representative list of topics a company might consider including in its codes for its own employees, suppliers, and joint ventures.

Each company should undertake a review of its code when issues and risks emerge that require adjustment of the coverage. For example, codes have been modified in reaction to the external shocks identified in Table 5.17.

Looking ahead, it is likely that codes will be modified to encompass the following:

▎ New antibribery statutes enacted in early 1999 by about 30 countries in the OECD who have responded to the call of Transparency International for standards that will outlaw bribery of foreign officials and allow cross-border investigation and litigation by competitors (see **www.cengage.com/accounting/brooks**).

▎ Adherence to company principles by suppliers, particularly in foreign operations with respect to child labor, fair wages, no forced labor, and so on.

▎ Integrity or values orientation.

▎ Self-control instead of only imposed control.

▎ Security of information.

▎ Environmental management and performance.

TABLE 5.16 Subjects Found in Codes

Ethical principles—honesty, fairness, compassion, integrity, predictability, responsibility.
Respect for stakeholder rights, and duties owed to each stakeholder.
Vision, mission, and key policies tied into the above.
Ethical decision-making frameworks, sniff tests, rules of thumb, and guidance on making trade-offs between competing objectives.
When to seek counsel, and whom to seek it from.
Specific topics found in over 5 percent of employee, supplier, and joint venture codes:

• Bribery/improper payments or influences	• Political activities
• Conflict of interest	• Community relations
• Security of proprietary information	• Confidentiality of personal information
• Receiving gifts	• Human rights
• Discrimination/equal opportunity	• Employee privacy
• Giving gifts	• Whistle-blowing and protection programs
• Environmental protection	• Substance abuse
• Sexual harassment	• Nepotism
• Antitrust	• Child labor
• Workplace safety	

Source: The Conference Board Research Report, *Global Corporate Ethics Practices*, 1999, 29.

TABLE 5.17	External Shocks & Influences Triggering Code Modification

Antibribery legislation—U.S. Foreign Corrupt Practices Act of 1977
  This Act provided an early motivation for codes
U.S. Sentencing Guidelines of 1991
  Brought provision for "Due Diligence" defense
Environmental responsibility:
  Acid rain, air pollution, ozone depletion
    (U.N. Brundtland Commission Report of 1987)
  New Environmental Protection Statutes
  Exxon Valdez oil tanker spill triggers Valdez (now CERES) Principles
Fair treatment for:
  Employees:
    Feminism: sexual harassment, equal opportunity for pay and promotion
    Minorities: discrimination[*]
    Health, safety, and well-being
      Supplier employees—no sweat shop or child labor
    Drug problems—privacy vs. safety
    Whistle-blowers[**]
  Customers—buyer beware slowly becomes seller beware
    Health & safety concerns—auto recalls (see Ford/Firestone case)
    Ethical consumerism, quality
  Shareholders:
    Misuse of inside information
    Conflict of interests
    Mandate and operations are ethical—Enron's banks engage in transactions without economic substance, designed to mislead

[*]See Texaco's Jelly Bean case in Chapter 7.
[**]See GE case described in reading by Andrew Singer in Chapter 1.

▌ Governance principles—clarification of accountability to the board of directors and stakeholders, transparency, risk management for regular and ethics risks.

▌ Ethicality of objectives and competitive practices.

These modifications will also be guided by the application of measures of the effectiveness of codes. Codes can be scored or reviewed for comprehensiveness of coverage and for the nature of control signaled. Other measures have been identified, such as surveys of employee awareness and understanding of key aspects covered in the code and in training programs, and their ability to apply these to the ethical dilemmas proposed.

Benchmarking of codes is done by many consultants. Company employees can also do so by comparing their code against the subjects that information services report upon or are included in the Global Reporting Initiative (GRI) discussed later.

Helpful advice on the preparation of codes can be obtained from several organizations, including the following:

▌ Institute of Business Ethics (IBE) http://www.ibe.org.uk

▌ CodesofConduct.com www.codesofconduct.org

▌ **Effective Implementation** ▌ Because a code of conduct is critical to organizational success for several reasons, it is important to ensure that a code is both effectively drafted *and implemented*. A properly functioning code is essential to the following:

▌ The development and maintenance of an ethical corporate culture.

▌ An effective internal control system.

▮ A "due diligence defense" for directors and officers.

▮ Effective empowerment for employees to make ethical decisions.

▮ Sending proper signals to external stakeholders.

In order to avoid implementation problems, the following issues should be kept in mind. First, *top management must endorse and support the code* and be seen to act in accord with it, or it will only be given lip service by management and workers. It is critical that management "walk the talk" or the entire program will be a waste of time and money.

The orientation, tone, and content of the code must be such that *general principles are favored instead of only specific rules*, or else employees will find the code oppressive and hard to interpret, and *background reasons must be given* to permit understanding sufficient for useful interpretation when specifics are not available. Experience has shown that codes designed as extensive rulebooks are rarely useful because they are too difficult to consult. If the underlying reason for a specific pattern of behavior is given, employees find it easier to understand and they buy-in, rather than fight the code or dismiss it. Getting the buy-in is essential.

Guidance should be provided for trade-offs between short-term profit and social objectives. If employees believe profit is to be earned at all costs, then unethical behavior based on short-term thinking can get the company into trouble.

A complete "due diligence" defense should be in place for environmental matters, including the items noted in Table 5.18.

Employees should be empowered to make ethical decisions. This should involve setting up *decision protocols* that will require employees to use and be able to defend their decisions against a set of criteria or questions that are outlined further in Chapter 6. Part of the decision process should involve the use of *sniff tests*—quick, simple questions that will alert the decision maker when to undertake an in-depth ethical analysis or to seek counsel. When in doubt over the proper conduct, *employees should be encouraged to seek counsel.* Rather than have them act inappropriately, or waste time needlessly, a company should encourage employees to consult their superior or an ethics officer, or use a hotline.

A *fair and confidential hearing process should be assured* or whistle-blowers will not come forward. They don't want to risk paying the price for snitching, even though it is in the best interests of the company. Nor do they want a person accused to be dealt with in a cavalier

---

TABLE 5.18 **Essential Features to Demonstrate a Due Diligence Defense in Respect to Environmental Matters**

1. A written environmental policy, made known to appropriate employees

2. Operating practices that guard against environmental malfeasance, including contingency plans to cover mishaps to ensure full-scale, timely clean-up

3. Employees briefed on their duties and responsibilities under the policy, as well as their potential personal liability, and the liability of others

4. Employees informed of legal requirements, including notice to government complete with a contact list

5. A person who is primarily responsible for environmental matters and monitoring compliance

6. Consideration of an environmental audit or consultation with an expert to start the protection process and monitor progress

7. Monitor pollution control systems and report of mishaps on a timely basis

8. Regular review of reports on: compliance, potential problems, environmental charges, conviction, and employee training

9. Management that keeps abreast of new legislation, makes an internal review of compliance and advises directors of the results, and allocates a real and satisfactory budget to achieve these features

way—they want a speedy, fair hearing process with protection for both parties. *Whistle-blowing should be legitimized*, and whistle-blowers that come forward should be protected.

Someone should be charged with the *ongoing responsibility for updating the code* so that issues can be referred as they come up. Otherwise, many issues will be lost in the pressures of day-to-day activity or because people won't know where to send their suggestions.

Distribution of the code should be to all employees so that none will be able to claim they were not told how to behave. It is surprising that many companies believe their line workers don't have responsibility for environmental acts, or for actions toward fellow workers, and so on. Not only do excellent suggestions come from the plant, but also bad actions are noticed, and support for the company's general activities is enhanced by bringing these employees into the distribution, in addition to management personnel.

Training in support of the code is essential. This training should focus on the awareness of issues, interpretation of the code in accord with top management wishes, approaches to ethical analysis to enable decisions beyond the code, realistic cases for discussion, and on legitimizing the discussion of ethical issues and of whistle-blowing. Codes are written by committees who spend long hours over each paragraph, so how is each employee supposed to know all the thought that went into its construction just by quickly reading the passage? Training is essential to help understand what is meant, and how the code applies to new problems.

Reinforcement of and compliance with the code should be furthered by mechanisms of encouragement, monitoring, and facilitation of the reporting of wrongdoing. These issues should not be left to chance, otherwise the organization might miss an opportunity to head off a disaster or to accomplish an ethical performance objective. These methods are summarized in Table 5.19.

Reinforcement of the code should be undertaken through measurement of the code's effectiveness; reporting of ethical performance for management purposes; featuring ethical performance in company publications; and ensuring that other company policies are supportive, including a linkage with the remuneration systems. If you can't measure performance (techniques are discussed in Chapters 4, 6, and 7), it is very hard to manage it. Reporting performance has the impact of producing a scorecard that people are induced to improve for the next report. Publicity of good results can have a salutary effect on subsequent performance as well, and including that performance in the corporation's reward systems will go a long way to underscore how important ethical issues are to top management.

The board of directors should actively review and monitor whistle-blower concerns on financial and nonfinancial matters, and ethics program activities and feedback. This will ensure the board is aware of problems and can take appropriate action before the company's reputation, activities, or stakeholders are compromised.

TABLE 5.19 | **Mechanisms for Compliance Encouragement Monitoring & Reporting Wrongdoing**

Compliance encouragement
    Awards, bonuses
    Inclusion in performance reviews, remuneration decisions, and promotion
    Reprimands, suspension, demotion, fines, dismissal
Monitoring
    Ethics audit or internal audit procedures
    Reviews by legal department
    Annual sign-off by all or some employees
    Employee surveys
Facilitation of reporting of wrongdoing
    Assurance of a fair hearing process
    Protection: absolute confidentiality, whistle-blower protection plan
    Counseling/information: ombudsperson program, hotline, human resources
    Committee oversight assured: ethics committee of board, Audit Committee

To have an effective corporate culture, not only do codes need constant upgrading under the watchful eye of an EO, but also constant attention must be given to improving training programs; measures and reports of performance; compliance; and whistle-blowing mechanisms. In addition, it is essential to have a formal external or internal review of the corporation's culture, code, and other mechanisms on a periodic basis. This is often referred to as an ethical audit, and although it may be undertaken by the internal audit staff, or a team of budding managers, such as in the Dow Corning case at the end of this chapter, an outside consulting service provides useful feedback.

Finally, it should be understood that it is unlikely that employees will see the merit of ethical behavior in regard to one area of the company's operations if they believe management want or are prepared to tolerate questionable behavior in other areas. Whistle-blowers will not come forward, for example, unless there is a feeling of trust that they and the parties they accuse will be dealt with fairly and confidentially. Consequently, the development of a broadly based ethical culture within the company is an essential precursor for an effective code of conduct, and vice versa.

| Ethical Leadership

One of the key elements of corporate governance and accountability is the "tone at the top" and the role leaders play in developing, nurturing, implementing and monitoring a desired corporate culture. If senior or junior leaders pay only lip-service to desired values, their followers—the rest of the employees—will consider those values as unworthy of attention. Although the corporation's formal culture specifies these values, if its informal culture does not support them, those values and the corporate culture implied by them is just "window-dressing."

Our understanding of ethical leadership and how it works has been developed through the publication of research studies such as that by Linda Treviño, Laura Pincus and Michael Brown.[25] Based on interviews with senior executives and corporate ethics officers, they argue that *an executive cannot develop a reputation as an ethical leader unless that individual is an ethical person who promotes ethical values and adherence to them.* In their terms, an executive must be a "moral person" and a "moral manager" to develop "a reputation for ethical leadership."[26]

Perhaps their most important finding is that it is not enough just to be an ethical person who makes good decisions, a reputation for ethical leadership requires the continuing, proactive communication of ethical values. Failure to develop a reputation for ethical leadership will likely result in a reputation for being "ethically neutral." The downside to being seen as "ethically neutral" is significant since, in the authors' view:

> . . . employees will believe that the bottom line is the only value that should guide
> their decisions and that the CEO cares more about himself and the short-term
> financials than about the long-term interests of the organization and its multiple
> stakeholders.[27]

According to Treviño et al. (2000), an executive must first be a moral or ethical person or else their followers will come to regard them as hypocrites when their true nature shows. The *character traits* associated with ethical leadership include: integrity, trustworthiness, honesty, sincerity, and forthrightness or candor, which are surprisingly similar to the dimensions in Frombrun's Reputation

---

25. Linda Klebe Treviño, Laura Pincus Hartman, Michael Brown, "Moral Person and Moral Manager: How Executives Develop A Reputation for Ethical Leadership" *California Management Review*, Vol. 42, No. 4, Summer 2000, 128–142.
26. Ibid., 129.
27. Ibid., 130.

Model (Figure 1.3) that was developed in Chapter 1. Character traits form the basis for *behaviors* that exhibit:

- Doing the right thing.
- Concern for people.
- Being open and approachable for discussion of concerns.
- Personal morality.

Similarly, executive *decision making* to be considered sound, should correspond by:

- Holding to desired values.
- Being objective and fair.
- Exhibiting concern for society.
- Following reasonable ethical decision rules.[28]

These traits, behaviors, and decision-making characteristics should be transparently evident, or else they may be misinterpreted, and the executive may not be viewed as a moral or ethical person.

Achievement of the reputation of a moral or ethical person does not, however, guaranty a reputation as a moral manager or leader—that depends upon how well and extensively an executive promotes his or her support for the corporation's ethics and values agenda. Treviño et al. (2000) found that this could be done effectively by:

- Serving as a visible role model.
- Communicating regularly and persuasively about ethical standards, principles, and values.
- Using the rewards system to hold all employees accountable to ethical standards.[29]

The authors summarize their findings in a schematic that is reproduced as Figure 5.8.[30] To be an ethical leader requires strong performance as both a moral person and a moral manager. To

FIGURE 5.8

Executive Reputation & Ethical Leadership

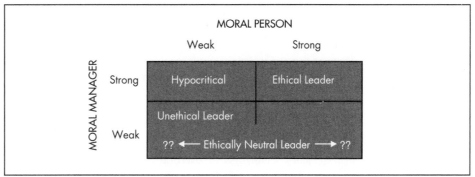

Source: "Moral Person and Moral Manager: How Executives Develop a Reputation for Ethical Leadership", L. K. Treviño et al, *California Management Review*, Vol. 42, No. 4, Summer 2000. Reprinted with permission.

---

28. Ibid., 131
29. Ibid., 134.
30. Ibid., 137.

attempt ethical leadership from a weak base as a moral person is highly risky as the likelihood of being discovered to be a hypocrite is high. An unethical leader is low on both dimensions, and a person who does not practice overt ethical guidance will be seen as an ethically neutral leader even if the individual is a highly moral or ethical person.

The key to ethical leadership is visible effective action stemming from an ethical base. This kind of leadership will greatly reinforce the corporation's ethics program and its attempts to develop and maintain an ethical corporate culture. Without strong ethical leadership from executives and supervisors, attempts to develop and maintain an ethical corporate culture are doomed to mediocrity and probably failure. The challenge of strong ethical leadership is not confined to the executive's own behavior, but must extend to the motivation of other executives and supervisory personnel using personal persuasion and the techniques discussed in earlier sections. Top management support is essential to any ethics program, and strong moral or ethical leadership is critical to effective support. Top executives should consider the adequacy of the support they offer through ethical leadership to their organization's ethics program in comparison to what they offer to their health and safety program, or their environmental responsibility program. Rarely has the effort directed to ethical leadership been sufficient in the past.

Director & Officer Liability

Corporate ethical governance and accountability is no longer just good business—it's the law.

The Sarbanes-Oxley Act (SOX) of 2002 triggered governance reform for SEC registrant companies around the world and spawned similar governance reform regulation in many other national jurisdictions. Section 404 of SOX requires companies to examine the effectiveness of their internal control systems with regard to financial reporting. The CEO, CFO, and auditors must report on and certify that effectiveness. Conscious miscertification by the CEO and CFO can lead to criminal as well as civil charges.

The mandatory review of internal control involves comparison of the corporation's systems with an accepted internal control framework, such as that developed for Enterprise Risk Management (ERM) by the Committee of Sponsoring Organizations (COSO) of the Treadway Commission. Further information on the COSO approach[31] is available in auditing texts or on the COSO website. The COSO ERM framework covers how an entity achieves its objectives on four dimensions: strategic, operations, reporting, and compliance. Within each of these dimensions or categories, the ERM framework involves eight interrelated components concerning the way management runs an enterprise and how they are integrated with the management process: internal environment, objective setting, event identification, risk assessment, risk response, control activities, information and communication, and monitoring.

Ethics and an ethical corporate culture are seen to play a vital role in setting the control environment, and thereby in creating an effective ERM-oriented internal control system and the behavior that results. Consequently, a COS ERM-oriented review will examine the tone at the top, codes of conduct, employee awareness, pressures to meet unrealistic or inappropriate goals, management's willingness to override established controls, code adherence in performance appraisals, monitoring of internal control system effectiveness, whistle-blowing programs, and remedial actions in response to code violations.[32]

---

31. See for example, *Enterprise Risk Management—Integrated Framework: Executive Summary*, Committee of Sponsoring Organizations (COSO) of the Treadway Commission, September 2004, **www.coso.org/ publications.htm**

32. Principle source, KPMG Forensic *Integrity Survey 2005–2006*, 2006.

Not surprisingly, some of these new governance requirements—tone at the top, existence of codes, adherence to policies, adequate disclosure, and so on—have been endorsed by stock exchanges that have required compliance of companies whose shares are listed. The governance requirements of the New York Stock Exchange, the Toronto Stock Exchange, and others can be accessed at **www.cengage.com/accounting/brooks**.

What happens if these new governance expectations are not met? Noncompliance with stock exchange regulations can result in fines, suspension, or delisting of the stock being traded, in addition to limitations being placed on offending directors or management. Noncompliance with SOX requirements laid down in SEC regulations, or in similar securities commission regulations around the world, can lead to civil and also criminal prosecution. The former can result in fines and personal limitations, while the latter can add *significant jail terms* for executives. A recent development is the requirement that executives and directors may be required to pay the fines *personally* rather than with company funds or through insurance plans. This frightening prospect was responsible for an article in the January 13, 2005, issue of the *Wall Street Journal,* titled, "Some outside directors consider quitting in wake of settlements"[33] which related that ten Enron and ten WorldCom directors had agreed to pay a total of $31 million of their own money to settle lawsuits.

When deciding whether to prosecute, the U.S. Department of Justice uses factors identified in guidance that it has published.[34] For example, important factors examined include whether:

| the compliance program is substantive or just a paper sham,

| management is enforcing the program or encouraging misconduct,

| there is staff sufficient to monitor and audit the compliance program,

| employees are aware of the program and convinced of the corporation's commitment to it.[35]

If convicted, management and directors will have to face penalties in the United States that meet the provision of the U.S. Sentencing Guidelines as amended on November 1, 2004. Penalties for SOX violations for misconduct in the preparation of financial statements and their reporting (Section 304) could include reimbursement of the issuer for any bonus or incentive payments or equity-based compensation received by the CEO and/or CFO in the year following, plus any profit on sale of stock during that period. Also, consciously certifying a statement knowing noncompliance is subject to a fine of $1 million and imprisonment up to ten years, and purposely certifying such a statement increases the penalties to $5 million and imprisonment for up to twenty years (Section 906). SOX also lowered the threshold for barring individuals from acting as a director or officer of an issuer from "substantial unfitness" to "unfitness" (Section 305).[36] As indicated in the study by KPMG Forensics, *"these guidelines now make more explicit the expectation that organizations promote a culture of ethical conduct,*

---

33. J. S. Lublin, T. Francis, and J. Weil, "Some outside directors consider quitting in wake of settlements," The *Wall Street Journal,* January 13, 2005, B13.

34. Ibid., KMPG *Integrity Survey,* 2005–2006, 21.

35. KPMG Forensic, *Integrity Survey.*

36. Principle source: *CEO and CFO Certification: Improving Transparency and Accountability, A Canadian Performance Reporting Board Discussion Brief,* Canadian Institute of Chartered Accountants, 2004, 41. Canadian penalties for securities act violations are fines up to $5 million, prison terms up to five years less a day, and for insider trading the fine would be up to the greater of triple the "profit" made (or loss avoided) and $5 million. Other fines involving disgorgement of ill-gotten gains are also possible.

tailor each program element based on compliance risk, and periodically evaluate program effectiveness."[37]

These penalties are so significant that misunderstanding and/or mitigating them is unattractive. Table 5.20 provides a list of specific ethics expectation guidelines that are to be considered in regard to the application of penalties per the U.S. Sentencing Guidelines, as amended on November 1, 2004.

Public Accountability Benchmarks

One of the recent developments that a board of directors and management need to consider when developing the values, policies, and principles that underpin their corporation's culture and the actions of their employees is the recent surge in stakeholder scrutiny and need for transparency and public accountability. Never before has there been such interest in what a corporation is doing, and how it is doing it.

In the United States, Canada, and the United Kingdom, rating services exist that examine and score corporate governance systems and performance against competitors and external benchmarks. New visibility is being given U.S., U.K., and Canadian companies through social rating services linked to the London Stock Exchange FTSE4Good service. New standards for social performance and disclosure are emerging that will provide comparisons that corporations will watch and build into their mechanisms, performance assessments, and public disclosures. It is doubtful that corporations will be regarded as responsible corporate citizens if their operations are seen not to compare well based on these new comparators. Therefore, at the very least, corporations should maintain a watching brief over developments identified in Table 5.21.

TABLE 5.20	U.S. Sentencing Guidelines Ethics Criteria per KPMG *Integrity Survey* 2005–2006

CRITERIA FOR DETERMINING DEGREE OF CULPABILITY & MITIGATION OF PENALTY

Specifically, the amended guidelines call on organizations to:

- Promote a culture that encourages ethical conduct and a commitment to compliance with the law

- Establish standards and procedures to prevent and detect criminal conduct

- Ensure the board of directors & senior executives are knowledgeable & exercise reasonable oversight of the compliance/ethics program

- Assign a high-level individual within the organization to ensure the organization has an effective compliance and ethics program, and delegate day-to-day operational responsibility to individuals with adequate resources authority, and direct access to the board

- Use reasonable efforts and exercise due diligence to exclude individuals from positions of substantial authority who have engaged in illegal activities or other conduct inconsistent with an effective compliance and ethics program

- Conduct effective training programs for directors, officers, employees & other agents & provide such individuals with periodic information appropriate to their respective roles & responsibilities relative to the compliance & ethics program

- Ensure that the compliance & ethics program is followed, including monitoring & auditing to detect criminal conduct

- Publicize a system, which may include mechanisms for anonymity and confidentiality, whereby the organization's employees & agents may report to seek guidance regarding potential or actual misconduct without fear of retaliation

- Evaluate periodically the effectiveness of the compliance and ethics program

- Take reasonable steps to respond appropriately to misconduct, including making necessary modification to the compliance/ethics program

- Promote and enforce consistently the compliance and ethics program through incentives and disciplinary measures

Source: Reprinted from KPMG *Integrity Survey* 2005–2006. Copyright © 2006 KPMG International.

37. KPMG Forensic, *Integrity Survey.*

| TABLE | 5.21 | **Emerging Public Accountability Standards & Initiatives** |

GRI—Global Reporting Initiative
  A framework for economic, social, and environmental reporting.
AA1000—AccountAbility
  An assurance standard designed to provide assurance on the quality of an organization's public reporting and the quality of its underlying systems and processes.
FTSE4Good
  FTSE4Good is an index made up of companies judged acceptable using an objective global standard for socially responsible investment. The FTSE4Good Selection Criteria cover 3 areas:

  • Working towards environmental sustainability

  • Developing positive relationships with stakeholders

  • Upholding and supporting universal human rights

Domini 400 Social index
  400 predominantly U.S. corporations are ethically screened on 11 criteria and included in the index for use by ethical investors.
The Jantzi Social Index
  Similar to the Domini and FTS4Good indices, 400 Canadian companies that are socially and environmentally screened.
SA 8000—Social Accountability International (SAI)
  SAI is developing the SA 8000 standard to provide guidance with regard to workplace conduct and specifically with regard to sweatshops. Auditors are also trained.

Conclusion

The need for ethical corporate governance is not just good for business—it is the law. Recent changes in governance regulation are shifting expectations significantly. In an era of increasing scrutiny, where ethical misbehavior can influence the achievement of corporate objectives profoundly, it is very much in the interest of shareholders, directors, and executives that their company's governance system provides appropriate guidance and accountability.

Directors must demonstrate due diligence in the management of the company's business and ethics risks. They need to ensure that an effective ethical culture prevails in their company. This requires the development of a code of conduct, and the essential means of creating an awareness of appropriate behavior, reinforcing that behavior, and making sure that the underlying values are embedded in corporate strategy and operations. The company's positions on conflicts of interest, sexual harassment, and similar topics need to be worked out in advance, with watchful updating to keep the company's culture abreast of current expectations.

If directors are able to recognize and prepare their company for the new era of stakeholder accountability through an effective, ethical governance system, they will not only reduce risks, but they will produce a competitive advantage among customers, employees, partners, environmentalists, and other stakeholders—which will surely be attractive to shareholders.

Questions

1. What is the role of a board of directors from an ethical governance standpoint?

2. Explain why corporations are legally responsible to shareholders but are strategically responsible to other stakeholders as well.

3. What should an employee consider when considering whether to give or receive a gift?

4. When should an employee satisfy his or her self-interest rather than the interest of his or her employer?

5. How can a company control and manage conflicts of interest?

6. What is the role of an ethical culture and who is responsible for it?

7. What is the most important contribution of a corporate code of conduct?

8. Are one or more of the fundamental principles found in codes of conduct more important than the rest? Why?

9. Why should codes focus on principles rather than specific detailed rules?

10. How could you monitor compliance with a code of conduct in a corporation?

11. How can a corporation integrate ethical behavior into its reward and remuneration schemes?

12. Other than a code of conduct, what aspects of a corporate culture are most important and why?

13. Is the effort being made to check on the effectiveness of internal control systems worth the cost? Why, and why not?

14. Why should an effective whistle-blower mechanism be considered a "failsafe mechanism" in SOX Section 404 compliance programs?

15. Descriptive commentary about corporate social performance is sometimes included in annual reports. Is this indicative of good performance, or is it just window dressing? How can the credibility of such commentary be enhanced?

16. Should professional accountants push for the development of a comprehensive framework for the reporting of corporate social performance? Why?

17. Do professional accountants have the expertise to audit corporate social performance reports?

Case Insights

- *Lord Conrad Black's Fiduciary Duty?* is a classic case of a domineering CEO/chairman who believes he did no wrong in managing his conflicts of interest, whereas many other shareholders and federal prosecutor Patrick J. Fitzgerald believe he ran a "corporate kleptography." With hindsight, his famous board of directors may agree.

- *Spying on HP Directors* explains how Patricia Dunn, chair of the Board of Directors at Hewlett Packard hired investigators to determine who had leaked sensitive information to the media, and the questionable techniques the investigators employed in order to identify the culprit.

- *Manipulation of MCI's Allowance for Doubtful Accountants* is the story of how Walt Pavlo, a junior manager at the telecommunications giant, hide $88 million of bad debts and only reported an allowance for doubtful accounts of $15 million.

- *A Minority-Controlling Shareholder: The Control of the New York Times by the Ochs and Sulzberger Families* describes some of the problems associated with a dual class share structure, where one class of shares has superior voting power. In the case of the *New York Times*, two families have a minority equity interest in the newspaper but a majority voting interest, and so they can control the newspaper and ignore the complaints of all the other shareholders.

- *Stock Options and Gifts of Publicly Traded Shares* explains how a CEO can strategically time the release of bad news so that he maximizes the tax benefit of donating shares of his company to his favorite charity.

- *The Ethics of Repricing and Backdating of Employee Stock Options* addresses several issues concerning employee stock options. Do they actually motivate employees? Do they encourage earnings management? Is manipulating the timing of the granting of stock options in the best interest of the shareholders?

- *Siemens' Bribery Scandal* describes how one of Germany's oldest multinationals developed a perverse organizational culture that condoned making bribery payments in foreign jurisdictions and the adverse consequence to both the company and many of its senior executives.

- *Société Générale Rogue Trader* explains how poor internal controls allowed Jerôme Kerviel, a derivative trader at one of the largest French banks, to engage in unauthorized transactions that cost the bank 4.9 billion Euros.

- *Barings Bank: Rogue Trader* reveals why Barings is no longer the oldest family owned bank in Britain. Was it the fault of a rogue trader in derivatives, or was it that the corporate culture sabotaged a greedy management?

- *Adelphia—Really the Rigas' Family Piggy Bank* presents the story of how Mr. Rigas formed a small cable company and grew it into a giant, while he and his sons used it as their own "piggy bank."

- *Tyco—Looting Executive Style* reveals how the CEO lived in style with million-dollar parties, $6,000 shower curtains, and a need to keep the money flowing.

- *Nortel Networks' Audit Committee was in the Dark* reveals the nature of manipulations spawned by a flawed incentive scheme and carried out under the noses of an unsuspecting Audit Committee.

- *Ford/Firestone Tire Recall* presents how two companies, with a history of earlier recalls, failed to learn from them, or use what they learned. Information was available, but not used. Risks were not assessed properly, nor were crises effectively dealt with. The tension between doing what is right to maintain the confidence of consumers and following advice to minimize legal liability is explored.

- *Conflicts of Interest on Wall Street* captures New York's Attorney General Elliot Spitzer's challenge of the traditional conflicted ways that brokers have been doing business on Wall Street. While purporting to act for their investing clients, they have been profiting by misleading investors with over-hyped investment analyses.

- *Loyalty, But to Whom?* Many people—particularly in the securities industry—have great difficulty understanding to whom they owe duty, and in what order of priority. This is a real case that offers a chance to explore the results of tough loyalty decisions in a modern governance framework.

- *Bankers Trust: Learning from Derivatives* is the story of how the competitive culture of an enterprise got out of control and affected the company's clients, personnel, and fortunes.

- *Dow Corning Silicone Breast Implants* illustrates the pitfalls of a company with an excellent code and a world-class, follow-up, monitoring procedure—yet they still had problems with effectiveness.

Reading Insights

Patrick Murphy provides a broad overview of the role of corporate codes and their impact on corporate culture, with reference to useful examples.

References

AICPA, *Statement of Auditing Standards* (SAS) No. 99, 2003.

Badaracco, J. L., and A. P. Webb. "Business Ethics: A View from the Trenches," *California Management Review* 60, no. 2 (Winter 1995): 8–28.

Berenbeim, R. E., *Corporate Ethics*, a report of The Conference Board, Inc., New York, 1987.

Brooks, L. J. "Ethical Codes of Conduct: = Deficient in Guidance for the Canadian Accounting Profession," *Journal of Business Ethics* 8, no. 5 (May 1989): 325–336.

Brooks, L. J. "A Survey on the Effectiveness/Compliance of Corporate Codes of Conduct in Canada," unpublished manuscript, 1990.

Brooks, L. J. "No More Trial and Error: It's Time We Moved Ethics Out of the Clouds and into the Classroom," *CAmagazine*, March 1993, 43–45.

Brooks, L. J. "Codes of Conduct: Trust, Innovation, Commitment and Productivity: A Strategic-Cultural Perspective," *Global Outlook: An International Journal of Business, Economics, and Social Policy* 12, no. 2, (2000): 1–11.

Brooks, L. J., and V. Fortunato. "Discipline at the Institute of Chartered Accountants of Ontario," *CAmagazine*, May 1991, 40–43.

Centre for Applied Ethics, University of British Columbia, www.ethics.ubc.ca/resources/business/codes.html.

CEO and CFO Certification: Improving Transparency and Accountability, A Canadian Performance Reporting Board Discussion Brief, Canadian Institute of Chartered Accountants, 2004.

Chatman, J. A. and K. A. Jehn. "Assessing the Relationship between Industry Characteristics and Organizational Culture:

How Different Can You Be?" *Academy of Management Journal* 37 (1994): 522–533.

CICA Handbook Section 5135, *The Auditor's Responsibility to Consider Fraud and Error in an Audit of Financial Statements*, 2002.

Clarkson, Max B.E., and M. Deck. "Applying the Stakeholder Management Model to the Analysis and Evaluation of Corporate Codes," Clarkson Centre for Business Ethics, University of Toronto, 1992.

Clarkson, Max B.E., and M. Deck. "Towards CSR4: Defining Economic and Moral Responsibilities," unpublished manuscript, November 1989.

Clarkson, Max, M. Deck, and R. Leblanc. *Codes of Ethics, Practice and Conduct*, The Society of Management Accountants of Canada, 1997. (An excellent practical guide that incorporates part of the material in Clarkson and Deck, 1992.)

Clarkson, Max, M. Deck, and R. Leblanc. "Towards CSR4: Defining Economic and Moral Responsibilities," unpublished manuscript, Nov. 1989.

Corporate Ethics Monitor, a bi-monthly publication published by EthicScan Canada, Toronto, Canada.

Council on Economic Priorities, *SA8000: Guideline for Social Accountability*, New York, updated continuously, **http://www .cepaa.org**.

Davis, Michael and Andrew Stark, eds. *Conflict of Interest in the Professions*. New York: Oxford University Press , 2001.

Enterprise Risk Management—Integrated Framework: Executive Summary, Committee of Sponsoring Organizations (COSO) of the Treadway Commission, September 2004. http:// www.coso.org/publications.htm.

Enterprise Risk Management: Trends and Emerging Practices, The Institute of Internal Auditors Research Foundation, 2001.

Global Corporate Ethics Practices: A Developing Consensus, The Conference Board, New York, 1999.

Guidance for Directors—Governance Processes for Control, Canadian Institute of Chartered Accountants, Toronto, Canada, December 1995.

IFAC Code of Ethics for Professional Accountants, International Federation of Accountants, November 2001. http://www.ifac. org/Ethics/index.tmpl.

Institute of Business Ethics (IBE). http://www.ibe.org.uk.

Integrity Survey 2005–2006, KMPG Forensic Advisory Service, 2005. http://www.kpmg.com/.

ISA 240, The Auditor's Responsibility to Consider Fraud and Error in an Audit of Financial Statements, International Accounting and Audit Standards Board (IAASB), 2001, rev. 2004.

Linda Klebe Treviño, Laura Pincus Hartman, Michael Brown, "Moral Person and Moral Manager: How Executives Develop A Reputation for Ethical Leadership" *California Management Review*, Vol. 42, No. 4, Summer 2000, 128–142.

Managing Risk in the New Economy, AICPA & CICA, 2001.

Maslow, A. *Motivation and Personality*, New York: Harper and Brothers, 1954.

Mathews, M. C. "Codes of Ethics: Organizational Behaviour and Misbehaviour," *Research in Corporate Social Behaviour*, JAI Press Inc., 1987, 107–130.

McGregor, D. D. *The Human Side of Enterprise*. New York: McGraw-Hill, 1960.

Paine, L. S. "Managing for Integrity," *Harvard Business Review*, March-April 1994, 106–117. (Reproduced as a reading in Chapter 1.)

Report of the Toronto Stock Exchange Committee on Corporate Governance in Canada, Toronto Stock Exchange, Toronto, December 1994, paragraphs 4.3 and 4.4, p. 17.

Report on The Role of The Board of Directors in the Collapse of Enron, U.S. Senate Permanent Subcommittee on Investigations, July 8, 2002. See **www.cengage.com/accounting/ brooks**.

Reschke, W. and R. Aldag. "A Model of the Impact of Organizational Culture on Individual/Team Outcomes and Organizational Effectiveness," *The Business Case for Culture Change*, Center for Organizational Effectiveness, August 2000, 14.

Statement of Corporate Governance, The Business Roundtable (September 1997).

Schien, E. H., *Organizational Culture and Leadership*, San Francisco: Jossey-Bass , 1985.

Treviño, L. K., G. Weaver, D. G. Gibson, and B. L. Toffler. "Managing Ethics and Legal Compliance: What Works and What Hurts," *California Management Review* 41, no. 2 (Winter 1999): 131–151.

U.N. Brundtland Commission Report, *Our Common Future*, World Commission on Environment and Development, Oxford University Press, Oxford, 1987.

U.S. Sentencing Guidelines, United States Sentencing Commission, Washington, D.C., November 1, 1991.

Valdez (CERES) Principles, Environmental management principles created by a coalition of environmental interest groups (hence CERES), including the Sierra Club, shortly after the Exxon Valdez went aground.

Weaver, G. R., L. K. Treviño, and P. L. Cochran. "Corporate Ethics Practices in the Mid-1990's: An Empirical Study of the Fortune 1000," *Journal of Business Ethics* 18 (1999): 283–294.

Weaver, G. R., L. K. Treviño, and P. L. Cochran. "Corporate Ethics Programs as Control Systems: Influences of Executive Commitment and Environmental Factors," *Academy of Management Journal* 42, no. 1 (February 1999): 41–57.

White, B. J., and R. Montgomery. "Corporate Codes of Conduct," *California Management Review*, Winter 1980, 80–87.

Ethics Case | *Lord Conrad Black's Fiduciary Duty?*

On November 17, 2005, Conrad Black and three other executives[1] of Hollinger International, Inc., were charged with eleven counts of fraud with regard to payments allegedly disguised as "non-compete fees," or in one case a "management agreement break-up fee," and the misuse of corporate perks. The payments were alleged to be a self-dealing "series of either secret or misleading transactions involving sales of a series of various newspaper publishing groups in the United States and Canada."[2] The sales involved several hundred newspapers, and the alleged misdirection of over $80 million of the proceeds.

Hollinger International, Inc., (International), a U.S. holding company traded on the New York Stock Exchange, had been built up by Black over the years to own hundreds of newspapers, including the *Chicago Sun-Times*, the *Daily Telegraph* in London, the *National Post* in Toronto, and the *Jerusalem Post* in Israel. Partly in recognition of his business acumen, in 2000 Black was knighted by Britain's Queen Elizabeth and accorded the title of Lord Black of Crossharbour and the right to sit in the British House of Lords. Prevented from receiving the lordship by Jean Chrétien, then Prime Minister of Canada, Black resigned his Canadian citizenship to become a British citizen in order to accept the honor.

Black did not own the majority of Class A shares of International held by the public, but he (as CEO and principal owner) and his associates controlled it through their majority of ownership of the Class B shares that carried a 10-1 voting preference over the Class A shares. He and his associates owned 98.5 percent of Ravelston Corporation Limited, a private Canadian company with headquarters in Toronto, which in turn owned at least 70 percent of Hollinger, Inc., a Canadian holding company traded on the Toronto Stock Exchange. Hollinger, Inc., (Inc.) owned 30.3 percent of the equity (Class A and B) of International, which gave it, and Black, 72.8 percent of the voting power at International.[3] This type of arrangement, which allows the control of a corporation with the ownership of less than a majority of the corporation's equity, is known as "multiple-voting rights," or "super-voting rights."

The directors of International—who should have been standing up to Black on behalf of the investing public—were hand-picked by Black, probably for reasons other than their business acumen. Henry Kissinger, former U.S. secretary of state and a "trophy director," was probably selected for his fame and knowledge of history, defense, and politics—all passions of Black. The same can be said about other directors, including Richard Perle, former assistant secretary of defense and chair of the Pentagon advisory board; Robert Strauss, former chairman of the Democratic National Committee and ambassador to the Soviet Union; Richard Burt, former ambassador to Germany; and James R. Thompson, a former governor of Illinois. These directors, who were "expected to act as corporate watchdogs," and particularly the Audit Committee "seemed to behave like an old basset hound."[4] Cardinal Capital Management, which sued International's board in 2004, "described the directors . . . as "supine"

---

1. U.S. Department of Justice, United States Attorney, Northern District of Illinois, *Former Hollinger Chairman Conrad Black and Three Other Executives Indicted in U.S.-Canada Corporate Fraud Schemes,* press release, November 17, 2005, available at http://www.usdoj.gov/usao/iln/pr/chicago/2005/pr1117_01.pdf. John A. Boultbee, Peter Y. Atkinson, and Mark S. Kipnis are the other three executives. Another colleague, F. David Radler, pleaded guilty to a fraud count on September 20, 2005, and thereafter cooperated with the further investigation (p. 4).

2. Ibid.

3. Opinion of Judge Strine, Vice Chancellor of the Chancery Court of the State of Delaware, in *Hollinger International, Inc., v. Conrad M. Black, Hollinger Inc., et al.,* C.A. No. 183-N (February 26, 2004) 6. Available at **www.cengage.com/accounting/brooks**.

4. Sinclair Stewart and Jacquie McNish, "Lord Black's cautionary lessons for executives," *Financial Times,* November 21, 2005.

and "quiescent" and accused them of "rubber-stamping" tens of millions of dollars in pay-outs to company executives."[5]

Black was no stranger to the public spotlight, or to public scrutiny. Earlier in his career, he had achieved notoriety for being spectacularly and arrogantly outspoken, for authoring acclaimed biographies of historically significant individuals, for pre-emptively engineering the recovery of employee surplus pension funds when their legal status was in doubt and, most recently, for running a corporate kleptocracy.[6] The allegation of running a corporate kleptocracy was made when Black sued for peace from aggrieved minority shareholders who were blocking his ability to sell the *Daily Telegraph* to the Barclay brothers. On that occasion, Judge Strine of the Chancery Court of Delaware found that Black was not credible, saying:

> Black also vigorously defended his failure to inform the International board of his discussions with the Barclays. But then again, he could hardly deny these facts. On more debatable points, I found Black evasive and unreliable. His explanations of key events and of his own motivations do not have the ring of truth.[7]

The evidence provided to Judge Strine was ultimately responsible for the fraud charges that are the subject of this case.

It is not unusual for a company selling a business unit to agree not to compete with that unit for a period of years. It is unusual, however, for an executive of the selling company to agree not to compete personally, and to be paid to do so. It is extremely unusual for that executive to decide how much of the selling price he should be paid—as Black did—and how much should be paid to the selling company. Making such a decision places the decision maker in the position of self-dealing—a conflict of interest that, at the very least, requires disclosure to the selling company and the receipt of its approval. In this case, Black should have disclosed his related-party, self-dealing to the board of International and obtained their approval. Black claimed he did, but the district attorney claimed he did not because he failed to provide sufficient information and/or misled the board on numerous occasions.

According to the indictment press release in one case—the sale of 50 percent interest in the *National Post* to CanWest Global Communications Corp. for approximately $2.1 billion:

> Black negotiated the deal, . . . while Boultbee, Atkinson and Kipnis participated in reviewing and finalizing the transaction, which allocated approximately $51.8 million to non-competition agreements. This was allegedly done as a mechanism to pay Boultbee and Atkinson a bonus to take advantage of tax benefits that legitimate non-competition payments receive under Canadian tax laws.
>
> Between May 2000 and May 2002, Black, Boultbee, and Atkinson allegedly fraudulently inserted Boultbee and Atkinson as promissors not to compete and fraudulently caused approximately $51.8 million of the sale proceeds to be allocated to the non-competition agreements. Black, Boultbee, Atkinson and Kipnis failed to disclose this self-dealing to International's Audit Committee, the indictment alleges, and caused false and misleading statements to be made to International's independent directors about the non-competition payments. Although International was the seller and signed a non-competition agreement, all $51.8 million, plus interest, was diverted from International and, instead, was distributed to Black, Radler, Boultbee, Atkinson and Ravelston.

---

5. Ibid.

6. The charge of running a corporate kleptocracy (thiefdom) was made in the *Report of the Special Committee of the Board of Directors of Hollinger International. Inc.,* August 30, 2004, to which Richard C. Breeden, former Chair of the U.S. Securities and Exchange Commission, served as special investigator. See page 4. This report is available at **www.cengage.com/accounting/brooks**.

7. *Hollinger International, Inc.,* C.A. No. 183-N, at 59.

After an outside attorney for a bank discovered and questioned these payments during the course of a due diligence inquiry, Black, Boultbee, Atkinson and Kipnis returned to International's Audit Committee and sought ratification of the payments on different grounds, claiming that the information previously provided to the directors misdescribed the transaction in a number of "inadvertent" respects. In fact, the previous submission's falsehoods were not inadvertent, and the second submission was also false and misleading. After International's independent directors ratified these payments, Black then lied to International's shareholders about the payments at International's 2002 annual shareholder meeting, according to the indictment.

The information first submitted to the Audit Committee on Sept. 1, 2000, was allegedly false in that:

❙ only $32.4 million, not $51.8 million, was allocated to non-competition agreements;

❙ CanWest had requested Boultbee and Atkinson to sign non-competition agreements when it had not done so;

❙ International would be paid $2.6 million when it actually received nothing;

❙ it proposed that Ravelston be paid $19.4 million as a break-up fee to end a long-term management agreement with International. In fact, Ravelston had no right to any payment if International terminated its management agreement with Ravelston; and

❙ it failed to disclose that although approximately $647 million of the CanWest consideration would go to HCNLP, Black, Boultbee and Atkinson had unilaterally decided that International would pay 100 percent of the non-competition consideration. The first submission also failed to disclose that this decision was made to avoid having to raise the non-competition payments with the HCNLP (Hollinger Canadian Newspapers, Limited partnership) Audit Committee, which Black and

the other two executives feared would ask more questions than the International Audit Committee. As a result, International bore 100 percent of the non-compete allocation attributable to the assets sold by HCNLP, rather than its 87 percent pro rata share, a difference of approximately $2.1 million.

When the CanWest transaction closed, and Ravelston, Black, Radler, Boultbee and Atkinson caused approximately $52.8 million to be disbursed to themselves—approximately $11.9 million each to Black and Radler, approximately $1.3 million each to Boultbee and Atkinson, and approximately $26.4 million to Ravelston. (The extra $1 million dollars was interest from July 30 to November 16, 2000.) Although the Audit Committee was told that International would receive $2.6 million for its non-competition agreement, in fact, International received nothing.[8]

In addition to allegations of fraud with regard to non-compete and other fee arrangements, Black has been charged with repeated breaches of fiduciary duty and abuse of power in the misuse of corporate assets between May 1998 and August 2002 at the expense of the corporation and its public majority shareholders, including the following:

❙ in the summer of 2001, Black fraudulently caused International to pay for his use of its corporate jet to fly himself and his wife on a personal vacation to Bora Bora in French Polynesia. The couple left Seattle for Bora Bora on July 30, 2001, and returned to Seattle on Aug. 8, 2001, logging a total of 23.1 hours in flight. There was little, if any, business purpose to this vacation. To lease and operate the jet for Black's personal vacation cost International tens of thousands of dollars. When International's accountants sought to have Black reimburse International for this cost, Black refused, stating in an e-mail to Atkinson that "[n]eedless to say, no such outcome is acceptable";

❙ in December 2000, Black fraudulently caused International to pay more than $40,000 for his wife's surprise birthday party on Dec. 4, 2000,

---

8. U.S. Department of Justice, *Former Hollinger Chairman,* 6–8.

at La Grenouille restaurant in New York City. The party cost approximately $62,000; related expenses included 80 dinners at $195 per person, and $13,935 for wine and champagne. The party was a social occasion with little, if any, business purpose. Yet Black, without any disclosure or consultation with International's Audit Committee, determined that International would pay approximately $42,000 for the party, and that he would pay only $20,000; and

Black and Boultbee defrauded International of millions of dollars in connection with International's renovation of the ground floor apartment, and his purchase from International of the second floor apartment at 635 Park Ave., which Black used when he was in New York City and which provided proximate quarters for his servants. Last month, the government seized approximately $8.9 million in proceeds from Black's sale of the two apartments and the indictment alleges that those funds are now subject to criminal forfeiture.[9]

Time will tell if the court finds the case is as Lord Black has indicated:

Absolute nonsense, . . . There's no truth or substance whatsoever to these charges. This has been one massive smear job from A to Z, and it will have a surprise ending. . . . a complete vindication of the defendants, and exposure of their persecutors . . .[10]

Or will it be as Patrick Fitzgerald, the U.S. District Attorney has said:

Officers and directors of publicly traded companies who steer shareholders' money into their pockets should not lie to the board of directors to get permission to do so, . . . The indictment charges that the insiders at Hollinger—all the way to the top of the corporate ladder—whose job it was to safeguard the shareholders, made it their job to steal and conceal.[11]

Questions

1. What conflicts of interest may have been involved in Black's activities?

2. Were Black's non-compete agreements and payments unethical and/or illegal?

3. What questions should have been asked by International's directors?

4. If the boards of directors of his various companies approved these non-compete agreements, are the board members on the hook and Black off?

5. Black controlled key companies through multiple voting rights attached to less than a majority of shares. Was this illegal and/or unethical?

6. What risk management techniques would have prevented Black's potential conflicts from becoming harmful?

9. *Hollinger International, Inc.,* C.A. No. 183-N, at 11.
10. Lauren La Rose, "Conrad Black calls charges of fraud 'one massive smear job' against him," *CBC News,* November 24, 2005. www.cbc.ca.
11. U.S. Department of Justice, *Former Hollinger Chairman,* 5.

Ethics Case | ## *Spying on HP Directors*

In January 2006, the chair of Hewlett-Packard (HP), Patricia Dunn, hired a team of independent electronic-security experts to determine the source of leaked confidential details regarding HP's long-term strategy. In September 2006, the press revealed that the independent experts spied on HP board members and several journalists. They obtained phone call records of HP board members and nine journalists, including reporters for CNET, the *New York Times,* and the *Wall Street Journal* using an unethical and possibly illegal practice known as pretexting. Patricia Dunn claimed she did not know the methods the investigators used to determine the source of the leak but resigned after the scandal. Ten days earlier, George Keyworth, the director responsible for the leak, had resigned from HP's board after 21 years of service.

Company Profile:

HP, founded in 1939, operates in more than 170 countries and is the world's largest seller of personal computers, offering a wide range of products and services such as digital photography, digital entertainment, computing, and home printing. In addition, HP provides infrastructure and business offerings that span from handheld devices to some of the world's most powerful supercomputer installations. HP is among the world's largest IT companies, with revenue totalling $107.7 billion for the four fiscal quarters ended January 31, 2008. In 2007 HP was ranked 14th in the Forbes 500 list. The company's corporate headquarters is in Palo Alto, California.

Leak of Confidential Information and HP's Investigation:

Patricia Dunn joined HP's board in 1998, and was elected non-executive Chair in February 2005. She was CEO of Barclays Global Investors from 1995 to 2002. In January 2006, the online technology site CNET published an article about the long-term strategy at HP. The article quoted an anonymous source inside HP and contained information only known by the company's directors. Following the CNET article, Mrs. Dunn, with the assistance of HP security personnel and the company's counsel's office, authorized a team of independent electronic-security experts to investigate the origin of the leak. The investigation targeted the January 2006 communications of HP's directors, including not only the records of phone calls and e-mails from HP but also the records from their personal accounts.

The consultants were not actually listening on the calls. They were just looking for a pattern of contacts. The investigation employed tactics that ranged from the controversial to the not-necessarily legal. These tactics included using private investigators to impersonate HP's board members and then to trick phone companies into handing over the calling records of those board members' personal phone accounts. The records of nine journalists were similarly obtained. This technique is known as pretexting. With no more than a home address, an account number, or other pieces of personal information, an investigator or pretexter may obtain personal information from phone companies pretending be somebody else.

Resignation of Tom Perkins:

The consultants discovered the origin of the leak, and in a board meeting held in May 2006, Patricia Dunn identified director George Keyworth, the longest serving HP director, as the alleged leaker. He apologized and said to his fellow directors, "I would have told you all about this. Why didn't you just ask?" On September 12, 2006, Keyworth's public resignation letter apologizes and states his reasons for leaking information to CNET:

> I acknowledge that I was a source for a CNET article that appeared in January 2006. I was frequently asked by HP corporate communications officials to speak with reporters - both on the record and on background—in an effort to provide the perspective of a longstanding board member with continuity over much of the company's history. My comments were always praised by senior company officials as helpful to the company—which has always been my intention. The comments I made to the CNET reporter were, I believed, in the best interest of the company and also did not involve the disclosure of confidential or damaging information.

Immediately following the accusations, Keyworth left the board room and another director, Tom Perkins, a renowned Silicon Valley venture capitalist and friend of the company founders, protested against the secret internal investigation, which he considered illegal, unethical and a misplaced corporate priority on Dunn's part. Perkins was chair of the board's nominating and governance committee but had not been informed by Dunn of the surveillance, even though he knew that Dunn was attempting to discover the source of the leak.

After the board passed a motion asking Keyworth to resign, Perkins announced his own resignation. The next day, the company publicly announced Perkins' resignation without disclosing the reasons for his departure. HP reported Perkins's resignation to the SEC four days later, again giving no reason for his resignation.

In early August, after HP ignored his requests to take action, Perkins formally asked the SEC, prosecutors in California and New York to force HP to publicly file his written explanation for resigning. By early September, HP could not delay disclosing the scandal, and made a filing to the SEC, laying out the pretexting story. At the same time, the story was released to the press by Perkins. On September 12, 2006, Keyworth publicly resigned from the board and HP announced that Mark Hurd, HP chief executive officer and president, would replace Dunn as chair after the HP board meeting on January 18, 2007.

Congressional Hearings and Charges:

On September 21, 2006, Mark Hurd, in an official HP press release, explained that "What began as an effort to prevent the leaks of confidential information from HP's boardroom ended up heading in directions that were never anticipated." A day later, Patricia Dunn resigned as a HP director, stating in her resignation letter the reasons for her departure and her involvement in the internal investigation:

> I have resigned today at the request of the board. The unauthorized disclosure of confidential information was a serious violation of our code of conduct. I followed the proper processes by seeking the assistance of HP security personnel. I did not select the people who conducted the investigation, which was undertaken after consultation with board members. I accepted the responsibility to identify the sources of those leaks, but I did not propose the specific methods of the investigation. I was a full subject of the investigation myself and my phone records were examined along with others. Unfortunately, the people HP relied upon to conduct this type of investigation let me and the company down.

A week later, on September 28, the parties involved appeared at the U.S. House of Representatives Energy and Commerce Committee Subcommittee on Oversight and Investigations. Ann Baskins, HP's general counsel resigned hours before she was to appear as a witness and refused to answer questions, invoking the Fifth Amendment, due to the ongoing criminal investigations. In the hearing, Dunn and Hurd testified extensively about the internal investigation. Dunn testified she never approved the use of questionable tactics, saying she wasn't aware that pretexting could involve the misrepresentation of someone's identity to obtain phone records until late June or July (2006).

In October 2006, the California attorney general filed civil and criminal charges against the company, Patricia Dunn and other HP employees. HP settled the lawsuit in December 2006 paying $14.5 million in fines and promising to improve its corporate governance practices. In June 2007, a California judge dismissed fraud charges against Patricia Dunn and other employees involved in the scandal.

At the same time, the journalists whose records were obtained by HP's external consultants filed a lawsuit against the company. Two years later, in February 2008, HP agreed to a financial settlement with the *New York Times* and three *Business Week* magazine journalists. The amount of the settlement was not disclosed and the proceeds were donated to charity.

Questions

1. Should the chair of the board of directors be allowed to initiate investigations into weaknesses in a company's internal control system?

2. Is the strategy of pretexting an acceptable means in order to obtain critical information that will strengthen a company's internal control system? The following legal advice was obtained on the subject by HP:

   > The committee was then advised by the committee's outside counsel that the use of pretexting at the time of the investigation was not generally unlawful (except with

respect to financial institutions), but such counsel could not confirm that the techniques employed by the outside consulting firm and the party retained by that firm complied in all respects with applicable law.[1]

3. Should the reasons for resignations from a board of directors always be made public?

References

Hewlett-Packard. CNN Archive. September 2006 to July 2008. http://money.cnn.com/

Hewlett-Packard. Newsweek Archive. September 2006 to July 2008. http://www.newsweek.com/

Hewlett-Packard. The New York Times Archive. September 2006 to July 2008. http://www.nytimes.com/

Hewlett-Packard press releases 2006. http://www.hp.com/hpinfo/newsroom/press/2006/index.html

Source: The authors thank Miguel Minutti for his contributions to this case.

---

1. "Euphemisms and Crimes at Hewlett-Packard," Floyd Norris, *New York Times*, September 7, 2006.

Ethics Case | *Manipulation of MCI's Allowance for Doubtful Accounts*

Walt Pavlo joined MCI in the spring of 1992. At that time, MCI was a growth company in the booming long-distance telecommunications industry that had 15 percent of the long-distance market, with revenues of $11 billion.

In the 1990s the major telecommunications companies all shared their fiber-optic networks. This was more efficient than having each company lay its own network to every corner of the country. Each company would use the others' networks in places where the former did not have cable and vice versa. The cost of routing a call through these fiber optic networks was measured in pennies per minute. However, MCI and the other telecommunication companies sold the right to use the network to their customers for dimes per minute. It was a lucrative business based on volume. The more the network was used, the greater the revenue for the telecommunication company. MCI's stellar revenue growth was due to its sales, and sales personnel were awarded lucrative commissions. Senior management was given generous stock options. It was heady times.

MCI had a wide array of clients that varied from major corporations, such as American Express, General Electric, and IBM, to small newly formed long-distance discount services. Called LDDS, these were primarily marketing firms that bought MCI long-distance capacity, which they resold to individuals and small businesses. Although these LDDS customers represented only 5 percent of MCI's annual sales, the profit margins for both MCI and the LDDS companies were quite substantial. For example, in 1992, Telephone Publishing Corp., or TCP, paid $600,000 to MCI for long-distance calls that TCP was charging its customers approximately $5 million per month. After paying its overhead, TCP was netting, before taxes, about $20 million per year. Meanwhile MCI was often charging a LDDS as much as 28 cents a minute for services that cost about 5 cents. Everyone was making money.

However, many of these LDDS companies were slow in paying MCI for the use of the long-distance service. Collections were a problem because these companies normally had no hard assets. Their offices were rented, the communication switch was leased, and they had no other assets other than cash. Without assets they were somewhat bullet-proof. They could be threatened, but there was nothing to collect in the event the LDDS was successfully sued by MCI. If MCI cut off access to the network, then the LDDS would fold its operations and disappear, often reappearing under a new name as a client of one of the other telecommunication companies.

Walt Pavlo was in charge of the finance unit, responsible for LDDS collections. Walt was also given some clear guidelines with respect to accounts receivable and bad debts. Accounts that were ninety or more days old should not exceed 7 percent of total receivables, and bad debt write-offs should be under 2 percent of total account receivables. For 1994, the bad debt ceiling was set at $12 million, and then reduced to $10 million in 1995 even though 1995 revenues had increased. Unfortunately, both delinquent accounts and bad debts exceed these guidelines. So, Walt gathered a small group of bright MBAs, and he tasked them to be creative. How could they stay within the MCI guidelines?

One strategy was to get delinquent accounts to sign promissory notes, thereby moving their balances out of accounts receivable. These customers were also required to pay interest on the note, but because they often had no intention of paying the principal, the interest charge was irrelevant. For example, Voicecom had its account converted to a $3.5 million promissory note. It paid $100,000 per month for ten months and then defaulted on the balance. Another strategy was to accept the customer's common stock instead of cash.

They lapped payments, posting one customer's payment to another's account in order to show activity in the latter's account. They amortized bad debts, writing off a portion and pretending that the balance would be collected. They also convinced the accounting department to accept a check-in-the-mail. This consisted of a fax of a check and a FedEx tracking

number of the check to prove that the check was on its way. When the check arrived, the previous entry would be reversed. None of these procedures was identified and/or challenged by internal audit or the external auditors.

However, these strategies were merely disguising rather than solving the problem. So, in January of 1996 Walt sent a note to his new boss saying that MCI's bad debts for 1995 were approaching $88 million. A month later, he was told that his budget for 1996 was $15 million. He was also reminded that there was speculation that MCI would be taken over, and so it was everyone's responsibility to make their targets and budgets. At the time, Walt was being well paid for running an efficient department, and staying within budget. He had a stay-at-home wife and two small children. If MCI was taken over, he would profit handsomely from his stock options.

Questions

1. After being told that the guideline for bad debts for 1996 was to be $15 million, what should Walt do?

2. What are the risks for MCI in setting an unrealistic allowance for doubtful accounts?

Source: Stolen Without a Gun: Confessions from inside history's biggest accounting fraud—the collapse of MCI WorldCom, Walter Pavlo Jr. and Neil Weinberg, Etika Books LLC, Tampa Florida, 2007.

| Ethics Case | *A Minority-Controlling Shareholder:* **The New York Times Company** *and the Ochs and Sulzberger Families* |

In 2007, forty-four-year-old Hassan Elmasry was a London-based portfolio manager for Morgan Stanley Investment Management. He was a successful manager; his American and Global Franchise Strategies Portfolio of $11.5 billion had an 18.6 percent compound annual growth rate over the previous 10 years compared to an 8.4 percent growth rate of the S&P 500 Index over the same period.

Morgan Stanley began buying stock in *The New York Times Company* in 1996 before Elmasry took over the portfolio. By 2007, the

fund held a 7.2 percent ownership interest in the newspaper. However, Elmasry felt that the newspaper was performing badly with poor management and poor managerial supervision. The stock was trading in the $24 neighborhood, down nearly 40 percent in the previous two years. *The New York Times Company* had reported a $648 million loss in the fourth quarter of the previous year because of an $814 million write-down in the value of its New England newspapers, including the *Boston Globe.* Elmasry believed that the newspaper's board of directors was not providing proper oversight of management. But there was little that he could do because of the newspaper's corporate governance structure.

The New York Times Company, that went public in 1969, has a dual class share structure. The Class A shares, that trade on the New York Stock Exchange, can vote on a limited number of company matters and are restricted to voting for 4 of the 13 directors. The superior-voting Class B shares, that are thinly traded, can vote on all company matters and are entitled to elect 9 of the 13 board members.

In 1896 Aloph O. Ochs bought a controlling interest in the newspaper that the Ochs and Sulzberger families continue to hold today through direct ownership and a voting trust. The trust is administered by eight Ochs and Sulzberger family members, six of whom must approve major decisions. The trust owns 88 percent of the Class B shares of *The New York Times Company*. The Sulzberger family owns 19 percent of the Class A shares. Combined, the Ochs and Sulzberger families are a minority-controlling shareholder group; they have a minority equity interest (through the Class A shares) but a majority or controlling voting interest (through the Class B shares). Therefore Elmasry's criticism of the *New York Times* could be easily spurned by Arthur O. Sulzberger Jr., the current chairman and publisher of the newspaper, and the great-grandson of Aloph O. Ochs.

Since June 2005, Elmasry had been writing to Sulzberger and meeting with the various officials at the newspaper to discuss the company's corporate governance structure as well as some of its strategies. His criticisms were to no avail. He unsuccessfully tried to have two shareholder resolutions put to a vote at the annual meeting; one abolishing the dual class share structure, and the other requiring the newspaper to separate the chair and publisher duties. However, the Securities and Exchange Commission ruled, in December 2006, that the newspaper was not required to put these proposals to a shareholder vote.

Elmasry was a thorn in Sulzberger's side with his constant criticism. Meanwhile, the Ochs-Sulzberger family assets, valued at approximately $690 million, were being administered by Morgan Stanley, Elmasry's employer. Even though Morgan Stanley had long been the custodian of the family's assets, Sulzberger said that he planned to move them to another financial institution, which he did in February 2007. Nevertheless, Elmasry continued his campaign.

The board of directors of *The New York Times Company* has to be elected annually by the shareholders, but a slate of candidates is put forward by the Ochs-Sulzberger families with only enough candidates for all the available directorships. The shareholders can vote either in favor of the candidates on the slate or withhold their vote. At the April 2007 shareholder meeting, 47 percent of the Class A shareholders withheld their votes for the directors. Although a rebuff, it was only a symbolic gesture—the Class A shareholders can only elect four of the thirteen members of the board of directors. But it was up from the 30 percent who withheld their votes the previous year. Still the newspaper did not change. In October 2007 Morgan Stanley sold its 7.2 percent interest in the newspaper.

Questions

1. Discuss the ethical aspects of a minority-controlling share structure.

2. Pyramid ownership occurs when a minority-controlling shareholder owns a controlling stake in another company. In this case, whoever controls the Ochs-Sulzberger voting trust controls *The New York Times* newspaper. Discuss the ethical aspects of pyramid ownership.

3. Does a pension fund manager have an ethical responsibility to actively campaign for corporate governance reforms at the firms that the fund invests in?

4. Should the system be changed so that directors are elected by popular vote? The directors who receive the most votes are elected to the board. Should there be a minimum number of positive votes that each candidate has to receive before she/he can be elected to the board?

5. If you were John Mack, CEO of Morgan Stanley, and Arthur Sulzberger phoned you to say he was planning on moving his family's assets from your bank, how would you respond?

Sources

Arango, Tim, "Sulzberger's Revenge," Fortune, CNNMoney.com, February 2, 2007. http://money.cnn.com/2007/02/02/news/companies/sulzberger_morgan.fortune/index.htm

Ellison, Sarah, "Paper Chase: How a Money Manager Battled New York Times," *The Wall Street Journal Online*, March 21, 2007. http://online.wsj.com/public/article/SB117441975619343135-n

166azU72Y6GkdTvlv4nWSeWWWo_20080319.html

Sorkin, Andrew Ross and Fabrikant, "Big Holder Sells Stake in Times Co." *The New York Times*, October 18, 2007. http://www.nytimes.com/2007/10/18/business/media/18paper.html?_r=1&pagewanted=print&oref=slogin

---

Ethics Case | *Stock Options and Gifts of Publicly Traded Shares*

Pierre Garvey, the CEO of Revel Information Technology, sat back in his chair and looked at his assistants. He frowned. "My son has been diagnosed with MLD," he said.

They all looked at him with shock. "Its proper name is metachromatic leukodystrophy and it's caused by an enzyme deficiency that will eventually destroy his nervous system."

"I'm so sorry, Pierre." "That's awful." "Oh, my God! Is there anything that can be done?" They all spoke at once.

"It's an extremely rare disease. There's no known cure and no standard form of treatment," he went on. "But there has been research into bone marrow and stem cell transplant therapies. So, what I would like you to do, Gloria, is have fifty percent of our corporate charitable contributions redirected to organizations that are working on stem cell research."

She stared straight at her boss and said, "There is a formal procedure for how we allocate our charity."

Before she could say anything further, Pierre stopped her. "You're in charge of that committee! Fill out all the necessary forms and paperwork, but I want fifty percent of our corporate contributions to go to stem cell research. Do I make myself clear?" She nodded and remained silent throughout the rest of the meeting.

"I've decided to exercise some of my stock options and then donate the stock to the Lascelles Institute that is working on bone marrow therapy." As CEO, Pierre had been given multiple stock options that varied in price from $17.51 to $29.87. Shares of Revel Information Technology have been trading in the $19 range for the last month. The current share price is $19.25. "I'm going to exercise 50,000 at $17.51 and then donate the stock to the Lascelles Institute. They'll then give me a tax receipt for the fair market value of the shares."

"Wouldn't it be easier for you to exercise the options, sell the shares, and then donate the cash proceeds to the charity?" asked Carol, the executive vice president.

"No," said Lin, the controller. "If Pierre exercises the options and sells the stock, he has to pay capital gains. But because of the recent changes to the Income Tax Act, there are no capital gains if shares are donated to a charity."

"But isn't this subject to insider trading rules?"

"That's right," said Pierre, "but, because I'm donating the shares, there are no proceeds to me, and so the securities commission is not interested because I'm not receiving any cash and there's no capital gain."

"This is all quite legal," added Lin.

"However, I'm concerned about this quarter's financial results and what it will do to our stock price. Our earnings and net income are down substantially from the analysts' forecasts. I think that our stock will take a beating after we release our results and my stock options may no longer be in-the-money."

"That's right, Pierre," said Carol. "We lost sales to cheap imports from China; our competitors lowered their prices and stole some of our customers; our obsolete machinery finally broken down and had to be replaced; and we got hammered on those security-backed investments we bought with our surplus funds."

"Once we release this quarter's results we should expect out stock to fall to about $17. Maybe a bit more," said Lin.

"Okay, this is what you do. Gloria, I want you to arrange that our corporate donations go to stem cell research. I also want you to contact the Lascelles Institute and let them know that I'm going to be donating 50,000 shares of Revel Information Technology to them tomorrow, on Thursday. I also want a tax receipt at whatever price our shares are trading at tomorrow, probably at about $19 per share.

"Carol, I want you to get in touch with legal and arrange for me to exercise 50,000 options at $17.51. I then want them to change the ownership on the certificates to the Lascelles Institute.

"Finally, Lin, I don't want you to release this quarter's financial statements tomorrow. Wait until Monday morning of next week.

"Everybody clear? Good. Off you go."

Questions

1. Is it right that a CEO can direct the charitable donations of his company to the charity of his choice?

2. Comment on the ethical aspects of Pierre's stock option/stock donation strategy.

3. If you were Gloria, what should you do? Would this change if you were a donations specialist, a lawyer, or a professional accountant?

References

Walker, Michael, "Publicly Traded Gifts," *CAMagazine,* June 2008, 38–40.

Ethics Case | *The Ethics of Repricing and Backdating Employee Stock Options*

Employee stock options allow company executives to buy shares of their company at a specified price during a specified time period. They are given to executives as a form of noncash compensation. The option or 'strike price' is normally equal to the market price of the stock on the day that the option is granted to the employee. The stock option is intended to motivate the executive to increase the stock price of the firm. If the stock rises, the investor is pleased. If the stock rises, the executive exercises the option, buys the stock from the company at the strike price and then immediately sells those shares on the stock exchange at the current (higher) market price to obtain a capital gain. This is considered to be a win-win situation. Both the investor and the employee gain from the increase in the market price of the company's stock.

However, sometimes the stock price falls and the current price is less than the strike price. Such stock options are referred to as "underwater" or "out of the money." In such cases, companies will sometimes reprice the stock options to a price that is less than the current market price, or cancel the underwater options and issue new options that are priced at the new current market price. Both repricing and backdating of stock options have effectively been curtailed as a result of Sarbanes-Oxley disclosure requirements. As a result, two new strategies are available. One is to "spring-load" the options by issuing them to employees just before good news is announced to investors. The other is to "bullet-dodge" by delaying the granting of stock options until after bad news has been released.

An analysis of the ethics of repricing, backdating, spring-loading, and bullet-dodging is contained in the article "Ethics of Options Repricing and Backdating: Banishing Greed from Corporate Governance and Management". In their article that was published in the October 2007 issue of *The CPA Journal,* Raiborn, Massoud, Morris, and Pier present four ethical arguments.

The *theory of justice* says that equals should be treated equally, and unequals treated unequally in proportion to their inequalities. All investors are equal, and executive investors should be treated no differently from all other investors in the company. As such, preferential treatment through the backdating of stock options is inappropriate and unethical. Spring-loading and bullet-dodging are grounded on management's inside knowledge of good and bad news that will have an impact on the company's stock price. Their inside knowledge discriminates against all the other shareholders who do not know the good or bad news.

Utilitarianism or consequentialism argues that the ethically correct decision must be of benefit to most shareholders in the long term. Backdating stock options benefits the executive at the expense of the other shareholders. It is not in the best interest of the majority of the shareholders of the company. Spring-loading and bullet-dodging are only in the short-term interests of a minority of the shareholders (i.e., executive shareholders) and not in the best long-term interests of all the other (majority) shareholders.

From a *deontological* perspective, backdating and repricing are akin to lies because the intention is to manipulate and deceive the other shareholders. Deontology does not accept that the end justifies the means. Furthermore, it does not allow exceptions to a rule. Spring-loading and back-dating treat one category of shareholders (management) differently than the other category of shareholders (all the current and future shareholders). As such it is unlikely that everyone in society would accept as a universal rule that management should be given preferential treatment.

It is difficult to say that manipulating stock options, through any of these four tactics, is the sign of a virtuous person. *Virtue ethics* does not accept discrimination and prudential treatment of insiders as the mark of an ethical businessperson.

The conclusion of the article by Raiborn et al. is that the repricing of stock options may be legal but it is certainly unethical. Their concluding paragraph reads:

> Stock options were designed as a way to provide pay for performance, not to reward poor performance by backwards-looking repricing or backdating. Such activities undermine the incentive justification for use of stock option plans. Executives deserve compensation packages that provide both short-run benefits and a long-run motivation to increase organizational value for all stakeholders. Compensation methods that cause the tone at the top to be perceived as a cacophony of greed should be banished from the orchestra.

Questions

1. Do you think that stock options actually motivate employees to work for the long-term good of the company?

2. Do you think that stock options inadvertently encourage managers to engage in questionable accounting activities, such as earnings management, to artificially increase the company's net income and thereby the value of the executives stock options?

3. Do you agree or disagree with the four ethical arguments summarized above and contained in more detail in the article by Raiborn, Massoud, Morris, and Pier? Explain why.

4. Should a board of directors approve repricing or backdating stock options for outstanding executives whose current stock options are underwater due to uncontrollable economic factors, and who will be lured away unless some incentives to stay are created? What other incentives might work?

Ethics Case | *Siemens' Bribery Scandal*

Siemens AG is a 160-year-old German engineering and electronics giant. It is one of Europe's largest conglomerates, with profits in 2007 of 3.9 billion euros on revenue of 72.4 billion euros, up 6 billion euros from its 2006 revenue. It has over 475,000 employees and operations worldwide. It had also developed a corrupt organizational culture in which hundreds of millions of Euros were put into slush funds that were then used to pay bribes in order to obtain lucrative contracts. The following details have come to light:

▌ In November 2006 Siemens' auditors, KPMG, completed a confidential report that detailed a number of payments that were impossible to verify. They could not identify who received the money or what services were provided. The suspicious payments, made from 2000 to 2006, totaled €1.3 billion (U.S.$1.88 billion). At the time, the company said that senior executives were unaware of these payments.

▌ In January 2007 the company paid a €418 million fine to the European Commission because the company was accused of heading a cartel that was dividing up the market for power station equipment. Siemens is challenging the fine.

▌ In October 2007 the company paid a €201 million fine related to bribery in its communication equipment business.

A number of senior executives were also accused and subsequently convicted of making bribery payments, including:

▌ Andreas Kley, CFO of the power-generating unit, was convicted (in May 2007) of channeling €6 million, from 1999 to 2002, to an Italian energy company to win gas turbine contracts. The judge also fined Siemens €38 million and required the company to forfeit the profit it made on the contract.

▌ Johannes Feldmayer, an executive board member, was convicted (in July 2008) of authorizing bribes to a labor union, the Association of Independent Employees, that was considered friendly to Siemens' management. The payments, made between 2001 and 2005, were intended to offset the power of IG Metall, the German union that controls almost half of the seats on Siemens' board of directors.

▌ Reinhard Siekaczek, a sales manager in the telecom division, was convicted (in July 2008) of building a slush fund system designed to make bribery payments. The judge said that Siekaczek acted at the behest of his superiors, and that he "was part of a system of organized irresponsibility that was implicitly condoned."

Although they were never accused of any wrongdoing, in April 2007, both Klaus Kleinfeld, CEO, and Heinrich von Pierer, supervisory board chairman, resigned. They were replaced, in July 2007, by an outsider, Peter Löscher, who came from drug maker Merck & Company. As the new CEO, Löscher began to change the organizational structure and culture. Formerly, each line of business had a managing director and a separate managing board. This structure inhibited accountability and allowed corruption to spread. Löscher reorganized the company into three sectors—industry, energy, and health care—with each of these three managers sitting on the central managing board in Munich. He also adopted a zero-tolerance policy, delivering a message that corruption must end.

Questions

1. The senior executives at Siemen's spent most of their working life in an environment that condoned bribery outside of Germany but not inside. However, they failed to take notice of the changes that Transparency International—championed by a German who was embarrassed by the double standard of his countrymen—was proposing, and that ultimately resulted in a new worldwide anti-bribery regime. Why did they ignore the change?

2. If you were Löscher, the new CEO, how would you show the employees and external stakeholders that you actually have a zero-tolerance policy concerning corruption?

References

Balzil, Beat, Dinah Deckstein and Jorg Schmitt, "New Report Details Far-Reaching Corruption," *Spiegel Online*, January 29, 2007. http://www.spiegel.de/international/0,1518, 462954,00.html

Dougherty, Carter, "Siemens's Prosperity Doesn't Obscure Bribery Scandal," *New York Times*, January 22, 2008. http://www.nytimes.com/2008/01/22/business/worldbusiness/22siemens.html

Hack, Jens, "Former Siemens Manager Convicted in Bribery Case," *International Herald Tribune*, July 28, 2008. http://www.iht.com/articles/reuters/2008/07/28/business/OUKBS-UK-SIEMENS-TRIAL.php

Matussek, Karin, "Ex-Siemens Executive Feldmayer Charged Over Bribery (Update 1)," *Bloomberg.com*, July 2, 2008. http://www.bloomberg.com/apps/news?pid=20601100&sid=an9FWLdc0pWs&refer=germany

Sims, G. Thomas, "2 Former Siemens Officials Convicted for Bribery," *New York Times*, May 15, 2007. http://www.nytimes.com/2007/05/15/business/worldbusiness/15siemens.html

Ethics Case   *Société Générale Rogue Trader*

Jérôme Kerviel joined the French bank, Société Générale (SocGen), in 2000 at the age of twenty-three as part of its systems personnel in its back office. In 2005 he became a junior derivatives trader with an annual limit of €20 million, which is just under U.S.$30 million. However, in November 2007, exchange officials questioned SocGen about why he had traded more than U.S.$74 billion worth of stock-index futures contracts. Kerviel was allowed to continue trading until mid-January 2008, when SocGen liquidated his trading positions and realized a loss of U.S.$7.62 billion (€4.9 billion). How did this happen? Who should be blamed? Was he different than other rogue traders?

Société Générale began operations in France in 1864 and is one of the main European financial institutions. It is the sixth largest French company and the third largest bank in the Eurozone. By the mid-2000s, it had developed a risk culture. In 2007, for example, trading-related activities represented 35 percent of the bank's revenue, up from 29 percent in 2004. Traders were well rewarded and it was not uncommon for then to briefly exceed trading limits.

Kerviel began working for the bank in its back office recording and reconciling trading activity. In 2005 he became a trader in the bank's arbitrage department, trading European stock futures. He took unauthorized positions in equities and futures and used his knowledge of the bank's control procedures to conceal his trading positions. Because he knew the timing of the nightly reconciliation of daily trades he was able to delete and re-enter his trades, or enter fictitious offsetting trades. Although the bank's risk-control department monitored the bank's overall position, it did not verify individual transactions and so his trades went undetected.

In November 2007, officials at Eurex, a derivatives exchange owned by the Duestsche Böerse, questioned SocGen about Kerviel's huge trading activity and position. But Kerviel "produced a faked document to justify the risk cover," according to prosecutor Jean-Claude Marin,[1] and he continued to trade.

By the end of 2007, his positions had generated a paper profit of €1.4 billion.[2] But because this was generated with positions well over his authorized limit, he used his knowledge of the bank's systems and controls to hide most of his success. At the time, Kerviel was making a salary and bonus of not more than €100,000 (approximately U.S.$145,000),[3] and no evidence indicated that he benefited other than through salary and bonus from his trades. Later, Kerviel did tell investigators that he had been promised a bonus of €300,000 for his efforts in 2007.[4]

On January 18, 2008, the bank's risk-control department started an investigation after a week of his suspicious trades reached a position on 49 billion euros. His unauthorized trades were identified, and on January 21 the bank began to unwind his future positions. It took three days, and represented 8 percent of all the trading activity on the Eurostoxx, DAX,

---

1. "Bank warned on Trades: Prosecutor," Andrew Hurst and Thierry Leveque, *Toronto Star*, B1, B4.
2. Ibid., B4.
3. Rogue trader's fall stuns old friends, neighbors," John Leicester, *Toronto Star*, January 26, 2008, B5.
4. Op. cit., B4.

and FTSE future indices. After it reversed all his unauthorized trading positions, the bank lost 4.9 billion euros. Although the bank received permission from French authorities to do this, they did not tell the public until after the positions had been fully unwound. When asked, the bank's CEO, Daniel Bouton, stated that "it didn't want to cause even more losses."[5] Interestingly, the losses could have been much less if the markets had not turned so negative on the three days of liquidation.

Apparently Kerviel circumvented six levels of control.[6] Later, a special committee of the board of directors revealed numerous weaknesses in the bank's internal controls, including:

| There was a large increase in the volume of transactions within the equities department, but there was not an increase in the corresponding support services, including the information system.

| The nominal value of trades, by traders, was not controlled.

| Duties were not clearly defined, reports were not centralized, and there was no feedback to the appropriate hierarchical level.

| Priority was given to the execution of trades, without an adequate degree of sensitivity to fraud risks.

| Internal audit bodies were insufficiently responsive.

According to a judicial official, Kerviel claimed that his "bank bosses were aware of his massive risk-taking on markets but turned a blind eye as long as he earned money."[7] He said: "I can't believe that my superiors were not aware of the amounts I was committing, it is impossible to generate such profits with small positions."[8]

Although Kerviel was initially accused of fraud, that charge was thrown out by an investigating judge and he was put under investigation for breach of trust, computer abuse and falsification.[9] He was later released on bail in March 2008, after the police and internal investigators highlighted the lack of internal controls at Société Générale.

Banks have been bedeviled by rogue traders on several occasions.[10] Kerviel was not the only rogue trader to use a lack of controls to cause huge losses. For example, due to a lack of proper internal controls at Barings Bank, which had been in business for 230 years, Nick Leeson bankrupted the English bank in 1995 after he lost £360 million (U.S. $1.38 billion) on Asian futures markets.

Questions

1. Did Jérôme Kerviel perpetrate a fraud? Why or why not?

2. When such mammoth unauthorized trades occur, and the bank is bankrupted or severely damaged financially, should the board of directors, who have the ultimate responsibility for the bank's activities, or its executives whose job it is to protect the bank, go to jail rather than the rogue trader?

3. Were the bank's actions in liquidating Kerviel's positions ethical?

4. Did the French officials who authorized the liquidation behave ethically?

5. There is considerable debate about whether better controls can ever stop a rogue trader. What is your opinion, and why?

6. If enhanced controls really can't stop all rogue traders, how are companies to be protected from them?

5. "Tough questions engulf SocGen," Paul Waldie, *The Globe and Mail*, January 26, 2008, B2.
6. "Trader used inside knowledge," Molly Moore, *Toronto Star*, January 25, 2008, B1, B4.
7. "Trader points finger at bosses," Angela Boland, *Toronto Star*, January 30, 2008, B3.
8. Ibid., B3.
9. "Bank warned . . . ," B1.
10. "Rogue trader's fall . . . ," B5. Other rogue traders have included: Brian Hunter, who lost U.S. $6.6 billion on natural gas futures in 2006; Yasuo Hamanaka, who lost U.S. $2.6 billion dealing in copper futures in 1996; and John Rusnak, who lost U.S. $691 million trading in currency options in 2002.

Barings Bank: Rogue Trader

It was early on a Friday morning in London—7:15 A.M. on February 24, 1995, to be exact—that the phone call came for Peter Baring from Peter Norris. Barings' family had been in banking since 1763. They enjoyed the patronage of the Queen of England and had financed the Napoleonic Wars and the transcontinental railway in Canada. Barings, London's oldest merchant bank, would soon be owned by foreign interests because of Norris's news.

Early on the previous day, Norris, the head of investment banking, had been summoned to Singapore by James Bax, the regional managing director of Baring Securities. Its star trader, Nick Leeson, hadn't been seen since Wednesday afternoon Singapore time and it appeared that he had left major unhedged securities positions that Barings might not be able to cover. If not, Barings would be bankrupt, or owned by others who could pay off what was owed when the uncovered commitments came due.

At the beginning, Barings officials weren't sure what had happened, or the extent of the potential losses and commitments. When they did discover the nature of their obligations, they realized that the securities contracts were still open, so that the upper limit of their losses would not be known until the closing date of the contracts. If the markets involved sank further by that time, Barings' losses would grow. This was a complete shock because Leeson was supposed to deal in fully hedged positions only, making his money on short-term price changes with virtually no chance of losing a significant amount of money. What had happened?

Norris found confirmation of what Bax had told him. Essentially, Leeson had built up two huge securities positions. He had arranged futures contracts committing Barings to buy US $7 billion worth of Japanese equities and US $20 billion or more of interest rate futures at future dates. Unfortunately, due to the Kobe earthquake in Japan, the Japanese stock market was falling, so the equity contracts were worth less than he had paid, and the projected losses were growing but not yet at their maximum. In fact, it was estimated that every 1 percent decline in the stock market raised the losses by US $70 million.

When Peter Baring, the chairman of the bank, advised the Bank of England on Friday at noon that his bank had a potential problem, he estimated the combined losses at £433 million (US $650 million), a figure that was close to the shareholders' equity of £541 million. The governor of the Bank of England, Eddie George, was recalled from his skiing holiday in France, and his deputy, Rupert Pennant-Rea, called other British bankers to meet at the Bank of England to pledge funds to help meet Barings' problem. Prospective purchasers were canvassed throughout Saturday, but the loss estimate rose to £650 million with no cap in sight. On Sunday, several options were pursued, including contacting the world's richest man, the Sultan of Brunei. The British bankers met again at the bank at 10 A.M. and by 2 P.M. they had agreed to provide £600 million. The question of what their return would be for advancing the money was being debated, but the issue of someone providing an upper cap to the losses remained. An offer arrived from the sultan to do so, which included the taking over of Barings. Unfortunately, this offer was withdrawn before a deal was consummated, and Eddie George had to sign an Administration Order that essentially put Barings under the administration of the Bank of England. At 10:10 P.M., the Bank of England announced that Barings had failed. Two hundred thirty-three years of stewardship by the Barings family was over.

One of the prospective buyers, ING, the second largest insurance firm in The Netherlands, was still interested and had sent a squad of at least thirty people to complete due diligence examinations. ING was particularly interested in assessing the degree of risk of other losses and of the complicity of personnel in the London and Singapore offices in the Leeson problems. And Jacobs, the chairman of ING, agreed to buy Barings for £1 two hours before the Japanese market opened on Tuesday, February 28. As part of the deal, he agreed to keep the Barings name on the bank. In addition, he subsequently agreed to pay out most of the £105 million in bonuses that the Barings management had agreed to give its staff two days prior to the famous phone call.

How did this debacle happen? Bits and pieces of the puzzle came out slowly until the Report of the Bank of England's Board of Banking Supervision emerged. On Tuesday the 28th, Nick Leeson still had not been found, and he would not be detained until he and his wife arrived in Frankfurt on Thursday, March 2, having spent time in Kuala Lumpur and Kota Kinabalu, Malaysia. He would ultimately make a deal to assist investigators but would still be sent back to Singapore to stand trial.

Nick Leeson had gone to Singapore as the head of a unit that traded in futures, and he had prospered. He made money by buying and selling futures contracts for baskets of Japanese stocks known as Nikkei 225 futures. These Nikkei 225 futures contracts were traded on both the Osaka stock exchange and the SIMEX, the Singapore financial futures exchange. Since the prices on each exchange were slightly different, a sharp-eyed trader could buy on one and sell on the other exchange, making money on the spread. This was relatively safe, since for every purchase there was an immediate sale—if not, Barings would be exposed to very large risks, since the transactions were highly leveraged. In 1992 his unit made £1.18 million, in 1993 £8.83 million, and in the first seven months of 1994 it made a total of £19.6 million, or more than one-third of the total profit for the whole group. Nick was a star.

Barings did send out its internal auditors to see that all was well. Although the twenty-four-page report condemned the lack of controls and particularly having one man in charge of both the front (investing) and back (record keeping) offices, it was not acted on for fear that Leeson would be aggravated and leave for a job at another broker. Leeson's profits, after all, provided bonuses for everyone. Even though Leeson's behavior was getting somewhat bizarre, no action was taken. For example, five months before, he was fined $200 (Singapore) for dropping his pants in a pub and daring a group of women to use his cell phone to call the police.

It appears that his ego and the pressure to make more and more profits pushed him in the direction of more risky investments, and he began to make unhedged transactions in which there was no immediate sale or purchase to offset the initial transaction. As a result, since the market was declining, his transactions required funds to meet margin calls. Since he did not report to Mr. Bax but directly to the head office in London, he contacted the head office, and £454 million was sent in late January and early February.

Somehow he had convinced them that his operations were safe—but how? It seems that his ability to control the back office provided him the opportunity to do so. Earlier, when he began to trade heavily, the back office was swamped with transactions that included lots of errors made in the trading pits at the stock exchanges. He had been allegedly advised by Gordon Bowser, former derivatives trading chief, to set up a fictitious account, Error Account No. 88888, to put trading problems through and not to send reports to London so that the auditors would not be aroused. Instead, Leeson used the account as the hiding place for his losses, which totaled £2 million in 1992, £23 million in 1993, £208 million by the end of 1994, and £827 million by February 27, after Barings went into receivership. When the computer reports came off the printer for the fake account, Leeson destroyed them.

By happenstance, Anthony Hawes, the treasurer of Barings, visited Singapore. Over a sumptuous lunch on Wednesday the 22nd, he told Leeson that he was to get a bonus of at least $2 million (Singapore) on Friday the 24th. In addition, he told Leeson that the bank had a new policy of control, that he wanted to review the back room operation and check the accounting operation. Pleading that his wife was having a miscarriage and needed him, Leeson rushed from a meeting with Hawes on Thursday and left for Kuala Lumpur. He had evidently realized that the jig was about to be up and he would be caught.

Later, after he was caught, Leeson's wife revealed that the pressure for profits had become too much and that he had begun to take more risks. At the end, he was just trying to make back the losses. Before he was caught, Leeson reportedly phoned a friend from his Malaysian hotel and said, "People senior to me knew exactly the risks I was taking. Lots of people knew. . . . But it went wrong and now they're trying to lump all the blame on me."[1] Will we ever really know for sure?

Questions

1. How would you deal with a star trader who would be extremely sensitive to additional controls that implied he or she wasn't trusted or would generate more time on paperwork and explanations?

2. What ethical and accounting controls would you advise ING to institute at Barings?

3. Who was more at fault—top management or Nick Leeson?

Sources

Financial Post, "Leeson Expected to Receive a Light Sentence," December 2, 1995, p. 12.

Financial Post, "Police Hunt Rogue Trader Who Torpedoed Barings," February 28, 1995, p. 3.

Financial Post, "Buyers Circle Barings' Corpse," March 1, 1995, p. 5.

Financial Post, "Death Came Sudden and Swift for Barings," March 4, 1995, pp. 6, 7.

Financial Post, "Leeson Says Barings Told Him to Set Up a Secret Account," February 14, 1996, p. 10.

Financial Post, "Ex-Barings Directors Sued by Auditors," November 30, 1996, p. 15.

Manchester Guardian Weekly, "Barings Bank Goes Bust in 17 Bn Scam," week ending March 5, 1995, p. 1.

The Observer, "Busting the Bank," March 5, 1995, pp. 23–25.

The Observer, "Barings' Dutch Master," March 12, 1995, p. 8/Business.

Toronto Star, "Leeson's Resignation," March 7, 1995, p. D1.

Toronto Star, "Barings Loss Expands 50% as Takeover Approved," March 7, 1995, p. D6.

Manchester Guardian Weekly, "Barings Saved, but City Faces Inquiry," March 12, 1995, p. 1.

The Observer, "Norris Was a Director in Singapore," March 12, 1995, p. 1.

---

1. The Observer, "Busting the Bank," March 5, 1995, p. 25.

Ethics Case | *Adelphia—Really the Rigas' Family Piggy Bank*

On June 20, 2005, "John Rigas, the 80-year old founder of Adelphia Communications Corp., was . . . sentenced to 15 years in prison and his son Timothy, the ex-finance chief, got 20 years for looting the company and lying about its finances."[1] These were the largest sentences handed out to CEOs and CFOs after the Sarbanes-Oxley Act (SOX) and before the sentencing of Bernard J. Ebbers, CEO of WorldCom, and Dennis Kozlowski, CEO of Tyco, and before the trial of Richard Scrushy, CEO of HealthSouth.

John and Timothy Rigas had faced a maximum sentence of up to 215 years each, but John's age, bladder cancer, and heart condition were taken into account. His lawyer argued as well that John had been very generous with Coudersport, his home town, but Judge Sand responded, stating that what Rigas had done, ". . . he had done with assets and by means that were not appropriately his, . . . To be a great philanthropist with other people's money is really not very persuasive."[2]

Adelphia was founded by John Rigas in 1952 in Coudersport, Pennsylvania, and incorporated in 1972. The company started as a cinema business that transformed into a cable television provider. By 1988, Adelphia had more than two million customers in the cable television service. The company also expanded

---

1. David Glovin and David Voreacos, "Rigas Duo Gets 35 Years," *Financial Post*, June 21, 2005, FP8.
2. Ibid.

rapidly into a new line of telecommunications products and services (e.g., high definition television, video on demand, high speed Internet, and home security). By 1989, Adelphia more than doubled its reach through acquisitions, extending into forty-one states and serving more than five million customers. At its peak, Adelphia employed 14,000 people in the United States.

Members of the Rigas family held four seats on the firm's seven-member board. John Rigas (chairman and CEO), his son Timothy Rigas (chief financial officer), and Michael Rigas (vice-president of operations) had control of the firm and access to its resources beyond the oversight mechanisms of its board of directors. In essence, they used Adelphia as their own family piggy bank, withdrawing funds when they needed for their own purposes such as golf club construction, property purchases, and stock dealings as noted in following sections.

Unfortunately, these cash withdrawals and other improper use of company resources, as well as rapid expansion, poor management, and improper use of company's resources to pay management's personal expenses led Adelphia into a tight financial position. Faced with the needs for meeting earnings and cash targets, and to keep the company's debt levels within market averages, the Rigas family members began to commit fraud, and those frauds finally came to light.

On March 27, 2002, the company announced $2.3 billion dollars in off-balance sheet debt previously undisclosed in the company's financial statements. Adelphia guaranteed as co-borrower $2.3 billion loans given to the Rigas family and entities controlled by them. On April 1, the company delayed filing Form 10-K, required under the U.S. Securities and Exchange Commission (SEC) rules for public companies in the U.S. markets. The delay was followed by a formal inquiry by the SEC. On April 15, the company announced that continuing review of its financial statements

would not result in material changes to historical filings.

However, on May 2, Adelphia changed its position, announcing a possible restatement. Two weeks later, John Rigas and his son Timothy resigned, and the company's auditors, Deloitte & Touche, suspended the 2001 financial statements audit. The trade of the company's shares in NASDAQ was suspended after the stock price went from $20.39 on March 26 to $0.79 on June 3.

On May 23, other members of the Rigas family resigned their positions in management and the board of directors. The Rigas family also agreed to transfer $1 billion dollars in assets back to the company. Nevertheless, Adelphia filled for bankruptcy in June 2002 and operated subsequently under bankruptcy protection.

The SEC's charged Adelphia and the Rigas family with massive financial fraud on July 24, 2002. Its complaint alleged (1) understatement of debt, (2) overstatement of financial performance, and (3) extensive self-dealing, which are summarized from the SEC Press Release[3] and Complaint[4] documents, as follows:

1. Between 1999 and the end of 2001, the Rigas' Family (John, Timothy, Michael and James) with other executives, caused Adelphia to fraudulently exclude over $2 billion in its bank debt by systematically recording liabilities on the books of unconsolidated affiliates. Some of those operations where backed by the company's management with fictitious documents. False documents showed that Adelphia repaid debts while those debts were just transferred to related companies.

   From 1999 the company relied heavily upon commercial credit issuance of notes and access to equity markets. As of June 1st, 2002 Adelphia and its consolidated Subsidiaries owed $6.8 billion in credit facilities, $6.9 billion in senior or convertible notes, and $1.6 billion in convertible preferred stock. Certain

---

3. U.S. Securities and Exchange Commission, "SEC Charges Adelphia and Rigas Family With Massive Financial Fraud," *Press Release 2002-110,* July 24, 2002.

4. United States District Court, Southern District of New York, *Complaint: SEC against Adelphia Communications Corporation, John Rigas, Timothy J. Rigas, Michael J. Rigas, James P. Rigas, James R. Brown and Michael C. Mulcahey,* July 24, 2002.

Adelphia subsidiaries also issued separately notes of which $2.6 billion was outstanding on June 1st, 2002. The company's true liabilities increased from $4.4 billion in Q2 1999 to $20.4 billion in Q3 2001.

Funds obtained from borrowing and from a series of public offerings since 1999 were deposited and disbursed from a cash management subsidiary Adelphia CMS. This third company was used to set up schemes to transfer and hide debt in related companies (i.e. Special Purpose Entities).

2. In the same period, the Rigas Family with other executives caused Adelphia to regularly misstate press releases, including earnings reports. The company reported inflated figures for the number of cable subscribers, the extent of its cable plant, and Earnings Before Interest, Taxes, Depreciation and Amortization (EBITDA).

Specifically, the company overstated its number of customers by 142,000 by including in Basic Cable Subscribers 43,000 customers from unconsolidated subsidiaries; 39,000 Internet service customers; and 60,000 Home Security customers. Adelphia also included in these statistics, subscribers from the months after the quarter end, and false counts of new subscribers for affiliated companies.

Adelphia added to reported EBITDA management fees paid by the Rigas Family entities that owned cable operations. But, since Adelphia did not provide any services to earn those payments, the only purpose for recording them on Adelphia's books was to inflate the company's earnings.

Adelphia entered into agreements with suppliers of digital converter boxes, asking the suppliers for a $26 per box advance to market a new digital service. The money would be repaid later when the boxes were sold to customers. Adelphia recorded those payments (totaling $91 million) as income. The suppliers lost the advanced payments when the company filed for bankruptcy.

Adelphia also shifted expenses improperly to unconsolidated related entities to decrease the company's operating expenses.

3. From at least 1998, Adelphia used fraudulent misrepresentations and omissions of material facts to conceal self-dealing by the Rigas Family.

The Rigas Family used company funds to finance open stock purchases, purchase timber rights to land in Pennsylvania, construct a golf club for $12.8 million on a family property, pay off personal margin loans and other debts, and purchase luxury condominiums in Colorado, Mexico, and New York City.

The fraud continued even after Adelphia acknowledged, on March 27, the $2.3 billion excluded liabilities from its balance sheet. In the following months, the Rigas family diverted $174 million to pay personal margin loans.

Not only were the Rigas' among the first to face post-SOX justice for their financial frauds, John who was 77 when arrested, and his sons were among the first to endure the famous "perp walk"—to be hand-cuffed and marched to a waiting car in front of reporters who were only too glad to spread the embarrassing photos over the media immediately. The "perp walk" came to be dreaded by executives who faced charges for perpetrating financial crimes.

The SEC charges were not the only ones leveled against the Rigas family. In August 2004, Adelphia, their own company, sued them in a civil action for the return of $3.2 billion that the Family misappropriated. In the earlier SEC-sponsored criminal trial, the Family had argued that "any debt or funds used from the company were 'borrowed' not stolen, 'and the intended to full repay the amounts.'"[5] Adelphia had not received the funds nor had the Rigas' assumed the debt involved, so Adelphia sued the Rigas' to force them to keep their word.

This action was not surprising since Adelphia had shored up its governance processes after the Rigas' left. For example, new executives were appointed to remove members of the Rigas Family and related parties, and six of the seven members of the new board of directors were independent of Adelphia and Rigas family interests. The company developed

---

5. Marc Hopkins, "Rigas family owes Adelphia US$3.2 B: suit," *Financial Post*, August 24, 2004, FP8.

a new code of ethics, and changed its mission to:

We will leverage our historical strengths of customer focus, community involvement, and employee dedication; address issues that limit profitability and growth; and act with a sense of urgency, accountability and teamwork to emerge from bankruptcy and to succeed as a broadband industry leader. We will develop a reputation as a company with outstanding corporate governance.

In November 2002, Adelphia sued its former auditor, Deloitte & Touche (D&T), accusing D&T of professional negligence, breach of contract, fraud, and other wrongful conduct "for failing to spot the problems that brought the company down. . . . For its part, Deloitte said it was the victim of deception just as much as Adelphia's shareholders, and that it would be able to answer any accusations more fully once it had examined the lawsuit. It also said that it would seek damages from whichever members of Adelphia's management proved to be complicit in any wrongdoing. At the moment, [Adelphia's] bankruptcy protects it from such action, however."[6]

Adelphia's bondholders also launched a US$5 billion lawsuit in July 2003 against 450 banks and other financial institutions that had "fuelled the massive fraud by lending billions of dollars to the company's founders."[7] The lawsuit stated: "'This action seeks to redress defendant's knowing participation, substantial assistance and complicity in one of the most serious cases of systematic corporate looting and breach of fiduciary duty in American history' . . . 'Aware of the obvious red flags, many of the co-borrowing lenders merely rubber-stamped the co-borrowing facilities so that their affiliated investment banks could earn hundreds of millions of dollars in fees.'"[8] While the Rigas family was busy using Adelphia as their own piggy bank, it appears they were not alone.

Questions

1. What breaches of fiduciary duty does the Adelphia case raise?

2. Why do you think the Rigas family thought they could get away with using Adelphia as their own piggy bank?

3. What allowed the Rigas family to get away with their fraudulent behavior for so long?

4. What concerns should have been raised in the following areas of risk assessment in Adelphia's control environment: integrity and ethics, commitment, Audit Committee participation, management philosophy, structure, and authority?

5. What concerns should have been raised in the following areas of risk assessment in Adelphia's strategy: changes in operating environment, new people and systems, growth, technology, new business, restructurings, and foreign operations?

6. What is your opinion on the importance of independence in corporate governance? What are the most recent rules on corporate governance for public firms?

7. Discuss which changes could be done to the Adelphia's control system and corporate governance structure to mitigate the risk of accounting fraud in future years.

8. What is the auditor's responsibility in case of fraud?

9. What is the proper audit procedure to ensure:

    a. completeness of liabilities in the financial statements?

    b. that all the related parties have been included or disclosed in the consolidated financial statements?

10. Do you think analytical procedures would aid the detection of fraud? What is the responsibility of the auditor applying analytical procedures?

11. What should the 450 lending institutions have done to protect themselves from subsequent lawsuit?

---

6. "Cable flop sues former auditor," *BBC News,* November 7, 2002, at http://news.bbc.co.uk/l/hi/business/2415145.stm

7. Keith Kalawsky, "US$5B Lawsuit Names Big Five," *Financial Post,* July 8, 2003, FP3.

8. Ibid.

References

BBC News. "Adelphia," BBC News Archive. January 2002 to December 2002. http://www.bbcnews.com.

Grover, Ronald. "Adelphia's Fall Will Bruise a Crowd." *Businessweek,* July 8, 2002. http://www.businessweek.commagazine/content/02_27/b3790025.htm.

The *New York Times.* "Adelphia," NY Times News Archive. January 2002 to December 2002. http://www.nytimes.com.

Adelphia website. http://www.adelphia.com.

U.S. Securities and Exchange Commission. *SEC Press Release 2002–110.* http://www.sec.gov/news/press.

U.S. Securities and Exchange Commission. *SEC Complaint 17627.* http://www.sec.gov/litigation/complaints.

Ethics Case | ## *Tyco—Looting Executive Style*

Dennis Kozlowski was a dominant, larger-than-life CEO of Tyco International, Ltd., a multibillion dollar company whose shares are still traded on the New York Stock Exchange (Symbol: TYC). His stature was huge and his appetite for excess knew no bounds. Noted author Tom Wolfe, who wrote *Bonfire of the Vanities,* that profiled such men, says that "If you feel you are a master of the universe, then a lot of rules just don't apply,"[1] and this quote seems to apply well to Kozlowski.

Kozlowski was rolling along—often using company money—having lavish parties, planes, cars, enjoying multiple homes with fittings such as a $6,000 shower curtain and a $15,000 umbrella stand, a yacht, and an impressive art collection. It was his interest in art that triggered the first investigation, in January 2002, by New York State officials who asked about the sales tax on several multi-million dollar paintings[2]. Kozlowski had evaded the payment of sales tax on them, and was subsequently first charged in a New York court.

For Dennis, this was most unfortunate because upon conviction, he would serve time in the New York prison system instead of a federal prison in which white collar criminals often are assigned to facilities known as "Club Feds", or "Camp Cupcake", for women like Martha Stewart. The New York prison system is very harsh. According to former New York prosecutor, David Gourevitch, "The fed system is unpleasant, but at least you're physically safe there . . . In the state system, nobody would say you are physically safe."[3] For Kozlowski and his associate Mark Swartz, his Tyco CFO, who faced up to 30 years in prison, this prospect was surely daunting.

On the other hand, Kozlowski had certainly enjoyed high living, so many observers would argue he got what he deserved. Take the $2 million dollar 40th birthday party for his new wife on the Mediterranean island of Sardinia, more than half of which was paid for by Tyco. Jurors were shown an edited 21-minute version of a 4-hour videotape covering the whole week with 75 guests. The short version did not show inflammatory scenes such as "an anatomically correct ice sculpture of Michelangelo's David spurting vodka"[4], scantly clad and unclad dancers, and so on. Music was provided

---

1. Brian Ross, "Greed on Wall Street: The Rise and Fall of Dennis Kozlowski," *ABC News,* November 11, 2005. Retrieved from http://abcnews.go.com/2020/story? id=1305010 on 21/3/2006.
2. Ibid.
3. Krysten Crawford, "For Kozlowski, an especially grim future," *CNNMoney,* June 21, 2005. Retrieved from http://money.cnn.com/2005/06/21/news/newsmakers/prisons_state/index.htm on June 6, 2005.
4. Samuel Maull of Associated Press, "Tyco jurors view birthday video," *Globe and Mail,* October 29, 2003, B7.

by Jimmy Buffet and his group at a cost of $250,000, and a rock band at a cost of $20,000.[5] No wonder Kozlowski was charged with looting the company.

The U.S. Securities and Exchange Commission (SEC) also took an interest and charges for civil fraud regard in looting of the company and other misdeeds were laid on September 12, 2002. By the time of the trial in October 2003, Tyco was estimated to have about 270,000 employees and $36 billion in annual revenue derived from many sources, including electronic and medical supplies, and the ADT home security business.[6] A full list of the charges against Kozlowski and CFO Mark Swartz as well against chief legal officer Mark Belnick is outlined in the SEC Complaint, which is available at http://www.sec.gov/litigation/complaints/complr17722.htm.

An abbreviated version of the improper conduct of management was published by Tyco in their SEC 8-K information filing with the SEC on September 17, 2002. The Tyco Press Release[7] states:

> The Company said that this pattern of improper and illegal activity occurred for at least five years prior to June 3, 2002, when former CEO L. Dennis Kozlowski resigned, and that this activity was concealed from the Board and its relevant committees. The nature of such conduct, to the extent it is now known by Tyco, is described in the filing. The areas covered in this filing include:
>
> - **Relocation Programs,** under which certain executive officers, including Mr. Kozlowski, former CFO Mark Swartz and former Chief Corporate Counsel Mark Belnick used the Company's relocation program to take non-qualifying interest-free loans and unauthorized benefits that were not generally available to all salaried employees affected by relocations. Under the program,

> Mr. Kozlowski improperly borrowed approximately $61,690,628 in non-qualifying relocation loans to purchase real estate and other properties, Mr. Swartz borrowed approximately $33,097,925 and Mr. Belnick borrowed approximately $14,635,597.
>
> - **The "TyCom Bonus" Misappropriation,** in which Mr. Kozlowski caused Tyco to pay a special, unapproved bonus to 51 employees who had relocation loans with the Company. The bonus was calculated to forgive the relocation loans of 51 executives and employees, totaling $56,415,037, and to pay compensation sufficient to discharge all of the tax liability due as a result of the forgiveness of those loans. This action was purportedly related to the successful completion of the TyCom Initial Public Offering. The total gross wages paid by the Company in this mortgage forgiveness program were $95,962,000, of which amount Mr. Kozlowski received $32,976,000 and Mr. Swartz received $16,611,000. These benefits were not approved by, or disclosed to, the Compensation Committee or the Board of Directors. However, the employees who received these bonuses were led by Mr. Kozlowski to believe that they were part of a Board-approved program.
>
> - **The "ADT Automotive Bonus" Misappropriations,** in which Mr. Kozlowski authorized Tyco to pay cash, award restricted shares of Tyco common stock, and purportedly forgive additional loans and make related tax payments to approximately 17 Tyco officers and employees—even though the relocation loans of each of these 17 persons had already been paid in full. Mr. Kozlowski and Mr. Swartz received cash bonuses, restricted shares and "relocation"

---

5. Ibid.
6. Ibid.
7. Tyco Press Release: Tyco files Form 8-K Report on Improper Conduct of Former Management at http://www.tyco.com/livesite/Page/Tyco/Who+We+Are/Press+Center/Press+Releases+Details/??&DCRID=1185862359. Retrieved on March 22, 2006.

benefits valued approximately $25,566,610 and $12,844,632 respectively. These benefits were not approved by or disclosed to the Compensation Committee or the Board of Directors. As with the TyCom unauthorized bonus, other senior executives were misled by Mr. Kozlowski to believe that the ADT Automotive award of restricted shares was a Board-approved program.

- **The Key Employee Loan (KEL) Program,** in which certain executive officers borrowed money for purposes other than the payment of taxes due upon the vesting of restricted shares, or borrowed in excess of the maximum amount they were permitted under the program. Mr. Kozlowski was, by a large margin, the greatest abuser of this program. By the end of 2001, Mr. Kozlowski had taken over 200 KEL loans—some for millions of dollars and some as small as $100—and his total borrowings over that time exceeded $250 million. Approximately 90% of Mr. Kozlowski's KEL loans were non-program loans, which he used to fund his personal lifestyle, including speculating in real estate, acquisition of antiques and furnishings for his properties (including properties purchased with unauthorized "relocation loans") and the purchase and maintenance of his yacht. Mr. Swartz also borrowed millions in non-program loans. Like Mr. Kozlowski, Mr. Swartz used those unauthorized loans to purchase, develop and speculate in real estate; to fund investments in various business ventures and partnerships; and for miscellaneous personal uses having nothing to do with the ownership of Tyco stock. Tyco is currently evaluating the KEL program in light of recent enactment of a prohibition upon loans by public companies to directors and executive officers.

- **Attempted Unauthorized Credits to Key Employee Loan Accounts,** in which Mr. Kozlowski and Mr. Swartz attempted to erase an outstanding $25 million KEL indebtedness to Mr. Kozlowski and $12.5 million in KEL indebtedness to Mr. Swartz without the knowledge or approval of the Compensation Committee. Mr. Kozlowski, through his attorneys, has acknowledged to Tyco that he sought no approvals for these credits and that, if they were entered as a credit to his KEL account, it was done so improperly, and that he is therefore obligated to repay these amounts to Tyco. Mr. Swartz has also agreed to repay his forgiven indebtedness with interest and has repaid most of the amounts. Tyco has reversed these entries and a related unauthorized entry, thereby increasing the outstanding balances for the key employee loan accounts of each individual involved.

- **Executive Compensation,** including authorized and unauthorized compensation to Mr. Belnick, which totaled $34,331,679 for the years 1999–2001. Belnick's compensation resulted from a secret agreement that tied Mr. Belnick's compensation to Mr. Kozlowski's compensation, thereby giving Mr. Belnick an undisclosed incentive to aid and facilitate Mr. Kozlowski's improper diversion of Company funds to Mr. Kozlowski's personal benefit. The undisclosed terms of Messrs. Kozlowski's and Belnick's agreement were incorporated in a letter dated August 19, 1998 and signed by Mr. Kozlowski. Mr. Kozlowski and Mr. Belnick agreed that the letter would not be disclosed to the Tyco Board, the Board's Compensation Committee or the Tyco Human Resources department. Mr. Belnick did, however, keep a copy of the undisclosed agreement in his personal office.

- **Perquisites** in excess of $50,000 per year for Mr. Kozlowski and Mr. Swartz. These perquisites were required to be reported in a proxy to the extent they exceeded $50,000. However, these amounts were not reported in the proxy because Mr. Kozlowski and Mr. Swartz represented that they would reimburse the Company for amounts in excess of

$50,000. However, in most cases Messrs. Kozlowski and Swartz failed to reimburse the Company for all perquisites in excess of $50,000. Mr. Kozlowski also caused Tyco to make available to him various properties that the Company owned for his purported business use. Tyco has now discovered that Mr. Kozlowski periodically made personal use of properties in North Hampton, NH, Boca Raton, FL, New York City and New Castle, NH.

- **Self-Dealing Transactions and Other Misuses of Corporate Trust,** including Tyco properties purchased by or from Mr. Kozlowski without disclosure to or authorization by the Compensation Committee. For example, Mr. Kozlowski and others caused a Tyco subsidiary to purchase property in Rye, New Hampshire from Mr. Kozlowski on July 6, 2000 for $4,500,000. After an appraisal in March 2002 valued the property at $1,500,000, Tyco wrote down the carrying value of the property to the appraised value and charged Mr. Kozlowski's $3,049,576 overpayment to expense. Mr. Kozlowski also used millions of dollars of Company funds to pay for his other personal interests and activities, including a $700,000 investment in the film "Endurance"; more than $1 million for an extravagant birthday party celebration for his wife in Sardinia; over $1 million in undocumented business expenses, including a private venture; jewelry, clothing, flowers, club membership dues and wine; and an undocumented $110,000 charge for the purported corporate use of Mr. Kozlowski's personal yacht, "Endeavour." Mr. Kozlowski also tampered with evidence under subpoena, purchased a New

York City apartment at its depreciated rather than its market value, and took personal credit for at least $43 million in donations from Tyco to charitable organizations.

Not surprisingly, Tyco announced that it had launched a civil lawsuit against Kozlowski for breach of fiduciary duties, fraud and other wrongful conduct, and other lawsuits against executives considered complicit in these schemes. This brings to three the major suits faced by Kozlowski launched by New York, the SEC and Tyco, but does not include class action suits by aggrieved investors. Tyco also began to replace its board members.

On June 17, 2005, 58-year old Kozlowski and 44-year old Swartz were each convicted of 22 of 23 counts including grand larceny, conspiracy, securities fraud and eight of nine counts of falsifying business records.[8] On September 21, 2005, Kozlowski and Swartz were sentenced to up to 25 years in prison. Many observers thought that was about right, but others, including business leaders thought it to be too much. In comparison, it was pointed out that some violent crimes like rape and manslaughter carried a sentence of 20 years in jail.[9]

In a related announcement, the SEC and the lead auditor of Tyco, Richard Scalzo a partner with PricewaterhouseCoopers (PwC) agreed that Scalzo was permanently barred from preparing financial statements of publicly traded companies. The Tyco account was reportedly worth $100 million per year to PwC, and they retained the audit. The SEC found that Scalzo "was 'reckless' and stood idle as the conglomerates leading figures manipulated accounting entries to conceal their lavish spending and pay."[10]

8. Chad Bray, Dow Jones Newswires, "Tyco's ousted top officers face fines and jail terms," *Toronto Star,* June 18, 2005, D1, D9.
9. Daniel Kadlec, "Does Kozlowski's Sentence fit the Crime?," *Time:* Business and Technology, September 20, 2005 at http://www.time.com/time/business/printout/0,8816,1106932,00.html. Retrieved March 22, 2006.
10. Tim McLaughlin, Reuters, "Tyco auditor barred for life by regulator," *Toronto Star,* August 14, 2005, D3.

Questions

1. The pattern of illegal and improper conduct described above took place for at least 5 years prior to June 3, 2002. What red flags or governance mechanisms should have alerted the following people to this pattern:

   a. Tyco management accountants?

   b. Tyco internal auditors?

   c. Tyco external auditors?

   d. Tyco board of directors?

2. Identify and discuss the most important weaknesses in Tyco's:

   a. internal controls, and

   b. governance systems.

3. Would a post-Sarbanes-Oxley Act whistle-blowing program to the Audit Committee of the board have eliminated the improper and illegal actions? Why or why not?

4. If you have been a professional accountant employed by Tyco during this time, and you wanted to blow the whistle, who would you have gone to with your story?

5. Why were so many Tyco employees willing to go along quietly with the looting by senior executives?

6. How many years in jail do you think Kozlowski should have received for his white-collar crimes?

Ethics Case

Nortel Networks Audit Committee Was In The Dark

By the late 1990s, Nortel Networks Corporation, headquartered in Brampton, Ontario, Canada, was one of the giants of the telecommunications industry. Seventy-five percent of North America's Internet traffic was carried by Nortel equipment,[1] which was manufactured by 73,000 employees around the world[2]. The company's shares were listed on both the New York Stock Exchange (NYSE) and the Toronto Stock Exchange (TSE). By July 2000, the company had issued over 3.8 billion shares worth C$473.1 billion in market capitalization at a peak price of C$124.50. So dominant was Nortel that it accounted for more than one-third the value of the S & P/TSE 300 Composite Index.[3]

Then the infamous dot-com bubble burst, and by September 2002, Nortel stock closed at C$0.63.[4] John Roth, named Canada's "business leader of the year" in 2000, indicated that he would step down as CEO in April 2001.[5] This may have been partly because he had not foreseen a coming slump in sales and as a result appeared to have misled the investing public. Until Roth's departure, Nortel was considered to have had an exemplary corporate culture and code of conduct.

Frank Dunn, a CMA who had been head of public affairs and then CFO, was named as replacement CEO in November 2001. He led Nortel through a radical restructuring that saw a reduction in its workforce by 50 percent to 45,000 in 2001 and a further 10,000 in 2002. Apparently as a result, Nortel's financial picture showed a profit of US$54 million in the first quarter of fiscal 2003, which ended on March 31, 2003. Profits were also reported in the second quarter.

However, on October 23, 2003, when Nortel reported profits in the third quarter, restatements affecting 2000, 2001, and 2002 financial statements were also announced. Concern over these restatements, delays in financial reports, and concerns over bonuses

---

1. *CBC.CA News,* "Nortel: Canada's Tech Giant," May 2, 2005.
2. *CBC.CA News,* "Northern Telecom buys American firm," Nov. 13, 1998.
3. *CBC.CA News,* "Nortel: The wild ride of Canada's most watched stack," May 2, 2005.
4. Ibid.
5. Nortel News Release, "Nortel Networks announces Frank Dunn as President and CEO," October 2, 2001, http://www.nortelnetworks.com/corporate/news/newsreleases/2001d/10_02_01_ceo.html.

paid to executives triggered the Audit Committee of Nortel Networks Corporation to authorize an independent review (IR) of the company's financial affairs by the Washington, D.C., law firm of Wilmer Cutler Pickering Hale and Dorr LLP.

The IR findings resulted in the need for a second restatement of Nortel's financial statements and the termination for cause of ten senior employees, including the CEO, CFO, and controller. All were asked to repay bonuses received. A further twelve senior employees were required to repay bonuses received and did so. They were not terminated.

Summary of Findings and of Recommended Remedial Measures of the Independent Review[6]

The following excerpts provide an overview of the IR and its findings:

In late October 2003, Nortel Networks Corporation ("Nortel" or the "Company") announced that it intended to restate approximately $900M of liabilities carried on its previously reported balance sheet as of June 30, 2003, following a comprehensive internal review of these liabilities ("First Restatement"). The Company stated that the principal effects of the restatement would be a reduction in previously reported net losses for 2000, 2001, and 2002 and an increase in shareholders' equity and net assets previously reported on its balance sheet. Concurrent with this announcement, the Audit Committees of the Boards of Directors of Nortel Networks Corporation and Nortel Networks Limited (collectively, the "Audit Committee" and the "Board of Directors" or "Board," respectively) initiated an independent review of the facts and circumstances leading to the First Restatement. The Audit Committee wanted to gain a full understanding of the events that caused significant excess liabilities to be maintained on the balance sheet that needed to be

restated, and to recommend that the Board of Directors adopt, and direct management to implement, necessary remedial measures to address personnel, controls, compliance, and discipline. The Audit Committee engaged Wilmer Cutler Pickering Hale and Dorr LLP ("WCPHD") to advise it in connection with its independent review. Because of the significant accounting issues involved in the inquiry, WCPHD retained Huron Consulting Services LLC ("Huron") to provide expert accounting assistance. Huron has been involved in all phases of WCPHD's work.

The investigation necessarily focused on the financial picture of the Company at the time that decisions were made and actions were taken regarding provisioning activity. Because of significant changes to financial results reflected in the Second Restatement, the restated financial results differ from the historical results that formed the backdrop for this inquiry.

In summary, former corporate management (now terminated for cause) and former finance management (now terminated for cause) in the Company's finance organization endorsed, and employees carried out, accounting practices relating to the recording and release of provisions that were not in compliance with U.S. generally accepted accounting principles ("U.S. GAAP") in at least four quarters, including the third and fourth quarters of 2002 and the first and second quarters of 2003. In three of those four quarters—when Nortel was at, or close to, break even—these practices were undertaken to meet internally imposed pro-forma earnings before taxes ("EBT") targets. While the dollar value of most of the individual provisions was relatively small, the aggregate value of the provisions made the difference between a profit and a reported loss, on a pro forma basis, in the fourth quarter of 2002 and the difference between a loss and a reported profit, on a pro forma basis, in the first and

6. Released January 11, 2005, as part of the MD&A to the 2003 Annual Report. This can also be found at http://www.nortelnetworks.com/corporate/news/newsreleases/collateral/independent_review_summary.pdf.

second quarters of 2003. This conduct caused Nortel to report a loss in the fourth quarter of 2002 and to pay no employee bonuses, and to achieve and maintain profitability in the first and second quarters of 2003, which, in turn, caused it to pay bonuses to all Nortel employees and significant bonuses to senior management under bonus plans tied to a pro forma profitability metric.

The failure to follow U.S. GAAP with respect to provisioning can be understood in light of the management, organizational structure, and internal controls that characterized Nortel's finance organization. These characteristics, discussed below, include:

▌ Management "tone at the top" that conveyed the strong leadership message that earnings targets could be met through application of accounting practices that finance managers knew or ought to have known were not in compliance with U.S. GAAP and that questioning these practices was not acceptable;

▌ Lack of technical accounting expertise which fostered accounting practices not in compliance with U.S. GAAP;

▌ Weak or ineffective internal controls which, in turn, provided little or no check on inaccurate financial reporting;

▌ Operation of a complicated "matrix" structure which contributed to a lack of clear responsibility and accountability by business units and by regions; and

▌ Lack of integration between the business units and corporate management that led to a lack of transparency regarding provisioning activity to achieve internal EBT targets.

Nortel posted significant losses in 2001 and 2002 and downsized its work force by nearly two-thirds. The remaining employees were asked to undertake significant additional responsibilities with no increase in pay and no bonuses. The Company's former senior corporate management asserted, at the start of the inquiry, that the Company's downturn, and concomitant downsizing of operations and workforce,

led to a loss of documentation and a decline in financial discipline. Those factors, in their view, were primarily responsible for the significant excess provisions on the balance sheet as of June 30, 2003, which resulted in the First Restatement. While that downturn surely played a part in the circumstances leading to the First Restatement, the root causes ran far deeper.

When Frank Dunn became CFO in 1999, and then CEO in 2001, he drove senior management in his finance organization to achieve EBT targets that he set with his senior management team. The provisioning practices adopted by Dunn and other finance employees to achieve internal EBT targets were not in compliance with U.S. GAAP, particularly Statement of Financial Accounting Standards Number 5 ("SFAS 5"). SFAS 5, which governs accounting for contingencies, requires, among other things, a probability analysis for each risk before a provision can be recorded. It also requires that a triggering event— such as resolution of the exposure or a change in estimate—occur in the quarter to warrant the release of a provision. Dunn and other finance employees recognized that provisioning activity—how much to reserve for a particular exposure and when that reserve should be released—inherently involved application of significant judgment under U.S. GAAP. Dunn and others stretched the judgment inherent in the provisioning process to create a flexible tool to achieve EBT targets. They viewed provisioning as "a gray area." They became comfortable with the concept that the value of a provision could be reasonably set at virtually any number within a wide range and that a provision release could be justified in a number of quarters after the quarter in which the exposure, which formed the basis for the provision, was resolved. Dunn and others exercised their judgment strategically to achieve EBT targets.

Third quarter, 2002. At the direction of then-CFO Doug Beatty, a company-wide analysis of accrued liabilities on the balance sheet was launched in early August 2002. The CFO and the Controller,

Michael Gollogly, learned that this analysis showed approximately $303M in provisions that were no longer required and were available for release. The CFO and the Controller, each a corporate officer, knew, or ought to have known, that excess provisions, if retained on the balance sheet, would cause the Company's financial statements to be inaccurate and that U.S. GAAP would have required either that such provisions be released in that period and properly disclosed, or that prior period financial statements be restated. Instead, they permitted finance employees in the business units and in the regions to release excess accruals into income over the following several quarters. They acted in contravention of U.S. GAAP by failing to correct the Company's financial statements to account for the significant excess accrued liabilities. Neither the CFO nor the Controller advised the Audit Committee and/or the Board of Directors that significant excess provisions on the balance sheet had been identified and that the Company's financial statements might be inaccurate, nor did either suggest such information should be disclosed in the Company's financial statements.

As a result of this company-wide review, senior finance employees recognized that their respective business unit or region had excess provisions on Nortel's balance sheet, and directed other finance employees to track these excess provisions. Nortel finance employees had their own distinct term for a provision on the balance sheet that was no longer needed—it was "hard." Each business unit developed, in varying levels of detail and over varying periods of time, internal "hardness" schedules that identified provisions that were no longer required and were available for release. Finance employees treated provisions identified on these schedules as a pool from which releases could be made to "close the gap" between actual EBT and EBT targets in subsequent quarters.

Fourth quarter, 2002. By mid-2002, employees throughout the Company were being recruited by other companies

and morale was low. Corporate management sought to retain these employees but recognized that other public companies had come under criticism for awarding "stay" bonuses in the face of enormous losses. At management's recommendation, the Board determined to reward employees with bonuses under bonus plans tied to profitability. One plan, the Return to Profitability ("RTP") bonus, contemplated a one-time bonus payment to every employee, save 43 top executives, in the first quarter in which the Company achieved pro forma profitability. The 43 executives were eligible to receive 20% of their share of the RTP bonus in the first quarter in which the Company attained profitability, 40% after the second consecutive quarter of cumulative profitability, and the remaining 40% upon four quarters of cumulative profitability. In order for the RTP bonuses to be paid, pro forma profits had to exceed, by at least one dollar, the total cost of the bonus for that quarter. Another plan, the Restricted Stock Unit ("RSU") plan, made a significant number of share units available for award by the Board to the same 43 executives in four installments tied to profitability milestones. Once a milestone was met, the Board had discretion whether to make the award.

Through the first three quarters of 2002, Nortel experienced significant losses, and management reported to the Board that it expected losses would continue in the fourth quarter. After the initial results for the business units and regions were consolidated, they showed that Nortel unexpectedly would achieve pro forma profitability in the fourth quarter. Frank Dunn, who had been promoted to CEO in 2001, understood that profitability had been attained from an operational standpoint but determined that it was unwise to report profitability and pay bonuses in the fourth quarter because performance for the rest of the year had been poor. He determined that provisions should be taken to cause a loss for the quarter. Over a two day period late in the closing process, the CFO and the Controller worked with employees in the finance organizations in the business units, the regions, and in global operations, to identify and record additional provisions totaling more than $175 million. All of these provisions were recorded "top-side"—that is, by employees in the office of the Controller based on information provided by the business units, regions and global operations—because of the late date in the closing process on which they were made. Nortel's results for the fourth quarter of 2002 turned from an unexpected profit into the loss previously forecasted by management to the Board of Directors. Neither the CEO, the CFO, nor the Controller advised the Audit Committee and/or the Board of Directors of this concerted provisioning activity to improperly turn a profit into a loss. Nortel has since determined that many of these provisions were not recorded in compliance with U.S. GAAP, and has reversed those provisions in the Second Restatement. The loss then reported by Nortel in the fourth quarter meant that no employee bonuses were paid for that quarter.

First quarter, 2003. While Nortel had announced publicly that it expected to achieve pro forma profitability in the second quarter of 2003, Dunn told a number of employees that he intended to achieve profitability one quarter earlier, and he established internal EBT targets for each business unit and for corporate to reach that goal. At Dunn's direction, "roadmaps" were developed to show how the targets could be achieved. These roadmaps made clear that the internal EBT targets for the quarter could only be met through release from the balance sheet of excess provisions that lacked an accounting trigger in the quarter. At the request of finance management in each business unit, finance employees identified excess, or "hard," provisions from the balance sheet, and, together, they determined which provisions to release to close the gap and meet the internal EBT targets. That release activity was supplemented by releases, directed by the CFO and by the Controller, of excess corporate provisions that had been identified in the third quarter

of 2002 as available for release. Releases of provisions by corporate and by each business unit and region, including excess provisions, totaling $361M, enabled Nortel to show a consolidated pro forma profit in the first quarter, notwithstanding that its operations were running at a loss. The Finance Vice Presidents of the business units and two of the three regions, the Asia Controller, the CFO, the Controller, and the CEO knew, or ought to have known, that U.S. GAAP did not permit the release, without proper justification, of excess provisions into the income statement. Nortel has since determined that many of these releases in this quarter were not in accordance with U.S. GAAP, and has reversed those releases in the First and Second Restatements and restated the releases into proper quarters. When presenting the preliminary results for the quarter to the Audit Committee, the Controller inaccurately represented that the vast majority of these releases were "business as usual" and in compliance with U.S. GAAP, and that the remaining releases were one time, non-recurring events and in compliance with U.S. GAAP. Further, the CFO and the Controller failed to advise the Audit Committee and/or the Board of Directors that release of excess corporate provisions was required to achieve profitability and make up for the shortfall in operational results; that such releases were needed to cover the cost of the bonus compensation; that no event in the quarter triggered the releases (as required by U.S. GAAP); that the releases implicated Staff Accounting Bulletin 99 (relating to materiality) because they turned a loss for the quarter into a profit; and that they retained a significant amount of excess provisions on the balance sheet to be used, when needed, in a subsequent quarter. In separate executive sessions held by the Audit Committee with the CFO and the Controller, neither the CFO nor the Controller raised quality of earnings issues nor questioned the payment of the RTP bonus. Based on management's representations, the Audit Committee approved the quarterly results, and the Board approved the award of the RTP bonus.

Second quarter, 2003. Seeking to continue to show profitability in the second quarter and meet the first RSU milestone and the second tranche of the RTP bonus, senior corporate management developed internal EBT targets to achieve pro forma profitability. As was the case in the first quarter, it became clear during the quarter that operational results would be a loss. At the request of finance management in each business unit, finance employees again identified "hard" provisions from the balance sheet, and, together, they determined which provisions to release to close the gap and achieve the internal EBT targets. Nortel has since determined that many of these releases were not in accordance with U.S. GAAP, and has reversed those releases in the First and Second Restatements and restated the releases into proper quarters. In both the first and second quarters of 2003, the dollar value of many individual releases was relatively small, but the aggregate value of the releases made the difference between a pro forma loss and profit in each quarter.

The CEO, the CFO and the Controller failed to advise the Audit Committee or the Board of Directors that operations of the business units were running at a loss during the second quarter and that the validity of many of the numerous provision releases, totaling more than $370 million, could be questionable. Based on management's representations, the Audit Committee approved the quarterly results, and the Board approved payment of the second tranche of the RTP bonus and awarded restricted stock under the RSU plan.

Third and fourth quarters, 2003. In light of concerns raised by the inappropriate accounting judgments outlined above, the Audit Committee expanded its investigation to determine whether excess provisions were released to meet internal EBT targets in each of these two quarters. No evidence emerged to suggest an intent to release provisions strategically in those quarters to meet EBT targets. Given the significant volume of provision releases in these two quarters, the Audit Committee

directed management to review provision releases, down to a low threshold, using the same methods used to evaluate the releases made in the first half of the year. This review has resulted in additional adjustments for these quarters, which are reflected in the Second Restatement.

Governing Principles for Remedial Measures

The Audit Committee asked WCPHD to recommend governing principles, based on its independent inquiry, to prevent recurrence of the inappropriate accounting conduct, to rebuild a finance environment based on transparency and integrity, and to ensure sound financial reporting and comprehensive disclosure. The recommendations developed by WCPHD and provided to the Audit Committee were directed at:

▌ Establishing standards of conduct to be enforced through appropriate discipline;

▌ Infusing strong technical skills and experience into the finance organization;

▌ Requiring comprehensive, on-going training on increasingly complex accounting standards;

▌ Strengthening and improving internal controls and processes;

▌ Establishing a compliance program throughout the Company which is appropriately staffed and funded;

▌ Requiring management to provide clear and concise information, in a timely manner, to the Board to facilitate its decision-making; and

▌ Implementing an information technology platform that improves the reliability of financial reporting and reduces the opportunities for manipulation of results.

These recommendations were grouped into three categories—people, processes and technology . . . [which] [a]fter thorough consideration, the Audit Committee has recommended and the Board of Directors has approved, adoption of each . . .

In summary form, these recommendations included:

People:

- Creation of an effective "tone at the top" through effective policies, procedures and an awareness and commitment to fiduciary duty, accountability and accuracy, particularly in financial reporting.

- Termination for cause of the CEO, CFO, Controller and seven additional senior officers.

- Return of RTP and RSU bonus payments

- Clarification through training and other means (appropriate experience) that failure to adhere to U.S. GAAP will not be tolerated.

- External recruiting of individuals with strong accounting and reporting skills and expertise, and proven records of integrity and ethical behavior, particularly in key finance positions.

- Enhancement and bolstering of often by-passed internal "technical accounting group."

- Review and improve the training function. Clarify through training the accounting issues that lead to restatement, confirm knowledge and understanding of the company code, and secure sign-offs testifying to reading and adherence. Introduce ongoing training requirements.

Processes:

- Remedial improvements to the control structure to permit sound corporate oversight—internal controls noted included: financial policies, organizational structure, systems, processes, employees, leadership and culture focused to foster accurate financial reporting and disclosure in a timely manner.

- Reexamination of the matrix structure, and the specification of key responsibility for liability provisions that has been unclear.

- Confirmation of the role of the Controller and the control structure—who should have the sole authority to release liability provisions—and the development of transparency of reporting standards.

- Reexamination and rewriting of Nortel's accounting policies.

- Strengthen internal audit function and standards to provide a check on the integrity of financial reporting.

- Recruitment of a Chief Ethics and Compliance Officer; active, overt commitment to the new Nortel Code of Conduct; and the direction of management to reinforce and enhance the compliance program carrying this message to all employees.

- The Board and Audit Committee should regularly review the activities of the compliance officer, and the related policies and performance involved.

- The Board is to receive all necessary information for adequate review of policies and activities in a timely manner. Reports should be received from more than just the CFO and meetings should be included with the chief operations and finance employees for each business unit.

Technology

- The announced installation of a SAP information technology platform should be implemented such that the necessary and needed control elements are incorporated.

Board of Directors and Audit Committee

Guylaine Saucier, who sat on the board and its Audit Committee, has since stated that "directors were shocked to learn after an internal review in 2004"[7] of the alleged manipulations that triggered the RTP bonus. She went on to say:

> "What was the board's reaction? First of all, it's emotional. You feel betrayed," Ms. Saucier said. "You trusted your management . . ."
>
> Since then, Ms. Saucier said she has reflected on how a board can scrutinize a CEO to decide whether he or she has the right standards for the job, but said it is difficult because it comes down to many small elements that occur outside the boardroom.

---

7. Janet McFarland, "Ex-Nortel director didn't see it coming," *Globe and Mail,* November 15, 2005.

"If the board had known that Frank Dunn was building a $12-million house for himself while we were letting go 60,000 people, would that be an element in our overall judgment? These are anecdotes. It's very difficult to say somebody is ethical or unethical."

Ms. Saucier also rejected the criticism that the company's compensation plan created too much temptation for manipulation. She said most companies have bonuses based on performance.

"It depends on the people. If you have people with good ethical values, you won't have any problems having a performance bonus."

She said she has begun to question whether chief financial officers should be paid bonuses based on corporate performance, given that they are responsible for preparing financial statements.[8]

The directors did not bail out on Nortel. They hired a former U.S. Admiral and member of the Joint Chiefs of Staff, Bill Owens, to be the new CEO and preside over the recovery of their company. This process was not without challenges since the directors were sued by aggrieved shareholders and by the company's insurer, Chubb Insurance Co. Chubb wanted to rescind $40 million insurance coverage for the legal costs of defending Nortel and 20 of its officials because Nortel's CEO (Frank Dunn), CFO (Douglas Beatty), and Controller (Michael Gollogly) "made material misrepresentations with stock market regulators with the intent to deceive Chubb . . .".[9]

One of the new hires, as Chief Ethics and Compliance Officer, was Susan E. Shepard, a former Commissioner for the New York State Ethics Commission and earlier, Assistant U.S. District Attorney for the Eastern District of New York. Interestingly, the company announced on January 13, 2005, that, "Ms. Shepard will receive a base salary of U.S.$375,000 (per annum) and will be eligible for a target annual bonus of 60% of base salary under the annual bonus plan of NNL (known as the SUCCESS Incentive Plan), based on the generally applicable performance criteria under such plan . . . ."[10]

"Susan Shepard is not the first Nortel ethics guru. That distinction belongs to Megan Barry, who served as Nortel's senior ethics advisor between 1994 and 1999."[11] As Megan noted, Nortel was once a world leader in ethics. "By the time she left, however, Nortel wasn't really a trailblazer in ethics anymore. When John Roth took over as CEO in 1997, her department grew increasingly invisible within the organization. "When the senior leadership changed, you definitely saw a de-emphasis of ethics," she says. "Roth's legacy is what Nortel has to deal with today."[12]

On February 8, 2006, Nortel announced that it had settled two shareholder lawsuits in relation to this accounting scandal for a maximum total of US$2.47 billion.[13]

Questions

1. Why would Nortel Networks, a Canadian company, hire a U.S. law firm to undertake an independent review of factors that led to restatement of accounting reports?

2. Why did the independent review focus on the "establishment and release of contractual liability and other related provisions" (also called accruals, reserves, or accrued liabilities)?[14]

---

8. Ibid.
9. Rick Westhead and Tyler Hamilton, "Insurer seeks to rescind Nortel coverage," Toronto *Star,* February 24, 2005, D1.
10. "Change in Directors or Principal Officers," *SEC Form 8-K,* January 13, 2005.
11. Steve Maich, "Selling ethics at Nortel," *Macleans.ca,* January 24, 2005. www.macleans.ca.
12. Ibid.
13. "Nortel settles lawsuits for $2.5 billion US," *CBC News,* CBC.ca, February 8, 2006.
14. Wilmer Cutler Pickering Hale and Dorr LLP, *Summary of Findings and of Recommended Remedial Measures of the Independent Review,* Washington, D.C., 2005, 2. See copy released on January 11, 2005, at http://www.nortelnetworks.com/corporate/news/newsreleases/collateral/independent_review_summary.pdf.

3. How did the failure to follow U.S. GAAP permit the manipulation of Earnings Before Taxes (EBT) and lead to fraudulent behavior?

4. Describe the Nortel Return to Profitability (RTP) and Restricted Stock Units (RSU) bonus plans. What did the board of directors expect these plans to achieve?

5. Were the misstatements of EBT and bonuses paid material in an accounting sense?

6. Why didn't Nortel's auditor discover the misstatements?

7. Why didn't the Audit Committee, or board as a whole, anticipate the manipulation?

8. What questions should the Audit Committee or board have asked?

9. What internal control flaws permitted the fraudulent manipulation to occur without detection?

10. Would the new requirements spawned by the Sarbanes-Oxley Act of 2002 (SOX) and its SEC Regulations have prevented the manipulation per se—why or why not?

11. How have the expectations of the Audit Committee changed since SOX with regard to corporate culture, why is this so, and how can the Audit Committee ensure that these are met?

12. Should the Audit Committee or the whole board be held legally liable for the weaknesses noted in the review? Why and why not?

13. In February 2005, Nortel hired a new Chief Ethics and Compliance Officer using an incentive compensation scheme based upon profits. Is this a sound arrangement?

14. Nortel has issued a new code of conduct with striking similarity to their previous version. Why might this new code be more effective than the last?

15. In retrospect, what were the major failings of the Nortel Audit Committee? Were they the same as those for the board as a whole?

Ethics Case

Ford/Firestone Tire Recall

On August 9, 2000, 6.5 million Firestone tires were recalled in the United States.[1] 15″ ATX, ATXII, and Wilderness AT tires installed on Ford Explorers were to be replaced at company cost due to evident defects, public outcry, government investigation, and earlier recalls in Venezuela, Malaysia, Thailand, Colombia, Ecuador, and Saudi Arabia. Early estimates of costs of the recall were in the range of $300 to $600 million,[2] but these did not include loss of future revenues due to loss of consumer confidence, nor costs of future litigation. Further recalls followed.[3] As of September 2001, an estimated 192 deaths and over 500 injuries had been attributed to these tires.[4]

As the prospect of having to recall faulty tires increased, Firestone and Ford had a falling out. Firestone, or Bridgestone/Firestone as it became known, alleged that the Ford Explorer suspension accounted for at least part of the problem. Ford charged that Firestone had failed to advise them of potential problems

---

1. 14.4 million tires were produced, but at the recall date only 6.5 million were estimated to still be on the road.

2. "Ford/Firestone Tire Recall Time Line," Virginia Trial Lawyers Association.

 3. Statement of Michael P. Jackson . . . before the Subcommittees on . . . U.S. House of Representatives, June 19, 2001, (see **www.cengage.com/accounting/brooks**). Mr. Jackson advises of the recall details as follows:

  ▌ On August 9, 2000, Firestone recalled all of its ATX and ATX II tires of the P235/75R15 size manufactured since 1991. It also recalled Wilderness AT tires of that size made at its Decatur plant, for a total of 14.4 million tires.

  ▌ On May 22, 2001, Ford announced a tire replacement program that includes all other Firestone Wilderness tires on certain Ford, Mercury, and Mazda SUVs and light trucks. This replacement action totals approximately 13 million tires.

 4. "Engineering Analysis Report and Initial Decision Regarding EA00-023: Firestone Wilderness AT Tires," National Highway Traffic Safety Administration (NHTSA) (see **www.cengage.com/accounting/brooks**).

and provide their data for analysis. Ultimately, both companies were "invited" to face questioning and testify before U.S. Congress and Senate Subcommittees.

Déjà vu, All Over Again

Firestone and Ford had been in recall debacles before.

Firestone had to recall tires in 1977, 1978, and 1980. The 1978 recall was so large (14.5 million units) that it threatened the financial viability of the company. In fact, Bridgestone, a Japanese company and the No. 3 tire maker in the world, had to rescue Firestone, then the No. 2 tire maker, from financial collapse in May 1988. Consequently, although most design and operating decisions preceded the takeover, much of the decision making with regard to the recall in 2000 was under the Bridgestone/Firestone regime. Many Firestone people, however, continued to be involved.

Ford had suffered significantly during the Pinto fires fiasco.[5] Introduced in 1970, the small Pinto would burst into flames when struck from the rear at a speed of 21 miles per hour. This was due to a design flaw that permitted the rupturing of the Pinto's gas tank. Many lawsuits persisted until the late 1970s.

Multiple failures of Ford and Firestone people—and of government regulators at the National Highway Traffic Safety Administration (NHTSA) to recognize such problems early, and to deal with them effectively—raise interesting questions, including: Why did the companies get involved in yet another recall debacle? Did the companies and the NHTSA know about the need to investigate and recall the Wilderness tires much earlier than their official investigations began? If not, why not? Did the companies deal with the recall ethically? What lessons can be learned about crisis management?

The key events of the recall are summarized in Table 1.

The Safety Problems: Firestone Tire Tread Separation and Ford Explorer Design

The tread separation problem and the related NHTSA findings were summarized in the Executive Summary of NHTSA's Engineering Analysis Report and Initial Decision,[6] as follows:

Belt-leaving-belt tread separations, whether or not accompanied by a loss of air from the tire, reduce the ability of a driver to control the vehicle, particularly when the failure occurs on a rear tire and at high speeds. Such a loss of control can lead to a crash. The likelihood of a crash, and of injuries or fatalities from such a crash, is far greater when the tread separation occurs on a SUV than when it occurs on a pickup truck.

Tread separation claims included in the Firestone claims database involving the recalled and focus tires have been associated with numerous crashes that have led to 74 deaths and over 350 injuries (as of March 2001). Tread separation complaints from all sources included in the ODI consumer complaint database (including the Firestone claims data) that can be identified as involving these tires have reportedly led to 192 deaths and over 500 injuries (as of September 2001).

The belt-leaving-belt tread separations in the recalled and focus tires generally occur only after several years of operation. Thus, since the focus tires have not been on the road as long as the recalled ATX tires, the absolute number of failures of those tires, and the unadjusted failure rate of those tires, are less than those of comparable ATX tires. Claims in the Firestone claims database involving the focus tires have been associated with 17 deaths and 41 injuries, with additional

---

5. See the Ford Pinto case in this book for additional information.
6. "Engineering Analysis Report"

TABLE 1

Ford/Firestone Tire Recall Time Line

November 1978: Firestone recalled 14.5 million of the Firestone 500 series tires after reports of accidents and deaths due to tread separation on steel-belted radial tires.

May 1988: Bridgestone, the world's No. 3 tire maker, acquired Firestone, the No. 2 tire maker. The takeover rescued Firestone from potential financial collapse due to the 1978 recall.

February 1989: Arvin/Calspan Tire Research Facility of Alexandria, Virginia, an independent research lab hired by Ford, measured the performance of 17 Firestone tires. The lab reported 3 belt-edge separation failures of the 17 tires tested.

March 1990: The Explorer was introduced as a 1991 model. The Explorer was redesigned to its current chassis design in 1995.

1991: Bridgestone/Firestone ATX, ATX II, and Wilderness AT tires became original equipment for the Ford Explorer (1991–2000), Ford Ranger (1991–2000), F-150 truck (1991–1994), Mercury Mountaineer (1996–2000), Mazda Navajo (1991–1994) and B-Series pickup truck (1994–2000). Eventually, over 14.4 million tires would be manufactured.

1992: Bridgestone/Firestone began investigating allegations of safety problems with its tires. Ford began receiving complaints regarding Firestone tires on its light truck models.

1994–1996: The workers at the Firestone Decatur Illinois, plant went out on strike. Firestone used replacement workers during this period to continue production.

July 1998: State Farm Insurance research analyst Sam Boyden sent an e-mail to the National Highway Transportation Safety Administration (NHTSA) reporting 21 tread separation cases involving the Firestone ATX tire. Boyden continued to send e-mails to NHTSA about subsequent Firestone tread separation accidents.

October 1998: Ford noted tread separation problems on Ford Explorers in Venezuela, and sent samples to Bridgestone/Firestone for analysis. A Ford-affiliated dealer in Saudi Arabia wrote to Ford Motor Co. complaining of problems with Firestone tires.

March 12, 1999: Ford memorandum noted that Ford and Bridgestone/Firestone executives discussed notifying U.S. safety authorities about a planned tire recall in Saudi Arabia. Ford decided to replace the tires overseas without telling federal regulators.

April 1999: NHTSA's Uniform Tire Grading Report gave Firestone ATX II and Wilderness AT tires the lowest grade on stress test temperature. The overwhelming majority of comparable tires received higher grades. It is believed that overheated tires lead to tread separation.

August 1999: Ford began replacing Firestone tires on Explorers sold in Saudi Arabia after reports of tread separation problems. Ford did not report the safety concerns, but called the replacement program a "customer notification enhancement action."

January 19, 2000: Internal documents showed Firestone executives knew about rising warranty costs due to accidents caused by the ATX, ATX II, and the Wilderness AT tires.

February 2000: Houston, Texas, TV station KHOU does a story on tread separation of Firestone tires used on Ford Explorers. The TV station gives the NHTSA 800 telephone number for consumers to report complaints. Consumers start calling in with reports of tread separations of Firestone tires.

March 6, 2000: Based on the information NHTSA received, primarily from complaints stemming from the Houston, Texas, TV story, the agency begins its Initial Evaluation (IE) of Firestone Tires.

May 2000: Ford changed Explorer's standard equipment to Goodyear tires in Venezuela while waiting for Firestone to come to a resolution regarding the tire separation problems. Ford recalled Firestone tires in Malaysia, Thailand, Colombia, and Ecuador. The entire overseas recall reached 46,912 SUVs.

May 2/8, 2000: NHTSA launched a formal investigation (PE-0020) into the tread separation cases involving the Firestone ATX and Wilderness tires.

May 10, 2000: NHTSA sends letters to Ford and Firestone requesting information in connection with PE-0020.

June 8, 2000: Ford requests that Firestone provide all information that they gave to NHTSA relating to PE-0020. This information includes the claims data that will demonstrate the high accident rate of the tires.

July 28, 2000: Ford receives Firestone's information, and begins an analysis.

August 4, 2000: Ford found a pattern in the data pointing to the 15" ATX, ATX II, and Wilderness AT tires made at the Decatur, Illinois, plant and called in the Firestone experts. They found that older tires produced late in each production year from 1994–1996 had a higher failure rate.

August 9, 2000: Bridgestone/Firestone announced a region-by-region recall of more than 6.5 million AT, ATX II, and Wilderness AT tires. Approximately 2 million Ford Explorers were named as subjects to the recall. The cost estimate for the recall ranged from $300 to $600 million. The hot weather regions were scheduled for tire replacement first, with other regions to follow. NHTSA reports that Firestone tire separations were responsible for 46 deaths.

August 10, 2000: Plaintiff attorneys involved with Firestone litigation over the past decade note they know of 107 related tire cases, with 90 of those having a direct link to the recalled tires.

August 10, 2000: Ford claimed it became aware of the tire separation problem one year ago, from anecdotal reports from Saudi Arabia.

August 16, 2000: NHTSA increased the number of deaths connected to the Firestone tread separations to 62.

September 1, 2000: NHTSA announced another 24 Firestone tire models showed rates of tread separation exceeding those of the recalled tires. NHTSA also increased the estimate of deaths attributed to Firestone tires from 62 to 88. Venezuelan authorities report that at least 47 people died because of the Firestone tires.

Source: "Ford/Firestone Tire Recall Time Line," Virginia Trial Lawyers Association, (see **www.cengage.com/accounting/brooks**). "Firestone Tire Recall Timeline," Democratic Staff of the Commerce Committee (see **www.cengage.com/accounting/brooks**).

crashes and casualties reported in the ODI complaint database, including reports of six additional fatalities. However, on a plant-by-plant basis, the focus tires manufactured at the Wilson and Joliette plants have exhibited tread separation failure trends that are similar to those experienced by the recalled ATX tires at similar service intervals.

These failure trends indicate that it is likely that, if they are not removed from service, the focus tires— at least those manufactured before May 1998—will experience a similar increase in tread separation failures over the next few years, leading to a substantial number of future crashes, injuries, and deaths. The tread separation failure experience of the focus tires is far worse than that of their peers, especially that of the Goodyear Wrangler RT/S tires used as original equipment on many Ford Explorers.

The belt-leaving-belt tread separations that have occurred and are continuing to occur in the recalled and focus tires begin as belt-edge separation at the edge of the second, or top, belt. This is the area of highest strain in a steel belted radial tire and is a region with relatively poor cord-to-rubber adhesion because bare steel is exposed at the cut ends of the cords. Once belt-edge separations have initiated, they can grow circumferentially and laterally along the edge of the second belt and develop into cracks between the belts. If they grow large enough, they can result in catastrophic tread detachment, particularly at high speeds, when the centrifugal forces acting on the tire are greatest.

ODI conducted a non-destructive analysis of numerous randomly collected focus tires and peer tires from southern states, where most of the failures have occurred, using shearography, which can detect separations inside a tire. This shearography analysis demonstrated that the patterns and levels of cracks and separations between the belts were far more severe in the focus tires than in peer tires.

Many of the focus tires that were examined were in the later stages of failure progression prior to complete separation of the upper belt. The shearography results for tires manufactured at Wilson were similar to those manufactured at Joliette.

A critical design feature used by tire manufacturers to suppress the initiation and growth of belt-edge cracks is the "belt wedge," a strip of rubber located between the two belts near the belt edges on each side of the tire. The belt wedge thickness, or gauge, in the ATX tires and the Wilderness AT tires produced prior to May 1998 is generally narrower than the wedge gauge in peer tires, and the wedge gauge in cured tires was often less than Firestone's target for this dimension. The tires with this wedge did not adequately resist the initiation and propagation of belt-edge cracks between the steel belts. During March and April 1998, Firestone changed the material composition and increased the gauge of the wedge in its Wilderness AT tires (and some other tire models).

Another important feature of radial tires related to the prevention of belt-leaving-belt separations is the gauge of the rubber between the two steel belts, or "inter-belt gauge." The inter-belt gauge initially specified by Firestone for the focus tires is generally narrower than the inter-belt gauges in peer tires and is narrower than Firestone's original specification for the ATX tires in the early 1990s. Moreover, the actual measured gauge under the tread grooves in several of the focus tires measured by ODI was far less than Firestone's minimum design specification. Since an inadequate inter-belt gauge reduces the tire's resistance to crack growth and its belt adhesion capabilities, this narrow inter-belt gauge may be partially responsible for the relatively low peel adhesion properties of the focus tires compared to peer tires. In August 1999, after becoming concerned about the adequacy of the inter-belt gauge in the cured Wilderness AT tires, especially in the regions directly under the tread grooves, Firestone changed the inter-belt gauge specification back to the original dimension.

Another relevant feature is the design of the shoulder pocket of the focus tires, which can cause higher stresses at the belt edge and lead to a narrowing, or "pinching," of the wedge gauge at the pocket. The focus tires exhibit a series of weak spots around the tire's circumference, leading to the initiation and growth of cracks earlier than in competitor tires and in other Firestone tires produced for light trucks and SUVs. In addition, many of the focus tires exhibited shoulder pocket cracking similar to that which Firestone identified as a significant contributor to the risk of tread detachment in the recalled ATX tires.

Because the tread separations at issue in this investigation occur only after several years of exposure, almost all of the failures on which ODI's analysis of field experience was based involved tires manufactured before May 1998, when Firestone increased the dimensions and improved the material of the belt wedge. In theory, these modifications to the wedge would tend to inhibit the initiation and propagation of the belt-edge cracks that lead to tread separations. If these modifications actually improved the resistance of the focus tires to belt-edge separations, the historical failure trends described above may not predict the future performance of the newer tires. However, because tread separation failures rarely occur in the focus tires until at least three years of use, it is not now possible to ascertain from field experience whether their actual performance has improved significantly.

The rate of tread separation failures on Ranger pickups is lower that the rate of such failures on Explorers for a variety of reasons, including the fact that the Explorer generally carries higher loads and is a more demanding application, and the tires on the Explorer had a significantly lower recommended inflation pressure (especially on the rear wheels). The

risk of such a separation on Rangers remains a cause for possible concern. Nevertheless, because the likelihood of a crash due to a tread separation, and of deaths and injuries resulting from such a crash, is substantially lower when the separation occurs on a pickup than on a SUV, NHTSA's initial defect decision does not apply to focus tires installed on pickup trucks.

Under the National Traffic and Motor Vehicle Safety Act, in order to compel a manufacturer to conduct a recall, NHTSA has the burden of proving that a safety-related defect exists in the manufacturer's products. The record of this investigation supports a determination that a safety-related defect exists in the focus tires manufactured by Firestone prior to its 1998 modifications to the belt wedge that are installed on SUVs. Although the agency has concerns about the possibility of future tread separations in focus tires manufactured after the wedge change, the available evidence at this time does not clearly demonstrate that a safety-related defect exists in those focus tires. NHTSA will, however, continue to closely monitor the performance of these tires.

Therefore, on the basis of the information developed during the ODI investigation, NHTSA has made an initial decision that a safety-related defect exists in Firestone Wilderness AT P235/75R15 and P255/70R16 tires manufactured to the Ford specifications prior to May 1998 that are installed on SUVs. These tires were manufactured primarily at Wilson and Joliette and, to a lesser extent, at Oklahoma City. The initial decision does not apply to the P255/70R16 tires produced at Decatur or any of the Wilderness AT tires produced at Aiken, since these tires were all manufactured after May 1998.

At the request of Bridgestone/Firestone's chairman, the NHTSA also investigated the claims that the Ford Explorer had a design defect, probably in its suspension, that contributed to the tread separation in Wilderness tires. In his Statement to the U.S. Congressional Committees, NHTSA Deputy Secretary, Michael P. Jackson, comments that: ". . . NHTSA has had no credible evidence that the Ford Explorer's design is in any way responsible for *causing* tread separation or other such catastrophic tire failure."[7]

When Did the Companies Know of Problems and What Did They Do About Them?

According to the time line information, both Ford and Firestone received information about tire tread separations as early as 1992. These investigations may have been limited in some way, perhaps focused on or influenced by legal liability considerations. In any event, they do not appear to have raised "red flags" for Ford or Firestone such that either company was actively following up looking for further evidence.

Actually, Ford had received an earlier warning in February 1989, when an independent testing lab it hired found 3 of 17 tires tested had tread separations. Again, this information does not appear to have been carried forward as part of an ongoing formal risk assessment program.

Interestingly, in 1992, Ford chose the P235 tires that were later recalled over the smaller P225 tires that had tested better in turning (a prelude to rollover) tests. A memo shows Ford management was aware of the potential risk. Moreover, in order to improve the stability of the Explorer, Ford lowered the recommended tire pressure to 26 p.s.i. from the normal 30–35 p.s.i. that Firestone usually recommended. Firestone later insisted that this low pressure recommendation increased tire heat and caused the tire separations. At the time, however, Firestone went along; when Ford found

that the mushier tires worsened fuel economy and asked for a fix, Firestone reduced the tire weight by about 3 percent.[8]

Unlike General Motors, which has their own in-house tire safety and research unit,[9] neither Ford nor Firestone had an ongoing tire safety, testing, and database analysis program. Perhaps, if they had, they would have been aware of and following the work of Sam Boyden, the State Farm insurance analyst who began to e-mail NHTSA and have person-to-person conversations with NHTSA about Firestone tire problems in July 1998. Unfortunately, these e-mails and conversations do not appear to have been followed up until May 2, 2000, when the official investigation started. Even the NHTSA has admitted that they did not have an ongoing database project. Ford had to wait for Firestone to send them data, and Firestone initially had only cursory warranty data and needed to build a more comprehensive and useful dataset. NHTSA had to assemble data from various sources, including the companies, as well. Neither of the companies nor NHTSA was putting together a complete picture on an ongoing basis—they were all reacting, focused on short-term concerns, and using makeshift resources.

Ford and Firestone became aware of tire failures in warm climates in October 1998. The companies discussed the problems and Ford proposed a recall in Saudi Arabia. According to an internal Ford memo dated March 12, 1999, Firestone had asked Ford to handle it on a case-by-case basis so that the U.S. Department of Transport would not have to be notified, and so that the Saudi government would not overreact.[10] Ford had apparently told Firestone that the recall should be reported since the tires were also sold in the United States, but ultimately did not do so. Later, Ford maintained that it was not

7. Statement of Michael P. Jackson.

8. John Greenwald, "Inside the Ford/Firestone Fight," *Time Online Edition,* May 29, 2001 (see **www.cengage.com/accounting/brooks**).

9. Information from a student.

10. Stephen Power, "Tire Check: The Recall Rolls On: Bridgestone Fretted About Replacements," *Wall Street Journal,* September 6, 2000.

obligated to report the foreign recalls to U.S. regulators.[11]

Ford asked Firestone to do some tests in November 1999. These tests, which became known as the "Southwest Study," were completed in April 2000, but no evidence of a problem was discovered.[12]

Ultimately, when facing inflamed public reactions in specific locales to mounting accidents and deaths, Ford recalled Firestone tires in Saudi Arabia, Venezuela, and four other countries between June 1999 and May 2000. Firestone continued to advise Ford that there were no problems with the tires, and recalls were unwarranted. Note that these recalls were undertaken before recalling the same tires in North America—a fact not lost on consumers and commentators when the salient facts began to surface.

A TV station in Houston, Texas, KHOU, aired a 10-minute story on the tread separations on tires on Ford Explorers in February 2000. They gave the 800 telephone number for the NHTSA and complaints started to roll in. The news secrecy bubble had finally burst in the United States, and on March 6 the NHTSA began its Initial Evaluation (IE) of Firestone tires.[13] Subsequent analysis of Firestone warranty claims and other data showed a high accident rate for the tires, and led to the recall on August 9. Again, actions were in response to public pressure.

Findings were ultimately identified, in part, from Firestone warranty data that could have been assessed much earlier. Whose responsibility should that have been? Who would have benefited? On Friday, July 28, 2000, Ford engineers picked up the Firestone warranty data and then set up a "war room" at Ford headquarters in Dearborn, Michigan.[14] Working with Firestone personnel, after ten long days the investigators decided that "the problem tires appear[ed] to have come from the plant in Decatur, Ill., during specific periods of production. The bulk of the tire-separation incidents had occurred in hot states: Arizona, California, Florida and Texas. This correlated with information from overseas."[15]

"The rate of warranty claims on tires for Explorers surged in the mid-1990s, and the bulk of them involved tires made at Decatur. For the three years from 1994 through 1996, tread-separation claims attributed to ATX tires produced at the Decatur plant came in at rates ranging from roughly 350 to more than 600 tires per million. During the same years, tires of the same model produced at all other Firestone plants had claim rates of 100 per million tires."[16]

At least two factors may have contributed to these higher tread separation rates at Decatur. In preparation for a product liability suit in Florida, a retired worker has sworn that he saw inspectors pass tires without inspecting them on a daily basis in 1993 and 1994.[17] Secondly, Firestone used 2,300 scab or replacement workers when United Rubber Workers local 713 went on strike from 1994 to 1996. After the very acrimonious strike was settled Firestone made the scab workers permanent hires.[18] An interesting question remains: Did Firestone fully appreciate and manage these risks effectively?

11. Ibid.
12. "Firestone Tire Recall Timeline," Democratic Staff of the Commerce Committee (see **www.cengage.com/accounting/brooks**).
13. Ibid.
14. Robert L. Simison et al., "Blowout: How the Tire Problem Turned into a Crisis for Firestone and Ford—Lack of a Database Masked the Pattern That Led to Yesterday's Big Recall—The Heat and the Pressure," *Wall Street Journal,* August 10, 2000.
15. Ibid.
16. Timothy Aeppel et al., "Road Signs: How Ford, Firestone Let The Warnings Slide By as Debacle Developed—Their Separate Goals, Gaps in Communication Gave Rise to Risky Situation—Bucking the Bronco Legacy," *Wall Street Journal,* September 6, 2000.
17. Ibid.
18. James R. Healey & Sara Nathan, "Could $1 Worth of Nylon Have Saved People's Lives? Experts: Caps on Steel Belts May Have Stopped Shredded Tires," *USA Today,* August 9, 2000.

Misunderstanding the Risks

Perhaps the tread separation problems were found earlier, and actions were suppressed in the United States due to concerns over potential legal ramifications and ensuing costs. Unfortunately, this is probably a correct line of reasoning, and it reflects an erroneous understanding of the significant risks of delay in dealing with a product safety matter.

Specifically, delay in dealing with a product safety matter can lead to a serious erosion of reputation and confidence among customers, and result in a loss of future revenues and profits. Frequently, the cost of opportunities lost is the largest item to be taken into account in a cost-benefit analysis of the decision to recall a product. Moreover, failing to remedy a problem at the earliest point of recognition can lead to an inflation of the number of claims and the cost of satisfying them. If the executives had seen the cost-benefit analysis in Table 2, they would have seen the logic in speeding up their analysis and recognition of the tread separation problem.

Using an Ethical Decision-Making Framework

Had Ford and Firestone executives used an ethical decision-making framework such as those discussed in Chapter 5, they would have recognized the risks allowing legal defense strategy to dominate their thinking. Moreover, they might have considered the application of alternative remedies such as the use of a nylon cap or safety layer between the steel belts and tread to keep the ends of the belts from chafing the tread rubber and contributing to tread separation. The nylon cap was apparently used in late-production Firestone tires in Venezuela at a cost of $1 per tire. According to engineers, the extra cost was the only reason not to use them widely.[19] Bridgestone does use them on some tire lines, as does Pirelli on nearly all of its U.S.-market tires.[20]

The Aftermath

Not surprisingly, the sales of Ford Explorers dropped, as did Firestone's sales. In Venezuela, for example, Ford Explorer sales dropped 37 percent in 2000. In December 2000, Saudi Arabia banned new and used vehicles with Firestone tires. Firestone announced that it believed the ban was unjustified.

Both the U.S. Congress and Senate held hearings, and a new act was passed on October 11, 2000, called the Transportation Recall Enhancement, Accountability, and Documentation Act (TREAD). The TREAD Act:

BRIDGESTONE'S STOCK CHART

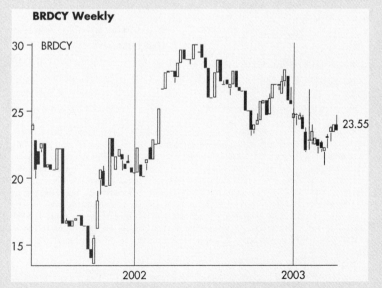

Reprinted courtesy of StatPro Canada, Inc.

---

19. Ibid.
20. Ibid.

FORD'S STOCK CHART

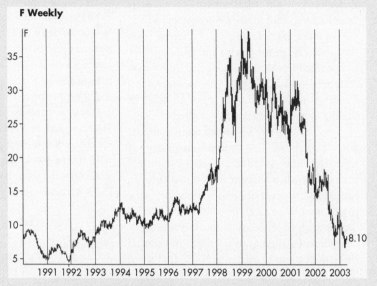

Reprinted courtesy of StatPro Canada, Inc.

TABLE 2

Cost-Benefit Analysis of Decision to Use a Nylon Cap Safety Layer

BENEFITS		
SAVINGS	**UNIT COST**	**TOTAL**
203 Deaths[1]	$977,000	$198,331,000
700 Injuries[2]	$327,925	229,547,500
Avoid Legal Fees & Settlements		
Avoid Recalling Tires		
Avoid Damage to Reputation[3]		1,272,121,500
Total Benefits		$1,700,000,000

COSTS		
COST	**UNIT COST**	**TOTAL**
Nylon Safety Cap for 10,000,000 recalled tires[4]	$1	10,000,000
Total Costs		$10,000,000

[1]The unit cost of death was obtained from an NHTSA study in 2000 on "The Economic Impact of Motor Vehicle Crashes" (see **www.cengage.com/accounting/brooks**).

[2]The unit cost of injury was determined by applying the percentage cost of injury/death in 1971 from the Ford Pinto case ($67,000/$200,000 = 33.5%) to the unit cost of death estimated by the NHTSA survey from 2000: $977,000 × 33.5% = $327,295.

[3]The investment banking firm of UBS Warburg estimated that the tire problems could cost Firestone and Ford between $719 million and $2.7 billion. We assumed the total cost to be $1.7 billion (a number in the middle). Therefore, since we know the total cost to Ford & Firestone is $1.7 billion, we can calculate the residual amount to be allocated to the avoidance of legal fees, settlement fees, cost of recalling tires, and the cost of the loss of reputation: $1,700,000,000 − $427,878,500 = $1,272,121,500 (see **www.cengage.com/accounting/brooks**).

[4]An article written in USA Today on August 9, 2000, by James R. Healey & Sara Nathan, proposed that a nylon safety cap could have prevented the tread separation problem. The article states that a nylon safety layer between the steel belts and the tread would keep the ends of the belts from chafing the tread rubber and contributing to tread separation. The article also cited that affidavits from tire engineers said that cost is the only reason not to use them. The estimated cost was $1 per tire to cover the radial piles with a nylon cap. We determined the number of tires affected as follows:

August 9, 2000	6.5 million tires were recalled	
September 4, 2000	3.5 million additional tires were recalled	
Total recalled	10.0 million	

Source: Master of Management & Professional Accounting (MMPA) degree students at the Rotman School of Management, University of Toronto: Meghan Davis, Theresa Yim, Paul Spitzen, Michael Krofchick, and Katy Yeung. Group project, Fall 2002.

| Strengthens the reporting requirements for manufacturers of motor vehicles and motor vehicle equipment (including the reporting of defects first discovered in a foreign country);

| Increases the civil penalties for violations of safety regulations (e.g., fines for certain violations of Title 49 were raised from $1,000 to $5,000 for each violation, and the maximum penalty for a related series of violations was raised from $800,000 to $15,000,000);

- Provides additional criminal penalties (e.g., for any knowing and willful false statement that was intended to mislead NHTSA with respect to a defect that causes death or grievous bodily harm, the possible prison term was raised from 5 years to 15);

- Requires NHTSA to revise and update its safety standards for tires;

- Increases the number of years that a defect must be remedied without charge to the owner (from three years to five for tires);

- Increases the authorization for funding NHTSA;

- Requires the Secretary of Transportation to report to Congress within a year on the criteria, procedures, and methods that NHTSA uses in determining whether to open an investigation of a possible defect; and

- Contains other safety-related provisions.[21]

Questions

1. Why didn't Ford and Firestone learn from their past recall debacles?

2. Why didn't Ford, Firestone, and the NHTSA discover the nature and seriousness of the tread-separation, product-liability problem earlier?

3. Why didn't Ford or Firestone report the problem to U.S. authorities earlier?

4. Ultimately, which was the largest cost to Ford and Firestone: fines, lawsuit settlements, or the loss of reputation leading to loss of future revenue and profits?

5. What errors should be corrected in the cost–benefit analysis presented?

6. What were the ethical risks, if any, involved in this tire recall situation?

7. If you were advising Ford and Bridgestone, what should each include in their risk management program?

---

21. "Lawyer's Silence and Highway Deaths," United States Republican Policy Committee, July 9, 2001 (see **www.cengage.com/accounting/brooks**).

Ethics Case | *Conflicts of Interest on Wall Street*

On December 20, 2002, New York's Attorney General, Eliot Spitzer, announced a $1.4 billion settlement ending a multi-regulator probe of ten brokerages that alleged that "investors were duped into buying over-hyped stocks during the '90s bull market."[1] But the settlement may represent only the tip of the iceberg as aggrieved investors review the findings and sue the brokerages for redress of their personal losses estimated to be $7 trillion since 2000.[2] Nonetheless, it promises an overdue start on the reform of Wall Street's[3] flawed conflict of interest practices. As such, the revisions ultimately adopted will provide a template for investment advisors around the world.

The story behind the probe is also an interesting one. It shows the capacity of a state's Attorney-General to force the U.S.

---

1. "Wall Street firms to pays fines of $1.4 billion U.S.," *Toronto Star*, December 21, 2002, D3.
2. Alex Berenson and Andrew Ross Sorkin, "How Wall Street Was Tamed," *New York Times*, December 22, 2003.
3. Wall Street is used in this case to signify the U.S. investment advisory/brokerage community, which is centered on Wall Street in New York City.

TABLE 1

Wall Street Brokers Settlement Payments[7]

FIRM	INDEPENDENT INVESTOR			
	FINES	RESEARCH	EDUCATION	TOTAL
Saloman Smith Barney parent, Citigroup Inc.	$300	$75	$25	$400
Credit Suisse First Boston	150	50	0	200
Merrill Lynch	100*	75	25	200
Morgan Stanley	50	75	0	125
Goldman Sachs	50	50	10	110
Bear Stearns	50	25	5	80
Deutsche Bank	50	25	5	80
J. P. Morgan Chase	50	25	5	80
Lehman Brothers	50	25	5	80
UBS Warburg	50	25	5	80
Total	$900	$450	$85	$1,435

*Merrill Lynch agreed to pay an additional $100 million seven months earlier in response to Spitzer's original charges.[8]

Securities and Exchange Commission (SEC), which has regulatory authority over U.S. capital markets, to act when they appeared reluctant to take on Wall Street in a direct, public, and serious manner. In fact, Spitzer was able to bring together his office, the SEC, the National Association of Securities Dealers, the New York Stock Exchange, and a group of state regulators, as well as the major brokerages involved, to arrange a settlement.

The accepted settlement, while indicating the complicity of the ten firms involved, will probably do more to restore lost confidence in the capital markets than to weaken it. Regulators have been seen to act, brokerages are on notice that the old practices will no longer be tolerated, and the right of investors to have unbiased advice is reinforced. The resulting sharpening of ethics awareness on the part of advisors, their firms, and the regulators, together with the emergence of more ethical practices, should assist in the restoration of investor trust in the capital markets.

The Settlement

Ten firms have agreed "to pay $1.435 billion, including $900 million in penalties, $450

million for research over the next five years and $85 million for investor education."[4] The list of payments, in millions, is shown in Table 1. Two other firms that had been part of the settlement talks did not participate in the announced settlement.

Some observers hailed the settlement and resulting changes to be "the dawn of a new day for Wall Street."[5] Others felt that the fines were a drop in the bucket. "Citicorp, for example, averaged about $65 million in profit each business day in the third quarter, meaning one good week would cover its payment."[6] If the payments turn out to be tax deductible, the impact would certainly be minor in size, but would possess a significant signaling value.

What Caused Concern?

Conflicts of interest have been common practice in the brokerage business since its inception. For example, most brokerages, and brokers, have investments upon which they take speculative positions, and upon which they make investment recommendations to investors. In the case of the brokerages, they are usually required to disclose to prospective investors when they are selling shares as a

---

4. Randall Smith, "Ten Firms Must Pay $1.4 Billion over Misleading Stock Research," *Wall Street Journal*, December 23, 2002.
5. Ibid.
6. "Wall Street firms."
7. Smith.
8. "Wall Street firms."

principal, but the presumption of unsuspecting investors has been that brokerage employees—analysts and investment advisers—were acting in the best interest of the investors they were advising. How wrong they were!

According to *Forbes.com,* Spitzer's office found emails showing Merrill Lynch (and other firms') analysts . . . privately trashing the stocks they publicly recommended."[7] In addition, "there is the widespread phenomenon of research departments commencing coverage of companies their (investment) banks recently took public. This coverage is always positive."[8] Moreover, ". . . analysts almost never say 'sell.' According to Thomson Financial/First Call, fewer than 2% of all financial analysts are 'sell' or 'strong sell.' . . . Third, there are cases like Enron that are not recent initial public offerings but companies that do massive and repeat business with Wall Street. The analysts can say they are not swayed by their firm's interests, and they can claim they were defrauded, but how do they explain the uniformity of their recommendations."[9]

Brokerages have long relied upon the notion of the Chinese wall or a firewall that they claim can stop information known to investment bank personnel who develop and price independent public offerings from reaching stock analysts or brokers serving retail clients. However, there are those who doubt that Chinese walls are fully effective. According to Richard Epstein, a law professor at the University of Chicago: "The only thing [the analyst] needs to know [about the investment banking client] if he is inclined to swing his recommendation is that it is a client."[10] Since analysts have been remunerated partly on the basis of underwriting revenues, and/or on the basis of retail commissions, or total brokerage revenues, there is built-in remuneration motivation for promoting the stock of known or potential underwriting clients.

On other occasions, the attempts to influence analysts have been quite direct. "Perhaps the most startling example came in mid-November, when Citigroup chief executive Sanford Weill said he told Jack Grubman to re-examine his rating of AT&T and admitted that he helped Grubman's children gain admission to a prestigious Manhattan nursery school."[11]

In addition to providing investment advice that lacked integrity, Wall Street firms have been playing favorites. They have been offering shares of hot public offerings to the executives of companies regarded as good prospects for investment banking deals. This is known as "spinning," and due to the pent-up demand for the new offerings, a profit is virtually assured.

Proposed Structural Reforms

In order to help ensure that "stock recommendations are not tainted by efforts to obtain investment banking fees"[12] and other benefits, the settlement proposes several changes in the way investment business is done, including:

▌ "Each firm's research unit will reside in a unit separate from the investment banking unit, with its own legal and compliance staff, and which doesn't report to investment banking, . . .

▌ . . . decisions to terminate [analyst] coverage must be made by research and not investment bankers, and can't substitute for a rating downgrade.

▌ . . . analysts can't be compensated based on investment banking work or input from bankers, and should be paid based partly on the accuracy of their stock picks. . . ."

Some problems still exist, and further framework changes will emerge, but a start has been made on cleaning up some of the conflicts of interest facing investors and the brokerage community.

---

9. Dan Ackerman, "Everyone Wants a Shot at the Analysts," *Forbes.com,* May 1, 2002.
10. Ibid.
11. Ibid.
12. Ibid.
13. "Wall Street firms."
14. Smith.

On April, 2003, a Joint Release was issued and lodged on the SEC Press website by the five regulatory agencies involved, which had the following headlines:

Ten of Nation's Top Investment Firms Settle Enforcement Actions Involving Conflicts of Interest Between Research and Investment Banking

Historic Settlement Requires Payments of Penalties of $487.5 Million, Disgorgement of $387.5 Million to Fund Investor Education and Mandates Sweeping Stuctural Reforms

Questions

1. Identify and explain the conflicts of interest referred to in this case.
2. What additional rules should the SEC make?
3. What should be included in the investor education that the settlement funds are earmarked for?
4. Was it appropiate for the New York Attorney General's Office to have become invloved in securities regulation, or should this have been left to securities regulators?

Ethics Case | *Loyalty, But to Whom?*

Glen Grossmith is an outstanding family man, a frequent coach for his children's teams, and a dedicated athlete who enjoys individual and team sports. One day, his boss at UBS Securities Canada Inc., Zoltan Horcsok, asked him to do a favor for a colleague, Mark Webb, with whom they had done business for awhile. Glen did the favour without asking why it was needed. Here is the story of what happened.

"At about 2:30 p.m." on February 4, 2004, "Mr. Webb called Mr. Horcsok. "I need your help with something badly right away," Mr. Webb told the Toronto trader. The two spoke soon after, working out a way to call one another without being taped. Mr. Webb, according to Mr. Horcsok, then told him: "You need to find a buyer for 10,000 Phelps Dodge. I may have a problem . . . you've got to be quick."

Mr. Horcsok then told Mr. Grossmith he needed a Canadian buyer for the Phelps Dodge shares.

Without knowing the details behind Mr. Webb's request, Mr. Grossmith got in touch with a client and asked the client to buy the shares. The client agreed.

Mr. Horcsok then spoke to about a dozen traders in the Toronto office, trying to find a trade ticket stamped at about

2:15 P.M. "Webb is in trouble," he told his traders, according to the settlement documents.

Eventually, a ticket time-stamped 9:43 A.M. was found. Mr. Grossmith, with Mr. Horcsok's knowledge, crossed out the stock trade that the ticket recorded and changed it to the Phelps Dodge symbol. Client information was also changed to reflect the Canadian buyer of the Phelps Dodge stock.

He also sent "fabricated" trade information to Mr. Webb, the settlement document states. Mr. Grossmith also created an electronic ticket reflecting the Phelps Dodge trade, while Mr. Horcsok later destroyed the altered paper trade ticket, according to the settlement.[1]

Unfortunately, for Glen and Zoltan, their activities were investigated and discovered by their employer. It turned out that Mark Webb needed the trade covered up because he was retaliating against a client and the client complained to UBS in the U.S. Regulators in the Market Regulation Services Inc. (RS) from the Ontario Securities Commission picked up the trail and subsequently claimed that:

". . . Mark Webb, a trader who worked at UBS's office in Stamford, Conn., received

---

1. Wojtek Dabrowski, "Former UBS brokers fined $75,000 and $100,000: Cover-up allegations," *Financial Post,* July 19, 2005, FP1,2.

an order from a client to buy 120,000 shares of Phelps Dodge Corp. However, once 6,000 shares were bought at about 2:18 p.m., the client cancelled the rest and moved it to another investment dealer.

Mr. Webb became angry and bought 10,000 Phelps shares for UBS's principal account in what RS alleges was "retaliation." After the client complained to UBS, Mr. Webb—who was fired along with Messrs. Horcsok and Grossmith in February— claimed the shares had been bought for a Canadian client, "when in fact they were not," RS said.[2]

Unfortunately for Horcsok and Grossmith, they

. . . were fired by UBS in late February over conduct that occurred earlier that month, [and] were denied their 2004 bonus by the investment dealer. The two brokers have sued UBS, with Mr. Grossmith seeking $1,053,000 and Mr. Horcsok seeking $1,750,000, which they claim is owed to them as bonus. Both claim they are owed the money because the conduct over which they were fired took place in 2005, not in 2004.

Additional court documents filed by Mr. Grossmith say UBS's reputation was "in tatters" by early 2005, following its settlement of unrelated allegations with RS in late 2004. He also claims UBS is improperly using him "as an example to try to enhance its reputation with the regulators."

But UBS spokesman Graeme Harris said yesterday the two men did not receive 2004 bonuses because of "misconduct, breach of UBS's policies and code of conduct and jeopardizing of UBS's reputation and business."

They were fired before the bonus payout date, and were therefore not entitled to one, Mr. Harris said.

Furthermore, the figures the two are claiming aren't the sums that would have been awarded to them even if they had received a bonus from UBS, Mr. Harris said.[3]

Ultimately, on July 18, 2005, the two brokers

. . . settled regulators' allegations that they falsified information and records to cover up a trade made by an angry U.S. colleague retaliating against one of his clients. Glen Grossmith, a former sales trader at UBS, and Zoltan Horcsok, his supervisor and former head of equity sales trading at the brokerage, have been fined $75,000 and $100,000 respectively. Each man will also pay $25,000 in costs to Market Regulation Services Inc. (RS) as part of the settlement deal approved yesterday.

"What we see here are two traders who falsified information and falsified trades to cover up the wilful action of a colleague and that's not acceptable," Maureen Jensen, RS's Eastern Region vice-president of market regulation, told reporters yesterday. "They need to bear the consequences."

Both senior traders have been suspended from trading on Canadian equity markets for the next three months, after which they must be strictly supervised for six months. Mr. Horcsok is also prohibited from acting as a supervisor for a year following his three-month trading ban.

Lawyers for the two men said yesterday that both regret their actions. Mr. Horcsok had not been disciplined in the past. In 2000, Mr. Grossmith was fined $35,000 and suspended for a month by the Toronto Stock Exchange for several high-close trades he executed.[4]

After over a year out of work, "Grossmith and Horcsok found employment at Scotia Capital Inc. following their ousters from UBS, but were fired last month, also in relation to the allegations settled yesterday."[5]

---

2. Ibid.
3. Ibid.
4. Ibid.
5. Ibid.

Questions

1. Loyalty is a highly desirable ethical value, and disloyalty is a serious unethical and often illegal activity. Explain how and to whom Grossmith, Horcsok, and Webb were disloyal.

2. Although Grossmith's actions did not negatively affect the wealth of any client, why did UBS fire him?

3. How should an employer like UBS encourage employee loyalty?

Ethics Case

Bankers Trust: Learning from Derivatives*

Bankers Trust (BT) was one of the most powerful and profitable banks in the world in the early 1990s. Under the stewardship of Chairman Charles Sanford, Jr., it had transformed itself from a staid commercial bank into "a highly-tuned manufacturer of high-margin, creative financial products—the envy of wholesale bankers."[1] BT prided itself on its innovative trading strategies, which used derivatives to manage risks; its performance-driven culture; and its profits: the bank made a profit of over $1 billion US in 1993.[2]

Key to BT success was the dominance of its business in derivatives—contracts in which companies make payments to each other based on some under-lying asset such as a commodity, a financial instrument, or an index.[3] The value of the payments—and thus the contract—is derived from those assets. Companies can use derivatives to lower financing costs, manage risk, or speculate on interest and currency rates. It is estimated that almost $400 million of BT's 1993 profits came from its leveraged derivatives business.

Derivatives, with their high margins, held a preeminent position with BT management, with their fervent focus on the bottom line. At BT, each product and each trader was given a value that was based on what income the product or trader could bring the firm.[1] The bank's intense focus on the bottom line decreased attention on products and services which had low margins but which fostered and nurtured client relationships. BT was known for courting customers only insofar as they would buy high-margin products.[1] In 1990 Charles Hill, former co-head of merchant banking, left with thirty members of his department because he saw no room at BT for offering clients impartial financial advice and deal structuring. One source within the company explained: "we got rid of the nurturers and builders—the defensive guys—and kept the offensive guys."[1] Those who remained describe a firm driven by intense internal rivalry, endless politicking, and discussions about profit and losses. They describe a "coliseum" mentality at the top level: "we look on while the guys are out there fighting the lions."[1] What remained was a bank where the customer's interests appeared to come second to the bank's.

It was within this context that BT, once one of the most powerful banks in the world, was disgraced by a series of highly publicized lawsuits brought forth by several of its clients in 1994 and 1995 over losses they incurred as a result of derivative products sold to them by BT. The clients contended that BT sold them the derivatives without giving them adequate warning and information regarding their potential risks. BT countered that these derivative deals were agreements between the bank and sophisticated clients who were now trying to escape from their loss-making contracts by crying foul.[2] At issue was whether the clients were naïve and should have known what they were getting into or whether BT deliberately deceived them (p. 110).[4]

---

* Prepared by L. J. Brooks, with assistance from student papers of Linda Rutledge, Deryk Angstenderger, Kelly Kang, Nilou Makarechian, Roman Masley, Khalid Rashid, and Chao Xu.

1. Shirreff, Y. D. "Can Anybody Fix Bankers Trust?" *Euromoney,* April 1995, 34–40.

2. "Bankers Trust Blurred Vision," *Economist,* April 8, 1995, 67–68.

3. Edwards, G. A., & Eller, G. E., "Overview of Derivatives Disclosures by Major US Banks," *Federal Reserve Bulletin,* September 1995, 817–31.

4. Holland, Kelly and Linda Himelstein and Zachary Schiller, "The Bankers Trust Tapes," *Business Week,* October 16, 1995, 106–111.

There were more than half a dozen companies that suffered losses as a result of derivatives due to BT's allegedly fraudulent sales practices (Appendix 1), but the Procter & Gamble (P&G) case is representative of the other cases.

The relationship between P&G and BT's derivatives unit was established in January 1993 when the company set up a broad agreement with the bank for derivatives contracts. In November 1993, P&G agreed to buy a leveraged derivative product; P&G would make large profits if interest rates decreased and would lose money if interest rates increased. Leveraged derivatives products are a complex type of derivative, and their value can fluctuate to a greater degree than ordinary derivatives. The derivative worked fine at first, and P&G was sufficiently satisfied to agree to a second leveraged derivative contract in February 1994. However, interest rates began to rise that same month, significantly increasing P&G's payments to BT.

It is unclear whether P&G knew the cost of getting out of the contract, and P&G has since acknowledged that its internal procedures were not followed when it agreed to this derivative. P&G claimed that Bankers fraudulently induced it to buy complex derivatives, misrepresented their value, and then induced P&G to buy more for alleged gains or to staunch losses. However, P&G appeared to be an active market player. It had $5 billion in long-term debt, and its treasury managed a large, sophisticated portfolio of derivatives. P&G has acknowledged that its internal procedures were not followed when it entered into the derivatives contracts in November 1993. Ed Artzt, P&G's CEO, said the executives who bought the derivatives ignored policies against such speculation and were "like farm boys at a country carnival." His treasurer, Ray Mains, didn't read the contract he signed, didn't ask the right questions, and didn't assess risk by seeking outside help. Artzt also said Mains "failed to tell his boss when he knew he had a problem, . . . delayed while losses piled up, . . .

and misled his boss into believing the loss was much smaller than it was."[5] P&G's CFO, Erik Nelson, relied on Mains instead of getting outside advice and did not inform Artzt or the board of the problems with the deal.

P&G's court filings include taped conversations that took place at Bankers Trust. In November 1993, Kevin Hudson, a managing director and salesman on the P&G deal, told his fiancee that the transaction would bring BT a profit of $7.6 million. She asked, "Do they understand that? What they did?" He replied, "No. They understand what they did but they don't understand the leverage." She warned Hudson that the deal would blow up on him. He replied, "I'll be looking for a new opportunity at the bank by then anyways." When the Fed raised interest rates in February 1994, P&G lost $157 million and when asked if "they were dying" Hudson replied, "They don't know." He was even then trying to sell P&G a second leveraged derivative and said, "Let me just get the deutsche mark trade done first; then they can ask." By April 12 that year, P&G announced a $157 million derivatives bath. Hudson's bonus for 1993 was $1.3 million. (He and his fiancee were married on November 5, 1994, live in London, and are still working for BT.[5])

P&G contended that, when it asked for an explanation of the costs, it learned that the bank was using a proprietary model to calculate the costs which it would not share with P&G.[4] P&G alleged that, in April, BT gave the company charts which showed that it would have had to pay a penalty to get out of its November contract almost from the day it was initiated.

Further evidence points to taped conversations between BT employees in which a BT salesman, discussing P&G's decision to enter into the November contract, says "we set 'em up."[4*] P&G finally locked in interest rates on both the derivatives; however, it claimed that by the time it finished doing so, its financing costs were $195.5 million higher than they should have been (p. 110).[4]

5. Loomis, C. J., "Bankers Trust Times—More Dirt About Derivatives," *Fortune Magazine,* November 27, 1995, 34.

Companies That Procter & Gamble Says Lost Money on Derivatives Due to Bankers Trust's Allegedly Fraudulent Sales Practices

COMPANY	LOSS (MILLIONS $US)
Procter & Gamble	195.5
Air Products	105.8
Sandoz	78.5
P.T. Adimitra Rayapratama	50.0
Federal Paper Board	47.0
Gibson Greetings	23.0
Equity Group Holdings	11.2
Sequa	7.5
Jefferson Smurfit	over 2.4

Source: Business Week, October 16, 1995.

P&G asserted that BT employees were trying to deceive it from the day the derivatives contract was initiated. As evidence, P&G points to a taped conversation between Bankers employees about the November contract where one asks: "Do they [P&G] understand that? What they did?"[4] The other employee replies: "No. They understand what they did but they don't understand the leverage, no."[4] The first employee then says: "But I mean . . . how much do you tell them. What is your obligation to them?"[4] The second employee responds: "To tell them if it goes wrong, what does it mean in a payout formula . . ."[4] P&G sued BT in October 1994, alleging that the bank "deliberately misled and deceived it, keeping the company in the dark about key aspects of the derivatives the bank was selling (p. 106)."[4]

BT countered that P&G was an active and sophisticated player in the financial markets and knew how its derivatives would perform. In court filings, BT described P&G as "sophisticated, experienced, and knowledgeable about the use of interest-rate derivative contracts and the risks presented by those contracts (p. 109)."[4] It added: "Although P&G would like this court to believe that it is a naive and unsophisticated user of derivatives transactions, the fact is that as part of its regular course of business and with authorization from top management, P&G's Treasury Department managed a large and sophisticated portfolio of derivative transactions (p. 109)."[4] BT asserted that P&G knew how the derivatives would perform and had included a taped conversation in its court filings in which a BT employee shows a P&G treasury employee how to calculate its rate on the November derivative.[4] BT also produced evidence in court filings that P&G top executives blamed their own personnel for the investments. "Rather than putting its own house in order, and accepting its losses, P&G chose instead to bring this lawsuit (p. 111)."[4]

On September 1, 1995, P&G filed a motion in the U.S. District Court, which was approved, to add RICO (racketeer-influenced and corrupt organization) charges to the allegations against BT. A company found guilty of RICO charges is liable for three times the damages and plaintiff's legal costs. Banker's counter-filing called this "blackmail", saying P&G was hoping to vilify BT by the sheer number of its charges.

The lawsuit was settled out of court in May 1996.

Questions

1. What do you think the basis of settlement should have been?

2. Did BT have a duty to disclose all the information it had regarding the transactions to P&G, including pricing, mark to market value, and risk, or should P&G, a multibillion-dollar company, have ensured that it knew and understood these figures and risks prior to engaging in the transactions?

3. Did BT have an ethical duty to ascertain the suitability of these products for P&G, or did its responsibilities end with providing its client with the product it demanded?

4. Was the maxim of "buyer beware" more appropriate than "seller beware"?

5. What other ethical issues are raised by the case?

Dow Corning Silicon Breast Implants

On January 6, 1992, the "growing controversy over the safety factor led the U.S. Food and Drug Administration to call for a moratorium on breast implants."[1] As January wore on, the crisis deepened until, on January 30, the Toronto *Globe & Mail* carried a New York Times Service report entitled "Dow Corning Fumbles in Damage Control." Among other critical points, that article stated:

> Regardless of whether Dow Corning Inc. ever convinces regulators its silicone-gel breast

---

Dow Cancels Implant Line
Rob McKenzie
Financial Post, March 20, 1992

Beseiged Dow Corning Corp quit the breast implant business yesterday, offering money to some women in the U.S. who need their implants removed, but leaving Canadian taxpayers to fund any medical costs here.

Bert Miller, president of subsidiary Dow Corning Canada Inc., said the number of medically necessary removals will not be as high as critics expect.

"I honestly don't think it's a huge amount," he said.

Dow Corning insisted its gel-filled sacs are no health hazard.

"Our reasons for not resuming production and sales, therefore, are not related to issues of science or safety, but to the existing condition of the marketplace," Dow Corning chairman and chief executive Keith McKennon said in a statement.

Miller told reporters in Toronto he was "personally quite convinced that there's been no unnecessary risk that wasn't worth the benefit."

He added: "We at Dow Corning stand by our product."

Many women say the company's silicone-gel implants maimed them or caused other health problems, either by leaking or bursting.

On Feb. 20, a panel of the U.S. Food and Drug Administration recommended use of the implants be sharply restricted. In Canada the Department of Health and Welfare has imposed a moratorium on their use.

Dow Corning, a Michigan-based joint venture of Dow Chemical Co. and Corning Inc., sold more than 600,000 breast implants, including an estimated 27,000 in Canada.

Besides ceasing production and sales, the company said it will spend US$10 million on research into breast implants. In the U.S., it will offer up to US$1,200 each to women who for medical reasons need their implants excised, but are not covered by private health insurance.

Miller said such surgery in Canada is covered by health-care programs.

Women who fear their implants will harm them, but as yet show no ill effects, are not eligible for aid.

"If she has no physical manifestation and the implant is not giving any problems, she should be calmed," Miller said.

Bryan Groulx, a manager of business development for the Canadian unit, added: "We're not here to provide unnecessary surgery."

One of Dow Corning's strongest critics, Ottawa consultant and breast-implant expert Dr. Pierre Blais, said yesterday's announcement was "a courageous and an appropriate decision."

Breast implants account for about 1% of Dow Corning's sales.

---

1. Feder, Barnaby, "Dow Corning Fumbles in Damage Control," *Toronto Globe & Mail,* January 30, 1992, 3.

implants are safe, the company seems likely to be branded as bungling in its handling of the problem, say public relations and crisis management experts.

"It's a textbook case of crisis management," . . . "it looks like the lawyers are in charge, trying to limit their liability." "But the damage is much worse to the corporation if they lose in the court of public opinion than if they lose in the court of law."

Consultants concede that, because Dow Corning argues there is little evidence supporting many of the injury claims, it is difficult for the company to act sympathetically without appearing to undermine its legal strategy. (p. B1)

The controversy escalated until, on March 20, one month after the U.S. authorities called for sharply restricted use and their Canadian counterparts opted for a moratorium, Dow Corning canceled its breast implant line. The company also offered up to $1,200 each to women in the U.S. not covered by private insurance who needed to have their implants removed. In addition, $10 million was to be spent by the company on research into breast implants.[2]

Among the issues raised by this unfortunate controversy is how faulty breast implants could come to be sold by Dow Corning, a company that had been lionized for almost a decade in three Harvard cases for its outstanding ethics program. The basic details of this program* are as follows:

> Six managers serve three-year stints on a Business Conduct Committee; each member devotes up to six weeks a year on committee work.

> Two members audit every business operation every three years; the panel reviews up to 35 locations annually.

> Three-hour reviews are held with up to 35 employees. Committee members use a code of ethics as a framework and encourage employees to raise ethical issues.

> Results of audits are reported to a three-member Audit & Social Responsibility Committee of the Board of Directors.[3]

Interestingly, although the silicone breast implant operation had been audited four times since 1983, and the ethics audit approach had failed to uncover any signs of problems, Jere Marciniak, an area vice president who is chairman of the Conduct Committee, has stated that "he has no plans to touch . . . the ethics program. . . . 'It will still aid and guide us through this difficult time.'"

Questions

1. Why didn't the Dow Corning ethics audit program reveal any concerns about the silicone-gel breast implant line?

2. What are the critical factors necessary to make such an ethics audit program work effectively?

3. Was the announcement on March 20 well-advised and ethical?

4. Are there any other ethical dilemmas raised by the case?

Source: "Dow cancels implant line," *Financial Post*, March 20, 1992.

---

* Further details of the program are described in "Dow Corning Corporation: Business Conduct and Global Values (A)," Harvard Business School case #9-385-018. See also pages 212 and 213 of the article by P. E. Murphy, which is a reading in this chapter.

2. McKenzie, Rob, "Dow Cancels Implant Line," *Financial Post*, March 20, 1992, 3.

3. Byrne, John A., "The Best Laid Ethics Programs," *Business Week*, March 9, 1992, 67–69.

Creating Ethical Corporate Structures

Patrick E. Murphy[*]

Sloan Management Review, Winter 1989, pp. 81–87

ETHICAL BUSINESS PRACTICES stem from ethical corporate cultures, the author writes. How does an organization go about developing that kind of culture? The most systematic approach is to build and nurture structures that emphasize the importance of ethical considerations. This paper outlines several companies' experiences with three types of ethics-enhancing structures: corporate credos, programs such as training workshops and ethics "audits," and codes tailored to the specific needs of a functional area. Ed.

WHAT IS AN ETHICAL COMPANY?

This question is not easy to answer. For the most part, ethical problems occur because corporate managers and their subordinates are *too* devoted to the organization. In their loyalty to the company or zest to gain recognition, people sometimes ignore or overstep ethical boundaries. For example, some sales managers believe that the only way to meet ambitious sales goals is to have the sales reps "buy" business with lavish entertaining and gift giving. This overzealousness is the key source of ethical problems in most business firms.

Employees are looking for guidance in dealing with ethical problems. The guidance may come from the CEO, upper management, or immediate supervisors.[1] We know that ethical business practices stem from an ethical corporate culture. Key questions are, How can this culture be created and sustained? What structural approaches encourage ethical decision making? If the goal is to make the company ethical, managers must introduce structural components that will enhance ethical sensitivity.

In this paper, I examine three promising and workable approaches to infusing ethical principles into business:

| corporate credos that define and give direction to corporate values;

| ethics programs where companywide efforts focus on ethical issues; and

| ethical codes that provide specific guidance to employees in functional business areas.

Below I review the virtues and limitations of each and provide examples of companies that successfully employ these approaches.

Corporate Credos

A corporate credo delineates a company's ethical responsibility to its stakeholders; it is probably the most general approach to managing corporate ethics. The credo is a succinct statement of the values permeating the firm. The experiences of Security Pacific Corporation (a Los Angeles–based national bank that devised a credo in 1987) and of Johnson & Johnson illustrate the credo approach.

Security Pacific's central document is not an ethical code per se; rather, it is six missionlike commitments to customers, employees, communities, and stockholders. The credo's objective is "to seek a set of principles and beliefs which might provide guidance and direction to our work" (see Table 1).

More than 70 high-level managers participated in formulating a first draft of the commitments. During this process, senior managers shared the analyzed examples of ethical dilemmas they had faced in balancing corporate and

Patrick E. Murphy is Associate Professor of Marketing at the College of Business Administration, University of Notre Dame. Dr. Murphy holds the M.B.A. degree from the University of Notre Dame, the M.B.A. degree from Bradley University, and the Ph.D. degree from the University of Houston. He is currently editor of the Journal of Public Policy and Marketing.

1. P. E. Murphy and M. G. Dunn, "Corporate Culture and Marketing Management Ethics," (South Bend, IN: University of Notre Dame, working paper, 1988).

TABLE 1

The Credo of Security Pacific Corporation

Commitment to Customer

The first commitment is to provide our customers with quality products and services which are innovative and technologically responsive to their current requirements, at appropriate prices. To perform these tasks with integrity requires that we maintain confidentiality and protect customer privacy, promote customer satisfaction, and serve customer needs. We strive to serve qualified customers and industries which are socially responsible according to broadly accepted community and company standards.

Commitment to Employee

The second commitment is to establish an environment for our employees which promotes professional growth, encourages each person to achieve his or her highest potential, and promotes individual creativity and responsibility. Security Pacific acknowledges our responsibility to employees, including providing for open and honest communication, stated expectations, fair and timely assessment of performance and equitable compensation which rewards employee contributions to company objectives within a framework of equal opportunity and affirmative action.

Commitment of Employee to Security Pacific

The third commitment is that of the employee to Security Pacific. As employees, we strive to understand and adhere to the Corporation's policies and objectives, act in a professional manner, and give our best effort to improve Security Pacific. We recognize the trust and confidence placed in us by our customers and community and act with integrity and honestly in all situations to preserve that trust and confidence. We act responsively to avoid conflicts of interest and other situations which are potentially harmful to the Corporation.

Commitment of Employee to Employee

The fourth commitment is that of employees to their fellow employees. We must be committed to promote a climate of mutual respect, integrity, and professional relationships, characterized by open and honest communication within and across all levels of the organization. Such a climate will promote attainment of the Corporation's goals and objectives, while leaving room for individual initiative within a competitive environment.

Commitment to Communities

The fifth commitment is that of Security Pacific to the communities which we serve. We must constantly strive to improve the quality of life through our support of community organizations and projects, through encouraging service to the community by employees, and by promoting participation in community services. By the appropriate use of our resources, we work to support or further advance the interests of the community, particularly in times of crisis or social need. The Corporation and its employees are committed to complying fully with each community's laws and regulations.

Commitment to Stockholder

The sixth commitment of Security Pacific is to its stockholders. We will strive to provide consistent growth and a superior rate of return on their investment, to maintain a position and reputation as a leading financial institution, to protect stockholder investments, and to provide full and timely information. Achievement of these goals for Security Pacific is dependent upon the successful development of the five previous sets of relationships.

constituent obligations. An outside consultant, hired to manage the process, helped to draft the language. Ultimately more than 250 employees, from all levels of the bank, participated in the credo formulation process via a series of discussion groups.

Once the commitments were in final form, management reached a consensus on how to communicate these guiding principles to the Security Pacific organization. Credo coordinators developed and disseminated a leader's guide to be used at staff meetings introducing the credo; it contained instructions on the meeting's format and on showing a videotape that explained the credo and the process by

which it was developed. At the meetings, managers invited reactions by posing these questions: What are your initial feelings about what you have just read? Are there any specific commitments you would like to discuss? How will the credo affect your daily work? Employees were thus encouraged to react to the credo and to consider its long-run implications.

Security Pacific's credo was recently cited as a model effort, and it serves internally both as a standard for judging existing programs and as a justification for new activities.[2] For example, the "commitment to communities" formed the basis for a program specifically designed to

2. R. E. Berenbeim, *Corporate Ethics* (New York: The Conference Board, research report no. 900, 1987), p. 15, pp. 20–22.

serve low-income constituents in the area. However, this credo should not be considered the definitive approach to ethics management. First, the credo could be interpreted simply as an organizational mission statement, not as a document about ethics. Indeed, the examples supporting the credo and the videotape itself do stress what might just be called good business practice, without particular reference to ethical policies. And second, the credo has not been in place long enough for its impact to be fully assessed.

Any discussion of corporate credos would be incomplete without reference to Johnson & Johnson, whose credo is shown in Table 2. This document focuses on responsibilities to consumers, employees, communities, and stockholders. (The current J&J president, David Clare, explains that responsibility to the stockholder is listed last because "if we do the other jobs properly, the stockholder will always be served.") The first version of this credo, instituted in 1945, was revised in 1947. Between 1975 and 1978, chairman James Burke held a series of meetings with J&J's 1,200 top managers; they were encouraged to "challenge" the credo. What emerged from the meetings was that the document in fact functioned as it was intended to function; a slightly reworded but substantially unchanged credo was introduced in 1979.

Over the last two years, the company has begun to survey all employees about how well the company meets its responsibilities to the four principal constituencies. The survey asks employees from all fifty-three countries where J&J operates questions about every line in the credo. An office devoted to the credo survey tabulates the results, which are confidential. (Department and division managers receive only information pertaining to their units and composite numbers for the entire firm.) The interaction at meetings devoted to discussing these findings is reportedly very good.

Does J&J's credo work? Top management feels strongly that it does. The credo is often mentioned as an important contributing factor in the company's exemplary handling of the Tylenol crises several years ago. It would appear that the firm's commitment to the credo makes ethical business practice its highest priority. One might question whether the credo is adequate to deal with the multitude of ethical problems facing a multinational firm; possibly additional ethical guidelines could serve as reinforcement, especially in dealing with international business issues.

When should a company use a corporate credo to guide its ethical policies? They work best in firms with a cohesive corporate culture, where a spirit of frequent and unguarded communication exists. Generally, small, tightly knit companies find that a credo is sufficient. Among large firms, Johnson & Johnson is an exception. J&J managers consciously use the credo as an ethical guidepost;

TABLE 2

Johnson & Johnson Credo

We believe our first responsibility is to the doctors, nurses, and patients, to mothers and all others who use our products and services. In meeting their needs everything we do must be of high quality. We must constantly strive to reduce our costs in order to maintain reasonable prices. Customers' orders must be serviced promptly and accurately. Our suppliers and distributors must have an opportunity to make a fair profit.

We are responsible to our employees, the men and women who work with us throughout the world. Everyone must be considered as an individual. We must respect their dignity and recognize their merit. They must have a sense of security in their jobs. Compensation must be fair and adequate and working conditions clean, orderly, and safe. Employees must feel free to make suggestions and complaints. There must be equal opportunity for employment, development, and advancement for those qualified. We must provide competent management, and their actions must be just and ethical.

We are responsible to the communities in which we live and work and to the world community as well. We must be good citizens—support good works and charities and bear our fair share of taxes. We must encourage civic improvements and better health and education. We must maintain in good order the property we are privileged to use, protecting the environment and natural resources.

Our final responsibility is to our stockholders. Business must make a sound profit. We must experiment with new ideas. Research must be carried on, innovative programs developed and mistakes paid for. New equipment must be purchased, new facilities provided, and new products launched. Reserves must be created to provide for adverse times. When we operate according to these principles, the stockholders should realize a fair return.

they find that the corporate culture reinforces the credo.

When is a credo insufficient? This approach does not offer enough guidance for most multinational companies facing complex ethical questions in different societies, for firms that have merged recently and are having trouble grafting disparate cultures, and for companies operating in industries with chronic ethical problems. A credo is like the Ten Commandments. Both set forth good general principles, but many people need the Bible, religious teachings, and guidelines provided by organized religion, as well. Similarly, many companies find that they need to offer more concrete guidance on ethical issues.

Ethics Program

Ethics programs provide more specific direction for dealing with potential ethical problems than general credos do. Two companies—Chemical Bank and Dow Corning—serve as examples. Although the thrust of the two programs is different, they both illustrate the usefulness of this approach.

Chemical Bank, the nation's fourth largest bank, has an extensive ethics education program. All new employees attend an orientation session at which they read and sign off on Chemical's code of ethics. (This has been in existence for thirty years and was last revised in May 1987.) The training program features a videotaped message from the chairman emphasizing the bank's values and ethical standards. A second and more unusual aspect of the program provides in-depth training in ethical decision making for vice presidents.[3]

The "Decision Making and Corporate Values" course is a two-day seminar that occurs away from the bank. Its purpose, according to a bank official, is "to encourage Chemical's employees to weigh the ethical or value dimensions of the decisions they make and to provide them with the analytic tools to do that." This program began in 1983; more than 250 vice presidents have completed the

course thus far. Each meeting is limited to twenty to twenty-five senior vice presidents from a cross-section of departments, this size makes for a seminar-like atmosphere. The bank instituted the program in response to the pressures associated with deregulation, technology, and increasing competition.

The chairman always introduces the seminar by highlighting his personal commitment to the program. Most of the two days is spent discussing case studies. The fictitious cases were developed following interviews with various Chemical managers who described ethically charged situations. The cases are really short stories about loan approval, branch closings, foreign loans, insider trading, and other issues.[4] They do not have "solutions" as such; instead, they pose questions for discussion, such as, Do you believe the individual violated the bank's code? Or, What should X do?

Program evaluations have yielded positive results. Participants said they later encountered dilemmas similar to the cases, and that they had developed a thinking process in the seminar that helped them work through other problems. This program, while it is exemplary, only reaches a small percentage of Chemical's 30,000 employees. Ideally, such a program would be disseminated more widely and would become more than a one-time event.

Dow Corning has a longstanding—and very different—ethics program. Its general code has been revised four times since its inception in 1976 and includes a seven-point values statement. The company started using face-to-face "ethical audits" at its plants worldwide more than a decade ago. The number of participants in these four-to-six-hour audits ranges from five to forty. Auditors meet with the manager in charge the evening before to ascertain the most pressing issues. The actual questions come from relevant sections in the corporate code and are adjusted for the audit location. At sales offices, for example, the auditors concentrate on issues such as kickbacks, unusual requests from customers,

---

3. A more detailed discussion of Chemical's comprehensive program, and of Johnson & Johnson's, appears in *Corporate Ethics: A Prime Business Asset* (New York: Business Roundtable, February 1988).

4. One of the case studies appears in "Would You Blow Whistle on Wayward Colleague?" *American Banker* 17, June 1988, p. 16.

and special pricing terms; at manufacturing plants, conservation and environmental issues receive more attention. An ethical audit might include the following questions.

I Are there any examples of business that Dow Corning has lost because of our refusal to provide "gifts" or other incentives to government officials at our customers' facilities?

I Do any of our employees have ownership or financial interest in any of our distributors?

I Have our sales representatives been able to undertake business conduct discussions with distributors in a way that actually strengthens our ties with them?

I Has Dow Corning been forced to terminate any distributors because of their business conduct practices?

I Do you believe that our distributors are in regular contact with their competitors? If so, why?

I Which specific Dow Corning policies conflict with local practices?

John Swanson, manager of Corporate Internal and Management Communications, heads this effort; he believes the audit approach makes it "virtually impossible for employees to consciously make an unethical decision." According to Swanson, twenty to twenty-three meetings occur every year. The Business Conduct Committee members, who act as session leaders, then prepare a report for the Audit Committee of the board. He stresses the fact that there are no shortcuts to implementing this program—it requires time and extensive interaction with the people involved. Recently the audit was expanded; it now examines internal as well as external activities. (One audit found that some salespeople believed manufacturing personnel needed to be more honest when developing production schedules.) One might ask whether the commitment to ethics is constant over time or peaks during the audit sessions; Dow Corning

may want to conduct surprise audits, or develop other monitoring mechanisms or a more detailed code.

When should a company consider developing an ethics program? Such programs are often appropriate when firms have far-flung operations that need periodic guidance, as is the case at Dow Corning. This type of program can deal specifically with international ethical issues and with peculiarities at various plant locations. Second, an ethics program is useful when managers confront similar ethical problems on a regular basis, as Chemical Bank executives do. Third, these programs are useful in organizations that use outside consultants or advertising agencies. If an independent contractor does not subscribe to a corporate credo, the firm may want to use an ethical audit or checklist to heighten the outside agency's sensitivity to ethical issues.

When do ethics programs come up lacking? If they are too issue centered, ethics programs may miss other, equally important problems. (Dow's program, for example, depends on the questions raised by the audit.) In addition, the scope of the program may limit its impact to only certain parts of the organization (e.g., Chemical Bank). Managers who want to permanently inculcate ethical considerations may be concerned that such programs are not perceived by some employees as being long term or ongoing. If the credo can be compared with the Ten Commandments, then ethics programs can be likened to weekly church services. Both can be uplifting, but once the session (service) is over, individuals may believe they can go back to business as usual.

Tailored Corporate Codes

Codes of conduct, or ethical codes, are another structural mechanism companies use to signal their commitment to ethical principles. Ninety percent of Fortune 500 firms, and almost half of all other firms, have ethical codes. According to a recent survey, this mechanism is perceived as the most effective way to encourage ethical business behavior.[5] Codes commonly address issues such as conflict of interest,

---

5. Touche Ross, *Ethics in American Business* (New York: Touche Ross & Co., January 1988).

competitors, privacy, gift giving and receiving, and political contributions. However, many observers continue to believe that codes are really public relations documents, or motherhood and apple pie statements; these critics claim that codes belittle employees and fail to address practical managerial issues.[6]

Simply developing a code is not enough. It must be tailored to the firm's functional areas (e.g., marketing, finance, personnel) or to the major line of business in which the firm operates. The rationale for tailored codes is simple. Functional areas or diversions have differing cultures and needs. A consumer products division, for example, has a relatively distant relationship with customers, because it relies heavily on advertising to sell its products. A division producing industrial products, on the other hand, has fewer customers and uses a personal, sales-oriented approach. A code needs to reflect these differences. Unfortunately, very few ethics codes do so.

Several companies have exemplary codes tailored to functional or major business areas. I describe two of these below—the St. Paul Companies (specializing in commercial and personal insurance and related products) and International Business Machines (IBM).

The St. Paul Companies revised their extensive corporate code, entitled "In Good Conscience," in 1986. All new employees get introduced to the code when they join the company, and management devotes biannual meetings to discussing the code's impact on day-to-day activities. In each of the five sections, the code offers specific guidance and examples for employees to follow. The statements below illustrate the kinds of issues, and the level of specificity, contained in the code.

▎ Insider Information. For example, if you know that the company is about to announce a rise in quarterly profits, or anything else that would affect the price of the company's stock, you cannot buy or sell the stock until the announcement has been made and published.

▎ Gifts and Entertainment. An inexpensive ballpoint pen, or an appointment diary, is a common gift and generally acceptable. But liquor, lavish entertainment, clothing, or travel should not be accepted.

▎ Contact with Legislators. If you are contacted by legislators on matters relating to the St. Paul, you should refer them to your governmental affairs or law department.

The "Employee Related Issues" section of the code is the most detailed; it directly addresses the company's relationship to the individual, and vice versa. This section spells out what employees can expect in terms of compensation (it should be based on job performance and administered fairly), advancement (promotion is from within, where possible), assistance (this consists of training, job experience, or counseling) and communications (there should be regular feedback; concerns can be expressed without fear of recrimination). It also articulates the St. Paul Companies' expectation of employers regarding speaking up (when you know something that could be a problem), avoiding certain actions (where the public's confidence could be weakened), and charting your career course.

The company also delineates employee privacy issues. The code outlines how work-related information needed for hiring and promotion is collected. (Only information needed to make the particular decision is gathered; it is collected from the applicant/employee where possible. Polygraphs are not used.) The St. Paul informs employees about what types of information are maintained. Finally, information in an individual's file is open to the employee's review.

The code covers other important personnel issues in depth, as well. It touches on equal opportunity by mentioning discrimination laws, but the emphasis is on the company recognition of past discrimination and its

---

6. Berenbeim (1987), p. 17.

commitments to "make an affirmative effort to address this situation in all of its programs and practices." Data acquired from the St. Paul supports this point. Between 1981 and 1986, hiring and promotion increased 60 percent for minorities in supervisory positions and 49 percent for women in management—even though overall employment rose only about 3 percent during this time. In addition, the code informs employees that the company will reimburse all documented business expenses. And it covers nepotism by stating that officers' and directors' relatives will not be hired; other employees' relatives can be employed, so long as they are placed in different departments.

Being an ethical company requires providing clear guidelines for employees. The St. Paul Companies' extensive discussion of personnel policies does just that. Employees may strongly disapprove of certain policies, but they are fully informed. The termination policy, for example, states that employment is voluntary and that individuals are free to resign at any time; the company, too, can terminate employees "at any time, with or without cause." Some people may consider that policy unfair or punitive, but at least the rules of the game are clear. One limitation of the code is that all sections are not uniformly strong. For example, the marketing section is only one paragraph long and contains few specifics.

The second illustration is of a code tailored to the company's major line of business. IBM's "Business Conduct Guidelines" were instituted in the 1960s and revised more recently in 1983. New employees receive a copy and certify annually that they abide by the code. It has four parts; the most extensive section is entitled "Conducting IBM's Business." Since IBM is, at its core, a marketing and sales organization, this section pertains primarily to these issues.

Six subsections detail the type of activities IBM expects of its sales representatives. First, "Some General Standards" include the following directives, with commentaries: do not make misrepresentations to anyone, do not take advantage of IBM's size, treat everyone fairly (do not extend preferential treatment), and do not practice reciprocal dealing. Second, "Fairness in the Field" pertains to disparagement (sell IBM products on their merits, not

by disparaging competitors' products or services). In addition, it prohibits premature disclosure of product information and of selling if a competitor already has a signed order. Third, "Relations with Other Organizations" cautions employees about firms that have multiple relationships with IBM (deal with only one relationship at a time, and do not collaborate with these firms).

The fourth and fifth sections address "Acquiring and Using Information for or about Others." The code spells out the limits to acquiring information (industrial espionage is wrong) and to using information (adverse information should not be retained). Employers must determine the confidentiality of information gathered from others. The final section outlines IBM's policy on "Bribes, Gifts, and Entertainment." The company allows customary business amenities but prohibits giving presents that are intended to "unduly influence" or "obligate" the recipient, as well as receiving gifts worth more than a nominal amount.

One might contend that it is easy for a large, profitable company like IBM to have an exemplary code. On the other hand, one could also argue that a real reason for the company's continued success is that its sales representatives do subscribe to these principles. Is this a perfect code? No. The gifts area could use more specificity and, even though the company spends millions of dollars a year on advertising, that subject is not addressed in any section of the code. Further, IBM's legal department administers the code, which may mean that problems are resolved more by legal than ethical interpretation.

When should a company use a tailored code of ethics? If a company has one dominant functional unit (like IBM), or if there is diversity among functional areas, divisions, or subsidiaries, then a tailored code might be advisable. It allows the firm to promulgate specific and appropriate standards. Tailored codes are especially useful to complex organizations because they represent permanent guidelines for managers and employees to consult.

When should they be avoided? If a firm's leaders believe specific guidelines may be too restrictive for their employees, then a tailored code is an unsatisfactory choice. Codes are not necessary in most small firms or in ones where a culture includes firmly entrenched ethical policies. If a credo is similar to the Ten Commandments, and programs are similar to religious services, then tailored credos can be considered similar to the Bible or to other formal religious teachings. They provide the most guidance, but many people do not take the time to read or reflect on them.

Conclusion

My research on ethics in management suggests several conclusions that the corporate manager may wish to keep in mind.

| **There Is No Single Ideal Approach to Corporate Ethics.** I would recommend that a small firm start with a credo, but that a larger firm consider a program or a tailored code. It is also possible to integrate these programs and produce a hybrid: in dealing with insider trading, for example, a firm could develop a training program, then follow it up with a strongly enforced tailored code.[7]

| **Top Management Must Be Committed.** Senior managers must champion the highest ethical postures for their companies, as James Burke of J&J does. This commitment was evident in all the companies described here; it came through loud and clear in the CEO's letters, reports, and public statements.

| **Developing a Structure Is Not Sufficient by Itself.** The structure will not be useful unless it is supported by institutionalized managerial processes. The credo meetings at Security Pacific and the seminars at Chemical Bank are examples of processes that support structures.

| **Raising the Ethical Consciousness of an Organization Is Not Easy.** All the companies mentioned here have spent countless hours—and substantial amounts of money—developing, discussing, revising, and communicating the ethical principles of the firm. And in fact there are no guarantees that it will work. McDonnell Douglas has an extensive ethics program, but some of its executives were implicated in a recent defense contractor scandal.

In conclusion, let me add that managers in firms with active ethics structures—credos, programs, and tailored codes—are genuinely enthusiastic about them. They believe that ethics pay off. Their conviction should provide others with an encouraging example.

The author would like to thank Bernard Avisbai, Gene Laczniak, Michael Mokwa, Lee Tavis, and Oliver Williams, C.S.C., for their helpful comments on an earlier version of this article.

Source: Reprinted from " Creating Ethical Corporate Structures," Patrick E. Murphy Sloan Management Review, Winter 1989, pp. 81–87, by permission of the publisher. Copyright © 1989 by Sloan Management Review Association. All rights reserved.

---

7. G. L. Tidwell, "Here's a Tip—Know the Rules of Insider Trading." *Sloan Management Review*, Summer 1987, pp. 93–99.

APPENDIX A
ALTERNATIVE GOVERNANCE THEORIES

A Traditional Governance Model— Agency Theory

Agency theory is an attempt to explain organizational behavior, and in particular corporate governance structures, based on the premise that there is an inherent conflict of interest between principals (who own the firm) and agents (who manage the firm). From this principle of a conflict of interest, it develops a comprehensive theory that addresses the importance of contracts, both formal and informal, and both written and tacit, that are used in monitoring, controlling, and motivating managerial behavior. It also explains the importance of financial reporting.

Agency theory is grounded on the concept of self-interest; this is not the cooperative self-interest of Thomas Hobbes and Adam Smith that leads to civil society and economic prosperity.[1] Rather, it is self-interest in a noncooperative fashion where the interest of the managers of the firm are not always aligned with the interest of the owners of the firm. Both investors and managers are interested in maximizing their personal utility. Investors want a reasonable return on their investment, either in terms of stock price appreciation resulting in a capital gain or in terms of cash distributions from the firm through dividends. Management, by contrast, is interested in compensation. Managers are motivated through self-interest to do a good job and learn new managerial skills so that they can either receive more pay, or move to another job where they can receive higher compensation. Agency theory makes the simplifying assumption that managers are motivated only by extrinsic tangible monetary-based rewards, such as direct cash compensation through regular pay and bonuses, and indirect compensation through fringe benefits such as pension plans, medical care, and stock options.

In a sole proprietorship, the owner of the business is also its manager. They are one in the same. However, in corporations, and especially in large publicly traded companies, there is clear separation of ownership from control.

The owners (called principals) have no desire to operate the firm; they simply want to earn a reasonable return on their investment. So, they hire and then delegate to management (the agent) the responsibility for operating the firm on the investors' behalf. Because they control the daily operations of the firm, management knows or has access to all the information about the firm. The investors, on the other hand, only know what they are told by management, normally through periodic financial statements and the annual report. As such there is a huge information asymmetry problem. Although they are the owners of the firm, they really don't know what is happening at their firm. This gives rise to two potential problems: adverse selection and moral hazard. Both of these problems occur because agency theory assumes that the manager will always act opportunistically; that is, when valid options are available the manager will choose the option that is in the best interest of management, even when that option might not be in the best interest of the investors.

Adverse selection occurs because management has better or more complete information about the firm than the investors. As such, management can make investment and credit decisions that may be profitable to managers but not to investors. A prime example is insider trading. Before management releases a piece of bad news that will negatively affect the price of the firm's stock, management might short the stock, and then buy the stock after the price falls. Management profits through a capital gain based on insider knowledge. This is why there are laws to prevent insider trading.

Moral hazard occurs because managerial behavior cannot be observed. All the investors see are the consequences of the decisions of management. As such, managers can shirk. They can avoid putting in effort without being detected by the investors. For example, all other things being equal, investors would prefer to see high net income rather than low net income. However, management, who choose and implement the accounting

---

1. For the ethical theories of Hobbes and Smith see Chapter 3.

policies of the firm, can artificially increase income by judiciously selecting specific income-increasing accounting policies. For example, straight-line amortization of long-life assets tends to show a lower expense in the early years of the assets' lives than double-declining balance. So, although neither policy has an impact on the cash flows of the firm, the straight-line method reports a lower expense and therefore a higher net income than the double-declining method. Management can also adjust discretionary accruals in order to manage reported earnings. Any accounting estimate that is determined by management, such as the allowance for doubtful accounts, inventory obsolescence and the provision for warranty expense, can be selected opportunistically in order to manipulate the reported earnings of the firm without altering the firm's actual cash flows. These discretionary accruals are not separately disclosed in the firm's set of financial statements, and so this form of managerial opportunism is not readily apparent to investors. Their manipulations cannot readily be observed by the investors.

In order to minimize the problems associated with moral hazard and adverse selection, investors implement various control mechanisms. The two most common are monitoring and bonding. Monitoring can occur by having the internal auditors check to ensure that the firm's control structures are operating efficiently and effectively. External accountants are hired by the investor to review and report on the financial statements that are prepared by management. But it is the board of directors that act as the key monitoring mechanism in most firms. The board represents all the investors. The board is to ensure that the decisions of management are in the best long-term interests of the firm and its owners. It does this by monitoring management and in particular by selecting and overseeing the CEO. However, monitoring can be costly, and not always effective. Enron had a blue-ribbon board of directors, and yet they failed to oversee and govern correctly.[2]

Bonding occurs through management compensation contracts. The idea is that a contract can be written to align the interest of management with those of the investor. For example, the investor is interested in a high net income. So, if the managers are given a share of the reported earnings, then they might be motivated to work very hard on the investors' behalf to increase reported earnings. Another contract might be to give management stock options. If management owns a piece of the firm then their interests as investors of the firm should be the same as the other investors of the firm. Because their interests are now aligned, managers will make decisions that are in the best interests of the investors.

There are obvious problems with this line of reasoning. First, management can increase net income without expending any effort by simply changing the accounting policies. Second, stock options can be abused and be quite costly to the other shareholders. After they exercise their options, managers rarely continue to hold their firm's stock. They prefer to obtain a capital gain, and then use the proceeds to purchase a diversified portfolio thereby mitigating their investment risk. Furthermore, prior to stock options being required to be reported as an expense in 2005, generous stock options were granted to employees on the basis that they were costless. In December 1997, Michael Eisner, then CEO of Disney Corporation, exercised stock options for $570 million. This was not recorded as an expense for Disney, but it was a cost to the other shareholders in terms of the dilution of their ownership by the amount of the options given to Eisner. This was not a costless transaction for the owners of Disney stock.

The primary weakness of agency theory is that it has a very narrow focus concerning human behavior. It views business activity as being conducted between atomistic principals and agents operating outside of a social context. Yet business is also a social activity conducted in a cooperative yet competitive manner as explained by Adam Smith.[3] People

---

2. See Chapter 2 for a richer analysis of the failure of the Board of Directors to govern Enron adequately and the inability of Arthur Anderson to objectively assess Enron's financial statements.

3. See Chapter 3 for a discussion of the importance of cooperation in economics, as per Adam Smith.

find satisfaction in work and an opportunity to utilize the skills and talents in a productive manner that contributes to their own well-being and, through the invisible hand, to the betterment of society. Stewardship Theory captures the social and cooperative aspects of work.

A More Holistic Approach to Governance—Stewardship Theory

Stewardship theory assumes no inherent conflict between principals and agents, between employees and investors, nor between subordinates and their supervisors. There is no trade-off between personal needs and organizational needs. Stewards identify with the goals of the firm, and strive to make sure those goals are achieved. The steward's interests are aligned with those of the investor and so the steward is less apt to engage in self-serving behaviors and actions that transfer wealth from the investor to the steward. As such, there is a lower need for monitoring and control mechanisms. Instead, in a stewardship environment, there is more emphasis placed on empowerment and structures that facilitate cooperative activities in a non-adversarial fashion.

Stewardship theory recognizes that there is often a very strong relationship between the success of the firm and the personal needs of the employees. Stewards take pride and satisfaction in working for the firm, and share vicariously in the success and failures of the firm as well as the steward's coworkers. Employees proudly wear their firm's company logo on their clothing, while saying "We just landed this great contract with a new supplier" even though they had no part in the contract negotiations.

Managers, under agency theory, are motivated by extrinsic monetary rewards. Stewards are motivated by both intrinsic and extrinsic rewards. Intrinsic rewards include recognition, advancement, growth, the opportunity to learn, and to become self actualized. However, stewards normally want more intrinsic rewards than extrinsic ones. A survey of public accountants in Canada revealed that most were interested in interesting work that is intellectually challenging.[4] The number one workplace priority for those surveyed was interesting work, followed by intellectual challenge, and then a good corporate culture. Of the top twelve priorities, high compensation (number four) and job security (number eight) were the only extrinsic rewards mentioned as being a priority. Canadian public accountants appear to be more aligned with stewardship than agency theory.

Most people acknowledge that there is an interdependent and interpenetrating relationship between business and society. Each influences and in turn is influenced by the other. The activities of business influence public policy which in turn influences business. For example, the Enron and WorldCom debacles lead to Congress passing the Sarbanes-Oxley Act in the United Sates. The rules and restrictions of SOX have, in turn, influenced business behavior as was mentioned in Chapter 2.

Stewardship theory acknowledges this interpenetrating relationship, and sees an interconnectedness among the individual, her or his work, and society. It has a more holistic concept of the individual, and the individuals place in business and society. Stewards want to contribute to the success and well-being of their firm. They also want to contribute to the success and well-being of society. They see no separation between these two activities. This may be why so many people want to work for socially responsible firms. An online 2006 survey by Care2[5] of nearly 1,600 people revealed that:

- 73 percent said that working for a socially responsible company was very important,

- 48 percent said that they would work for less pay if they could work for a socially responsible company, and

---

4. See "What CAs Want," in *CAMagazine*, August 2007. http://www.camagazine.com/index.cfm/ci_id/ 38627/la_id/1

5. See "Socially Responsible Companies Rank High with Job Seekers," January 31, 2006 press release by Care2. http://www.care2.com/aboutus/080206.html

- 40 percent said that they would work longer hours if they worked for a socially responsible company.

These are all aspects of a stewardship perspective that contends that that employees want to contribute to the success of their employer's business while at the same time contributing to the well-being of society.

The natural extension of this stewardship perspective into corporate governance was originally incorporated into the *laissez-faire* type of approach known as the original Carver Model[6] of board governance, which was based on boards of directors hiring the CEO and approving organizational policy, but essentially delegating ongoing monitoring to the CEO. However, many of those who subscribed to this approach found that the ethics and operational risks of "governance by policy"—of divorcing the board from ongoing monitoring—were too high and a revised Carver model was developed.

It is evident that the agency model—of top-down control that monitors opportunistic agents—still has a role to play today. The examples of unbridled greed and abuses of managerial power by unaccountable executives at Enron, WorldCom, Adelphia Communications, and Parmalat SpA illustrate the need for improved corporate governance structures. But the existence of rogue managers should not be used to stifle the creativity of other managers who have a stewardship perspective.

New governance structures are needed that balance the need for control with the need to create an innovative environment where talented managers can increase firm value in an ethically and socially responsible manner. This means that perspectives must be broadened. The firm is more than simply investors and managers. There are a variety of other stakeholders who have an interest, or stake, in the firm, and their interests cannot be ignored. The lessons of the last few years have shown that corporations are strategically accountable to numerous stakeholder groups, not just to shareholders. New perspectives on governance and accountability are required to meet this challenge.

TABLE 5.22   **Comparison of Agency Theory & Stewardship Theory**

	AGENCY THEORY	STEWARDSHIP THEORY
View of the individual Behavioral assumptions	Economic agent Opportunistic wealth maximizer	Complex and modern Holistic and rounded view of human nature
Behavioral characteristics	• self-serving—employees will choose the options that are in their own best interests • risk-averse—there is an increasing disutility for wealth • effort-averse—employees will shirk	• want to contribute • will choose to do right • strive to achieve • like to innovate • want to do competent work • interested in a work-life balance
Management philosophy Motivation Organizational identification Trust	Control oriented Extrinsic rewards Low value commitment Low—employees are work averse and so they will shirk	Involvement oriented More intrinsic than extrinsic rewards High commitment High—stewards have an inherent preference for honesty

Sources: James H. Davis, F. David Schoorman and Lex Donaldson, "Toward A Stewardship Theory of Management", *Academy of Management Review* 1997, Vol. 22, No. 1, 20-47. Steven E. Salterio and Alan Webb, "Honesty in Accounting and Control: A Discussion of 'The Effect of Information Systems on Honesty in Managerial Reporting: A Behavioral Perspective'", *Contemporary Accounting Research* 2006, Vol. 23, No. 4, 919-932.

---

6. See Carver, John, *Boards that Make a Difference,* Jossey-Bass, 2e, 1997, or visit http://www.carvergovernance.com/

6

PROFESSIONAL ACCOUNTING IN THE PUBLIC INTEREST, POST-ENRON

Purpose of the Chapter

When the Enron, Arthur Andersen, and WorldCom debacles triggered the U. S. Sarbanes-Oxley Act of 2002 (SOX), a new era of stakeholder expectations was crystallized for the business world and particularly for the professional accountants that serve in it. The drift away from the professional accountant's role as a fiduciary to that of a businessperson was called into question and reversed. The principles that the new expectations spawned and renewed resulted in changes in how the professional accountants are to behave, what services are to be offered, and what performance standards are to be met. These standards have been embedded in a new governance structure and in guidance mechanisms, which have domestic and international components. The influence of the International Accounting Standards Board (IASB) and the International Federation of Accountants (IFAC) will be as important as that of SOX in the long run because professional accounting bodies governing CPAs, CAs, CMAs and CGAs around the world have agreed to harmonize their standards and codes of ethics to IASB and IFAC pronouncements.

This chapter examines each of these developments and provides insights into important areas of current and future practice. Building upon the understanding of the new stakeholder accountability framework facing clients and employers developed in earlier chapters, this chapter explores public expectations for the role of the professional accountant and the principles that should be observed in discharging that role. This leads to consideration of the implications for services to be offered, and of the key "value added" or competitive edge that accountants should focus their attention on to maintain their reputation and vitality. Sources of ethical governance and guidance are also introduced. Prior reading of Chapter 2 is essential to understanding Chapter 6.

Stakeholder Expectations Accountability & Governance Framework

Both the increase in importance of traditional stakeholder concerns discussed in Chapter 1, and the impact of the Enron, Arthur Andersen, and WorldCom debacles discussed in Chapter 2, gave rise to a crisis of credibility for the business community, its reports and capital markets, and for professional accountants who were seen to be part of the problem. The public was looking for a return to credibility founded upon values such as trust, integrity, transparency of reports, and so on, and a rededication to the public interest.

SOX, which required the Securities and Exchange Commission (SEC) to create regulations bringing governance reforms for both corporations and the accounting profession, provided much of the answer. These reforms forced change upon those U.S. and foreign corporations (known as SEC registrants) and their auditors, that wish to access U.S. capital markets.

Enron-induced SOX reforms also triggered or reinforced the need for similar governance changes for corporations and professional accountants around the world.

A significant parallel development that benefited from the Enron-SOX concerns, was the development of a set of international accounting standards for corporations and a code of ethics for professional accountants to harmonize to worldwide. The International Federation of Accountants (IFAC) developed the IFAC Code of Ethics,[1] and released an initial version in 2001 and a revised version in 2005. The member organizations of IFAC—the professional accounting bodies around the world such as the American Institute of Certified Public Accountants (AICPA), the Institutes of Chartered Accountants, as well as Management Accountants, and Certified General Accountants—have agreed to bring their own codes of ethics into substantial agreement with the IFAC Code, which states that:

> A distinguishing mark of the accountancy profession is its acceptance of the responsibility to act in the public interest.[2]

The SOX and IFAC reforms called for business to be more openly accountable to the investing public, and for professional accountants to remember that they are professionals who are expected to protect the interests of investors and other stakeholders. Professional accountants are not expected to be involved in misrepresentations in order to assist management, or to avoid risk of losing audit revenues—or their jobs, if they are employees.

At the same time, the concerns of noninvestor stakeholders, such as customers, employees, or environmentalists, were becoming serious barriers to the achievement of corporate objectives. Damage to reputation caused by ethical problems was recognized to be so significant as to be potentially fatal, as in the case of Arthur Andersen.

Consequently, both business and professional accountants recognized that their future success depended upon meeting new regulations, and upon meeting the ethical expectations of stakeholders. Governance mechanisms for both business and the accounting profession now, more than ever, need to ensure that these expectations will be met.

Rededication of the Role of a Professional Accountant to the Public Interest

Fortunately, the Enron, Arthur Andersen, WorldCom and similar debacles have made clear that professional accountants owe their primary loyalty to the public interest. This rededication to the public interest is critically important. Unless professional accountants clearly and properly understand their role, they cannot consistently answer important questions in an ethically responsible way, and as a result will probably offer questionable advice and make decisions that leave them and their profession exposed to criticism or worse. For instance, a clear understanding of role is essential to respond appropriately to questions about ethical trade-offs encountered, as well as proper services to offer and at what levels, such as:

- Who really is our client—the company, the management, current shareholders, future shareholders, the public?

- In the event I have to make a decision with ethical ramifications, do I owe primary loyalty to my employer, my client, my boss, my profession, the public, or myself?

- Am I a professional accountant bound by professional standards, or just an employee?

---

1. IFAC Code of Ethics for Professional Accountants, 2005, http://www.ifac.org/store/Category.tmpl?Category=Ethics
2. Ibid., Section 100.1

▌ Is professional accounting a profession or a business? Can it be both?

▌ When should I not offer a service?

▌ Can I serve two clients with competing interests at the same time?

▌ Is there any occasion when breaking the profession's guideline against revealing confidences is warranted?

▌ **Public Expectations of All Professionals** ▌ There is little doubt that the public has different expectations of behavior for a member of a profession, such as a doctor or lawyer, than they do of a nonprofessional, such as a sales or personnel manager. Why is this? The answer seems to have to do with the fact that a profession often works with something of real value where trust in how competently they will function or how responsibly they will conduct themselves is particularly important. Ultimately, the public's regard for a particular profession will govern the rights it enjoys: to practice, frequently with a monopoly on the services offered; to control entry to the profession; to earn a relatively high income; and to self-regulation or to be judged by one's peers rather than government officials. If a profession loses credibility in the eyes of the public, the consequences can be quite severe, and not only for the offending professional.

What makes a profession? In the final analysis, it is a combination of features, duties, and rights all framed within a set of common professional values—values that determine how decisions are made and actions are taken.

The thoughts of Bayles (1981) and Behrman (1988), which are summarized in Table 6.1, are useful in focusing on the important features. Professions are established primarily to serve society. The services provided to society are so important that high levels of expertise are required, which, in turn, call for extensive educational programs focused primarily on intellectual rather than mechanical or other training and skills. Almost always the most highly regarded professions are licensed to practice on the public, and the degree of autonomy accorded a profession from government regulation, with its "red tape," is evident by the degree of control exerted over the education and licensing programs by the organization representing the profession.

It is worth noting the importance of autonomy to a profession. Autonomy, or freedom from government regulations and regulators, allows members of a profession to be judged by their informed, objective peers, rather than by politically appointed regulators, and sanctions to be meted out without raising the attention of the public. This allows a profession to manage its affairs efficiently and discretely, so that the public has the impression that the profession is

---

TABLE 6.1   **What Makes a Profession**

Essential Features (Bayles)
- Extensive training
- Provision of important services to society
- Training and skills largely intellectual in character

Typical Features
- Generally licensed or certified
- Represented by organisations, associations, or institutes
- Autonomy

Foundation of Ethical Values (Behrman)
- Significantly delineated by and founded on ethical considerations rather than techniques or tools

responsible and able to discharge its duties to members of the public properly. If, however, the public becomes concerned that these processes are not fair or objective, or that the public's interest is not being protected, the government will step in to ensure that protection. Here, as it is in dealings with clients, the maintenance of the credibility of the profession is extremely important.

This lack of credibility caused by recent financial scandals was responsible for the introduction in 2002 of the Public Company Accounting Oversight Board (PCAOB)[3] by the SEC in the United States, and the Canadian Public Accountability Board (CPAB)[4] by the Canadian Institute of Chartered Accountants (CICA). The PCAOB will oversee professional accountants who are able to practice before the SEC on large companies whose stock is traded on U.S. stock exchanges—which means that its oversight will affect the practice of large professional accounting firms worldwide—and the generally accepted accounting policies that are applied to those companies' accounts. CPAB will promote high-quality audits; inspect, report upon, and sanction auditing firms that audit Canadian securities issuing companies; refer problems to regulators; and make recommendations on auditing and accounting standards.

The services provided by a profession are so important to society that society is prepared to grant the profession the rights previously outlined, but it also watches closely to see that the corresponding duties expected of the profession are discharged properly. In general terms, the duties expected of a profession are the maintenance of:

- *Competence* in the field of expertise.
- *Objectivity* in the offering of service.
- *Integrity* in client dealings.
- *Confidentiality* with regard to client matters.
- *Discipline* over members who do not discharge these duties according to the standards expected.

These duties are vital to the quality of service provided, a condition made more significant because of the fiduciary relationship a professional has with his or her clients. A fiduciary relationship exists when service provided is extremely important to the client, and where there is a significant difference in the level of expertise between the professional and the client such that the client has to trust or rely upon the judgment and expertise of the professional. The maintenance of the trust inherent in the fiduciary relationship is fundamental to the role of a professional—so fundamental that professionals have traditionally been expected to make personal sacrifices if the welfare of their client or the public is at stake.

In the past, some have argued that to be a true professional the individual had to offer services to the public—that a person serving as an employee in an organization therefore did not qualify and could be excused from following the ethical code of the profession involved. It was presumed that the need to serve the employer should be dominant. Unfortunately, the failings of this limited perspective were exposed in cases where buildings and other structures collapsed due to cheap construction, and, as with Enron, the disclosure of financial results was favorable to current management instead of current and future shareholders. In both instances, the professions involved—engineering and accounting—lost credibility in the eyes of the public. As a

3. See PCAOB website. www.pcaobus.org
4. See CPAB website. www.cpa-ccrc.ca.

result, prior to Enron, some engineering and accounting professions had decided to make their responsibility to the public explicit in their code of conduct.

The U.S. Senate, SOX, the SEC and IFAC, and therefore its worldwide member professional accounting bodies, have made it clear that service to the public interest is paramount. The concept of *loyal agency* just to an employer has been refuted and is clearly out of step with the current expectations of the public. The conditions of a fiduciary relationship—the necessity to trust or rely on the judgment and expertise of a professional—are as applicable to professionals who serve within organizations as employees as to those who offer services directly to the public. The public considers the provision of services within organizations as indirectly for the public's benefit in any event.

In order to support this combination of features, duties, and rights, it is essential that the profession in question develop a set of values or fundamental principles to guide their members, and that each professional possess personal values that dovetail with these. Normally, desired personal values would include honesty, integrity, objectivity, discretion, courage to pursue one's convictions, and strength of character to resist tempting opportunities to serve themselves or others rather than the client. Without these values, the necessary trust required to support the fiduciary relationship cannot be maintained, so efforts are usually made by the profession to assess whether these values are possessed by candidates for the profession and by its members. Such screening is usually undertaken during the prequalification or articleship period, as well as by a discipline committee of the profession. Generally, criminal activity is considered cause for expulsion, and failure to follow the standards of the profession that are expressed in its code of conduct can bring remedial measures, fines, suspension of rights, or expulsion.

| **Public Expectations of a Professional Accountant** | A professional accountant, whether engaged in auditing or management, or as an employee or a consultant, is expected to be both an accountant and a professional. That means a professional accountant is expected to have special technical expertise associated with accounting and a higher understanding than a layman of related fields, such as management control, taxation, or information systems. In addition, he or she is expected to adhere to the general professional duties and values described above and also to adhere to those specific standards laid out by the professional body to which he or she belongs. Sometimes a deviation from these expected norms can produce a lack of credibility for or confidence in the whole profession. For example, when an individual or a profession puts their own interests before those of the client or the public, a lack of confidence can develop that can trigger public enquiries into the affairs of the profession in general. Such was the case with the Treadway Commission (1987) in the United States or the Macdonald Commission (1988) in Canada. Recommendations from such enquiries for the revision of professional accounting are difficult to ignore.

Not surprisingly, professional accounting conforms quite well to the combination of features, duties, and rights in a framework of values as previously described for professions in general. These have been summarized specifically for professional accounting in Table 6.2.

| **Dominance of Ethical Values Rather Than Accounting or Audit Techniques** | Many accountants, and most nonaccountants, hold the view that mastery of accounting and/or audit technique is the *sine qua non* of the accounting profession. But relatively few financial scandals are actually caused by methodological errors in the application of technique—most are caused by *errors in judgment* about the appropriate use of a technique or the disclosure related to it. Some of these errors in judgment stem from misinterpretation of the problem as a result of its complexity, whereas others are a result of lack of attention to the ethical

TABLE 6.2   **Features, Duties, Rights & Values of the Accounting Profession**

Features

- Provision of important fiduciary services to society
- Extensive knowledge and skill are required
- Training and skills required are largely intellectual in character
- Overseen by self-regulating membership organisations
- Accountable to governmental authority

Duties essential to a fiduciary relationship

- Continuing attention to the needs of clients and other stakeholders
- Development and maintenance of required knowledge and skills, including professional scepticism
- Maintenance of the trust inherent in a fiduciary relationship by behaviour exhibiting responsible values
- Maintenance of an acceptable personal reputation
- Maintenance of a credible reputation as a profession

Rights permitted in most jurisdictions

- Ability to hold oneself out as a designated professional to render important fiduciary services
- Ability to set entrance standards and examine candidates
- Self-regulation and discipline based on codes of conduct
- Participation in the development of accounting and audit practice
- Access to some or all fields of accounting and audit endeavour

Values necessary to discharge duties and maintain rights

- Honesty
- Integrity
- Objectivity, based on independent judgement
- Desire to exercise due care and professional scepticism
- Competence
- Confidentiality
- Commitment to place the needs of the public, the client, the profession, and the employer or firm before the professional's own self-interest

values of honesty, integrity, objectivity, due care, confidentiality, and the commitment to the interests of others before those of oneself.

Examples of placing too much faith in technical feasibility rather than proper exercise of ethical values or judgment are readily available. For example, a conceptually brilliant accounting treatment will lack utility if it is biased or sloppily prepared. Suppression of proper disclosure of uncollectible accounts or loans receivable prior to bankruptcy is often not a question of competence but one of misplaced loyalty to management, a client, or oneself rather than to the public, who might invest in the bank or savings and loan company.

It should be noted, however, that sometimes a disclosure problem is so complex or the trade-offs so difficult that suppression of disclosure seems a reasonable interpretation at the time the decision is made. For example, accountants are often confronted with the decision of when and how much to disclose about a company's poor financial condition. It is possible that the corporation may work out of its problem if sufficient time is allowed, but to disclose the weakness may trigger bankruptcy proceedings.

Particularly in these situations of uncertainty, accountants must take care that their decisions are not tainted by failing to observe proper ethical values. At the very least, ethical values must be considered on a par with technical competence—both qualify as *sine qua non*. However, the edge in dominance may be awarded to ethical values on the grounds that, when a professional finds a problem that exceeds his or her current competence, it is ethical values that will compel the professional to recognize and disclose that fact. *Without ethical values, the trust necessary for a fiduciary relationship cannot be sustained, and the rights allowed the accounting profession will be limited*—probably reducing the effectiveness an independent profession can bring to society.

From time to time, other members of other professions have made the mistake of doing something because it is technically possible without regard to the ethical consequences of doing so. Genetic cloning may be an example of this practice, which is referred to as the *technological imperative*—meaning if something can be done, it should be done. When this arises in accounting, it is usually because existing accounting standards do not prohibit the practice, and it is therefore presumed to be permitted. However, there are many examples of practices that were employed, such as pooling of interests or renegotiation of overdue mortgage loans that were then disclosed as current, only to be reversed, constrained, or changed when they were found not to satisfy the public interest fairly and objectively—in other words, in accord with fundamental ethical principles. Consequently, even though technical feasibility may govern the short-term decisions of some accountants, in the longer term, ethical considerations are dominant. Whether the interest of the profession is well served by adopting technical methods without thoroughly exploring their potential consequences is a question worth examining. Conceivably, the problems associated with pooling-of-interest merger consolidations or the 3-percent-outside investee special purpose entities (SPEs) of Enron fame could have been foreseen and constraints devised if an "ethical screen" had been explicitly in place.

| **Priority of Duty, Loyalty & Trust in a Fiduciary** | Who should be the real client of a professional accountant? Because the primary role of the professional accountant is to offer important fiduciary services to society, the performance of those services often involves choices that favor the interests of one of the following at the expense of the others: the person paying your fee/salary; the current shareholder/owner of the organization; potential future shareholder/owners; and other stakeholders, including employees, governments, lenders, and so on. A decision will have differing impacts in the short and long terms depending on the interest and situation of each stakeholder, and each should be examined carefully where a significant impact is anticipated. The intricacies of stakeholder impact analysis are discussed in depth in Chapters 3 and 4, but several general observations are worthy of mention for auditors and accountants.

A professional accountant is given the right to provide important fiduciary services to society because he or she undertakes to maintain the trust inherent in the fiduciary relationship. Not only must the professional accountant have expertise, but he or she must apply that expertise with courage, honesty, integrity, objectivity, due care and professional skepticism, competence, confidentiality, and avoidance of misrepresentation in order to ensure that those relying on the expertise can trust that proper care is taken of their interests.

History has shown, however, that these values, characteristics, and principles are not enough, on their own, to ensure predictability and best practice in the choice of accounting treatments or audit approach. Consequently, in order to narrow the range of acceptable choices of accounting treatment or auditing practice, professional accountants are expected to adhere to Generally Accepted Accounting Principles (GAAP) and Generally Accepted Auditing Standards (GAAS). These generally accepted principles and standards have been created so that the choices made according to them will be fair to the multiplicity of users of the resulting financial reports and audits (i.e., *fair to the public interest*). This means, for example, that audited financial statements are intended to be fairly presented from the perspectives of all of the current share-holders, future shareholders, lenders, management, government, and so on. If audited financial statements are biased in favor of one user group over another, the trust fundamental to that fiduciary relationship will have been broken. The professional accountant involved will not be worthy of the trust placed in him or her, and will bring his or her fellow professionals into disrepute, thus affecting the reputation and credibility of the profession.

The need to adhere to the ethical values previously articulated and to GAAP is as important for professional accountants working in management, as employees, or as consultants as it is for those who are auditing financial reports. The difference between a skilled manipulator of numbers and a professional accountant is that a user can rely upon or have trust in the integrity of the professional's work. Any involvement with misrepresentations, biased reports, or unethical activities will break the trust required in a professional's fiduciary relationships, and will bring other members of the profession into disrepute.

If a person wants to be a professional accountant, he or she must be prepared to act with integrity always, not just sometimes. He or she should not, for example, be involved with misrepresentations or illegalities caused by a misguided sense of loyalty to an immediate client or employer. Loyalty is owed first to the public interest and then to the accounting profession through the observance of the principles articulated in its code of conduct and its standards.

Auditors are specifically appointed by shareholders or owners as their agents to examine the activities of an organization and to report upon the soundness of the financial systems and the reasonableness of the annual statements. This is done to protect the interests of the shareholders/owners from a number of problems, including the unscrupulous conduct of management. Audited financial reports are used and relied upon both by existing and prospective shareholders and creditors, as well as by governments and others. This reliance is therefore critical to the effective running of commerce in general. The choice of accounting or disclosure treatment that maximizes current income at the expense of future income could breach the trust required for the fiduciary arrangement with the public—an outcome that could lead to charges of misrepresentation and loss of reputation for the auditor and the profession as a whole. Accordingly, *an auditor's loyalty to the public should not be less than the loyalty to existing shareholders/owners, but certainly not primarily to the management of the organization.*

In the case of accountants employed by organizations or by audit firms, there is no statutory or contractual duty to shareholders or the public. However, in the performance of their duties to their employers, professional accountants are expected to exercise the values of honesty, integrity, objectivity, and due care. These values prohibit a professional accountant from being associated with a misrepresentation, so improper acts by an employer should cause a professional accountant to consider their responsibility to other stakeholders, including those who would be disadvantaged by the act, and their professional colleagues whose reputation would be tarnished by association. From this perspective, the paramount duty of professional accountant employees is really to ensure the accuracy and reliability of their work for the benefit of the end user—the public. It is not surprising that professional codes of ethics or conduct require disassociation from misleading information and misrepresentations. Unfortunately, some current codes do this with the requirement of silence or confidentiality, thus leaving unsuspecting stakeholders to their fate. Logic would dictate that maintenance of the trust required in specific fiduciary relationships is based on the broader trust between the public and the profession as a whole; in the long term, codes should change to protect the public-at-large rather than a specific stakeholder.

In summary, if the interest of the public is not the prime motivator of actions by both professional accountants in public practice and those who are employees, and the codes of conduct of the profession were seen to permit this, confidence in and support for that profession would be eroded. Government pressure would be brought to bear to reform the profession or to create a new group of professionals free of bias and loyal to the public's interest. The Treadway and Macdonald Commissions are examples of such pressure, and each offered suggestions for change. As discussed in Chapter 2, the lack of credibility precipitated by the Enron, Arthur Andersen, and WorldCom disasters gave rise to the SOX reforms that brought new governance regulation and reinforced an IFAC-lead rededication of the accounting profession to the public interest.

Sometimes clients or employers are confused in their thinking that a professional accountant has a real or implied contract with them and must act only in the best interest of the client or employer. It is imperative to note, however, that the contract is one where the professional is understood to be answerable to the ethical codes of the profession, so it is unreasonable to expect absolute loyalty to the client or employer rather than the profession and ultimately to the public. By contrast, it is reasonable for the client/employer to expect that a professional accountant will place the client/employer interest before that of the professional's self-interest. To do otherwise would undermine the trust required for a fiduciary arrangement to work. Legitimate confidences about business problems would not be shared for fear the interest of the client/employer would be subverted or obviated by premature release, or misused for personal gain, so the professional accountant would not be able to work effectively or on sensitive matters. As a result, the scope of an audit could be constrained to the detriment of the auditor, the profession, and the public. To prevent the release of client/employer confidences, most codes of conduct require confidences not to be divulged except in a court of law or when required by the discipline process of the profession.

In the final analysis, a professional accountant facing a difficult choice should make that choice so as to preserve the trust inherent in the fiduciary relationships, first with the public, then with the profession, then with the client/employer, and finally with the individual professional. The usual practice of placing the client/employer's interests first is only valid if those interests will be overridden by the interests of the public and the profession in circumstances where a proposed treatment would not be in the public interest or profession's interest, either legally or ethically. Any doubt about the primacy of the public interest should be erased by remembering that the once-revered, mighty, 85,000-strong Arthur Andersen disappeared within a year of being discovered violating the public's trust at Enron.

| **Confidentiality: Strict or Assisted** | The previous analysis places the professional accountant in the unenviable position of having to keep confidential those aspects of his or her client/ employer that he or she might not agree with, but which may not impact on the financial activities of the company sufficiently to be of concern to the public. If, for example, the professional is dismissed for refusing to misrepresent the receivables as current, he or she would have to seek other employment but could not discuss the reason for leaving the former employer. He or she could not discuss client/employer problems with anyone not bound by a code of confidentiality (i.e., someone in the accounting firm or a lawyer hired specifically for the purpose). Unless the professional society has an ethics adviser (some now have) who could be called on, this leaves the professional accountant in a disadvantaged position from many perspectives. It also gives unscrupulous client/employers an opportunity to get away with wrongdoing.

Professional societies have begun to recognize that this strict level of confidentiality is not in the interest of several stakeholders, including the public, and have introduced a limited, confidential consultation service to ensure the professional has cost-free help to make the right decision, to call for a response from the client/employer and perhaps resolve the problem, and to reassure prospective employers. In its 2005 Ethics Code revision, IFAC has introduced the need for a professional accountant to resolve situations where there is a conflict between fundamental principles, which in this case could be between confidentiality and the public interest. The Code suggests, among other things, that the professional accountant consider obtaining "professional advice from the relevant professional body or legal advisors, and thereby obtain guidance on ethical issues without breaching confidentiality."[5] This recommendation will be introduced around the world as the codes of professional accounting bodies are harmonized to the IFAC Code.

It is also noteworthy that, generally speaking, professional accountants are not yet expected to report problematic accounting treatments to securities regulators, taxation authorities or their professional societies. It will be interesting to see if such a reporting responsibility emerges further. It has already done so in Canada where all Chartered Accountants must report apparent breaches of their rules of conduct and for auditors of financial institutions who must report viability problems to the Superintendent of Financial Institutions. Also in England and Wales, Chartered Accountants are required to report money laundering for drugs and terrorists. Professional accountants in doubt about such responsibilities should check with their society.

Implications for Services Offered

Assurance & Other Services | Professional accountants have developed fiduciary services in the following traditional areas:

- Accounting and reporting principles, practices, and systems
- Auditing of accounting records, systems, and financial statements
- Financial projections: preparation, analysis, and audit
- Taxation: preparation of tax returns and advice
- Bankruptcy: trustee's duties and advice
- Financial planning: advice
- Decision making: facilitation through analysis and approach
- Management control: advice and design of systems
- Corporate and commercial affairs: general advice

These services are all bounded by the professional accountant's primary area of competence, accounting. However, as the needs of management changed, it was recognized that accounting expertise in the measurement, disclosure, and interpretation of data could be applied to provide services outside of the traditional area of accounting. For example, nonfinancial indicators of quality have become an important part of control systems, which are far more timely than traditional financial reports.

More important, when examining the future vision of CPAs in the United States and CAs in Canada, it was realized that there were many so-called *assurance services* that could be offered *where the professional accountant could add value by adding credibility or assurance to a report or process.* In particular, the proper discharge of these services relies on the understanding possessed by professional accountants of fiduciary responsibilities, evidence-gathering and evaluation skills, skepticism, objectivity, independence and integrity, and reporting skills. In 1997, the AICPA Special Committee on Assurance Services estimated that whereas traditional audit services would generate approximately $7 billion per annum, new assurance services would generate $21 billion.

---

5. Ibid., Section 100.20

The Special Committee developed a list of over 200 possible new assurance services and then winnowed it down to assurance services concerning:

- Risk assessment;
- Business performance measurement;
- Information systems reliability;
- Electronic commerce (website seal of approval);
- Health care performance measurement;
- Eldercare.

Additional details can be obtained from the AICPA website.

| **SEC & IFAC Independence Rules** | What the AICPA Special Committee on Assurance Services did not anticipate was the inability of its members to manage the inherent conflict of interest situations that arise when audit and other services are offered to the same client. This failure was partly responsible for the Enron, Arthur Andersen, and WorldCom disasters, and the reaction in SOX, as discussed in Chapter 2, in setting limits on the services that could be offered by SEC auditors to their SEC registrant clients. Conflict of interest management was discussed in Chapter 5 and continues in this section.

The limitations introduced by SOX and ordered by the SEC restrict the auditor of an SEC registrant corporation—one that trades its stock on U.S. stock exchanges or raises funds from the U.S. public—from auditing his or her own work, or assuming an advocacy position for the client. This is to avoid those situations where the independent judgment that must be employed by an auditor to fairly judge the positions taken by an audit client is likely to be impaired or swayed from protecting the public interest. When auditing an information system installed by the audit firm, an auditor's self-interest (pride or wishing to retain the audit client revenue) may prevent him or her from pointing out an error or the result of an error. Advocating a client position may sway an auditor's position with regard to disclosure in accordance with GAAP to further the interests of current shareholders or management. Although most auditors have been managing most of these conflict situations successfully for decades, the Enron, WorldCom, and other disasters illustrate the serious consequences that can come from not properly managing the risks involved.

To avoid these conflict of interest risks in large company audits and thereby protect the public interest, SOX required the SEC to ban the following nonaudit services that would impair an accounting firm's independence from being offered by auditors to their SEC registrants:

- Bookkeeping or other services related to the accounting records or financial statements of the audit client;
- Financial information systems design and implementation;
- Appraisal or valuation services, fairness opinions, or contribution-in-kind reports;
- Actuarial services;
- Internal audit outsourcing services;
- Management functions or human resources;
- Broker or dealer, investment adviser, or investment banking services; and
- Legal services and expert services unrelated to the audit.

The Commission's principles of independence with respect to services provided by auditors are largely predicated on three basic principles, violations of which would impair the auditor's independence: (1) an auditor cannot function in the role of management, (2) an auditor cannot audit his or her own work, and (3) an auditor cannot serve in an advocacy role for his or her client.[6]

The SEC also adopted other measures beyond limiting the specific services offered, that will:

| require that certain partners on the audit engagement team rotate after no more than five or seven consecutive years, depending on the partner's involvement in the audit, except that certain small accounting firms may be exempt from this requirement;

| establish rules that an accounting firm would not be independent if certain members of management of that issuer had been members of the accounting firm's audit engagement team within the one-year period preceding the commencement of audit procedures;

| establish rules that an accountant would not be independent from an audit client if any "audit partner" received compensation based on the partner procuring engagements with that client for services other than audit, review, and attest services;

| require the auditor to report certain matters to the issuer's audit committee, including "critical" accounting policies used by the issuer;

| require the issuer's audit committee to pre-approve all audit and non-audit services provided to the issuer by the auditor; and

| require disclosures to investors of information related to audit and non-audit services provided by, and fees paid to, the auditor.[7]

These SOX/SEC limitations, as well as those subsequently approved[8], apply only to services offered to SEC registrants around the world. All services could continue to be offered to non-SEC registrant audit clients and to audit clients of other firms. Moreover, the vast majority of professional accounting firms around the world do not service large SEC registrant companies, or those trading securities on exchanges or in countries that will emulate the SOX/SEC position. The same criticism can be made of other governance regulations or guidelines around the world.

Fortunately, the standards of independence embedded in professional codes of ethics or conduct are in the process of being revised to apply these and other similar independence principles to all professional accountants. In this regard, the ethics codes for virtually all professional accountants are being harmonized to the IFAC Code.

Nevertheless, because the SEC and IFAC pronouncements are not perfectly specific, professional accountants will still have to use their best judgment to interpret them about which assurance service to offer, how to conduct them, and how to manage the conflict of interest risks involved.

| Critical Value-Added by a Professional Accountant | A professional accountant's judgment about what services to offer and how to do so should be based, in part, upon an understanding of the critical value added by a professional accountant. *Credibility* is the

---

6. *Final Rule: Strengthening the Commission's Requirements Regarding Auditor Independence,* U.S. Securities and Exchange Commission, http://www.sec.gov/rules/final/33-8183.htm, modified 2/6/2003

7. *Commission Adopts Rules Strengthening Auditor Independence,* U.S. Securities and Exchange Commission, http://www.sec.gov/new/press/2003-9.htm, January 22, 2003.

8. See for example, those related to provision of tax services, and contingent fees per PCAOB Release 2005-014 July 26, 2005.

critical value added by professional accountants in the newer assurance services as well as the traditional ones. This has become much more apparent during the recent visioning exercises.

Competence is, of course, a fundamental factor, and high levels of competence can and do provide a competitive advantage. But it is apparent that high competence can be acquired by nonprofessionals and is therefore not, by itself, the critical value added by a professional accountant. *Credibility to the immediate client/employer and to the public at large depends upon the reputation of the entire profession, and reputation stems from the professional values adhered to and the expectations those create in the people being served.* In particular, the critical value added by a professional accountant lies in the expectation that whatever services are offered will be based on integrity and objectivity, and these values, in addition to an assured minimum standard of competence, lend credibility or assurance to the report or activity. These individual ethical values, reinforced by the standards of the profession, provide a competitive advantage to professional accountants and ensure that their services are in demand. In the words of Stanton Cook, president of the (Chicago) Tribune Company, accountants, entrepreneurs, manufacturers, salespeople, and even lawyers all say, "The product we are ultimately selling is credibility" (Priest 1991).

| **Standards Expected for Behavior** | The public, and particularly a client, expect that a professional accountant will perform fiduciary services with competence, integrity, and objectivity. Although not obvious, *integrity* is important because it assures that whatever the service, it will be performed fairly and thoroughly. No detail will be omitted, understated, or misstated that would cloud the truth, nor would an analysis be put forward that misleads users. *Honesty,* or accuracy or truthfulness, is implied in all aspects of data gathering, measurement, reporting, and interpretation. Similarly, *objectivity* implies freedom from bias in the selection of measurement bases and disclosure, so as not to mislead those served. Objectivity cannot be maintained unless the professional accountant is *independent* minded, or free from undue influence from one stakeholder or another. Independence is an issue developed at greater length in the conflict of interest discussion that follows.

Integrity, honesty, and objectivity are essential to the proper discharge of fiduciary duties. They are, with competence, so important to the critical value added from belonging to a profession that they must be protected by the profession in order to assure its future. Consequently, professional accounting organizations take pains to investigate and discipline members whose conduct is questionable with regard to these ethical values.

| Judgment & Values

| **Importance to Value Added** | The proper discharge of the ethical values of competence, integrity, honesty, and objectivity relies substantially, if not primarily, upon the personal ethical values of the professional accountant involved. If the profession itself has high standards, the individual professional can choose to ignore them. Often, however, a professional is simply not sufficiently aware of potential ethical dilemmas or the appropriate values to properly discharge his or her duties. Additionally, a professional may err in her or his judgment about the potential outcome of an ethical dilemma or about the seriousness of the outcome for those who must bear the impact. The credibility of the profession, therefore, rests on the values it espouses, the personal and professional ethical values of each individual member, and the quality of judgment exercised.

| **Development of Judgment & Values** | How do professional accountants develop the judgment they must apply to ethical dilemmas? In the past, trial and error has been the

established mode—largely experienced when growing up, on the job, or by learning from others who have problems or pass on their own experience. But the limitations of trial and error are obvious as significant costs may be born by the learner, the client, society, and the profession. In addition, an orderly framework for thinking about future problems may never be developed, nor may the level attained by a professional be adequate to safeguard the profession's stakeholders, including the professionals themselves.

Trial and error can never be entirely supplanted by organized training or educational experiences, but many of the deficiencies previously noted can be remedied by a well-ordered, stimulating learning program that deals with the major issues to be faced and suggests practical, ethical approaches to their resolution. In this regard, it is helpful to consider how far a student's ethical reasoning capacity has progressed and how to advance that capacity. A model developed by Lawrence Kohlberg is helpful in this regard (Kohlberg 1981, 1984; Colby & Kohlberg 1987).

Kohlberg argues that individuals pass through the six progressive stages of moral development, which are described in articles on accountants by Ponemon (1992); Ponemon and Gabhart (1993); Etherington and Schulting (1995); Cohen, Pant, and Sharp (1995); and Thorne and Magnan (1998). These six stages and the motivation that leads individuals to make decisions at each can be helpful, as is pointed out by W. Shenkir (1990), in designing an educational program to expose students to the six levels. Such exposure can enable students to develop their awareness, knowledge, and skills for dealing with ethical problems and may, through understanding the motivations involved, shift their moral reasoning to higher stages. The motivations, which influence people at each of Kohlberg's stages of moral reasoning, are identified in Table 6.3.

Researchers have found that students in business facing ethical decisions are largely in cognitive stages 2 or 3, so there is quite a bit of growth that is possible and desirable (Weber & Green 1991). Other researchers have found that business students believe that their success is more dependent on questionable ethical practices than do nonbusiness students, so orderly ethics education would appear desirable lest these attitudes pervade the students who enter the ranks of professional accounting (Lane & Schaup 1989). Leaving the cognitive development of students for the accounting profession and graduate accountants to trial and error rather than significant thought and formal training could, in itself, be unethical. Exposure to educational material, linked traditional course work and particularly to realistic cases, should provide students and graduate practitioners with a better understanding of the ethical issues, dilemmas, approaches to their resolution, and the values necessary to make good ethical judgments than

TABLE 6.3   Motives Influencing People at Kohlberg's Six Stages of Moral Reasoning

STAGE DESCRIPTION	MOTIVE FOR DOING RIGHT
Preconventional	*Self-interest*
1. Obedience	Fear of punishment and authorities
2. Egotism—instrumental and social exchange	Self-gratification, concern only for oneself "Let's make a deal"
Conventional	*Conformity*
3. Interpersonal concordance	Role expectation or approval from others
4. Law and duty (social order)	Adherence to moral codes, or to codes of law and order
Post-conventional, Autonomous, or Principled	*Interests of Others*
5. General individual rights and standards agreed upon by society	Concern for others and broader social welfare
6. Self-chosen principles	Concern for moral or ethical principle

would the vicissitudes of trial and error. For further thinking on cognitive development, useful references may be made to the IFAC Education Committee's International Educational Standards (IES) No. 3 and 4,[9] and to the AACSB Ethics Education Committee Report of 2004.[10]

| Sources of Ethical Guidance

There are several sources of guidance available to professional accountants. The codes of conduct or ethics of their professional body and of their firm or employer rank as important reference points. However, many other inputs should also be taken into account when appropriate, because professional accountants must respond to a body of expectations and standards created by various professional accounting organizations in their own country and offshore together with standard setters, regulators, the courts, politicians, financial markets, and the public.

Expectations for behavior of professional accountants are and will be embodied in:

| Standard setters (IFAC, PCAOB, FASB, IASB, CICA, ICAEW, and so on)
- Generally accepted accounting principles (GAAP)
- Generally accepted auditing standards (GAAS)

| Commonly understood standards of practice

| Research studies and articles

| Regulator's guidelines (SEC, OSC, NYSE, TSX, etc.)

| Court decisions

| Codes of conduct from:
- Employer (i.e., corporation or accounting firm)
- Local professional accounting bodies
- International Federation of Accountants (IFAC)

No one organization has a monopoly on the creation of the environment of expectations or standards that a professional accountant in the United States, Canada, or elsewhere should meet. For example, as noted in Tables 6.4 and 6.5, there are five national and international professional

TABLE 6.4

National & International Accounting Organizations Operating in North America

NAME	DESIGNATION	PRIME MANDATE(S)	LOCATION
American Institute of Certified Public Accountants (AICPA)	CPA	Auditing, management accounting	United States, some Canadian provinces
Institute of Management Accountants (IMA)	CMA	Management accounting	United States
Canadian Institute of Chartered Accountants (CICA)	CA	Auditing, management accounting	Canada
Society of Management Accountants of Canada (SMAC)	CMA	Management accounting	Canada
Certified General Accountants Association of Canada (CGAAC)	CGA	Management accounting, auditing	Canada, some provinces

9. Downloadable from **www.cengage.com/acounting/brooks**
10. Downloadable from **www.cengage.com/acounting/brooks**

6.5   **Contributions to the North American Regulatory Framework for Professional Accountants**

ORGANIZATION	CONTRIBUTION GOVERNING ORGANIZATION'S MEMBERS/USERS
AICPA	Statements of Auditing Standards (SAS), research studies, journal articles, code of conduct
IMA	Statements of accounting practice, research studies, journal articles, code of conduct
Financial Accounting Standards Board (FASB)	Financial Accounting Standards (FAS)
CICA	Accounting and auditing standards in Canada, research studies, journal articles, code of conduct
SMAC	Statements of accounting practice, research studies, journal articles, code of conduct
CGAAC	Statements of accounting practice, research studies, journal articles, code of conduct
U.S. Securities and Exchange Commission (SEC)	Regulations related to U.S. public securities markets including corporate disclosure and governance, GAAP, GAAS, behavior of auditors and other professionals practicing before the SEC. Regulation in respect to disclosure for companies raising funds in the USA. Standards of independence for CPAs auditing SEC companies.
Ontario Securities Commission (OSC)	Regulations related to financial disclosure in Canada's principal securities market (Ontario), whose regulations are accepted by the SEC.
U.S. and Canadian courts	Common law decisions affecting legal liability
International Federation of Accountants (IFAC) and the International Accounting Standards Board (IASB)	International Code of Ethics, and accounting and auditing standards that may facilitate international harmonization
Public Accounting Oversight Boards PCAOB CPAB	Oversight in the U.S. (PCAOB) and Canada (CPAB) Issues Auditing Standards, inspections, sanctions Inspection reports, sanctions

accounting organizations operating in North America, plus their subsets in each U.S. state or Canadian province (e.g., The Institute of Chartered Accountants of Ontario or a state society of Certified Public Accountants) plus several regulatory units that are contributing to the North American regulatory framework. This multiplicity contributes to a strong desire for some global convergence, making it likely the IASB, and IFAC pronouncements will become increasingly more important sources of guidance, with the IFAC code emerging as the dominant ethics framework.

It is important to note that although a national body can develop a code of conduct, in North America the local state or provincial subset organization controls its own members by enacting its own code of conduct (using the national code as a guide but not always adopting all its provisions), and policing and disciplining its members. Consequently, the standard of ethical expectation varies somewhat from jurisdiction to jurisdiction, and from organization to organization. Fortunately, basic principles of ethical conduct apply to all organizations, and the convergence toward global ethics principles, accounting, and auditing standards holds considerable promise for promoting a common standard of performance.

Professional Codes of Conduct

Purpose & Framework | Professional codes of conduct are designed to provide guidance about the conduct expected of members in order that the services offered will be of acceptable quality and the reputation of the profession will not be sullied. If that reputation is sullied, some aspect of a fiduciary relationship has been breached, and a service has not been performed in a professional manner. Alternatively, it may mean that a member has offended the rules of society in some way so as to bring the profession's name into disrepute and thereby damage the public trust required for its members to serve other clients effectively.

To be effective, codes of conduct need to blend fundamental principles with a limited number of specific rules. If a code were drafted to cover all possible problems, it would be extremely voluminous—probably so voluminous that few members would spend the time required to become familiar with it and to stay abreast of the constant flow of additions. With practicality in mind, most professional codes have evolved to the framework outlined in Table 6.6.

Fundamental Principles & Standards

The fundamental principles and standards described in Table 6.7 are found in most codes.

IFAC, in its 2001 version of its Code of Ethics for Professional Accountants, articulated why professional accountants should *serve the public interest* when it stated:

> A distinguishing mark of a profession is acceptance of its responsibility to the public. The accountancy profession's public consists of clients, credit grantors, governments, employers, employees, investors, the business and financial community, and others who rely on the objectivity and integrity of professional accountants to maintain the orderly functioning of commerce. This reliance imposes a public interest responsibility on the accountancy profession. The public interest is defined as the collective well-being of the community of people and institutions the professional accountant serves. ... A professional accountant's responsibility is not exclusively to satisfy the needs of an individual client or employer. The standards of the accountancy profession are heavily determined by the public interest ...[11]

TABLE 6.6	Typical Framework for a Code of Conduct for Professional Accountants
	Introduction and purpose
	Fundamental principles and standards
	General rules
	Specific rules
	Discipline
	Interpretations of rules

TABLE 6.7	Fundamental Principles in Codes of Conduct for Professional Accountants
	Members should:
	• act in the public interest,
	• at all times maintain the good reputation of the profession and its ability to serve the public interest,
	• perform with:
	○ integrity
	○ objectivity and independence
	○ professional competence, due care, and professional skepticism
	○ confidentiality, and
	• not be associated with any misleading information or misrepresentation.

---

11. IFAC 2001 Code of Ethics for Professional Accountants, Sections 9 and 10.

IFAC left unsaid but implied that other professional groups would be granted standing to serve the public if any group of professional accountants were proven to be unreliable in discharging this mandate.

The maintenance of the *good reputation* of the profession is fundamental to the ability of the profession to continue to enjoy its current rights and privileges, including autonomy in the discipline of its members, the setting of accounting standards, and the recognition by the public and government that new competing professional organizations need not be created to serve the *public interest* more effectively. The phrase, *at all times*, is significant because the public will view any serious transgression of a professional accountant, including those outside business or professional activity, as a black mark against the profession as a whole. Consequently, if a professional accountant is convicted of a criminal offense or fraud, his or her certification is usually revoked.

Maintenance of standards of care is also imperative for the proper service to clients and the public interest. *Integrity*, or *objectivity* and *honesty*, in the preparation of reports, choice of accounting options, and interpretation of accounting data will ensure that the neither the client nor the public will be misled. Sometimes reports or opinions can lack integrity if the professional involved has failed to maintain *independence* from one of the persons likely to benefit or be harmed by the report, and this causes the professional to bias the report, decisions, or interpretations toward the favored party.

Charges of bias are very hard to refute, so professionals are often admonished to avoid any situation or relationship that might lead to the *perception of bias*. This is why, even though in the past many professionals have served successfully as bookkeeper, auditor, shareholder, and director of an organization, modern codes of conduct recommend against situations involving such apparent conflicts of interest. The prospect of an auditor misstating a report for their own gain, or that of their fellow shareholders, was judged to be too tempting a prospect to allow. Similar reasoning has lead to the introduction of the separation of duties within an organization and, wherever possible, between the bookkeeping and audit functions. In simplistic terms, from the profession's viewpoint, why leave freshly baked cookies on the open windowsill to cool if the temptation presented may someday lead someone to sneak one? It is interesting to speculate as to who is more at fault, the person leaving the cookies in a vulnerable position or the person succumbing to temptation.

It would be impossible for a professional accountant to offer services at the level a client or employer has the right to expect if the professional has failed to maintain their *competence* with regard to current standards of disclosure, accounting treatment, and business practice. However, beyond understanding and developing facility with current standards, a professional accountant must act with due care.

The exercise of *due care* involves an understanding of the appropriate levels and limits of care expected of a professional accountant in different circumstances. For example, a professional accountant is not expected to be all-knowing and all-seeing with regard to incidents of fraud that occur at a client or employer. However, if the professional becomes aware of these (and there are new expectations for auditors to search out fraud), there are expectations for follow-up and reporting that need to be observed. Similarly, audit procedures need not specifically cover 100 percent of an organization's transactions; judgment sampling and statistical sampling may be applied to reduce specific coverage to a level deemed appropriate according to professional judgment. That level will be set with reference to what other professionals regard as providing sufficient evidence for the forming of an opinion based on due care. In a court of law, expert witnesses will be called to testify as to what levels of judgment represent the exercise of due care.

An important aspect of the exercise of due care is the *professional skepticism* demonstrated. A professional accountant is not expected to accept everything she or he is told or shown as being accurate or true. The exercise of proper professional skepticism would involve the continuous comparison of representations and/or information received to what would be considered reasonable, and/or in line with other representations or information at hand or readily available. In addition, there should be a continuous questioning of whether the fact, decision, or action being considered is in the best interest of the client and is ethical, particularly with regard to the public interest. As evidenced by the actions of many accountants in recent financial scandals, without the continuous exercise of professional skepticism as described, an accountant will not be able to serve a client, society, profession, or him or herself at the level of a trusted professional.

Confidentiality is fundamental to fiduciary relationships from several perspectives. First, these relationships are very important to the well-being of the client or employer. They usually involve personal information, or information that is critical to the activities of the organization, and which would result in some loss of privacy or of competitive advantage if it were disclosed to specific individuals or to the public. Advice, for example, about a business transaction, could be used in bargaining if known by the other party to the transaction. Second, it is not beyond the realm of possibility that such information could be used for the professional's own purposes for profit or to gain some other advantage. Finally, if it were suspected that a professional accountant was not going to maintain a client's or employer's information in confidence, it is unlikely that full information would be shared. This would put an audit and other services on a faulty foundation, which could lead to substandard and potentially misleading opinions and reports.

Keeping information confidential should not, however, lead to illegal behavior. For example, codes of conduct usually specify that a professional accountant *should not be associated with any misrepresentations.* If the professional cannot induce revision by persuasion, then the professional is usually required by his or her code to disassociate from the misrepresentation by resignation. Professional accountants are also usually prohibited from disclosing the misrepresentation, except subject to a disciplinary hearing or in a court of law or to a legal adviser or an advisor from a professional accounting body.

For reference, the fundamental principles section of the IFAC 2005 Code of Ethics for Professional Accountants is reproduced as Table 6.8.

| **Rules: General & Specific** | Professional accountants are expected to apply the fundamental principles previously outlined in order to protect the public interest as well as the interest of the profession and of the member themselves. There are, however, matters that

---

TABLE 6.8

IFAC 2005 Code of Ethics for Professional Accountants Fundamental Principles— Section 100.4

A professional accountant is required to comply with the following fundamental principles:

(a) *Integrity*—A professional accountant should be straightforward and honest in all professional and business relationships.

(b) *Objectivity*—A professional accountant should not allow bias, conflict of interest, or undue influence of others to override professional or business judgments.

(c) *Professional Competence and Due Care*—A professional accountant has a continuing duty to maintain professional knowledge and skill at the level required to ensure that a client or employer receives competent professional service based on current developments in practice, legislation, and techniques. A professional accountant should act diligently and in accordance with applicable technical and professional standards when providing professional services.

(d) *Confidentiality*—A professional accountant should respect the confidentiality of information acquired as a result of professional and business relationships and should not disclose any such information to third parties without proper and specific authority unless there is a legal or professional right or duty to disclose. Confidential information acquired as a result of professional and business relationships should not be used for the personal advantage of the professional accountant or third parties.

(e) *Professional Behavior*—A professional accountant should comply with relevant laws and regulations and should avoid any action that discredits the profession.

lend themselves to coverage in general or specific rules, such as proper relations between members or the organization and conduct of a professional practice. The appropriate form of advertising would be one of the administrative matters covered in rules.

| **Discipline** | Customarily, codes of conduct provide information about the operation of the discipline process of the professional association. Members should know how and to whom to report a concern over conduct, what the process is for investigation of the concern, what the hearing process entails, how decisions will be made, what fines and other penalties are possible, how results will be reported, and how appeals will be considered. Unless these facts are known, together with some examples of sanctions levied, a professional is likely to misjudge how important the ethical conduct of its members is to the profession and to society.

Sanctions for unethical behavior can include any of the items listed in Table 6.9. It should be noted, however, that the sanctions identified are not all levied by every professional accounting body or regulatory agency.

Usually the discipline process begins with a complaint being lodged with the professional body about the ethical conduct of a member or firm. Alternately, the conviction on a legal charge of consequence (fraud, etc.) may also trigger the discipline process. The complaint or legal charge is investigated by staff, and a decision is made to lay a charge or not. Laying a charge necessitates a hearing to determine guilt or innocence, and the hearing process can be quite cumbersome. It can be held in camera or in public. It can involve lawyers for plaintiff (the staff of the professional body) and defendant, and a tribunal or panel to hear the case, which often includes an outside layperson to ensure that proper procedures are followed and the public interest is served.

The cost of the hearing can be substantial in terms of out-of-pocket costs and also lost work time, which could be billed to clients. In the end, the largest cost involved is the lost reputation of the guilty accountant—in the audit world, credibility is what professionals strive to protect the

TABLE 6.9   **Possible Sanctions for Unethical Behavior Under Professional Accounting Codes of Conduct & Regulatory Authorities**

	LEVIABLE ON THE	
	PROFESSIONAL	**ACCOUNTING FIRM**
Caution	Yes	Yes
Reprimand	Yes	Yes
Review by peer	Yes	Yes
Requirement to complete courses	Yes	No
Suspension:		
• for a specified period	Yes	No/Yes*
• for an indefinite period	Yes	No
• until specific requirements are completed	Yes	No
• from appearing before regulatory agencies (SEC, OSC)	Yes	Yes
• from auditing SEC or OSC registrant companies	Yes	Yes
Expulsion from membership	Yes	No
Compensation for damage	Yes	Yes
Fine	Yes	Yes
Costs of hearing	Yes	Yes
Ancillary orders		
• for community work	Yes	No
• financial support, etc.	Yes	Yes

*The SEC has suspended a firm's ability to audit SEC registrants and/or take on new clients
Source: Distillation of discipline cases from North American jurisdictions

most, since it is evidence of the value of their audit opinion. Without it, their audit services would be without demand.

When a professional accountant or firm is found guilty, the details of the case are made public, usually in the newsletter of the professional organization. It is essential that full details be published to warn other members of ethical problems and the sanctions they might encounter, and to preserve the profession's upstanding image as a profession worthy of policing itself (i.e., worthy of the trust of the public).

A guilty professional can look forward to more than one sanction. For example, he or she might receive a reprimand, a fine, and the bill for costs of the lawyers and hearing. Alternatively, the penalty might be a suspension from membership until a set of required courses are completed plus compensation for damages and costs. If the professional appears to need supervision for a while, the penalty might include the review of all work by a peer.

Fines can range in size from less than $1,000 to more than the damage done to the injured party. The amounts are growing over time, and in the United States, fines in the millions have been levied, particularly against Arthur Andersen and some of its partners, as was outlined in Chapter 2 (see Table 2.6). If the penalty involves the prohibition from practice, or appearance before the securities commissions, the lost revenue can be very large indeed. The inability to appear before the SEC or PCAOB appears to be a most powerful sanction to use against accounting firms, perhaps because of the potential for loss or suspension of the ability to audit SEC registrant companies, and/or the attendant notoriety and loss of reputation. It should be noted, however, that although Arthur Andersen was destroyed by the actions of the SEC, it is not as likely that this will happen again due to the public's perception that it would be fair if only the guilty few individuals were punished, not the whole firm.

| **Interpretations of Rules** | When the profession finds that a concern arises in the profession as a result of a debate over the proper application of a rule, a clarification is issued in the form of an interpretation. These interpretations are often an addendum or appendix to the code, which can be added to as circumstances require.

| **Motivation for Changes in Professional Codes** | The motivation for changes in professional codes has been surprisingly similar and cyclical over the years. An article by J. Michael Cook, "The AICPA at 100: Public Trust and Professional Pride" (May 1987), summarizes early professional pressures and developments. Usually, roughly every decade, pressure has come upon the accounting profession due to a financial or accounting scandal that has eroded the credibility of the profession.[12] Generally, the pressure has been greatest when the North American economy has been weak, and this weakness caused companies and individuals to engage in fraud, or misstatement of financial results, or the use of loopholes to take unfair advantage. In reaction, professional codes have been revised to provide more and stronger guidance to avoid such problems in the future.

Two factors are different with the motivations at the start of the new millennium. First, the Enron, Arthur Andersen, and WorldCom debacles occurred in good economic times—even though they gave rise to an erosion of credibility that drove confidence down and, in turn, the economy. This change suggests that ethics problems can and will play a more serious and significant role than earlier imagined. Second, the desire for global convergence or harmonization of standards to facilitate global business and capital flows is providing a driver of change beyond the previously normal, domestically dominated, political and corporate lobbying influences. As such, convergence may yield stronger standards and more rapid continuous changes than

---

12. Presentation of Mary Beth Armstrong, February 2, 2003, at the American Accounting Association Accounting Programs Leadership Group Conference in New Orleans.

heretofore possible. Time will tell, however, if the needed companion regulatory compliance and enforcement framework, best exemplified by the SEC and the OSC, will be replicated in Europe and around the world to realize the possible improvement fully.

To appreciate the potential of the future, an understanding of the similar issues facing the accounting profession in the late 1980s is useful. At that time, the Metcalf investigation,[13] the Treadway Commission (1987), and the Macdonald Commission (1988) were public or quasi-public processes of *investigation of how the members of the AICPA and the CICA were serving the public interest.* These investigations would not have been necessary unless some doubt existed about the service being provided. Although there were some specific problems that triggered these studies, concern over the credibility of financial reporting was essentially responsible—for reasons strikingly similar to those that became apparent in the Enron, WorldCom, and other financial scandals. From the perspective of the accounting profession, this manifested itself as an *expectations gap* "between what the public expects or needs and the auditors can reasonably expect to accomplish" (Macdonald 1988, iii).

In response to the Treadway Commission's *Report of the National Commission on Fraudulent Public Reporting,* a committee of the AICPA was struck under the chairmanship of W. Anderson, which redesigned the AICPA Professional Standards: Ethics and Bylaws (Anderson 1985, 1987). Paramount in the revisions proposed to the U.S. and Canadian codes by both the Anderson Committee and the Macdonald Commission was the desire for restoration of the public's faith that the profession was serving the public interest. The categorization of the principal recommendations of the Macdonald Commission, which follows in Table 6.10, makes this general objective abundantly evident.

| **Current Codes of Professional Conduct** | Current codes of the major industrial nations of the world—which have resulted from the concerns, investigations, commissions and

---

TABLE **6.10**   **The Macdonald Commission: Overview of Principal Recommendations**

Recommendations to strengthen auditor independence/integrity:

- Improvement of auditor relationships (11)
- Strengthen professional standards (7)
- Strengthen professional code of conduct (3)

Recommendations to strengthen auditor professionalism:

- Increase responsiveness to public concerns (6)
- Emphasize vital role of professional judgment (4)
- Improve self-regulation (2)

Recommendations to improve financial disclosure:

- Expand accounting standards and improve financial disclosures (13)
- Greater auditor responsibility for those disclosures (2)

Recommendations to lessen public misunderstanding of the auditor's role:

- Publish a statement of management responsibility (24)
- Expand audit report to clarify auditor's role and the level of assurance the audit provides (25)
- Audit committee to report annually to shareholders (3)

Source: The Macdonald Commission: *Report of the Commission to Study the Public's Expectation of Audits,* CICA, Toronto, June 1988.

---

13. "Why Everybody's Jumping on Accountants These Days," *Forbes,* March 15, 1977. http://www.forbes.com/forbes/1977/0315/037_print.html

committees of the late 1980s—are converging on the principles embedded in the *IFAC Code of Ethics*. However, because the process of change has begun recently and there is no obligation to replicate the IFAC Code exactly particularly if there are cultural or regulatory differences, it is worthwhile to study the existing representative codes from the AICPA and the ICAO, which are included in this chapter. Discussions of the provisions of each code are covered elsewhere in this book. For instance, discussion of the need to keep client information confidential is included in this chapter and in Chapter 5.

| **International Comparison of Professional Codes** | It is interesting for several reasons to compare the professional codes or rules of conduct from a variety of professional bodies drawn from around the world, and that is the purpose of Appendix A to this chapter. For instance, although these codes are to converge on the guidance offered in the IFAC Code, there are issues that may be slow in coming into particular code due to political, regulatory, or environmental considerations, but which a professional accountant should be aware of because of the need to observe the most rigorous code. Second, although most codes deal with the same issues, different wording can be used, and a review of that wording can provide an enriched understanding of the topic. Finally, as professional accountants become involved with foreign activities directly or indirectly through multinational reporting or capital markets, they would do well to be sensitive to professional accounting codes in foreign locales. For comparison purposes the Framework of the IFAC Code is presented in Table 6.11.

TABLE 6.11   **IFAC 2005 Code of Ethics for Professional Accountants Framework—Contents**

	Page
PREFACE	2
PART A: GENERAL APPLICATION OF THE CODE	
100 Introduction and Fundamental Principles	4
110 Integrity	9
120 Objectivity	10
130 Professional Competence and Due Care	11
140 Confidentiality	12
150 Professional Behavior	14
PART B: PROFESSIONAL ACCOUNTANTS IN PUBLIC PRACTICE	
200 Introduction	16
210 Professional Appointment	21
220 Conflicts of Interest	24
230 Second Opinions	26
240 Fees and Other Types of Remuneration	27
250 Marketing Professional Services	29
260 Gifts and Hospitality	30
270 Custody of Clients Assets	31
280 Objectivity—All Services	32
290 Independence—Assurance Engagements	33
PART C: PROFESSIONAL ACCOUNTANTS IN BUSINESS	
300 Introduction	79
310 Potential Conflicts	83
320 Preparation and Reporting of Information	85
330 Acting with Sufficient Expertise	86
340 Financial Interests	87
350 Inducements	89
DEFINITIONS	91
EFFECTIVE DATE	95

SUMMARY OF THE AMERICAN INSTITUTE OF CERTIFIED PUBLIC ACCOUNTANTS (AICPA)
*CODE OF PROFESSIONAL CONDUCT**

Principles:

Responsibilities: In carrying out their responsibilities as professionals, members should exercise sensitive professional and moral judgments in all their activities. (Section 52, Article I)

The Public Interest: Members should accept their obligation to act in a way that will serve the public interest, honor the public trust, and demonstrate commitment to professionalism. (S. 53, Article II)

Integrity: To maintain and broaden public confidence, members should perform all professional responsibilities with the highest sense of integrity. (S. 54, Article III)

Objectivity and Independence: A member should maintain objectivity and be free of conflicts of interest in discharging professional responsibilities. A member in public practice should be independent in fact and appearance when providing auditing and other attestation services. (S. 55, Article IV)

Due Care: A member should observe the profession's technical and ethical standards, strive continually to improve competence and the quality of services, and discharge professional responsibility to the best of the member's ability. (S. 56, Article V)

Scope and Nature of Services: A member in public practice should observe the Principles of the *Code of Professional Conduct* in determining the scope and nature of services to be provided. (S. 57, Article VI)

Rules:		Important Interpretations/Issues Covered:
101	Independence	• will be impaired by various transactions, relationships and interests, including: direct or material financial interests, performance of certain nonattest services, common investments, loans; family relationships, or official office such as: director, officer, employee, promoter, underwriter, trustee, or borrower (except under normal terms from a financial institution for auto, home, credit cards); and the threat of litigation.
102	Integrity and objectivity	• no conflicts of interest—see S 102-2 for definition • no misrepresentations of fact or subordination of judgment to others
201	General standards	• professional competence • due professional care • planning and supervision • sufficient relevant data
202	Compliance with standards	• necessary if service involves auditing, review, compilation, management consulting, tax, or other professional services
203	Accounting principles	• no departures from generally accepted accounting principles, *unless a misleading statement would result*; then must state why a departure is warranted and approximate effects—authorization of FASB, GASB, FASAB pronouncements
301	Confidential client information	• no disclosure without consent, except for proper court or CPA proceedings • no use for personal gain
302	Contingent fees	• not allowed for audit, review, compilation, examination of prospective financial information, or tax return or claim for tax refund—some exceptions listed
501	Discreditable acts	• not permitted: discrimination, harassment, deviation from gov. standards, negligence, disclosure or solicitation of CPA examination questions or answers, failure to file tax return or pay tax liability
502	Advertising and solicitation	• cannot be false, misleading, or deceptive, or involve coercion, over-reaching, or harassment
503	Commissions and referral fees	• not allowed for recommendations of services to or from a client of an audit, review, compilation, or examination of prospective financial information, otherwise requires disclosure • cannot be paid or accepted without disclosure to the client
505	Form of organization and name	• permits non-CPA minority ownership, provided CPA's remain ultimately responsible, financially and otherwise, for the attest work performed to protect the public interest, but cannot hold themselves out as CPA's, and must follow AICPA Code.

*Code of Professional Conduct, *AICPA, updated to June 2008. Full code is at http://www.aicpa.org/about/code/index.html*

SUMMARY OF *RULES OF PROFESSIONAL CONDUCT AND COUNCIL INTERPRETATIONS** *OF THE INSTITUTE OF CHARTERED ACCOUNTANTS OF ONTARIO (ICAO)*

Foreword . . . covering the philosophy underlying the Rules governing a Chartered Accountant's responsibilities for:

Characteristics of a profession	• 8 elements including the subordination of personal interest to the public good/interest
Principles governing the conduct of members and students	• derived from the public's reliance on sound and fair financial reporting, and competent advice on business affairs
	• maintenance of the profession's good reputation and its ability to serve the public interest
	• perform with integrity and due care, sustain professional competence, comply with *Rules*
	• no influences, interests or relationships which would impair professional judgment or objectivity, or appear to do so to a reasonable observer
	• duty of confidence, and no exploitative use, in respect information about a client's affairs
	• practice development based upon professional excellence, not on self-promotion
	• exhibit courtesy and consideration in dealings with professional colleagues
	• observance of fiduciary duties, and professional duties, where applicable
Principles governing the responsibilities of firms and responsible partners	• establish, maintain, and uphold policies and procedures in accord with the *Rules*
	• failure to comply may trigger sanctions for the whole firm or just the knowledgeable
Personal character and ethical conduct	• as per principles and *Rules*, honorable conduct beyond the letter of the prohibition
Application of the *Rules*	• to all members except where specific to those in public accounting *and/or* where the public and/or associates rely upon the individual based upon that person's membership in the ICAO
	• to non-members supervised by or in partnership with a member
	• in jurisdictions outside Ontario, a member must observe the local rules, but not bring disrepute upon the ICAO
Interpretation of the Rules	• Rules must be interpreted in light of the matters discussed in the Foreword.

Rules:		**Important Interpretations/Issues Covered:**
General		
101	Compliance with bylaws, regulations and rules	• is mandatory for members, students and firms.
102	Conviction of criminal or similar offenses	• duty to inform Institute of outcome after appeal period expires.
102.2	Reporting suspensions for disciplinary reasons	• promptly notify the Institute of any suspensions.
103	No association with misrepresentation	• on a letter, report, statement or representation, or related to candidacy as a student or member
104	Must reply in writing to Institute correspondence	
Standards Affecting the Public Interest		
201	Maintenance of the good reputation of the profession and its ability to serve the public interest	• at all times, both members and students
		• conviction in other Canadian jurisdictions results in charges by the ICAO
		• advocacy services requirements
202	Integrity and due care	• mandatory for all members, students, and firms
203	Maintenance of professional competence	• mandatory for members
203.2	Cooperation with inspections and investigations	• Must cooperate with the Institute's appointed personnel conducting practice investigations or investigating professional conduct
204	Independence and objectivity	• those members, firms, or members of firms who give opinions on financial statements or are undertaking an insolvency engagement must be free of any influence, interest or relationship which would impair professional judgment or objectivity, or has the appearance of doing so
		• there must be written disclosure of anything that a reasonable observer might consider impairs the member's independence and objectivity
205	False or misleading statements	• no association even where a disclaimer is given
		• covers letters, reports, representations, financial statements, written or oral
		• covers omissions, material misstatements, non-compliance

(CONTINUED)

SUMMARY OF *RULES OF PROFESSIONAL CONDUCT AND COUNCIL INTERPRETATIONS** *OF THE INSTITUTE OF CHARTERED ACCOUNTANTS OF ONTARIO (ICAO)* (continued)

Rules:		Important Interpretations/Issues Covered:
Standards Affecting the Public Interest (Continued)		
206	Compliance with professional standards	• with generally accepted accounting principles and generally accepted auditing standards as set out in the *CICA Handbook,* as auditor, preparer, approver or member of an audit committee or board of directors
207	No unauthorized benefits	• from client or employer
208	Maintenance of confidential information about a client's affairs	• no disclosure unless client has knowledge and consent, or pursuant to the proceedings of lawful authority, Council, or the Professional Conduct Committee or subcommittees
		• no improper use for personal advantage, advantage of a third party, or to disadvantage the client
		• responsibility for subcontracted agents
210	Conflict of interest	• responsibility to detect before accepting engagement
		• no acceptance of a conflicted (self vs. client, or client vs. client) engagement by a member, student, or firm unless all affected parties are advised and consent
211	Duty to report apparent breaches of member, student, or applicant or firm	• of rules of conduct
		• of any information raising doubt as to competencies, reputation or integrity
		• unless specific exemption, or would breach statutory duty or solicitor-client privilege, etc.
		• delay in reporting where engaged in criminal or civil investigation
212	Handling of trust funds and other property	• in accord with trust and trust law
		• segregation, records
213	No unlawful activity	• ensure no association of person, name, or services
214	Fee quotations	• only when requested by a client, after obtaining adequate information about the assignment
215	Contingent fees	• none allowed, except for an insolvency engagement, or under very specific conditions where there will be no real or apparent conflict of interest and where the client consents
216	No referral fees or compensation	• none allowed, except in sale or purchase of an accounting practice.
217	Advertising restrictions	• advertising cannot be false or misleading, in bad taste, contrary to professional courtesy; reflect unfavorably on competence or integrity, or includes unsubstantiated statements
		• no solicitation is permitted
		• endorsements are possible under strict conditions, and after suitable investigations
218	Retention of documentation and working papers	• for a reasonable time period
Relations with Fellow Members or Firms, and Non-members Engaged in Public Accounting		
302	Acceptance of appointment where there is an incumbent auditor	• not allowed without asking outgoing auditor if there are circumstances which should be taken into account
		• response is required from incumbent, fraud or illegal activity must be reported if suspected
303	Co-operation with successor	• timely response required if written request received
304	Joint appointments	• carry joint and several liability
		• must advise other accountant of activities
305	Communication of special assignments to incumbent	• must communicate with incumbent unless client makes such a request in writing before the engagement is begun, and CICA Handbook does not require
306	Responsibilities on special assignments	• no action to impair the position of the other accountant
		• no services beyond original referral terms, except with consent of referring member

SUMMARY OF *RULES OF PROFESSIONAL CONDUCT AND COUNCIL INTERPRETATIONS**
OF THE INSTITUTE OF CHARTERED ACCOUNTANTS OF ONTARIO (ICAO) (continued)

Rules:	Important Interpretations/Issues Covered:
Organization and Conduct of a Professional Practice	
401 Practice names	• in good taste, approved by institute, not misleading or self-laudatory
402 Descriptive styles	• must use "chartered accountant(s)" or "public accountant(s)" unless part of firm name
403 Association with firms	• restricted use of "chartered account(s)" if some partners are not CAs
404 Operation of offices	• offices must be under the charge of a licensed public accountant normally in attendance • no part-time offices except per regulations • cannot use "chartered accountants" if a non-CA shares a proprietary interest.
405 Office by representation	• not allowed if represented by another public accountant
406 Responsibility for non-members	• public accountants are responsible for the failure of non-members associated with the practice to abide by the *Rules of Conduct*
407 Related business or practice	• *Rules of Conduct* apply—cannot be designated "chartered accountant(s)" or "public accountant(s)"
408 Association with non-member in public practice	• only if maintains good reputation of profession, and adheres to *Rules of Conduct*, but cannot be designated "chartered accountant(s)" or "public accountant(s)"
409 Practice of public accounting in a corporate form	• prohibited except under specific circumstances—refer to current code
Rules Applicable Only to Firms	
501 Establish, maintain & uphold policies & procedures	• those necessary for compliance with professional standards per the *CICA Handbook*
502 Same	• those necessary for compliance with expected competence and conduct of members, students and any other persons contracted with
503 Association with Firms	• only if at least one partner of the other firm is chartered accountant

*ICAO, Toronto, Canada. Updated to February 22, 2008. ICAO Rules of Conduct are at http://www.icao.on.ca/Resources/Membershandbook/1011page5011.aspx

Appendix A is organized to review code provisions in comparison to those of the AICPA Code for the following professional accounting bodies:

▌ AICPA—American Institute of Certified Public Accountants;

▌ IFAC—International Federation of Accountants;

▌ ICAO—Institute of Chartered Accountants of Ontario (for Canada);

▌ ICAEW—Institute of Chartered Accountants of England and Wales;

▌ ICAA—Institute of Chartered Accountants of Australia;

▌ ICANZ—Institute of Chartered Accountants of New Zealand;

▌ IMA—Institute of Management Accountants (United States);

▌ SMAC—Society of Management Accountants of Ontario (for Canada);

Review of the *Comparison Table* will give rise to many observations, including the following:

▌ All of the codes identify serving the public interest as a primary obligation or responsibility, and some are moving to identify "stakeholders" as well. This is helpful in reminding professional accountants to consider their duty to stakeholder groups, thus adding specificity to the concept of the "public interest."

❙ All of the codes apply to members of the associations and are moving to apply to firms as well. This change signals the perceived or real responsibility of the governors of the firms from the level of "due diligence" required of corporation executives in building an ethical culture.

❙ Procedures for resolution of ethical conflicts vary. Most codes imply what the SMAC code states—which is that the Society's Code is to take precedence over management's code. Some suggest confidential counselling or legal advice, but increasingly propose consultation with the professional body. None of the codes have considered the interest of the public to be worthy of breaching a client or employer confidence to the attention of the public, although several require the reporting of breaches (presumably by members) of the code to the professional body (ICAO, ICAEW, IMA, SMAC).

❙ The IFAC code contains several provisions that are now coming into other codes as harmonization proceeds, including:

- An explicit standard approving the advancing of a client's best tax position, provided that does not conflict with any laws. Note that the ICAEW spells out that tax avoidance is legal, but tax evasion is illegal.

- A requirement for observing the most strict ethical code if required to work in multiple countries.

❙ The IFAC code specifies in Section 320.1 that information should be presented fully and honestly *to be understood in its context*. This extends the simpler prohibition against involvement with misrepresentations that is in many other codes. Sometimes the disclosure of an otherwise correct fact, out of context, results in a misinterpretation.

With the passage of time, it is possible that the professional codes of specific professional bodies will lag behind those of other countries, or of the expectations of the public. In those cases, other regulatory agencies will put forward requirements to protect the public interest, as has been done by the PCAOB as it enlarges on standards expected for independence and other matters.

❙ **Shortfalls with & in Professional Codes** ❙ In the past, most professional accountants have tended to view their codes as being less relevant than the technical material they were required to deal with. In some cases, lack of awareness of the significance of the code was at the root of the problem, whereas in other instances inability to interpret the general principles and rules was responsible. As our ethics environment has changed and ethical shortfalls have become recognized as serious threats to professional practice, there have been numerous calls for renewed interest, understanding, and commitment on the part of professionals themselves (see, for example, Gunning 1989; Brooks 1993; and a dedicated issue of *Accounting Education*, March 1994). Ethics education is now expected or an official requirement of the formal education of professional accountants according to the AACSB[14] and many professional bodies.

Although it would be theoretically attractive for professional codes of conduct to solve all the problems professional accountants face, in reality their application requires the use of judgment based on a full set of principles and rules. In this regard, many codes have the following deficiencies:

❙ Consultation on ethical matters may require the hiring of outside counsel rather than counseling through the professional association. This leaves both the professional and the profession involved at some risk that competent counseling will take place and/or appropriate action will be taken.

---

 14. See the AACSB *Ethics Education Committee Report*, 2004, available on the **www.cengage.com/accounting/brooks**.

| A fair reporting, investigation, and hearing process is not always indicated, so members are uncertain whether to come forward.

| Protection is not offered to a whistle-blower.

| Sanctions are often unclear and their applicability is not defined.

Aside from these flaws, there is a tendency for codes of conduct and the training related to them to focus on what may not be done rather than on how to do something positively. This negativism has been recognized, and recent revisions of codes, both professional and corporate, are beginning to stress the fundamental principles that are essential to the maintenance of strong ethical and fiduciary capabilities. The code of conduct, particularly of leading-edge corporations, is being seen as guidance to employees as to how to proceed, rather than a proscription on how not to act. It is being seen as a motivating document for action and consultation, rather than a list of rules.

One of the unresolved issues is the overlap between professional codes and those of the firm or corporation for which the professional works as an employee. The professional accountant is governed by both, and the internal control system and integrity of the organization depends upon its code, so an understanding of corporate codes in general, and of their employer's code in particular, is essential to the day-to-day activities of employed professionals. However, the professional accountant should ultimately be governed by his or her duty to protect the public interest.

| **Issues Not Usually Resolved in Corporate Codes of Conduct** | Having examined the nature, content, and shortcomings of both corporate and professional accounting codes of conduct, it is appropriate to turn to the overlap between them. Several issues are often not resolved in codes of conduct that could be faced by employees, including professional accountants. Accordingly, some thought should be given to the following matters when a corporate code is being set up or revised:

1. *Conflicts between codes*
   Occasionally a professional or some other employee will be subject to the company/employer's code and also another code, such as a professional code for engineers or accountants. To avoid placing the person in an ethical dilemma of debating which code to follow, at the very least, consultation with an ethics officer/ ombudsman should be advised.

2. *Conflicts between competing interests or corporate stakeholders*
   Sometimes the priority of competing interests can be made clear in training sessions. If not, then protected routes for consultation should be available. This subject is discussed at length in this chapter and in Chapter 5.

3. *When should a professional blow the whistle, and to whom?*
   A protected, internal route for discussion and reporting should be available for professional accountants. An employer should realize that every professional accountant has a professional duty to uphold, which could supersede loyalty to the employer. It would be helpful if the professional's accounting society were to provide consultation to the professional on a confidential basis to assist in these decisions, as is the case in the United Kingdom and some other jurisdictions.

4. *Adequate protection of whistle-blowers*
   The most successful arrangements for whistle-blowing involve reporting, in confidence, to an autonomous individual of high rank or to someone who reports to a person of very high rank in the organization, for example, an ombudsperson who will follow up on concerns without revealing the informant's name or

exposing the informant, and who reports, without informant names, directly to the Chair of the organization. With this level of apparent support, investigations can be undertaken without interference. The ombudsperson should report back to the informant.

5. *Service decisions involving judgment*

Codes of conduct should be fashioned so as not to rule out the exercise of a professional's values when those are required for the judgments they must make. In the final analysis, it is the exercise of these values and the judgments based on these that could save the individual, the firm or employer, the profession, and the public from ethical problems. The challenge is to develop codes and cultures that do not force the abandonment of personal values but rather foster the development and exercise of values and judgment processes that will credit the stakeholders when they really need it.

Conflicts of Interest & Global Independence Standards

One of the most bedeviling aspects of a professional accountant's life is the recognition, avoidance, and/or management of conflict of interest situations. This is because *conflict of interest situations threaten to undermine the reason for having an accounting profession—to provide assurance that the work of a professional accountant will be governed by independent judgment focused to protect the public interest.* For this reason, the independence standards that the accounting profession must live by are fundamental to the continued success of the profession, its members, and their firms.

A professional accountant is called upon in his or her professional code to "*hold himself or herself free from any influence, interest or relationship in respect of his or her client's affairs, which impairs his or her professional judgment or objectivity or which, in the view of a reasonable observer would impair the member's professional judgment or objectivity.*"[15] Consequently, there are two distinct aspects to be kept in mind: the reality of having a conflict of interests, and the appearance that one might be present. Therefore, the traditional definition—a *conflict of interest is any influence, interest, or relationship that could cause a professional accountant's judgment to deviate from applying the profession's standards to client matters*—covers only part of the conflict of interest risk faced by a professional accountant.

With one notable exception, a professional accountant's view of conflict of interest situations is very similar to that of a director, executive, or other employee as discussed in Chapter 5. Consequently, the discussion in Chapter 5 covering *basic concepts, terms—potential, actual, and apparent conflicts of interest—causes,* and Figures 5.5 and 5.6, and Table 5.4, should be reviewed because they are applicable to professional accountants and the environment they face.

The notable exception is that a professional accountant is a fiduciary for the public. A professional accountant must protect his or her client or employer, but not at any cost, and not if the public interest will suffer. *A professional accountant must adhere to a set of rules aimed at neutrality and at protecting the public interest—he or she should not go to absolutely any lengths to serve a specific client's interests, unless the public interest is also served.* The services rendered by a fiduciary must be able to be trusted, and the professional accountant's independence of judgment is essential to that trust.

---

15. *Rules of Professional Conduct and Council Interpretations,* Institute of Chartered Accountants of Ontario (ICAO), Toronto, 1997, Foreword, p. 5 05, updated continuously

| **A Global Perspective from the IFAC Code** | The IFAC Code of Ethics for Professional Accountants[16] provides a useful approach to examine because it offers the most up-to-date treatment of independence requirements and related conflict of interests problems to which IFAC member country codes will converge. The 2005 IFAC Code is structured as indicated in Figure 6.1.

The IFAC Code indicates, as noted previously, that the professional accountant should be dedicated to serving the public interest, and that this can be achieved by compliance with the fundamental principles: integrity, objectivity, professional competence and due care, confidentiality, and professional behavior (see Table 6.8 for details). Not only does this require understanding these fundamental principles, but also how to identify threats to compliance and to apply safeguards that can eliminate, avoid or mitigate these threats. Tables 6.12 and 6.13 identify the threats and safeguards involved.

Essentially the IFAC Code's discussion of threats to compliance with fundamental principles amplifies the need for a professional accountant to maintain independence so that the integrity and objectivity of service to the public and clients are not compromised. It is concerned not only with performance, but also the wholesome appearance of that performance, which might lessen the effective transmission of information and lower the reputation of the profession. This requires continued vigilance about the actual state of mind of the professional accountant, as well as about the appearance of independence. As Section 290.8 of the 2005 Code states:

Independence requires:
> *Independence of Mind*
>> The state of mind that permits the expression of a conclusion without being affected by influences that compromise professional judgment, allowing an individual to act with integrity, and exercise objectivity and professional skepticism.

FIGURE 6.1   **IFAC 2005 Code of Ethics Framework**

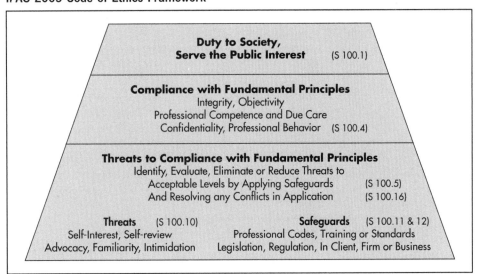

Source: *IFAC Code of Ethics for Professional Accountants*, June 2005 (Section number).

---

 16. IFAC 2005 Code is available at http://www.ifac.org/store/Category.tmpl?Category=Ethics and downloadable from **www.cengage.com/accounting/brooks**. Note the July 2006 revisions of Section 290 introducing Networks and Network Firms are also downloadable.

TABLE **6.12**

Threats to Noncompliance—Independent Judgement

Compliance with fundamental principles may be threatened by a broad range of circumstances. Many threats fall into the following categories:

(a) Self-interest threats, which may occur as a result of the financial or other interests of a professional accountant or of an immediate or close family member;

(b) Self-review threats, which may occur when a previous judgment needs to be reevaluated by the professional accountant responsible for that judgment;

(c) Advocacy threats, which may occur when a professional accountant promotes a position or opinion to the point that subsequent objectivity may be compromised;

(d) Familiarity threats, which may occur when, because of a close relationship, a professional accountant becomes too sympathetic to the interests of others; and

(e) Intimidation threats, which may occur when a professional accountant may be deterred from acting objectively by threats, actual or perceived.

IFAC 2005 Code of Ethics for Professional Accountants, Section 100.10

TABLE **6.13**

Safeguards Reducing the Risk of Conflict of Interest Situations

Safeguards Created by the Profession, Legislation, or Regulation

- Education, training, experience requirement for entry
- Continuing education
- Professional standards, monitoring, and disciplinary processes
- External review by a legally empowered third party of the reports, returns, communications or information produced by a professional accountant.
- External review of firm's quality control system
- Legislation governing independence requirements of the firm   *IFAC Code, S 100.12*

Safeguards Within a Client

- Appointment of auditors ratified/approved by other than management
- Client has competent staff to make managerial decisions
- Internal procedures to ensure objective choices in commissioning non-assurance engagements
- A corporate governance structure, such as the audit committee, that provides appropriate oversight and communications regarding a firm's services   *IFAC Code, 200.15*

Safeguards Within a Professional Accounting Firm's Own Systems and Procedures

- Leadership stressing importance of independence, and expectation of service/action in the public interest
- Policies and procedures to implement and monitor control of assurance engagements
- Documented independence policies regarding the identification and evaluation of threats to independence; applications of safeguards to eliminate or reduce those threats to an acceptable level
- Policies and procedures to monitor and manage the reliance on revenue from a single assurance client
- Using partners with separate reporting lines for the provision of non-assurance services to an assurance client
- Six other firm-wide and nine other specific items   *IFAC Code, 200.12*

Independence in Appearance

The avoidance of facts and circumstances that are so significant that a reasonable and informed third party, having knowledge of all relevant information, including safeguards applied, would reasonably conclude a firm's, or a member of the assurance team's, integrity, objectivity or professional skepticism had been compromised.

Diagrammatically, these components and relevance of proper judgment are represented in Figure 6.2.

Professional accountants must be alert to conflict of interest problems because they have the potential to erode independence. As noted in Table 6.12, the IFAC Code lists *five basic categories of threats or conflicts that could sway the professional accountant from acting in the public interest: self-interest; review of one's own work; advocating a client's position; familiarity with the management, directors, or owners of the client corporation; and intimidation by management, directors, or owners.* Self-interest, or the desire to protect or enhance one's position, certainly has been known to influence professional accountant's judgment. Arthur Andersen provides a glaring example of this, as they wanted to retain the audit revenue from several clients, including Enron, WorldCom, Waste Management, and Sunbeam. Auditing one's own work is a variant of the self-interest problem wherein auditors are reluctant to criticize themselves and lose face with client management. Advocacy of client's positions to a third party occasionally puts a professional accountant in a poor position to argue a different and better position with regard to GAAP or disclosure with the client. Familiarity with client personnel may create interpersonal bonds that leave a professional accountant not wanting to disappoint or offend the friends or close associates that familiarity has created. Finally, there are many cases whereby the senior management of a corporation has intimidated professional accountants working for the corporation, thereby forcing them into misrepresentations, illegalities, and/or poor accounting choices. The Sunbeam and WorldCom cases in Chapter 2 illustrate this problem vividly.

Identification of any of these potential conflict of interest situations should be followed by their avoidance, elimination, or reduction of their risk through the application of safeguards. The IFAC Code suggests that safeguards can be found in techniques and approaches detailed in professional guidelines, legislation, regulation, or within client or professional accounting firm systems and practices. The examples provided in the IFAC Code are listed in Table 6.13.

Most professional accountants take the proper handling of conflict of interest situations very seriously because that is fundamental to the maintenance of fiduciary relationships. Many professional accounting firms, including the largest, have additional codes of conduct or practice that offer the firm's guidance. Members of a multi-office firm often sign a document in which they promise not to discuss the affairs of, or trade in securities of, clients of any office in their firm, and a restricted list of client's names is maintained for reference. Members of the firm are

---

FIGURE 6.2

IFAC Code's Framework for Independent Judgment

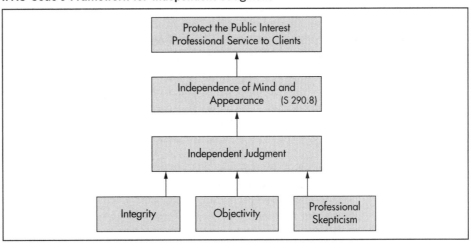

Source: *IFAC Code of Ethics for Professional Accountants,* 2005, S 290.8 and Independence Definition

told that, even if they do not personally possess information on a client's activities, they may be presumed to do so by interested public. Care must be taken to avoid the appearance of conflict as much as the reality. Reputation is too hard, and too costly, to restore. Consequently, most firms employ several techniques in the management of conflicts of interest to minimize potential harm, including:

| Firm codes, in addition to augment those of professional bodies;

| Training sessions and reinforcing memos;

| Client lists from all locales for reference and sign-off procedures signifying noninvestment;

| Scrutiny of securities trading, particularly related to new issues;

| Firewalls or Chinese walls to prevent information flows within firms;

| Reporting and consultation with senior officers;

| Avoidance;

| Rules for serving clients with potentially conflicting interests;

| Rules for taking on new clients or providing new services, and for termination of client relations.

| **Types of Conflicts of Interest Based on Stakeholder Impact** | With the foregoing background, it is useful to consider what the most common conflicts of interest are for accountants, which can be grouped into four categories as to stakeholder impact:

1. Self-interest of the professional conflicts with the interests of the other stakeholders.

2. Self-interest of the professional and some other stakeholders, conflicts with some other stakeholders.

3. Interests of one client are favored over the interests of another client.

4. Interests of one or more stakeholders are favored over the interests of one or more other stakeholders.

| **Spheres of Activity Affected** | The first category pits the professional accountant against the other stakeholders in several spheres of activity. The undermined independent judgment of the professional can be evident in the services offered, the improper use of influence, and the misuse of information. The second category, where the professional sides with some stakeholders to the disadvantage of others, also offers opportunities for poor judgment in terms of the services offered, as does the third category, which refers specifically to clients. Category four, which involves stakeholder groups but where self-interest may not come into play except sometimes on the disadvantaged side, focuses primarily on the proper use of information and particularly on issues of confidentiality. These relationships are summarized in Table 6.14, and it is to a discussion of how judgment can be undermined in each of these spheres of activity that we now turn.

| **Conflicts of Interest Affecting Services Offered** | Self-interest is a very powerful motivator that can disadvantage clients, the public and other stakeholders through a degradation of the services offered by a professional accountant, whether the professional is in the role of auditor or management accountant. Many of the temptations auditors succumb to arise because the auditor's "business" side dominates his or her "professional" side, and the drive for profit or personal gain dominates the values that are needed to maintain the trust expected in a fiduciary

6.14

Conflicts of Interest for Professional Accountants: Categories, Spheres of Activity Affected & Examples

STAKEHOLDER CATEGORY	SPHERE OF ACTIVITY AFFECTED	EXAMPLES
Self vs. others	Services offered Improper use of influence Misuse of information	Conflicting services, shaving quality Improper purchases of client goods Improper investments by relatives
Self and others vs. others	Services offered	Overinvolvement with management or directors erodes objectivity
Client vs. client Employer vs. employer	Services offered	Serving competing clients at the same time
Stakeholder vs. stakeholder	Misuse of information (confidentiality)	Whistle-blowing, reporting to government or regulators

relationship. When the needed trust breaks down, it does so because one or more of the essential aspects of professional service expected are not delivered in a manner that protects or furthers the interests that the professional should be serving before the professional's own interest.

For instance, the desire for profit can lead to services being performed at *substandard levels of quality*. Because of the pressures of rising costs, or in an effort to increase profit, services may be performed at substandard levels of quality. This may happen through the use of junior or unskilled staff, or if staff are not adequately supervised by senior, and more costly, personnel. It may lead to pressures on staff to increase their working hours beyond reasonable levels, or to encourage staff to work long hours but not to charge the clients for the total time spent. In either of these cases, the fatigue factor that results is not only unfair to staff but also can result in diminished capacity to detect errors on the audit. Although diminished services clearly affect clients and the public, these working conditions also present the staff involved with the very real ethical problem of how to react: should they complain, and if so, how much and to whom? These issues will be addressed later in this chapter.

The quality of services provided can suffer for other reasons, as well. A professional may be tempted to *lowball fee quotations* to clients in an effort to gain new business or retain old clients. Later, the reality of the low fee may present the dilemma of having to meet audit budgets that are too tight, which can again lead to substandard service quality and/or pressures on staff to bury or forget about time spent beyond budget allowances. Lowballing is occasionally justified on the basis of anticipated future price increases for audit services or the garnering of additional high margin work in tax or consulting services. This hope is not always incorporated into audit planning, so budgets are occasionally set too tight. Moreover, the anticipated high-margin revenue sources may not materialize in any event. These exigencies have been understood for a long time, and were the major reason why many professional societies prohibited the quotation of *fixed fees*. When something unexpected occurs, in a fixed or lowballed fee situation the additional time spent comes right out of the auditor's pocket—an obvious conflict of interest. Fees set on the basis of hourly rates per level of staff employed allow the need for quality service to be incorporated in the total fee even where unexpected problems arise during an audit.

Self-interest can also lead to the offer of services in situations leading to conflicts of interest with other stakeholders. For example, an auditor is in an excellent position to offer *management advisory services* or *assurance services* because the audit has developed a thorough knowledge of the client's affairs and personnel. On the other hand, if an auditor accepts an engagement to install an internal control system, there may be a reluctance to acknowledge its flaws when these become clear during a subsequent audit. Such reluctance can arise even where non-audit personnel from the same firm are used. Unfortunately, living with a faulty system of internal control is like living with a time bomb, with the enhanced risk being borne by the client and the public. Another example, which presents itself frequently, involves a partner who is negotiating with a client's chief financial officer (CFO) on the adequacy of a provision for bad debts, knowing that next week the CFO will be making a decision on whether to award his or her firm, or a competitor, a very large consulting assignment. The threat to objectivity is obvious and overwhelming, yet the partner is expected to be objective nonetheless.

What are the remedies for such situations involving so-called *conflicting services* that involve self-criticism? Refusal to provide such services is one option, but it could lead to the client incurring unnecessary costs and the professional losing revenue. At present, established position of the accounting profession has been to rely on the personal integrity of the professionals involved to be able to criticize themselves in the event they or their associates perform conflicting services. However, this reliance, which depends upon the values, strength of character, and ethical awareness of the professionals involved, is in the process of being replaced by the SOX-oriented limitations on the auditors of SEC registrant companies.[17]

The self-interest of professional accountants can cause the professional to want to side with certain stakeholder groups, to the detriment of others. Professional accountants can easily and inadvertently become overinvolved with clients or suppliers or other stakeholders. Sometimes this *overinvolvement* can make the professional's judgment susceptible to bias in favor of his or her newfound friends or compatriots. Gifts can create pressures for continuance. Involvement in management friendships and decisions can create the desire not to be critical, as can the continued, close involvement of an auditor with the board of directors. To borrow from the hierarchy of human needs developed by Maslow (1954), professionals can be subject to influence attempts directed at their ego, their social needs, or even their basic financial needs because of overinvolvement with other stakeholders, which threatens the professional's independence. Frequently, overinvolvement begins very innocuously and builds imperceptibly to a condition that the professional does not expect (the slippery slope problem noted earlier.). Constant vigilance is required to stay out of the difficulty of putting the interests of management and directors ahead of shareholders and the public.

Sometimes a professional accountant develops a mutuality of interest with a client or becomes overinvolved with senior management at a client, to the extent that the professional's skepticism and critical perspective is suspended. Friendship, partnerships, the desire to protect existing revenue streams or garner more, and the prospect of social interaction or admiration may all impact on the professional's independence of judgment to the detriment of the public interest. Care must be undertaken to ensure that a professional accountant or his or her firm does not become so dependent on the revenue from one client that decisions contrary to the public interest become difficult to make. This appears to have happened, as noted in Chapter 2, in the case of Arthur Andersen and several of its audit clients, including Enron, WorldCom, and Waste Management.

Concern over the impact of consulting and other services on the independence of professional accountants alarmed the accounting profession and its regulators, particularly in the United States prior to the demise of Arthur Andersen. In 1998, PricewaterhouseCoopers (PwC) discovered[18] in a postmerger review that its predecessor firms (Price Waterhouse and Coopers &

---

17. See discussion section on SEC and IFAC Independence Rules on pages 353 and 354.
18. SEC's Independent Consultant's *Report of the Internal Investigation of Independence Issues at PricewaterhouseCoopers LLP,* January 6, 2000. SEC website link at http://www.sec.gov/news/press/pressarchive/2000press.shtml.

Lybrand) had failed to properly supervise their consulting and audit partners and personnel and almost 50 percent of PwC's U.S. partners held improperly sanitized[19] investments in the firm's audit clients—thereby violating PwC and SEC conflict of interest guidelines. This led, in part, to the issuance of a proposed revision of the SEC's Auditor Independence Requirements[20] for auditors of companies that file SEC documentation in the United States. Among other guidance provided, the revised rule sought to clarify those services that an auditor of SEC registrant companies can and cannot engage in to preserve independence of judgment in fact, as well as the perception of independence. It should be noted that the matters dealt with in the proposed revision were overtaken by the SOX reforms and the resulting new SEC pronouncements[21] discussed on page 353 of this chapter.

Although embarrassed by the initial publicity of the PwC violations, PwC, the accounting profession, and regulators like the SEC have not required complete separation between audit or assurance services and consulting services. As previously noted, SOX has required the SEC to specify those services that can be offered to audit clients. However, even though some large firms have sold off service lines, they continue to operate multidisciplinary consulting practices.

The continuation in nonattest activity will require a strong set of guidelines and organizational culture to prevent the erosion of independent judgment and professional skepticism. Professional accountants will have to continue to resist the temptation of focusing on the development of high-profit services to the detriment of low-margin audit services. An instance of this might be a new perversion of risk management in tax matters, where the client is advised to take a questionable action based on the probability that government tax auditors are unlikely to appear because of other time demands, not because the tax treatment is in doubt. An additional aspect of a multidisciplinary firm that could cause difficulties is the potential conflict between the professional codes and practices of accountants, lawyers, and engineers. For example, accountants are not generally expected to blow the whistle on clients, but engineers are required to report any endangerment to life from a dangerous process or poorly maintained building[22]—which profession's rules should prevail? Similarly, lawyers have a different standard of confidentiality that prevents them from advising competing clients, whereas professional accountants do it frequently. We are also already seeing some assurance services downgraded to the status of a nonaudit review or consulting services to lessen the legal liability involved in an effort to bolster profits. Increased attention to ethical principles for managing such conflicts of interest will be essential to the maintenance of the accounting profession's reputation in the future, as well as the reputations of the other professions involved.

The examples of overindulged self-interest cited in Table 6.14 put the professional's reputation at risk because the interest of the client, employer, or public may not be considered before the professional's self-interest as is expected in a fiduciary relationship. The lure of personal profit from investment positions in clients may lead to the manipulation of accounting

---

19. Investment where PwC had precleared that no conflict of interests had or would occur.

20. See www.sec.gov/rules/proposed/34-42994.htm for the *Proposed Rule: Revision of the Commission's Auditor Independence Requirements,* July 17, 2000, pp.109. *A Final Rule* was released in January 2003.

21. See SEC website for *Final Rule: Strengthening the Commission's Requirements Regarding Auditor Independence,* U.S. Securities and Exchange Commission, http://www.sec.gov/rules/final/33-8183.htm, modified February 6, 2003, and Commission Adopts Rules Strengthening Auditor Independence, U.S. Securities and Exchange Commission, http://www.sec.gov/new/press/2003-9.htm, January 22, 2003.

22. Presumably, this difference in treatment is due to the higher priority attached by society (and therefore by engineers) to physical well-being as opposed to financial well-being. Society is willing to endorse the reporting of one, but not yet the other.

disclosure or the choice of accounting principles, which do not communicate the real state of affairs to shareholders because the stock price gains for the investor-professional accountant are too alluring to pass up. Fortunately such investment has been barred for years in most professional codes. Similarly, skimping on quality of service, particularly of audit service, has proven difficult to resist in the past. As competition on the basis of price of services becomes more intense, professionals would be well advised to consider the longer-term possibilities of loss of reputation, fines, and higher insurance premiums.

It is possible, but very risky, for a professional accountant and his or her clients to *represent more than one client in a transaction*. Even if a professional is very knowledgeable about the matter, such as would be the case if an audit client were being sold, and the buyer and seller are good friends, it is very difficult to do your best for one except at the expense of the other. Later, if the buyer or seller becomes disenchanted, they may suspect that their interest has been short-changed and launch a lawsuit. Therefore, even if more than one client who is party to a transaction wants a professional accountant to act on their behalf, the clients should at least be warned that each should have independent representation. Sometimes, it will be advisable to select and serve only one of the clients, even if they are insistent. Whenever more than one client is served in a transaction, the professional accountant must be able to show that all reasonable precautions were taken to avoid failing to act in the best interests of all parties.

For the accountant in management, it is similarly risky to consider *serving two or more employers*. Serving two or more masters has, over the years, proved very difficult because of the real, latent, and imaginary conflicts of interest that inevitably arise even where the employers are not competitors. Where the employers are competitors, it is sheer folly. A variant of this ethical problem surfaces when an accountant in management *invests in a competitor*. Care must be taken to ensure that conflicting interests do not influence judgment or work performance adversely for the employer.

Blind self-interest can prove to be the undoing of professional accountants, just as blind ambition has proven to be the bane of many managers. Frequently, however, professional accountants do not suffer from blind or rabid self-interest, but do lose sight of *whether they are in a profession or in business*. They would do well to remember that few businesses are accorded the privilege of engaging in fiduciary relationships. A balance is called for that involves placing the interest of the public, the client, the profession, and the firm or employer before the professional's own self-interest.

| **Conflicts of Interest Involving Improper Use of Influence** | The desire to improve the professional's own lot can lead to the improper use of influence such that the independent judgment of the professional can be undermined. For example, a professional accountant employed by a corporation might be successful in arranging for a friend to be hired by the company. In so doing, however, the professional may put themselves in a position to be approached by management who want a *favor in return,* which may take the form of nondisclosure of a financial matter, the delay of such disclosure, or the minimization of the disclosure. The public, shareholders, other management, and the auditors can be misled in the process.

An auditor may also be unsuspectingly trapped by use of his or her own influence. From time to time, auditors will want, and be encouraged by clients, to *purchase goods or services from the client* at substantial discounts beyond those available to the public. The risk is that the desire to do this or the satisfaction experienced will create a desire to subjugate public interests in favor of the interests of the management who control this privilege. Similarly, a professional employed by a corporation may wish to *buy goods or services from a supplier* at a discount. Is this a reasonable thing to do? The answer depends on the circumstances.

Alternatively, a professional in audit practice or employed by a corporation can be offered a *gift, a meal, entertainment, a trip, or preferential treatment* by a client or a supplier. Is it ethical to accept such a gift? Again, the answer depends on the circumstances. Fortunately, the guidelines outlined in Table 5.6 can be used to avoid the real or potential conflicts of interest that could develop when the giver expects a favor in return.

| **Conflicts of Interest Involving Use or Misuse of Information (Confidentiality)** | The misuse of information by a professional accountant can be detrimental to other stakeholders of the client or company involved. For example, the use of information by the professional before others have the right to use such information is unfair and considered unethical. This is the basic problem for anyone who is privy to *inside information* about a company by virtue of being the auditor or an employee—that is, an "insider"—to use that information personally or indirectly for *insider trading*. In order to ensure the basic fairness of stock markets so that the public and other noninsiders will wish to enter the market, regulatory bodies like the Securities and Exchange Commission or the Ontario Securities Commission require management insiders to wait until the information is released to the public before allowing insiders to trade, and then they must disclose these trades so the public will know what has happened. The prospect of a "rigged game" would not be in the public interest or in the interest of the corporations using the market for fund raising in the long run. Insider trading rules also apply to the families of the insider, extending to those who are not part of the immediate family but for whom the insider has an obvious ability to influence. Some individuals with high-profile jobs in the public service go even further to avoid such conflicts of interest. In order to be seen to be entirely ethical, some politicians have gone so far as to place their holdings, and those of their dependants, in so-called 'blind trusts', which are managed by someone else with instructions not to discuss trades or holdings with the politician.

The situation for auditors is somewhat different in that the ownership of shares or financial instruments of a client is forbidden based on the real or potential conflict of interest that would be created, as discussed in earlier segments of this book. Most auditing firms extend this ban in two ways. First, the ban is applied to the auditor's family and persons who would be considered significant dependants or subject to influence. Second, the ban may also apply for any client of the firm, even if that client is serviced through a wholly separate office (for international firms, even in another country) with which the individual does not have contact on a normally occurring basis. Where the ban is relaxed on trading in shares of the firm's clients for employees not directly involved in the client's affairs, extreme care should be taken through Chinese walls/ Firewalls and reporting/scrutiny mechanisms to manage the conflict of interest created. The extent of attention to the prevention of insider trading and the perception of it is indicative of the alarm with which most firms view its prospect.

Confidentiality is the term used to describe keeping confidential information that is proprietary to a client or employer. The release of such information to the public, or to competitors, would have a detrimental effect on the interests of the client, and it would be contrary to the expectations of trust of a fiduciary relationship. In the case of an auditor, this expectation of trust and privacy is vital to the client's willingness to discuss difficult issues, which are quite germane to the audit, to get the opinion of the auditor on how they might be dealt with in the financial statements and notes. How frank would the discussion of a contentious contingent liability be if there were a possibility the auditor would reveal the confidence? How could a contentious tax treatment be discussed thoroughly if there was the possibility of voluntary disclosure to the tax collection authorities? It is therefore argued that the maintenance of client confidences is essential to the proper exercise of the audit function, and to the provision of the best advice based on full discussion of the possibilities.

There are, however, limits to privacy that some professions have enshrined in their codes of conduct, or where these limits are spelled out in regulating frameworks. Engineers, for example, must disclose to appropriate public officials when they believe a structure or mechanism is likely to be harmful to the users, as in the potential collapse of a building due to violations of the building code. In Canada, the bankruptcy of two chartered banks resulted in the requirement to report lack of client-bank viability directly to the Federal Office of the Superintendent of Financial Institutions. In the United Kingdom, money laundering for drugs and terrorism must be reported. There appears to be an increasing focus on the public responsibility of auditors and an increasing expectation of action rather than silence.

This trade-off between the interests of client, management, public, regulators, the profession, and management promises to be a growing conundrum for accountants in the future. One issue that is not well understood is the consequences of a professional accountant observing strict confidentiality about the malfeasance of his or her employer, and being directed by the professional code to resign if the employer cannot be convinced to change their behavior. This would follow from the codes of conduct that require no disclosure of client/employer confidences except in a court of law or subject to a disciplinary hearing, and at the same time requiring resignation in order to avoid association with a misrepresentation. In the event of a resignation in silence, the ethical misdeed goes unrecognized by all stakeholders except the perpetrators and the silent professional. How does this protect the interests of the public, the shareholders, or the profession? A discussion of this issue earlier in the book gave rise to an argument for the modification of the strict confidentiality of codes and the introduction of assisted confidentiality involving consultations with officials of the relevant professional institute. Perhaps through such consultations, a means can be found to better judge what needs to be kept confidential, when and how disclosure ought to be made, and how the professional's and public's interests can be protected. For an auditor, the situation is different. When an auditor is discharged or replaced, the incoming auditor has the right to ask the outgoing auditor (and the client) what the circumstances were that led to the dismissal or resignation. In some jurisdictions, the removed auditor even has the right to address the shareholders at their annual meeting, or by mail, at the expense of the corporation involved.

One of the first items that ought to be examined is what action should be taken when a professional accountant realizes that a client or employer is engaging in *tax evasion*. Tax evasion involves the misrepresentation of facts to the taxation authorities, resulting in the commission of a fraud and the cheating of the public treasury. At present, the established practice is not to be involved in the misrepresentation, to counsel against it, but not to report the problem to the authorities. As a result, the perpetrators need not fear their misdeed will be reported by a *whistle-blower* to the tax authorities or the public. Consequently, the interests of the public and, when the deed is found out, the shareholders and the profession will suffer. Hopefully, the corporation will recognize the large cost of not encouraging whistle-blowers to come forward through protected internal channels so that unknown problems can be corrected and public disgrace, and fines, can be avoided.

Looking the other way when confronted with tax evasion doesn't appear to make ethical sense. In some cases, the professional involved may believe that the interpretation involved is debatable so that the problem is one of "*avoision,*" and its borderline nature is worthy of support until the authorities find and rule on the problem. Avoidance of taxes is, of course quite legal; avoision reflects borderline practices, and evasion is both illegal and unethical (Lynch 1987). The boundaries are blurred, so access to confidential consultation on these matters is essential to proper ethical action.

Enron's use of tax avoidance strategies that is reported in Chapter 2 offers an interesting case of avoidance and probably qualifies as avoision, according to a U.S. Senate Committee on

Finance report.[23] The reaction to Enron's tax avoidance transactions may lead to the closing of loopholes, such as using accommodation parties, to the increased scrutiny of the business purpose of transactions, and to increased sanctions for extra aggressive interpretations. The resulting publicity, potential loss of reputation, and potential for lawsuits have caused responsible advisers to consider ethical guidelines for limiting involvement with and the ethics risks inherent in such activities. This represents a significant change in thinking for many professionals engaged in tax practice.

In a subsequent related incident, in August 2005, KPMG paid $456 million and agreed to be monitored for three years to settle a potential U.S. criminal indictment triggered by the firm's admitted involvement with phony tax shelters (i.e., those without economic purpose other than to save tax). "Eight former partners and a lawyer who provided advice to KPMG were charged with tax-shelter fraud."[24] KPMG also put Jeffrey Eischeid, the former partner in charge of this area of service, on administrative leave some time after he had testified:

> The tax strategies being discussed represent an earlier time at KPMG and a far different regulatory and marketplace environment. . . . None of the strategies— nor anything like these tax strategies—is currently being offered by KPMG.[25]

It was argued that KPMG "scrambled" to avoid criminal prosecution as a firm, because conviction could have caused the same fate of collapse and bankruptcy Arthur Andersen suffered.[26] Other major accounting firms were also fined and settled out of court for similar tax service problems. The ethics case "Marketing Aggressive Tax Shelters" (on page 427) is about these issues.

Another tax practice, that of *risk management*, is worthy of comment here. If the risk management relates to a tax matter that is in doubt, that is an issue of avoision and worthy of estimation of the risks and support. However, if the risk management involves estimating if a known illegality will be found because tax auditors are few and far between, then the practice would appear to represent support for an evasion of tax.

Laws & Jurisprudence

Professional accountants can also refer to legal cases and lawyers for interpretations of their legal liability and potential defences. To assist the reader, an analysis of trends and a synopsis of important legal decisions is included in the Appendix to this chapter, "Trends in the Legal Liability of Accountants and Auditors and Legal Defenses Available." It documents an early trend to a broadening of liability from strict "privity of contract" with existing shareholders to "foreseeable parties" who might use the financial statements. Partly to counteract the trend to very excessive liability, more recent cases, such as *Hercules Managements Ltd. et al v. Ernst & Young* (1997), have been decided in favor of very limited liability for auditors. Since this case was defended on the rather bizarre basis that financial statements should not be used for investment purposes, and therefore an auditor has no legal liability to shareholders and investors, most

23. *Report of the Investigation of Enron Corporation and Related Entities Regarding Federal Tax and Compensation Issues, and Policy Recommendations, Volume 1: Report,* U.S. Senate Committee on Finance, February 2003, released February 22, 2003. (See **www.cengage.com/accounting/brooks**.)

24. Peter Morton, "KPMG pays US$456 million to settle fraud allegations," *Financial Post,* August 30, 2005, FP1.

25. Robert Schmidt, "Tax-shelter pressure sparks KPMG shakeup," Financial Post, January 13, 2004, FP4.

26. "KPMG scrambles to avoid criminal prosecution," *Financial Post,* June 17, 2005, FP4.

observers believe that it is a temporary diversion in a progression toward greater auditor liability. In fact, the U.S. Senate Permanent Subcommittee on Investigations stated in its *Report on the Collapse of Enron* that financial statements and auditor's independent opinions thereon were essential to the public investment process and its credibility.

To counter the trend to greater auditor liability, safe-harbor or limited liability arrangements are emerging for auditors. As noted in the later discussion of limited liability partnerships (LLP), these will limit the dollar value of legal damages each partner has to bear from each lawsuit. LLPs, however, will not stop lawsuits.

Caution should be exercised in the application of legal standards to ethical problems, however, for three reasons. First, the law appears to offer timeless wisdom when in reality it is continuously changing as it tries to catch up to the positions society believes are reasonable. In other words, the law generally lags what society views as ethically desirable.

Second, and more importantly, *what is legal is not always ethical.* According to former U.S. Supreme Court Justice Potter Stewart, ethics is "knowing the difference between what you have the right to do and what is right to do." There are plenty of examples of this difference between legal standards, moral standards, and ethical standards. For example, a company may be able to pollute in a way that is harmful to the health of its workers in a developing country because the local standards are less stringent than at home in North America. Sometimes the legal standard is clear, such as in tax matters or bribery, for example, but large portions of society do not adhere to it, so the mores or norms expected are different. What behavior is right? Legal, moral, and ethical standards are different and should be recognized as such.[27]

The third reason for caution in placing too much reliance on legal interpretations and remedies is that they appear not to be highly relevant to the launching of or final disposition of lawsuits, particularly in the United States. Of 800 allegations of audit failure during the period 1960–1990 against the 15 largest audit firms in the United States, only 64 were tried to a verdict (Palmrose 1991, 154). Although some cases were still underway, less than 10 percent were submitted to judge or jury, a rate that drops to 2.1 percent for the 1985–1989 period.

By far the highest percentage of cases cited in the Palmrose study were settled for practical reasons rather than legal precedent. Usually, audit firms found it cheaper to settle rather than fight in court. The cost to their pocketbooks in legal fees and lost billable time, and particularly to their reputation, rarely made recourse to the courts a sensible option, even where lawsuits were without legal foundation. This trend toward settlement has accelerated and shows no sign of reversal.

The reasons for this bizarre situation are outlined in a position statement authored by the Big 6 audit firms in August 1992, entitled *The Liability Crisis in the United States: Impact on the Accounting Profession.* This statement, which is included as a chapter reading, indicates that several quirks that have developed in the legal framework and process are responsible for an intolerable level of liability for audit professionals—a level that has resulted in individuals who have been offered partnerships hesitating or declining the offer, and in the bankruptcy in 1990 of one of the largest audit firms, Laventhol & Horwath. As the heads of the Big 6 said, "To restore equity and sanity to the liability system and to provide reasonable assurance that the public accounting profession will be able to continue to meet its public obligations requires substantial reform of both federal and state liability laws." Several reforms were suggested in the statement, but they have been slow to appear because of the multiple jurisdictions involved and the entrenchment of the practice of contingent legal fees and of the principle of joint and several liability.

---

27. For a fuller description of the differences between legal, moral and ethical standards, see Chapter 3.

Two developments are worthy of comment. In December 1995, the U.S. Congress enacted the *Private Securities Reform Act,* which changes auditor liability from having to share equally with his or her partners to having to bear a portion allocated by the jury involved (Andrews and Simonette 1996, 54). Secondly, the organizational form of the accounting firm was allowed to be altered to a limited liability partnership (LLP) in some jurisdictions to provide limited liability for nonculpable partners of the firm. Historically, accounting firms were required to be partnerships where, if the firm was sued, each partner was "jointly and severally liable" and was required to pay the full loss from their investment in the firm, plus any additional if required from their personal assets. Afterward, they could sue others who were also liable for recovery of their fortunes if these other people had resources left. This meant that partners could lose their investment in their firm and their personal assets as well, even though someone else was at fault. This was draconian, but it was considered an appropriate way to ensure that professional accountants were very focused on providing competent service. The LLP provided that the negligent partner would be required to settle up with both his or her investment in the firm plus his or her personal assets, whereas the "innocent" partners could only lose from the assets they had invested in the firm. Their personal assets were protected. Ernst & Young became the first LLP in New York on August 1, 1994. Other jurisdictions have enacted similar legislation.

Given this scenario, in which the legal "cure" for a problem is still unpalatable—where a lawsuit can bankrupt a firm, although most of the partner's personal assets are untouched—"preventative medicine," or not to get into the dilemma in the first place, is preferred if at all possible. Instilling high standards of professional ethics into the values and culture of accounting professionals and their organizations can prove to be a significant safeguard against getting into practice dilemmas. Even in legal jurisdictions such as Canada or the United Kingdom, where the liability crisis is not quite as alarming, high ethical standards and skilled judgment in their application can eliminate or reduce professional exposure.

When Codes & Laws Don't Help

Frequently, professional accountants find themselves facing situations that are not covered explicitly in codes of conduct, nor sufficiently close to jurisprudence to benefit from those sources of guidance. Sometimes a professional accounting body will provide its member with consultation services through a so-called Director of Ethics. Most often, however, the professional accountant will be left to his or her own devices. He or she may hire their own advisor from the ranks of legal or ethical experts, but ultimately the accountant will have to rely upon his or her own knowledge, values, and judgment to decide what is right. If they are fortunate enough, they will have an understanding of the frameworks discussed in Chapters 3 and 4 to facilitate ethical decision making.

Broadening Role for Professional Accountants

The need for integrity, independent judgment, expertise, and savvy in the preparation and presentation of financial analyses and reports is not abating; rather, it is increasing.

In addition to this traditional fiduciary role, professional accountants are best suited to play the dominant or supporting roles in *design, preparation, and management* of the following areas that are *vital to good governance* in the emerging era of stakeholder accountability:

❙ Stakeholder interests assessment

❙ Stakeholder-focused performance indicators and incentive systems

| Stakeholder-oriented reports for management, board, and public
| Ethical corporate culture
| Corporate codes of conduct
| Ethics compliance mechanisms and reporting to the board
| Ethical decision-making guidance frameworks
| Ethics risk management systems

Professional accountants understand the problems that caused the Enron, WorldCom, Arthur Andersen, and other recent fiascos, and understand the potential contribution of an organization's internal control system as well as the pitfalls of an unethical culture. While the professional accountant's focus has been on financial reporting, there is a need to refocus on future performance and how to guide and manage it to help ensure that ethics are built into strategic plans, board compliance reviews, and corporate incentive systems.

Boards of directors have not been equipped to consider and deal with these new necessities. That inability and lack of awareness resulted in the Enron problem and many others. Professional accountants can assist boards greatly in the new, ethics-sensitive era if they are ready to broaden their horizons.

Conclusion

Recent events such as the Enron, Arthur Andersen, and WorldCom disasters have rededicated the focus of professional accountants on their expected role as fiduciaries for the public interest. The reputation and future standing of the profession has suffered, and its distinction and success depends on this rededication.

The professional accountant must develop judgment, values, and character traits that embrace the public's expectations, which are inherent in the emerging stakeholder-oriented accountability and governance framework. Codes of ethics are being refined to better guide professional accountants, and assure that unrestrained self-interest, bias, and/or misunderstanding do not cloud the professional's independent state of mind or give rise to an appearance that independence may be lacking.

Globalization is influencing the development of codes and harmonization to IFAC standards and will surely continue. Just as governance mechanism for corporations has outgrown domestic jurisdiction and boundaries, stakeholders around the world will be more important in determining the performance standards for professional accountants. These professionals will increasingly serve global capital markets and global corporations, and their success will require the respect of employees and partners drawn from a much wider set than in the past.

Given their knowledge and skills, it will be interesting to see if professional accountants can seize the opportunities that present themselves for broadening their role. They are particularly well placed to assist in the further development of those mechanisms that will provide and ensure ethical guidance for organizations. They know that codes don't cover every possible challenge, nor are they sufficient on their own. Developing ethical decision-making frameworks developed in Chapters 3 and 4 and understanding the special issues covered in Chapter 7 will assist those who choose to make the most of future opportunities.

Questions

1. Answer the seven questions in the opening section of this chapter.

2. What is meant by the term "fiduciary relationship"?

3. Why are most ethical decisions accountants face complex rather than straightforward?

4. When should an accountant place his or her duty to the public ahead of his or her duty to a client or employer?

5. Which would you choose as the key idea for ethical behavior in the accounting profession: "Protect the public interest" or "Protect the credibility of the profession." Why?

6. Why is maintaining the confidentiality of client or employer matters essential to the effectiveness of the audit or accountant relationship?

7. What is the difference between exercising "due care" and "exercising professional skepticism"?

8. Why did the SEC ban certain nonaudit services from being offered to SEC registrant audit clients, even though it has been possible to effectively manage such conflict of interest situations?

9. Where on the Kohlberg framework would you place your own usual motivation for making decisions?

10. Why don't more professional accountants report ethical wrongdoing? Consider their awareness and understanding of ethical issues, as well as their motivation and courage for doing so.

11. Which type of conflict of interest should be of greater concern to a professional accountant: actual or apparent?

12. An auditor naturally wishes his or her activity to be as profitable as possible, but when, if ever, should the drive for profit be tempered?

13. If the provision of management advisory services can create conflicts of interest, why are audit firms still offering them?

14. If you were an auditor, would you buy a new car at a dealership you audited for 17 percent off list price?

15. If you were a management accountant, would you buy a product from a supplier for personal use at 25 percent off list?

16. If you were a professional accountant, and you discovered your superior was inflating his or her expense reports, what would you do?

17. Can a professional accountant serve two clients whose interests conflict? Explain.

18. If an auditor's fee is paid from the client company, isn't there a conflict of interests that may lead to a lack of objectivity? Why doesn't it?

19. Why does the IFAC Code consider the appearance of a conflict of interests to be as important as a real, but nonapparent, influence that might sway the independence of mind of a professional accountant?

20. What is the most important contribution of a professional or corporate code of conduct?

21. Are one or more of the fundamental principles found in codes of conduct more important than the rest? Why?

22. Was the "expectations gap" that triggered the Treadway and Macdonald Commissions the fault of the users of financial statements, the management who prepared them, the auditors, or the standard setters who decided what the disclosure standards should be?

23. Why should codes focus on principles rather than specific detailed rules?

24. Is having an ethical culture important to having an effective system of internal control? Why or why not?

25. What should an auditor do if he or she believes that the ethical culture of a client is unsatisfactory?

26. Are the governing partners of accounting firms subject to a "due diligence" requirement similar to that for corporation executives in building an ethical culture? Can a firm and/or its governors be sanctioned for the misdeeds of its members?

27. An engineer employed by a large multidisciplinary accounting firm has spotted a condition in a client's plant that is seriously jeopardizing the safety of the client's workers. The engineer believes that the professional engineering code requires that this condition be reported to the authorities, but professional accounting codes do not. How should the head of the firm resolve this issue?

28. Why don't codes of conduct or existing jurisprudence provide sufficient guidance for accountants in ethical matters?

Case Insights

The following cases have been selected to expose situations that shed light on the role of auditors and management accountants as they discharge their fiduciary duties. Specifically, the issues covered are as follows:

Famous Cases

- *Arthur Andersen, Enron, WorldCom, Sunbeam,* and *Waste Management* cases are located in Chapter 2, and the *Tyco* case is in Chapter 5.

- *HealthSouth—Can 5 CFOs be Wrong?* presents the strange case of Richard Scrushy who was the first CEO to be charged under the governance-reforming Sarbanes-Oxley Act of 2002. Although five HealthSouth CFOs testified that Scrushy had knowingly directed the fraud, the Alabama jury acquitted Scrushy of all 36 criminal charges. In contrast, the five CFOs were initially sentenced to receive a total of 115 years in prison and $11.2 million in fines. How did this come about, and what will the impact be on future prosecutions?

- *Parmalat—Europe's Enron* details how the world's seventh largest supplier of dairy products and Italy's seventh largest company—with 146 plants in 30 countries, employing 36,000 people worldwide—came to be placed under administration and declared insolvent in late December 2003. Because of its size and its involvement with special purpose entities (SPEs), off-balance sheet and sham transactions, many regard it as Europe's Enron. Lack of good governance, executive dominance, and sloppy auditing were again to blame.

- *Royal Ahold—A Dutch Company with U.S.-Style Incentives* required restructuring after several senior executives conspired with leading executives of U.S. and other suppliers to fraudulently boost profits and increase their personal wealth and position. Ahold's shares were traded on a U.S. stock exchange when disaster struck in late 2002 and early 2003. At the time, Ahold was the third largest food retail and foodservice group in the world.

Professional and Fiduciary Duty

- *Livent—When Maria... When?* reveals pressures that are often brought to bear on professional accountants who discover manipulation and fraud, and who must decide what they should do, and when they should blow the whistle.

- *The Lang Michener Affair* shows how legal professionals can take to the slippery slopes of shady deals, conflicts of interest, self-interest, passing the buck, failing to step forward when they should to protect themselves, their firm, and their profession. It also illustrates the frustrations of a whistle-blower and the workings of a self-regulating profession.

- *Strategic Roles* are presented that are beyond traditional financial preparation. Professional accountants must decide what their appropriate roles should be when facing these in the future.

- *Locker Room Talk* presents a fascinating case on confidentiality and its strange treatment in professional accounting codes.

- *Advice for Sam and Ruby* Frequently professional accountants are asked to get involved in activities that initially they don't perceive as questionable or illegal, or where they are trying to help out a friend and don't even take a fee. Facing the urgent real-life issues for Sam and Ruby will enable professional accountants to better understand the "red flags" involved, and consider appropriate actions to take if they find themselves already involved in a mess.

- *Biker Nightmare* involves a professional accountant, a single parent mom, who has been involved with some questionable activities and must decide what to do.

- *Budget Conflict* recounts how a professional accountant attends a Board meeting at which a strategically attractive but overly-aggressive proposal is about to be accepted even though she has privately advised the President against it. What should she do?

- *An Exotic Professional Accountant?* Is this something a professional accountant should be doing?

- *Freebie Services for Staff* presents a potential conflict of interest situation and asks if the professional accountant involved should stop providing the free services to their co-workers.

- *Summer Camp Holdback* portrays a professional accountant faced with a questionable instruction from the Executive Committee and must decide what is the best option for dealing with it.

- *Theft Reimbursement Twice* presents the case of a clerk who alters checks and steals the funds. When the theft is discovered, two reimbursements arrive: one from the bank and one from the check protector service company's insurance firm. What should a professional accountant do and when?

Accounting and Auditing Dilemmas

- *Dilemma of an Accountant* portrays an auditor who is caught between his principles and the desire of his superior to have a clean file and a clean opinion. What is he to do?

- *Management Choice* focuses on Sue, a management accountant who has a choice of accounting policy and practice to make. She can probably get away with it. Should she?

- *To Qualify or Not?* introduces the real-life dilemma of wanting to qualify an audit opinion, but realizing that doing so might cause the company to become insolvent.

- *Team Player Problems* deals with the situation faced by a professional accountant who is to be part of a team, but not the leader of it, when he or she disagrees with the use and presentation of data in the report. What would you advise?

- *Minimal Disclosure* investigates how an audit partner would deal with a client who wanted to avoid disclosing the amount of income made from derivative securities, details of a lawsuit, and the financial situation in a consolidated subsidiary.

- *Opinion Shopping* looks at some reasons for seeking a new auditor, and at the responsibility of an auditor likely to lose an audit to a firm willing to be more lenient in deciding on the acceptability of some accounting practices.

- *Lowballing a Fee Quotation* is a common temptation. Are there reasons why it is appropriate?

Fundamental Accounting and Auditing Issues

- *Societal Concerns* asks the reader to consider how realistic and shortsighted our traditional financial statements and reports are. Can accountants go beyond this traditional framework to take on environmental and other issues? Should they?

- In *Economic Realities or GAAP*, Stan Jones is asking penetrating questions about the fundamental utility of traditional financial reports and the role of the auditor.

- *Multidisciplinary Practices—Ethical Challenges* asks real questions about managing the new assurance service, expanded practices. If we don't get the answers right, the accounting profession could be in for a black eye.

Tax and Regulatory Cases

- *Italian Tax Mores* provides a priceless glimpse of the facilitating payments, bribery, and regulatory problems faced by businesses operating in foreign jurisdictions.

- *Tax Return Complications* introduces the prospect of "bending the rules" to keep the client happy, as well as having to decide to admit an error or attempt to hide it. This case provides a very good illustration of the "slippery slope" problem.

- *Marketing Aggressive Tax Shelters* has been done for years by some professional accounting firms. As the case recounts, Ernst & Young and KPMG were both in hot water for the very aggressive shelters they were marketing, so it is worth considering what distinguishes an acceptable from an unacceptable tax product or service, and why.

- *Providing Tax Advice* requires the consideration of some of the public policy and ethics issues associated with giving tax advice, and the conflicts of interest involved.

- *Risk Management of Taxes Payable—Is It Ethical?* spotlights a new practice that can get the accountant into trouble if he or she is not careful.

Reading Insights

The *Position Statement* of the six largest accounting firms in the United States on the legal liability crisis highlights the reality faced by the accounting profession and underscores the value of ethical behavior as an approach to the minimization of vulnerability to the legal process. Tom Lynch's article offers insights into the interesting and challenging world of tax advice. He examines trends in legal liability and defenses available to professional auditors in public practice.

References

Anderson, G. D. "A Fresh Look at Standards of Professional Conduct." *Journal of Accountancy*, September 1985, 93–106.

Anderson, G. D. "The Anderson Committee: Restructuring Professional Standards." *Journal of Accountancy*, May 1987, 77.

Andrews, A. R., and G. Simonette, Jr. "Tort Reform Revolution." *Journal of Accountancy*, September 1996, 54.

Bayles, M. D. *Professional Ethics*. Belmont, Calif.: Wadsworth, 1981.

Behrman, J. N. *Essays on Ethics in Business and the Professions*. New Jersey: Prentice-Hall, 1988.

Brooks, L. J. "Ethical Codes of Conduct: Deficient in Guidance for the Canadian Accounting Profession." *Journal of Business Ethics* 8, no. 5 (May 1989): 325–336.

Brooks, L. J. "No More Trial and Error: It's Time We Moved Ethics Out of the Clouds and into the Classroom." *CAmagazine*, March 1993, 43–45.

Brooks, L. J. "Codes of Conduct: Trust, Innovation, Commitment and Productivity; A Strategic-Cultural Perspective." "Business & the Contemporary World" *Global Outlook: An International Journal of Business, Economics, and Public Policy*, Vol. 12, No. 2, January 11, 2000.

Brooks, L. J., and V. Fortunato. "Discipline at the Institute of Chartered Accountants of Ontario." *CAmagazine*, May 1991, 40–43.

Cohen, J., L. Pant, and Sharp. "An Exploratory Examination of International Differences in Auditor's Ethical Perceptions." *Behavioural Research in Accounting* 7, (1995): 37–64.

Colby, A., and L. Kohlberg. *The Measurement of Moral Judgement: Theoretical Foundations and Research Validations, and Standard Scoring Manual*, Volumes 1 and 2. New York: Cambridge University Press, 1987.

Cook, J. M. "The AICPA at 100: Public Trust and Professional Pride." *Journal of Accountancy*, May 1987, 307–379.

Etherington, L. D., and L. Schulting. "Ethical Development of Accountants: The Case of Canadian Certified Management Accountants." *Research in Accounting Ethics*, 1, JAI Press, (1995): 235–251.

Final Rule: Strengthening the Commission's Requirements Regarding Auditor Independence, U.S. Securities and Exchange Commission, http://www.sec.gov/rules/final/33–8183.htm, modified February 6, 2003, and *Commission Adopts Rules Strengthening Auditor Independence*, U.S. Securities and Exchange Commission, http://www.sec.gov/new/press/2003–9.htm, January 22, 2003.

Gunning, K. S. "Completely at Sea." *CAmagazine*, April 1989, 24–37.

IFAC Code of Ethics for Professional Accountants, International Federation for Accountants, London, England, November 2001. Downloadable from **www.cengage.com/acounting/brooks**

IFAC Code of Ethics for Professional Accountants, International Federation for Accountants Ethics Committee, NY, NY, June 2005, http://www.ifac.org/Store/Category.tmpl?Category=Ethics&Cart=1215563035160178. Downloadable from **www.cengage.com/acounting/brooks**

IFAC Code of Ethics for Professional Accountants, Section 290 (Revised), International Ethics Standards Board for Accountants (IESBA), International Federation of Accountants (IFAC), NY, NY, July 2006, http://www.ifac.org/Store/Category.tmpl?Category=Ethics&Cart=1215563035160178. Downloadable from **www.cengage.com/acounting/brooks**

Kohlberg, L. *Essays on Moral Development. Volume I: The Philosophy of Moral Development.* San Francisco: Harper & Row , 1981.

Kohlberg, L. *Essays on Moral Development. Volume II: The Psychology of Moral Development.* Harper & Row, 1984.

Lane, M. S., and D. Schaup. "Ethics in Education: A Comparative Study." *Journal of Business Ethics* 8, no. 12, (December 1989): 58–69.

Lynch, T. "Ethics in Taxation Practice." *The Accountant's Magazine*, November 1987, 27–28.

Macdonald Commission, see *The Report of the Commission to Study the Public's Expectations of Audits*, Canadian Institute of Chartered Accountants, June 1988.

Metcalf, Lee, spearheaded a senatorial investigation of the large U.S. accounting firms and the AICPA in the 1970s. In response, the AICPA established the Cohen Commission.

O'Malley, S. F. "Legal Liability is Having a Chilling Effect on the Auditor's Role." *Accounting Horizons* 7, no. 2, (June 1993): 82–87.

Palmrose, Z. V. "Trials of Legal Disputes Involving Independent Auditors: Some Empirical Evidence." *Journal of Accounting Research* 29, Supplement (1992): 149–185.

Ponemon, L. A. "Ethical Reasoning and Selection-Socialization in Accounting." *Organisations & Society* 17, no. 3/4, (1992): 239–258, esp. 239–244.

Ponemon, L. A., and D. R. L. Gabhart. *Ethical Reasoning in Accounting and Auditing*, CGA-Canada Research Foundation, Vancouver, Canada, 1993.

Priest, S. "Perspective: The Credibility Crisis." *Ethics in the Marketplace*, The Centre for Ethics and Corporate Policy, Chicago, June 1991, 2.

SEC's Independent Consultant's Report of the Internal Investigation of Independence Issues at Pricewaterhouse Coopers LLP, SEC site, January 6, 2000. Press Release at http://www.sec.gov/news/press/2000–4.txt, link to Report at Press Release 2000–4 on http://www.sec.gov/news/press/press-archive/2000press.shtml.

Shenkir, W. G. "A Perspective from Education: Business Ethics." *Management Accounting*, June 1990, 30–33.

The Liability Crisis in the United States: Impact on the Accounting Profession, Arthur Andersen & Co., Coopers & Lybrand, Deloitte & Touche, Ernst & Young, KPMG Peat Marwick, Price Waterhouse, August 6, 1992.

Thorne, L., and M. Magnan. "The Generic Moral Reasoning Development and Domain Specific Moral Reasoning of Canadian Public Accountants." Unpublished manuscript, 1998. For a copy contact lthorne@bus.yorku.ca.

Treadway Commission, see the *Report of the National Commission on Fraudulent Public Reporting*, AICPA, 1987.

U.S. Sentencing Guidelines, United States Sentencing Commission, Washington, D.C., November 1, 1991.

Weber, J., and S. Green. "Principled Moral Reasoning: Is It a Viable Approach to Promote Ethical Integrity." *Journal of Business Ethics* 10, no. 5, (May 1991): 325–333.

Ethics Case

HealthSouth–Can 5 CFOs Be Wrong?

On March 19, 2003, the U.S. Securities and Exchange Commission (SEC) filed accounting fraud charges in the Northern District of Alabama against HealthSouth Corporation and its CEO, Richard Scrushy. Scrushy was also charged with knowingly miscertifying the accuracy and completeness of the company's financial statements. Consequently, Scrushy became the first CEO to be charged under the governance-reforming Sarbanes-Oxley Act of 2002. Although five HealthSouth CFOs testified that Scrushy had knowingly directed the fraud, on June 28, 2005, the Alabama jury acquitted him of all thirty-six criminal charges, and later some civil charges were initially dismissed. In contrast, the five CFOs were initially sentenced to receive a total of 115 years in prison and $11.2 million in fines. One of the CFOs, Weston Smith, had become a whistle-blower who had launched a *qui tam*[1] lawsuit under the False Claims Act against HealthSouth, and first told prosecutors about the financial statement falsification process. He was sentenced to twenty-five years and a $2.2 million fine. How did all this happen?

According to the SEC Complaint,[2] Health-South was founded in 1984 and grew to become the largest provider of outpatient surgery, diagnostic, and rehabilitative healthcare services in the United States. By 2003, it owned or operated over 1,800 different facilities with worldwide revenues and earnings of $4 billion and $76 million respectively in 2001. HealthSouth's stock was listed on the New York Stock Exchange (NYSE), trading under the symbol HRC. Scrushy, who founded HRC, served as its Chairman and CEO from 1994 to 2002. He relinquished the CEO title on August 27, 2002, but reassumed it on January 6, 2003.

The SEC claim states that Scrushy instructed that HRC earnings be inflated as early as just after the company's stock was listed on the NYSE in 1986. Specifically, during the forty-two-month period between 1999 and the six months ended on June 30, 2002, HRC's Income (Loss) before Income Taxes and Minority Interests was inflated by at least $1.4 billion.

Each quarter, HRC's senior officers would meet with Scrushy and compare HRC's actual results with those expected by Wall Street analysts. If there was a shortfall, "Scrushy would tell HRC's management to 'fix it' by recording false entries on HRC's accounting records."[3] HRC's senior accounting personnel then convened a meeting—referred to as

"family meetings"—to "fix" the earnings. How this was done, and how the auditors were deceived, is outlined in the SEC Complaint as follows.

At these meetings, HRC's senior accounting personnel discussed what false entries could be made and recorded to inflate reported earnings to match Wall Street analyst's expectations. These entries primarily consisted of reducing a contra revenue account, called "contractual adjustment," and/or decreasing expenses, (either of which increased earnings), and correspondingly increasing assets or decreasing liabilities.

The contractual adjustment account is a revenue allowance account that estimates the difference between the gross amount billed to the patient and the amount that various healthcare insurers will pay for a specific treatment. [This difference was, in reality, never to be received by HealthSouth.]

… HRC falsified its fixed asset accounts [at numerous of its facilities] to match the fictitious adjustments to the income statement. The fictitious fixed asset line item at each facility was listed as "AP Summary."

HRC's accounting personnel designed the false journal entries to the income statement and balance sheet accounts in a manner calculated to avoid detection by the outside auditors. For example, instead of increasing the revenue account directly, HRC inflated earnings by decreasing the "contractual adjustment" account. Because the amounts booked to this account are estimated, there

---

1. "*Qui tam* is a statute under the False Claims Act (31 U.S.C. § 3729 et seq.), which allows for a private individual, or whistleblower with knowledge of past or present fraud on the federal government to bring suit on behalf of the government. Its name is an abbreviation of the phrase "qui tam pro domino rege quam pro seipse," meaning "he who sues for the king as well as for himself." This provision allows a private person, known as a "relator," to bring a lawsuit on behalf of the United States, where the private person has information that the named defendant has knowingly submitted or caused the submission of false or fraudulent claims to the United States. The relator need not have been personally harmed by the defendant's conduct." Retrieved from "Qui tam," Wikipedia.com. http://en.wikipedia.org/wiki/Qui_tam.

2. *Securities and Exchange Commission v. HealthSouth Corporation and Richard M. Scrushy,* Complaint for Injunctive and Other Relief, Civil Action No. CV-03-J-0615-S (March 19, 2003). www.sec.gov/litigation/complaints/comphealths.htm.

3. Ibid.

HealthSouth's Five CFOs Qualifications and Penalties

PERIOD AS CFO	NAME	CPA/OR	YEARS IN PRISON	FINE $ MILL.
Jan. 1984–Oct. 1997	Aaron Beam	CPA		1.00
Oct. 1997–Feb. 2000	Michael Martin		15	1.25
Feb. 2000–Aug. 2001	Bill Owens	CPA	30	5.50
Aug. 2001–Aug. 2002	Weston Smith	CPA	25	2.20
Aug. 2002–Jan. 2003	Malcolm "Tadd" McVay	MBA	15	1.25
				$11.20

Principal Source: http://www.al.com.specialreport/birminghamnews/healthsouth/.

is a limited paper trail and the individual entries to this account are more difficult to verify than other revenue entries.

Additionally, each inflation of earnings and corresponding increase in fixed assets were recorded through several intermediary journal entries in order to make the false inflation more difficult to trace.

Furthermore, HRC increased the "AP Summary" line item at various facilities by different amounts because it knew that across the board increases of equal dollar amounts would raise suspicion.

HRC also knew that its outside auditors only questioned additions to fixed assets at any particular facility if the additions exceeded a certain dollar threshold. Thus, when artificially increasing the "AP Summary" at a particular facility, HRC was careful not to exceed the threshold.

HRC also created false documents to support its fictitious accounting entries. For example, during the audit of HRC's 2000 financial statements, the auditors questioned an addition to fixed assets at one particular HRC facility. HRC accounting personnel, knowing that this addition was fictitious, altered an existing invoice (that reflected an actual purchase of an asset at another facility that approximated the dollar amount of the fictitious addition) to fraudulently indicate that the facility in question had actually purchased that asset. This altered invoice was

then given to the auditors to support the recording of the fictitious asset in question. Also, when the auditors asked HRC for a fixed assets ledger for various facilities, HRC accounting personnel would re-generate the fixed asset ledger, replacing the "AP Summary" line item with the name of a specific fixed asset that did not exist at the facility, while leaving the dollar amount of the line item unchanged.

While the scheme was ongoing, HRC's senior officers and accounting personnel periodically discussed with Scrushy the burgeoning false financial statements, trying to persuade him to abandon the scheme. Scrushy insisted that the scheme continue because he did not want HRC's stock price to suffer. Indeed, in the fall of 1997, when HRC's accounting personnel advised Scrushy to abandon the earnings manipulation scheme, Scrushy refused, stating in substance, "not until I sell my stock."[4]

These manipulations were testified to during the trial by the five men who served as CFO during the interval under review, all of whom pled guilty to charges such as conspiracy to commit securities and wire fraud, and falsification of financial records. On "August 14, 2002, Scrushy and HRC's CFO certified under oath that HRC's 2001 Form 10-K contained no 'untrue statement of material fact'" even though "...this report overstated HRC's earnings ... by at least 4,700%."[5]

---

4. *Securities and Exchange Commission v. HealthSouth Corporation and Richard M. Scrushy,* at paragraphs 19–30, inclusive.

5. Ibid., para 38.

The SEC Complaint did not detail all of the fraud at HealthSouth, estimated to total $3.8–$4.6 billion, which was reportedly made up of:

Fraudulent entries	$2.5 billion
Acquisition accounting/goodwill	0.5 billion
Improper (non-GAAP) accounting	0.8–1.6 billion
Total	$3.8–4.6 billion[6]

The same special report[7] stated that HRC profit was overstated by $2.74 billion from 1996–2002 inclusive, and that Scrushy received $265 million in remuneration, consisting of $21.9 million salary, $34.5 million in bonuses, and $208.9 million from the sale of shares. In 2002, Scrushy's remuneration totalled $112.3 million, including $99.3 million from sale of shares.

The timing of Scrushy's 2002 stock sales is of interest. In May 2002, the U.S. Justice Department joined the *qui tam* whistle-blower lawsuit of Bill Owens, which accused Health-South of fraudulently seeking payments for services provided by unlicensed employees, including interns and students. On the same day, Scrushy exercised 5.3 million stock options at $3.78 and sold them for $14.05 for a gain of over $54 million.

The major Scrushy-directed HealthSouth fraud is not the first or only one to take place in Scrushy's companies. Earlier frauds, bankruptcies, or questionable business dealings are part of the history of several companies owned at least in part by Scrushy and/or HealthSouth, and controlled by Scrushy with interlocking boards of directors to HealthSouth. These companies include MedPartners, Caremark National, Integrated Health Services, Capstone Capital, and HealthSouth for Medicare

frauds ($1 million paid in 2000; $8.2 million in 2001).[8] It is alleged, however, that Scrushy began to "fix" earnings in the early 1990s, and it is evident that he became involved in questionable business dealings during the same time frame. Significantly, the people involved with Scrushy in these and other questionable business dealings were often current and/or former HealthSouth employees, or members of the HealthSouth board of directors.[9] Scrushy, however, appears to have been the common link among the corporations involved.

In spite of the SEC's evidence on Health-South manipulations, which was supported by the testimony of five CFOs and ten other employees (all of whom pled guilty to the fraud), the jury of seven black and five white jurors voted to acquit Scrushy. Why was this? According to the *Report on Fraud,* the reasons were multifaceted,[10] as follows:

Surrounded by reporters as he left the courtroom, an elated Scrushy said: "Thank God for this." It was not a throwaway line, for his acquittal was partly due to a defence strategy that focussed on Scrushy's religious devotion (in fuller flourish during the trial), an unusual racism tactic, smear campaigns against key witnesses, an overabundance of prosecution documents (six million) but no smoking gun, and a victory for southern charm over northern sophistication.

More than any contributing factor to Scrushy's acquittal, however, was location. . . . "New York juries, like those in other metropolitan areas, often include people who have worked in the financial field and are more skeptical of CEOs who claim ignorance." "One of the questions in a very

---

6. Everything Alabama website, "HealthSouth's Fraud." http://www.al.com.specialreport/birminghamnews/healthsouth/.

7. Ibid.

8. These misadventures are well chronicled on the HealthSouth web pages of the University of Wollongong at http://www.uow.edu.au/arts/sts/bmartin/dissent/documents/health/map_usa.html, and in Russell Hubbard, "Rocket-like ascent tumbles back with crushed investors," *Birmingham News,* April 13, 2003.

9. Ibid.

10. "The Strange Acquittal of Richard Scrushy," *Report on Fraud,* Navigant Consulting, The Canadian Institute of Chartered Accountants, and the American Institute of Certified Public Accountants Vol. 8, no. 2 (September 2005): 4–7.

complex case like this is: 'How much did they understand?'"

Another was: who did they believe?... Scrushy was a prominent and respected figure in Birmingham, where HealthSouth employed thousands of residents. Perceived as "local boy made good," as he was often described, he donated lavishly to community causes ...

Faced with the enormous evidence against their client, ... how could his defence team convince a jury their client was not guilty?

Step number one: combine race and religion. It was a strategy led by defence counsel Donald Watkins, a black civil rights lawyer turned energy tycoon and banker, ...

As part of the defence strategy, Scrushy, who is white, "left his suburban evangelical church and joined a black congregation in a blue-collar neighborhood," reported the *Washington Post*. The Guiding Light congregation was the recipient of a $1-million donation from Scrushy. "He bought a half-hour of local TV for a morning prayer show featuring himself and his wife, and frequent guest spots by black ministers. He had a prayer group praying for him every day of the trial." Also during the trial, Scrushy's son-in-law bought a small TV station and began broadcasting daily reports bolstering the defendant's case, says *USA Today*. Many members of Guiding Light turned up at Scrushy's trial and sat directly behind him....

At the same time ... his defence team successfully manoeuvred to have seven blacks on the jury and five whites, all from working class backgrounds.

Faced with five former CFOs testifying to Scrushy's guilt, his defence team decided to impugn their credibility, ... all negotiated lenient sentences prior to testifying ... characterized one witness as looking clean as a "Winn-Dixie chitlin"... portrayed prosecution star witness William Owens, ... as a rat "who squeals 'trust me, believe

me'" ... "A witness was ridiculed because he used antidepressants," ... "Another witness was accused of faking tears on the stand." Yet another was forced to admit that he often cheated on his wife and lied about it.... The defence team's goal ... was to treat the group of CFOs as one ... comprised [of] a group of liars and cheats ... a bold move, but it worked, according to jurors.

Several jurors speaking after the trial said they wanted to see fingerprints on any of the evidence documents, or a smoking gun that would tie Scrushy directly to the fraud. Two poorly made audio tapes were not sufficient, and "defence lawyers argued that Scrushy never employed words such as 'fraud' or 'illegal' and no documents or e-mails produced during the trial implicated their client."[11] It took twenty-one days for the jury to reach a verdict. Originally, seven jurors wanted acquittal, but the number grew to ten. One of the jurors who wanted a guilty verdict was replaced due to recurring migraine headaches, and since the replacement juror wanted an acquittal, only one holdout remained. She was finally convinced to vote for acquittal.

The issue of credibility—who to believe—seemed to be paramount. The words of one juror and one author probably captured the essence of the trial best:

> There were five CFOs who testified against Scrushy and they all seemed to have some reason to lie.... Based on that conclusion, he said, he had to vote to acquit.[12]

> [Scrushy] never took the stand. He chose, instead, to preach at his new congregation during the trial, although his pastor said he didn't attend the service following his acquittal.[13]

Expert observers do not view this verdict as a problem for the future enforcement of the Sarbanes-Oxley Act. They view it as "a defeat for these particular prosecutors in this particular case."[14]

---

11. Ibid., "The Strange Acquittal..."
12. Ibid.
13. Ibid.
14. Ibid.

Questions

1. What were the major flaws in HealthSouth's governance?

2. What should HealthSouth's auditors, Ernst & Young, have done if they had perceived these flaws?

3. How—in accounting terms—did the manipulation of HealthSouth's financial statements take place?

4. Why did all the people who knew about the manipulation keep quiet?

5. What is the auditor's responsibility in a case of fraud?

6. What are the proper audit procedures to ensure existence of assets in the financial statements? What are the proper audit procedures to validate estimates?

7. What areas of risk can you identify in HealthSouth's control environment before 2003?

8. What areas of risk can you identify in HealthSouth's strategy before 2002?

9. What changes could be made in Health-South's control system and corporate governance structure to mitigate the risk of accounting fraud in future years?

10. Was Scrushy's defense ethical?

Note: Assistance in the preparation of this case is greatly appreciated from Miguel Minutti Meza, Catherine Hancharek, Lily Ding, Lei Guo, Joanna Qin, Crystal Wu, and Michelle Wu, all of whom were students in the Master of Management & Professional Accounting Program of the Rotman School of Management at the University of Toronto.

Ethics Case   *Parmalat–Europe's Enron*[1]

Parmalat Finanziaria S.p.A. and its subsidiaries manufacture food and drinks worldwide. Parmalat is one of the leading firms in the long-life milk, yogurt, and juices market. The company became the world's seventh largest supplier of dairy products and Italy's seventh largest company, with 146 plants in 30 countries, employing 36,000 people worldwide. In 2002, the company reported 7.6 billion euros in annual sales. In late December 2003, however, Parmalat was placed under administration and declared insolvent.

Because of its size and its involvement with Special Purpose Entities (SPEs), off-balance sheet, and sham transactions, many regard it as Europe's Enron. In January 2004, it was reported that the company "had net debts of 14.3 billion euros (US$23.47 billion) shortly before its crisis erupted ... almost eight times the figure given by former managers."[2] PricewaterhouseCoopers also found that earnings for the nine months ended September 30,

2003, were only one fifth of what had been reported, and bondholders were expected to recover under 7 percent of their capital. Parmalat's failure is expected to have a stimulative effect on corporate governance reform in Europe for decades.

The company started in Parma, Italy, in 1961. By the 1970s, it expanded to Brazil and later diversified into the pasta sauces and soups markets. In the 1990s, Parmalat's need for cash made the company go public and sell 49 percent of its shares to be traded on the Milan Stock Exchange. Calisto Tanzi, Parmalat's founder, kept effective control of the company, and Tanzi family members held several key positions in Parmalat and its subsidiaries.

Parmalat's series of acquisitions in the 1990s left the company with a reported $7.3 billion of debt. The company acquired subsidiaries in Asia, southern Africa, and Australia, as well as adding to its North and South American holdings and moving into Eastern Europe. The

---

1. Much of this case was developed as a group assignment by the author's students in the Master of Management & Professional Accounting Program at the Rotman School of Management of the University of Toronto. The students included: Sandy Egberts, Shivani Anand, Amanda Soder, Dave Scotland, Ramandeep Shergill, Fiona Li, and Tamer Alibux.

2. W. Schomberg and G. Wynn, "Parmalat Debt Rises to €14.3 B," *Financial Post*, January 27, 2004, FP9.

acquisitions were done without planning. The company did not go through a process of consolidation. Many investments were done to support the Tanzi family in areas unrelated to Parmalat's core business, such as the acquisition of the soccer team Parma, A.C., investments in travel agencies and hotels, and sponsorship of Formula 1 racing teams.

Over the course of more than a decade, Parmalat Finanziaria S.p.A. misrepresented its financial statements by billions of dollars. The company's founder and former CEO, Tanzi, now stands accused of market rigging, false auditing, and misleading investors and stock market regulators.[3] Tanzi established a series of overseas companies to transfer money among, and conceal liabilities, in order to give the illusion of financial liquidity within the Parmalat group. The scheme was eventually uncovered when the company was unable to make a bond payment and was forced to admit to having fraudulent assets on its accounts. The case raises a number of ethical issues that impact all stakeholders. The rights of shareholders were violated, and the expectations of stakeholders, with respect to the integrity of company management, were not met.

On December 9, 2003, Parmalat defaulted on a 150 million euro (US$184 million) payment to bondholders. Rumors began to circulate that the company's liquidity had been overstated, and the credit rating agency, Standard & Poor's, downgraded Parmalat's bonds to "junk" status. As a result of the downgrade, the company's stock fell by 40 percent. On December 17, 2003, the Bank of America announced that a US$5 billion account that Parmalat claimed to have had with it in the Cayman Islands did not exist. In little more than a week, trading in the company's shares was suspended and it was taken under administration and declared insolvent.

The company initially claimed that the missed payment to bondholders had been as a result of a late payment from Epicurum, a customer that was not paying its bills. Parmalat was eventually forced to concede, under pressure from its auditor Deloitte & Touche, that Epicurum was in fact simply a holding company of Parmalat's, located in the Cayman Islands. Furthermore, it could not access the funds from Epicurum that were required.

Parmalat had begun a period of rapid expansion in 1997, deciding to expand its operations globally and reposition itself in the marketplace. Those expanded operations, however, did not prove to be as profitable as Parmalat had hoped, and the company incurred losses. As a result of those losses, Parmalat began to invest more of its operations into derivatives and other risky financial ventures. The company expanded into tourism with a company called Parmatour, and also invested in a soccer club, both of which generated further losses for the company.

As the company's expansion continued, its need for more funds, in the form of debt financing, grew. To give the appearance of greater liquidity to its bankers and other investors, the company created a series of fictitious offshore companies that were used to conceal Parmalat's losses. Parmalat disassociated itself with the companies by selling them to American citizens with Italian surnames, only to repurchase them later. The phoney liquidity generated by these actions gave investors the assurance that they needed to continue purchasing bonds from the company and enabled Parmalat to continue to issue debt to the public.

In a classic example of the type of fraudulent action that Parmalat perpetrated, one such company, Bonlat, alleged that it was owed $767 million dollars by a Cuban firm that had ordered 300,000 tons of powdered milk. This money was then alleged to be owed to Parmalat. The entire transaction, however, did not exist, and was created to maintain the illusion of liquidity in Parmalat.[4]

Auditors failed to properly determine that roughly 200 companies created by Parmalat,

---

3. "Q&A Parmalat's Collapse and Recovery," *BBC,* 2005, http://news.bbc.co.uk/1/hi/business/3340641.stm (accessed November 16, 2005).
4. David McHugh, "Parmalat's scandal not very clever." *Seattle Times,* January 20, 2004, http://seattletimes.nwsource.com/html/businesstechnology/2001839930_parmalat200.html (accessed November 16, 2005).

such as Bonlat, did not exist. The fraud was perpetrated by, among others, CFO Fausto Tonna, who produced fake documents that he faxed to the auditors in order to falsify the existence of the subsidiaries.[5]

Calisto Tanzi admitted to having falsified Parmalat's accounts for over a decade and to stealing at least $600 million from the publicly traded company and funneling it into family businesses. The Parmalat board of directors, which consisted mostly of family members of Tanzi and controlled 51 percent of Parmalat, did not raise any questions regarding how the company was run.

By 2003, some shareholders began lobbying Tanzi for an independent member, chosen by the minority shareholders, to be put on the company's audit committee. Even though it was their legal right, Tanzi refused this request, and the issue was dropped. This led some to become more suspicious of Tanzi. Many bankers, however, had been suspicious of the Parmalat since the mid 1980s because of the company's practice of continuously issuing debt, despite an abundance of cash. At the time of the Parmalat disaster, members of the audit committee of an Italian company were elected by the board in such a way[6] that the controlling shareholder could determine who was successful. They did not have to be either independent or a director of the company and, in fact, in Parlamalat's case they were neither.

In March of 2003, Tanzi sent a thirty-four-page complaint to Consob, the Italian regulatory agency, claiming that he was being slandered by Lehman Brothers, Inc., who had issued a report that cast doubt on Parmalat's financial status. Tanzi stated that Lehman Brothers were doing this to deflate the price of Parmalat's shares in order to buy them at a cheaper price. The stir led to the publication of a series of articles critical of Parmalat and its management, which in turn had forced Parmalat to cancel a $384 million dollar bond issue in February 2003.

Despite this, some banks, including Deutsche Bank and Citibank, were still optimistic about Parmalat and were willing to buy more debt and promote their bonds as sound financial assets. The actions of the banks raises questions about possible collusion between them and the management at Parmalat, and the nature of the fiduciary duty of the banks.

After the critical December 9th default to bondholders, Tanzi appointed a turnaround specialist named Enrico Bondi. It was Bondi who decided to liquidate the US$5 billion Bank of America account, which was revealed to be fictitious and which eventually led to the bankruptcy of the company.

Tanzi was accused of dealing in fraudulent complex financial deals and bond deals, creating nonexistent offshore accounts to hide losses, and false bookkeeping. He misled investors and stock market regulators into believing that Parmalat was not in crisis. By doing so, he ensured financing from individuals that believed Parmalat was a sound company. Tanzi claimed, in his defense, that he was too far up the hierarchy to have known what top executives were doing, whom he blames for all Parmalat's problems.[7]

The story of Parmalat reveals many weaknesses in governance, both at the corporate and the professional accounting levels. One major weakness in corporate governance was a lack of oversight on the part of the board of directors. Despite the many suspicious aspects of Parmalat's business, the board of directors never demanded answers to any questions that they may have had. Nor did they ever worry about the close relationship between management and its original auditors. By placing too much faith in the integrity of the Parmalat's managers and the competence of its auditors, the company became susceptible to fraud.

In several instances, flaws were also exposed in the accounting governance of the company. In 1999, Parmalat was required to change auditors, and did so—but only partially—from Grant Thornton to Deloitte. This was due to a new Italian law—the "Draghi" law, passed in

5. Ibid.
6. Michael Gray, "ITALY: Corporate Governance Lessons from Europe's Enron," CORPWATCH, http://www.corpwatch.org (accessed April 11, 2005).
7. "Q&A Parmalat's Collapse and Recovery."

1998 to improve corporate governance[8]— whereby a public company is required to change auditors every nine years. At the time of the auditor switch, Tanzi moved a series of offshore companies that he had created during the 1990s from the Dutch Antilles to the Cayman Islands. By effectively shutting down and re-opening those companies in the new location, Tanzi was able to retain Grant Thornton as his auditor for seventeen offshore companies, including Bonlat,[9] and not require any new eyes to view the transactions of them. Furthermore, the Grant Thornton audit managers who had been auditing Parmalat since 1990 had been auditing the company for six years prior to that as managers with another auditing firm.

The testing procedures that the auditors used while auditing Parmalat were inadequate. Many of the company's assets were overstated and its liabilities understated, which had not been noticed by the company's auditors. For example, when Deloitte sent a confirmation to the Bank of America in regard to the fabricated $5 billion account, they sent it through the Parmalat internal mail service. It was intercepted and a favorable response was forged by the CFO Fausto Tonna, or persons under his direction, on scanned Bank of America letterhead.[10] Another example involved Deliotte's apparent inability to locate and/or audit what is referred to as Account 999, which held a debit of €8 billion (US$12.83 billion) representing the "'trash bin' for all faked revenues, assets and profits that Parmalat had accumulated over the years. To cover up the fake transactions, the entries were transformed into intercompany loans and credits."[11] In December 2003, executives "took a hammer to a computer at headquarters" in an attempt to destroy Account 999—but a printout survived.[12]

Parmalat sponsored an American Depositary Receipts (ADR) Program to raise funds in the United States and therefore came under the scrutiny of the U.S. Securities and Exchange Commission (SEC). The SEC charged Parmalat with securities fraud on December 30, 2003, and filed amended charges on July 28, 2004, covering the following:

- Parmalat Finanziaria consistently overstated its level of cash and marketable securities. For example, at year-end 2002, Parmalat Finanziaria overstated its cash and marketable securities by at least 2.4 billion Euros ("†"). As of year-end 2003, Parmalat Finanziaria had overstated its assets by at least €3.95 billion (approximately $4.9 billion).

- As of September 30, 2003, Parmalat Finanziaria had understated its reported debt of €6.4 billion by at least €7.9 billion. Parmalat Finanziaria used various tactics to understate its debt, including: (a) eliminating approximately €3.3 billion of debt held by one of its nominee entities; (b) recording approximately €1 billion of debt as equity through fictitious loan participation agreements; (c) removing approximately €500 million of liabilities by falsely describing the sale of certain receivables as non-recourse, when in fact the company retained an obligation to ensure that the receivables were ultimately paid; (d) improperly eliminating approximately €300 million of debt associated with a Brazilian subsidiary during the sale of the subsidiary; (e) mischaracterizing approximately €300 million of bank debt as intercompany debt, thereby inappropriately eliminating it in consolidation; (f) eliminating approximately €200 million of Parmalat S.p.A. payables as though they had been paid when, in fact, they had not; and (g) not recording a liability of approximately €400 million associated with a put option.

- Between 1997 and 2003, Parmalat S.p.A. transferred approximately €350 million to

---

8. In 1999, Italian companies were also asked to **voluntarily** comply with a new noncomprehensive set of governance rules known as the "Preda Code."

9. Navigant Consulting, Canadian Institute of Chartered Accountants, and the American Institute of Certified Public Accountants, "Milk Gone Bad," *Report on Fraud* 6, no. 5, 6, March 2004.

10. Ibid.

11. F. Kapner, "Parmalat's Account 999 Points a Finger at Deloitte," *Financial Post,* April 12, 2004, FP16.

12. Ibid.

various businesses owned and operated by Tanzi family members.

- Parmalat Finanziaria transferred uncollectible and impaired receivables to "nominee" entities, where their diminished or nonexistent value was hidden. As a result, Parmalat Finanziaria carried assets at inflated values and avoided the negative impact on its income statement that would have been associated with a proper reserve or write-off of bad debt.

- Parmalat Finanziaria used these same nominee entities to fabricate non-existent financial operations intended to offset losses of its operating subsidiaries. For example, if a subsidiary experienced losses due to exchange rate fluctuations, the nominee entity would fabricate foreign exchange contracts to offset the losses. Similarly, if a subsidiary had exposure due to interest rate fluctuations, the nominee entity would fabricate interest rate swaps to curb the exposure.

- Parmalat Finanziaria used the nominee entities to disguise intercompany loans from one subsidiary to another subsidiary that was experiencing operating losses. Specifically, a loan from one subsidiary would be made to another subsidiary operating at a loss. The recipient then improperly applied the loan proceeds to offset its expenses and thereby increase the appearance of profitability. As a result, rather than have a neutral effect on the consolidated financials, the loan transaction served to inflate both assets and net income.

- Parmalat Finanziaria recorded fictional revenue through sales by its subsidiaries to controlled nominee entities at inflated or entirely fictitious amounts. In order to avoid unwanted scrutiny due to the aging of the receivables associated with these fictitious or overstated sales, the related receivables would be transferred or sold to nominee entities.[13]

On January 29, 2004, Pricewaterhouse-Coopers took over as the auditor of Parmalat. They discovered that cash had been misstated by billions of euros, and that Parmalat's debt was eight times what was claimed. Further reinforcing suspicions that the company had been altering its financial statements since the 1980s, an independent auditor for the prosecutor in Milan found that Parmalat had been profitable for only one year between 1990 and 2002. Parmalat had claimed to be profitable all of those years. This material misstatement had not been noticed by either Grant Thornton or Deloitte. It was also found that there were many instances where Deloitte's Italian office did not apply aggressive enough audit procedures despite being informed of irregularities with Parmalat, uncovered by other Deloitte offices around the world.[14]

It appears that at least some of Parmalat's auditors were in collusion with the company's managers to keep the fraud under wraps. By March 2004, 11 people from Grant Thornton had been arrested, and more arrests may follow.[15]

A number of large banks were also complicit in the fraud, according to Enrico Bondi, who was appointed as Parmalat's government-appointed administrator. His report stated:

A continued inflow of financial resources constituted the necessary condition for keeping the group going well beyond its natural capacity for survival. These were furnished directly by banks, or through them, by means of vehicles created for this purpose by Parmalat abroad, often in "tax havens" . . .

Foreign banks and investment banks used the particular laws of so-called "tax havens" to place bonds. They directly supplied financial resources by means of structured products that, de facto, contributed to the

---

13. U.S. Securities and Exchange Commission, "SEC Alleges Additional Violations by Parmalat Finanziaria S.p.A.," *Litigation Release No. 18803,* July 28, 2003, http://www.sec.gov/litigation/litreleases/lr18803.htm (accessed March 11, 2005).

14. Y. Richard Roberts, P. Richard Swanson, and Jill Dinneen, "Spilt Milk: Parmalat and Sarbanes-Oxley Internal Controls Reporting," *International Journal of Disclosure and Governance* 1, no. 3 (June 2004): 215–226.

15. Morgan O'Rourke, "Parmalat's Scandal Highlights Fraud Concerns. Risk Management," *New York* 51, no. 3 (March 2004): 44.

false representation of the economic and financial situation of the group's accounts.[16]

Bondi went on to estimate that Parmalat obtained:

€13.2 billion from banks between Dec. 31, 1998 and Dec. 31, 2003. International banks supplied 80% of the funding, with the rest from Italian lenders. By contrast, Parmalat generated only €1 billion in gross cashflow during the period.

Mr. Bondi calculates Parmalat spent about €5.4 billion on acquisitions and other investments, €2.8 billion on commissions and fees to banks, €3.5 billion on payments to bondholders, €900 million on taxes and €300 million on dividends. The remaining €2.3 billion was apparently siphoned off for other purposes . . . .

The Bondi Report suggests that, as early as 1997, there was sufficient information available about Parmalat's true condition for the financial community to have realized the company was in trouble. . . . As a result, while Parmalat might still have collapsed in 1997–98, the scandal would have cost investors less money . . .[17]

Under Italian law, banks and financial institutions can be sued for damage caused by and recovery of improper transactions. It is noteworthy that "Citigroup . . . had been instrumental in setting up the insolently named "Buco Nero" ("black hole") as an offshore account for Parmalat"[18] and has found "itself under investigation by the SEC and the subject of a class action lawsuit."[19]

Questions

1. What conditions appear to have allowed the Parmalat situation to get out of control?

2. What specific audit procedures might have uncovered the Parmalat fraud earlier?

3. What audit steps should Deloitte have taken with regard to the seventeen offshore subsidiaries that continued to be audited by Grant Thornton?

4. What impact will the Parmalat fraud have on Grant Thornton and on Deloitte & Touche?

5. How did the following areas of risk in Parmalat's control environment contribute to the fraud: integrity and ethics, commitment, audit committee participation, management philosophy, structure, and authority?

6. How did the following areas of risk in Parmalat's strategy contribute to the fraud: changes in operating environment, new people and systems, growth, technology, new business, restructurings, and foreign operations?

7. Should the banks and other creditors be legally responsible for so-called irresponsible lending that contributes to higher than necessary losses? If so, how can they protect themselves when dealing with clients whose viability is in doubt?

8. Do you think that applying bankruptcy projection models should be a regular tool used by auditors, creditors, and regulators to assess the reasonability of a company's financial statements?

9. Is independence important in corporate governance? What are the most recent rules on corporate governance for public firms?

10. Discuss which changes could be made to the Parmalat's control system and corporate governance structure to mitigate the risk of accounting and business fraud in future years.

Helpful References

BBC News. Parmalat. BBC News Archive. October 2003 to January 2005. http://www.bbcnews.com

BBC[1]. "Parmalat: Timeline to Turmoil." BBC News UK edition, updated September 28, 2005. http://news.bbc.co.uk/1/hi/business/3369079.stm (accessed November 17, 2005).

Celani, Claudio. "The Story behind Parmalat's Bankruptcy." *Executive Intelligence Review*, January 16, 2004. http://www.larouchepub.com/other/2004/3102parmalat_invest.html (accessed November 16, 2005).

---

16. T. Barber, "Parmalat chief slams big banks," T. Barber, *Financial Post*, July 23, 2004, FP12.
17. Ibid.
18. Navigant Consulting, "Milk Gone Bad."
19. Ibid.

CNN. "Timeline: Parmalat Fraud Case." CNN, September 28, 2005. http://www.cnn.com/ 2005/BUSINESS/09/28/parmalat.timeline/ index.html (accessed November 16, 2005).

CNN. "Tanzi 'Admits False Accounting.'" CNN, December 29, 2003. http://www.cnn.com/2003/ WORLD/europe/12/29/parmalat.tanzi/index. html (accessed November 16, 2005).

Cohn, Laura, and Gail Edmondson. "How Parmalat Went Sour." *Business Week Online,* January 12, 2004. http://www.businessweek.com/magazine/ content/04_02/b3865053_mz054.htm (accessed November 16, 2005).

Edmondson, Gail, David Fairlamb, and Nanette Byrnes. "The Milk Just Keeps On Spilling At Parmalat." *Business Week Online,* January 26, 2004. http://www.businessweek.com/magazine/ content/04_04/b3867074_mz054.htm (accessed November 16, 2005).

Knox, Noelle. "Parmalat founder might face more charges." *USA Today,* December 29, 2003. http://www.usatoday.com/money/world/2003-12-29-parmalat-int_x.htm (accessed November 16, 2005).

Parmalat website. http://www.parmalat.com.

"Special report Europe's corporate governance", *The Economist,* January 17, 2004, 59–61.

New York Times. Parmalat. *NY Times* News Archive. October 2002 to January 2005. http:// www.nytimes.com.

U.S. Securities and Exchange Commission. *Litigation Releases 18527, 18803,* http://www.sec.gov/ litigation/.

| Ethics Case | *Royal Ahold–A Dutch Company with U.S.-Style Incentives* |

According to the Royal Ahold company profile:

> Ahold is a global family of local food retail and foodservice operators that operate under their own brand names. Our operations are located primarily in the United States and Europe. Our retail business consists of retail chain sales, sales to franchise stores and sales to associated stores. The store format that we primarily use is the supermarket. Through our foodservice operations we distribute food, and offer services and expertise to restaurants and hotels, health care institutions, government facilities, universities, sports stadiums and caterers.
>
> In 2003, our consolidated net sales were Euro 56.1 billion, our retail trade and foodservice businesses representing approximately 70% and 30% of this total, respectively. At the end of 2003, Ahold's average number of employees in full-time equivalents totalled 256,649 worldwide.[1]

The company is listed on the Dutch and U.S.[2] stock markets. Ahold was one of the first big Dutch or European companies to implement U.S.-style large stock option compensation schemes for its managers, and that may have led to its downfall in late 2002 and early 2003.[3]

In 2002, Ahold claimed to be the world's third largest retail group. However, due to unfavorable market conditions the company had lower than expected U.S. sales. For years, the company outperformed its peers, expanding aggressively, but the expansion left Ahold with $12 billion in debt, one of the largest in the sector. In July, the company revised its full year EPS growth target to 5–8 percent. The company's figures revealed a 6 percent fall in its core foodservice business in the United States, and 10 percent fall in the value of Ahold shares. In October, some investors suggested that Ahold's chief executive, Cees van der Hoeven, leaked the sales numbers to certain analysts and the share price suffered a first drop.

In February 2003, the company announced that net earnings and earnings per share would be significantly lower than previously indicated for fiscal 2002. In the same month, the

1. From the Ahold website at http://www.ahold.com/index.asp?id=2 (accessed January 24, 2005).
2. As KONINKLIJKE AHOLD NV (AHODF.PK) on the PNK Exchange, and as Koninklijke Ahold NV American Depositary Shares (each representing one Ordinary Share) (AHO) on the NYSE.
3. Stephen Taub, "Royal Ahold in Dutch," *CFO.com,* February 25, 2003 (accessed January 24, 2005).

company disclosed that its financial statements for fiscal 2000 and fiscal 2001 would be restated. A press release indicated that the restatements primarily related to overstatements of income related to vendor promotional allowance programs at its subsidiary, U.S. Foodservice. Managers of the subsidiary booked much higher promotional allowances (provided by vendors to promote their merchandise) than the company was to actually receive. Ahold estimated the amount of the overstatement to be close to $500 million.

Other irregularities under investigation were the legality and accounting treatment of questionable transactions at the Argentine subsidiary, Disco. Certain joint ventures were consolidated based on misrepresentations to Ahold's auditors. CEO Cees van der Hoeven and CFO Michiel Meurs resigned immediately. The SEC and the Dutch stock exchange Euronext investigated the irregularities, requiring Ahold to present documentation from 1999 to 2003. The company said the irregularities only began in 2001.

In May 2003, Ahold named a new CEO, former executive of Ikea, Anders Moberg.[4] While waiting for the results of the investigations, the company started a restructuring program that involved divesting Indonesian and South American operations. The company also entered into an emergent credit facility from a syndicate of banks.

In May 2003, a forensic report from PricewaterhouseCoopers (PwC) indicated a total overstatement of pre-tax earnings of approximately US$880 million.[5] Offsetting the bad news of the report, Ahold said that no evidence of fraud was found at other operations. Later in the same month, Jim Miller,

president and CEO of U.S. Foodservice, resigned from his position. Ahold considered that he was not implicated. In July 2003, the regulator's inquiry ended and Ahold disclosed additional $84.4 million in accounting irregularities, bringing the total overstatement to $1.1 billion. The company declined to reveal when or where the latest accounting irregularities occurred.[6]

Ahold's auditors, Deloitte & Touche, insisted that they warned the firm about problems in its U.S. unit. The auditors also pointed out that Ahold did not supply them with full information. These problems were never disclosed to the public. Deloitte said during the inquiries that they identified the problems during the 2002 audit and gave the details to Ahold's board immediately before the audit was concluded in 2003.

In January 2005, nine executives were charged by the U.S. Securities and Exchange Commission (SEC)[7] with participating in a scheme of accounting fraud at U.S. Foodservice. All executives were accused of approving documents that claimed U.S. Foodservice was owed millions of dollars more in promotional allowances than was actually the case. Former U.S. Foodservice chief marketing officer Mark P. Kaiser faced charges of conspiracy and fraud, along with former chief financial officer Michael Resnick. Executives Timothy J. Lee, and William F. Carter pleaded guilty to similar charges in 2004. All the executives have been named in a civil case involving John Nettle, former vice president of General Mills; Mark Bailin, former president of Rymer International Seafood; and Peter Marion, president of Maritime Seafood Processors. Nettle confirmed to the auditors false amounts owed by

4. "Ahold turns to IKEA's ex-boss," *BBC News,* May 2, 2003, http://news.bbc.co.uk/l/hi/business/2995135.stm (accessed January 1, 2005).

5. "Ahold profits inflated by $880m," *BBC News,* May 8, http://news.bbc.co.uk/l/hi/business/3011103.stm (accessed January 1, 2005).

6. Gregory Crouch, "Royal Ahold's Inquiry Ends, Finding $1.1 Billion in Errors," *New York Times,* July 2, 2003, C2, New York Times Archive website at http://select.nytimes.com/gst/abstract.html?res=F60A11F7395E0C718CDDAE0894DB404482 (accessed January 21, 2005).

7. U.S. Securities and Exchange Commission, "Nine Individuals Charges by the SEC with Aiding and Abetting Financial Fraud at Royal Ahold's U.S. Subsidiary for Signing and Returning False Audit Confirmations. One Also Charged with Insider Trading," *SEC Litigation Release No. 19034,* January 13, 2005, http://www.sec.gov/litigation/litreleases/lr19034.htm (accessed January 26, 2005).

his company to U.S. Foodservice in 2001. Bailin and Marion benefited by buying U.S. Foodservice stock in 2000, ahead of the company's announcement that Royal Ahold was acquiring it.

According to SEC Litigation Release No. 18929 dated October 13, 2004,[8] the misdeeds were described as:

The Earnings Fraud at U.S. Foodservice

With respect to the fraud at U.S. Foodservice ("USF"), Ahold's wholly-owned subsidiary based in Columbia, Maryland, the Commission's complaint against Ahold alleges as follows:

| A significant portion of USF's operating income was based on vendor payments known as promotional allowances. USF executives materially inflated the amount of promotional allowances recorded by USF and reflected in operating income on USF's financial statements, which were included in Ahold's Commission filings and other public statements.

| USF executives also provided, or assisted in providing, Ahold's independent auditors with false and misleading information by, for example, persuading personnel at many of USF's major vendors to falsely confirm overstated promotional allowances to the auditors in connection with year-end audits.

| The overstated promotional allowances aggregated at least $700 million for fiscal years 2001 and 2002 and caused Ahold to report materially false operating and net income for those and other periods.

The Joint Venture Sales and Operating Income Fraud Ahold and the Top Officers

With respect to the fraudulent consolidation of joint ventures, the Commission's complaints against Ahold, van der Hoeven, Meurs, and Andreae allege as follows:

Ahold fully consolidated several joint ventures in its financial statements despite owning no more than fifty percent of the voting shares and despite shareholders' agreements that clearly provided for joint control by Ahold and its joint venture partners. To justify full consolidation of certain joint ventures, Ahold gave its independent auditors side letters to the joint venture agreements, signed by Ahold and its joint venture partners, which stated, in effect, that Ahold controlled the joint ventures ("control letters").

However, at the time or soon after executing the control letters, Ahold and its joint venture partners executed side letters that rescinded the control letters—and thus the basis for full consolidation (the "rescinding letters").

Meurs signed all but one of the control and rescinding letters on behalf of Ahold. He also knew that Ahold's auditors were relying on the control letters and were unaware of the existence of the rescinding letters.

Van der Hoeven cosigned one of the rescinding letters and he was at least reckless in not knowing that the auditors were unaware of its existence.

Andreae participated in the fraud by signing the control and rescinding letters for ICA, Ahold's Scandinavian joint venture, and by knowingly or recklessly concealing the existence of the ICA rescinding letter from the auditors.

As a result of the fraud, Ahold materially overstated net sales by approximately EUR 4.8 billion ($5.1 billion) for fiscal year 1999, EUR 10.6 billion ($9.8 billion) for fiscal year 2000, and EUR 12.2 billion ($10.9 billion) for fiscal year 2001. Ahold materially overstated operating income by approximately EUR 222 million

---

8. U.S. Securities and Exchange Commission, "SEC Charges Royal Ahold and Three Former Top Executives with Fraud: Former Audit Committee Member Charged with Causing Violations of the Securities Laws," *SEC Litigation Release No. 18929*, October 13, 2004, http://www.sec.gov/litigation/litreleases/lr18929.htm (accessed January 26, 2005).

($236 million) for fiscal year 1999, EUR 448 million ($413 million) for fiscal year 2000, and EUR 485 million ($434) for fiscal year 2001.

In February 2004, Ahold announced its plans with regard to the recommendations of the Dutch Tabaksblat Committee on Corporate Governance.[9] In order to restore trust in its governance processes, thirty-nine executives and managers were terminated, and an additional sixty employees faced disciplinary actions of different degrees. Members of the Corporate Executive Board will serve for a predetermined period, in which continuity and succession have been taken into account. According to the company, these measures will result in significant improvement in transparency and a far-reaching increase in the power of its shareholders.

The company is also replacing a decentralized system of internal controls with a one-company system with central reporting lines. The most important control, however, is making clear to Ahold's people what the company expects of them going forward. As a first step in this process, they initiated a company-wide financial integrity program. This is aimed at 15,000 managers, the entire middle and top ranks of the organization. The goal of the program is to underscore the importance of integrity and to help guide Ahold's people to apply its corporate business principles.

Questions

1. A vendor may offer a customer a rebate of a specified amount of cash or other consideration that is payable only if the customer completes a specified cumulative level of purchases or remains a customer for a specified period of time. When should the rebate be recognized as revenue? At what value should the rebate be recorded as revenue?

2. The SEC investigation found the individuals involved in the fraud "aided and abetted the fraud by signing and sending to the company's independent auditors confirmation letters that they knew materially overstated the amounts of promotional allowance income paid or owed to U.S. Foodservice." Is the confirmation procedure enough to validate the vendor's allowance amount in the financial statements?

3. The SEC investigation also revealed "a significant portion of U.S. Foodservice operating income was based on vendor payments known as promotional allowances." How might irregularities have been discovered through specific external audit procedures?

4. Royal Ahold made several changes in its corporate governance structure. Discuss how those changes will mitigate the risk of accounting fraud in future years.

---

9. From Ahold's company history at http://www.ahold.com/index.asp?id=14 (accessed January 24, 2005).

Ethics Case | *Livent—When Maria . . . When?*

Livent, once the world's premier live entertainment company, was sold in 1998 to buyers that soon found the value they had paid for was an illusion. Livent had thrilled audiences with performances of *Phantom of the Opera, Ragtime, Kiss of the Spider Woman, Sunset Boulevard, Showboat, Joseph and the Technicolor Dreamcoat, Fosse, Candide,* and *Barrymore.* Needless to say, Garth Drabinsky and Myron Gottlieb, the creators of Livent, were suspected of fraud, but justice was slow in coming in Canada.

Whereas the U.S. Securities and Exchange Commission pursued fraud charges in 1999[1], it wasn't until May 2008, over ten years after their alleged manipulation of earnings, that Drabinsky and Gottlieb finally went on trial in Toronto for two counts of fraud and one of

---

1. RELEASE 99-3 SEC Sues Livent and Nine Former Livent Officials for Extensive Accounting Fraud; U.S. Attorney Files Criminal Charges Washington, Size: 6419 Modified: 1/13/1999/news/press/pressarchive/1999/99-3.txt

forgery. The manipulations occurred from 1993 to 1998, and were reported to be significant. For example, according to the testimony of Gordon Eckstein, Livent's senior vice president of finance, an internal document showed a loss of $41 million for the third quarter of 1997 that was reported publicly as a $13.4 million profit after adjustments were made by accounting staff.[2] Eckstein also reported that: "Just before Livent was sold, its managers wrote down the value of its assets to "clean up the books" and declared a loss of $44 million for 1997."[3]

Maria Messina, Livent's chief financial officer, had joined Livent in May 1996 after having been a partner at Deloitte & Touche, Livent's auditors. Ms. Messina had worked on the audit but testified that she did not become aware of the manipulation until July 1997 "when she saw a set of internal statements showing a loss of about $20-million for the first six months of 1997, then later saw a subsequent set showing an $8-million profit."[4] Interestingly, she never revealed the fraud to her former colleagues at Deloitte. In fact, she didn't disclose Mr. Drabinsky's manipulative influence to any outsider until July 1998 when she met the new owner's chief executive officer, Roy Furman. She then revealed the fraudulent behavior on August 6, 1998, when she met with Robert Webster, the new executive vice president, who had asked for a report on construction costs, the area affected by many of the manipulations.

Why did Maria delay so long? At first she was shocked and numbed. She questioned her manager, Gordon Eckstein, who replied: " ... it's just income smoothing. Everybody does

it."[5] She was so shocked that she panicked and was "completely immobilized by fear ... didn't know how to get out of the situation and didn't have the courage to expose the fraud and "take on" Mr. Drabinsky and Mr. Gottlieb."[6] Drabinsky, in particular, was somewhat famous and had a reputation for being frighteningly intimidating. "Instead she settled on a campaign of 'baby steps,' and tried to persuade Mr. Eckstein to stop the fraud."[7] During this period, she did work on manipulated financial statements. Eckstein's proposal was presented at an Executive meeting in February 1998, but it wasn't accepted. In April 1998, she wrote a memo to Drabinsky and Gottlieb, indicating proposed adjustments were not in accord with GAAP and she would not support them. This worked: the manipulations were abandoned and some of the accumulated fraud was written down.[8] However, on June 30, when she met with Drabinsky to show him an estimate of Q2 earnings indicating a loss of $13-million, he said: " ... these numbers are all fucked up. You don't know what the fuck you are doing. You can't show these to anyone." Drabinsky then demanded that Q2 earnings be boosted from a loss of $13-million to just $200,000.[9] This was the situation that she disclosed to Roy Furman, but she didn't tell him about the earlier fraud. When asked why not, she replied: "How do you tell somebody that, when you are a chartered accountant? I was also obviously going to be destroying my own life. It just took me several weeks to find the courage to do it."[10] She paid a high price. On January 7, 1999, she pleaded guilty to a federal felony charge and as a "36-year-old single mother of a 10-year-old

2. "Livent hid large losses, court told," Peter Small, *Toronto Star*, May 21, 2008, A7.
3. Ibid.
4. "Former Livent CFO 'numb' over extent of fraud," Janet McFarland, *The Globe and Mail*, June 10, 2008, B3.
5. Ibid.
6. Ibid.
7. Ibid.
8. "Ex-Livent executive says she blew the whistle," Janet McFarland, *The Globe and Mail*, June 11, B3.
9. Ibid.
10. Ibid.

girl faced[s] up to five years in jail and fines as high as $250,000."[11] In addition, she lost her Chartered Accountant designation.

Questions

1. Did Maria blow the whistle at the right time? Why or why not?

2. Was her planned response appropriate? Why or why not?

3. How would you suggest she should have dealt with the problem?

4. Should whistle-blowing be encouraged? Why or why not?

---

11. "Is Fraud the Thing?," *BusinessWeek*, February 15, 1999, 104.

Ethics Case

The Lang Michener Affair

Martin Pilzmaker was a young, aggressive lawyer from Montreal who was invited in 1985 to join the law firm Lang Michener in Toronto. It was expected that his immigration law practice "could enrich the (firm's) coffers by $1 million a year catering to the needs of Hong Kong Chinese already starting to panic over the crown colony's 1997 return to China's control."

Although rumors of Pilzmaker's questionable practices began to surface and were reported to the firm's executive committee in December, it wasn't until early February 1986 that a senior colleague, Tom Douglas, "drew aside Ament and Wiseman (Pilzmaker's junior colleagues) and grilled them on their boss's activities. They told him that Pilzmaker not only smuggled regularly but that he was running a double-passport operation.... The scam involved the false reporting of lost Hong Kong passports by his clients, which, in fact, would be kept by Pilzmaker in Canada. On their replacement passports, the clients could travel in and out of the country at will. When the time came to apply for citizenship—which requires three years' residence—they could supply the original 'lost' passports to show few if any absences from Canada."

Douglas told the executive committee of this activity, by memo, on February 10. The executive committee "speculated that Pilzmaker's admissions may have constituted only knowledge of wrongdoing on the part of certain clients and not active complicity. The committee decided to send (two members) Don Wright and Donald Plumley back to Pilzmaker to ask him, in the words of

Farquharson's instructing memo, 'if he would be willing to agree' not to participate in any client violation of the Immigration Act."

Early in June 1986, angered that Pilzmaker had not been expelled, Tom Douglas sought advice from Burke Doran, "a colleague he regarded as a personal friend but moreover, one who was a bencher, or governor, of the Law Society. Doran went on to advise him to keep his head down and his mouth shut—a caution Doran later said he had no recollection of giving."

While mulling over this advice and some from another lawyer, Brendon O'Brien, a foremost authority on professional conduct, Douglas discovered a further problem. "This was a proposal by Pilzmaker to Brian McIntomny, a young associate lawyer, who was in the market to buy a house. The idea was that McIntomny would put up $50,000 for a $200,000 house, the balance supplied by a Pilzmaker client in Hong Kong. The client would officially own the house, have the phone and utilities registered in his name, while McIntomny lived in it and held a secret deed. After three years, he would pay the client the interest-free $150,000, register the deed to place title in his own name and benefit from the accrued increase in value. The client, meanwhile, would have 'proof' of having resided in Canada for the three years required for citizenship." Douglas arranged for Bruce McDonald, a member of the firm's new executive committee, now consisting of McDonald, Don Wright, Albert Gnat, Donald Plumley, and Bruce McKenna, to be informed.

An investigation was begun and "at a July 28th Executive Committee meeting, a vote was taken on whether or not to expel Pilzmaker." The vote was three to two in favor of his staying. Douglas was allowed to address the meeting only after the vote was finalized, and he was enraged.

"On August 6, the night before McKenna's report was submitted but in partial knowledge of what it would likely contain, Douglas had dinner with Burke Doran again, this time in the company of a mutual colleague, Bruce Drake. Drake and Douglas subsequently claimed that when he was asked whether the firm had an obligation to report at least Pilzmaker's double-passport scam to the Law Society, Doran said no, 'because no white men have been hurt.' (Neither man took this as a racist remark but as meaning it was a victimless crime, with the clients knowingly involved.) The following morning at the office, Drake said he asked Doran if his remarks of the night before could be taken as official advice from the chairman of the Law Society. Doran said yes."

Doran has always denied that, confining his explanation to the dinner and not the morning after: "It's far-fetched to say I was sitting at a social dinner in my capacity as chairman of discipline." Don Wright would later testify, however, that it was Doran's view throughout the period "that we did not have any obligation to report to the Society."

On August 7, McKenna filed a scathing fifteen-page report to the executive committee, listing fifteen breaches of unethical behavior both inside and outside the firm by Pilzmaker, noting that "I am not aware of any material statement of fact made by him to me that I have checked out and has proven to be true." Furthermore, "I am concerned that I now have a personal responsibility, as a member of the Law Society and an officer of the court, to report the situation. If each of you review the facts closely, you will have similar concerns about your own obligations." 'On August 20, the executive committee did finally decide Pilzmaker had to go, subject to confirmation by the entire partnership.'

After this, events proceeded at a faster pace:

September 4: Brendon O'Brien, hired to counsel the firm, advised that "they couldn't afford not to report to the Society."

September 5: A general meeting of the firm's partners is called to review the matter.

September 18: The requisite two-thirds of the 200 votes was obtained to force expulsion.

September 26: Pilzmaker's files were secured at the firm.

October 1: The Executive Committee debated the impact on the reputation of the firm and of high-profile partners "such as Jean Chretien (who is now the Prime Minister of Canada) and Burke Doran."

November 6: Douglas wrote Don Wright, urging the firm to report to the society.

November 18: Pilzmaker's lawyer filed suit to have Pilzmaker's files transferred to him.

November 21: The Law Society received a report from O'Brien "that (a) Pilzmaker had been expelled, (b) that he had been wrongly billing into the general, not trust, account and (c) that there was more than $300,000 in unpaid fees where Pilzmaker had either not done the work or had not even been retained in the first place." The society's investigator, Stephen Sherriff, began his investigation and subsequently called for a fuller report from the firm.

December 5: Pilzmaker's request for his files was granted by Justice Archibald Campbell, who "was given no hint that the files contained evidence that at some point might need to be looked at by the Law Society."

December 8: A fuller report is presented to the Law Society.

Twenty-five months later, "in January, 1989, Sherriff filed a lacerating 138-page confidential report that recommended a professional misconduct charge be laid against Burke Doran for placing himself in a conflict-of-interest situation in which he chose the interests of the firm over his responsibility as the Society's then chairman of discipline. Separate charges of professional misconduct were recommended against eight others in the firm. Sherriff contended that (a) they had failed to inform clients that Pilzmaker had likely given them unethical advice and to seek independent counsel and (b) they had failed to report in a timely manner what they knew about his behavior, indeed they reported only when Pilzmaker's lawsuit gave them no alternative."

An Ottawa lawyer, David Scott, was retained to help the society by analyzing what to do about Sherriff's recommendations. His report of March 2, 1989, was presented to Paul Lamek, the new chair of discipline for the society. "The ball was now in Lamek's court. He says he saw his job as twofold: To define who Scott meant by 'Managing partners and/or group' and to decide whether a charge could be made against Doran on a basis different from Sherriff's—namely, that as a bencher and chair of discipline, Doran had a 'higher duty' to report than did his colleagues. Although it wouldn't be officially disclosed until this spring, Lamek initially did opt to charge all eight, subject to clarifying just who exactly was on the executive committee from the crucial time on—a period Lamek pinned at June, 1986. That clarification consequently dropped several senior people out of the picture. As for Doran, 'after agonizing analysis' Lamek concluded that no complaint of any kind should be issued."

What was the outcome of these charges/ events?

In the Spring of 1989, when it became obvious that Douglas would have to testify against his colleagues that fall, he finally did resign—three years after he'd first threatened to.

On October 31, without waiting for the panel's ruling, a disillusioned Sherriff resigned from his job: "What could have been a testament to the integrity of the Society had ended up sullying it. I had no choice but to quit." His departure, coupled with growing media speculation that there might be a "whitewash of a cover-up" in process, had many other members of the Society adding to the chorus of concern.

At a convocation meeting of the benchers last September [1989], lawyer Clayton Ruby, who'd been given a copy of the investigation report by Sherriff, presented a motion that Lamek's decision be set aside and the original recommendations adopted. Ferrier ruled the motion out of order. "Douglas and Sherriff are right-wingish, not my kind of guys," [said] the notoriously left-leaning Ruby. "But I really felt that Lamek's decision to charge only five made it look as if we (the Society) were covering something up."

At a general members meeting the following month, former bencher Paul Copeland tried to table a motion demanding simply an explanation for why only five had been charged. He says he too was "cut off" by Ferrier.

On January 5 of this year [1990], the five who'd been charged were found guilty of professional misconduct for not reporting their concerns about Pilzmaker three months earlier than they did, specifically at the time McKenna made his damning report. The panel, however, found that the same concerns had not "imposed a duty on them" to inform clients that Pilzmaker had been expelled or that he might have given them unethical advice or that they should get independent legal advice.

Due to the ensuing controversy, on February 7, "the Society hired retired Manitoba former Chief Justice Archibald Dewar to review its handling of the entire affair." But his findings didn't please everyone. "Dewar did not find any evidence of impropriety or favouritism in Lamek's charges. The Doran decision was a judgment call, he wrote, and while debatable, to proceed with a charge now would only satisfy critics but "Not be seen as adding lustre to the discipline process."

What he did find, however, was a catalog of complaints against Sherriff. Sherriff was incensed. "The big deal, first," says Sherriff, "is that the real bad guy (Pilzmaker) almost went free. The big deal, second, is that the self-governing ability of this profession was compromised. 'Lawyers have special privileges, therefore, special responsibilities. Protecting the public is chief among them. That's the big deal. If you're a man of principle, you won't walk away from it.'"*

Questions

1. Are professionals bound to meet a higher standard of ethical behavior than nonprofessionals? If so, why?

2. In what respects were the actions of the lawyers involved in the Lang Michener Affair not up to the ethical standard you would expect? Consider:

    a. Pilzmaker's conduct,

    b. the conduct of members of the executive committee at Lang Michener—in particular, Burke Doran, and

    c. the investigation and proceedings by the Law Society.

What obligations did each owe to clients, the legal profession, the Law Society, the public?

3. Do the same considerations apply to other professionals as to lawyers?

4. Is the self-regulation of a profession on ethical matters effective from the perspective of

    a. the members of the profession?

    b. the public?

    c. clients?

5. Would you agree with the argument, which was used to exonerate members of the management team, that "when a professional makes a serious mistake, the error is of no consequence, if it is honestly made" (Bud Jorgensen, *Globe & Mail,* February 5, 1990, B9)?

---

*Martin Pilzmaker was disbarred by the Law Society of Upper Canada in January 1990. Five other partners of his firm—Lang, Michener, Lash, and Johnston—were also found guilty and reprimanded. But the scandal refused to die, culminating in a major article in the "Insight" section of the *Toronto Star* on Sunday, July 22, 1990. The quotations in the case are from that article. Postscript: Martin Pilzmaker committed suicide.

> **Ethics Case** | *Strategic Roles*

Assume that you are a professional accountant who is CFO of a medium-sized manufacturing company that plans to:

| Misrepresent products that come from environmentally irresponsible sources as environmentally friendly.

| Bribe officials of a foreign government.

| Use analyses and/or decision techniques that you know are faulty or unethical.

| Encourage an unethical corporate culture.

| Mislead the audit committee.

| Ignore important internal controls.

Question

1. What is your responsibility in each of these situations?

> **Ethics Case** | *Locker Room Talk*

Albert Gable is a partner in a CPA firm located in a small midwestern city, which has a population of approximately 65,000. Mr. Gable's practice is primarily in the area of personal financial planning; however, he also performs an annual audit on the city's largest bank.

Recently, Mr. Gable was engaged by Larry and Susan Wilson to prepare a comprehensive personal financial plan. While preparing the plan, Mr. Gable became personal friends of the Wilsons. They confided to him that they have had a somewhat rocky marriage and, on several occasions, seriously discussed divorce. Preparation of the comprehensive personal financial plan, which is nearing completion, has taken six months. During this period, Mr. Gable also performed the annual audit for the bank.

The audit test sample selected at random from the bank's loan file included the personal loan files of Larry and Susan Wilson. Because certain information in the loan files did not agree with facts personally known to Mr. Gable, he became somewhat concerned. Although he did not disclose his client relationship with the Wilsons, he did discuss their loan in detail with a loan officer. The loan officer is very familiar with the situation because he and Larry Wilson were college classmates, and now they play golf together weekly.

The loan officer mentioned to Mr. Gable that he believed Larry Wilson was "setting his wife up for a divorce." In other words, he was arranging his business affairs over a period of time so that he would be able to "leave his wife penniless." The loan officer indicated that this was just "locker room talk" and that Mr. Gable should keep it confidential.

Mr. Gable's compensation from his firm is based upon annual billings for services. If Mr. Gable resigns as CPA for the Wilsons, it would result in his losing a bonus constituting a substantial amount in annual personal compensation. Mr. Gable is counting on the bonus to contribute to support tuition and expenses for his youngest daughter, who will be starting as a freshman in college next fall.

Questions

1. What are the ethical issues?
2. What should Albert Gable do?

Source: Prepared by Paul Breazeale, Breazeale, Saunders & O'Neil Ltd., Jackson, Mississippi. Drawn from the Ethics Case Collection of The American Accounting Association.

| Ethics Case | *Advice for Sam and Ruby* |

Dear John:

I really appreciate your willingness to give me your opinion as a fellow professional accountant on what I should do, and on what I should advise the minority owner to do. Given that I was asked to help out Ruby, a family friend, and have found myself in the following situation, your advice is welcomed. Please take into account that I am not (and have not been) retained, nor am I being compensated in any manner related to the situation; I have not been providing accounting services in any shape or form related to the situation; and I have ensured that Ruby did seek out accounting advice from another party as events unfolded.

Approximately three years ago, Jimmy, an owner of a small auto body shop, approached Ruby to give her a 10 percent equity stake in the shop and asked her to provide day-to-day management functions for the entity. Jimmy wanted Ruby to allow certain cash receipts to bypass the books of the shop, and in return Ruby would directly receive a commission on these transactions. We do not know if these amounts were claimed as taxable income by Jimmy, but it is possible. This cash bypass requirement was incorporated into the shareholders' agreement, signed by both parties, and witnessed. I informed Ruby and her accountant that these amounts must be tracked and reported on Ruby's tax returns as taxable income without deduction.

Ruby was lax and followed Jimmy's advice in completing certain paperwork, so the incorporation documents and subsequent filings still reflect her as the sole director of the company, even though she merely set up the new company formed at the time of the initial transaction. Now, Jimmy has approached her to buy her out.

During the course of the negotiations, which I attended, Jimmy's accountant disclosed he was aware that the "off book" revenue was occurring, but I am still unaware of how it was treated for tax purposes. There is a high likelihood of premeditated tax evasion on Jimmy's part. Jimmy has had, and continues to have, various taxation "issues," including one for approximately $80,000 that caused him to approach Ruby in the first place. Jimmy was apparently attempting to hide assets from the tax authorities and used the then-unaware Ruby to effectively be a shield for him.

By the way, Jimmy's accountant has indicated that he is a professional accountant, and the negotiations for the sale of the minority shares have now been transferred to Ruby's lawyer. I am still providing some help through her lawyer.

I am looking forward to receiving your advice.

Sincerely,
Sam

Questions

1. Keeping in mind that no compensation, nor accounting services, were ever received or provided, has Sam stepped "out of bounds"?
2. What is your advice for Sam?
3. What is your advice for Ruby?
4. Given the alleged disclosure by Jimmy's accountant, has he crossed any boundaries? If so, does Sam have to take any actions and what would these actions be?

Ethics Case | *Biker Nightmare*

I need your advice on an anonymous basis. I am a professional accountant employed by a company that imports bikes from China. Before I get into the issue, I wish to advise you that I really need this job as I am a single mother of two teenagers, and jobs like the one I have are hard to come by in the area where I live.

The company deceptively avoids paying the mandatory import duty on the bikes it imports. Last week, the president of the company asked me to prepare and provide him with a statement of the duty avoided on the purchase of these bikes for the past three years. He also asked that I sign off on this statement. The statement that I prepared and presented to him showed that $200,000 in customs duties

has been avoided by the company in the period covered.

Since I prepared that statement, I am having trouble sleeping at night.

Questions

1. What does our professional code say about this?
2. If this issue is uncovered by the government regulatory authorities, will I be implicated?
3. Should I quit my job and then go and report this situation to the regulatory authorities?

Ethics Case | *Budget Conflict*

I have a question that I need a bit of help on, but I am not sure where to turn, and I hope you maybe able to help me out.

I am the CFO of a charitable organization, it is a paid position and I am a professional accountant. We are currently presenting our budget to the Board of Directors, which is a volunteer Board. There is a chance they may pass a budget that is not fiscally possible, that is, we do not have the cash flow to execute it. It is not the budget we are recommending, but they may have us spend to levels of 25 percent growth (stretch budgeting).

Both our treasurer and I have tried on numerous occasions to explain this to our President, but she and other Board members are not financially astute.

Our treasurer has stated that he will go on the record to advise against any such spending and budget, and may even resign over it.

Questions

1. What should the CFO do?
2. Beyond resigning, how can the CFO protect him or herself?

Ethics Case

An Exotic Professional Accountant?

Excuse me, we are both professional accountants, and I need some advice. I have a full-time management position with a company. I was wondering if I would be in violation of our Professional Code of Ethics, if I took on the role of an exotic dancer at night in order to fund my husband through university?

Question

1. What advice would you give?

Ethics Case

Freebie Services for Staff

I am a professional accountant and hold the position of Financial Analyst, Capital Projects, with the Town of Pinecrest. In my position, I deal with, among others, developers and their lawyers with respect to development agreements, costs sharing agreements, and financial agreements.

In the past, during lunch hours and after hours, I have provided informal financial advice to a fellow municipal employee with respect to her marriage separation, including a review of her ex-husband's personal tax returns (which included self-employment income). No issue arose in this regard. Currently, during lunch hours and after hours, I am providing informal financial advice to another fellow municipal employee with respect to her common-law separation.

A verbal "complaint" or "allegation" has been made to the Town Manager that I have a "conflict of interest" by being a municipal employee carrying out my duties as a public servant as paid for by the town and by helping a fellow municipal employee who is currently facing a common-law separation. The town does not have an internal "conflict of interest" policy for staff. I know of no basis for such a "complaint" or "allegation" except that the lawyer for a group of developers is also the lawyer for the ex-common-law spouse.

As there is no actual "complaint" or "allegation" to respond to, only rumors and innuendo, I am seeking your general advice at this time. In due course, as a municipal employee, I will be providing a written response to the Town Manager.

Question

1. What advice would you give to this professional accountant?

Ethics Case

Summer Camp Holdback

I think I have a problem. I am a professional accountant and work for a not-for-profit organization which operates a summer camp. We have obtained a legal opinion stating that a portion of our camp fees could be considered a charitable donation with respect to religious education costs for the 2007 summer and subsequent years.

When we originally invoiced parents for the 2007 summer (in January 2007) we billed the amounts as fees fully subject to sales tax and collected and remitted the tax to the government authorities. As a charitable donation, no sales tax needs to be collected, so we have since adjusted the 2007 invoices to reflect the amounts of taxes charged in error and are in the process of recovering these funds from the governments involved.

The question that arises is: as we are acting as an agent for the governments with respect to collection of taxes and therefore these funds are considered a 'deemed trust', it is my opinion that these recovered taxes rightfully belong to the parents who originally paid them and should be refunded. Our Executive Committee believes that we can simply keep these funds and issue donation receipts without ever telling the parents that they are entitled to this money. I strongly believe that their view is unethical and have indicated as such but they are intent on doing it regardless.

This leaves me in a difficult position in that I do not want to do anything that I feel is unethical, but I can not afford to lose my employment by refusing their demands. Any guidance or advice you could give me would be most appreciated.

Question

1. What is your advice?

Ethics Case

Theft Reimbursement, Twice

I am the assistant controller at a medium-sized, not-for-profit organization. I hired a new accounts payable clerk three months ago—let's call her Mary, which is not her real name—and then I fired her last week because she stole $16,583 from us by altering six checks. Mary's primary duties were to key in all the accounts payable information, and then, after the checks were printed, to match all the supporting documentation to each check. She then took the checks to the signing officers. After they were signed, she mailed the checks and filed the yellow copy with all the supporting documentation in the paid invoices filing cabinet.

We pay each member of our board of directors a $2,000 honorarium. I prepare the list of the directors and how much to pay each director, which I give to Mary for inputting into the computer. Each honorarium check simply has the name of the director and no address or other information. We normally hand them to the directors during the meeting. Similarly, our expense report reimbursement checks only have the names of the individuals and no address or other information on the checks. We send those to our employees through the interoffice mail.

Well, after they were signed, Mary took four honorarium checks and two expense report checks, and changed the names on the checks to her name. All of our checks are printed on light green paper. Well, Mary used White-Out to alter the names, but she wasn't very smart. It was obvious that the names had been changed from the White-Out used and her name wasn't even the same font as the typing on the rest of the check. She took the

checks across the street to an ATM machine and deposited them into her bank account. She then transferred the money to her family who live in another country.

I discovered the false checks last week when I was doing the bank reconciliation. She admitted what she did and we've had the police charge her with theft. Our bank was very apologetic and immediately reimbursed us the full $16,583. Our bankers admitted that the checks were so obviously falsified that they never should have cleared the bank in the first place.

Well, my problem is that, after I discovered the theft and before the bank reimbursed us, I decided to claim on our insurance policies. One of those policies is a check-protector service. Well, today we received a check for $16,583 from them. So, I took the check to my boss, the controller, and I was laughing saying that we've been reimbursed twice and that I was going to send the check back to the insurance company. Well, he said "No." He told me to deposit the check into a high-interest savings account. "We'll return the $16,583 to the insurance company after the court case is settled. In the meantime we'll earn interest on the money and since we're a non-profit organization we won't even have to pay tax on the interest."

He said the interest represents the aggravation we're going through. Well, there has been a lot of aggravation. The other accounting clerks felt terrible about Mary. They felt violated and abused because they had trusted her. We will also have to spend a lot of time with the lawyers and time in court at Mary's trial. My boss' attitude is that the interest on the extra $16,583 will cover all of these additional costs associated with the Mary fiasco. He also said that the bank deserves to pay the interest to us since they should never have cashed those doctored checks in the first place.

Well, I don't think that this is right. But I don't want to challenge him since I was the one who hired Mary. So, like, what do you think I should do?

Questions

1. How would you answer the assistant controller?
2. What advice would you give to the controller?
3. What aspects of the organization's governance process and/or internal controls were flawed?
4. Should the directors be told about the fraud and/or any other matters?

Ethics Case | *The Dilemma of an Accountant**

In 1976 Senator Lee Metcalf (D-Mont.) released a report on the public accounting industry which rocked the profession. Despite a decade of revisions in rules and regulations (variously established by the Securities and Exchange Commission, Accounting Principles Board, and Financial Accounting Standards Board), public accounting firms were still perceived by many on Capitol Hill as biased in favor of their clients, incapable of or unwilling to police themselves, and at times participants in coverups of client affairs. Senator Metcalf even went so far as to suggest nationalizing the industry in light of these activities.

Just prior to the Metcalf report, Daniel Potter began working as a staff accountant for Baker Greenleaf, one of the Big Eight accounting firms. In preparation for his CPA examination, Dan had rigorously studied the code of ethics of the American Institute of Certified Public Accountants (AICPA) and had thoroughly familiarized himself with his profession's guidelines for morality. He was aware of ethical situations which might pose practical problems, such as maintaining independence from the client or bearing the responsibility for reporting a client's unlawful or unreasonably misleading activities, and he knew the channels through which a CPA was expected to resolve unethical business policies. Dan had taken the guidelines very seriously; they were not only an integral part of the auditing

exam, they also expressed to him the fundamental dignity every independent auditor was obligated to maintain and calling of the profession—namely, to help sustain the system of checks and balances on which capitalism has been based. Daniel Potter firmly believed that every independent auditor was obligated to maintain professional integrity, if what he believed to be the best economic system in the world was to survive.

Thus, when Senator Metcalf's report was released, Dan was very interested in discussing it with numerous partners in the firm. They responded thoughtfully to the study and were concerned with the possible ramifications of Senator Metcalf's assessment. Dan's discussions at this time and his subsequent experiences during his first year and a half at Baker Greenleaf confirmed his initial impressions that the firm deserved its reputation for excellence in the field.

Dan's own career had been positive. After graduating in economics from an Ivy League school, he had been accepted into Acorn Business School's accountant training program, and was sponsored by Baker Greenleaf. His enthusiasm and abilities had been clear from the start, and he was rapidly promoted through the ranks and enlisted to help recruit undergraduates to work for the firm. In describing his own professional ethos, Dan endorsed the Protestant work ethic on which he had been raised, and combined this belief

---

*Copyright © 1980 by the President and Fellows of Harvard College. Harvard Business School case 380-185. This case was prepared by Laura Nash under the direction of John B. Matthews as the basis for class discussion rather than to illustrate either effective or ineffective handling of an administrative situation. Reprinted by permission of the Harvard Business School.

with a strong faith in his own worth and responsibility. A strong adherent to the assumptions behind the profession's standards and prepared to defend them as a part of his own self-interest, he backed up his reasoning with an unquestioning belief in loyalty to one's employer and to the clients who helped support his employer. He liked the clearcut hierarchy of authority and promotion schedule on which Baker Greenleaf was organized, and once had likened his loyalty to his superior to the absolute loyalty which St. Paul advised the slave to have towards his earthly master "out of fear of God" (Colossians 3:22). Thus, when he encountered the first situation where both his boss and his client seemed to be departing from the rules of the profession, Dan's moral dilemma was deep-seated and difficult to solve.

The new assignment began as a welcome challenge. A long-standing and important account which Baker had always shared with another Big Eight accounting firm needed a special audit, and Baker had reason to expect that a satisfactory performance might secure it the account exclusively. Baker put its best people on the job, and Dan was elated to be included on the special assignment team; success could lead to an important one-year promotion.

Oliver Freeman, the project senior, assigned Dan to audit a wholly-owned real estate subsidiary (Sub) which had given Baker a lot of headaches in the past. "I want you to solve the problems we're having with this Sub, and come out with a clean opinion (i.e., confirmation that the client's statements are presented fairly) in one month. I leave it to you to do what you think is necessary."

For the first time Dan was allotted a subordinate, Gene Doherty, to help him. Gene had worked with the project senior several times before on the same client's account, and he was not wholly enthusiastic about Oliver's supervision. "Oliver is completely inflexible about running things his own way—most of the staff accountants hate him. He contributes a 7:00 A.M. to 9:00 P.M. day every day, and expects everyone else to do the same. You've *really* got to put out, on his terms, to get an excellent evaluation from him." Oliver was indeed a strict authoritarian. Several times over the next month Dan and Oliver had petty disagreements over interpretive issues, but when Dan began to realize just how stubborn Oliver was, he regularly deferred to his superior's opinion.

Three days before the audit was due, Dan completed his files and submitted them to Oliver for review. He had uncovered quite a few problems but managed to solve all except one: one of the Sub's largest real estate properties was valued on the balance sheet at $2 million, and Dan's own estimate of its value was no more than $100,000. The property was a run-down structure in an undesirable neighborhood, and had been unoccupied for several years. Dan discussed his proposal to write down the property by $1,900,000 with the Sub's managers, but since they felt there was a good prospect of renting the property shortly, they refused to write down its value. Discussion with the client had broken off at this point, and Dan had to resolve the disagreement on his own. His courses of action were ambiguous, and depended on how he defined the income statement: according to AICPA regulations on materiality, any difference in opinion between the client and the public accountant which affected the income statement by more than 3 percent was considered material and had to be disclosed in the CPA's opinion. The $1,900,000 write-down would have a 7 percent impact on the Sub's net income, but less than 1 percent on the client's consolidated net income. Dan eventually decided that since the report on the Sub would be issued separately (although for the client's internal use only), the write-down did indeed represent a material difference in opinion.

The report which he submitted to Oliver Freeman contained a recommendation that it be filed with a subject-to-opinion proviso, which indicated that all the financial statements were reasonable subject to the $1.9 million adjustment disclosed in the accompanying opinion. After Freeman reviewed Dan's files, he fired back a list of "To Do's," which was the normal procedure at Baker Greenleaf. Included in the list was the following note:

1. Take out the pages in the files where you estimate the value of the real estate property at $100,000.

2. Express an opinion that the real estate properties are correctly evaluated by the Sub.

3. Remove your "subject-to-opinion" designation and substitute a "clean opinion."

Dan immediately wrote back on the list of "To Do's" that he would not alter his assessment since it clearly violated his own reading of accounting regulations. That afternoon Oliver and Dan met behind closed doors.

Oliver first pointed out his own views to Dan:

1. He (Oliver) wanted no problems on this audit. With six years of experience he knew better than Dan how to handle the situation.

2. Dan was responsible for a "clean opinion." Any neglect of his duties would be viewed as an act of irresponsibility.

3. Any neglect of his duties would be viewed as an act of irresponsibility.

4. The problem was not material to the Client (consolidated) and the Sub's opinion would only be used "in house."

5. No one read or cared about these financial statements anyway.

The exchange became more heated as Dan reasserted his own interpretation of the write-down, which was that it was a material difference to the Sub and a matter of importance from the standpoint of both professional integrity and legality. He posited a situation where Baker issued a clean opinion which the client subsequently used to show prospective buyers of the property in question. Shortly thereafter the buyer might discover the real value of the property and sue for damages. Baker, Oliver, and Dan would be liable. Both men agreed that such a scenario was highly improbable, but Dan continued to question the ethics of issuing a clean opinion. He fully understood

the importance of this particular audit and expressed his loyalty to Baker Greenleaf and to Oliver, but nevertheless believed that, in asking him to issue knowingly a false evaluation, Freeman was transgressing the bounds of conventional loyalty. Ultimately a false audit might not benefit Baker Greenleaf or Dan.

Freeman told Dan he was making a mountain out of a molehill and was jeopardizing the client's account and hence Baker Greenleaf's welfare. Freeman also reminded Dan that his own welfare patently depended on the personal evaluation which he would receive on this project. Dan hotly replied that he would not be threatened, and as he left the room, he asked, "What would Senator Metcalf think?"

A few days later Dan learned that Freeman had pulled Dan's analysis from the files and substituted a clean opinion. He also issued a negative evaluation of Daniel Potter's performance on this audit. Dan knew that he had the right to report the incident to his partner counselor or to the personnel department, but was not terribly satisfied with either approach. He would have preferred to take the issue to an independent review board within the company, but Baker Greenleaf had no such board. However, the negative evaluation would stand, Oliver's arrogance with his junior staff would remain unquestioned, and the files would remain with Dan's name on them unless he raised the incident with someone.

He was not at all sure what he should do. He knew that Oliver's six years with Baker Greenleaf counted for a lot, and he felt a tremendous obligation to trust his superior's judgment and perspective. He also was aware that Oliver was inclined to stick to his own opinions. As Dan weighed the alternative, the vision of Senator Metcalf calling for nationalization continued to haunt him.

Ethics Case | *Management Choice*

Anne Distagne was the CEO of Linkage Construction Inc., which served as the general contractor for the construction of the air ducts for large shopping malls and other buildings.

She prided herself on being able to manage her company effectively and in an orderly manner. For years there had been a steady 22–25 percent growth in sales, profits, and earnings per share, which she wanted to continue because it facilitated dealing with banks to raise expansion capital. Unfortunately for Sue Fault, the chief financial officer, the situation has changed.

"Sue, we've got a problem. You know my policy of steady growth—well, we've done too well this year. Our profit is too high: it's up to a 35 percent gain over last year. What we've got to do is bring it down this year and save a little for next year. Otherwise, it will look like we're off our well-managed path. I will look like I didn't have a handle on our activity. Who knows, we may attract a takeover artist. Or we may come up short on profit next year."

"What can we do to get back on track? I've heard we could declare that some of our construction jobs are not as far along as we originally thought, so we would only have to

include a lower percentage of expected profits on each job in our profit this year. Also, let's take the $124,000 in R&D costs we incurred to fabricate a more flexible ducting system for jobs A305 and B244 out of the job costs in inventory and expense them right away."

"Now listen, Sue, don't give me any static about being a qualified accountant and subject to the rules of your profession. You are employed by Linkage Construction and I am your boss, so get on with it. Let me know what the revised figures are as soon as possible."

Questions

1. Who are the stakeholders involved in this decision?
2. What are the ethical issues involved?
3. What should Sue do?

| Ethics Case | *To Qualify or Not** |

Jane Ashley was a staff accountant at Viccio & Martin, an accounting firm located in Windsor, Ontario. Jane had been a co-op student while in college and, during her first work term with the firm, she had the privilege of being on several audits of various medium-sized companies in the Windsor area, where she picked up some valuable audit experience. Fresh out of her final academic term, she felt ready to put her scholastic knowledge to work and show the seniors and partners of Viccio & Martin her stuff.

In her first assignment, Jane was placed on an audit team consisting of herself and a senior. This senior, Frankie Small, had been a qualified accountant for five years and had been on staff for over ten. He was well respected within the company and was known for his ability to continually bring engagements in under budget.

The client, Models Inc., which was Viccio & Martin's largest, was a private corporation which made its business in the distribution of self-assembly, replica models, toys, and other gaming products. It operated from a central

warehouse in Windsor but also distributed from a small warehouse in Toronto and had a drop-off point in Michigan as it purchased merchandise from companies in the United States. Its year-end was April 30. Since Jane had joined the firm on May 15, she had not been present for the year-end inventory count, which was taken on the year-end date. Frankie S. was present, along with another co-op student, who, incidently, had returned for her final academic term on May 11. Jane asked Frankie how just two people could simultaneously be present for an inventory count at three locations. Frankie responded by telling her that, since the inventory balances at the Toronto warehouse and Michigan drop-off sites were of immaterial amounts (based on representations by management, company records, and audits in prior years) audit staff had only been present at the Windsor warehouse count. Models Inc. was on a periodic inventory system.

Since she had not been on this engagement before, the evening before her first day of fieldwork, Jane stayed at work late to review the

*This case was adapted from an assignment submitted by Phil Reynolds, an MBA (accounting) student at the University of Toronto in the summer of 1994.

previous year's audit files, this year's audit programs, and the notes on this year's inventory count so she could gain a knowledge of the client's business. After an hour or so of reviewing the information, Jane gained a knowledge of the client, but she couldn't quite understand what was happening with the inventory section because the working papers were messy and disorganized. On reviewing the inventory sheets from this year's count, she found that many of the items were unfamiliar and were referenced only by general product names; there were no serial numbers, no order numbers.

The first day of fieldwork arrived, and Jane was given the responsibility of Accounts Payable Cut-off. On tracing invoices to the master accounts payable ledger, Jane found that she was having a hard time locating many of them. She brought this matter to the attention of the accounts payable clerk, who provided the explanation that invoices received after the year-end date were not yet entered in the current year but should have been. Jane was provided with this list and traced it to the journal entry made to pick up the extra payables. Jane then performed audit procedures on this extra list. She again found that it was incomplete. The total cut-off problem was, in her estimation (of sample to population figures), in excess of $400,000. She also noted that many of the invoices received had invoice dates after April 30, but title to these goods had changed hands (F.O.B. shipping point) prior to April 30.

The financial statements originally provided by management showed healthy profits of $150,000. The current accounts payable (trade) balance was $1.4 million, which was up over a half a million from last year. The current receivables balance was $800,000 which was up about $100,000 from the previous year. Sales had jumped from $8 million in 1988 to $10 million this year. The company had an operating (demand) line of credit with a lending institution of $1 million. The company owned its two warehouses, which had a net equity of approximately $1,600,000 at fair market.

Jane brought the cut-off problem to the attention of Frankie, who was perplexed and surprised by the whole issue. The two returned to the office that evening, and Jane was asked to prepare a memorandum explaining her findings. It was reviewed by the partner in charge, Mr. Viccio, who contacted the appropriate level of management of Models Inc. to explain the discrepancy.

The accounts payable clerk recorded the transactions Jane had found left out, and the audit testing was again performed on the accounts payable cut-off and the rest of the accounts payable section to the satisfaction of the auditors with respect to all financial statement assertions. The total corrections made to accounts payable were in the order of $350,000. The impact of the adjustments was partially to inventory, where traceable, and partly to cost of goods sold. The total effect on the profit figure was $300,000. The financial statements showed a loss of $150,000.

The head manager and 50 percent shareholder of the corporation, Mrs. Hyst, was astonished and panic stricken by the entire situation. She was sure something was wrong and that this problem would be rectified at some point throughout the remainder of the audit.

No problems were encountered throughout the remainder of the audit fieldwork; however, Jane did notice, when she was in the accounts payable clerk's office, that the clerk spent a great deal of time on the phone with suppliers, discussing how Models Inc. could pay down its over-90-day payables such that the company would not be cut off from purchasing further goods.

Toward the finalization of the audit, Mrs. Hyst came to the auditors and told them that there was most likely inventory that had been left out of the count. She provided a listing which amounted to approximately $200,000. In this listing were material amounts of inventory in the Toronto warehouse, the Michigan drop-off point, goods in transit, and goods stored at other locations.

The auditors, who were surprised by the list, decided to perform tests on it and found that it was very difficult and often impossible to track the inventory, given the poor system used by the company. Jane telephoned all of the companies that appeared on the list under "goods stored at other locations" and, in all cases, found that no inventory was being kept on behalf of Models Inc. Suppliers in the United States were telephoned for exact shipment dates, and, based on the evidence of how long it usually takes to bring goods across the border, it was determined that those goods were included in the year-end inventory count. As for the "extra" inventory stored in the Toronto and Michigan sites, there was no reliable evidence that anything not already accounted for was there. However, there was no way to tell for sure. From the items on this extra list, $50,000 was accounted for as either already counted in inventory as of the year-end date or included in cost of goods sold. The whereabouts of the other $150,000 was not determinable.

Mrs. Hyst was asked to discuss this listing. At the meeting, Mr. Viccio, Frankie, and Jane were all present. Mrs. Hyst stated that, if she showed these sorts of losses, the bank would surely call the company's operating loan of $1 million and it would "go under." Mr. Viccio asked the client whether there was any way of determining where the other $150,000 was. She explained that it was hard, given their inadequate inventory system, but she was pretty sure that it was not counted in the year-end inventory count.

After the meeting, Mr. Viccio explained that there was no reason to doubt management's good faith and that the $150,000 most likely should be added to inventory and taken out of cost of goods sold. Frankie went along with this. Jane, however, was astonished. She felt that, since there was no evidence backing up the claims made by the client, the firm should be conservative. She also related her experience to the other two concerning the problems the company was having with

keeping up with its trade payables. Mr. Viccio explained to her that the $150,000 should be added to back inventory and that, even if it was the cost of goods sold, the client will most likely recover in the near future, anyway. "In these situations, we must help the client; we cannot be responsible for its downfall. Who are we to say that there isn't an extra $150,000 in inventory—we're just guessing." Frankie added to this by saying that, if the loan were called, there would be plenty of equity in the buildings of the company to pay it off.

Jane went home that day very distraught. She felt that Mr. Viccio's decision was based on audit fees and that a poor picture on the financial statements would result in the loan being called and Mr. Viccio would not get his fees. Jane was also disappointed with the level of responsibility shown by Frankie, the senior. Jane couldn't believe what was happening, given the fact that the original reason for the audit was because the bank had requested it several years ago as the operating loan was increasing. Jane was also aware that Model Inc.'s major suppliers were requesting the year-end statements as well and, based on them, would make a decision whether or not to extend the company any more credit.

The next day, Jane expressed her opinion in a morning meeting held in Mr. Viccio's office. Frankie was also present. She was told that the $150,000 would be added back to inventory.

Question

1. What should Jane do? Why?

Ethics Case | *Team Player Problems*

"John, I have questions about that job you want me to do next week—the one where I am supposed to go and be part of that multidisciplinary team to study how the hospitals in Denver ought to be restructured for maximum efficiency, and how they should be reporting that efficiency in the future. As you know, I am a professional accountant, but I'm not going to be the study leader. What happens if I disagree with the study's findings or

recommendations? What do I do if I think they haven't used accounting data correctly and have recommended that a hospital be shut down when I don't think it should be? Do I go along? Do I blow the whistle?"

Question

1. Answer the questions put to John.

Ethics Case | *Minimal Disclosure*

Ted was the manager and Carl the partner on the audit of Smart Investments Limited, an investment company whose shares were traded on the NASDAQ exchange. They were discussing the issues to be debated at the upcoming Audit Committee meeting to finalize the financial statements and audit for the current year.

"As I see it, Carl, we have three problems that are going to be difficult because it's not in the interests of the CEO, CFO, and some directors to go along with us. Remember that all those stock options that may be exercised next month at $7.50 per share and with the stock trading at $9.50 now—well, they aren't about to upset the price with negative news."

"Anyway, the rules call for segmented disclosure of significant lines of business, and this year the company has made 55 percent of its profit through the trading of derivative securities. It's awfully high risk and I'm not sure they can keep it up, so I think they ought to add a derivative securities disclosure column to their segmented disclosure information. They are going to argue that they are uncertain how much profit relates to derivative securities trading by itself, and how much was realized because the derivative securities were part of hedging transactions to protect foreign currency positions."

"The second issue concerns their reluctance to reveal the potential lawsuit by their client, Bonvest Mutual Funds, for messing up the timing and placement of orders for several mining securities. I believe it should be mentioned in the Contingent Liabilities note, but they may be dragging their feet on calculating the size of the problem. They don't want to disclose an amount, anyway, because they argue that Bonvest will set that figure as the lower bound for its claim."

"Finally, as you know, the statements we are auditing are consolidated and include the accounts of the parent and four subsidiaries. One of these subs, Caribbean Securities Limited, is in tough shape, and I think they may let it go broke. That's the sub which is audited by the Bahamian firm of Dodds & Co., not our own affiliate there. There is no qualification on the Dodds & Co. audit opinion, though, but I know how these guys at Smart think."

"I realize that a lot of this is speculative, but each of these issues is potentially material. How do you want to play each of them?"

Question

1. What should Carl, the partner, plan to do?

Ethics Case | *Opinion Shopping*

"We have had Paige & Gentry as our auditors for many years, haven't we, Jane? They have been here since I became president two years ago."

"Yes, Bob, I have been the Chief Financial Officer for seven years, and they were here before I came. Why do you ask?"

"Well, they were really tough on us during the recent discussions when we were finalizing our year-end audited statements—not at all like I was used to at my last company. When we asked for a little latitude, our auditors were

usually pretty obliging. Frankly, I'm a little worried."

"Why, Bob, we had nothing to hide?"

"That's true, Jane, but let's look ahead. We're going to have difficulty making our forecast this year, and our bonuses are on the line. Remember, we renegotiated our salary/bonus package to give us a chance at higher incentives, and we have to be careful."

"Looking ahead, we've got a problem with obsolete inventory that's sure to come to require discussion for a second year in a row.

We've got the warranty problem with the electrical harness on mid-range machine which is going to cost us a bundle, but we want to spread the impact over the next three years when the customers discover the problem and we have to fix it up. And don't forget the contaminated waste spill we just had—how much is that going to cost to clean up, if we ever get caught?"

"These are potentially big ticket items. Bill Paige, the guy who is in charge of our audit, is not going to let these go by. He said the inventory problem was almost material this year and we had to argue really hard. You are a qualified accountant; how can we handle this?"

"Well, Bob, we could have some informal discussions with other auditors—maybe even the ones at your old company—to see how they would handle issues like these. The word will get around to Bill and he may be more accommodating in the future, and will probably shave his proposed audit fee for next year when he meets with our Audit Committee next month. If you really wanted to play hardball, we could talk the Audit Committee

into calling for tenders from new auditors. After all this time, it's logical to check out the market, anyway. We would have advance discussions during which we would sound them out on how they would assess materiality in our company's case. Our audit fee is getting pretty large—almost $50,000 this year—so some big firms will be really interested."

"Jane, let's play hardball. Get a list of audit firms together for the tender process, and I will approach the Audit Committee. Be sure to list some small firms, including Webster & Co., the firm auditing my old company."

Questions

1. Who are the major stakeholders involved in this situation?
2. What are the ethical issues involved?
3. Is this situation unethical? Why and why not?
4. What should Jane do if Webster & Co. looks like the choice the Audit Committee will make and recommend to the board of directors?

Ethics Case | *Lowballing a Fee Quotation*

"Look, Tim, I've been told that the competition for the audit of Diamond Health Services is really competitive, and you know what it would mean to the both of us to bring this one in. You would be a sure bet for the Executive Committee and I would take over some new audit responsibility as your back-up partner. Let's quote the job really competitively and get it."

"I'm not sure, Anne. After all, we have to make a reasonable profit or we're not pulling our weight. Anyway, you don't know what problems we may meet, so you should build in a cushion on the front end of the job."

"But, Tim, if we quote this job the usual way—on an hourly rate and estimated total time basis—we are going to miss it! The CFO as much as told me we would have to be lower than the current auditor, and we would have to

guaranty the fee for two years. Now, are we in, or not? I plan to put our best staff on the job. Don't worry; they won't blow it. What's the matter? Don't you think I can get the job done?"

"Well, Anne, I suppose there would be some overall saving to our firm because this audit is the only one of six companies in the Diamond Group that we don't audit. We certainly don't want any other auditors getting a foothold in the Diamond Group, do we? What are you proposing, anyway, a fee that's at a lower margin than normal, or one that's below the projected cost for this job? Either way, It's unethical, isn't it?

Question

1. Answer the question posed to Tim.

Ethics Case — *Societal Concerns*

Two accounting students, Joan and Miguel, were studying for their final university accounting exam.

"Miguel, what if they ask us whether the accounting profession should speak out about the shortcomings in financial statements?"

"Like what, Joan? We know they don't show the value of employees or the impact of inflation, or the economic reality or market value of many transactions—is that what you mean?"

"No, I mean the advocacy of disclosures which will lead to a better world for all of us. For example, if we could only get companies to start disclosing their impacts on society, and particularly our environment, they would be induced to set targets and perform better the next year. We know that lots of externalities, like pollution costs, are not included in the financial statements, but we could speak out for supplementary disclosures."

"Joan, you go right ahead if you like. But I'm going to stick to the traditional role of accountants—to the preparation and audit of financial statements. It got us this far, didn't it?"

"Yes, but do medical doctors refrain from commenting on health concerns, or do lawyers refrain from creating laws that govern our future? Why should we shy away from speaking out on issues that we know something about that mean a lot to our future?"

Question

1. Is Joan or Miguel right? Why?

Ethics Case — *Economic Realities or GAAP*

Stan Jones was an investor who had recently lost money on his investment in Fine Line Hotels, Inc., and he was anxious to discuss the problem with Janet Todd, a qualified accountant who was his friend and occasional adviser.

"How can they justify this, Janet? This company owns 19.9 percent of a subsidiary, Far East Hotels, which has apparently sustained some large losses. But these consolidated statements don't show any of these losses, and the investment in Far East hasn't been written down to reflect the loss either. I bought my shares in Fine Line just after its last audited statements were made available but just before the papers reported that the statements didn't reflect any of the losses. What should I do in the future—wait until the papers report the true economic picture? If I can't rely on audited figures, what's the sense of having an audit? And don't tell me that, if the ownership percentage had been 20 percent, the consolidated statements would have reported the loss. That's just outrageous."

Question

1. How should Janet Todd respond?

Ethics Case — *Multidisciplinary Practices—Ethical Challenges*

Multidisciplinary practices, or MDPs, are probably an inevitable development. Clients want "one-stop shopping," at a professional firm where they can go for all their needs, and where the partner responsible for their work can keep them briefed on new services that might be worth using. New services offered currently include:

▌ Legal services

▌ Actuarial services

▌ Engineering services

▌ Investment services

▌ Risk assessment services

▌ Ethics and integrity services

These new services, particularly in the area of legal services, have raised a high degree of controversy among existing accounting partners. Trevor, an older partner, and Dhana, a new and younger partner, were deep in discussion about the problems and benefits the new organization would bring.

"Trev, I don't really see what your problem is. We're going to be more helpful to our clients—that's the bottom line, isn't it?"

"I suppose so, D, but all these new services bring their own professionals. Are lawyers or engineers going to set aside their codes of conduct to live by ours? Whom do they report to—I don't have enough legal expertise or engineering expertise to supervise them, so how can I ensure they live up to our accounting standards of service and quality? Aren't I going to be holding myself out as their supervisor on false pretenses? If anything goes wrong, won't we be sued?

"Another thing, D, as the proportion of our operations from these new services grows, won't the entire firm take on a client focus just like any other business? As professional accountants, we are supposed to be serving the public—that's what keeps us from fudging the figures and our audit reports to benefit current management and current shareholders. Do you think that all these new professionals will buy into a 'public' focus rather than a 'client' focus where the bottom line drives decisions? How would we go about keeping them on the straight and narrow, even if we got them on it in the first place?"

"Trev, you sure do have a lot of worries. How close are you to retirement? Well, I just had a call from our CEO, Hajjad. He wants me to think about taking over our Ethics and Integrity practice. Say—you don't have anything I could read up on in that area, do you?"

Question

1. What are your answers to the questions raised in the case?

Ethics Case   *Italian Tax Mores**

The Italian federal corporate tax system has an official, legal tax structure and tax rates just as the U.S. system does. However, all similarity between the two systems ends there.

The Italian tax authorities assume that no Italian corporation would ever submit a tax return which shows its true profits but rather would submit a return which understates actual profits by anywhere between 30 percent and 70 percent; their assumption is essentially correct. Therefore, about six months after the annual deadline for filing corporate tax returns, the tax authorities issue to each corporation an "invitation to discuss" its tax return. The purpose of this notice is to arrange a personal meeting between them and representatives of the corporation. At this meeting, the Italian revenue service states the amount of corporate income tax which it believes is due. Its position is developed from both prior years' taxes actually paid and the current year's return; the amount which the tax authorities claim is due is generally several times that shown on the corporation's return for the current year. In short, the corporation's tax return and the revenue service's stated position are the operating offers for the several rounds of bargaining which will follow.

---

*This case, which is based on an actual occurrence, was prepared by Arthur L. Kelly. The author is the Managing Partner of KEL Enterprises L. P., a private investment partnership. He has been actively involved in international business for more than 40 years and has served as a member of the Boards of Directors of corporations in the United States and Europe. These currently include BASF Aktiengesellshaft and Bayerische Motoren Werke (BMW) A. G. in Germany as well as Deere & Company, Northern Trust Corporation, and Snap-on Incorporated in the United States. Copyright 1977. All rights reserved.

The Italian corporation is typically represented in such negotiations by its *commercialista,* a function which exists in Italian society for the primary purpose of negotiating corporate (and individual) tax payments with the Italian tax authorities; thus, the management of an Italian corporation seldom, if ever, has to meet directly with the Italian revenue service and probably has a minimum awareness of the details of the negotiation other than the final settlement.

Both the final settlement and the negotiation are extremely important to the corporation, the tax authorities, and the *commercialista.* Since the tax authorities assume that a corporation *always* earned more money this year than last year and *never* has a loss, the amount of the final settlement, that is, corporate taxes which will actually be paid, becomes, for all practical purposes, the floor for the start of next year's negotiations. The final settlement also represents the amount of revenue the Italian government will collect in taxes to help finance the cost of running the country. However, since large amounts of money are involved and two individuals having vested personal interests are conducting the negotiations, the amount of *bustarella*—typically a substantial cash payment "requested" by the Italian revenue agent from the *commercialista*—usually determines whether the final settlement is closer to the corporation's original tax return or to the fiscal authority's original negotiating position.

Whatever *bustarella* is paid during the negotiation is usually included by the *commercialista* in his lump-sum fee "for services rendered" to his corporate client. If the final settlement is favorable to the corporation, and it is the *commercialista's* job to see that it is, then the corporation is not likely to complain about the amount of its *commercialist's* fee, nor will it ever know how much of that fee was represented by *bustarella* and how much remained for the *commercialista* as payment for his negotiating services. In any case, the tax authorities will recognize the full amount of the fee as a tax-deductible expense on the corporation's tax return for the following year.

About 10 years ago, a leading American bank opened a banking subsidiary in a major Italian city. At the end of its first year of operation, the bank was advised by its local lawyers and tax accountants, both from branches of U.S. companies, to file its tax return "Italian-style," that is, to understate its actual profits by a significant amount. The American general manager of the bank, who was on his first overseas assignment, refused to do so both because he considered it dishonest and because it was inconsistent with the practices of his parent company in the United States.

About six months after filing its "American-style" tax return, the bank received an "invitation to discuss" notice from the Italian tax authorities. The bank's general manager consulted with his lawyers and tax accountants who suggested they hire a *commercialista.* He rejected this advice and instead wrote a letter to the Italian revenue service not only stating that his firm's corporate return was correct as filed but also requesting that they inform him of any specific items about which they had questions. His letter was never answered.

About 60 days after receiving the initial "invitation to discuss" notice, the bank received a formal tax assessment notice calling for a tax of approximately three times that shown on the bank's corporate tax return; the tax authorities simply assumed that the bank's original return had been based on generally accepted Italian practices, and they reacted accordingly. The bank's general manager again consulted with his lawyers and tax accountants who again suggested he hire a *commercialista* who knew how to handle these matters. Upon learning that the *commercialista* would probably have to pay *bustarella* to his revenue service counterpart in order to reach a settlement, the general manager again chose to ignore his advisors. Instead, he responded by sending the Italian revenue service a check for the full amount of taxes due according to the bank's American-style tax return even though the due date for the payment was almost six months hence; he made no reference to the amount of corporate taxes shown on the formal tax assessment notice.

Ninety days after paying its taxes, the bank received a third notice from the fiscal authorities. This one contained the statement. "We have reviewed your corporate tax return for 19____ and have determined the [the lira equivalent of] $6,000,000 of interest paid on deposits is not an allowable expense for federal purposes. Accordingly, the total tax due for 19____ is lira____." Since interest paid on deposits is any bank's largest single expense item, the new tax assessment was for an amount many times larger than that shown in the initial tax assessment notice and almost fifteen times larger than the taxes which the bank had actually paid.

The bank's general manager was understandably very upset. He immediately arranged an appointment to meet personally with the manager of the Italian revenue service's local office. Shortly after the start of their meeting, the conversation went something like this:

GENERAL MANAGER: "You can't really be serious about disallowing interest paid on deposits as a tax deductible expense."

ITALIAN REVENUE SERVICE: "Perhaps. However, we thought it would get your attention. Now that you're here, shall we begin our negotiations.

Questions

1. Should the Italian bank's general manager hire a *commercialista* and pay *bustarella?*

2. Should the general manager phone the bank's American CEO in New York and ask for advice?

3. If you were the bank's American CEO, would you want to receive the phone call for advice?

| Ethics Case | *Tax Return Complications* |

As Bill Adams packed his briefcase on Friday, March 15, he could never remember being so glad to see a week end. As a senior tax manager with a major accounting firm, Hay & Hay, on the fast track for partnership, he was worried that the events of the week could prove to be detrimental to his career.

Six months ago, the senior partners had rewarded Bill by asking him to be the tax manager on Zentor Inc., a very important client of the firm in terms of both prestige and fees. Bill had worked hard since then insuring his client received impeccable service and he had managed to build a good working relationship with Dan, the Chief Executive Officer of Zentor Inc. In fact, Dan was so impressed with Bill that he recommended him to his brother, Dr. Rim, a general medical practitioner. As a favor to Dan, Bill agreed that Hay & Hay would prepare Dr. Rim's tax return.

This week a junior tax person had prepared Dr. Rim's tax return. When it came across Bill's desk for review today, he was surprised to find that, although Dr. Rim's gross billings were $480,000, his net income for tax purposes from his medical practice was only $27,000. He discussed this with the tax junior, who said he had noted this also but was not concerned, as every tax return prepared by the firm is stamped with the disclaimer "We have prepared the return from information provided to us by the client. We have not audited or otherwise attempted to verify its accuracy."

On closer review, Bill discovered that the following items, among others, had been deducted by Dr. Rim in arriving at net income:

a. $15,000 for meals and entertainment. Bill felt that this was excessive and probably had not been incurred to earn income, given the nature of Dr. Rim's practice.

b. Dry-cleaning bills for shirts, suits, dresses, sweaters, etc. Bill believed these to be family dry-cleaning bills that were being paid by the practice.

c. Wages of $100 per week paid to Dr. Rim's twelve-year-old son.

Bill telephoned Dr. Rim and had his suspicions confirmed. When Bill asked Dr. Rim to review the expenses and remove all that were personal, Dr. Rim became very defensive. He told Bill that he had been deducting these items for years and his previous accountant had not objected. In fact, it was his previous accountant who had suggested he pay his son a salary as an income-splitting measure. The telephone conversation ended abruptly when Dr. Rim was paged for an emergency, but not before he threatened to inform his brother that the accounting firm he thought so highly of was behind the times on the latest tax planning techniques.

Bill was annoyed with himself for having agreed to prepare Dr. Rim's tax return in the first place. He was afraid of pushing Dr. Rim too far and losing Zentor Inc. as a client as a result. He could not anticipate what Dan's reaction to the situation would be. Bill was glad to have the weekend to think this over.

Just as Bill was leaving the office, the tax senior on the Zentor Inc. account informed him that the deadline had been missed for objecting to a reassessment, requiring Zentor Inc. to pay an additional $1,200,000 in taxes. The deadline was Wednesday, March 13. The senior said he was able to contact a friend of his at the Tax Department, and the friend had agreed that if the Notice of Objection was dated March 13, properly signed, and appeared on his desk Monday, March 18, he would process it. Bill left his office with some major decisions to make over the weekend.

Questions

1. Identify the ethical issues Bill Adams should address.

2. What would you do about these issues if you were Bill?

Source: Prepared by Joan Kitunen, University of Toronto, 1994.

Ethics Case | *Marketing Aggressive Tax Shelters*

Before 2002, accounting firms would provide multiple services to the same firm. Hired by the shareholders, they would audit the financial statements that were prepared by management, while also providing consulting services to those same managers. Some would provide tax advice to the managers of audit clients. However, the Sarbanes-Oxley Act of 2002 (SOX) restricted the type and the intensity of consulting services that could be provided to the management of audit clients because it might compromise the objectivity of the auditor when auditing the financial statements prepared by management on behalf of the shareholders. Nevertheless, both before and after the passage of SOX, Ernst & Young (E&Y) and KPMG were offering very aggressive tax shelters to wealthy taxpayers as well as to the senior managers of audit clients.

Ernst & Young

In the 1990s, E&Y had created four tax shelters that they were selling to wealthy individuals. One of them, called E.C.S., for Equity Compensation Strategy, resulted in little or no tax liability for the taxpayer. The complicated tax plan was a means of delaying, for up to thirty years, paying taxes on the profits from exercising employee stock options that would otherwise be payable in the year in which the stock options were exercised. E&Y charged a fee of three percent of the amount that the taxpayer invested in the tax shelter, plus $50,000 to a law firm for a legal opinion that said that it was "more likely than not" that the shelter would survive a tax audit.

E&Y had long been the auditor for Sprint Corporation. They also took on as clients William Esrey and Ronald LeMay, the top executives at Sprint. In 2000 E&Y received:

- $2.5 million for the audit of Sprint,

- $2.6 million for other services related to the audit,

- $63.8 million for information technology and other consulting services, and

- $5.8 million from Esrey and LeMay for tax advice.

In 1999 Esrey announced a planned merger of Sprint with WorldCom that potentially would have made the combined organization the largest telecommunications company in the world. The deal was not consummated because it failed to obtain regulatory approval. Nevertheless, Esrey and LeMay were awarded stock options worth about $311 million.

E&Y sold an E.C.S. to each of Esrey and LeMay. In the three years from 1998 to 2000, the options profits for Esrey were $159 million and the tax that would have been payable had he not bought the tax shelter amounted to about $63 million. The options profits for LeMay were $152.2 million and the tax thereon about $60.3 million.

Subsequently, the Internal Revenue Service rejected the tax shelter of each man. Sprint then asked the two executives to resign, which they did. Sprint also dismissed E&Y as the company's auditor.

On July 2, 2003, E&Y reached a $15 million settlement with the IRS regarding their aggressive marketing of tax shelters. Then, in 2007, four E&Y partners were charged with tax fraud. These four partners worked for an E&Y unit called VIPER, "value ideas produce extraordinary results," later renamed SISG, "strategic individual solutions group." Its purpose was to aggressively market tax shelters, known as Cobra, Pico, CDS, and CDS Add-Ons, to wealthy individuals, many of whom acquired their fortunes in technology-related businesses. These four products were sold to about 400 wealthy taxpayers from 1999 to 2001 and generated fees of approximately $121 million. The government claims that the tax shelters were bogus and taxpayers were reassessed for taxes owing as well as penalties and interest.

KPMG

On August 26, 2005, KPMG agreed to pay a fine of $456 million for selling tax shelters from 1996 through 2003 that fraudulently generated $11 billion in fictitious tax losses that cost the government at least $2.5 billion in lost taxes. The four tax shelters went by the acronyms FLIP, OPIS, BLIPS, and SOS. Under the Bond Linked Premium Issue Structure (BLIPS), for example, the taxpayer would borrow money from an offshore bank and invest in a joint venture that would buy foreign currencies from that same offshore bank. About two months later, the joint venture would then sell the foreign currency back to the bank, creating a tax loss. The taxpayer would then declare a loss for tax purposes on the BLIPS investment. The way that the BLIPS were structured, the taxpayer only had to pay $1.4 million in order to declare a $20 million loss for tax purposes. They were targeted at wealthy executives who would normally pay between $10 million and $20 million in taxes. Buying a BLIPS, however, effectively reduced the investor's taxable income to zero. They were sold to 186 wealthy individuals and generated at least $5 billion in tax losses. The FLIP and OPIS involved investment swaps through the Cayman Islands, and SOS was a currency swap similar to the BLIPS. The government contended that these were sham transactions since the loans and investments were risk-free. Their sole purpose was to artificially reduce taxes.

Some argued that the KPMG tax shelters were so egregious that the accounting firm should be put out of business. However, Arthur Anderson had collapsed in 2002, and if KPMG failed, then there would be only three large accounting firms remaining: Deloitte, PricewaterhouseCoopers, and Ernst & Young. KPMG Chairman, Timothy Flynn, said "the firm regretted taking part in the deals and sent a message to employees calling the conduct 'inexcusable.'"[1] KPMG remains in business, but the firm was fined almost a half billion dollars.

Questions

1. What differentiates very aggressive tax shelters from reasonable tax shelters?

2. As a result of the Ernst & Young and KPMG tax fiascos, the large accounting firms have become wary of marketing very aggressive tax shelters. Now, most shelters are being sold by tax "boutiques" that operate on a much smaller scale and so are less likely to be

---

1. "9 Charged Over Tax Shelters In KPMG Case: Accounting Firm Agrees to Pay As More Indictments Expected", Carrie Johnson, *Washington Post*, August 30, 2005; p. A01

investigated by the IRS. Is it right that accountants market aggressive tax shelter plans? Are tax shelter plans in the public interest?

References

Browning, L., "Four Charged in Tax Shelter Case," *New York Times*, May 31, 2007.

Gleckman, H., Borus, A., and McNamee, M., "Inside the KPMG Mess," *Business Week*, September 12, 2005.

Internal Revenue Service, *KPMG to Pay $456 Million for Criminal Violations.* IR-2005-83, August 29, 2005.

Johnston, D., and Glater, J., "Tax Shelter is Worrying Sprint's Chief," *New York Times*, February 6, 2003.

Ethics Case | *Providing Tax Advice*

Sophia and Maya were having a quiet after-work drink at the Purple Pheasant around the corner from their office. Both are professional accountants in their late twenties, and were talking about their futures in public accounting.

"I want to concentrate on the not-for-profit sector," said Sophia putting her glass of Chardonnay down on the table. "I really enjoyed the two months I spent at Save-a-Tree Foundation. And there's a huge demand for providing consulting advice to environmental groups and agencies."

"There's no money in that," said Maya. "They can't afford to pay you the big bucks. Not me. I like tax. That's where the money is; providing advice to wealthy clients who can easily afford to pay." She sat back in the booth sipping her Manhattan. "Do you know what my current billing rate is? It's outrageous, is what it is! But I've got a 94 percent recovery so I'm looking at being made a partner next year."

"It's not about money, it's about helping people. We're supposed to be upholding the public interest, not the interests of some fat cat executives." Sophia was leaning forward to make her point.

"Hey. I don't make the rules. I just follow them. The Income Tax Act is a rule book. I would never advise a client to break the law. But there's lots that's not covered. When the law doesn't prohibit something or when it's ambiguous, that's when we can advise them and come up with a plan. We always tell them there's a risk that the deduction might be disallowed. We cover our ass, and leave the ultimate decision up to them."

"But they're following your advice because you're the expert. They'd never come up with these schemes on their own. You're the one who found the loophole."

"We don't look for loopholes. We plan and offer sound advice that fits with the client's business objectives. Loopholes are outside the law."

"Whatever! You're the one who came up with the plan and how to implement it. You're telling them that it'll save them some money. They're not going to say no to that. They're like children, doing whatever mommy says."

"Yeah." Maya shrugged and smiled. "Occasionally they do ask for a second or third opinion."

Sophia was leaning forward again. "For many of them, tax is emotional. They don't want to pay anything and so they'd do anything to save a buck. They'd gladly pay you $350,000 in consulting fees if you could save them a million in tax."

"Yeah." Maya shrugged again and sipped her drink.

"But is that right? A million dollars that could have gone to the government for the good of society is now being siphoned off and thirty-five percent of it is being given to you. That can't possibly be in the public interest."

"Hey, the partners will pay tax on that three hundred and fifty, and the client will reinvest the remaining $650,000 in the business. Anyway many of my clients think that the government's wasteful. They don't want the government squandering their money."

"What the government does with the money is irrelevant." Sophia realized her voice was rising, so she settled back in the booth and had another sip of her wine. It was still early but the bar was beginning to fill up with the regular Friday night crowd.

"Tax is a redistribution system that is supposed to help everyone in society. And you're draining money out of that system, even if the partners are paying some tax on the money that should have gone to the government in the first place."

"Just a minute, Sophia." Maya was now leaning forward. "The poor are covered by tax relief and they're not my concern. As a tax specialist my first responsibility is to my clients. I'm being hired to save them money. That's what I'm supposed to do!"

"No, your first responsibility is to maintain the public interest; your second responsibility is to your clients. Anyway, why don't you look for tax loopholes for the poor?"

"First, the public interest doesn't pay me. And, second, poor people can't afford my billing rate. And third, we don't look for loopholes! We come up with tax plans that have a more likely than not chance of surviving a tax audit."

"Yeah. Whatever!"

Maya finished the last of her Manhattan. "What do you think I should do when I find a tax 'loophole'? Not advise my clients? What happens if some other tax specialist finds the same thing and comes up with a similar plan? If I remain silent, then they might steal my clients away by providing the tax advice that I should have been providing to them."

"If you find a loophole," Sophia was excited and talking very quickly, "then why don't you inform the government, and have them change the law to close the loophole?"

"Not a chance! You may be a do-gooder, Sophia, but this is my livelihood. I'm talented and professional. I charge top dollar to provide sound advice. That's how I make my living. I'm honest and candid with my clients. I'm straightforward when I explain the risks to them. I've got nothing to be ashamed about or to apologize for. So, let's order another round of drinks and talk about investment strategies instead."

Questions

1. Is there a basic conflict of interest between upholding the public interest and providing tax advice that reduces the amount of money taxpayers pay to the government? Why or why not?

2. How can professional accountants maintain the support of the public while giving tax advice? Is providing tax advice that only benefits the wealthy, who can afford to pay for tax advice, in the public interest? Is this fair? Is providing highly specialized tax advice to naïve clients being paternalistic?

3. If a tax specialist spends only one hour devising a tax plan that saves a client $1 million, is it ethically acceptable for the tax specialist to charge that client more than the one hour billing rate?

4. Is it ethically correct for a corporation to pay $350,000 to tax consultants so that the corporation can save a million in tax?

| Ethics Case | *Risk Management of Taxes Payable—Is it Ethical?*

"At the firm, we've got a new way of looking at tax issues. It's called 'risk management,' and, in your case, John, it means that we can be more aggressive than in the past. In the past, when there was an issue open to interpretation, we advised you to adopt a practice that was relatively safe, so that you would not get into trouble with the tax department. The thinking was that it would be better not to attract attention because that would lead to more audits and more difficult negotiations of questionable issues. We noticed, however, that there are fewer tax auditors now than in the past, particularly in remote areas, so it makes sense to take more chances than in the past—if you are audited, you can always pay up, anyway. It just makes good business sense to take advantage of all the possibilities open to your competitors. More and more of our clients are moving into this area of risk management, and you should think about it too."

Question

1. Is this new practice of risk management ethical?

Readings

The Liability Crisis in the United States: Impact on the Accounting Profession— A Statement of Position

Arthur Andersen & Co., Coopers & Lybrand, Deloitte & Touche, Ernst & Young, KPMG Peat Marwick, Price Waterhouse

The tort liability system in the United States is out of control. It is no longer a balanced system that provides reasonable compensation to victims by the responsible parties. Instead, it functions primarily as a risk transfer scheme in which marginally culpable or even innocent defendants too often must agree to coerced settlements in order to avoid the threat of even higher liability, pay judgments totally out of proportion to their degree of fault, and incur substantial legal expenses to defend against unwarranted lawsuits.

The flaws in the liability system are taking a severe toll on the accounting profession. If these flaws are not corrected and the tort system continues on its present inequitable course, the consequences could prove fatal to accounting firms of all sizes. But a liability system seriously lacking in logic, fairness and balance is not just the accounting profession's crisis. It is a business crisis and a national crisis.

This position statement describes these matters in more detail, as well as needed reforms that the American Institute of CPAs (AICPA) and the six largest accounting firms are advocating. In seeking these reforms, the firms are not attempting to avoid liability where they are culpable. Rather, the firms seek equitable treatment that will permit them and the public accounting profession to continue to make an important contribution to the U.S. economy.

An Epidemic of Litigation

The present liability system has produced an epidemic of litigation that is spreading throughout the accounting profession and the business community. It is threatening the independent audit function and the financial reporting system, the strength of U.S. capital markets, and the competitiveness of the U.S. economy.

The principal causes of the accounting profession's liability problems are unwarranted litigation and coerced settlements. The present system makes it both easy and financially rewarding to file claims regardless of the merits of the case. As former SEC Commissioner Philip Lochner recently pointed out in *The Wall Street Journal*, plaintiffs may simply be seeking to recoup losses from a poor investment decision by going after the most convenient "deep pocket"—the auditor.[1] In too many cases, moreover, claims are filed with the sole intent of taking advantage of the system to force defendants to settle.

The doctrine of joint and several liability makes each defendant fully liable for all assessed damages in a case, regardless of the degree of fault. In practical terms this means that, even with no evidence of culpability, a company's independent auditors are almost certain to be named in any action filed against that company alleging financial fraud, for no reason other than the auditors' perceived "deep pockets" or because they are the only potential defendant that is still solvent. A particularly egregious example of the abuses encouraged by joint and several liability is the common practice of plaintiffs' attorneys settling with the prime wrongdoers, who don't have a defense or money, at a fraction of what these parties should pay. The attorneys then pursue the case against the "deep pocket" professionals, who as a result of joint and several liability are exposed for 100 percent of the damages even if found to be only one percent at fault.

Other elements in the system also act as incentives for unwarranted litigation leading to forced settlements. For example, American judicial rules make no effective provision for recovery of legal costs by prevailing defendants, even if the plaintiff's case is meritless. In addition, judicial restrictions on the types of cases in which punitive damages may be

---

1. Philip R. Lochner, Jr., "Black Days for Accounting Firms," *The Wall Street Journal*, May 22, 1992, page A10.

awarded have been significantly relaxed in recent years, making solvent professional and business defendants a prime target. The prospect of having to pay all damages as a consequence of joint and several liability, the high costs of defense, and possible punitive damages are persuasive factors in coercing settlements.

Abusive and unwarranted litigation is a problem not just for the accounting profession, but for business and the economy generally. A small group of attorneys is reaping millions of dollars by bringing federal securities fraud claims (under SEC Rule 10b-5) against public companies whose only crime has been a fluctuation in their stock price. These attorneys use the threat of enormous legal costs, a lengthy and disruptive discovery process, protracted litigation, and damage to reputation to force large settlements.

The CEO of a high tech company that has been the target of 13 specious Rule 10b-5 suits calls these actions "legalized extortion" and their effects go far beyond the "payoffs" demanded. These meritless suits siphon off funds needed for research and development, capital investment, growth and expansion. They divert management's time, talent and energy from the principal mission of running the business. They send liability insurance premiums skyrocketing. Ultimately, the direct and indirect costs of these suits are borne by shareholders, along with employees, customers, and all of a company's stakeholders.

Joint and several liability encourages the inclusion of "deep pocket" defendants such as independent accountants, lawyers, directors and underwriters in these suits in order to increase the prospect and size of settlements. Prohibitive legal costs, the unpredictable outcome of a jury trial, and the risk of being liable for the full damages compel even blameless defendants to race each other to the settlement table. And they do this despite the realization that, to the uninformed public, "agreeing" to settle is seen as an admission of wrongdoing.

A survey by the six largest accounting firms of the cases against them involving 10b-5 claims which were concluded in fiscal year 1991 showed that: (i) the average claim subjecting the accounting firm to joint and several liability was for $85 million; (ii) the average

settlement by the firm was $2.7 million, suggesting there might have been little or no merit to the original claim against the accountant; yet, (iii) the average legal cost per claim was $3.5 million. It is not surprising that an accounting firm would agree to settle a case for less than what it had already spent in legal fees and, therefore, avoid the risk of liability of over twenty times the settlement by a jury that may be hostile to a business with "deep pockets." However, controlling risk by settling where you did nothing wrong becomes a very expensive strategy for "winning" the liability game.

Financial Crisis for the Accounting Profession

The financial impact of rampant litigation on the six largest accounting firms has been well-publicized. Numerous headlines and articles resulted from the firms' own disclosure that, in 1991, total expenditures for settling and defendant lawsuits were $477 million—nine percent of auditing and accounting revenues in the United States. This figure, a multiple of what other businesses spend on litigation, does not even include indirect costs. It covers only costs of legal services, settlements and judgments, and liability insurance premiums, minus insurance reimbursements. The 1991 figure represents a substantial increase over the 1990 figure of $404 million or 7.7 percent of audit and accounting revenues. And based upon reported settlements through June 30, 1992, there appears to be no end to the continuous upward spiral.

The litigation explosion has affected the entire accounting profession. It has been estimated that there are about $30 billion in damage claims currently facing the profession as a whole. A recent survey by the AICPA indicates that claims against firms other than the six largest rose by two-thirds between 1987 and 1991. Ninety-six percent of those firms having more than 50 CPAs reported an increase in exposure to l egal liability. The same group has experienced a 300 percent increase in liability insurance premiums since 1985. Smaller firms must now carry far more coverage, and high deductibles force them to pay even medium-sized claims out-of-pocket. The median amount for deductibles is now $240,000—nearly six times the 1985 median of $42,000. Forty percent of all the firms surveyed are "going bare," largely because liability insurance is simply too expensive.[2]

For the largest firms, the increase in insurance premiums was dramatically higher than that reported by the smaller firms, coupled with drastically reduced policy limits. Deductibles also have risen dramatically and now exceed $25 million for a first loss. The higher rate of increase in liability insurance for the largest firms generally reflects the larger proportion of audit work for publicly-held companies, thereby subjecting them to a greater liability risk.

Impact on Corporate Accountability and Economic Competitiveness

The heavy financial burden placed on accounting firms by runaway litigation affects business and the economy in two major ways: first, through the actual and threatened failure of accounting firms; and, second, through the "survival tactics" firms are forced to employ.

In 1990, Laventhol & Horwath, the seventh-largest firm, collapsed—the largest bankruptcy for a professional organization in U.S. history—necessitating that its former partners agree to pay $48 million to avoid personal bankruptcy. While other factors contributed to the firm's demise, the overriding reason was the weight of its liability burden. According to former CEO Robert Levine, L&H, like other accounting firms, was included as a defendant because of the perception of being a "deep pocket" rather than deficiencies in the performance of its professional responsibilities. "It wasn't the litigation we would lose that was the problem," he asserted. "It was the cost of winning that caused the greatest part of our financial distress."

The consequences of L&H's failure reverberated throughout the capital markets. Audits in process were interrupted. New auditors had to be found, with the inevitable time lag that occurs for start-up. Special rules had to be adopted by the SEC to deal with public companies whose prior year financial statements reported on by L&H had to be reissued in connection with public offerings and periodic public filings. Companies whose financial statements were audited by L&H were placed under a cloud through no fault of their own.

Furthermore, the failure undermined confidence in the ability of the profession to carry out its public obligations by creating concerns about the financial viability of other firms. It also created a deep sense of apprehension throughout the accounting profession that has only grown worse. During 1992, another prominent firm, Pannell Kerr Foster, closed or sold about 90 percent of its offices and opted to reorganize its offices as individual professional corporations. *Accounting Today* quoted a former PKF partner who indicated that liability was one of the reasons for this massive restructuring.

The magnitude of the six largest accounting firms' liability-related costs, as well as the size of some highly-publicized judgments and settlements, has fueled speculation about their survival. This is not surprising. A grim precedent has been set, and without decisive action the liability crisis will grow worse and the six firms' collective liability burden, enormous as it is, will increase.

This potential long-term threat to the survival of the six firms has serious implications for the independent audit function, the financial reporting system and the capital markets. As a group, the six largest accounting firms audit all but a handful of the country's largest and most prominent public companies in every category:

- 494 of the *Fortune* 500 industrials;
- 97 of the *Fortune* 100 fastest growing companies;
- 99 of the *Fortune* 100 largest commercial banks;
- 92 of the top 100 defense contractors; and
- 195 of the 200 largest insurance companies.

2. Survey of accounting firms (excluding the six largest), American Institute of Certified Public Accountants, 1992.

In each of these categories, at least one of the six firms audits more than 20 percent of the companies. According to figures from *Who Audits America,* the six firms audit 90 percent (4,748 of 5,266) of the publicly-traded companies in the U.S. with annual sales of one million dollars or more.[3]

The detrimental effects on auditing, financial reporting, and our capital markets are already very much in evidence. They are a natural consequence of the risky and uncertain practice environment which the litigation epidemic has created not only for the six largest firms, but for the entire accounting profession.

The "Tort Tax"

One obvious effect is what the media [have] called "the tort tax"—that is, the increased cost of goods and services caused by runaway litigation. To quote SEC Chairman Richard C. Breeden, "Accounting firms, in particular, pay substantial and increasing costs to litigate and settle securities cases. At some point, these increasing litigation costs will increase the cost of audit services and tend to reduce access to our national securities markets."[4] If companies must pay higher costs for services provided not only by auditors, but by underwriters, attorneys and other frequent "deep pocket" defendants, it will be more expensive for them to raise needed capital. Opportunities for investors will be reduced, and U.S. businesses will be placed at a competitive disadvantage *vis-à-vis* companies in countries with more rational liability systems—virtually every other country in the world.

The Impact of Risk Reduction

The liability burden cannot be measured only in dollars and cents. Other effects are less easy to detect, but are no less costly. For example, groups targeted by frequent litigation now practice risk reduction as a matter of professional survival. Doctors, for instance, are avoiding such fields as gynecology and obstetrics. The result is a scarcity of practitioners in crucial specialties.

Accountants are also practicing risk reduction. The six largest firms are attempting to reduce the threat of litigation by avoiding what are considered high-risk audit clients and even entire industries. High risk categories include financial institutions, insurance companies, and real estate investment firms. Also considered "high risk" are high technology and mid-size companies, and private companies making initial public offerings (IPOs). These companies are a ready target of baseless Rule 10b-5 suits because their stock prices tend to be volatile. Unfortunately, they are also the companies that most need quality professional services, are a key source of innovation and jobs, and play a crucial role in keeping this country competitive.

Risk avoidance is not confined to only the largest accounting firms. Smaller and medium-sized firms are dropping their public clients or abandoning their audit practices altogether. A recent survey of California CPA firms showed that only 53 percent are willing to undertake audit work. This creates serious problems for smaller companies (and their shareholders) that need viable alternatives to the major firms. Additionally, the survey showed that thirty-two percent of the reporting CPA firms are discontinuing audits in what they consider as high risk sectors. Another survey by Johnson & Higgins found that 56 percent of the mid-sized firms surveyed will not do business with clients involved in industries they consider high risk.

Impact on Professional Recruitment and Morale

Another troubling effect of the litigation explosion on the accounting profession, its clients and the public is one that cuts across all industries and services. The litigious practice environment is making it increasingly difficult to attract and retain the most qualified individuals at every level. The *Atlantic Monthly* has reported that fewer top business students are choosing to go to public accounting firms to do audit work because, among other things, they perceive it as risky.

---

3. *Who Audits America,* 25th Edition, Data Financial Press, Menlo Park, California, June 1991, pp. 393–396.
4. Letter from SEC Chairman Richard C. Breeden to Rep. John D. Dingell (D-MI), Chairman, Committee on Energy and Commerce, U.S. House of Representatives, May 5, 1992.

It is likely that the most serious impact on recruitment and retention of qualified people is yet to be felt, since widespread media and public attention have only recently begun to focus on the accounting profession's liability plight. Recruiters from the six largest firms report that they are encountering more awareness, more questions and more apprehension about the liability risk on college campuses across the country. Transforming public accounting from a secure and respected career to one in which becoming a partner carries with it the threat of personal financial ruin, is no way to ensure the profession's ability to meet its responsibilities to investors and the public.

Needed Reforms

To restore equity and sanity to the liability system and to provide reasonable assurance that the public accounting profession will be able to continue to meet its public obligations requires substantive reform of both federal and state liability laws.

Proportionate Liability

While other serious problems must also be addressed, the principal cause of unwarranted litigation against the profession is joint and several liability, which governs the vast majority of actions brought against accountants at the federal and state levels.

In arguing for an end to joint and several liability, the profession is in no way attempting to evade financial responsibility in cases where accountants are culpable. The profession is merely asking for fairness—the replacement of joint and several liability with a proportionate liability standard that assesses damages against each defendant based on that defendant's degree of fault. SEC Chairman Richard Breeden recently acknowledged that joint and several liability can lead to unfair results by forcing marginal defendants to settle even weak claims. He has also expressed support for reducing the coercive "effect of allegations of joint and several liability in cases of relatively remote connection by the party to the principal wrongdoing."[5]

Proportionate liability will help restore balance and equity to the liability system by discouraging specious suits and giving blameless defendants the incentive to prove their case in court rather than settle. By creating overwhelming pressure on innocent defendants to settle, joint and several liability gives plaintiffs' lawyers a strong incentive to bring as many cases as possible, without regard to the relative merits, include as many defendants as possible without regard to their degree of fault, and to settle these cases at a fraction of the alleged damages. Thus victims of real fraud receive no more (on average 5 to 15 percent of their alleged damages) than so-called "professional" plaintiffs and speculators trying to recoup investment losses. On the other hand, the lawyers bringing these suits typically receive 30 percent of the settlement plus expenses. If plaintiffs' lawyers were not able to use the threat of joint and several liability to compel innocent defendants to settle meritless cases, they would have to focus all of their efforts on meritorious claims. That, in turn, would result in more appropriate awards for true victims.

Current Reform Efforts

The six largest firms have joined with the AICPA and concerned businesses in calling for federal securities reform to curb unwarranted litigation brought under Rule 10b-5. Proposed remedies include replacing joint and several liability with proportionate liability and requiring that plaintiffs pay a prevailing defendant's legal fees if the court determines that the suit was meritless.

Curbing baseless Rule 10b-5 actions will, however, ease but not solve the liability problem. Of the total cases pending against the six largest firms in 1991, only 30 percent contained Rule 10b-5 claims. Of that 30 percent, less than 10 percent were exclusively 10b-5 claims.

The greatest liability exposure resides in the states. Reform of state liability laws affecting accountants is of critical importance to the future viability of the profession. The 10b-5 effort, if successful, will certainly serve as an important precedent for further reform.

---

5. Letter from SEC Chairman Richard C. Breeden to Sen. Terry Sanford (D-NC), June 12, 1992.

Beyond proportionate liability, reasonable limitations on punitive damages, as well as disincentives to filing meritless claims ought to be enacted. Reforms could be accomplished either through federal preemption or state-by-state modification of their statutes governing legal liability. The accounting profession will continue to participate in various state liability reform initiatives.

No less important is the need for the accounting profession to remove legislative, regulatory and professional restrictions on the forms of organization that may be used by accounting firms. Accountants must be free to practice in any form of organization permitted by state law, including limited liability organizations. The accounting profession is not seeking special treatment. Importantly, public accountants only seek to practice in forms of organization that are available to the vast majority of American businesses. Such changes will not relieve culpable individuals of legal responsibility for their own actions, but simply end the current inequity of full personal liability on all partners for all judgments against their firms resulting from the actions of others. The six largest firms will continue to aggressively pursue needed state-level liability reform.

The six largest firms are exploring all possible alternatives for reducing the threat that liability poses to their ability to meet their public obligations and to their survival. In this pursuit, the firms cannot support any legislative or regulatory proposal that increases the responsibilities of the profession unless these increased responsibilities are accompanied by meaningful and comprehensive liability reform. The firms will support initiatives at both the federal and state levels that will restore balance to the current system of justice.

August 6, 1992

J. Michael Cook
Chairman and Chief Executive Officer
Deloitte & Touche

Ray J. Groves
Chairman
Ernst & Young

Shaun F. O'Malley
Chairman and Senior Partner
Price Waterhouse

Eugene M. Freedman
Chairman
Coopers & Lybrand

Jon C. Madonna
Chairman and Chief Executive
KPMG Peat Marwick

Lawrence A. Weinbach
Managing Partner-Chief Executive
Arthur Andersen & Co., S.C.

Readings | *Ethics in Taxation Practice*

Tom Lynch

The Accountant's Magazine, November 1987

Tom Lynch draws attention to some problem areas where ethical standards come under pressure in particular tax situations.

Taxation practice is no different from any other professional practice in that it should be conducted in accordance with the highest ethical standards backed by the application of a high degree of skill, know-how and competence, to the affairs of clients whose interests will be foremost in the mind of the practitioner.

Taxation services fall broadly into two categories: compliance and advisory. There are, of course, other services such as advocacy before Tribunals, addressing the members of a trade association client and so on, but these are usually ancillary activities which can be ignored for present purposes.

When the word "ethics" is mentioned in taxation circles the first reaction is that it relates to evasion and avoidance. Evasion is illegal and therefore unethical, while avoidance is entirely in order and therefore ethical. It follows from this that if one does not positively evade taxes all is well, and since no self-respecting accountant would do so or assist others to do so, that is the end of the matter. Beyond this ethics may be ignored. There is, of course, a great difference between evasion and avoidance. One can lead to prison while the other leads only to disappointment.

But life is not quite as simple as that. On the one hand there are degrees of culpability in evasion, while in avoidance there is a distinction to be made between straightforward mitigation and complex artificial schemes of tax avoidance. Some writers on the subject have even referred to "avoision" as a hybrid word implying that evasion and avoidance may in some circumstances be indistinguishable. The ultimate effect may be the same in that revenue is lost to the Exchequer, but they are different and they are distinguishable. It is in compliance work that tax evasion is normally encountered while generally speaking advisory work is more likely to involve tax avoidance.

Evasion

Evasion can take many forms but the objective is the same: to evade in whole or in part the tax liabilities which arise on the actual expenditure income, gains and wealth of the taxpayer. Given that the accountant in practice would not consciously assist a client to evade taxes it may be argued that evasion does not concern him. But this is not so and, further, it is a dangerous assumption to make. He, or she, can still become involved in evasion—for example, by failing to notice discrepancies in books or accounts or perhaps by finding out after the event that the client has evaded some or all of his tax liabilities.

The practicing accountant must strive to ensure—as far as it is humanly possible to do so—that, as agent, no contribution is made to evasion of tax by a client. Compliance work is not a merely passive exercise when it is done by a professional accountant and it is by accepting unsatisfactory information and explanations that the accountant is most at risk. It must be borne in mind too that an accountant's contribution to evasion could be more reprehensible than the evasion itself.

If the accountant comes to the conclusion that his client is evading his tax liabilities, he must point out the risks and penalties; if the client fails to change his ways, the accountant

should cease to act for him. Similarly, if an omission in a return or set of accounts comes to light after they have been submitted (and possibly agreed), the client should be advised to report the error—the client is responsible for what is in the return—and if he does not do so the accountant should withdraw his services. It should be made clear to the client, before doing so, that the Inland Revenue's attitude is very different in cases of voluntary disclosure from those where evasion is discovered only after investigation.

Compliance

Not all taxpayers are both highly literate and highly numerate. Their accounts and financial records can be a mess. But this is no reason to refuse to act for them even if it is necessary to use estimates in order to complete their accounts and returns. The Inland Revenue acknowledges this as a fact of life and is prepared to settle for estimated assessments in many cases. Provided the extent of the estimation is clearly stated, the accountant cannot be faulted even if evasion on the part of the taxpayer is subsequently discovered. But it is necessary to apply professional skills and common sense to the information and explanations on which the estimates are based and to refuse to accept doubtful information.

When the proprietor of a small local business in a rural area in Scotland tells his accountants that his regular trips to Newmarket are solely for business purposes, it would not be prudent to accept this statement without further enquiry. It may well be that what he says is true—perhaps because it is the one place he can be sure to get hold of a certain important supplier or customer; apart from that he may loathe crowds in general and racegoing crowds in particular. But on the face of it further enquiry would be expected.

One of the most common problems is the danger of accepting unsatisfactory explanations (or none) in the preparation of accounts because of the pressure of work and time limits—"the General Commissioners' meeting is tomorrow!" The accountant must ensure that work is properly staffed and where there is client-caused delay the accountant must not be stampeded or tempted to "keep things tidy" by throwing fingers into accounts without weighing up their reasonableness and requiring further explanations where this is necessary. Indeed, the more incomplete the records and the greater the delay in getting information to supplement what is there the more watchful the accountant should be and the more inclined to seek to square the accounts and returns with the client's standard of living and wealth. This will often turn out to be a valuable service to the sort of client who is simply careless and who would otherwise get into deep financial trouble or worse over his tax liabilities.

Avoidance

"Avoidance" is rather an unfortunate word with a rather naughty connotation; in fact it covers everything from a simple and real rearrangement of affairs, which is eminently sensible and pure, to complex schemes where affairs are re-arranged with no real effect—i.e., with no substance other than to reduce tax liabilities. These artificial schemes are not illegal but are thought by many to be reprehensible and, more importantly, potentially ineffective.

Form and Substance

The *obiter dicta* in the Duke of Westminster's case about form being preferred to substance and Lord Tomlin's famous words about it being legitimate to arrange one's affairs so as to avoid the Inland Revenue putting its largest shovel into one's store still hold good despite *Furmiss v Dawson* et al. Form is still important. For example, a grandparent may give a grandchild a simple cash gift each year or may choose instead to pay the same cash under a valid deed of covenant. The gift is the same under either method, but the latter will have a tax saving effect solely because of the form in which the gift is made. The essential point is that the transaction between the grandparent and the grandchild has substance apart from tax saving. It is a real transaction in which real money passes from one person to another. The grandparent's finances would change for the worse after each payment while the grandchild's financial position would correspondingly improve. The form of the transaction is therefore vital.

Where the form of the transaction is not accepted by the courts it is not because the substance is preferred to the form but because there is no substance, no real transaction. Whatever form one may choose to give to a nothing, a nonentity, a fiction, it can never be a real transaction and it may therefore be ignored. Such transactions may conveniently be described as artificial avoidance schemes.

Advisory Services

Whatever may be said about artificial avoidance schemes, tax mitigation is not reprehensible. Taking advantage of loopholes (with real transactions) may not be quite so commendable, but they are available to all taxpayers and it is up to Parliament to avoid creating them and, where they occur, to close them up as soon as possible.

Clients expect to be given advice on tax planning and mitigation and there is nothing wrong in the accountant giving this sort of advice. A Royal Commission report put it very well:

> "there is no reason to assume that the situation of any one taxpayer at that moment is the fairest possible as between himself and others differently situated: and if there is not, it seems wrong to pronounce any principle that would have the effect of fixing each taxpayer in his situation without allowing him any chance of so altering his arrangements as to reduce his liability to assessment."

A wife who helps her husband in his business may decide not to take a salary. Nevertheless, the true situation is that any profits are jointly earned and if the wife becomes a paid employee or a partner it is possible that the tax liability on the jointly earned income may be less. That the profits are jointly earned is the real substance of a case such as this, but once again it is the form in which the profits are earned that will settle the tax position. The accountant should see that the most tax efficient form is in fact adopted.

The transfer of cash from a building society deposit account (taxed income) to National Savings Certificates (income not taxed) is an example of a transaction which is both tax efficient and entirely acceptable. HM Government itself publicizes the tax efficiency of National Savings Certificates using phrases such as "send the taxman away empty handed," phrases which accountants would think twice about using in the exercise of their profession.

On other slightly more complicated matters—such as the timing of an incoming or outgoing partner, or accepting shares rather than cash in a take-over bid—Lord Tomlin's dictum should be followed with enthusiasm, without risk of blame or stigma.

The situation is not so clear when it comes to artificial avoidance schemes. Certainly accountants should advise on them and indeed it is their duty to point out the risks associated with such schemes, the uncertainties and possible changes in the law which might negate them. It would not, however, be part of his duty to devise and promote such schemes if for no other reason than that the scheme so promoted not only has the blessing of the accountant but, because of his expertise, some sort of guarantee of success which if it fails to materialise may sour the relationship with the client. There is no question of morality here, at least so far as the adviser is concerned. Artificial schemes are best left alone simply because they bring trouble and expense in their wake, and often they do not work.

As regards morality, this is a question solely for the taxpayer. It is not the duty of the accountant as tax adviser to advise on what is or is not moral. Not everyone agrees that what is legal must necessarily also be moral or that any act within the law is not only permissible but even praiseworthy. Moral values are often rather higher than minimum legal requirements and it will be a matter for the individual's own conscience to determine which he or she prefers. The accountant/adviser may want, however, to avoid unduly influencing a client's moral judgment by vigorously promoting artificial schemes of tax avoidance.

Conclusion

In compliance work it is important not to be "used" either deliberately or willy nilly to assist evasion. It is all too easy to get caught up in this way and accountants must not allow pressures of any kind to distract them from working to a uniformly high standard. It is also necessary to be entirely firm about disclosing omissions in previous accounts and returns.

In advisory work, mitigation advice may and should be given. Advice should also be given on artificial avoidance schemes, but I suggest that accountants should not promote such schemes.

Tom Lynch, CA, FRSA, is visiting Professor of Taxation at the University of Glasgow and a former senior tax partner in Ernst & Whinney.

Source: *The Accountant's Magazine*, November 1987: 27, 28. Reprinted with the permission of the Editor of *CAmagazine*, published by the Institute of Chartered Accounts of Scotland.

Appendix A

INTERNATIONAL COMPARISON OF MAIN ASPECTS OF PROFESSIONAL CODES OF CONDUCT

(Consult **www.cengage.com/acounting/brooks** for Updated Table with hyperlinks. Effective to August 2008. Commentary on Professional Codes of Australia, New Zealand, Japan, and China is at the end of Table.)

	US AICPA	INTERNATIONAL IFAC	CANADA ICAO	UK ICAEW	US IMA	CANADA SMAC
DESIGNATION SOURCES	CPA American institute of Certified Public Accountants	International Federation of Accountants	CA Institute of Chartered Accountants of Ontario	CA Institute of Chartered Accountants in England and Wales	CMA Institute of Management Accountants	CMA Society of Management Accountants of Ontario
Org. Website	www.aicpa.org	www.ifac.org	www.icao.on.ca	www.icaew.com	www.imanet.org	www.cma-ontario.org
Code Website	http://www.aicpa.org/about/code/index.html	http://www.ifac.org/Store/ See also www.ifac.org// ethics/	http://www.icao.on.ca/Resources/Membershandbook/1011page2635.pdf	http://www.icaew.com/index.cfm/route/136011/icaew_ga/en/Technical_amp_Business_Topics/Topics/Professional_ethics/ICAEW_Code_of_Ethics	http://www.imanet.org/about_ethics_statement.asp	http://www.cma-ontario.org/index.cfm/ci_id/7409/la_id/1.htm
Effective date	Updated to June. 2007	Amended July 2006 Not Applicable	Feb. 2006	Sept. 1, 2006	Dec. 2002, on web Jan. 2006	Rev. Aug. 2008
Advisory Service	Yes		Yes	Yes	Yes	Yes
PRINCIPLES	SECTIONS 50-57 (52) Responsibilities In carrying out their professional responsibilities, members to exercise sensitive professional and moral judgment in all their activities.	PART A: General Application (100) Code is in three parts. Part A establishes the fundamental principles of professional ethics for professional accountants and provides a conceptual framework for applying those principles. Professional accountants (PA) are required to apply this conceptual framework to identify threats to compliance with the fundamental principles, to evaluate their significance and, if such threats are other than clearly insignificant. Parts B and C illustrate how the conceptual framework is to be applied in specific situations.	SECTION 200: Standards of Conduct Affecting the Public Interest See FOREWORD as well	Since the ICAEW *Code of Ethics* is declared to be derived from and wholly compatible with the principles of the *IFAC Code, the specific details are not listed below except where they offer additional guidance.* The ICAEW *Code of Ethics* maintains the same numbering of sections as the IFAC Code except where there.	Members of IMA shall behave ethically. A commitment to ethical professional practice includes: overarching principles that express our values, and standards that guide our conduct. IMA's overarching ethical principles include: Honesty, Fairness, Objectivity, and Responsibility. Members shall act in accordance with these principles and shall encourage others within their organizations to adhere to them.	A Member will act at all times with: (i) responsibility for and fidelity to public needs; (ii) fairness and loyalty to such Member's associates, clients and employers; and (iii) competence through devotion to high ideals of personal honour and professional integrity.
	(53) The Public Interest Members have an obligation to act in a way that will serve public interest, honor the public trust and demonstrate commitment to professionalism.	(100.1) The Public Interest A distinguishing mark of the accountancy profession is its acceptance of the responsibility to act in the public interest. Therefore, a professional accountant's responsibility is not exclusively to satisfy the needs of an individual client or employer.	(201) The Public Interest Maintenance of good reputation of the profession and its ability to serve the public interest.	(100.1) The Public Interest Same as IFAC.	The Public Interest Provide decision support information and recommendations that are accurate, clear, concise, and timely.	The Public Interest Members have a responsibility for and fidelity to public needs.

Column 1	Column 2	Column 3	Column 4	Column 5	Column 6
(54) Integrity To maintain and broaden public confidence, perform all responsibilities with highest sense of integrity.	**(110) Integrity** To be straightforward and honest in professional and business relationships. Integrity also implies fair dealing and truthfulness. Not be associated with misleading information.	**(202) Integrity and due care** Perform his or her professional services with integrity and due care.	**(110) Integrity** Same as IFAC.	**(III. 1-3) Integrity** Avoid influences and actual or apparent conflicts of interest. Advise of any gift, etc. that would influence or appear to influence Refrain from active or passive subversion	**Integrity and Personal Honour** Must perform duties with honour and professional integrity.
(55) Objectivity & Independence Be objective and free of conflicts of interest in discharging responsibilities. A member in public practice be independent in fact and appearance when providing auditing and other attestation services.	**(120) Objectivity** Not to compromise their professional or business judgment because of bias, conflict of interest or the undue influence of others.	**(204) Objectivity** Opinion on financial statements must be free of any influence and interest or relationship which may impair judgment.	**(120) Objectivity** It is the state of mind which has regard for all considerations relevant to task in hand, but no other. Same as IFAC.	**(I. 4) Competence** Communicate fairly and objectively. Disclose fully all relevant information that could reasonably be expected to influence an intended user's understanding.	**Objectivity** Must be objective and impartial.
	(220) Conflicts of Interest	**(204) Independence** Interests and relationships may weaken independence or appear to do so. Identify and document threats to independence, evaluate the significance of those threats and apply safeguards to reduce the threats to an acceptable level, otherwise eliminate the activity, interest or relationship creating the threat or threats, or refuse to accept or continue the engagement. Disclose prohibited interests and relationships.	**(220) Conflicts of Interest** A PA in public practice should take reasonable steps to identify circumstances that could pose a conflict of interest since such circumstances may give rise to threats to compliance with the fundamental principles. See IFAC Section 100, of discussion in Ch. 6 of IFAC assessment approach. See also Section 310 below. Where a conflict of interest poses a threat to one or more of the fundamental principles, including objectivity, confidentiality or professional behaviour, that cannot be eliminated or reduced to an acceptable level through the application of safeguards, the PA in public practice should		**Independence** Must maintain independence of thought and action. *See integrity above.*

(Continued)

Appendix A, continued

INTERNATIONAL COMPARISON OF MAIN ASPECTS OF PROFESSIONAL CODES OF CONDUCT

US AICPA	INTERNATIONAL IFAC	CANADA ICAO	UK ICAEW	US IMA	CANADA SMAC
(56) Due care Observe the technical and ethical standards, strive to improve competence and quality of services, and act to the best of ability.	**(130) Professional Competence & Due Care** To maintain professional knowledge and skill at the level required to ensure that clients or employers receive competent professional service.	**(203) Professional Competence & (202) Due Care** Sustain professional competence by keeping informed of, and complying with, developments in professional standards in all functions in which the member practices or is relied upon because of the member's calling. Co-operate with ICAO to arrange or conduct inspections, reviews or investigation on behalf of the professional conduct committee.	conclude that it is not appropriate to accept a specific engagement or that resignation from one or more conflicting engagements is required unless the client(s) involved agree(s). **(130) Professional Competence & Due Care** Competent professional service requires the exercise of sound judgement in applying professional knowledge and skill. Professional competence may be divided into two separate phases: (a) Attainment of professional competence; and (b) Maintenance of professional competence.	**(I. 2) Competence** To constantly develop professional knowledge and skills level	**Competence** Act with competence through devotion to high ideals of personal honour and professional integrity.
(57) Scope and nature of services Members in public service should observe the Principles of the *Code of Professional Conduct* in determining the scope and nature of the services to be provided.	**(130) Technical standards** To act diligently in accordance with applicable technical and professional standards when providing professional services. Attainment of professional competence; and maintenance of professional competence.	**(101) Compliance with Bylaws and Regulations** Observe all bylaws and regulations.	**(1.200-4) Performance** Employ due skill, care, diligence and expedition, with proper regard for technical and professional standards.	**(I. 1-3) Competence** Observe laws, regulations and technical standards. Prepare complete and clear reports and recommendations after appropriate analyses of relevant and reliable information.	**Scope of Service** Undertake only such work as competence allows, and advise that another person be engaged when appropriate.
(See below)	**(140) Confidentiality** To refrain from: disclosing outside the firm or employing organization confidential information acquired as a result of professional and business relationships without proper and specific authority or unless there is a legal or professional right or duty to disclose; and using such confidential information.	**(208) Confidentiality** No improper use of information received in the course of business Maintain confidentiality unless lawful authority requires such information.	**(140) Confidentiality** The principle of confidentiality is not only to keep information confidential, but also to take all reasonable steps to preserve confidentiality. Further treatment is extensive.	**(II. 1-3) Confidentiality** No improper disclosure or use of information. Inform subordinates and monitor. Refrain from misusing info, or appearing to misuse it.	**Confidentiality** No disclosure without proper authority, unless there is legal or professional right or duty to disclose.

	Courtesy Members must show courtesy to all in performing their professional duties.			**Independence** Maintain at all times independence of thought and action.	
	(150) Professional Behavior To comply with relevant laws and regulations and avoid any action that may bring discredit to the profession.	**(150) Professional Behaviour** Same as IFACConduct with courtesy and consideration towards all in professional work.	*Code of Ethics* is a 3 page statement of undertakings, attached to short statement on Professional Misconduct.		**(200) Independence** A professional accountant in public practice* should not engage in any business, occupation or activity that impairs or might impair integrity, objectivity or the good reputation of the profession and as a result would be incompatible with the rendering of professional services.* Same conceptual approach for risk-based analysis of independence matters as IFAC. For details see Ch. 6.
ORGANIZATION & APPLICABILITY	**INTRODUCTION** **SECTION 90** Divided into Principles and Rules for all members.	**(201) Maintenance of good reputation** Duty to maintain good reputation of the profession and its ability to serve the public interest.	*Standards of Ethical Conduct* is a 3 page document covering: Introduction, Competence, Integrity, Objectivity. **Resolution of Ethical Conduct** a) Discuss with supervisor, b) Escalate, c) Discuss with IMA d) Discuss with personal attorney.		**(204) Independence** **(210) Conflicts of Interest** Be free of any influences, relationship or interests, which may impair professional judgment or have the appearance of doing so. Disclosure requirement. Before accepting any professional engagement, determine whether there is any restriction, influence, interest or relationship which, in respect of the proposed engagement, would cause a reasonable observer to conclude that there will be a conflict.
		PART B: PA in Public Practice **PART C: PA in Business** A PA in public practice should not engage in any business, occupation or activity that impairs or might impair integrity, objectivity or the good reputation of the profession and as a result would be incompatible with the rendering of professional services. A PA in business has a responsibility to further the legitimate aims of their employing organization. The Code considers circumstances in which conflicts may be created with the absolute duty to comply with the fundamental principles.	**(1)** Approach, Scope, Authority & similarity to IFAC. **(100-150)** Introduction, Fundamental Principles. Conceptual Approach to assessment of non-compliance threats. Ethical conflict resolution Section on each fundamental principle **(200-290)** PA in Public Practice **(300-350)** PA in Business **(400)** Practice of Insolvency Definitions Index		**Independence** **(210) Professional Appointment,** **(220) Conflicts of interest** **(290) Assurance engagements** Before accepting a new client relationship, a PA should consider whether acceptance would create any threats to compliance with the fundamental principles. The PA should take reasonable steps to identify circumstances that could pose a conflict of interest. In the case of an assurance engagement it is in the public interest and, therefore, required by this Code of Ethics, that members of assurance teams, firms and,
APPLICABILITY TO MEMBERS & TO FIRMS	See above	Foreword gives characteristics and principles that inform the *Rules* for all members.		*Most principles are covered above*	
RULES				*Wholly compatible with IFAC Code*	**SECTION 100** Introduces a conceptual framework for risk-based analysis of independence matters to be used to determine whether the member's relationship to an attest client poses an unacceptable risk to the member's independence—by compromising the member's professional judgement—and if so, whether and how that risk can be mitigated or eliminated. For details, see discussion of IFAC approach in Ch. 6.

(Continued)

Appendix A, continued

INTERNATIONAL COMPARISON OF MAIN ASPECTS OF PROFESSIONAL CODES OF CONDUCT

US AICPA	INTERNATIONAL IFAC	CANADA ICAO	UK ICAEW	US IMA	CANADA SMAC
(101) Independence Required for all members in public practice. Considered impaired by various transactions, relationships and interests, including; direct or material financial interests, performance of certain non-attest functions, common investment, loans, family relationships, or official office such as director, officer, trustee, employee, underwriter, promoter, and the threat of litigation, and all other that may be included under significant influence over financial reporting, operations, and accounting policies.	when applicable, network firms be independent of assurance clients.		Approach considers the impact of the proposed engagement on the integrity and independence of the audit, by reference to the APB's to identify threats to independence, evaluate the significance of those threats, and, if the threats are other than clearly insignificant, identify and apply safeguards to eliminate the threats or reduce them to an acceptable level. Independence required of mind and in appearance. **(220) Conflicts of interest (280) Objectivity (290) Assurance engagements**		
(102) Integrity & Objectivity No conflicts of interest are allowed. No misrepresentations, must report to avoid subordination of judgment.	(110, See above)	**(202) Integrity** Perform professional services with integrity and due care. (103) No association with any form of misrepresentation. (205) No association even when a disclaimer is given with a false or misleading statements. (206) Disclosure of material facts and material misstatements covers omissions, non-compliance with GAAP & GAAS.		**(III. 1-3) Integrity** Avoid conflict of interest, gift, pressures, family influences, etc, which can affect decision-making. No form of misrepresentation of facts, etc.	**Professional integrity.** Not to be party to any unlawful act of employer or misrepresentation, etc. Disclose all material facts and departures from GAAP.
See above	**(280) Objectivity** Consider whether there are threats to compliance with the fundamental principle of objectivity resulting from having interests in, or relationships with, a client or directors, officers or employees. A PA who	**(204) Objectivity** Opinion on financial statements must be free of any influence and interest or relationship which may impair judgment, or appear to do so.		**(I. 4) Competence** Recognize and communicate professional limitations or other constraints that would preclude responsible judgment or successful performance of an activity.	**Impartiality.** Beware of pressures and conflicts, etc.

provides an assurance service is required to be independent of the assurance client. Independence of mind and in appearance is necessary to enable the PA to express a conclusion, and be seen to express a conclusion, without bias, conflict of interest or undue influence of others.

		Compliance Must follow the code of ethics. Personally accountable for their own ethical behavior.
SECTION 200 **(202) Compliance with standards** Necessary if service involves auditing, review, compilation, management consulting, tax or other professional services.	**(101) Compliance with Bylaws and Regulations** Observe all bylaws and regulations. (206) Compliance with professional standards. (130, See above)	**(I. 2) Competence** To perform in accordance with relevant laws, regulations and standards.
(201) General standards, Professional competence Due professional care Planning and supervision Sufficient relevant data	**(203) Professional Competence and** **(202) Due Care** Maintain professional competence and due care. (130, See above)	**(I. 1) Competence** To maintain appropriate level of competence by ongoing development of knowledge and skills. See above
(203) Accounting Principles No departure from generally accepted accounting principles, unless a misleading statement would result; then must state why a departure is warranted and its effects.	**(206) Accounting principles** Must comply with professional standards and GAAP. Those approving financial statements (i.e. Board of Directors) should carry out that responsibility with the care and diligence of a competent Chartered Accountant, enhanced by the skills and knowledge derived from the member's own career. (130.3) The maintenance of professional competence requires a continuing awareness and an understanding of relevant technical professional and business developments. Continuing professional development develops and maintains the capabilities that enable a professional accountant to perform competently within the professional environments. (140, See Above)	
SECTION 300 **Responsibility to Clients** **(301) Confidentiality** No disclosure without consent, except for court or CPA proceedings. Information from client not to be used for personal gain.	**(208) Confidentiality** No improper use of information received in course of professional duties. To maintain confidentiality of information unless a lawful authority requires such information. Responsible for agents.	**(II. 1-2) Confidentiality** No disclosure of information except when legally obligated Inform all relevant parties regarding appropriate use of confidential information. **Confidentially** No improper disclosure of information received in course of duties.

(Continued)

Appendix A, continued

INTERNATIONAL COMPARISON OF MAIN ASPECTS OF PROFESSIONAL CODES OF CONDUCT

US AICPA	INTERNATIONAL IFAC	CANADA ICAO	UK ICAEW	US IMA	CANADA SMAC
(302) Contingent fees Not allowed for audit, review, compilation, examination of prospective financial information or tax return or refund claim etc. – some exceptions	**(240) Fees and other types of remuneration** Contingent fees are widely used for certain types of non-assurance engagements. They may, however, give rise to threats to compliance with the fundamental principles in certain circumstances. They may give rise to a self-interest threat to objectivity. The significance of such threats should be evaluated and safeguards should be considered to eliminate or reduce them to an acceptable level.	**(215) Contingent Fees** Not allowed. No free services unless for charitable or benevolent organization. No unauthorized benefits allowed from client or employer.			
		SECTION 300: Relations with Members, Firms and Non-Members (302) Acceptance of appointment where there is an incumbent auditor. (305) Communication of special assignments to incumbent. (306) Responsibilities on special assignments.			**Relations with Members** Exhibit fairness and loyalty, courtesy and good faith. No review of other members except with the knowledge of the member, unless terminated.
SECTION 400 **(401) Responsibilities to colleagues** Reserved as at June 2007.					
SECTION 500 **Other Responsibilities** **(501) Discreditable acts** Not permitted, any form of discrimination, harassment, deviation from government standards, negligence		**(201) Maintenance of the good reputation of the profession** (213) No unlawful activities, association of person, name or services.		**(III. 3) Integrity** Abstain from engaging in or supporting any activity that might discredit the profession.	**Breach of principles discreditable act.** No discreditable acts Report breaches of *Code* to the proper tribunals of the Society.
(502) Advertising and solicitation Cannot be false, misleading or deceptive, or involve coercion, over-reaching or harassment.	**(250) Marketing professional services** Not bring the profession into disrepute when marketing professional services. Should be honest and truthful and should not:	**(217) Advertising and promotion** None that are false, misleading or in bad taste. Endorsement only under limited conditions. No solicitation. Do not bring disrepute to profession.			

- Make exaggerated claims for services offers, qualifications possessed or experience gained; or
- Make disparaging references to unsubstantiated comparisons to the work of another.

(503) Commission and referral fees

Not allowed for audit, review, compilation, examination of prospective financial information, otherwise requires disclosure. Cannot be paid or accepted without disclosure to client.

(505) Names and Forms of organization

Practice public accounting only in a form (see ET Appendix B) of organization permitted by state law or regulation whose characteristics conform to resolutions of Council.
Permits non-CPA minority ownership, provided CPA is ultimately responsible, financially and otherwise, for attest work performed to protect the public interest; non-CPA must abide by CPA code and requirements, and not hold themselves out as CPA's.

(240) Referrals

A PA in public practice should not pay or receive a referral fee or commission, unless the professional accountant in public practice has established safeguards to eliminate the threats or reduce them to an acceptable level. Disclose to client.

(216) Referral fees or Compensation

Other than in relation to the sale and purchase by a member or firm of an accounting practice, accountants shall not directly or indirectly pay to any person who is not an employee of the member or firm or who is not a public accountant a commission or other compensation to obtain a client.

SECTION 400: Organization and conduct of a professional practice

(401) Practice Names

Not allowed.
(404) Work for public interest must be under the charge of licensed public accountant.
(406) Sole and firm's names, Surnames in title limited to active or deceased partners.
(408) Practice of public accounting in corporate form limited in many provinces.

(100.16) Resolution of ethical conflicts

Consider, either individually or together with others, as part of the resolution process:

Resolution of ethical Matters

Resolve with superiors and follow the ethical guidelines of the Institute.
Resign if matter not resolved.

Commission or Non-standard Remuneration

None allowed without disclosure to employer/client and consent there from.

Resolution of Conflict

To follow policy of the organization and discuss such issues with superiors, obtain advice from recently IMA Ethics.

(Continued)

INTERNATIONAL COMPARISON OF MAIN ASPECTS OF PROFESSIONAL CODES OF CONDUCT

US AICPA	INTERNATIONAL IFAC	CANADA ICAO	UK ICAEW	US IMA	CANADA SMAC
	(a) Relevant facts;			Counseling Service available as a hotline, or if not resolved finally resign and present a memorandum to an appropriate representative of the organization. Depending on the nature of the ethical conflict, consideration should also be given to the notification of other parties.	
	(b) Ethical issues involved;				
	(c) Fundamental principles related to the matter in question;				
	(d) Established internal procedures; and				
	(e) Alternative courses of action.				
	Determine the appropriate course of action consistent with the fundamental principles. Should also weigh the consequences of each possible course of action.				
	(290.178) Tax Practice				
	When a firm, or a network firm, performs a valuation service for a financial statement audit client for the purposes of making a filing or return to a tax authority, computing an amount of tax due by the client, or for the purpose of tax planning, this would not create a significant threat to independence because such valuations are generally subject to external review, for example by a tax authority.				**Responsibility to others** To provide opportunities for professional development and adequate compensation to accountants employed.

(102) Conflict of interest May occur if a member performs a professional service for a client or employer and the member or his or her firm has financial or family relationship, in the member's professional judgment, be viewed by the client, employer, or other appropriate parties as impairing the member's objectivity.	**(320) Presentation of information** Maintain and present information in a manner that: (a) Describes clearly the true nature of business transactions, assets or liabilities; (b) Classifies and records information in a timely and proper manner; and (c) Represents the facts accurately and completely in all material respects.	**Presentation of Information** Members must report all material misstatements or departures from generally accepted accounting principles.
	(205) Presentation of Information No false reports or misrepresentation.	**(I. 3) Competence** Must disclose fully all relevant information, fairly and objectively.
(310) Potential Conflicts (In Business) Owe duty to employer and profession. Normally must support organization's legitimate objectives and ethics. Resolve any differences with superiors and professionals within the organization. Resign if no recourse left.	**(210) Conflict of interest** Must inform client of conflicting business connections, affiliations or interests, and obtain consent. Responsible for detection before accepting engagement.	**Conflict of interests** Inform the client or employers.
	(310) Potential Conflicts (In Business) Similar to IFAC. If the threat to non-compliance with fundamental principles is significant, and cannot be reduced or eliminated, and conflict resolution is unsuccessful, the PA should consider informing appropriate authorities in line with the guidance in Section 140. The professional accountant in business* may also wish to seek legal advice or resign.	**(III. 1) Integrity** Members must be aware of and avoid conflict of interest, and not be affected.
	(406) Responsible for the failure of non-members, Responsible for all associated with the practice to abide by the rules of conduct.	**(II. 2) Confidentiality** Responsible for subordinates work to maintain confidentiality of information etc.
	(211) Duty to report apparent breaches Report on conduct, competencies, regulations or integrity.	See above
See above	**1.17 Duty to report misconduct** Seeking advice from the Ethics Advisory Services does not discharge a PA's duty to report misconduct,	**Duty to report violations** Can not condone violations of ethical code. **Duty to report** Any deviation from code of ethics.

(Continued)

Appendix A, continued

INTERNATIONAL COMPARISON OF MAIN ASPECTS OF PROFESSIONAL CODES OF CONDUCT

US AICPA	INTERNATIONAL IFAC	CANADA ICAO	UK ICAEW	US IMA	CANADA SMAC
	(270) Custody of Clients Assets A professional accountant in public practice should not assume custody of client monies or other assets unless permitted to do so by law and, if so, in compliance with any additional legal duties imposed on a professional accountant in public practice holding such assets.	**(212.1) Handling of trust funds** Do so in accordance with the terms of the engagement, including the terms of any applicable trust, and the law relating thereto and maintain such records as are necessary to account properly for the money or other property; unless otherwise provided for by the terms of the trust, money held in trust shall be kept in a separate trust bank account or accounts. **(218) Retention of documents and working papers** For a reasonable period of time. **SECTION 500: Rules applicable only to Firms** (501-502) Maintenance of policies and procedures. (503) Association with firms.	including their own misconduct (see Section 2.7, 'The duty to report misconduct' in the *Members' Handbook*.		

Note: The Ethical Codes of Conduct for Professional Accountants in Australia, New Zealand and Japan were also reviewed. Their findings have been omitted from this table for lack of space. However, the main issues and points were:

- The New Zealand Institute of Chartered Accountants (www.nzica.com) released a Code of Ethics in 2003 and revised in Oct. 2006 that is designed to reflect the IFAC Code Principles. It is available at (http://www.nzica.com/AM/Template.cfm?Section=Search&section=Code_of_Ethics&template=/CM/ContentDisplay.cfm&ContentFileID=1465) Appendix 3 of the PDF version, contains a comparison with the IFAC and Australian Codes.

- The Australian Institute of Chartered Accountants (www.icaa.org.au) code matches the guidelines of IFAC Code. It is available in the ICAA Members Handbook on the ICCA website.

- The Japan Institute of Certified Public Accountants Code document dated 1987 contained general principles, and a brief list of responsibilities is available of the Institute's website at http://www.hp.jicpa.or.jp/english/e-code.html

- The Chinese Institute of Certified public Accountants (CICPA) became a member of IFAC in October 2006. The CICPA Law of the People's Republic of China on Certified public Accountants is viewable at http://www.cicpa.org.cn/english/law_regulations/2008804/t20080428_4184.htm

APPENDIX B

Trends in the Legal Liability of Accountants and Auditors and Legal Defenses Available

The traditional sources of legal liability for accountants and auditors have arisen under common law related to breach of contract or to torts for negligence. Recently, however, due to Enron and other financial fiascoes, there is a growing prospect of liability from statutory law particularly in the United States and probably in Canada. New constructs, such as proportionate liability and the Limited Liability Partnership (LLP), have provided some relief, but the advent of class actions and higher public expectations for auditors, such as for the finding of fraud and for auditor independence, have focused auditors on how to minimize their liability risk as well as the risk to their reputation and future viability.

The fact that there have been no law cases of significant principle for many years is probably because most—and a growing proportion—lawsuits and threatened lawsuits are settled before time is wasted in court, huge trial lawyers fees are incurred, and significant damage is done to professional reputation and the future flow of fees. The KPMG settlement of US $456 million in August 2005, where the firm was said to have "scramble[d] to avoid criminal prosecution,"[1] is a dramatic example. Based on comments from lawyers close to this area of law, there has been an increase in threats of lawsuits, demand letters, and lawsuits, even though relatively few lawsuits have proceeded to court or have become public knowledge. Avoidance of legal entanglements, and settlement when avoidance is impossible, have become the primary means of dealing with legal liability. Both avoidance and settlement strategies, however, rely heavily on an understanding of accountants' legal liability.

The burden of liability has shifted over time. As discussed later, early common law restricted liability to situations where there was privity of (a direct) contract between auditor and an investor/plaintiff in order to avoid "liability in an indeterminate amount for an indeterminate time to an indeterminate class" (*Ultramares 1931*). Subsequently, this bound was relaxed to allow liability to plaintiffs that could have reasonably been foreseen by the auditor (*Hedley Bryne & Co.* 1964; *Haig v. Bamford* 1976). However, more recent cases have reduced the exposure to liability by narrowing the "foreseeability" test (*Caparo Industries plc* 1991; *Hercules Management Ltd. et al. v. Ernst & Young et al.* 1997). The last case, in a bizarre twist by the Supreme Court of Canada, calls for a duty of care by auditors *only* "when they [audited financial reports] are used 'as a guide for the shareholders, as a group, in supervising or overseeing management.'"[2] On the other hand, a month earlier a lower Canadian court, the British Columbia Court of Appeal, held in *Stephen Kripps et al. v. Touche Ross* (now Deloitte & Touche) that the accounting profession could not hide behind "'according to GAAP' if the auditors know ... that the financial statements are misleading."[3] The words "present fairly" are particularly important in the auditor's opinion in determining auditor liability.

Auditors have been liable for malfeasance under statutory law for some time. For example, involvement with misleading statements in a prospectus has, for some time, been actionable under acts in both the United States and Canada. However, since 1997, the will of politicians and the impact of statutory law, regulators, and their agents have become greater. While dealing with Enron, the U.S. Senate has articulated that auditors are responsible to investors (see page 367) and has caused the SEC to create regulations and activate statutes that make this clear. The Public Company Accounting Oversight Board (PCAOB) is one result that has begun to

---

1. "KPMG scrambles to avoid criminal prosecution," *Financial Post*, June 17, 2005, FP4; Peter Morton, "KPMG pays us $456 million to settle fraud allegations," *Financial Post*, August 30, 2005, FP1; see also the earlier discussion on page 383 of this chapter. KPMG was reported to have earned at least US $130 million for selling the tax shelters.

2. Philip Mathias, "Auditors Not Legally Liable to Investors, Top Court Rules," *Financial Post*, May 24, 1997, p. 3.

3. Editorial, "Accounting Profession Has a Duty to Shareholders," *Financial Post*, May 20, 1997.

impact on auditor liability. In Canada, the Ontario Securities Commission has been given similar powers to oversee auditors, and a Canadian Public Accountability Board (CPAB) has been created.[4] A similar board also exists in Australia. Consequently, there is a strong likelihood that future developments in auditor and accountant liability will arise from statutory and regulatory authority rather than common law.

The burden of legal liability has also been affected by another development that sprang from the cry for reform of tort liability by the Big 6 firms on August 6, 1992 reproduced as a reading beginning on page 431. That cry for reform documents the debilitating state of affairs that prevailed in 1992. It suggests that the joint and several liability of audit firm partners should be replaced by a proportionate responsibility standard. This, it was argued, would remedy the unfairness of plaintiffs going after defendants with deep pockets who had very little, if any, direct culpability but had to pay and then look for recompense from others who were bankrupt. In fact, proportionate liability did come into being, and the construct of the Limited Liability Partnership (LLP) originated in 1994 in New York. In an LLP framework, "innocent" partners can lose their business investment but not their personal assets in the event of their firm losing a court case.[5]

The development of proportionate liability and the LLP is counterbalanced to some extent by the advent of class action lawsuits that were stimulated in part by plaintiff's lawyers, who were willing to take the case on a contingency fee basis. That is, for 30 percent of the final settlement, they will forgo other fees. Some even chase plaintiffs to get their business because the possibility of settlement or winning a large judgment is so high. The reading by the Big 6 accounting firms provides interesting information on the nature and extent of class action liability.

Over the decades, changes in legal liability have had a profound effect on the development of the accounting profession's governance framework and of generally accepted accounting and auditing principles and practices, as outlined in the following review.

Trends in Legal Liability of Accountants and Auditors

Contract experts contend that stakeholders (including employees, suppliers, customers, creditors) and their interests are protected adequately through explicit and implicit contracts with a business enterprise. However, there has been a progressive trend over the last 30 years, reflected through changes in the law, that has been predicated on the notion that contracts may be insufficient to protect the interests of certain stakeholders who rely upon the conduct of and statements made by governors of a corporation and the professionals associated with it. Public and stakeholder knowledge, expectations, and sophistication have been heightened, and the law has changed to reflect a third-party duty (foreseeable) owed beyond contract by virtue of the position held within the company and the standard of conduct expected of a professional, such as an auditor or an accountant. A precedent-setting Canadian case, *R. v. Bata Industries Ltd.* (1992), 70 C.C.C. (3d) 394 (Ont. Prov. Ct.), established that the courts will in fact pierce the corporate veil to determine the controlling mind and, more particularly, not merely what someone in a position of authority, such as a director, did or knew, but what that director could or ought to have done or known under the circumstances.

This broadening trend from that of contractual privity to a duty owed to foreseeable stakeholders is reflected in the common law for auditors and accountants. Both auditors and accountants are now being sued by stakeholders without privity of contract, such as investors, shareholders, suppliers, and creditors. This is sometimes referred to as a "foreseeability" or "fairness" principle and is actually one part of a test of negligence that

---

4. Peter Breiger, "New auditing watchdog recruits its first board", *Financial Post*, February 27, 2003, FP11.

5. See earlier discussion at page 384.

courts will use in determining whether an accountant or auditor's conduct has been negligent.

In very general legal terms, in order to establish auditor or accountant negligence, a duty of care must be owed by virtue of the relationship that is recognized in law; that standard of care must have been breached; that breadth of duty owed must have caused in a proximate and not remote way the actual damage to a third party (plaintiff), who relied to its detriment on the audit statements; the resultant damage must have been reasonably foreseeable (hence the "foreseeability" test); and, lastly, the conduct of the plaintiff must not be such so as to bar recovery, that is, the plaintiff must not have voluntarily assumed the risk, must not have contributed to the negligence, and must be able to show that he or she attempted to mitigate damages.

A significant increase in auditor and accountant litigation has occurred as a result of this trend in the law that broadens standing among third-party stakeholders, allowing them to sue auditors for negligence if the prior requirements are met. So now, in addition to the auditor or accountant being bound by contract and fiduciary duty of trust to the client, he or she must, as a result of the previously mentioned foreseeability or fairness principle, assume additional duties to third-party stakeholders.

The trend along the continuum between contractual privity on one end and stakeholder fairness and foreseeability on the other can be demonstrated by a review of how the common law has developed in Canada, England, and the United States. on this issue. Both the high courts in Canada and England have spoken on the foreseeability test of auditor liability, suggesting that the U.S. Supreme Court may soon speak on this point as well.

The leading Canadian case on auditor liability to foreseeable parties is *Haig v. Bamford et al.* (1976) 72 D.L.R. (3d) 68. The Supreme Court of Canada held in *Haig* that where an accountant has negligently prepared financial statements and a third party relies on them to his or her detriment, a duty of care in an action for negligent misstatement will arise in the following circumstances:

(i) The accountant knows that it will be shown to a member of a limited class of which the plaintiff is a member and which the accountant actually knows will use and rely on the statements.

(ii) The statements have been prepared primarily for guidance of that limited class and in respect of a specific class of transactions for the very purpose that the plaintiff did in fact rely on them.

(iii) The fact that the accountant did not know the identity of the plaintiff is not material as long as the accountant was aware that the person for whose immediate benefit they were prepared intended to supply the statements to members of the very limited class of which the plaintiff is a member.

In short, *Haig v. Bamford* stands for the proposition that an accountant will be found liable to a third party where the accountant had actual knowledge of the limited class of which the third party is a member, and that third party will use and rely on the statement.

In England, in a landmark case establishing the modern role governing liability for professional advisers whose negligence gives rise to economic loss, the House of Lords in *Hedley Byrne & Co. Ltd. v. Heller & Partners Ltd.* [1964] A.C. 562 (H.L.) held that a professional adviser has an implied duty of care in making an oral or written statement to another person who he or she knows, or should know, will rely on it when making a decision with economic consequences.

The "foreseeability" test in the previously mentioned Canadian *Haig* case was narrowed recently in *Caparo Industries plc. v. Pickman et al.* [1991] 2 W.L.R. 358 (H.L.). Although *Caparo* is an English case from the House of Lords, it is of precedential value to Canadian jurisprudence and has been followed in both Ontario and British Columbia courts. *Caparo* narrows the scope of the foreseeability doctrine by focusing on whether the auditor knew the "purpose" for which the third party was to use the financial statements. The *Caparo* foreseeability test is as follows: A duty is said to arise only where the auditor knew the *purpose* for which the financial statements were to be used by the person relying on them and knew that the statements would be communicated to that person either as an individual or as a member of an identifiable class, specifically in connection with a particular transaction or a transaction of a particular kind. The duty extends only to the particular transaction for which the accountants knew their accounts were to be used. Moreover, the advisee must reasonably suppose that he or she was entitled to rely on the advice or information communicated for the very purpose for which it was required. No duty arises in respect of statements put into general circulation and relied on by strangers to the maker of the statement for a purpose that the maker had no reason to anticipate, such as nonshareholders contemplating investment in a company.

Therefore, although both Canada and England have moved from contractual privity to a stakeholder foreseeability test of auditor liability, the British decision *Caparo* restricts *Haig*'s primary emphasis on foreseeability to that of knowledge of purpose. In other words, an auditor may be liable to a foreseeable third party under *Haig,* where the accountant had actual knowledge of the third party and that party's intention to rely on the statement. An auditor may be liable to a foreseeable third party under *Caparo,* where the accountant knew the purpose for which the third party was to rely upon and use the financial statements. The point is that the trend in auditor and accountant liability toward being liable to foreseeable third parties has been established in both Canada and England and has resulted in increased litigation for auditing firms.

Unlike Canada and England, the U.S. Supreme Court has never ruled on the duty owed to foreseeable third parties. In fact, state supreme courts are split between considering contractual privity (often termed *intended beneficiary)* versus foreseeable third parties as the required grounds for suit. Two cases are noteworthy here. *Ultramares Corporation v. Touche* 174 N.E. 441 (1931) stands for the proposition that experts who prepare statements or reports for a third party who is not a client will not be held accountable in negligence for any misstatement or misreport to that third party (nonclient). In other words, an immediate legal relationship (contractual privity) must exist between the parties in order for one to be liable in negligence to another.

The trend away from this contractual privity requirement in *Ultramares* to that of foreseeability was apparent in *Credit Alliance Corp. v. Arthur Andersen & Co.* 493 N.Y.S. 2d 435 (1985). In this case, the court reaffirmed yet relaxed the *Ultramares* principle. The court said that a legal relationship approaching that of a contract must exist for an auditor to be held liable in negligence to a nonclient. The court, however, stated that an auditor will meet the "contractual privity" test, where the auditor was aware that his or her statement would be used for a particular purpose and that a known party was intended to rely on it. In addition, some evidence must exist demonstrating a relationship between the auditor and the nonclient third party and demonstrating that the auditor knew that the nonclient third party was relying on the auditor's statement.

Despite the fact that the trend from contractual privity to foreseeable third parties is still not being applied uniformly in the United States, the forseeability doctrine for auditors and accountants is now good law in both Canada and England, as the high courts have spoken. The result of this trend has been "joint and several" liability exposure by auditors and accountants to third-party plaintiffs. Joint and several liability means that all codefendants, including the auditors, must account for all damages. If the client is insolvent, the audit firm's and its partners' assets are exposed, regardless of the degree of fault. This is often the case, as lawyers are trained to sue "deep pockets"—those entities believed to be most able to bear the burden of the loss, such as an accounting firm.

Legal Defenses Available

This litigation exposure has had a chilling effect on the auditing profession and has resulted in a reluctance to pursue risky engagements, such as environmental or social audits; exorbitant legal bills; increases in professional liability insurance premiums; increasing opportunity costs of the litigation; and adverse publicity for the profession as a whole.

Nevertheless, five defensive and proactive measures can be offered to auditors and accountants to limit their liability to foreseeable third-party litigants. These defenses include:

1. Due diligence and due care
2. Contributory negligence
3. Engagement letter provisions
4. Documentation and record keeping
5. Legal counsel

A cursory overview of each of these will be provided.

1. Due Diligence and Due Care

The defense of due diligence exists both in common law and statute. Due diligence entails a thorough and proper examination (reasonable investigation) of all relevant financial records prior to the rendering of an opinion, advice, or conclusion. Due care includes the application of auditing and financial analysis models and techniques to the existing subject matter. Due diligence is the principal means by which an accountant or auditor can defend against a negligence claim by a client for an alleged breach of a duty of care and skill.

In common law, there is no definitive law defining the standard of due diligence for an auditor or accountant. Each case is fact dependent. However, due diligence for an auditor is generally understood as requiring an auditor to make a complete examination of the matter to be audited before issuing any report or giving any advice.

To illustrate the judicial reasoning in this due diligence defense and the degree to which the courts will intervene in applying the law to the facts, the recent precedent-setting Canadian case *R. v. Bata Industries* (1992), 70 C.C.C. (3d) 394 (Ont. Prov. Ct.) hinged on the due diligence defense. Although the conduct involved applied to a company director, the judicial reasoning and degree of intervention illustrates profoundly the leaning of the courts in evaluating the due diligence defense; this reasoning could and likely would be as applicable in evaluating whether an auditor acted with due diligence. At page 427, Justice

Ormstrom addressed effectively the issue of due diligence:

I ask myself the following questions in assessing the defense of due diligence:

(a) Did the board of directors establish a pollution prevention "system" as indicated in *Regina v. Sault Ste. Marie*, i.e., Was there supervision or inspection? Was there improvement in business methods? Did he exhort those he controlled or influenced?

(b) Did each director ensure that the corporate officers have been instructed to set up a system sufficient within the terms and practices of its industry of ensuring compliance with environmental laws, to ensure that the officers report back periodically to the board on the operation of the system, and to ensure that the officers are instructed to report any substantial non-compliance to the board in a timely manner?

I reminded myself that:

(c) The directors are responsible for reviewing the environmental compliance reports provided by the officers of the corporation but are justified in placing reasonable reliance on reports provided to them by corporate officers, consultants, counsel or other informed parties.

(d) The directors should substantiate that the officers are promptly addressing environmental concerns brought to their attention by government agencies or other concerned parties including shareholders.

(e) The directors should be aware of the standards of their industry and other industries which deal with similar environmental pollutants or risks.

(f) The directors should immediately and personally react when they have noticed the system has failed.
Within this general profile and dependent upon the nature and structure of the corporate activity, one would hope to find remedial

and contingency plans for spills, a system of ongoing environmental audit, training programs, sufficient authority to act and other indices of a proactive environmental policy.

Applying the preceding judicial reasoning in the due diligence defense, auditors as well may limit their liability by adopting proactive and defensive measures to support a due diligence defense. These measures may include, but are not limited to:

- Educating and communicating with personnel as to the technical, regulatory, legal, and ethical standards required by the profession and the firm, and having reporting procedures implemented to ensure that this occurs

- Ensuring that all personnel are properly trained and supervised, and having reporting and information systems to facilitate prompt identification and bottom-up flow of difficulties, problems

- Maintaining confidentiality and independence, and avoiding conflicts of interest and judgment; conforming with one's fiduciary duty of trust to the client

- Understanding industry standards and familiarity with the client's business and reputation for integrity

- Obtaining the necessary engagement letter provisions

- Proper documenting and record keeping

- Supporting senior managing partners and other partners, and rewarding and compensating the previously noted behaviors

2. Contributory Negligence

Contributory negligence exists as a defense for the auditor in a negligence claim for a breach of a duty of care and skill. The auditor, in using this defense, submits to the court that the client (often company management) contributed to the breach through an act (or acts) of commission or omission. In other words, the client did or failed to do something, and this contributed to the loss. The contributory negligence defense by auditors exists notwithstanding the policy argument against it; namely, that the auditor should not be permitted to use this defense to reduce liability, for doing so would defeat the purpose of having an auditor act as a check on the conduct of managers of a company through the analysis of financial documents.

3. Engagement Letter Provisions

An engagement letter is an agreement between the auditor and the client identifying whether the audit and/or other services will be provided, due dates, and fees. To mitigate liability and potential litigation, auditors should attempt to include provisions in the engagement letter that:

- Narrow the scope of services to be provided in specific, rather than broad, general, terms. This limits liability to failure to perform the terms of the engagement letter.

- Indemnify the auditor for third-party claims arising from services rendered by the auditor to the client in accordance with the engagement letter.

- Enable the auditor to modify or withdraw the opinion or conclusion should circumstances warrant, such as, for example, the subsequent discovery of a material misstatement.

- Permit liability claims against the auditor to be released completely should litigation claims against the indemnitor be settled.

- Enable the auditor to participate fully in the preparation of a public offering document insofar as his or her opinion or conclusion is used or summarized in the final document. This participation would include the right to limit and qualify the scope of the opinion or conclusion prior to it reaching public investors via the public disclosure documents and/or the disclaiming of any fiduciary or agency relationship with shareholders should a public offering not be contemplated but the auditor's opinion or conclusion still used.

4. Documentation and Record Keeping

Due diligence, due care, and a reasonable investigation can be more effectively demonstrated to a court by an auditor during litigation when he or she has a documentary or computerized record of all working papers, tests, and procedures performed that preceded the opinion or report and all written communications with the client. Also, the auditor should not agree in advance to release original copies of confidential client information to third parties without first seeking legal counsel, for retaining copies of the original document for record-keeping purposes could aid in litigation defense and regulatory purposes.

5. Legal Counsel

Auditors and accountants should not wait to be sued but should take a proactive approach and seek legal counsel concerning their legal rights, exposure, and obligations. Competent and experienced legal counsel educates, communicates, limits exposure to client and third-party liability and costly litigation, and also aids in establishing due diligence evidence should litigation commence. More particularly, auditors should seek legal counsel in preparing and reviewing engagement and representation letters, developing the due diligence reviews, and reviewing the legal implications impacting and flowing from preliminary and final versions of the auditor's opinions and conclusions.

A Review of Cases

Ultramares Corporation v. Touche *174 N.E. 441 (1931)*

In *Ultramares,* the creditors of the insolvent Ultramares Corporation sued the accountants for negligence in relying on the financial statements to their detriment. In particular, the accounts receivable had been inflated by $700,000. The New York Court of Appeals held that the accountants had been negligent but were not liable to the creditors because of privity of contract. Only the contracting parties could sue the accountant(s) for negligent services. At page 444, Justice Cardozo held that "to hold the maker of the statement to be

under a duty of care in respect of the accuracy of statement ... is to find liability in an indeterminate amount for an indeterminate time to an indeterminate class." This case stands for the proposition that contractual privity is required in order to sue an accountant or auditor in negligence for any misstatement or misreport.

Hedley Byrne & Co. Ltd. v. Heller & Partners Ltd. *[1964] A.C. 562 (H.L.)*

In *Hedley Byrne,* the National Provincial Bank telephoned and wrote to Heller & Partners on behalf of Hedley Byrne to find out whether Easipower Ltd., a customer of Heller & Partners, was of sound financial position and thus a company with which Hedley Byrne would want to do business. Heller & Partners, disclaiming all responsibility to both inquiries by National Provincial Bank, said Easipower Ltd. was of sound financial shape. Hedley Byrne, in reliance on those statements, entered into a contract with Easipower Ltd., who subsequently thereafter sought liquidation.

The House of Lords, in deciding that Heller & Partners Ltd. would have been liable except for the disclaimer, established the modern role governing liability for professional advisers whose negligence gives rise to economic loss. A professional adviser has an implied duty of care in making an oral or written statement to another person whom he or she knows or should know will rely on it in making a decision with economic consequences.

Haig v. Bamford et al. *(1976) 72 D.L.R. (3d) 68*

In *Haig,* the Saskatchewan Development Corporation agreed to advance a $20,000 loan to a financially troubled company in part based on the conditional production of satisfactory audited financial statements. The company engaged Bamford's accountants to prepare the statements. The accountants knew that the statements would be used by Saskatchewan Development Corporation. Relying on the accountants' information, Saskatchewan Development Corporation advanced $20,000 to the company. Later investigation disclosed that a

$28,000 prepayment on two uncompleted contracts had been treated as if the contracts had been completed, thereby showing a profit instead of a loss, and the accountants failed to spot the error. The court held that where an accountant has negligently prepared financial statements and a third party relies on them to his or her detriment, a duty of care in an action for negligent misstatement will arise in the following circumstances: the accountant knows that it will be shown to a member of a limited class of which the plaintiff is a member and which the accountant actually knows will use and rely on the statements; the statements have been prepared primarily for guidance of that limited class and in respect of a specific class of transactions for the very purpose for which the plaintiff did in fact rely on them; the fact that the accountant did not know the identity of the plaintiff is not material as long as the accountant was aware that the person for whose immediate benefit they were prepared intended to supply the statements to members of the very limited class of which the plaintiff is a member.

Credit Alliance Corp. v. Arthur Andersen & Co. *493 N.Y.S. 2d 435 (1985)*

The contractual privity requirement in *Ultramares* was broadened somewhat by the same New York Court of Appeals, but has not approached in scope the stakeholder foreseeability test of *Haig* in Canada and *Caparo* in England. The court held that in order for a relationship to approach that of privity, the auditor must have been aware that the financial statement would be used for a particular purpose by a party known to the auditor, and the auditor must have had subjective knowledge that the third party had intended to rely upon the statement. Also, evidence, such as the auditor's conduct, must be presented demonstrating these requirements, and the third-party plaintiff carries this burden.

Caparo Industries plc. v. Pickman et al. *[1991] 2 W.L.R. 358 (H.L.)*

Caparo, in its takeover of Fidelity plc, had Touche Ross & Co. audit the financial statements of Fidelity. Caparo later alleged that its purchase of shares and subsequent takeover were made in reliance on the accounts, which they claimed were misleading and inaccurate in that they showed a pretax profit of £1.3 million instead of a loss of £400,000. Caparo sued Touche Ross for negligence, maintaining that Touche Ross owed them a duty of care as shareholders and potential investors with respect to the audit and certification of the accounts.

The House of Lords decided that Touche Ross owed no duty of care to Caparo, either as a potential investor before it was registered or as a shareholder thereafter for the following reasons:

> "While there is no general principle that will determine the existence and scope of a duty of care in all cases, in order for a duty of care to arise, there must be: the harm said to result from the breach of duty must have been reasonably foreseeable; there must be a relationship of sufficient "proximity" between the party said to owe the duty and the party to whom it is said to be owed; and the situation must be one in which, on policy grounds, the court considers it fair, just and reasonable that the law should impose a duty of a given scope on the part of one party for the benefit of the other."

In the case of negligent misstatements made by such a professional adviser as an accountant, a relationship of proximity sufficient to give rise to a duty of care typically arises where the advice is required for a purpose that is made known to the adviser when the advice was given; the adviser knows that his or her advice will be communicated to the advisee, either specifically or as a member of an ascertainable class, in order that it should be used by the advisee for that purpose; it is known that advice so communicated is likely to be acted upon for that purpose without independent inquiry; and it is so acted upon by the advisee to his or her detriment.

The duty extends only to the particular transaction for which the accountants knew their accounts were to be used. Moreover, the advisee must reasonably suppose that he or she was entitled to rely on the advice or information communicated for the very purpose for which it was required. No duty arises with respect to statements put into general circulation and relied on by strangers to the maker of the statement for a purpose which the maker had no reason to anticipate, such as a nonshareholder contemplating investment in a company.

Hercules Management Ltd. et al v. Ernst & Young. (1997) *146 D.L.R. (4th) 577 (S.C.C.)*

This judgment in this case—that Canadian auditors have owed essentially no duty of care to third parties including shareholders in cases of negligent misrepresentation—is very controversial. It flies in the face of common sense, and is contrary to statements made in Senate documents in respect of auditors for Enron and other U.S. companies that have experienced financial difficulties. Accordingly, informed observers expect that the impact of this decision will be greatly diminished over time.

The court took the view that "there may be a duty of care between auditors and shareholders—but [said this was] negated by "policy considerations". Paramount in these considerations [were] the "socially undesirable consequences" the court felt would result from exposing accounting firms to indeterminate economic liability to an indeterminate number of shareholders for an indeterminate length of time."[6] In other words, the court decided that Canadian audit would have difficulty bearing the liability of their duty of care without some limit to that liability.

"The court also found that the normal purpose for which auditors reports are used is to guide shareholders in supervising management—not for investment reasons."[7] This finding essentially limits the impact of shareholder class actions in Canada. Over time, now that the new Limited Liability Partnership (LLP) framework has been established, it is expected that new court cases will modify the Hercules findings, or that securities laws will be revised to reflect what is happening in the rest of the world.[8]

Source: Based in part on an earlier version by L. J. Brooks and R. LeBlanc.

---

6. Sandra Rubin, "Hercules shields auditors, *Financial Post*, July 17, 2002, FP10.

7. Ibid., Hercules shields . . .

8. Ibid.

Significant Ethics Issues Facing Business & the Accounting Profession

Introduction

Part 4 explores how directors, executives, and accountants should approach specific decisions and the ethical management of key aspects of a corporations activities within the frameworks for ethical awareness, behavior, governance, and accountability developed in Parts 1, 2, and 3.

Chapter 7 develops an understanding of several key ethics opportunities and risks facing corporations and a set of tools to deal effectively with them. Topics covered include:

- Ethics risk and opportunity management—a new concept;
- Ethics strategies and tactics for effective stakeholder relations;
- Corporate social responsibility/corporate citizenship;
- Workplace ethics;
- Fraud and white collar crime;
- International operations;
- Crisis management.

Chapter 8 discusses the ethics and governance issues associated with the recent subprime mortgage debacle and the associated meltdown of the worlds financial markets. It explains how the crisis occurred, including the effect of the mark-to-market financial reporting requirement for investments and derivative instruments that were based on the subprime mortgages. Other topics covered include an analysis of the roles of underwriters of subprime investments and of the credit rating agencies involved, as well as the lack of government regulation, poor decision making, as well as the evidence that greed, incompetence, dishonesty, conflicts of interest, non-transparency, lack of moral courage and poor risk management all contributed to the fiasco. The chapter concludes with a set of lessons learned, and a look into the future.

7

MANAGING ETHICS RISKS & OPPORTUNITIES

Purpose of the Chapter

Earlier chapters provided an understanding of the changing ethical expectations for business and professional accountants; the new frameworks of stakeholder accountability and governance stimulated by Enron, Arthur Andersen, WorldCom, and the Sarbanes-Oxley Act; and how to provide adequate guidance for ethical behavior in the future. Looking ahead, there are several areas that are worthy of specific discussion because of their current and potential significance to the successful future of corporations, directors, executives, and professional accountants. These areas hold risks and opportunities that modern businesspeople and professionals must consider to secure and maintain the support of their stakeholders.

This chapter develops an understanding of how to identify, assess, and manage ethics risks and opportunities effectively under the following headings:

▎ Ethics risk & opportunity identification & assessment
- Ethics risk & opportunity within traditional enterprise risk management
- Ethics risk & opportunity assessment

▎ Ethics risk & opportunity management
- Effective stakeholder relations
- Corporate social responsibility performance & accountability
- Workplace ethics challenges
- Fraud & white collar crime
- International operations
- Crisis management

Ethics Risk & Opportunity Identification & Assessment

▎ Ethics Risk & Opportunities within Enterprise Risk Assessment

▎ **Ethics Risks & Opportunities** ▎ The recent recognition of the need for corporate accountability to stakeholders, has brought a corollary recognition that modern governance systems need to reflect the importance of satisfying the interests of stakeholders. Stakeholder satisfaction, in turn, is based upon the respect a corporation shows for the interests of each stakeholder group from whom the corporation wants and needs support to reach its strategic objectives. Within this context, attention to ethics risks and opportunities—*since the* *risks of not meeting stakeholder expectations lead to a potential loss of support for a corporation's objectives, and where exceeding expectations leads to opportunities to garner support*—is critical to avoid potential loss of support for a corporation's objectives, and to discover opportunities of greater support. This requires a much broader framework for risk assessment than most corporations have employed.

To be fair, there has been some overlap in the traditional risk assessment approaches with the ethics risk/stakeholder interests' assessment (ERSIA) approach. However, even in cases of overlap, the focus of the non-ERSIA approaches and the mindset of investigators have not been as broad as now appears appropriate, because the focus has been on what is important from a shareholder perspective rather than a stakeholder perspective. *Without the stakeholder support perspective, an investigator may not recognize risks that could lead to loss of support or opportunities for the creation of support based on competitive advantage or attention to other stakeholder interests.*

| **Limitations with Traditional Enterprise Risk Management (ERM) Approaches** | Risk management has been a commonly used concept since the late 1990s, when major stock exchanges listed it as one of those matters that directors needed to oversee.[1] However, risk management as normally practiced rarely involves a full examination of ethics risks and opportunities. There is a growing focus on fraud-related matters, but this does not go far enough to prevent loss of reputation and stakeholder support.

During the 1990s, leading-edge corporations had employed some form of risk management, but most other corporations had not. The Sarbanes-Oxley Act of 2002 (SOX) effectively made risk management an integral part of good governance when it brought governance reform to SEC registrant companies around the world and spawned similar developments in many other national jurisdictions. Section 404 of SOX, for example, which is aimed at risk assessment and prevention, requires companies to examine the effectiveness of their internal control systems with regard to financial reporting, and the CEO, CFO, and auditors must report on and certify that effectiveness.

As noted in Chapter 5, the mandatory review of internal control involves comparison of the corporation's systems with an accepted internal control framework such as that developed for Enterprise Risk Management (ERM) by the Committee of Sponsoring Organizations (COSO) of the Treadway Commission. Further information on the COSO approach is available in auditing texts, or on the COSO website.[2] The COSO ERM framework represented in Table 7.1 assesses how an entity achieves its objectives on four dimensions. Within each of these dimensions or categories, the ERM framework involves eight interrelated components concerning the way management runs an enterprise and how they are integrated with the management process.

Ethics and an ethical corporate culture, which was explored in Chapter 5, are seen to play a vital role in setting the control environment, and thereby creating an effective ERM-oriented internal control system and influencing the behavior that results. Consequently, a COSO ERM-oriented review will examine the tone at the top, codes of conduct, employee awareness, pressures to meet unrealistic or inappropriate goals, management's willingness to override established controls, code adherence in performance appraisals, monitoring of internal control system effectiveness, whistle-blowing programs, and remedial actions in response to code violations.[3]

However, few corporations approach risk management within the full ethics risk management framework necessary to support the new era of stakeholder accountability and

---

1. The Toronto Stock Exchange identified risk management as a matter requiring oversight by directors in 1995.
2. See for example, *Enterprise Risk Management—Integrated Framework: Executive Summary,* Committee of Sponsoring Organizations (COSO) of the Treadway Commission, September 2004, http://www.coso.org/publications.htm.
3. Principle source: KPMG Forensic, *Integrity Survey* 2005–2006, 2005.

TABLE 7.1

COSO Enterprise Risk Framework – Basic Elements

FOCUS: HOW DOES AN ENTERPRISE ACHIEVE ITS OBJECTIVES?

	DIMENSION			
	Strategic	*Operations*	*Reporting*	*Compliance*
COMPONENT				
Internal Environment				
Objective Setting				
Event Identification				
Risk Assessment				
Risk Response				
Control Activities				
Information & Communication				
Monitoring				

Source: *Enterprise Risk Management – Integrated Framework: Executive Summary*, Committee of Sponsoring Organizations of the Treadway Commission, 2004

governance. Depending on the organization, *traditional risk management has focused on issues from the perspective of their financial impacts on shareholders, and not on nonfinancial impacts on stakeholders.* For example, financial institutions have tended to focus on financial risks, such as the bankruptcy of borrowers, or the risk of loss on loans and derivative investments. Other corporations have focused on broad business risks, such as those covered in recent studies by the Institute of Internal Auditors (IIA)[4] or in the jointly published study by the AICPA and CICA.[5] Table 7.2 provides a summary of the business risks identified in the two studies. Because of their focus, traditional ERM approaches have generally been limited in scope.

In addition, even within the financial impacts, traditional ERM approach there has been a mistaken reliance on external auditors. Some directors and executives have presumed that their

TABLE 7.2

Identification of Business Risks

RISK FOCUS/CATEGORIES		AICPA/CICA	INSTITUTE OF INTERNAL AUDITORS
Company Objectives		X	
Areas of Impact:	Reputation	X	
	Assets, Revenues, Costs	X	
	Performance	X	
	Stakeholders	X	
Sources of Risk:	Environmental	X	
	Strategic	X	X
	Operational	X	X
	Informational	X	
	Financial		X
Specific Hazards or Perils:	Lawsuits		X
	Fire	X	
	Theft	X	
	Earthquake/natural disasters	X	X
Degree of Control over the Risk	Little, Some, Great	X	
Documentation		X	

4. *Enterprise Risk Management: Trends and Emerging Practices,* Tillinghast-Towers Perrin and the Institute of Internal Auditors Research Foundation, 2001.
5. *Managing Risk in the New Economy,* American Institute of Certified Public Accountants and the Canadian Institute of Chartered Accountants, 2001.

external auditors, who were reviewing for risks, would bring any risks found to the attention of management and/or directors. This reliance, however, was and is misplaced.

Although, as part of their audit, external auditors review a corporation's internal controls and sometimes their business risks, the normal external audit mandate requires concern only if risks found would have resulted in a material misstatement of the results of operations or financial position of the company. Moreover, because external auditors are only testing, they are not expected to find every problem. In addition, until fiscal periods beginning on or after December 15, 2002, they were not expected to look seriously for fraud. It is noteworthy, however, that there never has been a requirement for external auditors to search for and report any ethics risks or opportunities.

The new Statement of Auditing Standards (SAS 99),[6] released by the AICPA in response to the Enron and WorldCom disasters, and the Sarbanes-Oxley Act of 2002, illustrates how external auditors have been redirected toward greater fraud awareness, examination, and reporting thereon. Specifically, SAS 99 requires:

- Mandatory discussion and brainstorming among the audit team of and about the potential and causes for material misstatement in the financial statements due to fraud before and during the audit.[7]

- Guidance to be followed about data gathering and audit procedures to identify the risks of fraud.[8]

- Mandatory assessment of the risks of fraud based upon the risk factors found, and under revised assumptions of management innocence to guilt,[9] as follows:
  - Presume ordinarily that there is a risk of manipulation of revenues due to fraud and investigate,
  - Always identify and assess the risks that management could override controls as a fraud risk.

- Increased standards for examination, documentation, and reporting on audit steps taken to assure that manipulation did not occur.

- Other measures, including:
  - Support of research on fraud,
  - Development of antifraud criteria and controls,
  - Allocation 10 percent of CPE credits to fraud study,
  - Development of fraud training programs for the public,
  - Encouraging antifraud education at universities, as well as appropriate materials.[10]

Even after the adoption of SOX reforms, external auditors will be looking for fraud and/or flaws in controls that will give rise to material misstatements of the financial statements. They will not normally be expected to pursue immaterial or other non-financial risks or opportunities. In other words, *they will not normally be expected to raise all ethical risks or opportunities* with management or the Audit Committee, or any other committee or the board. Consequently, directors and

---

6. "SAS 99," Official Releases column in the *Journal of Accountancy,* January 2003, 105–120.
7. "Auditor's Responsibility for Fraud Detection." *Journal of Accountancy,* January 2003, 28–36.
8. Ibid., 30–32.
9. Ibid., 32.
10. Ibid., 36.

executives, who are responsible for monitoring *all* ethics risks, must design in-house audit or review processes, or specifically contract with designated outsiders to perform those reviews.

| Ethics Risk & Opportunity Identification & Assessment

Ethics risk and opportunity identification and assessment can be undertaken in several ways, but the three-phase approach presented in Figure 7.1 and discussed below offers a comprehensive approach.

Phase 1 of a sound ethics risk identification and assessment process should begin with the identification of the corporation's major stakeholders and their interests using the techniques discussed in Chapter 4. Investigators should then rank stakeholder interests in importance using the urgency, legitimacy, and power framework[11] and dynamic influence analysis[12] also developed in Chapter 4. After completion of these steps, investigators should have a projected under-standing of which stakeholder interest issues are sensitive and important, and why.

Next, the investigator should confirm these projections by interacting with a representative stakeholder panel and with important stakeholder groups. This will show concern for their interests and open a dialog that should build trust that could be helpful if unfortunate problems arise later. At the end of this process of stakeholder consultation, a confirmed grid of important stakeholder expectations for performance should emerge.

In Phase 2, against this mosaic of important stakeholder expectations, investigators should consider their corporation's activities and assess the risks of not meeting or the opportunities of exceeding expectations. When considering whether expectations have been met, comparisons should be made of relevant input, output, quality, and other performance variables.

FIGURE 7.1 **Ethics Risk and Opportunity Identification and Assessment**

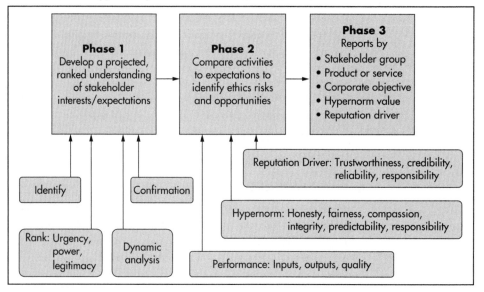

11. R. K. Mitchell, B. R. Agle, and D. J. Wood. "Toward a Theory of Stakeholder Identification and Salience: Defining the Principle of Who and What Really Counts," *Academy of Management Review* 22, no.4, (1997): 853–886.

12. T. Rowley. "Moving Beyond Dyadic Ties: A Network Theory of Stakeholder Influences," *Academy of Management Review* 22, no. 4 (1997): 887–910.

In addition, comparison should be made of company activities and stakeholder expectations using the *six hypernorm values* identified in Chapter 1 that are universally respected in most cultures: *honesty, fairness, compassion, integrity, predictability, and responsibility.*[13] If corporate activities respect these values, there is a good chance that those activities will also respect the expectations of the corporation's important stakeholders, domestic and foreign, now and in the near future.

Finally, the comparison of corporate activities and expectations should be reassessed from the perspective of potential impacts on the corporation's reputation. Charles Fombrun's model,[14] also developed in Chapter 1, where *reputation depends upon four factors—trustworthiness, credibility, reliability, and responsibility*—can be a helpful framework to organize the comparison needed.

Phase 3 involves preparation of the reports generated by the process. Specific corporate needs should dictate the nature of the reports presented, but consideration should be given to at least the following reports of ethics risks and opportunities:

- By stakeholder group
- By product or service
- By corporate objective
- By hypernorm value
- By reputation driver

This set will provide data that will allow directors and executives to monitor ethics risks and opportunities, to plan to avoid and mitigate risks, and to strategically take advantage of opportunities.

A significant company official, such as the corporate ethics officer or corporate social responsibility officer, should be charged with the ongoing responsibility of monitoring the assumptions and inputs to the ERSIA model, and for reporting to the relevant subcommittee of the board on a periodic basis. Letting down the corporate guard on this continuing oversight could have very serious consequences, as corporations such as General Motors, Ford and Chrysler have recently discovered relative to Toyota in the area of environmentally sustainable products.

Ethics Risk & Opportunity Management

Once the organization's ethics risks and opportunities have been identified and assessed, strategies will need to be developed and tactics employed to best manage them to mitigate problems and to align activities with stakeholder interests. Discussions follow covering tools and techniques to employee, and how to approach significant problem areas facing directors, executives and professional accountants.

Effective Stakeholder Relations

Strategies and tactics can be developed for dealing with each stakeholder or group, based upon an assessment of stakeholder interests and possible changes in them. One approach originated by

13. Ronald E. Berenbeim, Director of the Working Group on Global Business Ethics Principles, discovered in research for the Working Group's Report, *Global Corporate Ethics Practices: A Developing Consensus.*, The Conference Board, New York, May 1999.
14. C. J. Fombrun. *Reputation: Realizing Value from the Corporate Image.* Boston: Harvard Business School Press, 1996.

Savage et al. (1991) focuses on the potential for stakeholders to pose a threat to the organization, or to cooperate with it. Stakeholders can be susceptible to invitations to collaborate or become cosupporters or, if they are not amenable to the company's position, consideration may be given to their need for monitoring or when a defense is needed against them. Figure 7.2 presents a useful model for considering such decisions.

The model suggests that the most desirable stakeholder group (called Type 1) is likely to pose a low threat to an organization's objectives and a high degree of cooperation with them. If possible, it makes sense to *involve* this group more closely with the organization because they are likely to be *supportive*. A stakeholder group that is ranked high on cooperation and high as a potential threat holds some promise (i.e., is a *mixed blessing*), and it is probably wise to try to *collaborate* with them to keep them as supporters. Where a stakeholder group is ranked as probably a high threat and a low cooperator, they are considered *nonsupportive* and should be *defended* against. A group low in potential to threaten and low in potential to cooperate is *marginal* to the development of support for company objectives, but it may be wise to *monitor* their expectations in the event that conditions change.

It should be noted that this is a somewhat static analysis. Consequently, any strategy for improving the support of stakeholders should be confirmed through periodic re-analysis that considers possible alliances of stakeholder groups through the use of the urgency, power, legitimacy framework, and particularly the position of and trends in media coverage. Surprise embarrassment can erode support very quickly. Where possible, advance communication with supporters is attractive in maintaining their support. Of course, the creation of rapport and trust will assist in providing an opportunity to explain problems or tactics if necessary.

It is also worth considering how stakeholders in one cell of the model can be moved to a more supportive position. Even if one group is being defended against, continuing to consider how to convert the group to supporters is very worthwhile. The interests of all stakeholder groups should regularly be reconsidered as input to the development of strategies for improved support.

This regular or continuous reconsideration of stakeholder interests and potential gaps from corporate behavior could be part of the organization's *environmental scanning or issues management programs*, and could provide input into its *business–government relations program*. Although

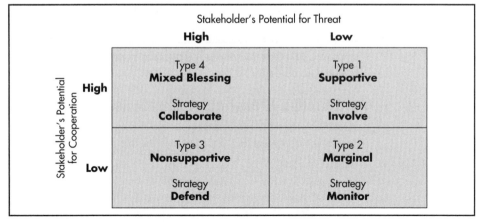

| FIGURE 7.2 | **Diagnostic Typology of Organizational Stakeholders** |

Source: G. Savage et al., "Strategies for assessing and managing organizational shareholders," *The Executive, Vol. 5,* no. 2, May 1991, 65.

issues management programs have been in place for decades, their focus has not traditionally been organized on a comprehensive stakeholder interests, gap analysis framework.

The same is true for business–government relations programs where the focus has been on specific issues, and only recently has turned to the creation and maintenance of overall support from which the management of specific issues is facilitated. Additionally, there has been a change in the framing of successful proposals to government—to stress the proposed impact on the public interest (i.e., all stakeholders) rather than on a select group—perhaps because of a greater awareness of lobbyist scandals, or a more mature awareness of the need for government to protect the public interest. Without doubt, stakeholder gap analysis can be of great utility in both framing proposals as well as in creating and maintaining overall stakeholder support.

Corporate Social Responsibility & Corporate Citizenship

Corporations have been thought to be legally accountable only to shareholders or owners, but in reality they are also strategically accountable to a broader range of stakeholders if they wish to garner the support necessary for achievement of strategic objectives. *To this extent, a paradigm shift is underway, from accountability to shareholders to accountability to stakeholders.*

As a result, organizations are increasingly interested in what stakeholders expect of them, and how they are performing and perceived as performing against those expectations in order to enhance stakeholder support. There are also investors, directors, executives and employees who, from an altruistic perspective, are interested in their organization's performance on non-financial matters. Both groups—those from an instrumental perspective and those from an altruistic perspective—are interested in the organization's *corporate social responsibility* (CSR) plans and performance or, as some prefer to describe it, as a *corporate citizen.*

Regardless of which label—CSR or corporate citizenship—is chosen, both refer to the degree to which an organization takes the interests of stakeholders into account, and takes actions which respect those interests. High praise is no longer just for high profit, it depends how the profit is earned and how stakeholder interests are respected in the process. The key questions are: "How does our organization want to be known?" and "How do we plan for it and make it happen?"

Consequently, there is a growing interest in assessing stakeholder interests, planning for their integration into corporate governance, decision and action processes, and in the measurement, reporting, and audit of corporate impacts on stakeholders. To manage the ethics risks and opportunities involved, organizations should decide which elements of CSR are important, how these are to be incorporated, and how performance is to be measured and reported internally and externally. The precise nature and degree of action and CSR disclosure will determine the image of corporate citizenship that the corporation will take on.

| **Organizational Objectives for CSR** | To develop a comprehensive plan or framework for CSR an organization should consider its strategic goals, both as an operation and how it wishes to appear as a corporate citizen, the cultures its operations will encounter, and the interests of its stakeholders, both in domestic and foreign theatres. These considerations, with an understanding of available measures of CSR, will allow the architect of the corporation's systems to match its aspirations with measures that will allow monitoring and reinforcement. Perhaps of equal or greater importance, they will also enable the organization's strategic planners to formulate objectives that are ethical and respectful of the interests of the stakeholders and cultures to be dealt with.

| **Establishing a Corporate Social Responsibility Framework** | New initiatives are being developed to assist with the involvement of stakeholders in corporate planning and

decisions, organize corporate activities and report on them, and audit what the corporation is doing and reporting.

The Sustainability Reporting Guidelines developed by the Global Reporting Initiative (GRI)—a cooperative venture of many stakeholders, including professional accounting bodies—offers the most comprehensive reporting framework and is instructive for those who are considering improving their CSR or Corporate Social Performance (CSP) planning, delivery, and reporting.[15] The GRI guidelines are being refined continuously. The framework for the G_3 Version is outlined in Table 7.3. Further detail can be found on the GRI website. GRI and AccountAbility have formed a strategic alliance in which AccountAbility provides information on stakeholder engagement and GRI on the aspects to be considered in the managed and reportable set. Companies that report using the GRI framework are able to benchmark or compare their activities to other enterprises or targets.

It would also be appropriate to create a CSR framework that responded to the actual stakeholder interests likely to be encountered. These could be developed using stakeholder survey, analysis, and focus group techniques developed in Chapter 5 in connection with the design of codes of conduct, ethical decision making, and corporate culture.

| **Measurement of CSR Performance** | It will also be helpful to review other CSR frameworks that have been created by consultants who screen corporate activities for ethical investors—both individuals and institutional investors who wish to invest with a social purpose or in companies where activities are socially responsible. Consultancies that are active in CSR screening include:

| KLD Research & Analytics Inc. at http://www.kld.com (U.S. companies)

| EthicScan Canada Limited at http://www.ethicscan.ca (Canadian companies)

TABLE 7.3

Global Reporting Initiative Sustainability Reporting Guidelines Standard Disclosure Framework – G_3 Version [Draft]

Strategy and Analysis – CEO statement, key risks & opportunities
Organizational Profile – 8 items
Report Parameters – 17 items
Governance, Commitments, & Stakeholder Engagement – 17 items
Management Approach & Performance Indicators:

Economic Performance (EC) – econ. perform., market presence, indirect impacts

Environmental Performance (EN) – materials; energy; water; biodiversity; emissions, effluents & waste; products & services; compliance; transport

Social Performance:

- Labor Practices & Decent Work (LA) – employment; labor/manage. relations; occupational health & safety; training & education; diversity & opportunity

- Human Rights (HR) – manage. practices; non-discrimination; freedom of assoc.; child labor; forced & compulsory labor; security practices; indigenous rights

- Society (SO) – community; corruption; public policy; anti-competitive behavior

- Product Responsibility (PR) – customer health & safety; products & services; marketing communications; customer privacy

Source: Sustainability Reporting Guidelines [Draft], G_3 version, Global Reporting Initiative, January 2006.

---

15. GRI developments can be viewed at http://www.globalreporting.org

▌ Michael Jantzi Research Associates Inc. at http://www.jantzisocialindex.com/ (Canadian companies)

▌ FTSE at http://www.ftse.com/Indices/FTSE4Good_Index_Series/index.jsp (mostly U.K. and European companies)

Measurements or indicators of CSR can take many forms. A selected set of eighty of those that have been used by EthicScan Canada's *Corporate Ethics Monitor* in its "Comparisons of Ethical Performance" is provided in Appendix A. These *measures of fact* are grouped into categories covering:

▌ Codes or statements of guidance, their currency, and their reinforcement;

▌ Job creation: overall and with regard to women and minority groups;

▌ Relations with communities and local stakeholders, including charitable donations.

▌ Treatment of employees:

- Progressive staff policies: family, health, training, communications, retirement, benefits programs,

- Gainsharing programs: stock options, profit sharing,

- Labor relations: unionization, safety.

▌ Environmental management programs;

▌ Environmental performance;

▌ Ethical sourcing and trading practices.

There are other measures that may be useful in revealing attitudes of managers and employees toward ethical issues. These may be useful in capturing information about actions that are about to happen, or about changes in attitude due to certain signals sent voluntarily or involuntarily by management or perceived by employees. Examples of such *anticipatory measures* are:

▌ Employee attitude surveys;

▌ Customer or other stakeholder surveys;

▌ Evaluation by paid "shoppers" or solicited customer complainants;

▌ Media commentary assessment.

Other measures concentrate on the operational merit of the organization's fundamental building or support blocks for ethical behavior. This could include *quality assessments* of:

▌ Code of conduct;

▌ Training programs;

▌ Reinforcement mechanisms, including:

- Newsletters, correspondence,

- Pay and reward systems,

- Promotion.

▌ Whistle-blowing atmosphere/protection:

- Follow-up on reported problems,

- Speed of response,

- Fairness of hearing process and of the penalty assigned.

Measures are also available to indicate:

I The level of understanding that employees have of ethical issues[16]

I The principal motivator for an employee's ethical behavior[17]

I Whether an employee is disposed to raise ethical concerns due to the individual's perception of his or her ability to affect the outcome of such debates (locus of control tests[18])

I The degree of inclusion of ethical concerns in, "the development of plans, setting of goals, search of opportunities, allocation of resources, gathering and communication of information, measurement of performance, and promotion and advancement of personnel"[19]

A further source of a measurement scheme can be found in the New York–based Social Accountability International SA8000 standard for working conditions. It can be accessed at **www.cengage.com/accounting/brooks**.

I **Monitoring CSR** I After the CSR measurements have been identified, the data gathered, and the report fashioned, the next step is monitoring how the corporation is doing. As with most measurement schemes, comparison can be helpful with:

I Strategic objective key success factors

I Similar organizations

I Best-practice alternatives for benchmarking

I Published standards such as those described earlier

I Industry statistics and averages

I Management by objective targets

I Results obtained in earlier periods

Ethical performance could also be selectively monitored by reference to external studies. These may be found in books such as *The 50 Best Ethical Stocks for Canadians,*[20] or in industry studies published in the *Corporate Ethics Monitor.* Alternatively, several annual studies are published such as the "100 Best Corporate Citizens" in *Business Ethics* magazine, or as it has now been absorbed into the *CRO, The Corporate Responsibility Officer* magazine. This publication also features its Annual Business Ethics Awards that identifies companies judged to be outstanding

---

16. See, for instance, the Defining Issues Test (DIT) as discussed in James R. Rest, *Development in Judging Moral Issues* (Minneapolis: University of Minnesota Press, 1979.)

17. According to the subject's stage of moral reasoning per the schema developed by L. Kohlberg in *Essays in Moral Development, Volumes I and II: The Psychology of Moral Development* (San Francisco: Harper & Row, 1981 and 1984).

18. "Locus of control is a self-regulatory aspect of character that captures individuals' tendency to feel that control of their lives rests in their own hands (internal locus of control) or in the hands of others (external locus of control). Those who are "internals" take responsibility for their actions, and are therefore more likely to act upon their ethical judgment. "Externals" are less likely to take responsibility for their actions and, therefore, are more susceptible to the pressures of the situation, feeling somewhat powerless." from Joanne Jones, Dawn W. Massey and Linda Thorne, "Auditors' Ethical Reasoning: Insights From Past Research And Implications For The Future," *Journal of Accounting Literature* 2003.

19. Lynn Sharp Paine, "Managing for Organizational Integrity," *Harvard Business Review* March–April (1994): 112. (Reprinted as a reading at the end of Chapter 1).

20. Deb Abbey and Michael C. Jantzi, *2001 Edition* (Toronto: Macmillan Canada, 2000.)

performers.[21] Even general business publications like *The Economist* offer useful, and sometimes skeptical information on CSR in surveys and editorials such as those in their January 22, 2005, issue. Organizations also exist, such as Toronto's Social Investment Organization (SIO), that provide information derived from CSR matters. On a specific company level, it is possible to obtain a specific report on the CSR performance of a company from research organizations like Jantzi Research or EthicScan Canada that are providing these to the corporate and investment community. Hiring a consultant specializing in ethical performance measurement may also be beneficial, especially if the consultant has extensive experience with ethical processes in other organizations that can be of use, on a confidential basis, for benchmarking purposes.

Reports will be most useful when reviewed and analyzed on a continuing basis. The chief ethics officer and other individuals carrying out the review and analysis should be familiar with the ethical performance process, and should be committed to its improvement. They should be formally charged with, and known throughout the organization to have, the responsibility for improving the process and should also have the responsibility to report to senior levels of management and/or a subset of the board of directors. These individuals may be part of, or report to, an ethics advisory committee with ongoing responsibility and authority to revise the company's ethics program, and/or to a subcommittee of the board of directors.

| **Reporting of CSR** | The corporation that embarks on a CSR measurement program needs to consider how it will report on performance, and whether the report will be internal only or available to the public. Internal reports can take on any form, but should be focused on the program's performance objectives.

Recently, several organizations have created and published standards for CSR reports. They are currently testing and refining their creations and will be modifying them further. Consequently, it would be wise to maintain a watching brief on the following:

| Global Reporting Initiative (GRI) involves a comprehensive reporting framework (G$_3$) covering economic, environmental and social performance that is being developed by a global group including noted stakeholder environmentalists, accountants and others—see http://www.globalreporting.org and Table 7.3

| AccountAbility, a UK group, is developing the (AA1000) sustainability reporting framework that provides guidance on how to, "establish systematic accountability processes and how to assure that the underlying systems, processes and competencies live up to the AA1000 Assurance Standard"—see http://www.accountability.org.uk and Table 7.4

| Social Accountability (SA) and Audit (SAA) has developed SA8000, a "comprehensive and flexible system for managing ethical workplace conditions throughout global supply chains," and SAI, a system for auditing SA8000 performance—see http://www.sa-intl.org

The G3 and AA1000 are particularly promising frameworks. Tables 7.3 and 7.4 offer summaries of them.

Public reports are becoming more common. Reporting ethical performance can:

| Heighten awareness of ethical issues within an organization

| Provide encouragement for employees to adhere to ethical objectives

---

21. Another awards program providing similar sources of best practice is organized by *Corporate Knights Magazine*. The Best 50 Corporate Citizens in Canada Annual Survey can be found at http://www.corporateknights.ca/special-reports.html

7.4

AA1000 Accountability Assurance Standard Summary

Purpose, Sustainability Reporting and Assurance:

- The AA1000 Assurance Standard is a generally applicable standard for assessing, attesting to, and strengthening the credibility and quality of a reporting organizations' sustainability reporting, and its underlying processes, systems and competencies. It provides guidance on key elements of the assurance process (is a standard guiding the audit of sustainability reporting).

- The AA1000 Assurance Standard is primarily intended for use by assurance providers in guiding the manner in which their assurance assignments are designed and implemented.

- Assurance should provide confidence in the report's underlying information to the reporting organization's stakeholders, particularly the direct users of the report.

Assurance of sustainability reporting prepared in accordance with generally accepted standards:

- The AA1000 Assurance Standard supports assurance (whether made public or not) of reporting that adheres to specific standards and guidelines, and is customised by the reporting organisation. It is specifically designed to be consistent with, and to enhance, the Global Reporting Initiative Sustainability Reporting Guidelines, as well as other related standards.

Commitment by reporting organizations:

- Reporting organizations commit to (1) identify and understand their environment, (2) respond to their stakeholders' aspirations, and (3) provide an account to their stakeholders regarding the organization's decisions, actions and impacts.

Assurance principles:

- Materiality: the assurance provider must evaluate if the report contains all the important information about the reporting organization's sustainability performance required by the organization's stakeholders for making informed judgements, decisions and actions.

- Completeness: the assurance provider must evaluate the extent to which the reporting organization can identify and understand material aspects of its sustainability performance.

- Responsiveness: the assurance provider must evaluate whether the reporting organization has responded to stakeholders' concerns, policies, and relevant standards; and adequately communicated these responses in the report.

Evidence (supporting the reported figures and disclosures):

- The assurance provider must evaluate whether the reporting organization has provided adequate evidence to support the information contained in the report.

Assurance statement (i.e. auditor's opinion):

- The assurance statement should address the credibility of the report and the underlying systems, processes, and competencies that deliver the relevant information, and underpin the reporting organization's performance.

- Elements of the assurance statement (i.e. auditor's report):

  - Statement on use of AA1000

  - Description of work performed

  - Conclusion on the quality of the report and underlying organizational processes, systems, and competencies

  - Additional comments if necessary

Assurance provider standards (i.e. auditor's independence and competencies):

- The credibility of a report's assurance relies on the assurance provider's competencies, independence, and impartiality.

  - The assurance provider should aim to be independent of the reporting organization and impartial with respect to the organisation's stakeholders. Any interests that detract from this independence and impartiality need to be transparently declared by the assurance provider.

  - The assurance provider must be impartial in its dealings with the reporting organization's stakeholders.

  - Assurance providers and the reporting organization must ensure that the individuals involved in any specific assurance process are demonstrably competent.

  - The organisations through which individuals provide assurance must be able to demonstrate adequate institutional competencies.

* For a full version of this report, visit: http://www.accountability21.net/

> | Inform external stakeholders

> | Enhance the image of the company

Internal reporting of ethical performance can take several forms. Newsletters can provide full or partial reports, scorecards as well as recognition of exemplary behavior by employees. Other internal reporting systems could include charts or progress reports on bulletin boards, partial or full reports as stand-alone documents, and verbal or video reports by senior management. Written reports can be prepared by internal staff and certified by external agents like auditors, professors, or editors of ethics publications. Alternatively, reports can be prepared entirely by individuals independent of the corporation. Several organizations, including The Council on Economic Priorities Accreditation Agency (CEPAA) in New York and EthicScan Canada in Toronto, train auditors to review CSR/CEP activity; and large public accounting firms offer related services including Ethics and Integrity (KPMG), Reputational Assurance (PricewaterhouseCoopers), Governance Review (Ernst & Young) and Corporate Responsibility and Sustainability (Deloitte & Touche). Details are available on each organization's website.

Large corporations are releasing ethical performance reports to the public with greater frequency on a continuing basis. Such reports may be a few paragraphs in the annual report and may, or may not, be specifically identified as ethical performance reports. For example, an annual report may separately comment on corporate governance issues, gender equality, employment of minorities, charitable donations programs, environmental issues, and health and safety issues. More companies are publishing separate reports specifically devoted to ethical conduct or specific components thereof. General Motors, Dow Chemical and BP were early examples of this. More recent examples are Shell, Placer Dome, and Royal Bank of Canada (among many others). Readers may access the website for any significant public company and in many cases find public reporting of some kind on ethical issues. Such information can be particularly useful for companies wishing to start down this road, or to improve their reporting if they have already started. Reference to **www.cengage.com/accounting/brooks** will provide ready access to lists of companies, including:

> | 25 companies with recent CSR reports per the GRI website

> | 100 companies included in The 2007 AccountAbility Ranking

> | 30 companies with CSR reports and related website addresses

> | Over 300 companies included in the Dow Jones Sustainability Index World October 2007

The reports from Shell and VanCity Credit Union, which are both audited or externally reviewed, make very useful reading and can be accessed at http://sustainabilityreport.shell.com/servicepages/welcome.html and https://www.vancity.com/MyMoney/AboutUs/WhoWeAre/CorporateReports/AccountabilityReport/, respectively. Environmental performance reports, it should be noted, are mandatory disclosure in some parts of Europe.

Senior management may not support reporting, especially to external parties, if the results to be reported are unfavourable or if the possibility of legal action is significant. This is, however, an evolving area. Stakeholders are becoming increasingly interested in ethical performance, and leading companies are responding. Organizations are recognizing that it can be to their benefit to report even when the results are unfavourable. By contrast, even when unfavorable results are not reported, the motivation for improvement remains in that if corrective action is taken, favorable results can be reported in future.

| **Audit Assurance of CSR Reports** | The spread of so-called audits of CSR reports has been growing, particularly in Europe. European initiatives in environmental protection and

through the International Standards Association (ISO) have had a driving influence on corporate behaviour and have required public disclosure of environmental performance. As a result, many individuals, and some large public accounting and other firms have become involved in attesting to the reports issued. Reports by BP, Shell, and VanCity Credit Union, for example, have been audited in whole or in part. Independent audits of labor practices in undeveloped and developing countries have become rather common for retailers and their manufacturers whose products come significantly from such sources, for example, Nike, Adidas, and Umbro. Care should be taken when relying on certifications in this area because auditing standards have not yet become generally accepted for this kind of reporting. Increasingly, however, international accounting bodies and other organizations such as CEPAA and AccountAbility are focusing on the need for appropriate auditing standards, including standards for the content of audit reports and certifications. National and international professional accounting bodies are beginning to take a greater interest in these areas. As well, the next phase of ISO reporting may well push currently registered firms beyond documentation of systems to the reporting and audit levels. Articles are appearing that review different aspects of CSR disclosure.

It is possible for a corporation to have company personnel audit CSR reports. Internal audit staff may be used, as may managers from other divisions of a company. This managerial audit approach was used by Dow Corning and was lionized in Harvard Business School cases before the unfortunate breast implant scandal. It should be pointed out that the Chairman of the Conduct Committee of Dow Corning remains convinced of the worth of the company's ethics audit program, but acknowledges that audit improvements were warranted.[22]

| **Concluding Thoughts** | The strategic accountability of corporations to stakeholders, managers, and professional accountants has become so evident that it would be short-sighted for an organization not to develop an effective concept of corporate citizenship and an effective program of corporate social responsibility. They will greatly facilitate better management of an organization's ethical culture and performance, and the degree of support garnered from stakeholder groups. More important, providing guidance to employees and others about the corporation's intended CSR or Corporate Citizenship expectations will reduce the ethics risks and enable the taking of ethics opportunities in an orderly way.[23]

| Workplace Ethics

The increasing levels of social conscience and the pressures of activist groups that have been documented elsewhere have had a significant impact on both the internal and external operations of organizations. Consequently, it is appropriate for businesspeople to have an appreciation of the major ethical themes and issues that have emerged or are emerging in regard to the conduct of employees in North American workplaces. The comments that follow are not intended to provide an exhaustive review, but they will raise awareness of the issues and provide some guidance, including when to seek more informed advice.

| **Employee Rights** | Since the early 1970s, there has been an increasing awareness that the rights of individual workers were worthy of more respect relative to the rights of the employer than had been the case before. For example, the rights of an employer have

---

22. See, for example, the quotation of the Chairman of the Conduct Committee of Dow Corning in the Ethics Case: *Dow Corning Silicon Breast Implants*" at the end of Chapter 5 on page 329.
23. Parts of this segment on CSR and Corporate Citizenship are reprinted with permission from *Ethics & Governance: Developing and Maintaining an Ethical Corporate Culture*, 3rd ed., L. J. Brooks & D. Selley, Canadian Centre for Ethics & Corporate Policy, Toronto, 2008.

changed; the employer can no longer order his/her employees to pollute, risk their health or safety or that of others, or say nothing when the truth was being distorted. Some of the changed rights have become protected by new legislation, while others have been influenced by common law cases, union contracts, and corporate practices that have been sensitive to stakeholder pressures.

Table 7.5 identifies those employee themes in North America that have lead to new expectations by employees.

| **Privacy & Dignity** | The right of an employer to search the person of a North American employee, to access any personal information desired, or to search any property has become significantly curtailed. North American society now endorses the position that an *individual's personal rights are more important than those of an employer,* unless it can be shown that, in a particular circumstance, the employer's interest is reasonable, legitimate, and morally acceptable. For example, in most locales it is not acceptable to place a surveillance camera in a washroom unless there is a threat to life and health, such as through violent attacks or drug dealing. Even in these cases, outside legal authorities should be consulted before the surveillance, and in some cases notification of the intent to use a camera may be called for.

It should be noted, however, that simply notifying workers should not be taken to imply that they had consented to the procedure. Specific conditions must be met before the courts will agree that proper procedures have been followed. In fact, workers must be allowed what is called *informed consent,* wherein they have time to deliberate, have a free choice among reasonable alternatives, and have adequate information to understand the problem and options. In addition, the choice must be one that the courts consider possible to agree to make. An employee, for

---

TABLE 7.5   **Employee Rights Themes in North America**

Privacy and dignity of person, personal information and property:

- Boundaries of personal rights, employers rights and right of the public
- Proper procedures: notification and consent
- Testing for substance abuse
- Harassment, sexual and otherwise

Fair treatment:

- Discrimination: age, race, sex, employment, pay
- Fair policies
- Is equal treatment fair?

Healthy and safe work environment

- Expectations: reasonability, right to know, stress, family life, productivity
- Quality-of-life concerns: smoking, health
- Family-friendly workplaces

Ability to exercise conscience

- Blind loyalty
- Whistle-blowing

Trust – the key to leadership, innovation, loyalty, and performance – depends on ethics

- Operations: downsizing, contingent workforce

instance, cannot bargain away his or her right to life or to take on extremely serious health risks. Legal advice is vital before action is taken.

Testing for substance abuse is a related area in which North American society has been reluctant to accept invasion of privacy without compelling reason, usually involving the life and health of coworkers or others. Indeed, random drug testing for airplane pilots was only approved by the U.S. Supreme Court in the late 1990s. Drug testing has been relatively inaccurate when measured against the potential harm done to the falsely accused, so that discrete, repeat testing is desirable if an initial test is positive before any accusations are made. Confidentiality should be maintained throughout this time period if at all possible. There have been some testing programs for office workers, but several have been struck down by the courts as being unreasonable. For example, the Exxon program of random testing (started in response to the Exxon Valdez shipwreck, see Ethics Case: *The Exxon Valdez* at the end of this chapter) was considered to be too unreasonable because it resulted in a reassignment/suspension from the employee's position for up to seven years. The Toronto-Dominion Bank program for new recruits—if offered a job, a positive mandatory substance abuse test would lead to a required remediation program from which a cured person could have the job—was considered not to be sufficiently justified by the bank's desire to make sure that its employees would protect customer's assets properly to warrant allowing the personal intrusion involved. It appears, however, that the stigma associated with drug and alcohol testing programs can be circumvented. Some trucking companies achieve the same ends (protection of the public and their assets) by requiring their drivers to score well on computer games (which feature hand-eye coordination) before they will be given their truck keys. Society does not regard such testing as sufficient invasion of privacy to object to its use.

Harassment is, of course, not only objectionable on grounds of dignity and privacy, but also on grounds of fairness. Definitions of harassment vary depending on the locale, but the trend is toward more stringent tests than most businesspeople or professionals initially contemplate. *Harassment can be defined as any improper behavior directed at you that you find offensive, and that the other person knew or ought reasonably to have known would be unwelcome.* Note that the test is not what the person doing the harassment thought about the act—the important test is what the offended party thought and whether the local authorities think it is reasonable behavior. Usually they side with the offended person. It is therefore imperative if an employee alleges harassment that the claim be investigated immediately and discretely. If the claim is justified, then the perpetrator should be warned, or dismissed if already warned, and dismissed subject to the due process rules of the company involved. If prompt action is not taken, the manager receiving the complaint and the company can be subject to legal proceedings for failing to provide a harassment-free workplace. In fact, if a traveling salesperson or visiting auditor is harassed, his or her organization must contact the management of the offending company and see that appropriate action is taken, otherwise the manager and company of the complainant can be subject to legal proceedings.

| **Fair Treatment** | Discrimination is considered to be unethical and is considered illegal if it involves age, race, gender, and sexual preference. In addition, it is generally held that there should be equal opportunity for employment, and equal pay for equal work, particularly for women and minorities. Many leading-edge companies strive to hire sufficient representation into their workforce so that it reflects the population that they are operating in. "Breaking the glass ceiling" is a term that is used to describe overcoming the barrier women face to promotion within their organizations, and some firms have found a competitive advantage by removing barriers and creating a level playing field for women and men. The Bank of Montreal, for example, found that many outstanding women managers applied for jobs when the bank did so, thus leaving the rest of the Canadian banks facing a dearth of promotable women.

Workers in North America believe that they are entitled to fair policies. These would include fair wages, fair hours, fair consideration for promotion, and for downsizing (see the Ethics Case: *Texaco's Jelly Beans* at the end of this chapter), and fair hearing. If dismissal is required, then employees expect that it will be according to appropriate or due process, including adequate notice or pay in lieu of notice. Unjust dismissals are those that do not follow fair due processes, and reinstatement, remedial payments, and/or fines can result.

It should be noted that people with disabilities are frequently accorded more than an equal chance for employment. This treatment is more than fair, and it is considered ethical in view of their disabilities.[24]

| **Healthy & Safe Work Environment** | The balance between the rights of workers and owners has shifted to the point that it is considered ethical for workers to expect that their health and safety will not be unreasonably compromised. They must know what the risks are in advance, and many jurisdictions have created right-to-know laws to ensure that organizations make information on hazardous substances, processes, and related treatments readily accessible.

Concern is presently being expressed over extending these arguments to the less tangible areas of excessive stress in terms of hours of overtime expected, extreme levels of productivity and degradation of family life. No guidelines have emerged as yet, but the pressure for them in these areas will grow, so a watch should be kept for future developments in this regard.

It is apparent that responsible companies are showing respect for the preferences of their workers before they are forced to do so by changing regulations. Smoke-free workplace areas are a case in point. In addition, other companies are recognizing the need for fitness and recreation by establishing centers for theses on-site. The desire to improve the family-friendliness of workplaces has lead to the provision of on-site daycare for children of employees, the institution of flexible work hours, and other similar arrangements.

A 2006 survey of chartered accountants who were 35 years and younger revealed that after interesting work, the most important factor in attracting and retaining employees is offering them a work/life balance. Not only must employers give employees the opportunity to take advantage of a work/life balance, they must also make a shift in their organizational culture. They should not make employees feel guilty about not working excessive hours, nor penalize them through their performance evaluations.[25]

| **Ability to Exercise One's Conscience** | As noted elsewhere, the argument that a worker just did what he or she was ordered to do will no longer provide the worker with protection in many jurisdictions, so the worker should exercise his or her own conscience. The concept of *blind loyalty* is not one that many employees would be comfortable with, in any case. They would prefer to bring their concerns forward and speak out against pollution or other misdeeds, but they are frequently prevented from doing so by their caution in exposing themselves to the wrath of their coworkers or managers.

Whistle-blowing, although it could contribute to a more ethical organization, is none-theless something most North Americans were taught not to do when they were growing up, and a stigma continues to be attached to it. To encourage whistle-blowers to come forward within the organization, rather than have them report their concerns outside the enterprise, many are creating a whistle-blower protection program. In these programs, an inquiry or allegation is handled by an individual who has credibility with employees to undertake a speedy, fair

---

24. A discussion of justice as fairness is also provided in Chapter 3.
25. *CAMagazine*, "The Price of Happiness," September 2006. http://www.camagazine.com/index.cfm/ci_id/33539/la_id/1

investigation without revealing the name of the inquirer. If it becomes necessary for the inquirer to testify against the accused, then the inquirer is asked to do so and may decline. Reports of inquiries received are made on an aggregate basis, without revealing the names of the whistle-blowers. Some companies are calling these services Ethics Inquiry Services, rather than more pejorative terms such as a "hotline" or "whistle-blowing" service.

There are also a growing number of statutes that seek to protect whistle-blowers. There-fore, and because secrets almost always become public, it would be wise for organizations to facilitate the exercise of employee conscience within the organization, where appropriate action can be taken without ruining the company's reputation. In order to facilitate corporate whistle-blowing programs, many law firms, specialized consultancies, and corporations are now offering telephone and/or email hotlines. Details on whistle-blower programs are available from KPMG's Integrity Survey.[26]

| **Trust & Its Importance** | Only recently have researchers begun to document what far-sighted owners and managers have known for some time. As noted earlier, the ethics of an organization are directly related to how leaders are perceived, to whether there is sufficient trust for people to share ideas without fear of losing jobs or the respect of their coworkers and managers, and to whether they believe that the organization is worthy of loyalty and hard work (Brooks, 2000). In our current North American workplaces, it is increasingly unlikely that employees and managers will be willing to follow the instructions of an untrustworthy or unethical leader if they have any choice. Workers are not willing to contribute to innovation if they fear retribution or erosion of their position in some form, and they may not take the initiative on behalf of the company. Therefore, the organization will find that it may fall behind competitors whose employees trust the company and its leaders.

If employees have sufficient trust in their situation, they will participate wholeheartedly in restructuring sessions (this has been called a process of *ethical renewal*) that even involve downsizing, and may accept the necessity of shared work assignments or part-time work contracts with greater understanding (this creates what is called a *contingent workforce*). To maintain the trust necessary for these steps, an organization would have to be prepared to make trustable commitments to recall employees to full-time status when possible or to provide fair termination or contracting arrangements. Continuation of benefits could be one such way of maintaining trust with a contingent workforce.

| **Overall Benefit** | Many experts and successful practitioners subscribe to the belief that *the way employees view their own treatment by the company determines what the employees think about their company's ethics program.* Consequently, if an organization wants employees to observe a set of corporate ethical values, the workers must be convinced that the organi-zation really means what it says, and there must be a level of trust that permits this belief to flourish. Treating employees right is not only ethical, it is essential to them carrying out the organization's ethics program and to achieving its strategic objectives.

Fraud & White Collar Crime

One of the challenges facing all organizations is the prospect of unethical employees who commit acts of fraud and white collar crime. Executives are expected to ensure that they take all reasonable steps to guide, influence and control employees who might be inclined to become involved, and external auditors are expected to be alert for potential problems. Experience has suggested that an understanding of the circumstances leading to and enabling fraud and white collar crime, and the

---

26. KPMG Forensic, *Integrity Survey,* 2005–2006.

motivation for it, provides a useful foundation for preventative measures. In order to provide that understanding, an analysis is offered of the motivation of a white collar fraudster, Walt Pavlo, who was a star at MCI, and who was a key enabler of a $6 million fraud at MCI. His story is told in the Ethics Case*: Manipulation of MCI's Allowance for Doubtful Accounts* at the end of Chapter 5, and in the Ethics Case: *Walt Pavlo's MCI Scams/Frauds* at the end of this chapter.

| **Walt Pavlo's Motivation & Rationale for Fraud as MCI's Star**[27] | **The Fraud Triangle—A Framework for Understanding Fraudsters**   Investigative and forensic accountants use a helpful framework—The Fraud Triangle[28]—to identify potential fraudsters and situations that have potential for fraud. As shown in Figure 7.3, potential for fraud is said to be a function of the presence of three factors: *need*—financial or otherwise, *opportunity*—poor controls or overaggressive culture, and the willingness and ability to *rationalize* the fraudulent act.

Analysis of these factors can be facilitated by using the additional frameworks Maslow's Hierarchy of Needs[29] and Heath's Seven Rationalizations of Unethical Behavior,[30] which are discussed later, based on facts gleaned from Walt Pavlo's book *Stolen Without A Gun*[31] about his frauds on MCI and its customers.

Walt Pavlo Story—Brief Version   Walt Pavlo joined MCI in 1992, and rapidly became second in command at the company's Finance or long distance collections unit. Walt left MCI in 1996, and ultimately resigned in early 1997. During the four years and just afterward, he participated in several frauds on MCI and on customers who were dealing with MCI. These frauds are detailed in the two cases noted earlier.

Walt was found out and, in January 2001, pleaded guilty to obstruction of justice, money laundering and wire fraud. He was sentenced to 41 months in prison, and ordered to pay over

FIGURE 7.3   **The Fraud Triangle**

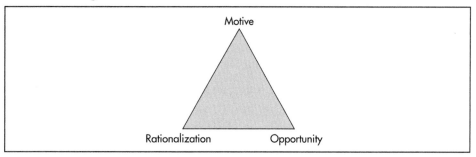

Source: D.L. Crumbley et al., 2005, pp. 3–131.

---

27. All details used in this case are taken from *Stolen Without A Gun: Confessions from Inside History's Biggest Accounting Fraud—The Collapse of MCI WorldCom*, Walter Pavlo Jr. and Neil Weinberg, Etika Books LLC, Tampa Florida, 2007.

28. Fraud Triangle—see CICA Handbook Section 5135 or the new CAS 240; see also W. S. Albrecht, C. C. Albrecht and C. O. Albrecht, *Fraud Examination*, 2nd ed. (Mason, OH: South-Western Cengage Learning, 2006), 31.

29. "The Hierarchy of Needs", from A. H. Maslow, "A Theory of Human Motivation," *Psychological Review*, American Psychological Association, vol. 50, 1943, pp. 394–395, as reprinted in *The Maslow Business Reader*, edited by Deborah C. Stephens (New York: John Wiley & Sons, 2000), pp. 3–4.

30. "7 Neutralization/Rationalization Techniques," a speech by Joseph Heath at the Centre for Ethics at the University of Toronto, April 9, 2007.

31. Ibid.

$5.7 million in restitution to MCI, AT&T and BTI. In addition, the banks won a $5.5 million judgment against him. Walt ultimately served 24 months in a federal prison, and was released in 2003. The outcome was particularly hard on his two sons and his wife, who divorced him in 2003.

Walt was a great looking blond, athletic, MBA graduate, with a young wife and two young sons. He had the capacity to become a star at MCI. So what happened? What motivated Walt to become involved in fraudulent behavior, and how did he rationalize the actions he took?

Understanding Fraudster Motivation—Maslow's Hierarchy of Needs   Like many newly graduated MBAs, Walt had a super strong drive to succeed. He wanted to fulfill his dreams:

I To prove himself to his mother and father, and to his wife and her well-off family.

I To earn enough remuneration to live comfortably and have enough for some indulgences.

I To be recognized for his contributions at work, and be

- paid what he thought he was worth, and

- have job security.

I To be respected by and friendly with his boss, Ralph McCumber, a former military man.

These desires led Walt to behave in ways he thought would lead to his success, including:

I Obeying orders unquestioningly, as if he was in a military culture,[32] such as by "making his numbers" by any means possible, including misrepresentation of the condition of bad debts through lapping, and worse.

I Behaving ultra aggressively, and even though some actions were distasteful, come in the next day ready to "bite the heads off chickens."

I Setting aside company policy, such as the "zero tolerance" policy for allowing customer credit positions to deteriorate to which company executives paid lip service.

I Creating apparently helpful mechanisms without the knowledge of his boss, and for which he did not disclose the risks. An example of this is the Rapid Advance "factoring" program to speed up collections, where Walt signed an unauthorized guaranty of bank loans on behalf of his company.

I Consorting with shady individuals to rip off his company and its customers.

I Emulating his boss in terms of approaches for encouraging his subordinates, and in encouraging them "not to worry about ..."

I Once on the slippery slope,[33] ultimately succumbing to the "blinding powers of desperation and greed" (p. 127).

Walt's desires fit neatly into Maslow's Hierarchy of Needs,[34] which is shown in Figure 7.4. Maslow asserted that an individual's needs could be categorized, and would be responded to in

---

32. At one point when Ralph and Walt were discussing how to "whitewash' a $55 million debt, McCumber barked: "Don't tell me what I can and can't do! Orders are orders. You've got yours." p. 92.

33. The term "slippery slope" refers to a situation in which a person starts by doing something slightly unethical, but follows with subsequent acts of growing significance, only to find that he or she must continue on to more highly unethical acts to cover up the earlier ones, or because someone else who knows of the earlier transgressions threatens to reveal them in order to coerce further unethical or illegal acts.

34. Op. cit.

FIGURE 7.4 **Maslow's Hierarchy of Needs**

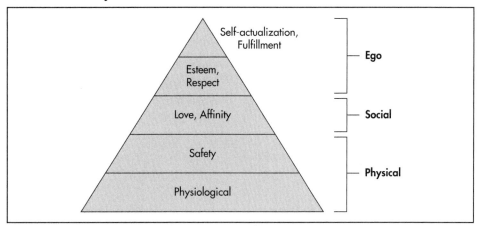

priority from the bottom of the pyramid. Later researchers[35] disagreed with this bottom-up priority sequence, citing many instances where needs at the top of the pyramid exerted a stronger influence than those at the bottom. Nonetheless, Maslow's categorization is widely respected and useful for understanding human needs, and can be applied to the understanding the motivation of white collar criminals and fraudsters.

Walt's desires show that he was motivated by the need for money to maintain his family (a *physiological need*), and by job security (a *safety need*). In addition he wanted to earn the respect of his boss and other MCI employees and higher-ups. When it came time to create the Rapid Advance factoring program, he signed a guaranty for the financing bank without advising his superiors because he wanted to feel like he was really contributing—he wanted to feel the joy of *fulfillment or self-actualization*. His bosses certainly played upon Walt's need for *affinity*—to be seen as a worthy employee, one who was "making his numbers," or "biting the heads off chickens." Walt was subject to the influence of needs at all levels. Only he can say which category, or which level—*ego, social, or physical needs* played the dominant role. It is safe to say, however, that modern management can and will use all levels to motivate employees; and that both management and the individual employee should understand the vulnerabilities involved.

Understanding the Rationalization of Fraud—Heath's Seven Rationalizations   According to Joseph Heath, the seven rationalizations identified in Table 7.6 are customarily used to justify unethical behavior.

Walt Pavlo's behavior conforms to Heath's set of seven rationaliztions. In his book, we see that Walt explains that he is just taking orders for the accounting chicanery he leads, and that someone else at a higher pay grade is responsible for determining whether the actions involved are ethical or not. Similarly, when considering the monies he siphons off, he states that "you can't steal, what they're not going to get" indicating that he doesn't believe that there is any real injury caused by his action. Moreover, Walt takes the position that by hiding the true state of MCI's bad debts, he is supporting a pending buyout, thus helping the executives and current shareholders to get a good price for their shares rather than making them victims of his crime. He also views the money he helps skim from MCI's shyster customers (the ones he considers unethical) is a "victimless hustle" because it is stealing from crooks and scammers (p. 165).

---

35. See discussion in Wahba, A; Bridgewell, L (1976). "Maslow reconsidered: A review of research on the need hierarchy theory." *Organizational Behavior and Human Performance* (15): 212–240.

| TABLE | 7.6 | **Heath's Seven Rationalizations of Unethical Actions** |

- Denial of responsibility.
- Denial of injury.
- Denial of the victim.
- Condemnation of the condemners.
- Appeal to higher loyalties.
- Everyone else is doing it.
- Entitlement.

Source: "7 Neutralization/Rationalization Techniques," a speech by Joseph Heath at the Centre for Ethics at the University of Toronto, April 9, 2007.

Walt begins to realize that he is not being recognized for his good work and that he has been taken advantage of because he has to hire staff who report to him for more than he is being paid. By demanding that he "make his numbers" in terms of hiding the real state of the bad debts, Walt believes he is being asked to do the impossible. Consequently, he condemns the senior executives and the company in general. He feels that the company owes him, and that he is entitled to help himself by engaging in fraud. He takes the view that many senior executives know what is going on and are turning a blind eye to the hiding of the size of the bad debt problems. He believes they know that the accounting and reporting systems are a mess—a veritable black hole—and are taking advantage of it. He reasons that everyone else is doing it, so why shouldn't he?

Walt justifies some of his behavior by his loyalty to his family. He arranges for his father to buy a company, and for his family to have a higher lifestyle that they would otherwise have. His loyalty to family takes precedence over loyalty to MCI.

Opportunity to Commit Fraud Even though there may be a need to commit fraud, and the action can be rationalized, there must also be opportunities to commit fraud with acceptable levels of risk of getting caught and punished severely.

In Walt's case, he views the MCI accounting system as a veritable black hole—an "absolute shambles," as someone later described it. Reports are inaccurate, and no one seems to mind. There are no apparent controls over the accuracy of payment postings to the correct accounts. No one has taken the time to understand the fundamental nature and economic substance of the Rapid Advancement and other schemes that are being put in place. Ultimately the economic value falsely created in MCI's financial statements is removed in a huge write-off attributed to other problems. Clearly, senior management was not performing their oversight role properly, the organizational culture did not support whistleblowers and they were not encouraged to come forward, and internal audit functions were not effective.

These failings provided the opportunity that Walt was looking for and the belief that he wouldn't get caught. He was particularly susceptible when one of his bosses or one of his cofraudsters told him "not to worry about it right now." Perhaps it was also his belief that he could control the situation, so he wouldn't be found out. Ultimately he realized that he couldn't control his greedy colleagues, and he lost sight of the fact that he had ripped off a bank not just scammers. Both misjudgments came back to haunt him.

In the end, for Walt the slippery slope proved uncontrollable. Walt would have been wise to be more suspicious at the start when he heard: 'I'll make it worth your while." He should have listened to Ralph McCumber, his first boss whom he idolized, who had a keen "bullshit detector" and was fond of saying: "Don't make any promises you can't keep."

| **Lessons Learned** | When executives and auditors engage in a process of considering where fraud and white collar crime might emerge, they would do well to use the Fraud Triangle, Maslow's Hierarchy of Needs, and Heath's Seven Rationalizations of Unethical Acts as frameworks to spot red flag problems before they cause or allow significant harm. Such a process of consideration might be part of an annual or periodic brainstorming session as is now required of auditors in some jurisdictions. These frameworks should also be considered when planning for or instituting new incentive and reward systems because they present opportunities for introduction of dysfunctional pressures. Similarly, when assessing the performance of supervisory staff, it would be useful to consider using the frameworks to assess if the motivational methods used, while productive in the short run, were potentially harmful in the longer term. Finally, in order to assure adequate awareness and knowledge of the frameworks, their use should be discussed in supervisory training sessions. A sensitized supervisor, for example, should be able to red flag and correct potentially harmful rationalizations used by employees.

The analysis presented here shows how vulnerable accounting systems are to employees who are intent on taking advantage. It is also apparent that several people in addition to Walt suspected that something was not right, but they did not question or report their concerns. This was because MCI's corporate culture did not encourage such inquiries or whistle-blowing. In fact, it accepted and even encouraged a culture of manipulation rather than ethical behavior. There is a definite advantage installing an ethical corporate culture with a whistle blowing mechanism, and to instilling an expectation of an ethical corporate culture from the beginning of employment as well as reinforcing these expectations periodically.

In addition, there was a military-like micro-culture, in which employees were expected to follow orders rather than exercise their own conscience. Although this looks attractive in the short run, it prevents longer-term benefits from surfacing and raises risk for the enterprise as a whole.

Finally, the analysis of Walt's activities underscores the need to embed ethics concerns in the strategic and operational aspects of a company, and have a senior corporate official designated to champion the ethics portfolio in a company as well as in each significant division of that company. Monitoring these concerns should be an important ongoing function of a committee of the board of directors. Only by integrating ethics concerns into the governance structure of a company can ethics risks and opportunities be managed effectively.

International Operations

When any corporation operates outside of its domestic market, the normal guidance offered employees must be reconsidered as to:

| How their usual operating practices will impact on the local economy and culture;

| Whether different local foreign practices, such as widespread gift-giving or even bribery, should be endorsed or banned;

| The reaction to these changes by domestic stakeholders and particularly by primary stakeholders, including major customers and capital markets.

| **Impacts on Local Economies & their Cultures** | Multinational corporations may have a significant impact on local cultures that they would not have domestically. They must be careful not to have unfavorable impacts on local:

| Labor markets: wage rates, availability of supply;

| Raw material and other input markets;

- Political and legal processes;
- Religious and social customs.

If, for example, a multinational corporation decides to ignore local religious and/or social customs, it and its workers may be accused of *cultural imperialism*, and may find it difficult to obtain cooperation for future activities. Similarly, by virtue of its size, a multinational may so dominate the locale that there may be an unintended domination of local governments, courts, or elections that, again, may produce a backlash at some point.

| **Conflicts Between Domestic & Foreign Cultures** | Perhaps the most difficult problems arise when the values of the primary corporate stakeholders differ from those in the local foreign country. Differences noted in the media in recent years have included:

- Approval of bribery (Southeast Asia);
- Use of child labor (Dominican Republic, Southeast Asia);
- Use of slave labor;
- Unhealthy labor conditions;
- Treatment of women;
- Support of repressive regimes through location of operations (apartheid, Chile, Sudan);
- Lack of freedom of association;
- Respect for environment;
- Dealings with family members are expected, not avoided.

Often corporations locate operations in a country just because they want access to cheap labor, lower environmental protection costs, or less governmental red tape, and they are invited to come by the local politicians who do what they can by way of inducements. Why, then, should business-people worry about taking advantage of these opportunities when they find them? The reason lies in the new broader and global accountability the stakeholders expect and demand of corporations. Putting it simply, influential stakeholder groups have made it very difficult for corporations caught offending the values of the group anywhere in the world. Examples include:

- Boycott of clothing made in offensive labor situations:
  - Kathy Lee Gifford's line,
  - Nike, Reebok, Adidas, and other shoe manufacturers.
- Frustration of the intended scuttling of Shell's Brent Spar oil storage vessel in the depths of the North Sea (see case *Brent Spar Decommissioning Disaster* at the end of this chapter), and boycott of Shell products in Europe.
- Worldwide boycott of Nestle products for distributing powdered baby food to mothers in South Africa, who mixed the powder with contaminated water and harmed their babies.
- Activist investors in North America have pursued many mining companies for their poor environmental protection practices elsewhere.
- Boycott of beef grown on land cleared in the Amazon rain forest.

In addition, environmental and personal disasters such as at Bhopal have resulted in lawsuits launched by the same foreign politicians that invited the companies in and even entreated them to stay in adverse circumstances. Lawsuits have also arisen in the these cases in domestic jurisdictions where the offending company's stock has been traded because of investors' and/or foreigners' claims that management was negligent and should have issued warnings of heightened risk caused due to reduced safeguards. Although it seems that some customers want cheap goods and some investors rejoice in high profits, there are others who care about how these are produced, and/or are willing to sue if an opportunity presents itself.

More important than the costs of a trial in terms of time lost, fines, and legal fees paid, companies should realize that the damage to their reputation is usually the most significant impact they suffer. The impact of lost reputation may not be seen for a while, but there is no doubt that it translates into lost future revenues of a very large magnitude.

Finally, there is an impact on the morale of domestic employees to be considered from engaging in practices not considered worthy. Their desire to be productive, and to produce at high levels of quality, may be undermined with serious consequences.

| **Bribery, Facilitating Payments** | In their foreign operations, multinational corporations are likely to be asked for facilitating payments or bribes. A *facilitating payment* is usually nominal in value and made to speed up a result that would have happened anyway given enough time. A bribe is usually larger than nominal, and without which the desired result would not occur. Both payments are intended to influence outcomes, but some observers believe that a facilitating payment is of lesser ethical consequence than a bribe. Others can't see any difference between them.

One or both types of payment may be illegal, depending on the jurisdiction. Because of the instigation of a multinational group, Transparency International, the United States and other leading Organization for Economic Development (OECD) countries decided to agree to an OECD protocol whereby each signatory country would enact legislation similar to the U.S. Foreign Corrupt Practices Act during late 1998 and early 1999. It is expected, once the international mechanisms are in place, that these acts will allow a corporation that believes their foreign competitor is bribing officials in a third country to pursue the offending corporation through their domestic legal systems. For example, a U.S. corporation that suspected that a German company was bribing the officials in a South American country could apply to their U.S. legal system, which would, in turn, contact German authorities, who would search the German company's records for proof of the alleged transactions to be put forward in court. This initiative will make it much more risky to make payments to officials of foreign governments. It is a dramatic change from earlier positions where, for example, Germany considered a bribe outside of their country to be ethical and tax deductible, but a bribe inside Germany was considered unethical and illegal.

It should be clear that facilitating payments or bribes are problematic for reasons other than illegality, including:

| Adding to the cost of the operation, good, or service;

| Undermining the practice of purchasing based on merit in a country or firm;

| Risking possible negative consequences from stakeholder groups should they find out;

| Impossibility of enforcing performance (obtaining a contract) after bribes are paid;

| Impossibility of assessing sales force effectiveness;

| Indicating to employees elsewhere in the multinational corporation, that bribes are acceptable in spite of what codes of conduct say;

| Indicating to seekers of bribes elsewhere that bribes are possible if they ask.

As a result, some multinational corporations have banned the giving of bribes or facilitating payments. All corporations should have a policy on paying bribes and facilitating payments, rather than leaving employees to make up their own minds as to when payment is appropriate.

| Apparent Cultural Conflicts with Banning Gifts, Bribes, or Facilitating Payments | In some cultures, particularly in Southeastern Asia, China, and Japan, there is a long tradition of gift giving to cultivate long-term relationships that facilitate business dealings. In addition, it has been popularly believed that a corporation cannot do business in some countries unless payments are made to officials. Consequently, it has been said that if a corporation wants to do business in certain markets, bribery or facilitating payments is necessary.

In fact, however, some corporations have found that they have been able to do business without such payments, primarily because their products or services are excellent. Allis Chalmers and Citibank are examples of such corporations.

| Moral Imagination | In other corporations, managers have used their *moral imagination* to devise alternatives that answered needs in the host culture but conformed to North American norms for acceptable behavior. For example (see the Illustrative Ethics Case: *Bribery or Opportunity in China Case* in Chapter 4, a manager in China refused to pay officials of a potential host city, citing company policy. When the officials insisted repeatedly, the manager sought and received approval for a corporate contribution toward the establishment of a community center in a local park that would offer services to senior citizens. This appealed to Chinese cultural values and was in line with the corporation's North American policy of community support. It was differentiated from a bribe in that no payment was made to an individual for their personal benefit, and all payments were made in public rather than in secret.

| Guidelines for Ethical Practice | Two authors have made an extensive study of the ethics of foreign operations, and have written excellent books on the subject. Tom Donaldson (1989) and Richard DeGeorge (1993) have each put forward guidelines that may be useful for corporations to take note of. Their views are summarized in the end-of-chapter reading by Nancy Roth et al. (1996). Tom Donaldson's (1996) excellent article on bribery and foreign cultures is also reproduced as a reading.

| Consultation Before Action | The presumption that an organization is best served by a monolithic and rigid ethical culture may not be correct. Dunn (2006) and Dunn and Shome (2009) show that cultural differences contribute to Chinese and Canadian business students holding different attitudes towards the appropriate action to take when confronted with questionable accounting and business situations. Leaving employees to figure out how to deal with the various cultures encountered in international operations is a high-risk strategy. All organizations with international operations should sensitize their employees to cultural differences and equip them with an understanding of how the organization wants them to deal with the major issues likely to come up. At the very least, there should be an avenue of consultation with home office officials and a clear understanding of when to use it.

Crisis Management

Crises are pervasive in the current business environment. In the *1997 Crisis Management Survey of Fortune 1000 Companies*, 71 percent of the respondents companies had a crisis management plan and/or program in place, and almost a further 12 percent indicated that one was in development. A crisis has the potential to have a very significant impact of a crisis on the reputation of the company and its officers, on the company's ability to reach its objectives, and its ability to survive.[36] As a result, executives have learned that crises are to be avoided, and if avoidance is not

---

36. O. Lerbinger, *The Crisis Manager: Facing Risk and Responsibility*, Mahwah, New Jersey: Lawrence Erlbaum Associates, 1997, 4.

possible, that the crisis is to be managed so as to minimize harm. Directors have learned that crisis assessment, planning, and management must be part of a modern risk management program.

Unfortunately, the urgent nature of a crisis causes a focus on survival, and ethical niceties are largely forgotten. According to Lerbinger, a crisis *"is an event that brings, or has the potential for bringing, an organization into disrepute and imperils its future profitability, growth, and, possibly its very survival."*[37] Effective management of such events involves minimization of all harmful impacts. In reality, crisis-driven reactions rarely approach this objective unless advance planning is extensive and is based upon a good understanding of crisis management techniques, including the importance of maintaining reputation based upon ethical behavior.

If ethical behavior is considered to be of great importance by a corporation in its normal activities, ethical considerations should be even more important in crisis situations, since crisis resolution decisions usually define the company's future reputation. Not only are crisis decisions among the most significant made in terms of potential impact on reputation, opportunities may also be lost if ethical behavior is not a definite part of the crisis management process. For example, avoidance of crises may be easier if employees are ethically sensitized to stakeholder needs; phases of the crisis may be shortened if ethical behavior is expected of employees; and/or damage to reputations may be minimized if the public expects ethical performance based on past corporate actions. Moreover, the degree of trust that ethical concern instills in a corporate culture will ensure that no information or option will be suppressed and not given to the decision maker. Finally, constant concern for ethical principles should ensure that important issues are identified and the best alternatives canvassed to produce the optimal decision for the company.

Fundamental to the proper management of a crisis is an understanding of four phases of a crisis: precrisis, uncontrolled, controlled, and reputation restoration. These are outlined in Figure 7.5. The main goal of crisis management should be to avoid crises. If this is not possible, then the impacts should be minimized. This can be done by anticipating crises or recognizing early warning signs as soon as possible, and responding to soften or minimize the impact and shorten the time during which the crisis is uncontrolled. These goals can best be achieved by proper advance planning, by continued monitoring, and by speedy, effective decision making during the crisis. Figure 7.5 shows two cost

FIGURE 7.5 **Phases of a Crisis**

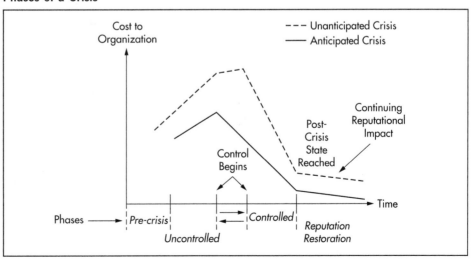

37. Ibid., 4.

curves, where the lower one reflects the benefits of earlier control being applied, thus minimizing the overall cost and the ongoing damage to reputation.

Advance planning for a crisis should be part of a modern enterprise risk assessment and contingency management program because of the growing recognition of the potential negative impact of an unanticipated crisis. It can be done effectively by brainstorming for potential problem areas, assessing those identified, and devising contingency plans for effective action. Second, red flags or warning indicators can be picked out that will identify what is developing so that the earliest action can be taken to minimize cost. In the 1997 Crisis Survey noted earlier, 73 percent of the companies reporting had a senior-level management and corporate-level crisis management team that would focus on the crisis, and 76 percent had a crisis communication plan, which could include notification of the public, employees, government, and the media.

The process of brainstorming to identify crises should address problems that could arise from the seven types identified by Lerbinger:[38]

1. Natural disasters

2. Technological disasters

3. Differences of expectations between individuals, groups, and corporations leading to confrontations

4. Malevolent acts by terrorists, extremists, governments, and individuals

5. Management values that do not keep pace with environmental and social requirements and obligations

6. Management deception

7. Management misconduct

Managing the crisis effectively once it has happened is vital to the achievement of crisis management goals. Quick identification and assessment of a crisis can be instrumental in influencing the outcome efficiently and effectively. One of the key characteristics of a crisis is that it will degenerate if no action is taken,[39] so delay in identification and action can have serious consequences.

Of the Fortune 1000 companies responding to the survey, 73 percent indicated that internal training was part of preparing for crisis awareness, identification, and management, and 48 percent used outside contract trainers. Major factors listed by respondents as needing improvement in crisis management included internal awareness (51 percent), communication (46 percent), drills/training (38 percent), vulnerability/risk assessment (36 percent), information technology (33 percent), planning/coordinating (32 percent), and business continuity (25 percent).

Undivided attention to the crisis and avoidance of other problems that can befuddle decision makers will result in better decisions, just as will the making of plans on a contingency basis and the integration of ethics into the decision-making process.

One of the most important aspects to keep in mind during the assessment of crises, and the avoidance or minimization of their impact, is the immediate and ongoing impact on the organization's reputation. By reflecting on how the organization's response to the crisis will affect the perception by stakeholders of it trustworthiness, responsibility, reliability, and credibility, decision makers can make choices that benefit all stakeholders and often *enhance* the organization's reputational capital or shorten the period of diminishment.

---

38. Ibid, 10-14.

39. C. F. Hermann, "Some Consequences of Crisis Which Limit the Viability of Organizations." *Administrative Sciences Quarterly* 8, no. 1 (1963): 62–82. Noted in Lerbinger, 1997, p. 7. 1963.

Ethics can be integrated into the decision-making process for crisis management in many ways. Specific instances involving prevention and warning, inclusion in an analytical approach, focusing a decision, and framing communications are outlined in Table 7.7.

Conclusion

Modern corporations and other organizations are successful because they create, sustain, or inform upon value. Ultimately, success depends upon the support they engender from their stakeholders, and that depends upon the respect shown for stakeholder expectations. Appropriate or ethical behavior is therefore circumscribed by the expectations of stakeholders, and care should be shown for the creation of guidance and other means for encouraging employees to "do what is right."

In this new era of stakeholder accountability, organizations would do well to observe the six hypernorms: honesty, fairness, compassion, integrity, predictability, and responsibility. These values should be built into governance, risk management, strategy, operations, ethical decision making, disclosure, and crisis management. Reputation and success depend upon it whether you are a director, executive, or professional accountant.

| TABLE | 7.7 | **How to Incorporate Ethics into Crisis Management** |

Prevention and warning:

- Code of conduct: identify values, adopt, emphasize and make effective
- Identify potential ethics problems and warning indicators, and pre-plan responses, as part of an ongoing enterprise risk management and contingency planning program
- Ethical "red flags" or warning indicators:
  - Training to emphasize how to identify and what to do about them
  - Check as part of an ongoing enterprise risk management system
- Encourage by publicizing good examples, and awarding paper medals

Analytical approach:

- Apply a stakeholder-analysis framework as discussed in Chapter 5:
- External ethics consultant
- Checklist or specific time to consider:
  - ethics issues, alternatives & opportunities

Decision itself:

- Ethics/company's values: integrate into the decision making:
  - Consider how the crisis or its impact can be influenced ethically—timing, cost, mitigation?
  - Specific consideration of how to improve the organization's reputation drivers including—trustworthiness, responsibility, reliability, and credibility
  - Specific ethical communications objectives
  - Assign ethics watch-dog responsibility
  - Use a checklist or template with specific ethics objectives
  - Apply moral imagination as discussed in Chapter 5

Communications on ethical intent to:

- Media, employees, customers, government, public & other stakeholders

Questions

1. In what ways do ethics risk and opportunity management, as described in this chapter, go beyond the scope of traditional risk management?

2. If a corporation's governance process does not involve ethics risk management, what unfortunate consequences might befall that corporation?

3. How will the U.S. external auditor's mindset change in order to discharge the duties contemplated by SAS 99 on finding fraud?

4. How could a corporation utilize stakeholder analysis to formulate strategies?

5. What would you list as the five most important ethical guidelines for dealing with North American employees?

6. Is trust really important—can't employees work effectively for someone they are afraid of, or at least where there is some "creative tension"?

7. Should a North American corporation operating abroad respect each foreign culture encountered, or insist that all employees and agents follow only one corporate culture?

8. What should a North American company do in a foreign country where women are regarded as secondary to men, and are not allowed to negotiate contracts or undertake senior corporate positions?

9. Descriptive commentary about corporate social responsibility performance is sometimes included in annual reports. Is this indicative of good performance, or is it just window dressing? How can the credibility of such commentary be enhanced?

10. Why should a corporation make use of a comprehensive framework for considering, managing, and reporting corporate social responsibility performance? How should they do so?

11. Do professional accountants have the expertise to audit corporate social performance reports?

12. Why should ethical decision making be incorporated into crisis management?

Case Insights

The cases provided to illuminate the issues developed in this chapter are surprisingly realistic and engage the reader quickly. The specific scenarios, with notation of the chapter section to which they primarily apply, are as follows:

Cases on Workplace Ethics

- *Texaco's Jelly Beans* is the story of how Texaco's discrimination against black workers ended up costing a $300 million fine and lost respect. Why did it happen?

- *Downsize or Bonus Allocation Decisions* confronts the reader with realistic, tough choices among staff, thus forcing decisions about what values the decision maker holds and which values ought to be communicated to the work team.

Case on Fraud & White Collar Crime

- *Walt Pavlo's MCI Scams/Frauds* explains how a young junior executive at MCI managed to defraud his employer of $6 million that he then transferred to the Cayman Islands.

Cases on International Operations

- *Jail and the German Subcontractor* is a real story about a U.S. executive who went to Germany to supervise a project, only to be jailed due to the actions of a German subcontractor.

- *AIDS Medication in South Africa* causes students to face the reality corporations face when they deal in a country that has a low standard of living and disposable income, and where the local government sets aside property/patent rights and forces low prices or arranges for generic drugs, thus impacting negatively on corporate profits.

Cases on Crisis Management

- *Digoxin Overdose—The Need for Skepticism, Courage, and Persistence* involves the death of a child that could have been avoided if only one of the many people involved had demonstrated sufficient skepticism, courage, and persistence. These deficiencies of character are frequently responsible for business and professional crises and scandal.

- *The Exxon Valdez* reviews the event of the shipwreck and oil spill that galvanized the public and environmental activists to pressure companies for better environmental protection. It is an exceptional lesson of what can go wrong to lead to a crisis and during the crisis.

- *The Brent Spar Decommissioning Disaster* deals with the crisis management fiasco Shell faced when dealing with the outrage created by Greenpeace to stop a questionable environmental practice.

- *Crisis at Wind River Energy Inc.* is about a relatively small firm where the majority owner and CEO faces multiple crises critical to the financial and physical well-being of the company's stakeholders. What would you do if you were the CEO?

Reading Insights

The readings are intended to provide background on areas that will prove to be significant to future businesspeople and professional accountants. The drive to manage corporate social performance better will not subside, so articles by Roth et al., Donaldson, and Mitroff et al. should be essential reading. Appendices A and B on CSR/CSP programs and reporting provide useful benchmarks and frameworks.

References

1997 Crisis Management Survey of Fortune 1000 Companies conducted by The George Washington University Institute for Crisis, Disaster, and Risk Management and The Corporate Response Group. The Survey had 105 respondents.

AccountAbility. The Institute of Social and Ethical Accountability. United Kingdom. http://www.accountability.org.uk/.

Albrecht, W.S., Albrecht, C.C. and Albrecht, C.O. *Fraud Examination*, 2nd ed. (Mason, Ohio: South-Western Cengage Learning, 2006), 31

"Auditor's Responsibility for Fraud Detection." *Journal of Accountancy*, January 2003, 28–36.

Berenbeim, R. E. The Conference Board, Director, Working Group on Global Business Ethics Principles, 1999.

Brooks, L. J. "A Partial Preliminary Report on a Survey on the Effectiveness/Compliance of Corporate Codes of Conduct in Canada." Unpublished manuscript, 1990.

Brooks, L. J. "Codes of Conduct, Trust, Innovation, Commitment, and Productivity: A Strategic-Cultural Perspective." *Global Focus* 12, no. 2, (2000): 1–11.

Brooks, L. J., and Selley, D., *Ethics and Governance: Developing and Maintaining an Ethical Corporate Culture*, Canadian Centre for Ethics & Corporate Policy, 3rd ed., Toronto, 2008.

Corporate Ethics Monitor, EthicScan Canada, Toronto, Canada.

De George, R. T. *Competing with Integrity in International Business.* New York: Oxford University Press, 1993.

Donaldson, T. *The Ethics of International Business.* New York: Oxford University Press, 1989.

Donaldson, T. "Values in Tension: Ethics Away from Home." *Harvard Business Review*, September–October 1996, 48–62.

Dunn, P. "The Role of Culture and Accounting Education in Resolving Ethical Business Dilemmas by Chinese and Canadians." *Accounting and the Public Interest* 6, no. 1, (2006): 116–134.

Dunn, P., and Shome, A. "Cultural Crossvergence and Social Desirability Bias: Ethical Evaluations by Chinese and Canadian Business Students, *Journal of Business Ethics* (forthcoming).

Enterprise Risk Management: Trends and Emerging Practices, Tillinghast-Towers Perrin and the Institute of Internal Auditors Research Foundation, 2001.

Fombrun, C. J. *Reputation: Realizing Value from the Corporate Image.* Boston: Harvard Business School Press, 1996.

Gellerman, S. W. "Why Good Managers Make Bad Choices." *Harvard Business Review* 64, no. 4, (1986): 85–90.

Heath, Joseph, "7 Neutralization/Rationalization Techniques", speech at the Centre for Ethics at the University of Toronto, April 9, 2007

Hermann, Charles F. "Some Consequences of Crisis Which Limit the Viability of Organizations." *Administrative Sciences Quarterly* 8, no. 1 (1963): 62–82. Noted in Lerbinger, 1997, p. 7.

Jones, Joanne, Massey, Dawn W., and Thorne, Linda, "Auditors' Ethical Reasoning: Insights From Past Research And Implications For The Future," *Journal of Accounting Literature* 2003.

KPMG Forensic, *Integrity Survey 2005–2006*, 2005.

Lerbinger, Otto. *The Crisis Manager: Facing Risk and Responsibility.* Mahwah, New Jersey: Lawrence Erlbaum Associates, 1997.

Managing Risk in the New Economy, American Institute of Certified Public Accountants and the Canadian Institute of Chartered Accountants, 2001.

Maslow, A. H. *Motivation and Personality.* New York: Harper and Row, 1954. See also Maslow, A.H., "A Theory of Human Motivation", *Psychological Review*, American Psychological Association, vol. 50, 1943, pp. 394–395, as reprinted in *The Maslow Business Reader*, edited by Deborah C. Stephens. New York: John Wiley & Sons, 2000, pp. 3–4.

Mitchell, R. K., B. R. Agle, and D. J. Wood. "Toward a Theory of Stakeholder Identification and Salience: Defining the Principle of Who and What Really Counts." *Academy of Management Review* 22, no. 4 (1997): 853–886.

Mitroff, I. I., P. Shrivastava, and F. E. Udwadia. "Effective Crisis Management." *Academy of Management Executive* 1, no. 3, (1987): 283–292.

Nitkin, D., and L. J. Brooks. "Sustainability Auditing and Reporting: The Canadian Experience." *Journal of Business Ethics*, Vol. 17, 1998, 1499–1507.

Nudell, Mayer, and Norman Antokol. *The Handbook for Effective Emergency and Crisis Management.* Lexington, Mass: Lexington Books, 1988.

Paine, Lynne Sharp, "Managing for Organizational Integrity," *Harvard Business Review* March–April (1994): 112.

Pavlo, Walter, Jr., and Weinberg, N. *Stolen Without A Gun: Confessions from Inside History's Biggest Accounting Fraud—The Collapse of MCI WorldCom*, Etika Books LLC, Tampa FL, 2007.

Pellizzari, P. *Conscious Consumption: Corporate Social Responsibility and Canada's Grocery Giants.* Toronto: EthicScan Canada, 2002.

Rest, James R., *Development in Judging Moral Issues.* Minneapolis: University of Minnesota Press, 1979.

Rowley, T. "Moving Beyond Dyadic Ties: A Network Theory of Stakeholder Influences." *Academy of Management Review* 22, no. 4, (1997): 887–910.

Roth, N. L., T. Hunt, M. Stravropoulos, and K. Babik. "Can't We All Just Get Along: Cultural Variables in Codes of Ethics." *Public Relations Review* 22, no. 2 (Summer 1996): 151–161.

"SAS 99," Official Releases column in the *Journal of Accountancy*, January 2003, 105–120.

Sethi, S. P. "Codes of Conduct for Global Business: Prospects and Challenges of Implementation," in *Principles of Stakeholder Management*, The Clarkson Centre for Business Ethics, 1999, 9–20.

Social Accountability International, previously the Council on Economic Priorities. *SA8000: Guideline for Social Accountability*, New York, 1997.

Sustainability Reporting Guideline, Global Reporting Initiative, G_3 version, January 2006. http://www.grig3.org.

"The Price of Happiness," *CAMagazine*, September 2006. http://www.camagazine.com/index.cfm/ci_id/33539/la_id/1.

Wartick, S. L., and P. L. Cochran. "The Evolution of the Corporate Social Performance Model." *Academy of Management Review* 10, no. 4, (1985): 758–769.

Ethics Case | *Texaco's Jelly Beans*[1]

In March 1994, six African Americans employed at Texaco Inc. filed a class action lawsuit on behalf of 1,400 current and former African American employees. They alleged that Texaco had systematically discriminated against them in terms of promotions and had fostered a hostile corporate environment for minority employees.[2]

Richard Lundwall was the senior coordinator of personnel services in the Finance Department at Texaco's office in Harrison, New York. During an August 5, 1994, deposition,[3] he testified that he and other officials in Texaco's Finance Department retained records relating to the promotion of minority employees. He was asked to produce these documents. On August 14, 1994, Lundwall attended a meeting with other members of the Texaco Finance Department to discuss the production of these requested documents. Among the officers attending this meeting were Robert Ulrich, treasurer; David Keough, senior assistant treasurer; and various division heads such as Peter Meade, Brian Ashley, Pete Wissel, and Steve Carlson.[4] Prior to entering the meeting,

---

1. Prepared from a case submission by students: Sudha Kutty, Philip Malin, Yasmina Miller, Shelley Pancham-Candler, and David Wong.
2. *Roberts et al. v Texaco Inc.*, 94 Civ. 2015.
3. U.S. Attorney, Southern District of New York. Press release. November 19, 1996.
4. Affidavit of Cyrus Mehri, sworn October 28, 1996, citing deposition of R. Lundwall.

Lundwall placed a small tape recorder in his pocket and turned it on. When later asked why he had taken such action, he stated that "over the years I've seen a number of people thrown to the wolves when something went wrong, and I didn't want to be fodder for the wolves."[5] On a more practical level, however, Lundwall was also in charge of taking minutes of the meeting and found that recording the meetings ensured the accuracy of the minutes.[6] He stated that after the meeting he placed the tapes in his desk and forgot about them.[7]

In the spring of 1996, Lundwall was informed that he was being downsized out of his job and had to leave Texaco by the end of August 1996. After thirty-one years of loyal service to Texaco, he expected more; he had seen other employees being pushed out when they reached fifty-five years of age and realized that the same thing was now happening to him.[8] It was not until he was in the hospital recovering from surgery in March 1996 that he remembered the tapes and had time to listen to them.[9] Lundwall maintains, on an interview on *60 Minutes,* that he had only to mention his possession of the tapes to a senior executive and his job would have been secure. When asked why he did not take such an action, he responded, "It's not the right thing to do. That's called extortion and that's illegal. And . . . the world's a crummy enough place without adding to it."[10]

By July 1996, Lundwall realized that there would be no job at Texaco. On his last day of work, he approached one of the employees who had launched the suit and informed her that "depending on how my situation turns out, you might have an ally."[11] Lundwall's reasoning was that, if a job did surface, then he would not have been able to come forward with the tapes, not for a while, anyway.[12] On August 1, 1996, Lundwall contacted Cyrus Mehri at the law firm of Cohen, Milstein, Hausfeld, and Toll, lawyers for the plaintiffs. He informed Mehri that he had in his possession information that would be useful in the lawsuit against Texaco. In subsequent conversations, Lundwall informed Mehri that such information included tape recordings. On August 12, 1996, Lundwall met with Mehri and informed him that the tape recordings, created after the litigation began, revealed himself and other senior officials in the Finance Department discussing the destruction of documents relevant to the plaintiffs' case.[13] After this meeting, Lundwall retained a lawyer and in September 1996 handed over copies of two tapes to attorneys for the plaintiffs. On October 25, 1996, Lundwall met again with Mehri and listened to the tapes. He confirmed that the tapes were the same ones he had provided to his counsel to hand over.[14] He admitted that one of the purposes for the meeting of August 14, 1994, was to review the materials requested by the plaintiffs after the deposition and to hide documents from the plaintiffs. He admitted that he and others had shredded portions of the requested evidence, that handwritten comments were deleted from certain documents, and that certain finance officials were told to say that they did not retain their own copies of such information.[15] In one part of the tape, the following was revealed:

Ulrich: You know, there is no point in even keeping the restricted version any more. All it could do is to get us in trouble. That's the way I feel. I would not keep anything.

5. *60 Minutes* interview, p. 2 transcript.
6. Affidavit of Cyrus Mehri, p. 6.
7. *60 Minutes.*
8. Ibid.
9. Ibid., p. 3.
10. Ibid.
11. Ibid.
12. Ibid.
13. Affidavit of Joseph Magan, special agent with the FBI, sworn November 19, 1996.
14. Ibid.
15. Ibid.

Lundwall: Let me shred this thing and any other restricted version like it.

In another segment:

Keough: They'll find it when they look through it.

Lundwall: Not if I take it out they won't.

Matters did not end here. The tape recording of the August 14, 1994, meeting contained other interesting bits of conversation. The initial transcript of the recordings which hit the *New York Times* on November 4, 1996, indicated the use of expletives and racist terms such as niggers and "black jelly beans." According to the *Times*, at one point in the tape the treasurer states, "It's this diversity thing. You know how black jelly beans agree . . . ," To which Lundwall responds, "That's funny. All the black jelly beans seem to be glued to the bottom of the bag." At another point in the tape, Lundwall states, "I'm still having trouble with Hanukkah. Now we have Kwanzaa. These f—ing niggers, they s— all over us with this."[16]

Texaco was quick to act over the revelation of these tapes. At a news conference held on November 4, 1996, Texaco chairman, Peter Bijur, apologized for the remarks on the tape, stating that such remarks represent not only a profound contempt for the law but also a contempt for Texaco's values and policies. Bijur indicated that the company was taking six steps to reinforce company policy and its code of conduct. Such measures included visits by senior executives to company locations to apologize to employees, the expansion of Texaco's "diversity learning experience," and a renewed emphasis on the company's core values. Two current employees were suspended with pay, and the benefits of Lundwall and former treasurer Robert Ulrich (who had retired in March 1995) were cut off. Texaco retained the services of Peter Armstrong, former Assistant U.S. Attorney for the Southern District of New York, to conduct an independent investigation into the matter. In his report released November 11, 1996, Mr. Armstrong notes that by using digital processing techniques, he was able to obtain a clearer version of the recording.[17] After listening to this version, he concluded that the word *nigger* was never used, as initially alleged in the plaintiffs' transcript. The relevant portion of the tape is actually

Ulrich: "I've heard that diversity thing, we don't have black jelly beans or green . . ."

Lundwall: " . . . that's funny, all the black jelly beans seem to be glued to the bottom of the bag."

Through his attorney, Mr. Ulrich indicated that the term *jelly bean* was not meant to be pejorative and actually was a reference from a speech given by a gentleman later identified as Doctor R. Roosevelt Thomas Jr. who uses a jelly bean analogy as a means of describing diversity.[18]

Armstrong's conclusion was that the terms "f—ing nigger" were never used and that the references to jelly beans do not appear to have been intended as a racial slur. Bijur was quick to indicate that these preliminary findings merely correctly identified what words were actually spoken in the conversation but by no means changed the unacceptable context or tone of the conversation. The report's findings were published in the *New York Times* on November 11, 1996. Civil rights leaders interviewed on November 12, 1996, felt that the distinction in the transcript made little difference, as the tone of the conversation indicated a clear disdain for both Hanukkah and Kwanzaa and revealed intolerant overtures.[19] Bijur spent most of the day meeting with civil rights leaders, such as Kweisi Mfume of the National Association for the Advancement of Colored People and Reverend Jesse Jackson, many of whom called for a national boycott of Texaco.

---

16. *Court TV* Library: *Texaco Suit—Order to Show Cause,* Transcript. Kwanzaa is an African American cultural festival.
17. Interim report, p. 2.
18. Ibid.
19. "Civil Rights Leaders Issue Call for a National Boycott of Texaco." Kurt Eichenwald, November 13, 1996.

On November 15, 1996, Texaco announced it had reached an Agreement in Principle to settle the *Roberts et al. v Texaco* lawsuit. The terms of the settlement were as follows:

| Provide payment to the plaintiff class in the amount of $115 million, in addition to a one-time salary increase of approximately 11 percent for current employees of the plaintiff class effective January 1, 1997[20]

| Create an Equality and Tolerance Task Force, which will be charged with determining potential improvements to Texaco's human resources programs and monitor the progress of such programs

| Adopt and implement companywide diversity and sensitivity, mentoring and ombudsperson programs

| Consider nationwide job posting of more senior positions

| Monitor its performance on the programs and initiatives provided for in the settlement agreement

The total cost of the agreement was said to be $176.1 million, making it the largest settlement for a race discrimination suit in history.[21] Texaco's problems, however, are far from over. On November 13, 1996, two Texaco shareholders launched a shareholder's derivative action lawsuit, stating that Texaco's directors and officers breached fiduciary duty and damaged Texaco's name.

Some would say that it was about time Texaco was finally caught. In 1991, Texaco paid a record $17.7 million in compensatory and punitive damages to an employee who sued for sex discrimination after the company denied her a promised promotion and gave her job to a man.[22] Others say that Texaco was forced to settle the case not on its legal merits but due to the inaccurate transcript published by the *New York Times*.[23] Some have argued that what the Texaco case proves is that "if you can create enough bad publicity, depicting a company as hopelessly racist, you can win without ever going to trial."[24] This may not be entirely correct. Had this matter gone to trial, damages in the Roberts action were estimated at $71 million in back pay and damages for each plaintiff in the amount of $300,000, resulting in a total liability of $491 million.[25] Furthermore, in June 1996, Spencer Lewis, Jr., a district director of the Equal Employment Opportunity Commission for the New York City District, found against Texaco for failing to promote blacks and pursuing a companywide pattern of racial bias.[26] Lewis held that Texaco used an evaluation system to promote employees that did not comply with EEOC guidelines. Questions about Texaco's corporate culture exist. In a company whose core values state that "Each person deserves to be treated with respect and dignity,"[27] and where it is within the corporate conduct guidelines to report known or suspected violations of company policy to supervisors, some say that such a conversation could not have arisen if it were not prevalent for such written policies to be undermined by the actions of senior executives.

When Lundwall was questioned as to why he turned over the tapes, he indicated that it was

---

20. For the sake of accuracy, it should be noted that the plaintiff class had yet to be certified as a class and was to appear before the court on December 6, 1996, for a hearing regarding class certification. In the Agreement in Principle, the parties agree for the sake of the settlement to the certification of a class consisting of all African Americans employed in a salaried position in the United States by Texaco or its subsidiaries at any time from March 23, 1991, to November 16, 1996 [Agreement in Principle. November 15, 1996].

21. *60 Minutes,* p. 1.

22. *Texaco's White Collar Bigots,* by Jack E. White.

23. John Leo, "Jelly Bean: The Sequel," *US News Online.*

24. Ibid.

25. Derivative Action Complaint filed November 13, 1996, p. 7.

26. "Texaco Discrimination Lawsuit Sparks National Dialog on Racism in Corporate America."

27. "Texaco Apologizes for Racist Remarks of Senior Executives but Questions About Culture Remain."

not to get back at Texaco but, rather, to maintain a job.[28] In retrospect, he admits that he was naive bordering on stupid to think that handing over the tapes would help his cause. If anything, handing over the tapes apparently hurt his cause. On November 19, 1996, Robert Lundwall was arrested and charged with obstruction of justice in that, from July 1994 to August 1994, he corruptibly destroyed, concealed, and withheld documents requested by attorneys for the plaintiffs. As of December 17, 1996, Lundwall was involved in discussions with the prosecuting attorneys to possibly resolve the charge without going to trial by either pleading to a lesser charge or offering help in exchange for immunity.[29] As a result of Lundwall's criminal subpoena before the grand jury, further questionable actions on the part of Texaco's executives have come to light. In addition to the documents pertaining to the promotion of minority employees, the grand jury records included a draft memo dated June 24, 1994, summarizing the results of an employee survey in Texaco's Finance Department. The results were distinctly unfavorable toward the criteria for promotions of employees. The draft results were forwarded by Lundwall to a lawyer in Texaco's Legal Department on June 30, 1994, requesting advice on publication of the survey results. A handwritten reply on Lundwall's covering memo from the lawyer dated July 26, 1994, advised delaying publication of the survey results to avoid its becoming part of the discovery process in the class action suit.[30] While Texaco lawyers state that this draft memorandum was not subject to discovery, the plaintiffs' lawyers claim that it did fall within the time frame.

When asked why it appears on certain portions of the tape that he took the initiative to shred documents, Lundwall would not comment.[31] His attorney indicates that the transcripts of the tape make it clear that Lundwall was directed to shred and destroy the evidence.[32] When asked what he would do if he had to do it all over again, Lundwall stated that he would "slip quietly into the night with my benefits and let the system stay as screwed up as it is."[33]

Questions

1. In a company as progressive as Texaco, what permitted such discrimination to occur?
2. How could such discrimination have been prevented?
3. Is whistle-blowing ethical?
4. Could a protected whistle-blowing mechanism or conscientious ombudsperson have helped?

Sources

Cohen, Milstein, Hausfeld, and Toll. *Texaco Discrimination Lawsuit Sparks National Dialog on Racism in Corporate America.* Internet Bulletin, (see **www.cengage.com/accounting/ brooks**), November 1996.

Court TV Library. *The Texaco Suit.* Internet Bulletin. See **www.cengage.com/accounting/ brooks**, 1996.

Eichenwald, K. *Texaco Lawyers Reportedly Tried to Conceal Damaging Documents.* Internet Bulletin. (See **www.cengage.com/ accounting/brooks**). November 15, 1996.

Leo, J. *Jelly Bean: The Sequel.* Internet Bulletin. (See **www.cengage.com/accounting/brooks**)

Sixty Minutes. The Texaco Tapes. Livingston, NJ: Burrelle's Transcripts. April 13, 1997.

Stepshow, *Ex-Texaco Exec May Avoid Trial.* See **www.cengage.com/accounting/brooks**, December 17, 1996.

White, J. B. *Texaco's White Collar Bigots.* Internet Bulletin, Volume 148. Number 123, November 18, 1996.

---

28. *60 Minutes,* p. 4.
29. "Ex-Texaco Exec May Avoid Trial," December 17, 1996.
30. "Texaco Lawyers Reportedly Tried to Conceal Damaging Documents," Kurt Eichenwald, November 15, 1996.
31. *60 Minutes,* p. 5
32. Ibid.
33. Ibid., p. 6.

Ethics Case

Downsize or Bonus Allocation Decisions

Assume that you have just been placed in charge of the Claims Investigation Unit of a small insurance company based in Minneapolis. Your personnel department has provided the following details on your personnel. However, because your insurance company is in the midst of takeover discussions, you have been asked to decide whom you would terminate if you were called on to downsize by one person and, alternatively, how you would allocate a bonus of $20,000 if no one were to be dismissed. You really want your team to function well after the decision is made because your future depends on it.

Question

1. What would your answers be, and what would your reasoning be for each?

Personnel Characteristics of Claims Investigation Unit

NAME	SALARY	TITLE	YEARS OF SENIORITY	PERFORMANCE	PERSONAL
Carol	$84,000	Analyst	5	Acceptable, misses deadlines	Married, many dependents
Gord	$72,000	Analyst	2	Outstanding, pushy, suggestions	Single, no dependents
Jane	$68,000	Junior	8	Consistent, excellent, dependable	Married to successful architect
Ralph	$86,000	Senior	15	Acceptable, plodder	Married, two children in University
Hilary	$64,000	Junior	6	Acceptable, costly mistakes	Single, dependable, chronically ill mother

Ethics Case

Walt Pavlo's MCI Scams/Frauds[1]

Walt Pavlo joined MCI in 1992, and rapidly became second in command at the company's Finance or long-distance collections unit as is documented in the *Manipulation of MCI's Allowance for Doubtful Accounts* case in Chapter 5 on page 285. Walt left MCI in 1996, and ultimately resigned in early 1997. During the four years and just afterward, he participated in several frauds on MCI and on customers who were dealing with MCI. The frauds against MCI are detailed in the case noted earlier, and the frauds he perpetrated against others are detailed here. Walt's motivation, opportunity for and rationalization of these frauds are analyzed in the illustration on page 481.

Walt initially became caught up in an attempt to cover up the fact that many of the accounts receivable from companies that resold MCI's telephone connection time to consumers were far past due, and collection ultimately unlikely. Senior executives at MCI were reluctant to show the true state of MCI's bad debts because they wanted to isolate the company's earnings and assets in order to attract a favorable takeover bid buy-out of shares that would make them rich. Consequently, although total bad debts approached $120 million, upper management encouraged MCI finance staff to use a number of techniques to minimize the visibility of the problem and limit the annual write-off of bad debts

1. All details used in this case are taken from *Stolen Without A Gun: Confessions from Inside History's Biggest Accounting Fraud—The Collapse of MCI WorldCom*, Walter Pavlo Jr. and Neil Weinberg, Etika Books LLC, Tampa Florida, 2007.

to only $15 million. The minimization techniques included:

▎ Restructuring a $55 million account receivable into the form of a promissory note—but one without collateral—so that the amount would not appear old in an aging analysis.

▎ Restructuring other bad debts into notes in a similar fashion.

▎ Lapping—applying checks from one creditor to the account of another to make it appear that bad accounts were being paid. The accounting system was notorious for its delays and inaccuracies, so if a customer complained about his account, it was "fixed" by a transfer from another customer's account with only a few accounting staff knowing what was going on.

▎ Disappearing an account—an extension of lapping where the balance on an account is eliminated by spreading it into the accounts of others through lapping.

▎ Recording "cash in transit" and using it to reduce problem accounts receivable—large payments of $50–60 million per month from WorldCom, for example, were picked up by a clerk, faxed in, and recorded as a debt to cash in transit with the credit to a problem account. When the real check arrived, the entries would be reversed and proper entries made, but the interval of a few days allowed some "management" of accounts receivable.

▎ Misapplying vagabond payments—millions of dollars per month were sent in which MCI's inefficient accounting system could not figure out which account the money belonged.

Walt was encouraged to "make his bad debt aging numbers," as he says in his own words: "Instead of gaming the system, MCI Finance had turned the system into a game, going so far as to send around a monthly internal report, grading departments on how well they did in sticking to their "aging" numbers. Pavlo got a hearty pat on the back from his superiors, and he passed on the favor by praising his staff for

their heroism in battle."[2] Walt was seen, and saw himself, as a "solutions provider" for MCI in managing the exposure to and of its bad debts.

One of Walt's customers, Harold Mann, introduced him to Mark Benveniste, the owner of a company called Manatee Capital, who had a proposal for "factoring" MCI's accounts receivable—paying MCI up front for a portion of certain receivables, and collecting the entire receivable when it was paid. MCI would get their money much faster in return for a factoring discount or fee. It sounded great except that Manatee would not do the deal unless MCI guaranteed any accounts that proved to be uncollectible.[3] In Walt's terms, Manatee would, in effect advance or loan money to MCA's clients to allow them to pay early, provided MCI guaranteed these loans—and Walt was sure that MCI wouldn't.[4]

Nonetheless, as time went on, Walt was under increasing pressure to "make his numbers" in terms of collections which meant hiding overdue accounts receivable. Hoping a solution would emerge, Walt agreed to meet with Manatee's bankers from the National Bank of Canada. The meeting went well. Walt felt great—in charge—and he continued discussions with Benveniste over the coming months until the day came to sign off the legal documents. Although he had not discussed the Manatee arrangements with anyone at MCI, and he knew that only company officers were authorized to sign such documents, he went ahead anyway and signed the bank documents committing MCI to guaranty up to $40 million if Manatee could not collect.[5] The bank took Walt at his word after checking with a switchboard operator that he was employed at MCI. Walt's bosses didn't find out until it was too late, and by then they were on the hook for millions.

Needless to say, Walt took the factoring scheme forward within MCI under the banner of the Rapid Advancement Program for financing sales. It made him extremely popular

2. Ibid., p. 103.
3. This is known as factoring "with recourse" because the risk of loss stays with the account owner, MCI.
4. Ibid., p. 97.
5. Ibid., p. 110.

with both the sales and collections people. Walt was a hero, and no one investigated how it worked sufficiently to question the economics involved or uncover the MCI guaranty.

During one of his meetings with Harold Mann, Walt told Harold that Robert Hilby, whose shady MCI reseller operation, Simple Access, had offered Walt a job, and that he was considering it. Not wanting to lose Walt as a potential co-operator within MCI, Mann proposed that Walt play "hardball" with Hilby by threatening to cut him off from the network (essentially stopping his business) unless he came up with a $2 million payment to eliminate his overdue account. Mann further suggested that Walt tell Hilby that Mann would help him raise the money for a fee. Mann had earlier told Walt that he would make their relationship "worth his while," so Walt told Hilby the MCI's new zero tolerance policy would require him to pay up, and that he should talk to Mann. Hilby did call Mann, who told him that Mann would take over Hilby's company's $2 million debt in return for an up-front payment of $300,000, plus monthly payments to Mann until the $2 million was fully paid. Walt questioned Mann about where the money was actually going to go, and Mann proposed that if Walt would write off or "disappear" the $2 million account, he and Walt could split the money. Mann rationalized this saying: " ... if we don't pay MCI, it's not really out anything. I mean, you can't steal money MCI wasn't going to get anyway, right?"[6] Walt protested, but Mann countered: "You guys're cooking the books over there and you know it. Everybody cheats. That's the way the world works."[7]

Walt decided to think about it. It "was no worse than what MCI customers were doing to MCI, or what MCI was doing to its shareholders. Embezzlement was the legal term for Mann's proposal. But it wasn't like he was going to trick old ladies out of their savings or

bash anyone over the head. It was victimless embezzlement—unless you counted hustlers as victims."[8] In the end, Walt decided to go for it.

Walt went on to play hardball with other MCI customers. They would pay Mann and his company, Walt would make the amount owing MCI disappear, and he and Mann would split the money. At least that was how it should have worked. Ultimately Walt found that Mann was taking more than his share. In addition, Walt had to work through others in MCI Finance, who became accomplices. Unfortunately for Walt, one of these decided to deal with Mann directly, and Walt lost control of the operation. Ultimately, between the bilked clients, and the National Bank wanting its guaranty, the house of cards that Walt built came tumbling down.

Questions

1. What aspects of the schemes described in this case were:
   a. Unethical
   b. Illegal
   c. Fraudulent?

2. When would a healthy skepticism by senior management, or professional skepticism by an accounting or legal professional have been useful in combating the opportunities faced by Walt?

3. Was the Hilby caper a victimless crime, and therefore okay?

4. What ethical issues should have occurred to Walt and MCI in regard to the schemes described?

5. What governance measures might have protected MCI if they had been in place and enforced?

6. What is the role of internal auditors in regard to such schemes?

---

6. Ibid., p. 118.
7. Ibid., p. 120.
8. Ibid., p. 120.

Ethics Case

Jail and a German Sub-Contractor (Names are fictitious)

Harold Johns found himself in jail in Germany. He was a vice-president of Baranca Industries Inc., a U.S. firm that constructs and installs factory equipment. Unfortunately he was the highest-ranking Baranca official in Germany while he was in Germany overseeing the installation of some equipment. Much to his surprise, there was a problem with the way a subcontractor paid his workers. Apparently, the way the subcontractor calculated the pay was illegal. In Germany, when a subcontractor does something illegal, it is assumed that the company hiring the subcontractor had knowledge and was also guilty. In addition, the highest-ranking officials with the subcontractor and the firms who hired him are held legally responsible. Therefore Harold and the head of the subcontractor were arrested—as well as the head of the enterprise that owned the factory.

Questions

1. Is this a fair law?
2. If you were Harold Johns, how would you ensure that Baranca executives and Baranca itself would never be vulnerable to such problems again?

Ethics Case

AIDS Medication in South Africa

"South Africa and the drug companies have changed for ever, say David Pilling and Nicol degli Innocenti.[1]

South Africa is to the drug pharmaceutical industry what Vietnam was to the U.S. military. Nothing will be quite the same again.

That, at least, is the view of Oxfam, the U.K. charity that has mounted a campaign for affordable medicines in poor countries. With other activist groups, it has championed the cause of the South African government, which has been in a three-year legal tussle with the drug industry about national legislation making it easier to override patents.

Yesterday, the drug industry, exhausted by the vitriol that has been heaped upon it, threw in the towel.

In return, they appear to have won certain assurances from the government that it will respect the World Trade Organization's Agreement on Trade Related Intellectual Property Rights (TRIPS), ... [which they had earlier argued] allows the health minister to ignore patents without due process.

The threat of such wholesale disregard for patents—the lifeblood of the research-based drug industry—has prompted it to take some extraordinary steps. Several companies, ... have offered to sell AIDS medicines to the developing world at manufacturing cost, slashing the price of triple therapy from at least $10,000 in the West for an annual supply to about $600.

[This differential price strategy] carries several risks. Drugs may flow back into Western markets. The scheme also exposes the companies to political pressures in Western markets, where consumers may start asking for similar discounts ... [whereas the drug companies will] ... "need some markets in which to recoup our development costs."

The article went on to raise questions about the way in which the government of South Africa was not waging an all-out war on AIDS, as follows. "The government doesn't have a good record with HIV, " says Glenda Gray, an HIV specialist in Soweto's enormous Barawanath hospital. "We have a president who questions whether HIV causes AIDS ... and a program that raises awareness but can't get condoms to people. It's difficult to see how winning this court case would be translated into treatment."

---

1. "A Crack in the Resolve of an Industry," *Financial Times*, April 19, 2001, 15.

Questions

1. Is it legal, moral, or ethical for South Africa to override AIDS medication patents?

2. Is it legal, moral, or ethical for drug patent holders to resist?

3. If you were a senior executive in an affected drug patent holder, what solution would you suggest?

Ethics Case

Digoxin Overdose—The Need for Skepticism, Courage, and Persistence

A two-month-old child was accidentally given a drug overdose at a Texas hospital despite the fact that seven health care professionals reviewed the prescription order before the drug was given to the baby. The following excerpts from a *New York Times* article[1] illustrate how important it is that individuals continually question actions and their outcomes rather than assume that others have gotten it right. Although the setting is health care, most businesspeople and professionals have or will find themselves in situations in which skepticism, courage, and persistence are vital. All too often in business and professional situations, and particularly in those that escalate into crises, individuals suspect there is something that is not right, but they don't do anything, or enough, about it. As a result, the problem or crisis gets worse.

> On a Friday afternoon last summer, tiny Jose Eric Martinez was brought to the outpatient clinic of Hermann Hospital in Houston for a checkup. The 2-month-old looked healthy to his parents, and he was growing well, so they were rattled by the news that the infant had a ventricular septal defect, best described as a hole between the pumping chambers of his heart.
>
> He was showing the early signs of congestive heart failure, the doctors said, and those symptoms would need to be brought under control by a drug, Digoxin, which would be given intravenously during a several-day stay. The child's long-term prognosis was good, the doctors explained.

> Time would most likely close the hole, and if it did not, routine surgery in a year or so would fix things. The Digoxin was a bridge between here and there. There was nothing to worry about.
>
> On the Friday afternoon that the boy was admitted, . . . , the attending doctor discussed the Digoxin order in detail with the resident. First, the appropriate dose was determined in micrograms, based on the baby's weight, then the micrograms were converted to milligrams. They did those calculations together, double-checked them and determined that the correct dose was .09 milligrams, to be injected into an intravenous line.
>
> They went on to discuss a number of tests that also needed to be done, and the resident left to write the resulting list of orders on the baby's chart. With a slip of the pen that would prove fatal, the resident ordered 0.9 milligrams of Digoxin rather than .09.
>
> The list complete, the resident went back to the attending doctor and asked, "Is there anything else I need to add on here?" The attending scanned the list, and said no, there was nothing to add. The error went unnoticed.
>
> A copy of the order was faxed to the pharmacy, and a follow-up original copy was sent by messenger. The pharmacist on duty read the fax and thought that the amount of Digoxin was too high. The pharmacist paged the resident, and then put

---

1. "How Can We Save The Next Victim?." Lisa Belkin, *New York Times*, June 15, 1997.

the order on top of the pharmacy's coffee-pot, site of the unofficial "important" pile. What the pharmacist did not know was that the resident had left for the day and did not receive the page.

Sometime later, the backup copy of the as-yet-unfilled order arrived at the pharmacy. This time a technician looked at it and filled a vial with 0.9 milligrams of Digoxin. The technician then set the order and the vial together on the counter so that the pharmacist could double-check the work.

The pharmacist verified that the dosage on the prescription matched the dosage in the vial, and did not remember questioning the dosage in the first place. The order of the digoxin was sent up to the pediatric floor.

A nurse there took the vial, read its dosage, and worried that it was wrong. She approached a resident who was on call but had not personally gone over the drug calculation with the attending.

"Would you check this order?" she asked. Or maybe she said, "Is this what you want me to give?"

The resident took out a calculator, redid the math, and came up with .09, the correct dose. Looking from the calculator to the vial, the resident saw a "0" and "9" on both and did not notice the difference in the decimal point.

There was one remaining step. Following procedure, the first nurse asked a second nurse to verify that the order in the chart was the same as the label on the vial. She did, and it was.

At 9:35 P.M., a troubled nurse gave Jose Martinez a dose of Digoxin that was 10 times what was intended. It took 20 minutes for the entire dose to drip through his IV tube. At 10 P.M., the baby began to vomit while drinking a bottle, the first sign of a drug overdose.

Digoxin works by changing the flux of ions in the heart, altering the cell membranes. Too much allows the heart to flood with calcium, so it cannot contract. There is an antidote, called Digibind, and the nurse,

her fears confirmed, called for it immediately. But even immediately was too late.

"They killed my son," the boy's father, Jose Leonel Martinez, sobbed on the local TV news. "Those people who work there are not professional and they shouldn't be there." A restaurant worker who had moved his family from Mexico a few years earlier, Martinez was shocked that the world's best health care system could make such a mistake.

"When I asked the doctor if the medicine they were going to put in him was strong, the doctor said no, that it was normal," he said through an interpreter. "That it was just so the child would function better."

The residents and the nurse were "given some time off" during the investigation, Walts [the hospital CEO] says; no one was fired. "It sobered us to realize that we've always dealt with errors as a discipline problem, yet we're not eliminating errors by firing people," she adds.

All those in the chain of error are back at work, and all are still haunted by the death of Jose Martinez. When the system fails, the patient is not the only victim. "It was an absolutely devastating thing," the attending doctor says. "The loss to the parents was indescribable. There are no words. . . . The only thing that made it possible for me to struggle through was my concern for these young people"—meaning the two residents. "I had to make them understand that this did not mean they were bad doctors."

Questions

1. What should the individuals involved have done?

2. How can the Hermann Hospital ensure that individuals do what they should?

3. Should the doctor, residents, pharmacist, and nurses involved in this tragedy be fired? If not, should they be sanctioned, and if so, how?

4. Should such health care failures be made public?

Ethics Case

The Exxon Valdez

Shortly after midnight on March 24, 1989, the oil tanker *Exxon Valdez* ran aground on Bligh Reef in Alaska's Prince William Sound, spilling 11 million gallons of crude oil. Ecological systems were threatened, and the lives and livelihood of area residents were severely disrupted. For the tanker's owner, New York-based Exxon Corporation, the effects were profound.

How did such a tragedy occur? Opinions vary considerably. One oil company executive put it this way: "Its simple. A boat hit a rock." On the other hand, the evidence shows a much more complex picture of human and technical errors.

At the time of the grounding, the vessel had departed from normal shipping lanes to avoid ice in the water and had failed to make a corrective turn in time to avoid the submerged reef. The ship was piloted by third mate Gregory Cousins, who did not hold a required license; the captain, Joseph Hazelwood, was in his quarters. Hazelwood, whose driver's license was at the time suspended for driving while intoxicated, later failed a sobriety test. At the time, the pipeline was opened and strict traffic lanes were established in the Sound to guarantee safe tanker passage. But, in recent years, disintegration of the Columbia Glacier had filled the lanes with ice. To avoid slowing down to dodge icebergs—thereby delaying the oil's delivery to market—tanker captains routinely moved out of the shipping lanes.

On shore, no one was keeping watch. Although the Coast Guard was charged with monitoring vessels through Prince William Sound, in fact, its outdated radar system did not reliably track vessels as far out as Bligh Reef. An earlier proposal to upgrade the radar system had been rejected as too expensive. And the Coast Guard's oversight, to say the least, was lax: at the time of the *Valdez* grounding, the only radar man on duty had stepped out for a cup of coffee.

Other corners had also been cut. The Coast Guard had reduced the use of specially trained harbor pilots to guide tankers out the sound and had withdrawn a proposal for tugboat escorts. Rules, such as those governing the number of crew members on the bridge, were not enforced.

The response to the accident was also fraught with difficulties. Alyeska, the consortium of oil companies that built and operate the Trans-Alaska pipeline, is responsible for cleaning up oil spills that occur in Prince William Sound. At the time of the accident, Alyeska's contingency plan promised to reach a stricken vessel within five and a half hours and to recover half of a 200,000-barrel spill within seventy-two hours, yet, when the event occurred, Alyeska's plan was revealed, as Alaska's Commissioner for Energy Conservation later put it, as "the greatest work of maritime fiction since *Moby Dick*." The cleanup crew had no instructions, the barge was in dry-dock for repairs, needed boom and skimmers were buried under tons of other equipment in a warehouse, and lightering supplies were lost under a snowdrift.

Alyeska did not even reach the *Valdez* until almost twelve hours after the accident and in the first three days was able to pick up only 3,000 barrels of oil—2 percent of what it had promised. Incredibly, a group of local fishermen, later dubbed the "mosquito fleet," managed to retrieve more oil with their fishing boats and five-gallon buckets than did Alyeska with all its money and equipment.

When Alyeska's cleanup collapsed, a response effort had to be hastily jury-rigged by Exxon and the federal and state governments. Federal law called for an interagency team effort in which Exxon was responsible for cleaning up the oil, and different federal agencies were responsible variously for providing scientific advice, protecting the parks, and safeguarding birds and animals. The U.S. Coast Guard and Alaska's Department of Environmental Conservation were supposed to supervise the whole effort, yet no established procedures existed for bringing these organizations together into a working crisis management team under unified leadership. The result was a response effort "paralyzed by indecision, a struggle over authority, and vastly different and conflicting expectations as to which measures would work."

The debate over the use of dispersants, detergent-like chemicals that break up oil into droplets that descend below the water's surface, illustrates the costs for this paralysis. Exxon wanted to use dispersants and immediately flew in planes and chemicals. But, under Alaskan guidelines, dispersants would be used in an oil spill only if less harmful to the environment than the crude itself. Since no one knew whether they were or not, the Coast Guard ordered tests, which were inconclusive. After two days of indecision, the government finally approved the dispersants—but that night the weather turned, and a spring blizzard whipped the oil into an impervious, frothy mousse. The opportunity had been lost.

The reaction of the public was predictable. A complete cleanup was demanded, which cost Exxon a reported $2 billion in 1989 and a further $200 million in 1990, with more out-of-pocket cost to come. More than 150 civil lawsuits were filed, not including those on behalf of the state and federal governments. The state and federal claims may be settled for a reported $1.2 billion.

Not surprisingly, Exxon's profits and stock price have remained flat since the accident. Shareholder groups have, however, been very active, particularly the institutional investors who as a group own 35 percent of Exxon's shares. With the support of the administrators of the New York City pension funds (which own 6 million Exxon shares) the Coalition for Environmentally Responsible Economies (CERES) brought pressure to bear on the company during 1990 to accept and endorse a code of conduct, known as The Valdez Principles (see below), for dealing with the corporation's environmental behavior.

The company resisted accepting The Valdez Principles on several grounds, including that the principles were not sufficiently developed to be workable, that they went too far, and that further study was needed. In 1990 Exxon did, however, appoint an outside environmentalist to the board of directors and placed a senior officer in charge of environmental matters. The tanker was rechristened the *Exxon Mediterranean* and will operate henceforth in the Pacific Ocean. It was not refitted with a double hull that would have cost about $20 million. Observers have also reported that Exxon has bought back substantial amounts of its stock: a move possibly made to support the stock price and pressure investors.

The Valdez (CERES) Principles

Leading environmental organizations—including the Sierra Club, National Audubon Society, and National Wildlife Federation—joined with the Social Investment Forum to form the Coalition for Environmentally Responsible Economics (CERES), whose first act was to draft the Valdez Principles for corporations to sign. The idea is to make the Valdez Principles a litmus test of corporate behavior. Companies are being pressured to abide by the following prescripts:

1. Protection of the Biosphere
We will minimize the release of any pollutant that may cause environmental damage to the air, water, or earth. We will safeguard habitats in rivers, lakes, wetlands, coastal zones, and oceans and will minimize contributing to the greenhouse effect, depletion of the ozone layer, acid rain, or smog.

2. Sustainable Use of Natural Resources
We will make sustainable use of renewable natural resources, such as water, soils and forests. We will conserve nonrenewable natural resources through efficient use and careful planning. We will protect wildlife habitat, open spaces, and wilderness, while preserving biodiversity.

3. Reduction and Disposal of Waste
We will minimize waste, especially hazardous waste, and wherever possible recycle materials. We will dispose of all wastes through safe and responsible methods.

4. Wise Use of Energy

We will make every effort to use environmentally safe and sustainable energy sources to meet our needs. We will invest in improved energy efficiency and conservation in our operations. We will maximize the energy efficiency of products we produce or sell.

5. Risk Reduction

We will minimize the environmental, health, and safety risks to our employees and the communities in which we operate by employing safe technologies and operating procedures and by being constantly prepared for emergencies.

6. Marketing of Safe Products and Services

We will sell products or services that minimize adverse environmental impacts and that are safe as consumers commonly use them. We will inform consumers of the environmental impacts of our products or services.

7. Damage Compensation

We will take responsibility for any harm we cause to the environment by making every effort to fully restore the environment and to compensate those persons who are adversely affected.

8. Disclosure

We will disclose to our employees and to the public incidents relating to our operations that cause environmental harm or pose health or safety hazards. We will disclose potential environmental, health, or safety hazards posed by our operations and we will not take any retaliatory personnel action against any employees who report on any condition that creates a danger to the environment or poses health or safety hazards.

9. Environmental Directors and Managers

At least one member of the board of directors will be a person qualified to represent environmental interests. We will commit management resources to implement these Principles, including the funding of an office of vice president for environmental affairs or an equivalent executive position, reporting directly to the CEO, to monitor and report on our implementation efforts.

10. Assessment and Annual Audit

We will conduct and make public an annual self-evaluation of our progress in implementing these Principles and in complying with all applicable laws and regulations throughout our worldwide operations. We will work toward the timely creation of independent environmental audit procedures which we will complete annually and make available to the public.

For more information, please visit **www.cengage.com/accounting/brooks**

Questions

1. Who was responsible for the accident?
2. What were the responsibilities of the company, the government authorities, and the employees of the company, which were not properly discharged?
3. Should Exxon abide by The Valdez Principles?
4. Could a better code of conduct have prevented this accident?
5. If Exxon had known, before the accident, about the captain's alcohol problem, what actions should have been taken, if any?

Sources

Barnard, J.W. "Exxon Collides with 'Valdez Principles.'" *Business & Society Review* (Fall 1990): 32–35.

Gehani, R. "Will Oil Spills Sink Exxon's Bottom Line." *Business & Society Review*, (Fall 1990): 80–83.

"Lawsuits Proliferate from Grounding of the Exxon Valdez." *Globe & Mail* (G&M), November 29, 1989, p. B2.

Lawrence, A.T. "An Accident Waiting to Happen." *Business & Society Review* (BSR) (Fall 1990): 93–95.

"Shareholders' suggestions get Exxon nod." *G&M*, May 12, 1989, p. B2.

"Exxon Looking at Offer to Settle Oil Spill Suits." *Financial Post*, February 8, 1991, p. 7.

The Brent Spar Decommissioning Disaster

According to the Greenpeace webpage,

> On 16 February last year (1996), Green-peace learned that the UK government had granted permission for Shell Oil to dump a huge, heavily contaminated oil installation, the 4,000 tonne Brent Spar, into the North Atlantic despite it being loaded with toxic and radioactive sludge. Dumping operations, just west of Ireland and Scotland, were expected to begin in May. Greenpeace went into action with plans to take over and occupy the rig to prevent the dumping. More than two dozen activists from six North Sea countries pulled operations together. Video and photo staff were called upon to document the Brent Spar platform and the occupation. The Moby Dick delivered activists to the platform (on April 30) and remained in the area to provide back up.
>
> ... Greenpeace believes that if this platform were to be dumped at sea, with some 400 others at work in the North Sea alone, this would have set a dangerous precedent.

Without doubt, this act of piracy caused serious consternation at the headquarters of Shell UK, and at the parent company's head office in The Netherlands.

Shell UK had been studying options for decommissioning the oil storage and tanker loading platform since 1991, but no perfect option had emerged. The Brent Spar was 140 meters in length, with 109 below the water level, so tearing it apart would be likely to cause leakage of hazardous substances. Consequently, for reasons of cost as well as environmental safety, Shell had chosen to apply to the UK government for a permit to sink the platform in the deep ocean. This decision was based on extensive assessments of the following options:

- Horizontal dismantling (and onshore disposal)
- Vertical dismantling (and onshore disposal)
- In-field disposal
- Deep water disposal
- Refurbishment and re-use
- Continued maintenance

Deep water disposal (at roughly $60 million) was expected to be between 5 percent and 40 percent cheaper than other options, and, since the structure would not leak for 1,000 years, it was expected to be so buried by silt at that point as to be harmless.

The problem faced by Shell UK was what to do? The UK government was expected to issue a dumping permit momentarily. The Fourth North Sea Conference was scheduled to debate the issue of deep sea disposal on June 8–9, and rumor had it that eleven of the thirteen countries involved could call for a moratorium on such dumping.

The following events transpired on or just after April 30, 1995:

- April 30: Greenpeace charged that large amounts of hazardous and radioactive oil were stored on the Brent Spar.
- May 5: The UK government issued deep sea disposal permit.
- May 13: Shell failed to evict Greenpeace from oil platform.
- May 19: Shell failed to obtain court consent to evict Greenpeace.
- May 22: Shell failed to evict Greenpeace.
- May 23: Shell removed activists from Brent Spar.
- June 7: Greenpeace re-boarded and occupied tow tug.
- June 9: Greenpeace revealed leaked document about cheap land option.
- June 10: Greenpeace battled to prevent tow to dump site.
- June 11: Shell postponed tow due to bad weather, tangled wire.
- June 12: Shell begins tow.
- June 14: Protesters in Germany threatened to damage 200 Shell service stations—50 were

Structure of Brent Spar

- Helideck
- Accommodation
- Overall height to turntable = 137 m
- Column
- Chain fenders
- Overall weight = 14,500 tonnes
- Buoyancy tanks
- Anodes
- Anchor chains
- Oil storage tanks (Volume = 300,000 bbl)
- Ballast
- Main body diameter = 29 m

subsequently damaged, two fire-bombed, and one raked with bullets—unrest continued until June 20.

- June 15: Protesters in continental northern Europe strongly opposed — Chancellor Kohl protested deep water disposal at G7 Summit to 17th.

- June 16: Greenpeace re-occupied Brent Spar.

- June 20: Several governments opposed.

- June 20: Shell UK aborted deep water proposal and sought onshore disposal.

- June 21: Shell UK apologized to Prime Minister Major for any embarrassment.

- Late June: Support grew for Shell's early scientific approach.

- July 7: Permission granted to moor in Erford, Norway, temporarily.

- August 26: UK television executives admitted to lack of objectivity and balance in their coverage using dramatic film footage supplied by Greenpeace.

- September 5: Greenpeace apologizes to Shell UK for sampling errors and inaccurate claims that Spar contained 5,500 tonnes of oil in three of six tanks, and so on.

Questions

1. What would you have done if you were calling the shots at Shell UK? When?

2. What would you have done if you were calling the shots at the parent Shell head office?

Crisis at Wind River Energy Inc.

Lynn James was in the vortex of a set of crises. Lynn, an entrepreneur and the president, CEO, and 75 percent owner of Wind River Energy Inc., was one week away from closing a deal to secure much-needed financing for existing and new operations via an independent public offering (IPO) on NASDAQ under the sponsorship of prominent stockbrokers in New York and Toronto. All Lynn had worked for was in danger of going up in smoke, and there was grave risk to the lives of innocent workers and citizens. What on earth could and should Lynn do?

Over the last nine years, Lynn had been very successful. Initially Lynn had been intrigued by the possibility of developing small, freestanding energy installations that fed their power into regional electrical grids or provided power to small isolated towns. It had been possible to acquire and refurbish several small hydroelectric generating stations that had been mothballed by large northeastern energy producers or the small cities that still owned them. Due to the rise in the cost of fossil and nuclear fuels, these waterfall plants made a rate of return on invested capital of roughly 22 percent. Over the years, Lynn and various associates had bought and refurbished five plants, sold two, and continued to operate three in Ontario and Vermont. Based on successful operations in the east, Lynn had arranged for the incorporation of Wind River Energy Inc. into which energy holdings were transferred to provide collateral for bank loans and vendor mortgage financing.

During the last six years, Lynn became interested in the generation of energy using windmills. After visiting "wind farms" in California and off the shore of Denmark, Lynn realized that the wind conditions were exceptionally favorable just east of portions of the Rocky Mountains. He began to investigate providing energy needs to small isolated towns in that area. Four years ago, a ten-windmill installation was developed outside of Freeman, Alberta, which initially contributed to the town's energy needs. The town owned an old hydroelectric plant on the local river and had a back-up oil generator system for emergencies.

Two years ago, Wind River acquired the town's energy generation systems and became the sole source of energy for Freeman. Four years ago, Freeman was a town of 2,000 homes that was using all the energy it could produce, so it welcomed the windmill installation. Since that time, 750 more homes were built to house the workers at two new mines in the area, and the town's hospital was enlarged. Further investment was now needed to provide additional generating capacity.

Based on favorable operations in Freeman, Wind River Energy had developed a reputation for reliability. The company took pride in keeping its commitments—a fact that attracted the attention of the mayor and leaders of West Fork, a neighboring town to Freeman. They approached Wind River, and Lynn signed a contract to provide energy to West Fork on the same basis as for Freeman. Part of the anticipated financing was to provide funds for the purchase of West Fork's electrical generating capacity.

Disaster struck during the last week. On Monday the Wind River manager in Freeman, Ben Trent, called Lynn in Toronto to say that something had gotten stuck in one of the water input pipes to the hydro station, and he wanted to know what to do. Summer was just starting, and air conditioning needs would go beyond Wind River's capacity. Wind River's chief engineer was away on holiday, but Lynn checked with his assistant who suggested that, if the input door could be closed, someone could enter the clean-out pipe that intersected the input pipe. When this was relayed to Ben, he said that he didn't think that the input door had ever been shut and might not work, nor had the clean-out pipe been used during the forty years the plant had been in service. He would check on them and call back. On Tuesday, Lynn received a notification from the Province of Ontario stipulating that Wind River's Ontario hydro station would have to be shut down no later than Thursday. The court order stated that the stagnant water at the edges of the pond where the water intake pipe was located was likely to allow the breeding of mosquitoes that would spread the West Nile

Virus. The stagnant water situation would have to be remedied before the plant could restart, and Wind River would be liable to any persons from the local community who were diagnosed with West Nile Virus from Tuesday to five days after the stagnant water problem was remedied. When Lynn went to consult the chief engineer's assistant (the only other real engineer on staff), he found that the man had just gone home sick with a SARS-like attack of the flu. Unfortunately, the chief engineer was in the middle of a backpacking trip in the Rockies and would be unreachable unless he activated the satellite phone that Lynn had insisted he take.

Ben called back on Wednesday to say that they had finally closed the input door and had just sent a small, thin man into the clean-out pipe to crawl up the intake pipe and clear the obstruction. Because the fellow was so keen, Ben told him to crawl all the way up to the intake door and try to grease the hinges on the inside.

On Thursday morning Ben called to say that the fellow had done a great job of clearing the input pipe and had examined the hinges on the inside of the input door. He had just gone back in to try to remove the hinge pins, replace the bushings around the pins, and grease the bushings and pins. The mayor was pleased because the fellow was his brother-in-law who had never really done anything else very well.

At about noon on Thursday, Lynn's lawyer called to remind him of the meeting on the following Tuesday during which Lynn, the CFO, and the chief engineer would have to sign off documents attesting to the excellent status of the company so the IPO could go ahead. Any delay would jeopardize the financing deal. Lynn didn't know what to say. He just thanked his lawyer and hung up.

In the early afternoon, Ben called to say that the fellow had gotten out of the pipe all right, but had jammed one of the hinge pins when reinserting it and didn't think the input door would open to allow water into the generating equipment. Someone bigger and stronger would have to go into the pipe to fix the hinge. Ben didn't know what to do. He wasn't a real engineer, having been promoted to be manager on the basis of long service and personal connections with the city council, and he wanted Wind River's chief engineer to take responsibility and tell him what to do.

In addition, Ben said that the transformer station regulating the power from the company's windmills had been hit about a month ago by lightning and was operating only partially on an intermittent basis. The mayor of Freeman was getting calls about the intermittent "brown-outs" of electricity and was putting pressure on Ben. Ben was really fed up. He also had a call from the mayor of West Fork, but he hadn't returned it yet.

Question

1. What would you do if you were Lynn?

Readings | *Can't We All Just Get Along: Cultural Variables in Codes of Ethics*

Nancy L. Roth, Todd Hunt, Maria Stavropoulos, and Karen Babik

Ethical issues in the practice of public relations become increasingly complex when international borders are crossed. Differences in what "counts" as public relations as well as what "counts" as ethical practice abound. Rather than taking the position that a specific, "objective" code of ethics can be developed or arguing that cultural diversity makes ethical standards impossible, this paper argues that an international set of principles for practice is feasible. Such a set of principles can only be agreed upon if representatives of diverse organizations and cultural values will work together to understand each others' perspectives. This approach is consistent with the goal of "mutual understanding" that increasingly characterizes public relations practice. It is also consistent with recent theoretical work in ethics and post-colonialism. (Reprinted by permission of the publisher.)

Rodney King's plaintive plea "Can't we all just get along?"—voiced at a rally of his supporters after a notorious California trial that split Americans along cultural lines—may be a phrase with multiple utility. It is a question we should be asking at this point in the discussion about whether or not cultural variables make it impossible to construct a code of ethics that would govern the behaviors of public relations practitioners in global settings—people from countries with very diverse cultures. Are we really so different that we "can't all just get along?"

Arguing that such a code is possible, Hunt and Tirpok proposed that initial steps should be an attempt "to put forth a general code and let its interpretation and use suggest further refinements that will help adapt it to the nuances of the global community."[1] Kruckeberg seconded the motion, observing that "cultural relativism is not problematic for a universal ethics code" and that "globally … there is a plenitude of shared ethical values, and those which are within differing areas of moral 'taste' can be discussed, universally accepted or negotiated."[2] Wright dissented, noting that cultural differences cannot be accommodated by a code of ethics. According to Wright, "With or without professional codes of conduct most who practice public relations will choose to be ethical because they believe in themselves and want others to respect them," and thus an attempt at forging a universal ethics code is unnecessary.[3]

This paper extends the debate by exploring recent research about the meaning of "public relations" in cross-cultural settings, calling into question simplistic conceptions of cultural variability, and reviewing codes of ethics in use in global settings. We suggest ways that the door can be kept open to discussion of a "universal" approach to ethical behavior that will be useful in the emerging era of Multi-National Enterprises (MNEs).[4] With increased globalization in all aspects of social life, it is essential for public relations practitioners to engage in ongoing discussions about ethical practice with international colleagues. While all may not agree to a specific ethics "code," there might be agreement to a set of principles that contain enough ambiguity to allow for differing interpretations and practices. Such a set of principles might move international public relations practice closer to the goal of "mutual understanding" that is the foundation for many of the "two-way" models of public relations currently in use.[5]

Multicultural Meanings of Public Relations

When questions of multicultural differences arise, it is easy to establish one type of practice or principles as the model against which all others are compared. In public relations, the United States model has played that role in the literature. In this section we will present examples of discussions of the public relations practices of "others" viewed from the perspective of United States practice. We will argue that it is dangerous to establish one mode of practice as the norm and thereby label all other practices as deviant. In the following section, an alternative perspective is proposed.

Over 25 years ago, a practical book called *The Public Relations Man Abroad* sketched out cultural differences in major trading partners of the United States, including Japan and Germany.[6] The Japanese, it was noted, say

1. Todd Hunt and Andrew Tirpok, "Universal Ethics Code: An Idea Whose Time Has Come," *Public Relations Review 19* (1993), p. 141.
2. Dean Kruckeberg, "Universal Ethics Code: Both Possible and Feasible," *Public Relations Review 19* (1993), pp. 21–31.
3. Donald K. Wright, "Enforcement Dilemma: Voluntary Nature of Public Relations Codes," *Public Relations Review 19* (1993), pp. 13–20.
4. We have chosen MNEs rather than MNCs—Multi-National Corporations—because of our belief that nonprofit groups and governmental groups face most of the issues that for-profit organizations must deal with in a global setting.
5. James Grunig and Todd Hunt, *Managing Public Relations* (New York: Harcourt, Brace, Jovanovich, 1984).
6. Geoffrey Kean, *The Public Relations Man Abroad* (New York: Praeger; 1968).

"yes" when they mean "no" out of politeness (p. 182). The Germans think it appropriate to serve champagne during a press conference, while Americans think drinking should wait until later (p. 97).

American companies are hyper-cautious about admitting any responsibility for causing a disaster, because company lawyers convince management that the courtroom is the only place to assess blame. The Japanese, however, are conditioned to ask forgiveness and even to express a willingness to resign ... or even die. After a 1985 air crash, the company's president offered personal apologies to the families of the dead, made speedy financial reparations, and attended memorial services. A technician responsible for preparing the doomed plane for flight committed suicide to atone for his part in the disaster.[7] Indeed, a Japanese scholar studying in the United States suggests that the Japanese government's non-practice of public relations was responsible for a bungling of relationships with the international community following the Kobe earthquake. Unlike in America where crisis communication plans are in place, in Japan it was days before the government appeared to be in control and before correct information was provided to key publics.[8]

On the other hand, American practices do not always serve well in foreign settings. One U.S. public relations agency lost an account in London because its budget for entertaining the media was too low, suggesting that the agency was not good at cozying up to the press and entertaining lavishly—practices frowned upon in America and specifically forbidden by the ethics codes of the Society of Professional Journalists and the Public Relations Society of America.[9]

As easygoing and casual as Americans are reputed to be both at home and abroad, Americans tend to think of business as just that—not to be confused with friendship or intimacy. Most other cultures are different. Culbertson notes that Confucian values emphasize personal relationships that govern business relationships to the point that "interpersonal relationships serve as the main basis for strong public relationships" (p. 38).[10]

In the Arab world, "public" is not even linked with "relations"; the preferred term is "general relations" or "general affairs" because the word "public" cannot be translated literally in Arabic. Al-Enad (p. 24) suggests that the semantic problem "may have contributed to the persistent vagueness of the nature, goals, roles, and functions of public relations" in the Arab countries.[11] In a similar vein, Signitzer suggests that "public diplomacy" may be a more palatable label for influence and persuasion in Europe, where "public relations" is seen as a tough-minded attempt to influence foreign attitudes through the use of rapid-fire media messages instead of slow debate.[12]

Americans often assume that media-use patterns are the same in other countries as they are in the U.S., and thus media relations can follow the same pattern. Even in neighboring Canada, there are far fewer "local" newspapers and several regional or national newspapers, so the concept of a "hometown news release" does not work as well north of the border as it does at home.[13]

A communications company executive in Hong Kong discovered that the colony, with

7. Marion K. Pinsdorf, "Flying Different Skies: How Cultures Respond to Airline Disasters," *Public Relations Review 17* (1991), pp. 37–56.

8. Junko Taguchi, "Japanese Officials and PR Mentality," *Public Relations Quarterly 40* (1995), pp. 31–37.

9. David M. Grant, "Cross-Cultural Crossed Signals," *Public Relations Journal 44* (1988), p. 48.

10. Ni Chen and Hugh M. Culbertson, "Two Contrasting Approaches of Government Public Relations in Mainland China," *Public Relations Quarterly 37* (1993), pp. 36–41.

11. Abdulrahman H. Al-Enad, "Public Relations' Roles in Developing Countries," *Public Relations Quarterly 35* (1991), pp. 24–26.

12. Benno H. Signitzer and Timothy Coombs, "Public Relations and Public Diplomacy: Conceptual Convergences" *Public Relations Review 18* (1992), pp. 137–147.

13. Melvin L. Sharpe, "The Impact of Social and Cultural Conditioning on Global Public Relations," *Public Relations Review 18* (1992), pp. 103–107.

approximately the same population as the Chicago area, is served by more than 40 newspapers and over 600 magazines, making media placement a nightmare.[14] "People tend to forget that Asia is even more complex than Europe because of the autonomous development of small geographies," said the executive. "Each has its own laws, business styles, ethics, history of business development. If you find anyone who really understands the media of Japan, China, India, Thailand, Vietnam, Malaysia ... they are indeed a novelty" (pp. 1–15).

The views expressed in this literature establish United States customs as the "norm" and those of practitioners in other countries as the "other." This approach leads to development of ethics codes that attempt to impose U.S. standards on practitioners from other countries and on U.S. nationals working elsewhere. Such an approach is problematic because U.S. standards are highly specific and legalistic and leave little room for cultural variation. It also establishes the U.S. method of conducting business as the most ethical without calling into question U.S. practices. For example, this literature might be viewed as suggesting not only that U.S. and Japanese practitioners might handle an airplane crash differently, but also that the U.S. tendency to protect the company name and wealth from lawsuits is more ethical than the Japanese desire to apologize and make restitution to affected families.

Rethinking Cultural Variables

Too often in the past, cultural variables were thought of as "quaint customs" that one merely had to "learn about" in order to succeed in foreign settings—don't show the bottom of your shoes to people in Arab lands, remember to bow when meeting the Japanese, take a gift when you are entertained in someone's home, and don't make this or that gesture that means something-or-other lewd in such-and-such country. The idea that knowledge about customs makes it possible for different cultures to overcome differences is simplistic. Recent writings by communication scholars—and, indeed, recent actions taken by companies and countries engaged in global commerce—indicate that cross-cultural sophistication is increasing.

Botan suggests that "what has been called international public relations may not actually be the two-way multicultural exercise that its name implies.[15] The practice of public relations across borders often ... is controlled and directed from the home country based on assumptions inherent to the home country. As a result, business practice often may not really be international public relations but might better be called trans-border public relations" (pp. 151–152). He proposes (p. 157) that overcoming ethnocentrism and viewing public relations "in different ways than many of us in developed countries have in the past" is the key to formulating a truly global approach.

L. Grunig suggests that too often what organizations try to perform on a global scale, public relations is equated with media relations.[16] She proposes (p. 129) that a new name might be in order—publics relations rather than public relations—to emphasize the "strategic constituencies" approach that is necessary when working on a global scale. In that way of thinking, the media would fall behind several other publics—most notably the local, regional and national governments of the host country—when laying plans for helping the MNE adjust to their many publics in a multinational setting.

Examples of how specific organizations are rethinking cultural variables abound:

> | Wal-Mart, long accustomed to sending out English-only information in Canada, where it had little presence in the

---

14. Geoffrey L. Martin, "West Unraveling Mysteries of Culture," *Advertising Age International* (Oct. 16, 1995), pp. 115–116.

15. Carl Botan, "International Public Relations: Critique and Reformulation," *Public Relations Review 18* (1992), pp. 149–159.

16. Larissa A. Grunig, "Strategic Public Relations Constituencies on a Global Scale," *Public Relations Review 18* (1992), pp. 127–136.

French-speaking areas, now has 22 Quebec stores operated entirely in French, including internal communications. The leader of Wal-Mart's transition team in Quebec was responsible for making the company "culturally correct" as well as legally correct.[17]

| Chubb, the American insurance company, is one of many firms that has learned how to cope with the routine expectation of bribes to public officials in many countries. The U.S., of course, forbids American companies from paying bribes to win international business. Chubb satisfied the Chinese expectation of "sweetening the pot" in order to do business there, and stayed within U.S. regulations, by agreeing to set up a $1 million program to teach insurance at a university in Shanghai. Disney flies people from other countries for free training at its Disney World educational facilities, a perk that includes lodging and entertainment at the theme parks. Another enticement: scholarships to American universities for the children of foreign officials.[18]

| European companies have long had difficulty understanding why American companies reveal so much about their condition and their plans on a quarterly basis. The norm in Europe is to keep silent about short-term decisions, because that is seen as impeding the flexibility of management decision-making. The norm is changing however, as European companies—eager to seek capital on the world stage—are moving toward the American system of full, open and frequent disclosure.[19]

These examples characterize a practice of public relations that takes into account local standards and values. Yet, rather than suggesting that differences among such standards mitigate against universal ethical standards, we argue that such a guideline is possible. In the following sections we review existing codes and suggest that their power lies in "authority" rather than "enforcement." We suggest that a universal set of principles based on authority with sufficient ambiguity to account for cross-cultural differences is feasible.

"Authority" Underlies Association Codes

The two major ethics codes adopted by professional public relations associations in the U.S. are the "IABC Code of Ethics" that applies to all members of the International Association of Business Communicators and the "Code for Professional Standards for the Practice of Public Relations" that applies to all members of the Public Relations Society of America. The codes also apply to the student groups affiliated with the professional associations. Because about one public relations professional in ten in the United States belongs to these associations, it is fair to say that only 10 percent of American practitioners are bound by the codes and subject to penalty if they are charged with a violation.

Officers of the professional organizations have authority and responsibility to hold hearings, determine culpability, and expel from the association members who violate the code. In practice, very few violations are reported. In fact, when the president of one of the associations was charged publicly with a violation in the 1980s, he resigned his presidency and his membership, continuing the practice of public relations in the large regional firm that bears his name.

Thus it can be seen that while the power to expel members who violate their codes of ethics gives professional associations "authority" it really does not serve to give them control over the profession or its members.

---

17. Jon Kalina, "'Vive la Difference': Learning Trade North of 49th Parallel," *Advertising Age International* (Sept. 18, 1995), pp. 123, 130.
18. Dana Milbank and Marcus W. Brauchli, "Greasing Wheels: How U.S. Concerns Compete in Countries Where Bribes Flourish," *The Wall Street Journal* (Sept. 29, 1995), p. A1.
19. Editors, "Governance Goes Global," *Inside PR V* (1995), pp. 18–20.

Indeed, ethics codes are not controllers of behavior, they are merely models for behavior. That raises the issue of whether they should even be called "codes," since a code usually implies enforcement, as in the military's codes of conduct or the code of laws enacted by governments. We are one step along the semantic trail of abandoning the term "ethics code."

Another problem with prescribing and proscribing through the use of a code is the need for completeness. The PRSA code is under 400 words long, and it highlights (literally, in boldface type) such overarching and generic concepts as public interest, honesty, integrity, deal fairly, accuracy, truth that it appears at first to be steering clear of cultural contexts. But the PRSA code does not stand alone. It is accompanied by a section called "Interpretations of the Code" that gets into very specific prohibitions on compensating or entertaining the media—rules that are counter to the norms in many countries. Other lengthy interpretative sections are provided for those who engage in the practice of political and financial public relations. In its attempt to account for all of the code violations that are likely to occur in specific settings, the PRSA code becomes increasingly ethnocentric, and increasingly difficult to apply to the work done by MNEs.

In the past two years, Russian public relations practitioners have moved to organize and to promote ethical behavior.[20] In 1994, a professional association was formed in Moscow, and on August 16, 1994, the St. Petersburg Association of Public Relations Specialists adopted a "Professional Code" that is remarkably similar to the IABC and PRSA codes. The St. Petersburg code calls for "protecting, preserving, and respecting freedom of speech, freedom of the press, and existing legislation." It states that public relations practitioners must provide "objective and reliable information," that they must not violate the fairness and objectivity of the mass media, that they must inform clients if there is a conflict of interest stemming from working for more than one client, and that they must report violations of the code to the Association.

In contrast, the Code of Athens—the International Code of Ethics that applies to members of the International Public Relations Association—is much more general, avoids interpretations, and bases its moral authority on the "Universal Declaration of Human Rights," which was adopted in 1948 by the United Nations General Assembly. In its simplicity, it probably is a much better starting place for understanding how we can "all get along" than are the ethics codes stamped "Made in America."

New Thinking about Ethical Conduct

In the past decade, analysis of the role of MNEs engaged in global communication has led to new thinking about how best to articulate basic expectations of ethical behavior.

Donaldson identified ten "minimal" human rights that can be applied or honored by all international moral agents.[21] His list does not explicitly refer to any local culture:

1. The right to freedom of physical movement. 2. The right to ownership of property. 3. The right to freedom from torture. 4. The right to a fair trial. 5. The right to non-discriminatory treatment (on the basis of race or sex). 6. The right to physical security. 7. The right to freedom of speech and association. 8. The right to minimal education. 9. The right to political participation. 10. The right to subsistence.

DeGeorge suggested that despite differences in culture and values among nations, there are moral norms that can be applied to

20. Alexandre G. Nikolaev and A. G. Gorgin, "The Value of a PR Association to Russians," International Association of Business Communicators *Communication World 12* (1995), pp. 7–9.

21. Thomas Donaldson, *The Ethics of International Business* (New York: Oxford University Press, 1989).

multinational enterprises. He proposed seven principles to guide MNEs in ethical conduct:

1. MNEs should do no international direct harm.

2. MNEs should produce more good than bad for the host country.

3. MNEs should contribute by their activities to the host country's development.

4. MNEs should respect the human rights of their employees.

5. MNEs should pay their fair share of taxes.

6. To the extent that local culture does not violate moral norms, MNEs should respect the local culture and work with it, not against it.

7. MNEs should cooperate with the local government in the development and enforcement of just background institutions.[22]

Perhaps the first international code of ethics crafted by business leaders for business is the CAUX Round Table Principles, the result of a collaborative effort by business leaders from Japan, Europe, and the United States. The CAUX Round Table was established in 1986 in Caux-sur-Montreux, Switzerland, to bring together global business leaders to reduce trade tensions. The Principles reflect two ideals, Japan's concept of Kyosei—living and working together for the common good—and the Western concept of human dignity.[23] The Principles address the following concerns:

1. The responsibilities of businesses (which are further outlined in a lengthy section titled "Stakeholder Principles" that specifies behaviors toward customers, employees, owners/ investors, suppliers, competitors, and communities).

2. The economic and social impact of business.

3. Business behavior that is based on trust.

4. Respect for rules.

5. Support for multilateral trade.

6. Respect for the environment.

7. Avoidance of illicit operations.

The CAUX Round Table Principles were based, in part, on the Minnesota Principles crafted by business leaders who are members of the Minnesota Center for Corporate Responsibility. Bob MacGregor, president of the Center, helped draft the CAUX Round Table Principles. MacGregor says acceptance of the Principles has been widespread and that "enlightened business leaders know that all stakeholders profit under a common set of values."

To reach the skeptics, however, MacGregor believes that business leaders who subscribe to the Principles will have to show how abiding by the precepts will open markets, increase productivity, and affect the bottom line of profits positively. The Principles do not explicitly acknowledge the need to respect the cultural diversity of each group of stakeholders—an issue MacGregor says was raised but not dealt with. With the addition of that perspective, the CAUX Round Table Principles would serve as a good model for a document of utility to MNEs as they pursue their global communications. The Principles also could and should be extended to include the ethical behavior of government, since business behaviors so often reflect compliance with the laws of home and host countries.[24]

Conclusion

The question of whether or not it is possible to develop a set of ethical principles that is

---

22. R. T. DeGeorge, "Ethical Dilemmas for Multinational Enterprises: A Philosophical Overview." In Hoffman, Lange and Fedo (Eds.) *Ethics and the Multinational Enterprise: Proceedings of the Sixth National Conference on Business Ethics* (New York: Oxford University Press, 1986), pp. 39–46.

23. Joe Skelly, "The Rise of International Ethics," *Business Ethics,* unnumbered reprint.

24. MacGregor was interviewed by one of the authors in August 1995.

meaningful across cultures in the current global business and political environment raises issues about objectivity. Do standards need to take into account cultural differences of what "counts" as "moral?" Does objectivity mean that cultural differences cannot be recognized?

Too often, as we noted in the introduction to this article, the debate about objectivity is reduced to a question of whether it is better to subscribe to a rigid, culturally specific value system that does not account for cultural difference ("weak objectivity") or to subscribe to a system of "judgmental relativism" where there are no standards. A third possibility, "strong objectivity," calls for an analysis of historically situated local beliefs—both those of "others" and those of the United States.[25] By looking at U.S. generated codes of ethics from the standpoint of "others" we might begin to understand and critique our own system of values, rather than trying to impose it uncritically on others.

From the perspective of "other," United States and other Western countries are seen as subscribing to an ethical position that values autonomy over most other principles. The individual has the privilege of ownership and autonomous action. In contrast, other cultures (including some women's cultures in the West) value connection. This might account for the differences mentioned above between the handling of air disasters in Japan and the United States, for example. Neither of these ethical positions accounts for the relative differences in power wielded by different countries in the world economy.[26]

Recent post-colonial literature suggests that issues of relative power ought to be addressed as well. A universal set of ethical principles should take into account the differing power exerted by countries and organizations in the global economy.[27] Future work on international ethical principles should explore thoroughly the issue of power in the international practice of public relations.

Viewing Western values from the standpoint of others may lead to the ability to create or modify universal standards that account for cultural difference by using wording that allows for flexibility in interpretation,[28] but does not impose ethnocentric standards.[29] Such a move is consistent with the goal of "mutual understanding" that increasingly characterizes the practice of public relations in the global environment.[30]

American professional associations, particularly IABC and PRSA, should consider reviewing their codes of ethics from the standpoint of the "others" with whom practitioners are increasingly doing business. They should take into account differing cultural variations of autonomy and connectivity as well as differences in global power. Finally, they should consider the ramifications of carrying "codes" of "ethics" across national borders and consider instead the development of mutually agreed upon principles to guide global practice. Adoption of such practices is not only ethical, but it also might result in a move toward international cooperation— perhaps we can "get along."

Acknowledgment: The authors are indebted to Alexandre G. Nicolaev, a member of the board of directors of the Russian Public Communications Company, for providing a translation of the St. Petersburg Code. Mr. Nicolaev spent the 1995–1996 academic year

25. Sandra Harding, *Whose Science? Whose Knowledge?* (Ithaca, New York: Cornell University Press, 1991).

26. Seyla Benhabib, *Situating the Self: Gender, Community and Postmodernism in Contemporary Ethics* (New York: Routledge, 1992).

27. Edward Said, *Orientalism* (New York: Routledge, 1978).

28. Eric Eisenberg, "Ambiguity as Strategic Organizational Communication," *Communication Monographs 51* (1984), pp. 227–242.

29. Heddy R. Dexter, Kathy Drew, Jolanta A. Drzewiecka, Barbara M. Gayle, Dreama G. Moon, Sami Reist, Richard A. Rogers, Nancy L. Roth, Michelle T. Violanti, and Kathleen Wong, "Reconceptualizing Identity and Agency in Communication Theory," paper presented at the Speech Communications Association Annual Conference, San Antonio, TX, 1995.

30. James Grunig and Todd Hunt, *Managing Public Relations,* 1984.

as a visiting scholar at the Center for International Trade Development at Oklahoma State University. In a personal communication with the second author, he reported that while in the United States, he visited with Ray Gaulke and Elizabeth Allan, the top administrators of the PRSA and IABC respectively, and found "that there were more similarities than differ-ences between us; we shared the same human values."

Nancy L. Roth is Assistant Professor of Communication, Todd Hunt is Professor of Communication, Maria Stavropoulos is a Ph.D. student, and Karen Babik is completing her Masters Degree in the School of Communication, Information, and Library Studies at Rutgers University.

<table><tr><td>Readings</td></tr></table>

Values in Tension: Ethics Away from Home
Thomas Donaldson

> **When is different just different and when is different wrong?**

When we leave home and cross our nation's boundaries, moral clarity often blurs. Without a backdrop of shared attitudes, and without familiar laws and judicial procedures that define standards of ethical conduct, certainty is elusive. Should a company invest in a foreign country where civil and political rights are violated? Should a company go along with a host country's discriminatory employment practices? If companies in developed countries shift facilities to developing nations that lack strict environmental and health regulations, or if those companies choose to fill management and other top-level positions in a host nation with people from the home country, whose standards should prevail?

Even the best-informed, best-intentioned executives must rethink their assumptions about business practice in foreign settings. What works in a company's home country can fail in a country with different standards of ethical conduct. Such difficulties are unavoidable for businesspeople who live and work abroad.

But how can managers resolve the problems? What are the principles that can help them work through the maze of cultural differences and establish codes of conduct for globally ethical business practice? How can companies answer the toughest question in global business ethics: What happens when a host country's ethical standards seem lower than the home country's?

Competing Answers

One answer is as old as philosophical discourse. According to cultural relativism, no culture's ethics are better than any other's, therefore there are no international rights and wrongs. If the people of Indonesia tolerate the bribery of their public officials, so what? Their attitude is no better or worse than that of people in Denmark or Singapore who refuse to offer or accept bribes. Likewise, if Belgians fail to find insider trading morally repugnant, who cares? Not enforcing insider-trading laws is no more or less ethical than enforcing such laws.

The cultural relativist's creed—When in Rome, do as the Romans do—is tempting, especially when failing to do as the locals do means forfeiting business opportunities. The inadequacy of cultural relativism, however, becomes apparent when the practices in question are more damaging than petty bribery or insider trading.

In the late 1980s, some European tanneries and pharmaceutical companies were looking for cheap waste-dumping sites. They approached virtually every country on Africa's west coast from Morocco to the Congo. Nigeria agreed to take highly toxic polychlorinated biphenyls.

Unprotected local workers, wearing thongs and shorts, unloaded barrels of PCBs and placed them near a residential area. Neither the residents nor the workers knew that the barrels contained toxic waste.

We may denounce governments that permit such abuses, but many countries are unable to police transnational corporations adequately even if they want to. And in many countries, the combination of ineffective enforcement and inadequate regulations leads to behavior by unscrupulous companies that is clearly wrong. A few years ago, for example, a group of investors became interested in restoring the *SS United States*, once a luxurious ocean liner. Before the actual restoration could begin, the ship had to be stripped of its asbestos lining. A bid from a U.S. company, based on U.S. standards for asbestos removal, priced the job at more than $100 million. A company in the Ukranian city of Sevastopol offered to do the work for less than $2 million.

In October 1993, the ship was towed to Sevastopol.

A cultural relativist would have no problem with that outcome, but I do. A country has the right to establish its own health and safety regulations, but in the case described above, the standards and the terms of the contract could not possibly have protected workers in Sevastopol from known health risks. Even if the contract met Ukranian standards, ethical businesspeople must object. Cultural relativism is morally blind. There are fundamental values that cross cultures, and companies must uphold them. [For an economic argument against cultural relativism, see the insert, "The Culture and Ethics of Software Piracy."]

At the other end of the spectrum from cultural relativism is ethical imperialism, which directs people to do everywhere exactly as they do at home. Again, an understandably appealing approach but one that is clearly

The Culture and Ethics of Software Piracy

Before jumping on the cultural relativism bandwagon, stop and consider the potential economic consequences of a when-in-Rome attitude toward business ethics. Take a look at the current statistics on software piracy: In the United States, pirated software is estimated to be 35% of the total software market, and industry losses are estimated at $2.3 billion per year. The piracy rate is 57% in Germany and 80% in Italy and Japan; the rates in most Asian countries are estimated to be nearly 100%.

There are similar laws against software piracy in those countries. What, then, accounts for the differences? Although a country's level of economic development plays a large part, culture, including ethical attitudes, may be a more crucial factor. The 1995 annual report of the Software Publishers Association connects software piracy directly to culture and attitude. It describes Italy and Hong Kong as having "'first world' per capita incomes, along with 'third world' rates of piracy." When asked whether one should use software without paying for it, most people, including people in Italy and Hong Kong, say

no. But people in some countries regard the practice as less unethical than people in other countries do. Confucian culture, for example, stresses that individuals should share what they create with society. That may be, in part, what prompts the Chinese and other Asians to view the concept of intellectual property as a means for the West to monopolize its technological superiority.

What happens if ethical attitudes around the world permit large-scale software piracy? Software companies won't want to invest as much in developing new products, because they cannot expect any return on their investment in certain parts of the world. When ethics fail to support technological creativity, there are consequences that go beyond statistics—jobs are lost and livelihoods jeopardized.

Companies must do more than lobby foreign governments for tougher enforcement of piracy laws. They must cooperate with other companies and with local organizations to help citizens understand the consequences of piracy and to encourage the evolution of a different ethic toward the practice.

inadequate. Consider the large U.S. computer-products company that in 1993 introduced a course on sexual harassment in its Saudi Arabian facility. Under the banner of global consistency, instructors used the same approach to train Saudi Arabian managers that they had used with U.S. managers: the participants were asked to discuss a case in which a manager makes sexually explicit remarks to a new female employee over drinks in a bar. The instructors failed to consider how the exercise would work in a culture with strict conventions governing relationships between men and women. As a result, the training sessions were ludicrous. They baffled and offended the Saudi participants, and the message to avoid coercion and sexual discrimination was lost.

The theory behind ethical imperialism is absolutism, which is based on three problematic principles. Absolutists believe that there is a single list of truths, that they can be expressed only with one set of concepts, and that they call for exactly the same behavior around the world.

The first claim clashes with many people's belief that different cultural traditions must be respected. In some cultures, loyalty to a community—family, organization, or society—is the foundation of all ethical behavior. The Japanese, for example, define business ethics in terms of loyalty to their companies, their business networks, and their nation. Americans place a higher value on liberty than on loyalty, the U.S. tradition of rights emphasize equality, fairness, and individual freedom. It is hard to conclude that truth lies on one side or the other, but an absolutist would have us select just one.

The second problem with absolutism is the presumption that people must express moral truth using only one set of concepts. For instance, some absolutists insist that the language of basic rights provide the framework for any discussion of ethics. That means, though, that entire cultural traditions must be ignored. The notion of a right evolved with the rise of democracy in post-Renaissance Europe and the United States, but the term is not found in either Confucian or Buddhist traditions. We all learn ethics in the context of our particular cultures, and the power in the principles is

What Do These Values Have in Common?

NON-WESTERN	WESTERN
Kyosei (Japanese): Living and working together for the common good.	Individual liberty
Dharma (Hindu): The fulfillment of inherited duty.	Egalitarianism
Santutthi (Buddhist): The importance of limited desires.	Political participation
Zakat (Muslim): The duty to give alms to the Muslim poor.	Human rights

deeply tied to the way in which they are expressed. Internationally accepted lists of moral principles, such as the United Nations' Universal Declaration of Human Rights, draw on many cultural and religious traditions. As philosopher Michael Walzer has noted, "There is no Esperanto of global ethics."

The third problem with absolutism is the belief in a global standard of ethical behavior. Context must shape ethical practice. Very low wages, for example, may be considered unethical in rich, advanced countries, but developing nations may be acting ethically if they encourage investment and improve living standards by accepting low wages. Likewise, when people are malnourished or starving, a government may be wise to use more fertilizer in order to improve crop yields, even though that means settling for relatively high levels of thermal water pollution.

When cultures have different standards of ethical behavior—and different ways of handling unethical behavior—a company that takes an absolutist approach may find itself making a disastrous mistake. When a manager at a large U.S. specialty-products company in China caught an employee stealing, she followed the company's practice and turned the employee over to the provincial authorities, who executed him. Managers cannot operate in another culture without being aware of that culture's attitudes toward ethics.

If companies can neither adopt a host country's ethics nor extend the home country's standards, what is the answer? Even the traditional litmus test—What would people think of your actions if they were written up on the front page of the newspaper?—is an unreliable guide, for there is no international consensus on standards of business conduct.

Balancing the Extremes: Three Guiding Principles

Companies must help managers distinguish between practices that are merely different and those that are wrong. For relativists, nothing is sacred and nothing is wrong. For absolutists, many things that are different are wrong. Neither extreme illuminates the real world of business decision making. The answer lies somewhere in between.

When it comes to shaping ethical behavior, companies might be guided by three principles.

| Respect for core human values, which determine the absolute moral threshold for all business activities.

| Respect for local traditions.

| The belief that context matters when deciding what is right and what is wrong.

Consider those principles in action. In Japan, people doing business together often exchange gifts—sometimes expensive ones—in keeping with long-standing Japanese tradition. When U.S. and European companies started doing a lot of business in Japan, many Western businesspeople thought that the practice of gift giving might be wrong rather than simply different. To them, accepting a gift felt like accepting a bribe. As Western companies have become more familiar with Japanese traditions, however, most have come to tolerate the practice and to set different limits on gift giving in Japan than they do elsewhere.

Respecting differences is a crucial ethical practice. Research shows that management ethics differ among cultures; respecting those differences means recognizing that some cultures have obvious weaknesses—as well as hidden strengths. Managers in Hong Kong, for example, have a higher tolerance for some

forms of bribery than their Western counterparts, but they have a much lower tolerance for the failure to acknowledge a subordinate's work. In some parts of the Far East, stealing credit from a subordinate is nearly an unpardonable sin.

People often equate respect for local traditions with cultural relativism. That is incorrect. Some practices are clearly wrong. Union Carbide's tragic experience in Bhopal, India, provides one example. The company's executives seriously underestimated how much on-site management involvement was needed at the Bhopal plant to compensate for the country's poor infrastructure and regulatory capabilities. In the aftermath of the disastrous gas leak, the lesson is clear: companies using sophisticated technology in a developing country must evaluate that country's ability to oversee its safe use. Since the incident at Bhopal, Union Carbide has become a leader in advising companies on using hazardous technologies safely in developing countries.

Some activities are wrong no matter where they take place. But some practices that are unethical in one setting may be acceptable in another. For instance, the chemical EDB, a soil fungicide, is banned for use in the United States. In hot climates, however, it quickly becomes harmless through exposure to intense solar radiation and high soil temperatures. As long as the chemical is monitored, companies may be able to use EDB ethically in certain parts of the world.

Defining the Ethical Threshold: Core Values

Few ethical questions are easy for managers to answer. But there are some hard truths that must guide managers' actions, a set of what I call *core human values*, which define minimum ethical standards for all companies.[1] The right to good health and the right to economic advancement and an improved standard of living are two core human values. Another is what Westerners call the Golden Rule, which

---

1. In other writings, Thomas W. Dunfee and I have used the term *hypernorm* instead of *core human value*.

is recognizable in every major religious and ethical tradition around the world. In Book 15 of his *Analects*, for instance, Confucius counsels people to maintain reciprocity, or not to do to others what they do not want done to themselves.

Although no single list would satisfy every scholar, I believe it is possible to articulate three core values that incorporate the work of scores of theologians and philosophers around the world. To be broadly relevant, these values must include elements found in both Western and non-Western cultural and religious traditions. Consider the examples of values in the insert, "What Do These Values Have in Common?"

At first glance, the values expressed in the two lists seem quite different. Nonetheless, in the spirit of what philosopher John Rawls calls *overlapping consensus*, one can see that the seemingly divergent values converge at key points. Despite important differences between Western and non-Western cultural and religious traditions, both express shared attitudes about what it means to be human. First, individuals must not treat others simply as tools; in other words, they must recognize a person's value as a human being. Next, individuals and communities must treat people in ways that respect people's basic rights. Finally, members of a community must work together to support and improve the institutions on which the community depends. I call those three values *respect for human dignity, respect for basic rights*, and *good citizenship*.

Those values must be the starting point for all companies as they formulate and evaluate standards of ethical conduct at home and abroad. But they are only a starting point. Companies need much more specific guidelines, and the first step to developing those is to translate the core human values into core values for business. What does it mean, for example, for a company to respect human dignity? How can a company be a good citizen?

I believe that companies can respect human dignity by creating and sustaining a corporate culture in which employees, customers, and suppliers are treated not as means to an end but as people whose intrinsic value must be acknowledged, and by producing safe products and services in a safe workplace. Companies can respect basic rights by acting in ways that support and protect the individual rights of employees, customers, and surrounding communities, and by avoiding relationships that violate human beings' rights to health, education, safety, and an adequate standard of living. And companies can be good citizens by supporting essential social institutions, such as the economic system and the education system, and by working with host governments and other organizations to protect the environment.

> **Many companies don't do anything with their codes of conduct; they simply paste them on the wall.**

The core values establish a moral compass for business practice. They can help companies identify practices that are acceptable and those that are intolerable—even if the practices are compatible with a host country's norms and laws. Dumping pollutants near people's homes and accepting inadequate standards for handling hazardous materials are two examples of actions that violate core values.

Similarly, if employing children prevents them from receiving a basic education, the practice is intolerable. Lying about product specifications in the act of selling may not affect human lives directly, but it too is intolerable because it violates the trust that is needed to sustain a corporate culture in which customers are respected.

Sometimes it is not a company's actions but those of a supplier or customer that pose problems. Take the case of the Tan family, a large supplier for Levi Strauss. The Tans were allegedly forcing 1,200 Chinese and Filipino women to work 74 hours per week in guarded compounds on the Mariana Islands. In 1992, after repeated warnings to the Tans, Levi Strauss broke off business relations with them.

Creating an Ethical Corporate Culture

The core values for business that I have enumerated can help companies begin to exercise ethical judgment and think about how to operate ethically in foreign cultures, but they are not specific enough to guide managers through actual ethical dilemmas. Levi Strauss relied on a written code of conduct when figuring out how to deal with the Tan family. The company's Global Sourcing and Operating Guidelines, formerly called the Business Partner Terms of Engagement, state that Levi Strauss will "seek to identify and utilize business partners who aspire as individuals and in the conduct of all their businesses to a set of ethical standards not incompatible with our own." Whenever intolerable business situations arise, managers should be guided by precise statements that spell out the behavior and operating practices that the company demands.

Ninety percent of all *Fortune 500* companies have codes of conduct, and 70% have statements of vision and values. In Europe and the Far East, the percentages are lower but are increasing rapidly. Does that mean that most companies have what they need? Hardly. Even though most large U.S. companies have both statements of values and codes of conduct, many might be better off if they didn't. Too many companies don't do anything with the documents; they simply paste them on the wall to impress employees, customers, suppliers, and the public. As a result, the senior managers who drafted the statements lose credibility by proclaiming values and not living up to them. Companies such as Johnson & Johnson, Levi Strauss, Motorola, Texas Instruments, and Lockheed Martin, however, do a great deal to make the words meaningful. Johnson & Johnson, for example, has become well known for its Credo Challenge sessions, in which managers discuss ethics in the context of their current business problems and are invited to criticize the company's credo and make suggestions for changes. The participants' ideas are passed on to the company's senior managers. Lockheed Martin has created an innovative site on the World Wide Web and on its local network that gives employees, customers, and suppliers access to the company's ethical code and the chance to voice complaints.

Codes of conduct must provide clear direction about ethical behavior when the temptation to behave unethically is strongest. The pronouncement in a code of conduct that bribery is unacceptable is useless unless accompanied by guidelines for gift giving, payments to get goods through customs, and "requests" from intermediaries who are hired to ask for bribes.

Motorola's values are stated very simply as "How we will always act: [with] constant respect for people [and] uncompromising integrity." The company's code of conduct, however, is explicit about actual business practice. With respect to bribery, for example, the code states that the "funds and assets of Motorola shall not be used, directly or indirectly, for illegal payments of any kind." It is unambiguous about what sort of payment is illegal: "the payment of a bribe to a public official or the kickback of funds to an employee of a customer . . . ." The code goes on to prescribe specific procedures for handling commissions to intermediaries, issuing sales invoices, and disclosing confidential information in a sales transaction—all situations in which employees might have an opportunity to accept or offer bribes.

> **Many activities are neither good nor bad but exist in moral free space.**

Codes of conduct must be explicit to be useful, but they must also leave room for a manager to use his or her judgment in situations requiring cultural sensitivity. Host-country employees shouldn't be forced to adopt all home-country values and renounce their own. Again, Motorola's code is exemplary. First, it gives clear direction: "Employees of Motorola will respect the laws, customs, and traditions of each country in which they operate, but will, at the same time, engage in no course of conduct which, even if legal, customary, and accepted in any such country, could be deemed to be in violation of the accepted business ethics of Motorola or the laws of the United States relating to business ethics." After laying down such absolutes, Motorola's code then makes clear when individual judgment will be necessary. For example, employees may sometimes accept certain kinds of small gifts "in rare circumstances, where the refusal to accept a gift" would injure Motorola's "legitimate business interests." Under certain circumstances, such gifts "may be accepted so long as the gift inures to the benefit of Motorola" and not "to the benefit of the Motorola employee."

Striking the appropriate balance between providing clear direction and leaving room for individual judgment makes crafting corporate values statements and ethics codes one of the hardest tasks that executives confront. The words are only a start. A company's leaders need to refer often to their organization's credo and code and must themselves be credible, committed, and consistent. If senior managers act as though ethics don't matter, the rest of the company's employees won't think they do, either.

Conflicts of Development and Conflicts of Tradition

Managers living and working abroad who are not prepared to grapple with moral ambiguity and tension should pack their bags and come home. The view that all business practices can be categorized as either ethical or unethical is too simple. As Einstein is reported to have said, "Things should be as simple as possible—but no simpler." Many business practices that are considered unethical in one setting may be ethical in another. Such activities are neither black nor white but exist in what Thomas Dunfee and I have called *moral free space*.[2] In this gray zone, there are no tight prescriptions for a company's behavior. Managers must chart their own courses—as long as they do not violate core human values.

Consider the following example. Some successful Indian companies offer employees the opportunity for one of their children to gain a job with the company once the child has completed a certain level in school. The companies honor this commitment even when other applicants are more qualified than an employee's child. The perk is extremely valuable in a country where jobs are hard to find,

and it reflects the Indian culture's belief that the West has gone too far in allowing economic opportunities to break up families. Not surprisingly, the perk is among the most cherished by employees, but in most Western countries, it would be branded unacceptable nepotism. In the United States, for example, the ethical principle of equal opportunity holds that jobs should go to the applicants with the best qualifications. If a U.S. company made such promises to its employees, it would violate regulations established by the Equal Employment Opportunity Commission. Given this difference in ethical attitudes, how should U.S. managers react to Indian nepotism? Should they condemn the Indian companies, refusing to accept them as partners or suppliers until they agree to clean up their act?

Despite the obvious tension between nepotism and principles of equal opportunity, I cannot condemn the practice for Indians. In a country, such as India, that emphasizes clan and family relationships and has catastrophic levels of unemployment, the practice must be viewed in moral free space. The decision to allow a special perk for employees and their children is not necessarily wrong—at least for members of that country.

How can managers discover the limits of moral free space? That is, how can they learn to distinguish a value in tension with their own from one that is intolerable? Helping managers develop good ethical judgment requires companies to be clear about their core values and codes of conduct. But even the most explicit set of guidelines cannot always provide answers. That is especially true in the thorniest ethical dilemmas, in which the host country's ethical standards not only are different but also seem lower than the home country's. Managers must recognize that when countries have different ethical standards, there are two types of conflict that commonly arise. Each type requires its own line of reasoning.

In the first type of conflict, which I call a *conflict of relative development*, ethical standards

---

2. Thomas Donaldson and Thomas W. Dunfee, "Toward a Unified Conception of Business Ethics: Integrative Social Contracts Theory," *Academy of Management Review*, April 1994, and "Integrative Social Contracts Theory: A Communitarian Conception of Economic Ethics," *Economics and Philosophy*, Spring 1995.

conflict because of the countries' different levels of economic development. As mentioned before, developing countries may accept wage rates that seem inhumane to more advanced countries in order to attract investment. As economic conditions in a developing country improve, the incidence of that sort of conflict usually decreases. The second type of conflict is a *conflict of cultural tradition*. For example, Saudi Arabia, unlike most countries, does not allow women to serve as corporate managers. Instead, women may work in only a few professions, such as education and health care. The prohibition stems from strongly held religious and cultural beliefs; any increase in the country's level of economic development, which is already quite high, is not likely to change the rules.

To resolve a conflict of relative development, a manager must ask the following question: Would the practice be acceptable at home if my country were in a similar stage of economic development? Consider the difference between wage and safety standards in the United States and in Angola, where citizens accept lower standards on both counts. If a U.S. oil company is hiring Angolans to work on an offshore Angolan oil rig, can the company pay them lower wages than it pays U.S. workers in the Gulf of Mexico? Reasonable people have to answer yes if the alternative for Angola is the loss of both the foreign investment and the jobs.

> If a company declared all gift giving unethical, it wouldn't be able to do business in Japan.

Consider, too, differences in regulatory environments. In the late 1980s, the government of India fought hard to be able to import Ciba-Ceigy's Entero Vioform, a drug known to be enormously effective in fighting dysentery but one that had been banned in the United States because some users experienced side effects. Although dysentery was not a big problem in the United States, in India, poor public sanitation was contributing to epidemic levels of the disease. Was it unethical to make the drug available in India after it had been banned in the United States? On the contrary, rational people should consider it unethical not to do so. Apply our test: Would the United States, at an earlier stage of development, have used this drug despite its side effects? The answer is clearly yes.

But there are many instances when the answer to similar questions is no. Sometimes a host country's standards are inadequate at any level of economic development. If a country's pollution standards are so low that working on an oil rig would considerably increase a person's risk of developing cancer, foreign oil companies must refuse to do business there. Likewise, if the dangerous side effects of a drug treatment outweigh its benefits, managers should not accept health standards that ignore the risks.

When relative economic conditions do not drive tensions, there is a more objective test for resolving ethical problems. Managers should deem a practice permissible only if they can answer no to both of the following questions: Is it possible to conduct business successfully in the host country without undertaking the practice? and Is the practice a violation of a core human value? Japanese gift giving is a perfect example of a conflict of cultural tradition. Most experienced businesspeople, Japanese and non-Japanese alike, would agree that doing business in Japan would be virtually impossible without adopting the practice. Does gift giving violate a core human value? I cannot identify one that it violates. As a result, gift giving may be permissible for foreign companies in Japan even if it conflicts with ethical attitudes at home. In fact, that conclusion is widely accepted, even by companies such as Texas Instruments and IBM, which are outspoken against bribery.

Does it follow that all nonmonetary gifts are acceptable or that bribes are generally acceptable in countries where they are common? Not at all. (See the insert, "The Problem with Bribery.") What makes the routine practice of gift giving acceptable in Japan are the limits in its scope and intention. When gift giving moves outside those limits, it soon collides with core human values. For example, when Carl Kotchian, president of Lockheed in the 1970s, carried suitcases full of cash to Japanese politicians, he went beyond the norms established by Japanese tradition. That incident galvanized opinion in the United States Congress and helped lead to passage of the Foreign Corrupt Practices Act. Likewise, Roh Tae Woo went beyond the norms established by Korean cultural tradition when he accepted $635.4 million in bribes as president of the Republic of Korea between 1988 and 1993.

Guidelines for Ethical Leadership

Learning to spot intolerable practices and to exercise good judgment when ethical conflicts arise requires practice. Creating a company culture that rewards ethical behavior is essential. The following guidelines for developing a global ethical perspective among managers can help.

Treat corporate values and formal standards of conduct as absolutes. Whatever ethical standards a company chooses, it cannot waver on its principles either at home or abroad. Consider what has become part of company lore at Motorola. Around 1950, a senior executive was negotiating with officials of a South American government on a $10 million sale that would have increased the company's annual net profits by nearly 25%. As the negotiations neared completion, however, the executive walked away from the deal because the officials were asking for $1 million for "fees." CEO Robert Galvin not only supported the executive's decision but also made it clear that Motorola would neither accept the sale on any terms nor do business with those government officials again. Retold over

---

The Problem with Bribery

Bribery is widespread and insidious. Managers in transnational companies routinely confront bribery even though most countries have laws against it. The fact is that officials in many developing countries wink at the practice, and the salaries of local bureaucrats are so low that many consider bribes a form of remuneration. The U.S. Foreign Corrupt Practices Act defines allowable limits on petty bribery in the form of routine payments required to move goods through customs. But demands for bribes often exceed those limits, and there is seldom a good solution.

Bribery disrupts distribution channels when goods languish on docks until local handlers are paid off, and it destroys incentives to compete on quality and cost when purchasing decisions are based on who pays what under the table. Refusing to acquiesce is often tantamount to giving business to unscrupulous companies.

I believe that even routine bribery is intolerable. Bribery undermines market efficiency and predictability, thus ultimately denying people their right to a minimal standard of living. Some degree of ethical commitment— some sense that everyone will play by the rules—is necessary for a sound economy. Without an ability to predict outcomes, who would be willing to invest?

There was a U.S. company whose shipping crates were regularly pilfered by handlers on the docks of Rio de Janeiro. The handlers would take about 10% of the contents of the crates, but the company was never sure which 10% it would be. In a partial solution, the company began sending two crates—the first with 90% of the merchandise, the second with 10%. The handlers learned to take the second crate and leave the first untouched. From the company's perspective, at least knowing which goods it would lose was an improvement.

Bribery does more than destroy predictability, it undermines essential social and economic systems. That truth is not lost on businesspeople in countries where the practice is woven into the social fabric. CEOs in India admit that their companies engage constantly in bribery, and they say that they have considerable disgust for the practice. They blame government policies in part, but Indian executives also know that their country's business practices perpetuate corrupt behavior. Anyone walking the streets of Calcutta, where it is clear that even a dramatic redistribution of wealth would still leave most of India's inhabitants in dire poverty, comes face-to-face with the devastating effects of corruption.

the decades, this story demonstrating Galvin's resolve has helped cement a culture of ethics for thousands of employees at Motorola.

Design and implement conditions of engagement for suppliers and customers. Will your company do business with any customer or supplier? What if a customer or supplier uses child labor? What if it has strong links with organized crime? What if it pressures your company to break a host country's laws? Such issues are best not left for spur-of-the-moment decisions. Some companies have realized that. Sears, for instance, has developed a policy of not contracting production to companies that use prison labor or infringe on workers' rights to health and safety. And BankAmerica has specified as a condition for many of its loans to developing countries that environmental standards and human rights must be observed.

Allow foreign business units to help formulate ethical standards and interpret ethical issues. The French pharmaceutical company Rhône-Poulenc Rorer has allowed foreign subsidiaries to augment lists of corporate ethical principles with their own suggestions. Texas Instruments has paid special attention to issues of international business ethics by creating the Global Business Practices Council, which is made up of managers from countries in which the company operates. With the overarching intent to create a "global ethics strategy, locally deployed," the council's mandate is to provide ethics education and create local processes that will help managers in the company's foreign business units resolve ethical conflicts.

In host countries, support efforts to decrease institutional corruption. Individual managers will not be able to wipe out corruption in a host country, no matter how many bribes they turn down. When a host country's tax system, import and export procedures, and procurement practices favor unethical players, companies must take action.

Many companies have begun to participate in reforming host-country institutions. General Electric, for example, has taken a strong stand in India, using the media to make repeated condemnations of bribery in business and government. General Electric and others

have found, however, that a single company usually cannot drive out entrenched corruption. Transparency International, an organization based in Germany, has been effective in helping coalitions of companies, government officials, and others work to reform bribery-ridden bureaucracies in Russia, Bangladesh, and elsewhere.

Exercise moral imagination. Using moral imagination means resolving tensions responsibly and creatively. Coca-Cola, for instance, has consistently turned down requests for bribes from Egyptian officials but has managed to gain political support and public trust by sponsoring a project to plant fruit trees. And take the example of Levi Strauss, which discovered in the early 1990s that two of its suppliers in Bangladesh were employing children under the age of 14—a practice that violated the company's principles but was tolerated in Bangladesh. Forcing the suppliers to fire the children would not have ensured that the children received an education, and it would have caused serious hardships for the families depending on the children's wages. In a creative arrangement, the suppliers agreed to pay the children's regular wages while they attended school and to offer each child a job at age 14. Levi Strauss, in turn, agreed to pay the children's tuition and provide books and uniforms. That arrangement allowed Levi Strauss to uphold its principles and provide long-term benefits to its host country.

Many people think of values as soft; to some they are usually unspoken. A South Seas island society uses the word *mokita*, which means, "the truth that everybody knows but nobody speaks." However difficult they are to articulate, values affect how we all behave. In a global business environment, values in tension are the rule rather than the exception. Without a company's commitment, statements of values and codes of ethics end up as empty platitudes that provide managers with no foundation for behaving ethically. Employees need and deserve more, and responsible members of the global business community can set examples for others to follow. The dark consequences of incidents such as Union Carbide's disaster in Bhopal remind us how high the stakes can be.

Thomas Donaldson is a professor at the Wharton School of the University of Pennsylvania in Philadelphia, where he teaches business ethics. He wrote The Ethics of International Business *(Oxford University Press, 1989), and is the coauthor, with Thomas W. Dunfee, of* Ties that Bind: A Social Contracts Approach to Business Ethics. *Harvard Business School Press (1999).*

Source: Donaldson, T., "Values in Tension: Ethics Away From Home," *Harvard Business Review*, Sept.–Oct., 1996, 48–62.

Readings

Effective Crisis Management

Ian I. Mitroff, *University of Southern California*

Paul Shrivastava, *New York University, Industrial Crisis Center*

Firdaus E. Udwadia, *University of Southern California*

Academy of Management Executive, 1987

Managers, consultants, and researchers have traditionally focused on problems of financial performance and growth, but have paid little heed to the effective management of corporate crisis. The negative effects of organizational and industrial activities have been treated as minor "externalities" of production. It can be argued that until recently, it was unnecessary to focus on such crises. Today, however, such crises as pollution, industrial accidents, and product defects have assumed greater magnitude. The consequences for many corporations—like Johns-Manville and A. H. Robins—have been near or actual bankruptcy.

Corporate crises are disasters precipitated by people, organizational structures, economics, and/or technology that cause extensive damage to human life and natural and social environments. They inevitably debilitate both the financial structure and the reputation of a large organization. Consider the following examples:

- In 1979, the Three Mile Island Nuclear Power Plant had an accident leading to the near meltdown of the plant's reactor core. The accident not only cost Metropolitan Edison—the company that owned the plant—billions of dollars; it altered the fate of the nuclear power industry in the United States.[1] The plant owners and operators paid $26 million in evacuation costs, financial losses, and medical surveillance; the estimated cost of repairs and the production of electricity via other means was $4 billion.

- In 1982 an unknown person or persons contaminated dozens of Tylenol capsules with cyanide, causing the deaths of eight people and a loss of $100 million in recalled packages for Johnson & Johnson. In 1986 a second poisoning incident forced J&J to withdraw all Tylenol capsules from the market at a loss of $150 million. The company abandoned the capsule form of medication and consequently had to redesign its production facility. The full cost of switching from the production of capsules to the production of other forms of medication was in the range of $500 million.

- In December 1984 the worst industrial accident in history occurred: Poisonous methyl isocyanate gas leaked from a storage tank at a Union Carbide plant in Bhopal, India, killing 2,000 people and injuring another 200,000. The accident caused unknown damage to flora and fauna in the area. Union Carbide was

---

1. C. Perrow, *Normal Accidents.* New York: Basic Books, 1984.

sued by victims for billions of dollars; compensation settlement is likely to be between $500 million and $1 billion. In addition, the company was forced to sell 20% of its most profitable assets to prevent a takeover attack mounted by GAF Corporation, which had acquired Carbide's undervalued stock after the accident.[2]

| In May and June 1985 deadly bacteria in Jalisco cheese caused the deaths of 84 people. The company that produced the product was forced into bankruptcy.

The list of recent corporate disasters is virtually unending. It includes executive kidnappings; hijackings, both in the air and at sea; hostile takeovers; and such acts of terrorism as the bombing of factories and warehouses. Most recently, slivers of glass have been found in Gerber's baby food. Contac—an over-the-counter cold remedy—has also been the object of product tampering.

Such incidents now happen on an ever-increasing basis. Further, the interval between major accidents is shrinking alarmingly.[3] The number of product-injury lawsuits terminating in million-dollar awards has increased dramatically in the past decade: In 1974 fewer than 2,000 product injury lawsuits were filed in U.S. courts; by 1984, the number had jumped to 10,000. In 1975, juries had awarded fewer than 50 compensation awards of greater than $1 million each; in 1985, there were more than 400 such awards. The costs of product- and production-related injury is one factor in the current liability insurance crisis. Many forms of liability insurance have simply vanished, and all forms of liability insurance have become so expensive, they are available only for small coverages.

The purpose of this article is to argue that while the situation is grave, it is far from hopeless for managers, researchers, and consultants who are prepared to confront the problem directly. While no one can prevent all disasters—let alone predict how, when, and where they will occur—organizations can adopt a systematic and comprehensive perspective for managing them more effectively. Anything less than such a perspective virtually guarantees that an organization will be less prepared to cope and recover effectively from a crisis.

The Essential Phases of Crisis Management

Exhibit 1 presents a basic model of crisis management. It identifies as many of the phases necessary for effective crisis management as we have been able to discern through our research and consulting. The model, reflecting the variety of organizational patterns possible, can be entered at and exited from any point, and the action can proceed in any direction. We shall discuss this model by starting at the entry point labeled "detection" and proceeding clockwise.

The circle labeled "detection" stands for the organization's early warning systems. Those systems—including computerized process control systems, plant/equipment monitoring systems, management information systems, and environmental scanning systems—scan both the external and the internal environments for signals of impending crises.

We have placed "detection" before the sloping line labeled "prevention/preparation" to indicate that it is difficult, both systematically and comprehensively, to prevent or prepare for crises that one has not detected. For most people and most organizations, detection logically occurs before prevention. Although one may unintentionally prevent what one has not detected, prevention in such instances is based on luck and happenstance, not on deliberate organization intervention.

Point II of the model indicates that no organization can prevent every crisis from occurring. Indeed, prevention of all crises is not the basic purpose of planning and crisis management. But constant testing and revision of plans should allow an organization to cope more effectively with crises that occur, because

2. P. Shrivastava, *Bhopal: Anatomy of a Disaster*. New York: Harper & Row, 1987.
3. B. A. Turner, *Man-made Disasters*. London: Wykeham Publications, 1978; Shrivastava, 1987.

EXHIBIT 1

A Model of Crisis Management

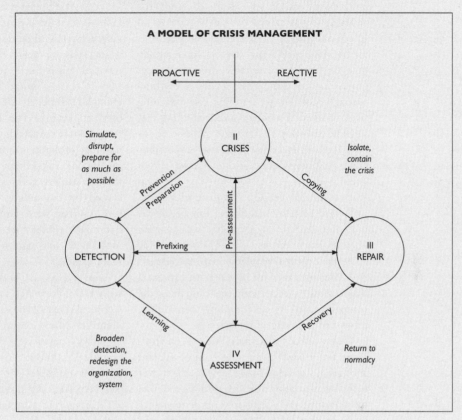

such efforts help it learn how to "roll with the punches." Prevention and preparation take the form of safety policies, maintenance, procedures, environmental-impact audits, crisis audits, emergency planning, and worker training.

Point III represents the major structures and mechanisms an organization has in place for guiding recovery. These include emergency plans, public relations plans, crisis management teams, etc. At Point IV, the organization asks itself what it has learned from its past crises and how it can use that knowledge in the future. It also assesses the effectiveness of its crisis handling strategies and identifies areas in which better crisis management capabilities need to be developed.

The more an organization denies its vulnerability, the more it will be focused on the right-hand side of Exhibit 1—the more it will respond *reactively* to crises it anticipates and

the more potential crises it prepares for, the more it engages in *proactive* behavior.

The model allows us to draw some vital lessons for effective crisis management. First, and perhaps most important, is that most crises are preceded by a string of early warning signals. To prevent some major crisis, organizations need only learn to read these early warning signals and respond to them more effectively. For example, we have seen that for a year and a half before the Bhopal tragedy, messages repeatedly passed back and forth between Union Carbide's parent company in Danbury, Connecticut, Union Carbide Eastern in Hong Kong, a similar Union Carbide plant in West Virginia, and the Indian plant. The messages warned Bhopal plant management to fix potential problems that could cause a catastrophic explosion.[4] The signals were sent, but the system chose either to ignore

---

4. Shrivastava, 1987.

them or not to act on them. This assessment holds even if, as Union Carbide contends, the catastrophe was caused by a deliberate act of on-site sabotage by a disgruntled employee.

The jury is still out, but Union Carbide may be legally accountable for the disaster unless it can show that it did everything humanly possible to read the early warning signs of internal sabotage and everything reasonable to lessen the chances of sabotage— even if complete prevention was impossible. (Editor's note: Courts in India have subsequently decided that Union Carbide was guilty.) Indeed, because complete prevention may have been impossible, it will be all the more important for legal experts to assess what organizational mechanisms Union Carbide could have actually implemented (not just left on a shelf in paper form) to try to prevent a major disaster, cope with one, and help the company and its surrounding community recover in the event of a disaster.

Given today's extremely litigious environment and a news media that is more vigilant and aware of worldwide events than ever before, organizations can regard it as a virtual certainty that their plans for and performance on every phase of the model in Exhibit 1 will become available to the press.

The field of crisis management is still in its infancy, yet available data seem to indicate that the more potential crises an organization can anticipate and prepare for (regardless of whether it can completely prevent them or not), the more quickly and successfully it will recover from any crises that strike.[5] While planning cannot prevent every crisis, the process of planning teaches an organization how to cope more effectively with whatever does occur. In fact, a cardinal rule of crisis management is that no crisis ever unfolds exactly as it was envisioned or planned for. For this reason, effective crisis management is a never-ending process, not an event with a beginning and an end.

There is, in fact, a fundamental paradox connected with crisis management: The less vulnerable an organization thinks it is, the fewer crises it prepares for; as a result, the more vulnerable it becomes. Conversely, the *more* vulnerable an organization thinks it is, the more crises it prepares for; as a result, the less vulnerable it is likely to be. The tragic explosion of Space Shuttle Challenger should be enough to dispel any doubts about the validity of this paradox. The Presidential Commission's report painstakingly examined the contending, probable causes of the disaster and, one by one, ruled them out. Slowly but surely the true cause was revealed: the explosion was caused by the failure of two large, critical O-rings that were supposed to keep highly flammable rocket fuel from spilling over its incasement and igniting with the shuttle's main engines.

The real causes, however, had little to do with technology per se. Having located the technical cause of the disaster, the report then identifies the accompanying human and organizational causes. This part of the report graphically exposes how one of the nation's premier examples of a highly successful and respected organization—NASA—became accident prone through multiple organizational failures.

One of the most powerful aspects of the report is its well-stocked supply of pictures. The report not only recounts, frame by frame, the hundredths and thousandths of seconds leading up to the accident; it also contains detailed photographs of recovered parts from the ocean floor. Although there can be no doubt that the failure of O-rings led to the disaster, the most striking evidence pertains to faulty organization—the underlying cause of the accident. This evidence consists of a seemingly endless series of reproduced memos revealing the anguished cries from deep within NASA's flawed bureaucracy and the bureaucracy of one of its prime subcontractors, Morton Thiokol. If NASA had listened and attended to these early warning signals, in all likelihood it could have prevented the disaster. One of the most striking memos starts with the cry. "Help!"

---

5. S. Fink, *Crisis Management*. New York: AMACOM, 1986; and I. Mitroff and P. Shrivastava, "Strategic Management of Corporate Crises," *Columbia Journal of World Business*, Vol. 22, No. 1, Spring 1987, pp. 5–12.

The memo goes on to say that if the shuttle continues to fly with the O-rings as they are designed, then NASA is almost guaranteed a disaster. The evidence shows an organization impervious to bad news. Instead of deliberately designing monitoring systems to pick up danger signals NASA designed, in effect, a management system that would intentionally tune out danger signals or downgrade their seriousness.

The early warning signals associated with crises are not only different for different types of organizations, but are seldom perfectly clear. Rarely, if ever, will a signal say, "The presence of such and such a defect automatically guarantees or invariably leads to disaster Y." Rather, signals will read, "It *appears* that there is a *good chance* that X will cause Y or is associated with its occurrence," or, "The numbers of Xs have been growing noticeably in recent months."

In addition, a big difference exists between warning signals external to an organization and its industry and those internal to them. Those internal to the organization and its industry are more likely to be taken seriously because they "fit in" with the business.

For these reasons, it should not be surprising to find that, based on what preliminary data we have, only 50% of *Fortune* 1000 organizations surveyed have any kind of contingency plan in place to cope with any kind of crisis.[6] Further, those organizations that are prepared have a narrow focus. They are preparing to "fight the last war" because they know how to read the signals and prepare for, cope with, and recover from those crises.

Yet this narrow focus stands in sharp contrast to what we have begun to learn about modern crises and disasters. Unlike previous crises and disasters, modern ones link up with one another and defy accepted truths. For instance, consider the recent finding of glass in Gerber's baby food. The food industry has long experienced such events, so they are historically well known to the industry. But what happened during the week that slivers of glass were found in Gerber's baby food was not part of the typical historic pattern. That week the

Challenger exploded and Tylenol was poisoned for the second time. These events shattered the twin myths that "The worst can and won't happen twice to any organization" and "Lightening won't and can't strike twice in the same place."

As a consequence of these events, the media focused on Gerber's CEO as perhaps never before. Although he may have been right in not withdrawing his products—because withdrawing them may have encouraged "copycat killers"—he was wrong in another, more important sense. By being unwilling to withdraw the products, Gerber's CEO appeared callous toward the most fragile and most precious of all consumers—babies! Contrast this with the behavior of Johnson & Johnson's CEO, who unequivocally withdrew Tylenol from the shelves to demonstrate the company's long-standing commitment to the safety and well-being of its consumers.

An Expanded Typology of Crises

Clearly, every organization must attend not only to crises that are well known to it and its industry, but to the many disasters that can now happen to any organization and all industries. Such an expanded list of crises is presented in Exhibit 2.

Exhibit 2 differentiates between crises that arise within the organization and those that arise outside it. This distinction is critical because the warning signals will be different for each type of crisis. Exhibit 2 also differentiates between crises caused by technical/economic breakdowns and those caused by people/organizational/social breakdowns. This is because nearly every technical/economic breakdown is associated with a people/organizational/social breakdown, and vice versa. Thus, if we look at only one part of the chain, we miss valuable potential lessons for preparing and correcting the whole system.

Exhibit 3 shows various causes of each type of crisis listed in Exhibit 2. Finally, Exhibit 4 shows the wide variety of actions organizations can take to prepare for, cope with, reduce the effects of, and recover from the various kinds of crises we've identified.

---

6. Fink, 1986.

EXHIBIT **2**

Types of Corporate Crises

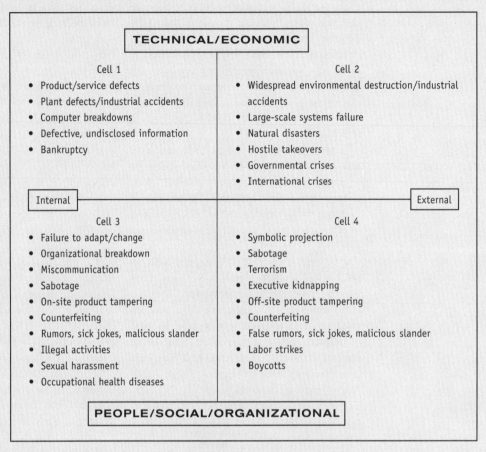

Exhibit 4 shows that when it comes to taking action, we are faced with the problem of choosing between too many options, none of which can guarantee us prevention or complete containment. But then again, perfection is not an appropriate criterion for judging the success of crisis management.

Indeed, if an appropriate goal for crisis management is to learn to prepare for as many crises as possible, then a reasonable way of approaching this goal is to form a crisis portfolio based on Exhibits 2, 3, and 4. One way to do this is to select a minimum of one crisis from each of the cells in Exhibits 2 and 3. This way, organizations can avoid the tendency to prepare mainly for the crises listed in Cell 1 of these exhibits and can thus begin to broaden their perspective about potential crises. In the same way, organizations can form a portfolio of coping and recovery mechanisms based on a

selection of at least one element from each of the cells in Exhibit 4.

Concluding Remarks

To manage crises effectively, organizations must first be aware of all the phases and steps involved in the entire process of crisis management. Next, they must be aware of the differences between the phases. For instance, the purpose of the "preparation and prevention phase" in Exhibit 1 is for organizations to ask themselves, "What can/cannot be prevented and/or prepared for?" The goal of this phase is to prepare for as many of the crises and causes of them listed in Exhibits 2 and 3 as possible.

Furthermore, because crises are becoming increasingly complex, a secondary step must be to prepare for the simultaneous occurrence of crises. Again, the purpose is to broaden the

EXHIBIT 3

Uses and Sources of Corporate Crises

TECHNICAL/ECONOMIC

Cell 1

- Undetected, unanalyzed, unsuspected product defects
- Undetected plant/manufacturing defects
- Faulty detection systems
- Faulty backup design/controls

Cell 2

- Unanticipated, unanalyzed environmental conditions
- Faulty technical monitoring systems
- Faulty strategic planning
- Poor societal planning
- Poor global monitoring

Internal | External

Cell 3

- Faulty organizational controls
- Poor company culture, information/communication structure, rewards
- Poor operator training
- Poor contingency planning
- Human operator failures/errors
- Internal saboteurs
- Faulty employee screening

Cell 4

- Failure to design and implement new societal institutions
- Faulty social monitoring of criminal stakeholders
  - Disgruntled ex-employees
  - Assassins
  - Kidnappers
  - Terrorists
  - External saboteurs
  - Copycat killers
  - Psychopaths

PEOPLE/SOCIAL/ORGANIZATIONAL

---

organization's outlook. Preparing for and attempting to prevent crises means constantly testing and simulating as many breakdowns as possible.

The breadth demanded in the prevention and preparation phase stands in sharp contrast to the narrow scope required in the "coping" phase. The goal of the "coping" phase is to draw a tight, narrow net around a crisis that has occurred. This will contain the crisis and prevent it from spreading either inside or outside the organization. To accomplish this, growing numbers of organizations have seen fit to establish special organizational units known as crisis management units or crisis teams. Their full-time responsibility is to prepare for and handle special, emerging situations. They are free to do this because they are buffered from the normal daily demands of the organization.

Finally, one of the many lessons emerging from the still new field of crisis management is worth stressing. For this lesson, consider an analogy with patients who have been informed that they have terminal cancer. It is believed that people go through four distinct phases upon being informed that their condition is terminal. The first is denial. When denial is no longer effective, one becomes angry at the universe, at God, for "letting this happen to me." At some point deep depression sets in. Most patients who live long enough to make it to the fourth and last stage: acceptance. This stage is accompanied by the feeling. "This may be it for me, but at least I can make a last, positive statement with my life and pass something of value on to others."

These steps also apply to organizations managing crises. Keep in mind that denial, anger, and depression are powerful human emotions that are difficult to manage, particularly during a crisis. For this reason, organizations are well advised to raise their anxiety levels when they prepare for the worst, so that

EXHIBIT

4   **Preventive Actions for Organizations**

TECHNICAL/ECONOMIC

One-Shot (Short Term)
- Preventive packaging
- Better detection
- Tighter system security
- Tighter internal operations
- Better operator/management controls
- Tighten design of plants/equipment
- Install chain of command
- Install crisis management units

Repeated (Long Term)
- Design expert monitoring systems, networks
- Hold "continental" planning workshops
- Bring in outside experts; form permanent networks
- Design stores of the future
- Install systems-wide monitoring
- Establish crises command centers
- Perform periodic, mandated reviews

TIME and SPACE

Immediate Environment (Limited Individual Parts)
- Ensure emotional preparation
- Provide psychological counseling for employees
- Provide security training for all employees
- Provide detection training
- Install social support groups
- Provide media training

Extended Environment (Systematic)
- Develop profiles of psychopaths, terrorists, copycats, etc.
- Establish preventive hot lines
- Sponsor community watch groups
- Provide consumer education
- Establish political action groups
- Sponsor mental-health programs
- Establish counseling groups
- Re-examine organizational culture
- Establish permanent crisis management units
- Perform organization redesign
- Appoint ombudsmen, whistle-blowers
- Establish outside auditing teams to inspect vulnerabilities
- Provide media programs/training for all executives
- Work with industry associations
- Work with research centers
- Establish programs on business ethics

PEOPLE/SOCIAL/ORGANIZATIONAL

they will be able to cope when a real crisis occurs.

No one should ever underestimate the emotional costs of a disaster. While the two Tylenol poisonings cost the company approximately half a billion dollars in total, there were the formidable emotional costs as well. Many executives associated with Tylenol still awake with nightmares on the anniversaries of the poisonings. Also, consider the fact that NASA had to set up special medical hotlines to help its personnel handle the emotional trauma associated with the Challenger disaster. In addition to the explosion itself and the tragic loss of the seven astronauts' lives, more than one member of NASA couldn't handle the question posed by their own children: "Daddy (Mommy) were you responsible for killing the astronauts?"[7]

Is your organization prepared to handle the financial and emotional costs of a major disaster? For those who work in the field of crisis management it is no longer a question of whether a major disaster will strike any organization, but only a matter of *when, how, what form will it take, and who and how many will be affected.*

Because we started with a simple model (Exhibit 1) that stressed the positive steps organizations can take to blunt crises, we will close with a simple model (Exhibit 5) that shows the steps that almost guarantee an organization will experience a major crisis from which it will not recover. Every organization therefore has a fundamental choice: Practice insurance against disaster or follow almost a guaranteed design for disaster.

Ian I. Mitroff is the Harold Quinton Distinguished Professor of Business Policy and codirector of the Center for Crisis Management at the Graduate School of Business, University of Southern California. He received a B.S. in engineering physics, an M.S. in structural mechanics, and a Ph.D. in engineering science and the philosophy of social science, all from the University of California, Berkeley.

EXHIBIT 5   **Steps for Crisis Management**

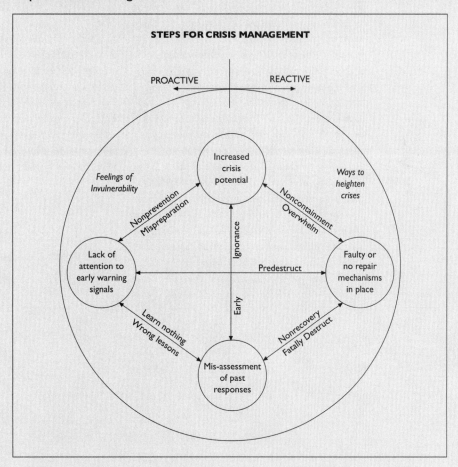

---

7. As reported to the first author in direct interviews with NASA officials.

Professor Mitroff is a member of the American Association for the Advancement of Science, Academy of Management, American Psychological Association, American Sociological Association, Philosophy of Science Association, and the Institute for Management Science. He has published over 200 papers and eight books in the areas of business policy, corporate culture, managerial psychology and psychiatry, strategic planning, and the philosophy and sociology of science, and has appeared on numerous radio and television programs. His most recent book is Business Not As Usual: Rethinking Our Individual Corporate, and Industrial Strategies for Global Competition, *published by Jossey-Bass in 1987.*

Paul Shrivastava *is associate professor in the Graduate School of Business Administration, New York University. He has a bachelor's degree in mechanical engineering and Master's and Ph.D. degrees in management. His management research interests include the strategic management of organizations, crisis management, policymaking processes, design of information and learning systems for strategic decision making, and management and administrative problems of developing countries. He has spoken on these topics at national and international meetings and has published over three dozen articles on these topics in professional and scholarly journals.*

Dr. Shrivastava has special expertise in managing decision-making processes in crises, and has chaired and conducted decision meetings and conference meetings in both corporate and professional environments. He was engaged in several major conflict resolution efforts that involved mediating conflicts between corporate, public, and government agencies. He now serves as executive director of the Industrial Crisis Institute, Inc., a nonprofit research organization devoted to resolving industrial crisis problems.

Dr. Shrivastava is the editor of Industrial Crisis Quarterly, *a coeditor (with Robert Lamb) of* Advances in Strategic Management, *and a contributing editor to the* Journal of Business Strategy. *He has received numerous awards and grants for his research from agencies such as the National Science Foundation, and is currently writing a book entitled* Bhopal: Anatomy of a Crisis, *to be published by Ballinger Publishing Company in 1987.*

Firdaus E. Udwadia *received his M.S. and Ph.D. from the California Institute of Technology and his M.B.A. from the University of Southern California, where he is presently professor of business administration, civil engineering, and mechanical engineering. He is director of the Structural Identification Facility and codirector of the Center for Crisis Management at USC.*

Professor Udwadia has received numerous awards, including the NASA Award for Outstanding Contributions to Technological Innovations, and has been a consultant to government and private industry in the areas of economic and engineering systems modeling, technology transfer, and project management and command, control and communications. His current research interest is in the area of crisis management.

Source: Reprinted with the permission of the Academy of Management, PO Box 3020, Briar Cliff Manor, NY 10510–8020. *Effective Crisis Management*, Mitroff, I. I., et al., *Academy of Management Executive*, 1987, Vol. 1, No. 3. Reproduced by permission of the publisher via Copyright Clearance Center, Inc.

Appendix A

CORPORATE ETHICAL PERFORMANCE INDICATORS USED IN THE CORPORATE ETHICS MONITOR SEPT.–OCT. 1998

Ethical Performance of Telecommunications Companies

	BELL CANADA	BC TELECOM	BRUNCOR	MANITOBA	MT&T	QUÉBEC TEL	ROGERS CANTEL	SASK TEL	TELUS
Code of Ethics									
Existence	Yes	Yes	Yes	Yes	Yes	Yes	No	No	Yes
Date (Original/Most Recent Update)	1893, 1998	1980, 1992	No info, 1997	1979, 1998	1980, 1998	1988, 1996	Not applic	Not applic	1988, 1995
Reinforcement/Ethics Training	Yes	Yes	No	No	No info	Yes	No	No	Yes
Annual Sign-off	Yes	Yes	No	No	No info	No	Not applic	Not applic	Yes
Direct Job Creation									
Current Employment Canada	32,688	12,246	2,924	3,614	3,269	1,635	2,050	No info	8,972
Current Employment Worldwide	32,688	No info	2,924	3,614	3,269	1,635	No info	No info	No info
One Year Change (1998/97) Canada (%)	21.0%	No info	17.7%	Nil	8.4%	Nil	No info	No info	No info
Five Year Change (1998/93) Canada (%)	31.9%	(15%)	29.3%	18.0%	23.9%	4.3%	(35%)	No info	(15%)
Employment of Women									
Directors (#)	1 of 15	2 of 14	2 of 14	2 of 11	2 of 14	1 of 11	No info	2 of 7	2 of 13
Senior Management (%)	13%	12%	14%	No info	16%	17%	No info	No info	2%
Management (%)	47%	No info	No info	No info	28%	21%	No info	No info	24%
Workforce (%)	56%	No info	No info	No info	43%	43%	No info	No info	45%
Hiring and Promotion Programs									
Employment Equity	Yes	Yes	Yes	Yes	Yes	Yes	No info	Yes	Yes
Affirmative Action	Not applic	Yes	Yes	No	Yes	Yes	No info	Yes	Yes
Gender Programs & Policies	3	4	2	3	3	4	No info	1	3
Charitable Donations									
Total Amount 1997 ($)	$7.5 million	No info	No info	$600,000	No info	$220,541	No info	No info	$7.39 million
% Profit Before Taxes	0.5%	No info	No info	No info	1% +	0.4%	No info	No info	1% +
'Imagine Campaign' Pledge	Yes	No	No	Yes	Yes	No	No	No	Yes
Community Relations									
Scholarship Fund for Employees	No	No	No	No	Yes	No	No info	No	No
Scholarship Fund for Employees' Children	Yes	Yes	Yes	No	No	Yes	No info	No info	No
Matching Gift Program	Yes	Yes	No	Yes	Yes	No	No info	Yes	Yes
Sports/Athletic Support	Yes	Yes	Yes	Yes	Yes	Yes	No info	Yes	Yes
Health/Medical Support	Yes	Yes	Yes	Yes	Yes	Yes	No info	No info	Yes
Arts/Cultural Support	Yes	Yes	Yes	Yes	Yes	Yes	No info	Yes	Yes
Social/Welfare Support	Yes	Yes	Yes	Yes	Yes	Yes	No info	Yes	Yes
Progressive Staff Policies									
Corporate Sponsored Daycare (On-Site or Referral)	No	Yes, referral	No	No	Yes, referral	Yes, referral	No info	No	Yes, referral
Extended Maternity Leave	Yes	Yes	Yes	Yes	Yes	Yes	No info	Yes	Yes

(Continued)

Appendix A, continued

CORPORATE ETHICAL PERFORMANCE INDICATORS USED IN THE CORPORATE ETHICS MONITOR SEPT.–OCT. 1998

	BELL CANADA	BC TELECOM	BRUNCOR	MANITOBA	MT&T	QUÉBEC TEL	ROGERS CANTEL	SASK TEL	TELUS
Employee Assistance Program (EAP) (#)	4	4	1	3	4	4	No info	4	4
Health Program Plan (HPP) (#)	1	3	2	3	1	3	No info	2	3
Company Training Programs (1997 Amount $/Per Employee)	$1,774	$1,800	$1,333	No info	$1,539	$43	No info	No info	No info
Tuition/Book Compensation	Yes (1)	100%	100%	100%	100%	100%	No info	100%	100%
Communications Programs (#)	5	3	5	3	2	4	No info	3	6
Retirement Counselling	Yes	Yes	Yes	Yes	Yes	Yes	No info	Yes	Yes
Same Sex Benefits	No info	Yes	No info	No	Yes	Yes	No info	No info	Yes
Gainsharing Programs									
ESOP—Yes/No/Employer Contribution	Yes, up to 6% of salary	Yes, 25% of share value	Yes, 25% of share value	Yes, 25% of share value	Yes, 25% of share value	Yes, 33% of share value			Yes, 30% of share value
Stock Option Plan - Yes/No	Yes	Yes	Yes	Yes	Yes	Yes	No info		Yes
- Who Eligible	Officers	Senior managers	Key executives	Senior managers	Senior managers	Officers	No info	Not applic	Officers
Profit Sharing - Yes/No	Yes	No	Yes	No	Yes	No	No info	No	No
- Who Eligible	Senior management	Not applic	Non-unionized	Not applic	All	Not applic	No info	Not applic	Not applic
Labor Relations/Health and Safety									
Unionized (% of Workforce)	80%	70%	30%	95%	67%	93%	No info	80%	70%
Decertification Cases (#, Yr)	None	None	No info	None	None	None	No info	No info	None
Unjust Dismissals	No info	None	None	None	2	None	No info	No info	None
Strikes/Lockouts in Last 10 Years	1	3	Nil	No info	1	1	No info	2	Nil
Workplace Accidents and Injuries Data Supplied	Yes	Yes	No	Yes	Yes	No	No info	No	Yes
Lost Time Accidents (Per Million Hours Worked)	7.86	No info	No info	No info	12.43	No info	No info	No info	3.92 (2)
Occupational Health & Safety Cases (#, Fines)	None	No info	No info	No info	None	None	No info	No info	None
Occupational H&S Awards	None	Yes	No info	Yes	None	None	No info	No info	None
Environmental Management									
Formal Environmental Code	Yes	Yes	Yes	Yes	Yes	No	No info	No	Yes
Date (Original/Recent Update)	1990, 1993	1989, ongoing	1990, no info	1992, 1994	1990, 1994	Not applic	No info	Not applic	1992, 1996
Undertaken Environmental Audits (Yes/No; Internal Staff/External Staff/Both)	Yes, both	Yes, internal	Yes, both	Yes, both	Yes, internal	No	No info	No info	Yes, both
Frequency of Environmental Audits	2 year cycle	Not regular	Annual	No info	Yes	Not applic	No info	No info	Annual
Employees with Full Time Environmental Responsibility	14	29	Nil	2	1	Nil	No info	No info	4

Senior Position with Full Time Environmental Responsibility	Director	Director	Manager	Manager	None	No info	No info	Manager
Staff Environment Committee	Yes	Yes	Yes	Yes	No	No info	No info	Yes
Environmental Committee of the Board of Directors	Yes	No	No	No	No	No info	No info	No
Environmental Reports to the Board of Directors (#/year)	2	2	Not regular	4	No	No info	No info	4
Issue Public Environmental Report (Yes/No; Frequency)	No	No	Yes (3)	No	No	No info	No	Yes
Charitable Giving to Environmental Organizations	Yes	No info	Yes	Yes	No	No info	No info	Yes
Annual Report on Recycled Stock	Yes	Yes	Yes	Yes	No	No info	Yes	Yes
Environmental Section in Annual Report	No	No	No	No	No	No info	No info	No
Environmental Performance								
Environmental Prosecutions in Last 10 Years (#, Fines)	None	None	None	None	No info	No info	No info	None
Environmental Awards (#)	11	10	No info	1	None	No info	No info	1
Recycling Programs (#)	7	7	6	8	5	No info	2	7
Report Quantities Waste Recycled	Yes	Yes	Yes	Yes	No	No info	No info	Partial
Environmental Expenditures 1997 ($)	$5–7 million	No info	$100,000	$60,000	No info	No info	No info	$924,000
Ethical Sourcing and Trading								
Commercial Relations with Repressive Regimes	China	China, Indonesia	No	No	No	No info	No info	No
Candor Quotient (%)								
1998 Current Review	85%	80%	88%	96%	95%	3%	49%	92%
1995 Previous Review	96%	88%	87%	90%	100%	Not applic	66%	89%

Information for this comparison is drawn from the files of EthicScan Canada. Where the performance of a company is described as "No info," the company may have a salutary record, but the facts are not known to EthicScan researchers. The regular fact checking process involves corporate database reviews, interviews, and two requests that the company review, update and validate the major findings on file.

Notes:

(1) Limit of $1,500 per year for tuition.

(2) Frequency of disabling injuries, accounting for hours of exposure.

(3) One report published in 1996.

Research Report filed by Jason Potts

APPENDIX B

Ethics Audit Program Annual Audit Questions

Questions to be Asked at Each Business Unit

Responsibility

- Is there a person at the business unit who is responsible for answering questions on and administering the *Code?* Who is this?

- Do the employees know of this person's responsibility with regard to the *Code?*

Awareness and Commitment

- Has the *Code* been distributed to all employees and managers?

- Have all managers signed the Representation Letter confirming that "during the past year, [they] and, to the best of their knowledge after due inquiry, [their] immediate subordinates who hold management responsibilities have complied with the *Code* and have taken appropriate actions to ensure compliance by other employees (who are [their] subordinates) and by contractors and consultants (who [they] have engaged or are responsible for)?

- Have all employees signed-off during the past year that they have observed the *Code* and will continue to do so, and that they know of no unreported breaches of the *Code?*

- Are all new employees signing-off when they join the company?

- Do all suppliers, contractors, and consultants receive a written notification that it is understood they will abide by the *Code* or specific provisions of it such as those on gifts or inducements, conflicts of interest, health and safety, or environmental protection?

Training

- Do new employees receive training on the *Code* when they join before they sign the *Code* sign-off?

- Have existing employees received training on the *Code* during the past year? What is the nature of this training?

- Do suppliers, contractors, and consultants receive a briefing on the *Code* and their need to observe it?

Commitment and Support Provided by Management

- Has management above the business unit shown personal commitment and support for the *Code* and the values on which it is based? How? (Speeches, memos, news articles, etc. . . .)

- Has the management of the business unit shown personal commitment and support for the *Code* and the values on which it is based? How? (speeches, memos, use in screening merit and promotion decisions, etc.)

- Has there been reinforcing publicity in newsletters, or through publicity of good or bad examples of behavior?

Operations

Regarding the business unit's systems for answering ethics inquiries, bringing ethics concerns forward for investigation, and investigation and sanction:

- Do employees and managers have confidence in these systems?

- Survey ten employees and five managers.

- What are the annual usage statistics of each system?

- Were any significant ethical problems not handled appropriately?

- Were actions taken on a timely and appropriate basis?

- Do any items or issues require clarification to avoid further problems?

- Are there any suggestions for improvement of the *Code* or the processes involved?

- Do timely periodic reports to division management exist covering the activities of these systems?

- Are all items reported?

Questions to Be Asked of Each Division Operation, Assessment, and Continuous Improvement

- Are there personnel assigned (specify who) and systems in place to monitor and ensure:

    - compliance with the *Code* in each business unit and at the division level?

    - effectiveness of the procedures for complying with the *Code* in such matters as training, sign-off, inquiry, investigation and sanction?

    - assessment of operations and risks?

    - reinforcement and support?

- Are necessary actions taken on timely and appropriate bases?

- Are timely reports prepared for and reviewed by division management?

- Are objectives related to the *Code* built into the divisional and business unit yearly operating objective statements?

- Are appropriate actions taken/reinforced by division management?

- Is there appropriate feed-forward reporting to head office to allow remedial action and solutions to be shared across the company?

- Does head office react and respond to feed-forward or requests for clarification?

- Has management above the division shown personal commitment and support for the *Code* and the values on which it is based? How? (speeches, memos, news articles, etc. . . .)

- Are there any issues needing further clarification and/or suggestion?

- Are there any issues that should be reported to the board for information or action?

8

SUBPRIME LENDING FIASCO—ETHICS ISSUES

Purpose of the Chapter[1]

The subprime lending crisis began to be felt in earnest in 2008. As the number of mortgage foreclosures and walk-aways grew, huge investor losses followed that threatened the vitality of financial institutions, intermediary companies, investors, and many individuals. Questions about how this situation developed, who was to blame, and what can be done to avoid similar occurrences in the future gave way to questions about the ethics, or lack of ethics, that underlay the actions causing so much distress. This chapter explores those questions and proposes lessons to be learned to help protect the future from similar fiascos.

The Economic Train Wreck

The subprime lending fiasco has brought the United States and world financial markets to their knees by precipitating a liquidity crisis and economic downturn so severe that major financial stalwart corporations have had to be rescued from insolvency by governments and private investors. U.S. stock prices declined in excess of 40 percent in company with extreme volatility. Russia offered to bail out several of Iceland's banks and save that country from financial ruin. Several countries including Iceland, Hungary, and Ukraine applied to the International Monetary Fund (IMF), the lender of last resort for countries, for financial assistance amid discussions that the IMF's capitalization of U.S.$250 billion might not be sufficient to meet the demand. European governments also pumped funds into several of their banks to keep them afloat.

All of this turmoil is principally[2] because financial institutions, pension funds, corporations, and private investors purchased mortgage-backed securities that ultimately have turned out to be worth a lot less than anyone ever imagined possible. The decline in value of these investments and an inability to accurately estimate their worth undermined the liquid funds or capital available to do business, to make loans, or to settle commitments. Although the value of the homes mortgaged could return to pre-fiasco levels in the long run,[3] it is impossible to find enough investors who want to wait that long even at depressed valuations. Consequently, the United States and other governments announced their desire to buy the depressed securities with

---

1. This chapter was prepared in early November 2008, well before the dust had settled on the subprime lending crisis and the related fallout and remediation. Consult **www.cengage.com/accounting/ brooks/** for discussion of subsequent events.
2. An additional but related cause was that derivative securities such as credit default protections/swaps grew significantly, based largely on computer-generated valuation models that incorporated unsound risk projection/calculations.
3. They may not return to previously high levels (for a very long time) if new regulatory and managerial conservatism prevent a return to recent debt ratios.

the intent to hold them until their value goes up, and/or to inject liquid funds through loans, equity investments or other means to keep the banks and other enterprises afloat. Some major financial firms have, however, been allowed to go bankrupt or have been taken over by stronger companies in forced, eleventh-hour, fire-sale transactions.

Nonfinancial firms also have been affected because borrowing became very difficult as a result of the lack of liquidity of normal financial sources, and the lack of desire by others to lend in uncertain times. It became very difficult for financial institutions to get normal overnight loans, even at very high rates of interest. More important, it became difficult or next to impossible for their customers to obtain longer-term financing as a result of the loss of trust.

The impact of this liquidity crisis on individuals has been brutal. Many lost their homes, or have seen their house, their major asset, decline in value when they needed it to remain high to support their retirement, lifestyle, or other borrowings. Entrepreneurs, businesses, car purchasers, and others who needed credit were unable to secure financing, so business activity is declining with the inevitable effect of reducing employment. Indeed, car manufacturing has declined so dramatically that the merger or bankruptcy of the largest automakers is in prospect. U.S.-owned auto manufacturers have sought financial assistance from government agencies. Inevitably, the lack of credit slowed economies worldwide, causing layoffs of workers who, in turn, were unable to pay their credit card and other debts, ultimately forcing banks and other lenders to suffer and disclose increased credit losses.

The economic engine of society is sputtering, not just in the United States but also around the world. European leaders have agreed "to provide capital for banks caught short of funds because of frozen money markets and to ensure or buy into new debt issues."[4] From their perspective, the "root cause of the crisis was a U.S. housing boom that went bust, and with it a market in mortgage-related debt, and derivatives that turned toxic with the downturn. That marked the start of a credit squeeze that snowballed worldwide."[5] According to French President and European Union President Nicholas Sarkozy, the crisis is so grave that "This needs concrete measures and unity—none of our countries acting alone could end this crisis."[6]

How Did The Subprime Lending Crisis Happen?

Opinions differ on the root cause of the creation and bursting of the U.S. mortgage bubble that led to the worldwide economic train wreck. Some observers claim that the U.S. Federal Reserve Board's (the Fed) policy of very "deep cuts in interest rates earlier in this decade, together with its lack of regulation on subprime mortgages—ultimately estimated to total 33% of the total U.S. mortgage market—fueled the housing and credit bubbles."[7]

In response, former Federal Reserve Chairman Alan Greenspan stated that the situation was "being driven by global forces . . ." and that "There's really nothing we could have done about it."[8] He said that:

> the Fed cut interest rates to stave off a deflation threat, but once it started raising short-term interest rates again, the long-term rates didn't follow suit. He said the globalization of debt markets and a glut of savings from booming emerging economies undermined the Fed's efforts.

---

4. "European leaders pledge aid for banks in crisis," *Toronto Star*, October 13, 2008, B1, B4.
5. Ibid.
6. Ibid.
7. "A train wreck? Greenspan says he didn't see it coming," David Parkinson, *The Globe and Mail*, November 8, 2008, B2.
8. Ibid.

He said the Fed first became concerned about the subprime lending market around 2000, but adopted a "wait-and-see" approach as the market remained healthy for the next five years. It was only when global demand for U.S. mortgage-backed instruments began to boom in 2005 did the quality of mortgage products deteriorate, . . .

"We hadn't the slightest inclination at the time that the securitization problems would become so large.[9]"

Regardless of where the blame for the creation of a U.S. housing bubble lies—overstimulation as a result of very low interest rates or excessive foreign savings, or both—the main vehicle involved in the financial and economic train wreck was the securitization and resale of U.S. mortgage-backed securities to investors, which lost value when house prices plummeted and homeowners walked away without obligation to repay. It is also the case that U.S. regulations were insufficient to prevent the creation of highly risky mortgages and the transfer of this risk to unsuspecting investors.[10]

Moreover, the conditions that allowed the subprime lending fiasco to happen began developing before the period identified by Greenspan. Banks and other financial intermediaries that were central to the creation and transfer process played an active role in encouraging the modification of preventive regulation.

Bankers are usually very careful. They want to ensure that their loans are protected, so they assess the prospects for repayment (based on the financial strength of the borrower through earnings and other investments), or—if the borrower cannot repay—then the bank's ability to recover its loss from the value of the underlying collateral (the value of the house), which could be sold for enough to cover the loan. Why weren't U.S. bankers prudent with the subprime mortgages that fueled the current crisis?

The breakdown in prudent lending practices actually started with the repeal in 1999 of the 1933 Glass-Steagall Act (GSA). The GSA had originally been put in place to force banks to choose between commercial and investment bank activities. The Act was to protect depositors' funds from the more speculative risks of securities underwriting, except for government bonds, by limiting the income derived from underwriting to 10 percent of total bank income. In other words, the U.S. banks' participation in mortgage lending was restricted. This GSA protection concept was extended in 1956 (by the passage of the Bank Holding Company Act) to preclude banks from underwriting insurance, although they were permitted to sell insurance products underwritten by others. In 1999, however, the Gramm-Leach-Billey Act was passed, allowing banks to become heavily involved in investment bank activities. It permitted banks to underwrite, trade, and invest in mortgage-backed securities and collateralized debt obligations, and to develop structured investment vehicles (SIVs) to facilitate this.

These developments spurred competition in the mortgage markets and stimulated the creation of investment vehicles that allowed the transfer of mortgage risks from the issuer to the ultimate investors in these SIVs. This freed the initial mortgagors (and the banks and other financial intermediaries that bundled mortgages up in the securitization process and resold them) from the normal risks of credit collection losses. At the same time, low interest rates were set by the Fed to stimulate housing starts, and huge polls of foreign savings increased the demand for securitized mortgage-backed investments. These two factors kept rates low and stimulated housing prices. In order to fill the investment demand, competitive lending practices were unleashed that had not been seen before, such as lending to mortgagees, without any deposit, without proper documentation, and without proper concern for their ability to pay.

---

9. Ibid.
10. Other derivatives were also to blame, including credit default swaps, in which executives relied on faulty risk valuation tools and flawed rating agency judgments.

| Mortgagors were advancing 100 percent of the purchase price instead of requiring a deposit of 10–25 percent of the purchase price, thus requiring the borrower to have some capital at risk to prevent walk-aways when repayment becomes difficult. Often, a borrower would be able to get a low-rate or subprime mortgage for 90–95 percent of the house value, and a second mortgage for the remaining 5–10 percent. These loans were sometimes referred to as *teaser loans* because the combination of no deposit and low interest lured many borrowers into arrangements that contemplated higher interest rates on renewal that were to be met from increased salaries or increased borrowing as house prices rose—two prospects that did not materialize.

| *No document* or *liar loans* attracted people with poor credit histories.

| *Ninja loans* were common, in which the mortgagee had no income, no job, and no assets.

These practices initially made it far easier to obtain mortgage financing and the housing market boomed as house prices soared, but ultimately the ticking time bomb blew up. When it came time to renew the teaser mortgages, many individuals could not meet the higher interest and payment costs, and because house prices had not gone up as expected, they chose to walk away from their mortgage obligations—creating the term "jingle mail" when they mailed their keys to the mortgagor—and let the mortgagor/bank foreclose and sell the house. In the United States, turning over the house to the lender extinguishes house mortgage commitments by the mortgagee. However, as the number of foreclosures grew, the selling value of homes declined past the point where lenders could recoup their capital.

Many lenders, however, bundled up their mortgage loans or sold them to second party consolidators (banks and others such as Fannie Mae and Freddie Mac) who would create larger units, which they might guarantee the collection of, and resell the larger sets called SIVs or other pass-through type vehicles to companies, pension plans, and individual investors. In other words, the risk of noncollection was passed from the original lender to a counterparty and then to investors who thought they were getting very sound, high-yield investments for their portfolios. In fact, the increasing walk-aways and falling house prices meant that repossession and resale did not recoup the original principal, and the guarantee of the counterparties was often worthless, so the ultimate investors had to face the fact that their investments had fallen dramatically in value.

In the case of banks and other publicly owned investors who were complying with mark-to-market accounting standards, this decrease in value had to be reflected in the company's financial statements as a provision for a significant loss. To complicate this scenario, the speed of the fall in value and the uncertainty created meant that even the reduced values were very difficult to estimate. Investor company share prices naturally fell adding further to the financial unrest. Faced with losses and uncertainty, most lenders were unwilling to lend to anyone until matters settled down, and a worldwide liquidity or credit freeze occurred.

The fate of the Federal National Mortgage Association (NYSE: FNM) and the Federal Home Loan Mortgage Corporation (NYSE: FRE) is worth understanding. Known as Fannie May and Freddie Mac, respectively, they were two giant purchasers and resellers of home loans. As a result of the loss of value of the homes mortgaged and guaranteed, FNM and FRE also suffered huge losses, to the point where they were unable to continue to buy mortgages. Rather than allow this inability to freeze the mortgage market, in early September 2008 the U.S. government essentially took over both publicly traded firms and injected as much as $200 billion to keep the mortgage markets flowing.[11]

---

11. "U.S. seizes Fannie and Freddie," David Ellis, CNN Money.com, September 7, 2008, 8:28 pm, Downloaded Nov. 9, 2008.

The CEOs of both firms were replaced, but they agreed to continue to assist and were allowed to keep significant severance packages. FNM's Daniel Mudd and FRE's Richard Syron left with $7.3 and $6.3 million, respectively, after earning $11.6 and $18.3 million, respectively, in the previous year. The severance payments raised the ire of many, including then-Senator Barack Obama, who wrote Treasury Secretary Henry Paulson, saying: "Under no circumstances should the executives of these institutions earn a windfall at a time when the U.S. Treasury has taken unprecedented steps to rescue these companies with taxpayer resources."[12] The ousted CEOs record speaks for itself. When Mudd took over FNM in December 2004, its stock was trading at about $70, but it closed at 73 cents on September 8. Syron took over FRE in December 2003 when its shares sold at about $55, later sinking to 88 cents on September 8.[13] More important, if these two men had had the foresight and/or moral courage to speak out and act against the subprime lending characteristics that ultimately led to the fiasco rather than attempt to take advantage of it, the fiasco might have been avoided, and their companies might have been able to continue to serve their purpose without government intervention. Did these men not understand the risks and unethical processes involved in the subprime lending chain even as their companies were becoming less profitable and losing their vitality? Even if these CEOs could be excused for focusing only on short-term profit, which they can't, it is definitely the role of their boards of directors to be concerned with strategy—a concern that should involve both the long term and ethics.

Banks, mortgage companies, and other financial intermediaries were not the only ones complicit in this transfer of explosive risk onto unsuspecting investors. The credit rating agencies (Moody's Corp., Standard & Poor's [S & P], and Fitch Ratings) also played a major role[14] because they, at least initially[15] bestowed sound investment grade ratings on the collateralized debt obligations (CDOs) and mortgage-backed securities (MBSs) bought by reliant investors even though some personnel knew and others should have known their ratings did not capture and signal all the risk involved. Emails and transcripts released in October 2008 by a U.S. House of Representatives panel[16] are illustrative:

| From a series of S & P structured finance division employees about to rate a structured deal: "That deal is ridiculous, . . . I know right . . . [our rating] model does not capture half of the [risk]. . . . We should not be rating it. . . . We rate every deal. It could be structured by cows and we would rate it."[17]

| From an S & P employee: "Let's hope we are all wealthy and retired by the time this house of cards falters."[18]

| Raymond McDaniel, chair and chief executive of Moody's, described the slippery slope of events. "What happened in '04 and '05 with respect to subordinated tranches is that our competition, Fitch and S & P, went nuts. Everything was investment grade. We tried to

12. "Fannie Mae and Freddie Mac CEOs to get golden parachutes," William Heisel, *Los Angeles Times*, September 8, 2008.

13. Ibid.

14. "Who Should be Blamed the Most for the Subprime Loan Scandal?," Curtis C. Verschoor, *Strategic Finance*, December, 2007, 11, 12, 59.

15. Moody's and S & P stopped rating SIVs and MBSs as the crisis deepened.

16. See website of the Committee on Oversight and Governance Reform of the U.S. House of Representatives for references to a hearing entitled "Credit Rating Agencies and the Financial Crisis," Wednesday, October 22, 2008 at http://oversight.house.gov/story.asp?ID=2250

17. "Rating agencies face the music," Paul Waldie, *The Globe and Mail*, October 23, 2008, ROB page B10.

18. "Debt raters ripped for 'colossal failure'," Lorraine Woellert and Dawn Kopecki, *Toronto Star*, October 23, 2008, B3.

alert the market. We said we're not rating it. This stuff isn't investment grade. No one cared because the machine just kept going."[19]

| When Mr. McDaniel was queried over potential conflicts of interest involved in the process of rating—rating agencies are paid by investment firms who create the securities and then use the ratings to sell the securities—he said: "Our ratings are not influenced by commercial considerations, . . . that is a conflict that has to be identified, managed properly and controlled."[20]

| But a Moody's employee said: It "seems to me that we had blinders on and never questioned the information we were given. It is our job to think of the worst-case scenarios and model them. Combined, these errors make us look either incompetent at credit analysis, or like we sold our sole to the devil for revenue."[21]

| When he briefed his Board of Directors in 2007, "Mr. McDaniel told directors that the agencies are pushed to provide high ratings to clients in order to win business and generate fees. 'It turns out that ratings quality has surprisingly few friends: Issuers want high ratings; investors don't want rating downgrades.'"[22]

It is also noteworthy that several "watchdog" regulators also tried to blow the whistle and were thwarted. According to *Businessweek*, in April 2003 the attorneys general for North Carolina and Iowa went to Washington to warn officials about "predatory real estate financing" and seek help in limiting the practices involved.[23] Instead, the Office of the Comptroller of the Currency (OCC) and the Office of Thrift Supervision (OTS) "sided with lenders." The OCC then argued that, in accord with the Preemption Doctrine, Federal regulation dominates or preempts State legislation when the two conflict. This led to banks being outside state regulation, and saw "state-chartered mortgage firms sell themselves to national banks and then declare that they [were] . . . sheltered from state oversight." States were then unable even to examine the records of mortgage lenders operating in their state that were subsidiaries of a national bank. National regulations and regulators were comparatively quite lax, and irresponsible lending practices continued unchecked and developed into a frenzy. As events turned out, the OCC and other national officials were not acting in the public interest.

Governments were forced to step in to save large companies from becoming insolvent and to inject liquidity capital to restart the lending process. For example, on October 3, 2008, the U.S. Senate and Congress voted for a $700 billion–plus rescue package,[24] and the U.S. Treasury Department under Secretary Henry Paulson and the U.S. Federal Reserve Bank under Chairman Ben Bernanke bailed out essentially insolvent companies such as Fannie Mae, Freddie Mac,[25] and AIG,[26] forced buyouts of others such as Merrill Lynch & Co,[27] and provided billions to buy up

---

19. Ibid.
20. Ibid.
21. Ibid.
22. Ibid., p. B6
23. "They warned us: The watchdogs who saw the subprime disaster coming—and how they were thwarted by the Banks and Washington," Robert Berner and Brian Grow, *Businessweek*, October 20, 2008, 36–42.
24. The Emergency Economic Stabilization Act of 2008 was finally approved on October 2, 2008 http://en.wikipedia.org/wiki/Emergency_Economic_Stabilization_Act_of_2008
25. "U.S. Seizes . . .," op. cit.
26. Also see the two ethics cases on AIG at the end of this chapter, "Mark-to-Market Accounting and the Demise of AIG" and "The Ethics of AIG's Commission Sales."
27. "Lehman Files for Bankruptcy, Merrill Sol, AIG Seeks Cash," C. Mollenkamp, S. Craig, S. Ng, and A Lucchetti, *Wall Street Journal*, WSJ.com, September 16, 2008, downloaded November 9, 2008.

distressed mortgage investments that the Fed could hold until housing prices recovered. Would these actions and similar actions by most nations around the world prove to be enough?

A Subprime Mortgage Example—Goldman Sachs' GSAMP Trust 2006-S3

In an excellent *Fortune* article,[28] Allan Sloan presents the story of GSAMP Trust 2006-S3 to illustrate the creation, sale, and aftermath of an SIV. He describes how GSAMP 2006-S3 was created in 2006 by Goldman Sachs' Alternative Mortgage Products (GSAMP) when it purchased 8,274 ultra-risky second mortgage loans worth $492 million on California homes. *On subsequent analysis, it was revealed that the average homeowner's equity in these mortgages was only 0.71 percent—or less than 1 percent—and 58 percent of these had little or no documentation.*

The mortgages were allocated into thirteen tranches or smaller bundles with different risk characteristics to appeal to different buyers, which were then rated by S & P and Moody's, and offered for sale to investors, as follows:

Investment-grade-rated tranches:

- $336 million—lowest interest and least risk—3 tranches—named A-1, A-2, A-3
- $123 million—next to be paid, progressively higher risk—7 tranches, M-1 to 7

Non-investment-grade-rated tranches:

- $35 million—last to be paid—highest risk—3 tranches, B1 to 3

The rating agencies have a lot to answer for. Moody's and S&P rated the top three tranches as AAA (which is government grade), and the second set of seven tranches were rated from AA to BBB–. Ninety-three percent of the dollar value of GSAMP 2006-S3 was rated as investment grade, even though they were "backed by second mortgages of dubious quality on homes in which the borrowers (most of whose income and financial assertions weren't vetted by anyone) had less than 1% equity and on which GSAMP couldn't effectively foreclose."[29]

There is an uneven distribution of risks associated with these securities. Any losses are first to be born by the lowest tranche, and when it is exhausted, the next lowest, and so on. Stated differently, the highest tranche, A-1, is first to be paid, followed by A-2 and so on, so the lowest ranked tranches are extremely risky. Goldman sold the B-1 tranche ($13 million) to the UBS Absolute Return Fund, headquartered in Luxembourg, and the B-2 tranche ($18 million) to the Morgan Keegan Select High Income Fund, but apparently kept the B-3 tranche as a fee for putting the deal together.

Most buyers would rely on the underwriter, Goldman Sachs, and the rating agencies to do their due diligence and examine the deal and the tranches to see what could go wrong and build it into the ratings. Some investors might examine the 315-page prospectus in detail, and/or the SEC filings. Others might want to go further and review the original documents or check out the mortgage/homeowner. Alas, there was no access to these original documents, or even to the names[30] of the borrowers involved, so there was really no alternative but to rely on the underwriter and credit rating agencies. Anticipating such reliance and to protect Goldman Sachs from liability, the GSAMP 2006-S3 documents warned against virtually every possible risk.

---

28. Allan Sloan, "House of Junk," *Fortune*, New York, Oct. 29, 2007, Vol. 156, Iss. 9, 117–118, 120, 122, 124
29. Ibid.
30. Ibid. Sometimes lists of postal codes were included.

That said, many investors in GSAMP 2006-S3 might not have realized that the underlying investments were second mortgages, and, as such, GSAMP could not foreclose on a property unless the first mortgagor also foreclosed. If the property was foreclosed then whatever money remained after paying out the first mortgagor would be available to pay out the second mortgagor. However, "if a borrower decided to keep on paying the first mortgage, but not the second, the holder of the second would get bagged."[31] In fact, in the first eighteen months, GSAMP had recovered almost nothing through foreclosure proceedings.

As the subprime lending crisis deepened, and housing prices began to fall, the rating agencies did downgrade their ratings from AAA to BBB, but it was too late for the original investors. *What is even more remarkable is that Goldman Sachs made more by betting against its customers during the wind-down period than it lost on the mortgage-backed securities it held.*[32] Goldman Sachs subsequently profited by short-selling an index of mortgage-backed securities but, in doing so, undermined the market value of securities such as those of GSAMP 2006-S3.

In retrospect, investors really had to be unjustifiably optimistic to invest in GSAMP-like securities that were backed by subprime mortgages, and the underwriters and rating agencies should have known it.

Ethics Issues—The Subprime Lending Fiasco

Greed, Incompetence, Dishonesty, Conflicts of Interest, Nontransparency, Lack of Moral Courage, & Poor Risk Management

Why did *sophisticated and experienced* lenders such as banks and large pension funds invest in subprime mortgages when the prospect for renewal was so unlikely and the underlying property value was so vulnerable? To be fair, some lenders understood the risks and decided not to invest at all. The TD Bank is one example of this.[33] However, most of the lenders simply put too low a probability on the risk of default and too low an estimate of loss. They might have been misled into thinking that the counterparties who guaranteed the mortgages may have been robust enough to cover the losses, but this proved not to be the case. In some instances, these poor aspects of risk management were honest miss-estimates, or the result of the nontransparency of the risks, but in most instances lenders really didn't do a good enough review to surface the underlying inadequacies. In other cases, investors knew the risks but decided to take the chance because of the possibility of high returns—they were greedy.

In either case, because AAA investment yields were very low, many institutional investors and individuals "chased yield" and blinded themselves to risk because of their desperation to achieve what they considered reasonable or attractive returns. To do otherwise would have risked dismissal. Fund managers who opted instead for the best (safest, or best-understood) credits would have had lower returns that would have led to lost market share. It would have taken a farsighted board of directors to put up with such apparently suboptimal behavior.

In the case of the original lenders, some may have believed in the possibility of renewal of teaser or liar loans, but most would have understood the risks. Those who understood the risks were part of the chain of those who aided and abetted transferring those risks onto ill-informed or

---

31. Ibid.
32. Ibid.
33. See the ethics case at the end of this chapter "Moral Courage: Toronto-Dominion Bank CEO Refuses to Invest in High Risk Commercial Paper."

unsuspecting investors. That chain included many investment advisers and others who pocketed very large gains from bonuses and stock options and holdings based on overstated earnings.

The investment advisors and executives involved were supposed to be acting in the best interest of others—investors or shareholders—but did they act only in their own interest? Were these facilitators dishonest? Did they understand and guard against harmful affects of conflicts of interest? Did they do something illegal? Should they be punished? How?

From a governance perspective, it is apparent that no one—including the mortgage lending units, the banks, and intermediaries that legitimized the process and pipeline for selling the SIVs, MBSs, and CDOs to the ultimate investors, or the executives who pocketed large bonuses and stock option gains—bore any significant risk until the subprime lending scandal erupted. The U.S. banks, for example, were not required to retain any risk (as they are to a limited extent in Canada[34]), and therefore the U.S. executives involved could afford to be reckless without fear of reprisal, and they were. There simply was insufficient regulation—governmental or self-interests—to balance the unbridled greed let loose on the public.

Lack of Regulation & Sound Decision Making

In September 2008, Hilary Clinton, appearing on CNN during the Obama-McCain Presidential Election Campaign, was asked if the Democratic Party didn't bear some blame for the subprime fiasco because her husband had signed the Gramm-Leach-Billey (GLB) Act that replaced the Glass-Steagall Act into law when he was president. She answered that although he had signed the bill into law, there had always been a second phase of stronger regulation in mind but that no one had an appetite for after the GLB Act was signed. Unfortunately, the extra level of robust regulation never came into being. Was this because of greed, ignorance, or lack of moral fiber or courage to stand up to corporate interests and argue that unbridled markets are too poor or slow at self-regulation to protect the public interest?

Others argue that U.S. regulators at the Federal Reserve, the OCC, or the Securities & Exchange Commission (SEC) had the mandate to protect the public interest and failed to do so. Although this is literally true, it has not been a popular philosophy politically-speaking to argue for increased regulation when stock and housing markets appear to be healthy. The problem with this line of thinking is that it focuses on the short term and not on the risks, costs, and benefits of the longer term—a flawed perspective that produces many bad ethical decisions. Moral courage is a rare commodity, and should be appreciated for its true worth.

It is also evident that, without promptly enforced and effective regulation, the subprime lending crisis illustrates that the ultimate free-market adjustment meltdown comes too late to protect many from loss, and has been judged too horrific to be allowed to happen. As we have seen, governments have stepped in to bail out the system rather than allow the ultimate free-market sanction to operate fully. Moreover, the principle of allowing the market to operate on self-interest is under question. Even Alan Greenspan has stated that "I made a mistake in presuming that the self-interests of organizations, specifically banks and others, were such that they were capable of protecting their own shareholders and their equity of the firms."[35] Perhaps, given the problems noted, it is time to integrate ethical thinking—to introduce for consideration interests beyond the short-term interests of current shareholders and executives—into corporate decision-making processes that are normally based on profit, shareholder returns such as

---

34. Guideline D3: Accounting for NHA Mortgage Backed Securities gives the accounting treatment for securitization which requires that, on sale, the net present value of the future spread is set up as a balance sheet asset.

35. "Greenspan admits "mistake" on bank regulation; Ex-U.S. Fed chief wrongly thought that self-interest would mitigate risk," Barrie McKenna, *Globe and Mail*, October 24, 2008, 1, 16.

dividends, and legal considerations. Because some legal jurisdictions preclude such consideration, a first step would be to make it permissible, at least, for boards of directors to specifically include ethics in their financial decision making. This would allow them to broaden their considerations beyond the short-term interest of current shareholders and executives.

Are Mark-to-Market Accounting Standards to Blame?

As the subprime mortgage meltdown escalated, financial institutions were required to record more and more losses on their income statement as they wrote-down the value of their mortgage-backed derivative assets because of mark-to-market accounting. The accounting rule, FAS 157 on *Fair Value Measurements*, issued by the Financial Accounting Standards Board (FASB) required that, effective November 15, 2007, financial assets, such as derivatives, are to be revalued each reporting period at their current market or best estimate values. In the case of financial institutions, this means that every three months, when the financial institution issues its quarterly financial statements, it is required to revalue its investment portfolio, including the derivatives it owns. If the market rises, then an unrealized gain is reported on the income statement, thereby increasing the firm's net income. However, if the market value of the portfolio falls during that three-month period, then the institution records an unrealized loss, which reduces net income. In the case of the financial institutions during the subprime meltdown, FAS 157 increased the losses reported on their income statements.

Not only did falling investment values negatively affect profits but also the valuation of the company's investment assets declined thus reducing the overall assets of the enterprise. For many, this meant that they were in jeopardy of falling below the capital requirements needed to meet bank protection limits or to fund operations. Banks chose to restrict new loans to conserve their capital, thus contributing to the credit freeze. Stock brokers and insurance companies such as Merrill Lynch,[36] Bear Stearns,[37] Wachovia,[38] and AIG[39] were taken over at fire sale prices. Lehman Brothers went bankrupt.[40]

Many affected executives and investors were calling for a change to this accounting rule. On September 29, 2008, at the Manulife Financial's Investors Day, Domenic D'Alessandro, the longtime and well-respected CEO of Manulife, Canada's largest insurance company, launched into an impromptu five-minute tirade on fair value accounting. He said that the mark-to-market (M2M) accounting rules "are wrong theoretically. They're wrong operationally. They make no sense for anybody."[41] A chartered accountant himself, he contended that the rule exaggerates the tendency toward greed and short-term thinking. Similar sentiments were being expressed in the United States and Europe.

On September 30, 2008, the Securities and Exchange Commission (SEC) issued a joint statement with FASB, saying that if there is no ready market for a firm's derivative portfolio, then instead of using the mark-to-market rule, management could estimate the value of its portfolio.[42] A few days later, the International Accounting Standards Board (IASB) said that firms could reclassify

36. "Lehman Files . . .," op. cit.
37. J.P. Morgan acquired Bear Stearns in September 2008 for a fraction of its earlier worth.
38. Wells Fargo acquired Wachovia in October 2008 at a fraction of its earlier value.
39. "U.S. to Take Over AIG in $85 Billion Bailout; Central Banks Inject Case as Credit Dries Up," M. Karnitschnig, D. Solomon, L Pleven, and J. Hilsenrath, *Wall Street Journal*, WSJ.com, September 17, 2008, downloaded November 10, 2008.
40. "Lehman Files . . .," op. cit.
41. Domenic D'Alessandro, "Mark-to-Market Madness," *National Post*, October 3, 2008, FP 13.
42. SEC Office of the Chief Accountant and FASB Staff, "Clarifications on Fair Value Accounting," September 30, 2008. http://www.sec.gov/news/press/2008/2008-234.htm

their damaged financial assets (to signal their condition) so that fair value changes would not have to be recognized immediately in net income.[43] On October 17, the CICA announced that it was rushing through new accounting rules, similar to the IASB rules, for Canadian firms.[44]

The accounting profession has been quick to change the rules after stubbornly insisting that M2M were good accounting rules. What happened? Did the accounting rules contribute to the subprime mortgage problem? Did they exacerbate the problem, as D'Alessandro contends? The answer depends on whether you are looking at financial statements from the investor's point of view or the perspective of management. These two viewpoints are not always the same.

The objective of financial reporting is to provide information that is useful to investors and creditors in helping them make their investment and credit decisions. In particular, they want to be able to assess the amount, timing, and uncertainty of the future cash flows of the firm. M2M was introduced to speed up the signaling of potentially lower future cash flows by reflecting them as a current loss or reduction in profits. Assets have long been valued conservatively by using the lower of cost or market value rule which forces the recognition of losses when they are thought to be permanent, but which allows for some judgment and permits some delay. M2M accounting is more stringent, requiring the *relatively immediate recognition* of those losses and the expectation of lower cash flows on the ultimate sale or liquidation of the assets.

It is interesting to note that M2M requires the relatively immediate recognition of gains on investments as well as the losses. Not surprisingly, many executives who did not complain about the recognition of gains that gave rise to performance bonuses and rising share prices, are now upset over the recognition of losses.[45] Executives' self-interest of this nature, however, is not reason enough to cause M2M accounting to be set aside in favor of other means of disclosure.

The more important objection to M2M accounting is that the current depressed valuations of mortgage-backed securities were believed to be temporary, so that losses estimated at present are expected to be reversed and probably eliminated in the longer term when housing prices recover. Because it is also very difficult to accurately estimate the current fair value of the depressed assets in question, it was argued that forcing losses to be recognized immediately would be misleading. Hence, M2M accounting was set aside in favor of separate, specific disclosure of the doubtfully collectible assets in question.

It should be clear that there isn't a perfect method of disclosure of the risks inherent in the mortgage-backed securities when the reality of ultimate collection is extremely uncertain. At the same time, M2M essentially sped up the recognition of losses that would have been required under the conservative lower of cost or market approach. The wisdom of delaying recognition of worst-case bad news is questionable, and could ultimately lead to a different kind of misrepresentation. Time will tell.

From a sophisticated investor perspective, it should also be noted that M2M treatment of projected potential losses on mortgage-backed securities is not expected to have much influence on short-term cash flows, except for the potential tax impact involved and triggering of management bonuses or of clients/depositors withdrawing their money. This is because the real direct cash flows involved take place when the assets are bought and sold, not when the losses are estimated. These estimates give rise to non-cash charges that affect profits but not direct cash flows.

43. International Accounting Standards Board, Press Release, October 17, 2008. http://www.iasb.org/NR/rdonlyres/7AF46D80-6867-4D58-9A12-92B931638528/0/PRreclassifications.pdf

44. Canadian Institute of Chartered Accountants, Media Release, "Canada Announces Important Changes in the Accounting for Financial Assets," http://www.iasb.org/NR/rdonlyres/7AF46D80-6867-4D58-9A12-92B931638528/0/PRreclassifications.pdf

45. "Mark-to-market: Great on the way up, very painful on the way down," Harry Koza, *Globe and Mail*, Nov. 7, 2008, B12.

However, from the perspective of management, accounting polices matter. Management performance and corresponding bonuses are often based on financial numbers. If net income rises, management is presumed to have done a good job, and they expect to be rewarded. However, management can increase net income without improving the firm's operations or cash flows, by simply changing non-cash-oriented accounting policy. As if by magic, net income increases, and management can claim a reward for good performance. Mark-to-market is such a non-cash-oriented accounting policy.

In summary, M2M accounting is not responsible for the subprime lending fiasco. It provides more immediate information to investors about the firm's probable future cash flows, but the information may not be accurate. Management, however, favors mark-to-market accounting during boom times when prices are rising and unrealized gains are reported on the income statement; but, in contrast, management is loath to report unrealized losses that may adversely affect how their stewardship is assessed and that may have a negative effect on their bonuses that are based on reported earnings.

Did M2M accounting contribute to the subprime lending problem and ensuing credit freeze? The answer is that it might have sped up the recognition of the magnitude of the problem and thereby contributed to its solution. The meltdown in the marketplace was caused by irresponsible lending, and the passing on of the risks, both leading to a credit freeze.

For some, M2M accounting was a distraction. As D'Alessandro said with respect to his own firm, "We've been able to run our business constantly with the view as to what is the best economic decision; not what is the best accounting decision."[46] This is the best decision-making perspective. However, the subprime lending crisis was caused by poor business decisions, not by poor accounting policies. Mark-to-market accounting provides useful information that simply highlighted the fact that financial institutions were holding onto investments that were rapidly loosing their value. The real problem was greed and poor risk management.

The Ultimate Risk Bearers

So often when greed, lack of transparency about risks, and flawed focus on the short term are poorly regulated and allowed to foment into financial fiascos, governments have to step in to prevent unreasonable harm to the public. As a result, the ultimate bearers of the risk are not those who made the early returns or bonuses or stock gains—rather, it is the public, the taxpayer, those workers who lose their job, and so on, who have to pay to pick up the pieces and put them back together. It's too bad that those who made money unethically cannot be made to pay restitution or give up their ill-gotten gains. It's too bad that those regulators who failed in their duties cannot be held accountable. It's too bad that the politicians who failed to consider and act in the long term interest of the public cannot be identified. It's too late to repair the damage anyway.

Lessons

The best outcome possible now that substantial damage has been done is to learn the ethics lessons identified and act on them well enough that the tragedy will not be repeated. These lessons include:

> *Realistic expectations and responsible behavior:*
> - Potential homeowners must remember that taking on debt is only realistic if they can afford to make the monthly mortgage payments. Because owning a home and having a mortgage are the largest asset and liability that most people will have, they should make these purchases based on their current, realistic financial prospects. Homeownership

---

46. D'Alessandro, op. cit.

should not be based on speculation that the debt can be repaid only if house prices increase.

- Lenders should be prudent in their lending practices; not talking naïve homeowners into taking on more debt than they can reasonably afford. Because there was little or no down-payment requirement, these homeowners had insufficient equity interest in their homes to motivate them to continue to make mortgage payments when their mortgage loans were to be refinanced at higher interest rates. It was easier for them to walk away from their homes and their debt. To avoid this *adverse selection problem*, lenders have a responsibility to verify the suitability of people to take on sizeable homeownership debts.

| *Full risk assessment, due diligence, and virtues expected:* Investors must always *consider fully the risks* associated with their investments. Because these mortgage-back securities were supposedly insured, investors had little motivation to monitor their investments. Because the securities had been repackaged so often, it was difficult for investors to identify, and therefore monitor, the initial borrower/homeowner—investors were relying on the expectation that the original lenders and financial intermediaries had done their *due diligence* in this regard. The tragedy is that they had not, and investors forgot that they must take personal responsibility for understanding their investment vehicles and the risks associated with those investments.

| *Ethics risks, including conflicts of interest, are ever-present, and require constant vigilance, especially in boom times.* It is wise to understand that it's not just how much profit you make, it's equally important how you make it that matters.

| Simply acting within *existing laws and regulations may not be a good guide for decisions because these can be shortsighted and manipulative,* which does not effectively serve the public interest—their ultimate purpose. Ethical assessments refocusing attention on key long-run issues are critical.

| Risk management assessment of subprime lending techniques failed to consider the fundamental *unfairness* involved for the mortgagees, the ultimate investors and the public.

| Insufficient consideration was given to the *virtues expected* by executives and firms in the lending market, by the credit rating agencies, and by regulators. They probably had no understanding of virtue ethics and mistakenly believed that maximizing profit in the short term was sufficient.

| Corporations have been known to take advantage of unsuspecting nations with low environmental standards, but in the case of the subprime lending crisis, they took advantage of unsuspecting mortgagees and investors in supposedly sophisticated markets. Don't the unsuspecting have *the right to transparent disclosure of the risks involved in corporate activities?*

| *Compensation schemes should be based on a balance between financial incentives, on one side, and financial*[47] *and ethical risks, on the other. In addition, full details of compensations schemes should be disclosed to the public.* Schemes should not just be based on profit earned at any cost.

| *Moral courage*—to speak up against unethical acts—is a rare and needed virtue.

| *Corporate governance systems have again proven to be inadequate to contain self-interest and short-term thinking, and to focus on the medium and longer term with the view to producing lasting value for the public.*

---

47. "Jarislowsky blames financial mess on lax governance rules," *Globe and Mail*, October 24, 2008, B12.

In conclusion, it is clear that the decision-making processes of the executives involved in the subprime lending fiasco would have benefited from the ethics and governance frameworks discussed in earlier chapters. There has been an evident lack of consideration for the full consequences of subprime lending activities, particularly on investors and other stakeholders including the public. In addition, there was little regard for the rights of investors, as well as the fiduciary duty and fairness owed them. Finally, the ethical expectations or virtues expected from the investment community were hopelessly submerged by its self-interest. What options are there to remedy this fiasco—self-regulation involving the institution of ethical cultures, or increased external regulation mandating greater attention to the public interest, or both? As with the Enron disaster, expectations for business and professional governance and personal ethics will rise. Time will tell if the lessons of the subprime lending fiasco have been learned, and how well.

Perhaps governments are now ready to move to global standards for business governance and ethical performance, as they have begun to do for the accounting profession.

The finishing touches to this chapter are being penned in mid-November 2008, in the middle of the aftermath of the subprime lending fiasco. We still don't know what will turn up on investigation by the authorities, and what their ultimate reactions will be. We will endeavor to keep the companion website at **www.cengage.com/accounting/brooks** up to date, and we encourage all readers to be on the alert for new developments.

Incongruous as it may seem, the future of business and professional ethics has probably never been brighter.

Questions

1. How much and in which ways did unbridled self-interest contribute to the subprime lending crisis?

2. How could increased regulation improve the exercise of unbridled self-interest in decision making?

3. How could ethical considerations improve unbridled self-interest in ethical decision making?

4. How much should the exiting CEOs of Fannie Mae and Freddie Mac have received when they were replaced in September 2008?

5. The government bailout of the financial community included taking an equity interest in publicly traded companies such as American General Insurance (AIG). Is it right for the government to become an investor in publicly traded companies?

6. Should CEOs who made large bonuses by having their firms invest in mortgage-backed securities in the early years have to repay those bonuses in the later years when the firm records losses on those same securities?

7. Should the CEOs who refused to have their firms invest in mortgage-backed securities in the early years because the risks were too great receive bonuses in the latter years because their firms did not incur any mortgage-backed security losses? How would determine the size of these bonuses?

8. Should organizations that have a risk-taking culture, such as the one developed by Stan O'Neil at Merrill Lynch, enjoy the gains and suffer the losses, without recourse to government bailouts?

9. Are the criticisms that mark-to-market accounting rules contributed to the economic crisis valid?

10. The global economic crisis was caused by the meltdown in the U.S. housing market. Should the U.S. government bear some of the responsibility of bailing out the economies of all countries that were harmed by this crisis?

11. Given that the marketplace for securities is global, and that the risks involved can affect people worldwide, should there be a global regulatory regime to protect investors? If so, should it be based on the regulations of one country?

12. What are the current estimates of the total dollar value and the percentage of all subprime lending that will default?

13. Although adjustable rate mortgages (ARMs) were not considered to be subprime mortgages, they were affected by the general economic downturn and other pressures caused by the subprime lending fiasco. Almost $750 billion of options ARMs were issued from 2004 to 2007. Describe what an ARM is, and provide the current estimates for the percent expected to default.

14. What significant events or developments in combating the subprime lending crisis occurred after November 15, 2008? Indicate the date of each and why you consider it to be significant.

Case Insights

The cases that follow capture important aspects of the subprime lending fiasco that businesspeople and professionals should be alert to identify and avoid in the future, including: the impact of accounting rules, appropriate risk-taking and reward systems, and astute risk management and moral courage:

- *Mark-to-Market Accounting and the Demise of AIG* is a case in which the CEO of AIG argues that the make-to-market accounting rule contributed to the collapse of the company. Do you agree?

- *Subprime Lending—Greed, Faith & Disaster* presents the story of a CEO who changed the corporate culture at Merrill Lynch to an aggressive risk-taking institution and how the purchase of subprime mortgage backed securities lead to huge losses for the brokerage house but a large termination payment for the CEO, Stan O'Neil.

- *Moral Courage: Toronto-Dominion Bank CEO Refuses to Invest in High Risk Commercial Paper* explains how the CEO of a major Canadian bank refused to invest in subprime mortgage derivatives when all other banks were doing so, on the basis that the instruments were too risky.

- *The Ethics of AIG's Commission Sales* describes how huge commissions and bonuses were paid to Joe Cassano for work that was ultimately responsible for the unprecedented losses incurred by AIG and its eventual bailout by the Federal Reserve.

Useful References

Many individuals and organizations have contributed to the current debate and have offered useful comments and recommendations, including:

- The Caux Round Table, "Global Prosperity at Risk: The Current Crisis and the Responsible Way Forward", cauxroundtable@aol.com Draft cited
- Lewis D. Johnson and Edwin H. Neave, "The subprime mortgage market: Familiar lessons in a new context", *Management Research News*, Vol. 31 No. 1, 2008, pp. 12–26
- *The Finance Crisis and Rescue*, Rotman School of Management, University of Toronto Press, Toronto, 2008.

- Consult **www.cengage.com/accounting/brooks/** for further references.

As Johnson and Neave indicate, the lessons to be learned have been evident in past. Will they be learned well enough this time? Those who are alert to ethics issues should have a better chance at long-run success.

References

Berner, Robert, and Brian Grow, "They warned us: The watchdogs who saw the subprime disaster coming—and how they were thwarted by the Banks and Washington," *Businessweek*, October 20, 2008, 36–42.

Canadian Institute of Chartered Accountants, Media Release, "Canada Announces Important Changes in the Accounting for Financial Assets," retrieved from http://www.iasb.org/NR/rdonlyres/7AF46D80-6867-4D58-9A12-92B931638528/0/PRreclassifications.pdf

Committee on Oversight and Governance Reform of the U.S. House of Representatives, "Credit Rating Agencies and the Financial Crisis," Wednesday, October 22, 2008, retrieved from http://oversight.house.gov/story.asp?ID=2250

D'Alessandro, Domenic, "Mark-to-market madness," *National Post*, October 3, 2008, FP 13.

Ellis, David, "U.S. seizes Fannie and Freddie," CNN Money. com, September 7, 2008, 8:28 pm, Downloaded Nov. 9, 2008.

Emergency Economic Stabilization Act of 2008, http://en. wikipedia.org/wiki/Emergency_Economic_Stabilization_Act_ of_2008

"European leaders pledge aid for banks in crisis," *Toronto Star*, October 13, 2008, B1, B4.

Heisel, William, "Fannie Mae and Freddie Mac CEOs to get golden parachutes," *Los Angeles Times*, September 8, 2008.

International Accounting Standards Board, Press Release, October 17, 2008. Retrieved from http://www.iasb.org/NR/rdonlyres/ 7AF46D80-6867-4D58-9A12-92B931638528/0/PRreclassifica tions.pdf

"Jarislowsky blames financial mess on lax governance rules," *Globe and Mail*, October 24, 2008, B12.

Karnitschnig, M., D. Solomon, L Pleven, and J. Hilsenrath, "U.S. to take over AIG in $85 billion bailout; Central banks inject cash as credit dries up," *Wall Street Journal*, WSJ.com, September 17, 2008, downloaded November 10, 2008.

Koza, Harry, "Mark-to-market: Great on the way up, very painful on the way down," *Globe and Mail*, Nov. 7, 2008, B12.

McKenna, Barrie, "Greenspan admits "mistake" on bank regulation; Ex-U.S. Fed chief wrongly thought that self-interest would mitigate risk," *Globe and Mail*, October 24, 2008, 1, 16.

Mollenkamp, C., S. Craig, S. Ng, and A Lucchetti, "Lehman files for bankruptcy, Merrill Sol, AIG seeks cash," *Wall Street Journal*, WSJ.com, September 16, 2008, downloaded November 9, 2008.

Parkinson, David, "A train wreck? Greenspan says he didn't see it coming," *The Globe and Mail*, November 8, 2008, B2.

SEC Office of the Chief Accountant and FASB Staff, "Clarifications on Fair Value Accounting," September 30, 2008. Retrieved from http://www.sec.gov/news/press/2008/2008-234.htm

Sloan, Allan, "House of junk," *Fortune*, New York, Oct. 29, 2007, Vol. 156, Iss. 9, 117–118, 120, 122, 124.

The Finance Crisis and Rescue, Rotman School of Management, University of Toronto Press, Toronto, 2008.

Verschoor, Curtis C., "Who Should be Blamed the Most for the Subprime Loan Scandal?," *Strategic Finance*, December, 2007, 11, 12, 59.

Waldie, Paul, "Rating agencies face the music," *The Globe and Mail*, October 23, 2008, ROB page B10.

Woellert, Lorraine, and Dawn Kopecki, "Debt raters ripped for 'colossal failure'," *Toronto Star*, October 23, 2008, B3, B6.

Ethics Case

Mark-to-Market Accounting and the Demise of AIG

American International Group, Inc. (AIG) was the world's largest insurance company with major offices in New York, London, Paris, and Hong Kong. From 2005 to 2008, the company had a series of accounting problems. First, it was convicted of fraudulent financial reporting, and, then, of reporting mammoth unrealized losses that led to the company being taken over by the government. Throughout this period, it went through four CEOs.

On June 6, 2005, the Securities and Exchange Commission (SEC) laid charges against executives at AIG and General Re alleging that they committed securities fraud by engaging in two reinsurance sham transactions that artificially increased the loss reserves of AIG by $500 million, thereby making the financial results of AIG look better than they were in the fourth quarter of 2000 and the first quarter of 2001. According to the SEC, "The transactions were initiated by AIG to quell criticism by analysts concerning a reduction in the company's loss reserves in the third quarter of 2000."[1] Billionaire Warren Buffet, who owns General Re, was not involved in the SEC suit, but Maurice Greenberg, the then CEO of AIG, was identified as an unindicted coconspirator who was aware of the sham transactions.[2] Afterward, Greenberg was pressured to leave the company.

1. "SEC Charges Gen Re Executive for Aiding in AIG Securities Fraud," Securities and Exchange Commission, June 6, 2005. http://www.sec.gov/news/press/2005-85.htm

2. Voreacos, David and Mills, Jane, "Former AIG, General Re Officials Convicted of Fraud," *Washingtonpost.com*, February 26, 2008. http://www.washingtonpost.com/wp-dyn/content/article/ 2008/02/25/AR2008022502722.html

In February 2006, AIG agreed to pay a $1.6 billion fine,[3] and two years later five former executives of General Re and AIG were found guilty of securities fraud.[4] Meanwhile, AIG began replacing its CEO. In 2005, Greenberg was replaced by Martin Sullivan, who was replaced in June 2008 by Robert Willumstad after AIG recorded mammoth losses and its stock price plummeted. Willumstad was replaced three months later by Edward Liddy, after the government took over AIG.

Although its primary business is selling insurance, in 1987 AIG began to sell financial products through its subsidiary, AIG Financial Products Corp. One of its major products was a credit default swap contract designed to protect investors against defaults on fixed-income investments such as mortgage-backed securities and other mortgage-backed derivatives. However, internal controls at the subsidiary were weak. In late November 2007, AIG's auditors PricewaterhouseCoopers raised concern with Sullivan about material weaknesses in the risk management areas. In March 2008, the Office of Thrift Supervision said, "We are concerned that the corporate oversight of AIG Financial Products . . . lacks critical elements of independence, transparency, and granularity."[5]

Nevertheless, the subsidiary continued to sell its financial products, including credit default swap contracts on $441 billion of asset-backed securities, $57.8 billion of which related to mortgage-backed securities. When the subprime mortgage meltdown occurred in 2007, AIG began to record losses on these credit default swaps as result of FASB 157. The Financial Accounting Standards Board (FASB) issued Statement No. 157 on Fair Value Measurements in 2006 that became effective in 2007. The fair value measurement rule, referred to as the "mark-to-market" rule,

requires that financial assets and liabilities be revalued to their market values each reporting period. In the case of a financial instrument, this would be at the quoted price of the instrument in an active market. As the market for subprime mortgages deteriorated, so, too, did the market for financial instruments that were backed by those mortgages.

In February 2008, the unrealized losses were $4.8 billion, which were increased to $11 billion by the end of the month. In June, Sullivan resigned as CEO but was given a $15 million "golden parachute."[6] On September 16, AIG reported losses of $13.2 billion for the first six months of 2008. Its shares were trading at $3.14, down more than 90 percent from its peak of $190 billion market value at the end of 2006.[7] The federal government decided that AIG, one of the five largest financial companies in the world, was "too big to fail," and so it announced a bailout for the company. The government would provide a credit-liquidity facility of $85 billion, which was later increased, in return for receiving warrants that in essence gave the government a 79.9 percent equity interest in AIG. On September 17, AIG drew down $28 billion of the credit-liquidity facility. By October 24, it had drawn down $90.3 billion of the $122.8 billion bailout.

In testimony before the House of Representatives Committee on Oversight and Government Reform on October 7, 2008, Willumstad laid part of the blame for the company's failure on the accounting rules that forced AIG to record unrealized losses on its credit default swaps.

However, when the market for the underlying bonds froze toward the end of 2007, accounting rules required AIG to "mark to market" the value of its swaps. But the

3. Masters, Brooke, "AIG Agrees to $1.6 Billion Fine to Settle Fraud, Bid-Rigging Case," *Seattle Times*, February 10, 2006.

4. Voreacos and Mills, op. cit.

5. Ross, Brian and Shine, Tom, "After Bailout, AIG Exec Heads to California Resort," *ABC News Internet Ventures*, October 7, 2008.

6. Ross and Shine, op. cit.

7. Son, Hugh, "AIG Plunges as Downgrades Threaten Quest for Capital", *Bloomberg.com*, September 16, 2008. http://www.bloomberg.com/apps/news?pid=20601087&sid=amuMN6feT0kE&refer= home

market was not functioning. The way the accounting rules were applied in this unprecedented situation forced AIG to recognize tens of billions of dollars in accounting losses in the fourth quarter of 2007 and the first two quarters of 2008, even though, as far as I am aware, AIG has made very few payments on any of the credit default swaps it wrote and the vast majority of the securities underlying the swaps are still rated investment grade or better by the rating agencies.[8]

So, according to Willumstad, the collapse of AIG and the subsequent bail out were the result of mark-to-market accounting. In a speech the next day, Lynn Turner, the former chief accountant of the SEC, said, "AIG is blaming its downfall on accounting rules which require it to disclose losses to its investors. That's like blaming the thermometer, folks, for a fever."[9] On October 10, 2008, FASB loosened the mark-to-market accounting rule, permitting companies to forgo writing down their securities if there is no ready market for them, provided that the existence and nature of the securities is disclosed.

Questions

1. The argument is that market-to-market accounting caused AIG to record huge unrealized losses. These losses led to a downgrade in the quality of AIG stock. The downgrade and frozen credit markets led to eventual bailout. So, do you agree that the accounting rules contributed to AIG's demise?

2. The government said that AIG was "too big to fail." It was concerned that if AIG declared bankruptcy, then individuals holding personal insurance as well as other investments would have no insurance and would be in danger as the financial and liquidity crisis deepened. But many felt that the federal government should not be investing in publicly traded companies. There is risk in the marketplace, and one such risk is that occasionally businesses go bankrupt. Should the federal government have bailed out AIG, especially when it had not rescued Lehman Brothers and had let Merrill Lynch be taken over by Bank of America?

---

8. *Statement of Robert B. Willumstad before the United States House of Representatives Committee on Oversight and Government Reform*, October 7, 2008. http://oversight.house.gov/documents/20081007101054.pdf

9. de la Merced, Michael and Otterman, Sharon "AIG's Spending Scorned," *The San Diego Union-Tribune*, October 8, 2008. http://www.signonsandiego.com/uniontrib/20081008/news_1b8aig.html

---

| Ethics Case | *Subprime Lending—Greed, Faith, & Disaster* |

In December 2002, Stan O'Neal became CEO of Merrill Lynch & Co Inc, the world's largest brokerage house. Known as "Mother Merrill" to insiders, the firm had a nurturing environment that accepted lower profit margins so that veteran employees could remain with the firm. O'Neal changed that culture. He laid off one-third of the workforce—24,000 employees—and fired nineteen senior executives while eliminating senior management perks. He put in a new young management team, expanded the firm's overseas activities, and made Merrill a more aggressive, risk-friendly organization. In 2006, for example, the firm made $7 billion in trading securities, compared with $2.2 billion in 2002. Under O'Neal's leadership Merrill became the most profitable investment bank in America, making more money per broker than any of its competitors. O'Neal was rewarded well—in 2007 he became one of Wall Street's best-paid executives, earning $48 million in salary and bonuses.

He pushed the company into new lines of business, including investing in collateralized debt obligations (CDOs). Merrill led the industry in its exposure to CDOs. Over an eighteen-month period, to the summer of 2007, its investment in these subprime mortgage-backed CDO pools rose from $1 billion to more than $40 billion. Then the subprime mortgage bubble burst.

The term "subprime" does not refer to the interest rate changed on the mortgage but, rather, to the risk associated with the borrower. Subprime mortgages are given to high-risk customers who are charged an interest rate that is greater than prime. These mortgages are typically given to people who would not normally qualify for a mortgage from a conventional lender such as a bank. From the lender's point of view, as long as house prices increase, the risk of a loss on the mortgage is low. As such, the mortgages became low-risk, high-yield investments. The lenders of these subprime mortgages would then package these mortgages as bundles of asset-backed synthetic securities, such as CDOs, which were sold to third parties, including individuals, corporations, pension funds, banks, insurance companies, and brokerage houses.

The subprime mortgage bubble bust when house prices in the United States began to fall. People could no longer refinance their homes nor pay off their mortgages by selling their homes. By late 2006, one in eight subprime mortgages was in default. Throughout 2007, nearly 1.5 million American homeowners lost their homes. As the housing market imploded, mortgage payment defaults increased and the value of subprime mortgages fell as did the value of the subprime mortgage-backed CDOs. By the summer of 2007, subprime-related losses were being reported by all the major financial institutions.

In the third quarter of 2007, Merrill announced a loss of $2.3 billion, compared with a profit of $3.05 billion for the third quarter in 2006. It also announced a $7.9 billion provision for losses on mortgage-related investments, larger than the warning of a possible $5 billion write-down that it had made a month earlier. Within a week of reporting the largest quarterly loss in the company's ninety-three-year history, O'Neal resigned as Chairman and Chief Executive Officer of Merrill Lynch. Although he did not receive any severance, O'Neal did receive $161 million in stock and retirement benefits.

Questions

1. Subprime mortgages targeted lower-income Americans, new immigrants, and people who had a poor credit history. The customers were told that because house prices had been rising, the borrower would be able to refinance the loan at a later date with the increased equity in the house. Was this an ethically correct sales pitch? Were the lenders taking advantage of financially naïve customers?

2. O'Neal transformed Merrill Lynch from a conservative bank into an aggressive risk-taking institution. Risk-taking means that there is the potential for high rewards as well as large losses. From 2002, when O'Neal became CEO, Merrill's share rose 53 percent. Should the investors now be upset that, as a result of the subprime mortgage meltdown, Merrill's stock price fell by about 30 percent in 2007?

3. As a result of the subprime mortgage debacle, the CEOs at Merrill Lynch, Citigroup, Bear Stearns, and Morgan Stanley all resigned or were fired. Their departure packages were $161 million, $68 million, $40 million, and $18 million, respectively. Are these settlements unreasonably high, given the huge financial losses and write-downs that their companies recorded?

Sources

McFarland, Janet, "Amid Billions in Writedowns and Plunging Stocks, Attention Turns to Executive Paycheques," *Globe and Mail*, March 21, 2008, B1.

"Merrill Lynch Chief Set to Resign," *Seattle Post-Intelligencer*, October 28, 2007. http://seattlepi. nwsource.com/business/337204_merrill29.html

Rosenbush, Steve, "Merrill Lynch's O'Neil Takes the Hit," *Business Week*, October 24, 2007. http://www.businessweek.com/bwdaily/dnflash/content/oct2007/db20071024_830456.htm

"The U.S. Subprime Mortgage Meltdown," *CBC News*, August 31, 2007. http://www.cbc.ca/news/background/personalfinance/mortgage-meltdown.html

Weiner, Eric, "Stan O'Neal: The Rise and Fall of a Numbers Guy," *NPR.org*, October 29, 2007. http://www.npr.org/templates/story/story.php?storyId=15768986

Ethics Case

Moral Courage: Toronto-Dominion Bank CEO Refuses to Invest in High-Risk Asset-Backed Commercial Paper

Although the Canadian banks have not suffered as much as other financial institutions around the world, they have not been immune from the economic consequences of the subprime mortgage meltdown. In Canada, the earliest crisis concerned the liquidity of asset-backed commercial paper (ABCP) that was affected by the precipitous decline of U.S. housing prices and the related mortgage-backed securities on which those prices were based.

ABCP are short-term debt obligations, generally issued by a specially formed entity or a trust and secured by a bundle of assets such as mortgages and other types of consumer loans. The repayment and maturity of these ABCPs is dependent on the cash flow of the underlying assets. The ABCPs were issued to investors by trusts that were sponsored or managed by either banks or nonbank financial institutions. The nonbank-sponsored portion of the Canadian market was approximately $35 billion.

In July 2007, as the U.S. subprime mortgage market began to deteriorate, the Canadian issuers began to fear that they, too, could face a liquidity crisis that would prevent the recovery of capital or refinancing of borrowings when they came due. As such, in August, a number of nonbank ABCP sponsors agreed to a sixty-day standstill period, called the Montreal Accord, during which the holders (those who had invested in the ABCP) promised not to roll over or redeem their paper at maturity, and the issuers agreed not to make any collateral calls. A committee, chaired by Toronto lawyer Purdy Crawford, then began to work out a deal whereby the short-term ABCP could be converted into long-term floating-rate debt that would have a much greater likelihood of recovery or refinance, because the underlying assets would eventually recover their value.

The agreement required the support of the five major banks in Canada. They were each to pay $500 million in order to shore up the country's debt market. However, Canada's third largest bank, the Toronto-Dominion Bank (TD), balked at the suggestion on the basis that, three years earlier, the bank intentionally had moved to eliminate its exposure in the nonbank ABCP market.

In May 2005, Edmund Clark, CEO of the TD, announced that the bank would exit the structured loans products market, including interest rate derivatives and collateralized debt obligations such as ABCPs. The Bank decided that it would focus on consumer banking rather than the securities business. Clark, who has a Ph.D. in economics from Harvard, contended that the securities business was too risky. He had been briefed by experts who traded these securities on the nature of credit and equity products and concluded the risk was too great. "The whole thing didn't make sense to me. You're going to get all your money back, or you're going to get none of your money back. I said 'wow!' if this ever went against us, we could take some serious losses here." The TD generates 80 percent of its profit from consumer lending and money management. "I'm an old school banker. I don't think you should do something you don't understand, hoping there's somebody at the bottom of the organization who does."[1]

Meanwhile, all of the other major Canadian banks were investing in the ABCP market. They collectively controlled two-thirds of the ABCP market.[2] The yields were high and everyone was on the bandwagon. It took great courage for Clark to go against the tide. As David Baskin of Baskin Financial Services said, "He's absolutely to be commended for not getting caught up in the subprime frenzy."[3]

---

1. Pasternak, Sean, "Toronto-Dominion Avoids Subprime as Banks Costs Rise," *Bloomberg.com.*, May 26, 2008. http://www.bloomberg.com/apps/news?pid=newsarchive&sid=aeAsOI6GUU1Y
2. "Credit Crunch Could be 'Quite Ugly' for Months: TD CEO," *CBC News*, September 11, 2007. http://www.cbc.ca/money/story/2007/09/11/credit.html?ref=rss
3. Pasternak, op. cit.

And Clark was right. When the ABCP market collapsed, the other banks reported large write-downs on their securities, estimated to be in excess of $2 billion.[4]

As the commercial credit market began to collapse, the Montreal Accord was being extended. The liquidity of the ABCP market was drying up, and only the major chartered banks could help solve the problem. TD was under a lot of pressure to help participate in the repair of the credit market, but Clark's attitude was "that it would not be in the best interest of TD shareholders to assume incremental risk for activities in which we were not involved."[5] TD was not part of the problem, so he thought it should not be part of the solution. Finally, the federal government, through its agency the Bank of Canada, weighed in saying that it wanted the problem solved, and that it was in both the public interest and the interest of the financial marketplace that all the banks participate in restructuring the commercial paper segment of the market. Since TD was part of the financial community, although it had not created the problem, it had a moral and financial obligation to help.

TD could have held out, but as one analyst said, "It's like protesting going to your mother-in-law's house for Christmas. Despite your protest, you know you're going because it's been determined that it's in your best interest to do so. In my view, the Bank of Canada will win the argument."[6] On March 13, 2008, the five major Canadian banks, including TD, said that they would provide $950 million to support the newly restructured credit market, in which $32 billion of short-term commercial paper would be swapped for long-term notes.[7]

Questions

1. Because the Toronto-Dominion Bank was neither a manufacturer nor a distributor of ABCP products, did the bank have a moral responsibility to assist in the restructuring of the commercial paper market?

2. If you were Edmund Clark, how would you explain to the board of directors that you were having the bank exit a market in which your competitors were making a lot of money?

3. The banks in Canada are highly regulated by the federal government. If the banks could not come to a voluntary agreement, should the federal government have forced the banks through legislation to providing $950 million financial support to help solve the ABCP liquidity crisis?

4. "TD Bank will Consider Montreal Accord Proposals on ABCP but Won't Take Risks," *The Canadian Press*, December 17, 2007.

5. Mordant, Nicole, "TD Bank Throws Wrench into Canada ABCP Repair," *Reuters*, December 17, 2007.

6. Critchley, Barry, "TD May Join ABCP Bailout," *Financial Post*, December 19, 2007.

7. Alexander, Doug and Pasternak, Sean, "Canada Commercial Paper Group Gets Credit Protection, *Bloomberg.com*, March 17, 2008. http://www.bloomberg.com/apps/news?pid=newsarchive&sid=aO.ysqLVjxUc

---

Ethics Case | *The Ethics of AIG's Commission Sales*

The advantage of commission sales is that if the salesperson puts in effort and makes a sale, then both the company and the salesperson benefit. The salesperson receives a commission and the company receives the proceeds of the sale, net of the commission. Referred to as a first-best contract, it supposedly aligns the interests of both the company and its salesforce. In addition, companies often reward their leading salespeople with expensive trips and holidays. They are considered thank-you gifts for generating so much revenue for the company. But commissions and holidays can be problematic. Consider the case of AIG.

American International Group, Inc. (AIG) was among the five biggest financial companies in the world.[1] A diversified company, its primary business was selling both personal and corporate insurance, but it was also involved in businesses such as lease financing, real estate, and selling financial products. With respect to insurance, AIG did not have agents but, rather, sold insurance through independent brokers. In this way, AIG only had to pay a commission if the broker was successful at selling one of AIG's products. If the independent broker was unsuccessful at making a sale, then there was no cost to AIG. Only successful sales were rewarded with a commission.

In 1987 the company formed a subsidiary, AIG Financial Products Corp., to sell a variety of financial products including credit default swap contracts. These products were designed to protect investors against defaults on fixed-income investments.[2] This business flourished under the leadership of Joe Cassano. At one point, it had sold protection on $441 billion of asset-backed securities, including $57.8 billion that were related to subprime mortgages.[3] Cassano and his team were paid a commission of 30 percent on every dollar of business generated. As the market for these credit default swaps increased, the sales staff received more and more commissions. In the eight-year period from 2000, Cassano was paid $280 million.[4]

In 2007, the subprime mortgage market turned as the housing crisis in the United States deepened. As a result, losses in the Financial Products subsidiary on credit default swaps began to increase. In February 2008, AIG said that the swaps lost $4.8 billion in October and November 2007. By the end of February, the losses had reached $11 billion, and Cassano was replaced as CEO of the division. He collected his bonuses of $34 million, and was then hired back as a consultant at $1 million per month to oversee winding-down the credit default swap business.[5] But the losses generated by Financial Products kept increasing. On September 16, AIG reported losses of $13.2 billion for the first six months of 2008. That same day, the government announced that it was prepared to pay $85 billion to bail out the company.

Meanwhile, at the beginning of October, as the company was being supported by the government to forestall bankruptcy, AIG paid $444,000 for a California holiday for its senior sales personnel. Although relatively small, the optics of this was questionable. The cost of their weeklong retreat at the St. Regis Resort, a luxury resort and spa, was $200,000 for rooms, $150,000 for meals, $23,000 in the spa, $7,000 in greens fees, $1,400 in the salon, and $10,000 in the bar.[6] Congressional leaders were appalled. "This is unbridled greed. It's an insensitivity to how people are spending our dollars." said Congressman Mark Souder. "They're getting pedicures and their manicures and the American people are paying for that," said Congressman Elijah Cummings.[7] When asked why Cassano, who had been responsible for the losses incurred by the Financial Products subsidiary, had been hired back as a consultant after he had been fired, Martin Sullivan, the former CEO of AIG, said "I wanted to retain the twenty-year knowledge of the transactions."[8]

1. Son, Hugh, "AIG Plunges as Downgrades Threaten Quest for Capital," *Bloomber.com*, September 16, 2008.
2. Karnitschnig, Matthew, Solomon, Deborah, Pleven, Liam, and Hilsenrath, Jon, "U.S. to Take Over AIG in $85 Billion Bailout; Central Banks Inject Cash as Credit Dries Up," *Wall Street Journal*, September 16, 2008.
3. Son, op. cit.
4. Ahrens, Frank, "Joe Cassano: The Man Who Brought Down AIG?," *Washingtonpost.com*, October 7, 2008.
5. Champ, Henry, "Lawmakers Fume at Excess of Failed Firm's Execs," *Washington File*, October 8, 2008.
6. Champ, op. cit.
7. Ross and Shine, op. cit.
8. Ahrens, op. cit.

Questions

1. Commission salespeople are paid their commission after they write successful insurance policies or consummate the sale of financial products. Should their commissions be recovered if the company subsequently suffers a loss as a result of the business written by the sales staff? Should there be an upper limit placed on commissions, so that no one employee receives $280 million in commissions over an eight-year period? How could such an upper limit be selected if a company wished to establish one?

2. Is it right that perks such as holidays at luxury resorts are only provided to senior executives and the sales staff but not to the other employees of the firm?

3. Should senior officers who have extensive firm-specific knowledge be hired back as consultants to help rectify their mistakes?

INDEX

Note: Symbols *t* and *f* in the index have been used for the terms found in tables and figures, respectively.